McClure of Idaho

McClure of Idaho

William L. Smallwood

Caxton Press
Caldwell, Idaho
2007

Library of Congress Cataloging-in-Publication Data

Smallwood, William L.
McClure of Idaho / William L. Smallwood.
p. cm.
Includes bibliographical references and index.
ISBN 978-0-87004-458-8
1. McClure, James A. 2. Legislators--United States--Biography. 3. United States. Congress. Senate--Biography. 4. United States. Congress. House--Biography. 5. Legislators--Idaho--Biography. 6. Idaho. Legislature--Biography. 7. Idaho--Politics and government--20th century. 8. Payette (Idaho)--Biography. I. Title.
E840.8.M4673S63 2007
973.924092--dc22
[B]

2006102368

Printed in Canada

CAXTON PRESS
Caldwell, Idaho
175098

THIS BOOK IS DEDICATED TO:

My wife, Patricia, who sustains me in every way

and

My son, William M., who has always been my best and most faithful critic.

Table of contents

Illustrations

Introduction and Acknowledgements

I was walking toward the Idaho State Capitol Building when I heard a voice calling my name. I turned and it was Roy Eiguren, a Boise attorney whose father had been a wonderful friend of mine. We talked and in the conversation he asked if I would give some thought to doing a Jim McClure biography. I discouraged him, pleading that I do not even know the man, I am in the middle of several projects, and, most importantly, I am not a biographer.

Roy waved aside my protests. "Just think about it," he said. A little over a year later, in almost the same location, I saw a man in jogging clothes coming toward me. It was Roy Eiguren again. And he immediately brought up the subject of me doing a McClure biography. This time I hesitated before nixing his idea.

I had done some thinking about McClure, especially after talking to some friends about him—particularly Secretary of State Pete Cenarrusa and his wife, Freda, who swore that Jim McClure was a unique human being who deserved to have his life and political career recorded for all Idahoans to appreciate. Roy sensed my wavering thoughts and said, "Would you consider going up to McCall and spending a weekend with Jim and his wife Louise just to meet them and get to know them?" "Yes, we can do that," I replied without hesitation.

My curiosity about Jim McClure had been piqued. I really did want to meet the man. A few weeks later, with my wife, Patty, I went to McCall. It was late August and I had at least a bushel of tomatoes fresh from my garden for the mountain dwellers, a gift that brought wide smiles from Louise when she saw them. And we spent a wonderful weekend. Great conversations. Beautiful sunsets over Payette Lake. And finally, late Sunday just before we were ready to leave, discussion of a biography. Then some agreements.

If I wrote it, he could read it when I was finished and I would listen carefully to any comments about accuracy, fairness and completeness. While the work was in progress, he would give me the "hundreds" of hours of his time that would be required without making me feel guilty of imposition. And he would answer without equivocation any fair question that I asked. Soon it was a done deal with a hand shake. Ready or not, I was going to do a McClure biography.

Now, almost six years later, I am sitting at my desk trying to do justice to the many kind souls who so generously gave their time to assist me with this endeavor. The first person who comes to mind is the subject himself.

He did give me the "hundreds" of hours that I had anticipated needing. Most important, to me at least, was the good cheer that emanated from the other end of the line (most of our discussions were over the telephone—a medium that his staffers said he hated) whenever I contacted him. The subject was a man of his word; never once did I get the feeling that I was imposing on him when I called. Thanks for all that, Jim. And thanks, too, to your lovely live-in who listened to many of our conversations. We have both benefited from her wisdom.

Next is a thank you to another Jim—*Jim Goller*. Read the latter two-thirds of this book and Goller's name is on perhaps one-third of the pages. Jim Goller was the master mind behind Jim McClure's election victories and he was, for most of McClure's political career, his closest aide and confidant. He, too, endured "hundreds" of hours on the telephone, always, when contacted with my words, "Have you got a few minutes?" he would reply with a cheery, "You betcha." (At Goller's 80th birthday I joked with his son that I was surprised his middle name was not "betcha" because his father used it so often.) Goller also read the entire manuscript and gave several helpful comments.

Next come the other McClure staffers. At the head of that list is *Dick Thompson* who, for the first thirteen years of McClure's congressional career was his chief aide in Washington and who, from his subsequent senate job, was a close observer of his former boss. We did not spend "hundreds" of hours on the telephone but he graciously endured at least a dozen protracted conversations. And most memorable was his passion for accuracy, evidenced several times when he would call me back or send an e-mail with comments to ensure that I would not stray from the facts. Right on Thompson's heels is Thompson's successor, *Tod Neuenschwander*, who responded enthusiastically to my every query. Also, both Thompson and Neuenschwander read the complete manuscript and gave helpful criticism.

Now comes the hard part. In what order does one name the other McClure staffers who gave generously of their time in assisting with this project? My sense of fairness suggests that, in the order I think of their names, I should acknowledge those who endured multiple interrogations. So here they are; meet some of McClure's finest.

Margo Carlisle. This wonderful lady (who, tragically, left us some months ago) was so patient during numerous interviews when I claimed ignorance of some of the most elementary Senate procedures.

Scootch Pankonin. Not only did she endure the phone calls, she spent one and one-half days with me in Idaho!

Nancy Carlile. I interviewed this nice lady in her home; then she made a special trip to Sun Valley just to give me an extended account of the Teton Dam disaster with which she had been extensively involved.

Mike Hathaway. We spent hours on the telephone together, him telling me about McClure's early days on the Senate Energy and Natural Resources Committee and their trips together to the Middle East. He also read and critiqued parts of the manuscript.

Martha Solodky. McClure's "token liberal" who repeatedly gave her good-humored version of events that, were I confined only to the papers in the McClure archives, I would never have understood. She also read parts of the manuscript and gave helpful comments.

Jim Norell. A talented writer who generously supplied his unique perceptions of McClure when he first went to the Senate.

Chuck Trabant. A very knowledgeable and perceptive staffer who had unique insights and experiences.

Ron Shiflett. Great stories of McClure and his passion for electric cars.

Jeff Silek. From an intern in the mail room to McClure's legislative director, Jeff's perspective and knowledge was wide-ranging and most helpful.

Frank Cushing. Extremely busy now as the staff director of a major committee, he was always willing to interrupt his work to answer my queries.

Kit Caples Kimball. Another staffer now busy with major responsibilities whose observations can be found in several textboxes scattered throughout the book.

Jack Gerard. A Mud Lake, Idaho farm boy who went on to do outstanding things with McClure, both in the senate and, later, when they, with Neuenschwander, founded their own Washington, D.C. consulting firm.

Susan Tackish. A McClure aide while he was in the senate and the "glue" who held together the new consulting firm founded after McClure left the Senate.

Mike Hammond. This brilliant staffer most patiently explained some of the more esoteric activities in which he was involved with McClure and, even though he was wrung out from current tasking, always made himself available to answer what must have seemed to him inane questions.

Tom Hill. Let actions reveal character—that is the admonition that every writer has to keep tucked away in his subconscious. But how do you learn of the actions of a subject? The gift of remembering and telling of those actions is what I will remember most about Tom Hill.

Ruthie Johnson. I spent many hours with this "Mother Hen of North Idaho" staffer who served McClure during his entire twenty-four years in Congress. She, herself, is worthy of a book.

Other staffers, aides and interns who granted me an interview or consulted with me on specific McClure activities are due thanks. They are: *Bobbie Butler, David Coombes, Gary Ellsworth, Patty Wendstrom Franden, Paula Forney, Mike Field, Debbie Field, Susan Fagan, Jim Fields, Bill Fay, Shirley Goller, Jim Harris, Al Henderson, Dorothy Hanford, Deborah Hartwell, Dave Leroy, Bill Livingstone, Nancy Norell, H. D. Palmer, Phil Reberger,*

Diane Rolig, Orrie Sinclair, Pat Sullivan, Jim Streeter, Al and Helen Timothy, Linda Turner, and Valorie Watkins.

Prior to starting on this book I consulted with numerous folks who knew McClure and from whom I sought advice on what to include in his biography. Generous with their time and comments were: *Steve Ahrens, former Governor Phil Batt, Steve Crump, Roy Eiguren, Carolyn Erickson, Judy Felton, Steve Hartgen, Lindy High, Peter Johnson, Marc Johnson (who also helped me by arranging a joint interview with Cecil Andrus and Jim McClure), Randall Morgan, Ken McClure, Laird Noh, Kaye O'Riordan, Dorothy Reynolds, John Rosholt, former state senator and PUC Commissioner Perry Swisher, and Randy Stapilus*. Another person consulted was *Bill Hall*, former editor of *The Lewiston Morning Tribune,* whom, throughout the writing of the book, I could always count on, in person or in his writings, for a fair and balanced opinion from the liberal side of the issues McClure dealt with during his career.

During the years I worked on this biography, I spent many weeks in the McClure archives in the special collections department of the University of Idaho Library. I wish to thank all of those in that department and at the university who were of special assistance: *Dr. Terry Armstrong, former President Bob Hoover, Curator Terry Abraham, Director of Residences Michael Griffel, Professor Wilma Davis Woods, Librarian Lynn Baird*, and *Special Collections Administrator Anar Imin*. In addition, thanks are due the history department, especially *Nancy DeFoe*, for finding me graduate students, *Stacey Karn, Bob Bobier,* and *Ed Papenberg*, who spent many hours digging out documents that I needed.

While at the University of Idaho I was fortunate to have a long luncheon with *Dr. LeRoy Ashby*, Washington State University professor and senior author of the Frank Church biography, *Fighting the Odds*. Among his words of wisdom I especially took to heart was his confession and admonition: "I'm afraid that, to some extent, I had my academic colleagues in mind when I was writing that book. You are lucky; you are not an academic and you do not have that hanging over you. My advice is to write strictly for the reader. Try to make it interesting. Try to make it flow. If the reader keeps turning the pages and learns what they should about the Senator, you will have done your job."

Special thanks are also due Jim McClure's classmates and friends with whom he spent his growing-up and professional years in Payette, Idaho. They were a special pleasure to interview as they dredged up the nostalgic days when life was hard, but simple in their little Idaho city. They are *Dave Bivens, Jack Bowman, Don Borgholthaus, Charles Couper, Mary Meechan Davis, George Fiddler, Ike and Ken Frazier, Bill Glover, Bob Hanigan, Ellis Hallman, Bill Kosesan, Lucy Cobb Lingel, Warren McCain, Cliff and Shirley Massingill, Tobe Massingill, Ron Manser, Larry Monroe, Gilbert Norris,*

Harold Preston, Bill and Jean Peterson, Barbara Pence, Fred Rabinau, Helen Ross, Jeanette Rutan, Hudson and Shirley Shake, Verne Swanson, Gifford Shaffer, Oscar Stauff, Margaret Smith Watson, and Duane Welch.

Many others assisted me with interviews and research: *Harry Anderson, former governor and Secretary of the Interior Cecil Andrus, Miren Artiach, Tim Alden, Barbara Gregory, Tom Allison, John Amonson, Bart Brassey, Deborah Baker, John Brandt, Gloria Brown, Jim Brown, Stewart Brandborg, Janet Bahara, Dick Bieber, Dick Bingham, Jim Bruce, John Carley, Margaret Church, Edward Coffman, Pete Cenarrusa, Dale Costa, Hank Crowley, Linda Culver, former Congressman Hugh Carey, Mindy Cameron, Ellomae DeMond, Dorothy Dolby, Jim Davis, Louise Dunlop, Bud Davis, Gary Edwards, Mike Everett, former Congressman Marvin Esch, Brock Evans, Blanche Evans, former Ambassador Herman Eilts, Debbie Farnsworth, Pat Ford, former Speaker of the House Tom Foley, Dale Fisk, Scott Freehafer, Lauren Fins, Don Ferguson, Ed Fournier, Ron Force, Celia Gould, Billy Grammer, Kelly Trammell Gayman, Dave Graham, LuVern Gruessing, Sharon Hawkins, former Congressman Orval Hansen, Dolly Hartman, Gene Hyde, Al Henderson, Fred Hutchinson, Bruce Hickey, Dick Hughes, Bob Hooper, Kathryn Ineck, Peter Johnson, Berne Jensen, John Jordan, Rick Johnson, Jerry Johnson, former Senator Bennett Johnston, Dwight Jensen, Dick Kading, Wayne Kidwell, Bill Kizer, Al Kiser, Ralph Kizer, Ed Kennedy, Roderick Kagen, Logan Lanham, Glen Lockery, Dale LaVigne, Norm Logan, Perk Lyda, Charlie Leppert, Jim Lundquist, Larry LaRocco, Duane Miller, Dawn Mattmiller, Ed Merrick, Janet Moore, Cleora Murphy, Lee McElvain, former Congressman Lloyd Meeds, Joel Markel, Tim Mahoney, Ivar Nelson, Alice Nelson, Barbara Shissler Nosanau, Tim Olson, Billie Odberg, Bob Purcell, Marty Peterson, Susan Peterson, Allen Porter, J. T. Peterson, Watt Prather, Former State Senator Ray Rigby, Bob Robson, George Russell, Helen Ross, Gray Reynolds, P. T. Rathbone, Eric Redman, Louise Shadduck, former Senator Steve Symms, Kirk Sullivan, Jay Shelledy, Court Sims, Ken Snyder, Bill Sweet, Shelby Scates, Ben Strohbehn, Sarah Sheehy, Bill Schroder, Gus Schade, Doug Scott, Stan Sloss, Ed Sheets, former Congressman Fletcher Thompson, Roger Vincent, Former Representative Jerome Waldie, Sarah Wilson, Dennis Wheeler, Mike Wetherell, Bill Wulf, Duane Williams, Pete Wilson, Jim Wheeler, Paul Weyrich, Elizabeth Wasiutynski, Andy Wiessner, C. Robert Yost, Ben Ysursa, and Leslee Yaryan.*

And a special thank you to McClure family members: *Raymond McClure, Jean Parton, Marilyn McClure Roach, Ken and Sally McClure, and Dave McClure*, all of whom were eager to help me understand their brother/father/father-in-law.

Another special thank you to old friend *Lois Widell* who introduced me to GOOGLE several years ago. Many days while researching and writing this book I was on GOOGLE at least five or six times. I cannot imagine taking on a project this size without the help of this online wonder. And I should not leave out the young computer guru who bailed me out of all kinds of technical problems with my software. Thanks, Andrew Hall.

One other person needs to be acknowledged. *Chris Carlson*, journalist, long-time aide to former Governor and Secretary of the Interior Cecil Andrus, and founder of the Gallatin Group, became interested in this project after our families shared a campfire during a pack trip into the White Clouds. Since then, Chris has consulted with me on several issues with which he was involved with McClure, and he has read every page of the manuscript and given me much valuable criticism and encouragement.

Finally, the two people to which this book is dedicated should also be given thanks here.

My oldest son, William M. Smallwood, has, over the past twenty-five years been my most faithful critic and adviser, and I always look forward to his input even when we disagree. When I was doing the pre-research interviews, he said something to the effect: "What I would like to know when I read that book is what it is like for a man who has grown up and lived his life in Payette, Idaho to go to Washington, D.C. and take on the job of being a congressman and senator. What were his challenges? What were his frustrations? What were his disappointments? It is the human side of his story that will interest me. That advice lingered in my thoughts, particularly when I was winnowing the mountains of material that could realistically be included in the biography without burying the reader. Yes, I wanted the reader to understand how the Sawtooth National Recreation Area became a reality. Yes, I wanted the reader to understand the significance of the Strategic Petroleum Reserve. And, yes, I wanted every reader to appreciate McClure's prescience relative to our nation's energy future. But, always, I was questioning whether I was also following my son's advice. *Am I telling the human side of the McClure story?*

Finally, I want to thank my wife, Patricia, who stood by me patiently during the nearly six years it took to complete this work, and always with a critical eye on the copy. Thank you, wife of thirty-three years, for sustaining me in every way.

WLS

Senator Jim McClure

Prologue

The Wild Man

Before McClure there was a wild man running loose in the First Congressional District. No history of Jim McClure would be complete without the story of the legendary character who preceded him. This is his story.

During World War II he was bored in the Marine Corps and volunteered for "extreme, extra-hazardous overseas duty"[1] with the U.S. Navy. After intensive frogman-type training, he parachuted into China as one of Admiral Milton "Merry" Miles' guerrillas, swam out into Amoy Harbor at night, and with one of his recruited Chinese guerillas, placed explosives all the way around a Japanese ship at anchor, then sat naked on the shore and blew the charges. The claim was made that this was the most totally destroyed Japanese ship during World War II and he won a Silver Star for that effort.

Back home in Kellogg, Idaho, in a Studebaker Avanti, he set a speed record on the winding road between Kellogg and Coeur d' Alene—a record that has probably never been broken.[2]

At night, coming from Missoula, Montana, he flew his Piper Tri-Pacer into a snowstorm, and with no blind-flying instruments and no training to fly in such conditions, tried to climb out of it and crashed into the rising terrain. He severed both Achilles tendons, lost a toe, but bought another airplane as soon as he was out of the hospital.[3]

One night he took the manager of his insurance agency in Kellogg on a wild 80 and 90 miles per hour ride down the winding, mountainous road to Boise, after which the manager refused to ever get in a car with him again.[4]

One afternoon in Grangeville he jumped out of a car, got directly into his Piper Comanche, started it, gunned it, and took off from the taxiway.[5]

Former Idaho Attorney General and close friend, Bob Robson, called him a wild man.

Who was this wild man?

John Mattmiller was his name. He was six feet tall, lean and muscular and, said Bob Robson, ". . .had the brightest blue eyes and darkest skin I ever saw on a white man. He was also smarter than hell."[6]

And in April, 1964 John Mattmiller was unhappy with his country.

In Washington, D.C., after five months in his presidency, Lyndon B. Johnson was using the nation's emotional trauma and guilt feelings over John F. Kennedy's tragic assassination as a hammer to drive massive new federal programs through Congress. Conservatives, led by presidential candidate Barry Goldwater, seemed to be helpless within the beltway of Washington in slowing the momentum building toward Lyndon Johnson's vision of a "Great Society," but they were generating outrage among concerned citizens in the hinterlands, particularly in the South and West. Thousands of new conservatives, inspired by Goldwater's public speeches railing against expansion of the federal government, were cropping up in these regions. John Mattmiller and his wife, Dawn, were two of them and they found soul mates like themselves in the Young Republican Club in their hometown of Kellogg, the county seat of Shoshone County.

Actually, Dawn Mattmiller was more active with the Young Republicans than her husband, because he was heavily involved with his insurance, real estate and development business and was also serving as a member of the Idaho State Real Estate Commission. However, one day, "out of the blue," John asked his wife what she thought of his running for Congress in Idaho's First District. He said, "I'm only one person, but maybe I can do something back there.

"I told him that the decision was entirely up to him—that I would go along with whatever he decided. After a few days, when he finally decided to do it, we were both enthusiastic. I was as gung ho as he was."[7]

Dawn had also attended meetings with the Young Republicans in the neighboring city of Coeur d' Alene and had met a young man named Dick Bieber who had started the club and who was as much or more passionate and intense as her husband. Now, as she and John discussed their needs for putting together a congressional campaign, she brought up Bieber's name as someone who might help them—a conversation that led to a dinner invitation to Bieber and his wife.

Dick Bieber had immigrated to Coeur d' Alene from Sioux City, Iowa via the U.S. Army and Fairchild Air Force Base in nearby Spokane, Washington. He had met and married his wife, Suzy, while she was in nurse training at Deaconess Hospital in Spokane. Now, in April 1964, after finishing college and majoring in hotel management, he was working for a resort owner in Coeur d' Alene and Suzy was working for a doctor who just happened to be Kootenai County chairman of the Republican Party. Dick and Suzie accepted the dinner invitation to the Mattmiller house in Kellogg even though they had not the slightest idea why they were invited.

"I think we were just finishing dinner when John said to me, 'Dick, I want to run for Congress in the First District if you'll be my campaign manager.' That really surprised me because I didn't have any qualifications for that kind of job. I told him that I'd never run a campaign before and he

John Mattmiller

quickly replied, 'I've never run for Congress before.'"[8]

Bieber and his wife went home and thought about the offer "for a day or two" and both decided that his career in hotel management could wait. With Lyndon B. Johnson at the helm the country was going to hell. It would be just one little battle in a war, but the Biebers were ready to fight. Suzy would continue to contribute her income as a nurse and Bieber would earn a token salary of $400 a month—money Mattmiller raised by selling an uncirculated collection of silver trade dollars the U.S. government had sent to China during the war—a collection he had somehow obtained while he had served in Chiang Kai-shek's guerilla army.

Bieber's first task was to assess his candidate's assets and liabilities. And, because his liabilities were far greater than his assets, those came to mind first. John Mattmiller was a complete unknown outside Shoshone County, except among realtors who knew him because of his position on the Idaho Real Estate Commission. Moreover, he had no political experience of any kind and no ideas on how a candidate should approach the voters of his district. Then there was the district itself, which at that time consisted of the northern and westernmost counties of Idaho—mostly the tall part of the "L" if the state's geography can be generously compared to that letter of the alphabet. From the Canadian border southward, with the exception of a few counties in the southern part of the district, the First District of Idaho was traditionally Democratic. In the predominantly mountainous counties, lumbering was the major industry and the loggers and lumber-mill workers were heavily attracted to the Democratic Party. In Mattmiller's Shoshone County, known as the "Silver Valley," there were several thousand unionized miners and smelter workers who were considered a certain block of Democratic votes. In mid-state, in Nez Perce County, the huge pulp mill near Lewiston employed thousands more unionized workers whose Democratic votes were also taken for granted. Clearly, the debit side of the ledger looked like heavy red ink when it was assessed by Bieber.

On the asset side, Bieber had a candidate who was "very very intelligent"[9] and who had committed himself to work twenty-four hours a day if that was necessary. He also had an airplane, which he was willing to fly any time of the day or night and anywhere in his district where he could meet "four or five people or four or five hundred."[10]

Bieber recalls that neither he nor Mattmiller spent any serious time trying to analyze their opponent. Of course, they knew that the incumbent Congressman, Compton White, Jr., was the son of Compton White who had served as First District congressman from 1932 to 1946 and again from 1948 to 1952. Both were considered to be traditional Western Democrats—more conservative than the Democratic mainstream, and mainly interested in capturing federal dollars for conservation and reclamation measures as well as support for the mining and lumbering industries of their district. However, Junior's current politics were particularly offensive to both Mattmiller and Bieber because he was unashamedly marketing himself as a confident of the president—LBJ had been friends with his father—and was a consistent supporter of LBJ's liberal legislation.

Clearly, Bieber had a lot of work to do and not much time to do it. He immediately started on his first task, which was to travel through the district and find good Republicans who would chair Mattmiller committees in each of the counties, and who would advise him on ways that he could get exposure for his candidate. As he proceeded with this task he found willing supporters who firmed his belief that his candidate would be the only Republican seeking the nomination. According to Bieber, his candidate was considered to be a "sacrificial lamb" because of the perceived strength of the Democrats in general and the incumbent in particular. If Mattmiller wanted to make that sacrifice, the Republican stalwarts in the counties would do what they could for him.

In most cases that did not mean they could raise money for him. The "big money" for Republican causes had traditionally been raised in the Boise area, but Ada County was in the Second Congressional District. And besides, with one exception, Mattmiller was a complete unknown among the traditional supporters of Republican candidates. The exception was realtor and investor, Don Day, a well-known and respected Boise Republican. Day was serving on the Idaho Real Estate Commission with Mattmiller and was enthusiastic about his candidacy.

No opposition rose against Mattmiller for the nomination and he obtained 38 percent of the total votes cast in the August 4, 1964 nominating election. Said Bieber, when asked about the dismal showing, "I don't think we ever even talked about the vote. We expected about a 60/40 split—that was tradition in that district. The main thing we accomplished that summer was to eliminate competitors in our party and avoid a battle [for the nomination]."[11]

Then how did either the candidate or his manager ever hope to win an election in the First District?

Both men were churning with energy and determination and Bieber had a conviction, which, almost forty years later, he still expressed with passion. "We had two things going for us. First, I had a candidate who was willing to get out and meet people and I felt that was the most important thing he could do. Second, we had an opponent who was both lazy and complacent. Comp would go into a town and have a drink at the bar, then dinner with the Democrat bigwigs, but he wouldn't go out and meet the people. He was well known in the district because of his father; he was in a strongly Democratic district; and he was an incumbent with ties to the president. Gracie Pfost, his predecessor, was all over the district—a real worker—she really got out and met people. I think Comp felt he didn't need to do that. Our strategy was simply to outwork him."[12]

Then Bieber had a fortuitous discussion with Bill Kirsch, the husband of a nurse who worked with Bieber's wife, Suzy. While Bieber was lamenting his problems getting exposure for his candidate, Kirsch, who was in the business of promoting country/western bands, proposed a series of Grand Ole Opry-type shows throughout the district—shows where Mattmiller could be introduced. Bieber liked the idea instantly and asked Kirsch to come up with a plan. Shortly afterward, Kirsch had a genuine Grand Ole Opry star as a headliner and a local country/western band to accompany him. The Mattmiller campaign was now about to go into high gear.

The star, Billy Grammer, had fond reminiscences of that campaign:

> *"One day I got this call from Bill Kirsch and he said he needed a Grand Ole Opry star to go around Idaho and do shows to give this political candidate—a good man, he said—the exposure he needed. He said he could pay me a nominal fee—nothing like I got on the road—and I told him that it sounded interesting and that I believed I would do it. I wanted the opportunity to see Idaho and I'll tell you, after those shows, I was a convert. I was an avid hunter and fisherman and if I were to be born again, I'd be born in Idaho."*[13]

They started in Bonners Ferry, twenty-eight miles from the Canadian border, in the gym of the high school, which was packed with farmers and loggers—folks who had never had a chance to see a big-name entertainer. Grammer, who was one of the most accomplished guitarists in the business and who played lead for Patsy Cline, sang some of his current hits such as *Detroit City* and *Bonaparte's Retreat*, but the real crowd-pleaser began with the refrain, ". . .*I've laid around and played around this old town too long. . .*"—words from the song that first catapulted Grammer to fame.

"People loved it," said Bieber, "and at the intermission, Billy would introduce John and his family and John would say, 'Now don't worry, I'm not going to give you a political speech. I'm Johnny Mattmiller and I'm running for Congress and all I want is a chance to meet you. I appreciate you coming and after the show, I'll be in the back of the gym and I would like to shake your hand.' That was the total of his speech, and then the show would resume. We also handed out programs—nice programs with information about the star and the band, and one page about John and his wife. We knew they would keep them for the souvenir value and, of course, they would also have something about John."[14]

Down the state they went, drawing huge, enthusiastic crowds at every one of the shows. At Orofino a local fishing guide named Perk Lyda, who later took Grammer fishing for steelhead trout, said that, ". . .tons and tons of people turned out for those shows and they absolutely persuaded people [to vote for Mattmiller]. He really persuaded me. I liked John. He was friendly. He was intelligent. He was not a country hick."[15]

The momentum toward Mattmiller was building. Bieber sensed that and so did the candidate as the crowds grew more and more enthusiastic. And, as they moved south into the agricultural region of the state and traditional Republican territory, their hope grew. Then, they hit a speed bump. In Canyon County, which was a Republican stronghold, the central committee scheduled a speech by the California Governor, Goodwin Knight, on the same evening as the Billy Grammer concert. "That hurt us a lot," said Bieber. "We were expecting a real strong showing in Canyon County to offset our losses in the north. I'm still mad at them over that."[16]

When the concerts were over, both Mattmiller and Bieber were running on adrenaline. "Bieber was so intense," said Billy Grammer, "that when we were in the Hotel Boise (after finishing one of the concerts), Bill Kirsch and I were jumping up and down on the bed and singing, trying to get his attention, and Herman (Grammer's nickname for Bieber) just sat there in his chair shuffling his papers over and over. He didn't even know what we were doing. His mind was a million miles away."[i 17]

The general election was held November 3 and when the votes were counted, practically everybody but Mattmiller and Bieber was surprised. Mattmiller lost by a scant 3,735 votes and garnered 48.3 percent of the total vote. They did not celebrate, of course, but the closeness of the election and the might-have-dones, including the Canyon County fiasco, energized the two men and set them planning for the next election two years down the road.

And then they got some help—real help. Not only were the rank-and-file Republicans of the state itching to help Mattmiller take on Compton White, Jr. in the next election, but the state legislature, itself, came through with a gift of great significance. Ada County (Boise), Idaho's most populous county and one that voted overwhelmingly for Goldwater in the 1964 general election, was moved into the First Congressional District as the result of the one-man, one-vote court-ordered redistricting by the legislature. And, since Goldwater out-polled Lyndon B. Johnson by almost 6,000 votes in the county, and Mattmiller lost by less than 4,000 votes, it was reasonable to expect that, things being equal through the rest of the district, Ada County could put Mattmiller over the top in the 1966 election.

Dick Bieber moved to Boise after the election and began working for the legislature. And, throughout all of 1965, he and Mattmiller stayed in touch, planning the next campaign. Both were enthusiastic, but Bieber especially. No longer did he have an unknown candidate. His sacrificial lamb had turned into a hard-charging elephant ready to trample LBJ's acolyte into the dust of the Great Society. And, he would have money this time around. Bieber knew who the Boise fat cats were now and he was not going to be bashful when it came time to tap them.

Mattmiller had also been recognized by the National Republican Congressional Campaign Committee and in late January, 1965, he was invited to Washington, D.C. for a one-week seminar with the campaign professionals. When he returned to Boise (he had flown down from Kellogg in his Piper Comanche), he stayed over with Don Day, his realtor friend and the next evening Bieber organized a strategy meeting held at the Day Realty office. His goal was to get a finance committee organized early and during the meeting, he was able to convince Don Day to chair such a committee. Bieber felt that was a big step forward. "Donnie Day knew the people with the money and how to approach them," said Bieber. "I didn't."[18]

The meeting also produced the first discord between the candidate and his campaign manager. Mattmiller had always been passionately opposed to Communism, probably because of his exposure to the Chinese Communists during World War II. Indeed, one of his long-term goals, according to Bieber, was to win a congressional seat, hold it for a term or two, then run against incumbent Senator Frank Church, who Mattmiller believed was a bedrock Socialist. Thus, when the subject of the now-raging Vietnam War somehow came up during the strategy meeting, Mattmiller began explaining why he should personally visit Vietnam and see for himself what the Communists were doing there. Then, said Bieber:

> *John drove me home about one o'clock in the morning and the discussion continued in the car. And when I saw that he was serious—and when John was serious, you knew it was really going to happen—I told him he was crazy—that he should stay here and tend to the home fires. John wasn't very forgiving and we exchanged words. Finally, as we pulled up in front of my house, I told him that if he was going to leave and go to Vietnam, he could get himself a new campaign manager. He didn't reply but he didn't blow his cork.*
>
> *The next morning about five-thirty or six o'clock there is John at the door. Rarely did he smile or chuckle, but that is what he was doing. He said, "Pack your bag and fly to Kellogg with me today. I'm sorry about last night." I said, "John, when I got home last night,*

> *I decided to forget about the blowup, but, I'm not going to Kellogg with you today. You've been gone for eight days and you're going to be tied up with your business. Were not going to have time to do anything up there and my time would be better spent down here. I need to go to Caldwell and see Bake Young* [a potential contributor] *and ride herd on this new committee. You're coming back down here in two or three days* [to fly on to Mexico with a group of pilots] *and we can do some work then." He said, "No, come ride along with me; we can talk in the plane." I said,"No, John I'm not going. It'll work better for us to get together when you get back down." Finally, he said, "Well, at least go out to the plane with me,"and I did.*
>
> *We were having breakfast in the airport restaurant and who walks in but Donnie Day with another fellow with him. He introduces a man named Lloyd* [William H. Lloyd] *to us and asks John if he could take him along—he was a realtor working for Donnie and was working on a land exchange in northern Idaho. Donnie said, "He can work up there for a couple of days and ride back down to Boise with you." John agreed, then left to check the weather with the FAA—it was kind of soupy looking that morning. When he came back, I walked out to the plane with them. John did his inspection; then they got in and I closed the door.*[19]

John Mattmiller flew to Kellogg that morning and found it obscured with fog. He called on the unicom radio and Duane Williams, a pilot/mechanic answered his call. Said Williams, "He asked how it looked down here and I told him that looking up through the fog I could see an outline of the sun which meant that it was a thin layer and about to burn off. I told him, 'If you just wait around for fifteen or so minutes I think it will burn off and you can get in.' That's the last I said. Sometime—not too long after that—the lights flickered and I didn't think anything about it at the time. It was just a brief interruption in the power flow."[20]

Kellogg was notorious for fog because the particulate matter spewing from its silver and lead smelter served as condensation particles for the tiny droplets of water. Mattmiller knew this and flew east up the valley where he expected to run out of the fog. He either found a clear area or saw a hole in the undercast. In either event he descended to a very low altitude and headed back toward the west. About four and one-half miles from touchdown on runway 25 at the Kellogg airport, and at an estimated 150 feet of altitude, John Mattmiller hit the unmarked main power line that ran up Big Creek to the Sunshine Mine. The collision somehow jammed an aileron and the Comanche rolled over and nosed into the ground. Both men were killed instantly.

> DICK BIEBER ON THE WILD MAN
>
> *His friend, Bob Robson, confided to me that he told John the only way he would agree to help him in his campaign was for him to park his Studebaker Avanti in the garage and pledge that he wouldn't drive it—that he had to agree to leave his car keys at home. . .*
>
> *I remember one night at the Cascade airport—it was after one of the Grand Ole Opry concerts—there were no lights at the airport and John wanted to take off. So we took a few cars out to the airport and put two facing each other about a third of the way up* [the runway] *and another at the end and he took off in the dark. . .*
>
> *I flew all over with John and I'm remembering some of the ungodliest weather we got into. . .I remember one time we were in a canyon and there was fog* [clouds] *and it just kept pushing us closer and closer to the ground and finally John had to fly into the fog and he wasn't even cleared for instruments. John was a wild man—he didn't have a death wish; I don't think he ever thought he would get killed. . .*

John Mattmiller died on Wednesday, February 2, 1966. On the following Saturday, after the funeral, a group of Mattmiller's supporters were gathered at his home. Dick Bieber, feeling like he was "shell shocked" and deeply depressed over the tragic loss of his close friend, decided that he had one final task to accomplish. Moving about the house he asked "fourteen or fifteen" of Mattmiller's closest supporters—including "several county chairmen" to meet with him in one of the bathrooms of the house. "When I got them all in there—it wasn't too crowded; it was a big bathroom—I said, 'Okay, what do you think we should do? Let's just hear it. The best thing is if we could stick together and get one person we could all support and elect a Republican from the First District.' Dawn's name came up but she couldn't be the candidate because she had two girls to raise and she now had to run John's business. Then my name was brought up and I could see that a decision semi-rested on my shoulders and they wanted to hear what I thought. I told them I didn't want to run but that there was one man in the district I could enthusiastically support. After some more discussion, they agreed with me and that ended the meeting. I then went to talk with Dawn."[21]

Without disclosing the results of the meeting just concluded, Bieber went to the widow and asked her whom she could support as a replacement candidate for her husband. Dawn Mattmiller's thoughts turned back to the late 1940s when one of her fellow students at the University of Idaho, a handsome young man with bright blue eyes and who was a "deep thinker," gave her a ride to southern Idaho on the way to her home in Rupert. She had developed a respect for this young man and had followed his career as an attorney, state senator, and, lastly, as a dedicated county chairman for her late husband. Now, with Bieber's question before her, she did not hesitate with her answer. "I think we should support Jim McClure"[22] Then Bieber told her of the recent meeting and the decision of that group. Bieber and John Mattmiller's close supporters were in total agreement with Dawn Mattmiller: Jim McClure was the man they wanted to see elected as the next congressman of Idaho's First Congressional District.

Prologue Notes

i When Bieber was told of Grammer's comment, he growled, "That nonsense wasn't getting Mattmiller any votes. I was only worried about getting votes."

Chapter 1

The McClures

On April 1, 1865, General Ulysses S. Grant, Union Army commander, had just spent 293 miserable, frustrating days outside Petersburg, Virginia where 40,000 of his soldiers had fallen in failed attacks against the Confederates barricaded in that city. The siege had begun in the late summer of 1864 and had continued through March 1865. Armchair generals throughout the north were shaking their heads in disgust at Grant's failure, and President Abraham Lincoln himself had harbored doubts that he would be reelected the past November. What probably saved him was the good news coming in from the far South. General Sherman had captured Atlanta, marauded his way to Savannah, Georgia and the sea, and had burned out the heartland of the Confederacy as he went.

Sherman's victories had given hope to the war-weary Union. Now, if only Grant and the Army of the Potomac would finally take care of General Robert E. Lee and his Army of Northern Virginia now barricaded inside Petersburg, the damned bloody war would soon be over. What the armchair generals could not understand was why Grant did not move his lines south and then west, a movement that would enable him to encircle Petersburg and cut off the railroad supplying General Lee's army from the south. Those on the sidelines were asking: Why doesn't Grant just surround Lee? He far outnumbers Lee in manpower and guns. Why doesn't he just tighten the damned noose and strangle the traitors? That's all that needs to be done. Starve Lee out if nothing else.

President Lincoln, General Grant, and every other Union general knew that such an encircling movement would mean the end of General Robert E. Lee's army. But, they had a problem beyond their control. It had rained hard during the fall months and it had continued to pour throughout the winter. So how was the Army to move on the unpaved roads? Wagon wheels, thin and hard, became buried when they set out on such roads. Likewise, with the thin, hard wheels of the heavy cannons and caissons. Then there were the thousands of horses that were needed to pull the wagons, cannons, and caissons plus the horses needed by Grant's cavalry divisions. When they began to move down a wet, sandy loam road, the churning action of their hooves soon created a quicksand-like porridge that literally sucked the animals into

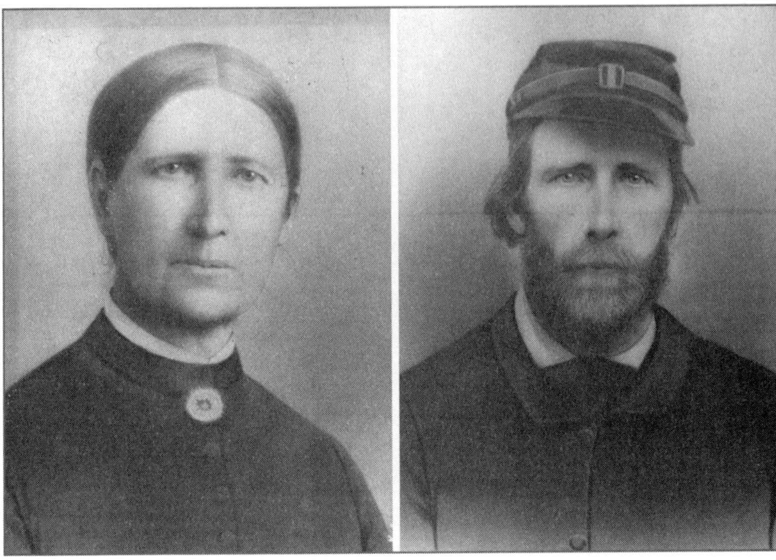

Courtesy McClure family

Catharine Gamble McClure was left to raise six children on her own after her husband, Andrew Robertson McClure, died of wounds received in one of the final battles of the Civil War. Their last child, Andrew Robertson McClure, Jr., born three month's before his father's death, would become the grandfather of Jim McClure.

the earth. So Grant's army was stalled because there was no way he could move it.

But time was on Grant's side and it was running out for Lee. Toward the end of March the roads were starting to dry and when they did, Lee knew that it was just a matter of time before the overwhelming numbers of Federal infantry and cavalry would crush him. On March 25, Lee attacked what he considered to be a weak point in the Federal line, hoping to get into the rear, destroy supplies, and cause Grant to bring reinforcements from the south of his line—the direction from which he felt threatened. But, the assault was stopped, several thousand Confederates were captured, and Grant, thinking that Lee had stripped his lines to the south for his assault, started 30,000 of his men moving in that direction under the command of General Phil Sheridan. By the evening of April first, one whole division of Confederates had been pulverized and over 3,000 prisoners had been taken. When Grant heard that, he ordered an immediate assault all along the lines for the following morning.

The Confederates held against a vicious onslaught with artillery, but Lee knew that he was on borrowed time and ordered an evacuation of his lines the next evening. His plan was to escape south and link up with General Joe Johnston who had another Confederate army trying to stop Sherman who was moving up through North Carolina. It was a desperate plan, but Lee's only hope. The Federal troops assaulted Petersburg the next morning but found a deserted city. Lee had pulled off the evacuation and was now heading south and west through the Virginia countryside, hoping to find a train of food and forage he had ordered for his men and horses. But, his plans were cruelly dashed. The Federals had captured his train. Men, half starved while they were barricaded in Petersburg, had to keep marching when they had had nothing at all to eat for two days. Horses, like skeletons and barely able to walk in the muddy roads, just dropped in their harnesses and died.

And the Federals were marching with renewed energy on roads corduroyed with fallen timbers and even with captured Confederate muskets.[1] They knew they were close to closing the trap on the Army that had caused them so much misery. They knew that there was no point in conserving energy now; it was either trap the old gray fox and his Army now or the war would just keep going on forever, especially if Lee and his troops decided to go west into the mountains and become an irregular guerrilla force. And even when the Union commanders ordered a night march on top of a day's best effort, there was little complaining or malingering. The boys in blue sensed that it was finally about over and no exertion was too much for them. "Stretch those legs out, boys. We've got to trap those damned Rebs before they can get away. That's the only way we're ever gonna get home."

One of the boys in blue who was stretching his legs out in early April was named Andrew Robertson McClure. Robertson, as he was known by those close to him (his father had been named Andrew), was the half-owner of a 130-acre farm in Franklin County, Pennsylvania near the town of Doylesburg. Six months earlier he had been living on that farm with his pregnant wife, Catharine, and their five children.[i] The farm was along Conococheague Creek which formed the two-mile wide Pass Valley at the base of the Tuscarora Mountains in the south-central part of the state.[2] However, the Union was desperate for men to replace the thousands of casualties experienced during the past two bloody years of conflict and despite the fact that Robertson McClure was 37 years old and sole supporter of a family of six—soon to be seven—totally dependent upon his efforts on the farm, he was drafted and ordered to report to the 82nd Pennsylvania Regiment on November 28, 1864. And, at the time, he must have felt there was bitter irony in the fact that the regiment proudly called itself the "82nd Pennsylvania Volunteers."

By March 9, 1865, Robertson's regiment was attached to the First Division, Sixth Corps under General Horatio G. Wright, which was holding down a sector of the Union line outside Petersburg. Robertson wrote to his wife on that day (original spelling retained):

> *Dear Wife I again seat myself to rite you a few lines to let you no that I am well at present and I hope that those few lines may you enjoying the same blessing. . .I have got along this far a great deal better than I expected when I left home. I do not no how the balance of the time*

go but I hope that I may not have any fighting to do. I have had fine easy time since I came here. . .it is likely that we may stay here for some time yet if the wedther keeps wet it will keep us here as there will be no move made as long as the roads are bad and it rains every other day or so it is raining like forty now while I write. . .
. . .I know that you have purty hard getting a lone which is a great dissatisfaction to me. . .but we will have to do the best we can and trust to an all mighty providence that this unjust war may soon be over and that we may have the unspeakable pleasure of meeting again in peace and joy and not have the dread of war on our mind more. . .your ever true and affectionate husband or til death.

Andrew R. McClure [3]

General Robert E. Lee ordered the evacuation of Richmond at the same time he pulled his troops out of Petersburg. Moving south and west along the Appomattox River he knew he was in a desperate race and that if he lost, he would stand no chance in head-to-head combat with the superior Union forces coming after him. But, he was losing the race. Not only were his men starving, his wagon trains were being continually harassed by General Phil Sheridan's cavalry. And the roadside where his troops marched was littered with discarded muskets abandoned by men so weak they could barely walk.

Then, on April 6, after President Lincoln had made a walking tour of Richmond and the citizens of Washington, D.C. were recovering from the greatest celebration in their history[4], with headlines blaring: "HAIL COLUMBIA!!! HALLELUJAH!!! RICHMOND OURS!!!", Lee's troops were to stumble into a debacle that became known thereafter as the "Black Thursday of the Confederacy."

Two of General Longstreet's divisions were intercepted by General Sheridan's cavalry and infantry from the Third and Fourth Corps between two forks of Saylor's Creek near their confluence with the Appomattox. The division commanded by General Anderson lost over 3,000 killed, wounded, or captured although General Anderson and some of his senior officers managed to escape. The commander of the second division, General Richard Ewell, was not so lucky. Surrounded by infantrymen of Robertson McClure's Fourth Corps, he and most of his troops surrendered to make the Battle of Saylor's Creek the worst debacle of the Civil War. It was also the last battle, for three days later, Lee, now completely encircled and having earlier vetoed the advice of some of his commanders to escape in small groups and continue the war as guerilla bands, agreed to surrender to General U. S. Grant at Appomattox Court House. Thus, on April 9, the bloodiest war in American history was near its end.[ii]

But Private Andrew Robertson McClure was not able to celebrate the great Union victory. Sometime in the late afternoon of April 6, probably on a flat area on the eastern bank of Saylor's Creek, he received a gunshot wound in his right ankle—a wound that shattered the bones. He probably laid in great agony where he fell because remnants of Confederate units were still fighting at nightfall. And his problem was not only the pain of his wound. During the night, blowing rain, then snow, fell on the battlefield and the temperature dropped to near freezing. At least by the next day, he was probably taken by stretcher to a field hospital, and by April 12 we know that he arrived at the City Point Hospital just northeast of Petersburg. There it was determined that he had a compound fracture of the ankle and that amputation was the only way to save his life. He was transported to the General Hospital in Annapolis, Maryland and on April 17, his right leg was amputated below the knee. A letter to Catharine McClure from his nurse, Mrs. Mary A. Fay, tells what happened after that.

> *Mrs. Catherine McClure*
> *My Dear Madam*
>
> *Among the painful duties incumbent on those women who devote themselves to the care of our sick and wounded soldiers there is one from which the heart shrinks and the trembling hand almost refuses its office it is to bear to the family at home the sad tidings of bereavement to tell a loving anxious wife that the object of her affections will return to her no more that her children are fatherless. Can you dear friend bear this message which comes to you from a strangers hand. It is hard enough as I know by my own experience when death comes to the home and we may take the last look of affection and shed out tears over the sod which covers our dead from our sight. But unspeakably more bitter is the anguish when we may not have their last solace.*
>
> *Dear friend may the loving Father enfold you in his arms and bear you up in this your hour of agony. May he send you great strength and peace and that resignation which is due to the will of him who doth all things well. I will try to tell you of your husband now no more a suffering creature of earth, but rejoicing in the presence of God. I do not know how recently you have heard from him by letter, though I remember having directed one for him not very long ago. His wound was doing extremely well and no danger was apprehended in his case. His appetite was so good that in serving the diet I sent him double rations. But about ten days ago diarrhea set in with vomiting which could not be checked by medicine. At this time orders were received to send all patients who could be moved from St. Johns* [Annapolis, Maryland] *to Hicks Hospital Baltimore preparatory to breaking up our hospital. All but a few badly wounded men were sent on Wednesday June 28th by boat. I felt anxious about your husband and saw his surgeons and requested that he might be*

left till he was better but he said that he thought the change of air would be beneficial to him. Not yet satisfied, I went to the Surgeon in charge who told me that it was quite best for him to go. He would be carried on a stretcher to the boat without fatigue and the sea air might work a favorable change. He left therefore on that day with most of my other patients. Yesterday on my way home I decided to stop a day in Baltimore for the purpose of going to the hospital and seeing the friends so long the object of my care. As I entered the ward there were calls from one bed and another in joyful accent Mrs Fay - Mrs Fay but one place was vacant, one head did not turn upon the pillow and I missed the quiet smile which I always expected when I came to the bedside of your husband. And then I learned that he had died a few hours before at 4 o'clock in the morning of July 3rd. I asked to be taken to the place where he had been carried and saw that. . .[remainder of letter lost][5]

The remains of Private Andrew Robertson McClure were buried in plot number 831 in the Loudon Park National Cemetery in Baltimore, Maryland. According to one authority on Civil War medicine, the most likely agent that caused his death was water contaminated by *Shigella dysenteria* or *Entamoeba histolytica*.[6]

Meanwhile, back on the farm, on May 14, the sixth child was born to the McClure family. It was a boy and he was given his father's name: Andrew Robertson McClure. This boy, who in less than two months would be fatherless, was destined to be the grandfather who would play a major role in the development of a future United States senator.

Catharine McClure, with six children to feed and clothe, was destitute and probably survived on a day-to-day basis on the charity of her neighbors and relatives. (Her family, the Gambles, still lived in the valley.) The United States Congress had made a widows and orphans pension available—twelve dollars a month for a widow; two dollars a month for each child—but Catharine was not receiving it. First, there was a problem with her marriage. It was not recorded anywhere and the minister who had conducted the ceremony in his parsonage had disappeared. In addition, she had no evidence that she had lost her husband—the letter that Nurse Fay had written had vanished into some relative's hands. Slowly, with the help of a local judge and an attorney in Chambersburg, she was able to locate a witness to her wedding ceremony and obtain from the United States Surgeon General an account of her husband's combat wounding, his amputation surgery, mode of death, and place of interrment, which, in 1868, finally enabled her to claim her pension. Sometime before that, or perhaps after she obtained her first income from the pension, she left the farm and on an 1868 plat of the village, she is shown living in one of the houses along the main street of Doylesburg.[7]

The state of Pennsylvania also aided her plight. After the war, the state legislature established Soldiers Orphan Schools which the McClure children were entitled to attend—boarding schools where the children were housed, fed, clothed, and educated until age 16. Records show that the two oldest girls, Margaret and Nancy, were admitted to the White Hall School at Camp Hill, three miles west of Harrisburg, on September 4, 1867. At the same time the fourth child, James, was admitted to the Andersonburg School in Sherman's Valley, also west of Harrisburg. There is no record of the third child, Amanda, attending a boarding school and the two youngest, Rebecca and Andrew, ages four and two, were too young to leave their mother.[8]

About fifteen years later the widow Catharine and her six children left Pennsylvania, bound for Rich Hill, a new boom town in western Missouri about seventy miles south of Kansas City and fourteen miles from the Kansas border. Rich Hill was a joint venture between the Missouri Pacific Railroad and its subsidiary, The Rich Hill Coal Mining Company. In 1880 the town site was platted by the joint venture and in the census of that year it had zero population. One year later there were probably 4,000 residents in the town and in three or four years there were several thousand more living in settlements outside the town. Right after Rich Hill was settled, there was a need for a mayor and other elected officials, but there were no citizens of the community who met the necessary time-in-residence requirement. To solve the problem, the state legislature in Jefferson City was petitioned on behalf of the town and it required special legislation to enable a legal election to be held.

It is not known how the McClure family learned about the new boom town, but according to Randy Bell, author of the local history, *The Town That Coal Built*, "The railroad and coal companies did a lot of advertising for miners and there was a lot of hype that Rich Hill would soon be the nation's largest city west of the Mississippi. It didn't work out that way, of course. The major mines began to close down about twenty years later."[9]

The McClure family settled in Carbon Center, a settlement about four miles from Rich Hill that was near one of the largest mines. It is not known whether James ever worked in one of the deep-shaft mines, but Andrew, known in the family as "Rob," later told his grandsons that he had never done that kind of work. All of the McClures met and married locals, and, except for Rob, they raised their families in the area and are buried, along with their mother, in local cemeteries. Rob, who for a time worked in a lumberyard and for a rancher near Woodward, Oklahoma, married Daisy Goodman on January 1, 1890. This union produced a daughter, Mary Belle McClure—ever after known as Mamie—who was born November 13, 1890, and a son, William Robertson McClure—known as Will—born October 11, 1893. Sometime later, Daisy contracted malaria, a common disease in that era, and it left her a semi-invalid. Her condition was so bad, in fact, that her

Courtesy McClure family

Robert and Daisy McClure with children Willie and Mamie.

doctor suggested that if she wanted to continue living, the family should move to a better climate.

Rich Hill, by 1907 or 1908 when Rob and his family were thinking of leaving, was a depressed area and a lot of residents had already moved on to more prosperous locations. The Kidwells, who were friends of Rob and Daisy and who would later have an Idaho Attorney General and State Supreme Court Judge in their heritage, had settled in Council, Idaho and had reported back to Missouri that there were abundant opportunities in their new state. In addition, some of Daisy's relatives were now living near Kuna, Idaho, just south of Boise, and the McClures probably received favorable reports on Idaho from them. These reports, and probably others like them, proved persuasive. In 1908 the McClure family left Rich Hill bound for Idaho.

They traveled there aboard an Immigrant Car which was a boxcar divided into three sections. The family cooked, ate, and slept in one end section; the middle section carried their household goods; and at the opposite end from their living quarters rode their livestock which included a team of horses, a pony, and an unknown number of milk cows. The railroad put their car off on a siding near Kuna and they lived with or near Daisy's relatives, a family named Scrivner. Young Will, who was 14 at the time, vividly remembered one of their first jobs in Idaho. There was an orchard being planted near Ustick, just west of Boise, and they were hired to dig the holes for the trees. However, because of the layers of caliche in the area, they had to use a half stick of dynamite to blast out each hole.

The town of Council, which was in Washington County at that time, was being touted by chamber of commerce-type promotions as the new garden spot of Idaho. Rob McClure, undoubtedly influenced by his friends, the Kidwells, visited the area and purchased a 163-acre farm from a man who was said to have won it in a poker game. The farm, located about a mile west of town, borders the Weiser River and is bisected by Hornet Creek. It was not an irrigated farm, but the valley land bordering the river was sub-irrigated by capillary action from the high water table. Rob later regaled his grandchildren with tales of the land's productivity, saying, for example, that the oats on the farm when he bought it were four feet high.

Mamie stayed in the town of Meridian to finish her schooling, but Will moved to Council with his parents and enrolled in school there. Both of them had suffered interruptions in their schooling and neither of them graduated from high school until they were 21 years old. In 1913, after Mamie had graduated and moved to Council, Adams County was created with Council as its seat. Mamie was hired by the new county to go to Weiser, the county seat of Washington County from which the new county was created, and transcribe all the records. Consequently, all of the old records of Adams County are in her handwriting. After completing that chore, she was hired to work for the Adams County clerk or the assessor for the next thirty years.

Mamie and her brother worked hard during their years in Council. Mamie took over what then was considered to be the farm wife's work—the cooking and clothes laundering—because of her mother's very limited physical capability. And she would never marry; she always felt it was her first obligation to look after her mother and do her mother's work.

Will was a robust six footer, weighing 190 pounds, but needing every ounce of his strength for the work that had to be done on the farm. One of his first chores was to use a team of horses dragging a railroad rail to grub out the sagebrush on the hillside part of the farm—dryland that was soon to produce one to two crops of alfalfa each year and, in certain years, excellent alfalfa seed.

Courtesy Wayne Cornell

The Kuna, Idaho railroad station, south of Boise as it looked when the Robert McClure family arrived about 1908 in an "Immigrant Car."

The two of them also found time for other enterprises. Photography was just becoming a home enterprise and they began developing film and making photo enlargements. Sometime in those early years they also, on their own or with an agency, sold insurance.

Mamie could not go to college after high school graduation because of her responsibility to her mother. But Will was not so encumbered. After he graduated in 1914 as, in his words, valedictorian and class dunce—he was a class of one that graduated from Council High School in that year—he was strongly motivated to go to college. His motive was literally romantic. He had fallen in love with a girl, five years younger, whose father was an attorney in the town and a famous state senator. And despite what an itinerant phrenologist told him after feeling the bumps on his head: "You're too dumb to go to college," Will headed to the University of Idaho. He, too, was going to be a lawyer and despite being a dirt-poor farmer's son, he was going to prove that he was worthy of the intelligent and regal-looking young lady who was the object of his affections. And the young lady? That is another story.

Chapter 1 notes

i Margaret 7 ½, Nancy 6, Amanda 4, James 3 ½, and Rebecca 1 ½

ii General Joe Johnston in North Carolina and other smaller Confederate units did not surrender until a few days later.

Chapter 2

The Freehafers

Albertus Leroy Freehafer was born in 1868 in Richland County, Ohio, the son of Andrew and Martha Freehafer. Nothing is known of his childhood; however one of his grandchildren vaguely remembers hearing that he attended some kind of military school, ". . . and his bearing would certainly suggest that—he was always ramrod straight."[1] Later, he attended Ohio Northern College in Ada, Ohio and graduated[i] as valedictorian of his class. He must have been a prescient young man for his valedictory speech, *The Role of the Independent in Politics*, was a theme that would reoccur throughout his life.

A. L., as he was always known, married a fellow graduate of Ohio Northern, Olive L. Robinson, whose family had a heritage in America going back to the Puritans who originally settled New England. Her father, Sam Robinson, had served in the Union Army during the Civil War, and although he purchased and was able to develop a beautiful 210-acre farm in Richland County, Ohio, a wound he received during the War created problems for him for the rest of his life.

What A. L. and Olive Freehafer did during the early years of their marriage is unknown. However, five years after the birth of their daughter, Marie Caroline Freehafer, on May 26, 1898, the family moved to northern Utah where both of them taught school. They stayed in Utah for two years, then in 1905 moved to Council, Idaho to take similar jobs. At that time Council was a vigorous small town enjoying a boom like many other towns of the West had experienced decades earlier. A contemporary account published in the December, 1905 issue of *Idaho Magazine* gives a description of the town:

> *Its present population is about 1,000 hardy, self-reliant, intelligent people, grown thus from a population of about a quarter of a hundred ten years back. It is now a youth of only seventeen, but it is conservatively estimated that five years hence when it shall have reached the age of manhood it will be the home of at least 5,000 prosperous inhabitants.*
>
> *On Council's commercial, industrial and professional calendar we find six general stores, one drug store, one planing mill, three saw mills, one harness shop, one hotel, three livery stables, three*

Courtesy McClure family

A. L. and Olive Freehafer in their later years.

time for an attorney to be licensed—for he was now practicing law with Burtenshaw in his little white frame building on the north side of Illinois Avenue.[ii] Among his activities was the negotiation of land contracts in the new development of Mesa for one of the major investors.[8] Sometime later he acquired a partner named Carr and, in a weekly display advertisement in the *Adams County Leader*, announced that they were agents for "Farm and Fruitlands, Stock Ranches, Loans and Insurance."[9]

More significant was his election in 1906—just one year after his arrival in town—as one of two representatives from Washington County to the state legislature. But, even more significant was his election two years later to be the state senator from Washington County. At that time Washington County was huge and its major population center was the city of Weiser at the south end of the county. Not only was Council 60 miles away from the population center, but Freehafer's law partner, Burtenshaw, was known as an outspoken critic of Weiser's domination and was actively campaigning for his north end of the county to secede from Washington County. Despite this handicap, in 1910 Freehafer was elected to a second term in the state senate and while serving this term, pushed through a bill that did, in fact, carve a new county out of northern Washington County.

A. L. Freehafer was awarded a finely engraved watch and a diamond stick pin by the grateful residents of Council—gifts that would be totally illegal today. And, according to one account, Burtenshaw was honored by the residents who allowed him to name the county. Burtenshaw reasoned that since Washington was the first president and he was followed by Adams, then the new county that followed Washington should also be named Adams.[10] It became official on March 3, 1911 when Governor James Hawley signed the bill creating Adams County. Later, during a big celebration to commemorate the new county, Burtenshaw was further honored by being presented with the pen used to sign the bill.[iii]

The "prim, and proper" Olive Freehafer may also have been active while her husband was leading the political scene. From various issues of the *Adams County Leader* we learn that the wild and wooly days of Council were drawing to a close. One saloon after another closed and finally a countywide election was held to determine whether the county would go dry—meaning that an affirmative vote by the majority would make the sales of alcoholic beverages illegal. Whether Olive Freehafer was active in the campaign is not known. But surely she was, even if she was in the background. And she must have rejoiced at the results. Despite strong opposition from the small mining towns of Cuprum and Landore, Council voters by a margin of two to one approved the measure—and a new cottage industry of making and selling "moonshine" was born.

Something else was born about this time, only it involved A. L. and Olive Freehafer's comely, sandy-haired daughter, Marie. She was falling in love with a boy five years her senior, a boy who lived on a farm on Hornet Creek about a mile from town. He was a student in Council High School, a tall, athletic young man who had moved to the Council Valley from Missouri just after she had arrived from Utah. The young man, Will McClure, was also falling in love with her, although in those times his feelings could not have been overtly demonstrated because of their age difference. Nevertheless, even though he graduated in 1914 and left for the University of Idaho, and she was sent away to the Intermountain Institute, a boarding high school in Weiser, the romance, once established, continued to grow.

Chapter 2 notes

i No one is sure whether it was a two- or four-year program.

ii This building has been moved, but still exists as a storage shed at the Council Cemetery.

iii This pen is now in the Council Valley Museum.

Chapter 3

WILL AND MARIE

In 1914 Will McClure was a young man in a hurry. Because of the family's moves from Missouri to southern Idaho and then to Council, he had missed a lot of school and was not able to graduate from high school until he was almost 21 years old. But now that he had graduated and had the goals of his life set—he was going to get a law degree and marry Marie Freehafer—he was not going to waste any more time. Somehow he managed to save enough money to buy a wagon and a team of horses. Then he drove that team and wagon to the University of Idaho in Moscow—a journey of about 200 miles on a winding dirt road that probably took him eight to ten days. After he arrived in Moscow, he sold the team and wagon and used that money to finance his first year of college.[1]

The pre-law curriculum at that time was a two-year program. The records show that he started on it on September 16, 1914, completed it in two years, and then enrolled in the law school, a three-year program. Meanwhile, the girl of his dreams was finishing her high school education at the Intermountain Institute, a private boarding school in Weiser,[2] and then, in September, 1916 she, too, began her college studies at the University of Idaho. They probably shared a lot of happy moments for two years, but trouble was brewing for all the young men of Will's age.

> MARIE'S SCHOOL
>
> The Intermountain Institute was founded in 1892 and was known throughout the nation as an outstanding "progressive" school. It was unique in that the boarding students attended classes and also worked up to five hours a day grubbing sage, milking cows, cooking, and gardening. It attracted idealistic teachers from some of the best eastern colleges, including Cornell, Yale, Oberlin, Mount Holyoke, and Bryn Mawr, and it was partly financed by nationally known supporters such as George Eastman (Kodak), Andrew Carnegie, the Kimball Piano Company—they donated eleven pianos—and the Kellogg Company. There were many outstanding graduates, but the best known was probably Jim Stevens who invented Paul Bunyan and Babe the Blue Ox. The Institute closed in 1933 because of financial difficulties.

The Great War, as it was known then, had been raging in Europe since Will had started college in 1914. By April 8, 1917, when America formally declared war

Courtesy McClure family
W. R. McClure 1918.

against Germany, it had already claimed several million lives. Yet, Americans everywhere, especially on college campuses, volunteered enthusiastically for military service and Will McClure was one of them. He enlisted in the Army and for reasons unknown, volunteered for flight training and was accepted into the Signal Corps, which was the Army branch responsible for aviation operations. He reported for three months of academic pre-flight training at the University of California at Berkeley on May 18, 1918. From there he went to Camp Dick, Texas, which was a personnel holding pool for graduates of ground training schools. It was located on the State Fairgrounds in Dallas and was known to the future aviators as the "Camp Dick Aviation Concentration Camp". Will was held in the "concentration camp" for a little over a month before he was released for flight training at Park Field, which was just outside Memphis, Tennessee. About a month later, on November 4, 1918, he flew his first solo which was seven days before the Armistice was signed. After the war ended, he had the option of completing his flying training and getting an officer's commission or being discharged. He chose the latter and left the Army on November 30, 1918.[3]

Soon Will was back studying law at the University of Idaho, but time with his girlfriend would be short. The following June, after only three years, Marie graduated with a Bachelor of Arts Degree in Education with "high honors."[4]

While Will was completing his last year of law school, Marie took a teaching job in Aberdeen, a small town in southeastern Idaho near Pocatello. Will graduated June 9, 1920 and 18 days later they were married in Boise where her father, A. L. Freehafer, was serving a six-year term as one of the first commissioners of the newly created Idaho Public Utilities Commission. The newlyweds then went back to Council, and purchased a small house on five acres on the edge of town and began housekeeping with a minimum of furniture augmented with orange crates and apple boxes.[5]

Will immediately opened a law practice with the other attorney in town, James A. Stinson, and within a year was elected prosecuting attorney for Adams County. Shortly afterward, Stinson left Council to practice law in Oregon, and Will brought in one of his law school classmates, Carl Swanstrom, as his partner, who he had appointed as his deputy.[6]

Courtesy McClure family
Marie Freehafer.

While Will was busy establishing his law practice, Marie was busy with her own new projects. The first one, born April 17, 1921, was a boy given the name of William Robertson McClure after his father, but who would be called "Bob" throughout his life. The second, also a boy, was born February 1, 1923, and was named Raymond Andrew McClure.

By this time Marie's father had finished his term as a P.U.C. commissioner and, for reasons unknown, decided to move to the town of Payette and open a law practice there. At the time, Payette was an agricultural community near the confluence of the Payette and Snake Rivers and a mainline station on the Union Pacific Railroad. Will and Marie must have found the town attractive when they visited her parents there and we know they were impressed by the better quality of the schools.[7] About a year after the birth of their second son, Will closed his practice in Council, moved his family to Payette, and opened a new law practice with his father-in-law as a partner. About ten months later, on December 27, 1924 their third son was born: James Albertus McClure.

Historians generally date the beginning of the Great Depression to October, 1929 when the stock market collapsed. By most accounts the years preceding that date were known as the "Roaring Twenties", which implied that the country was in a boom period and enjoying great prosperity. Nothing could be further from the truth, especially in Idaho. There had been a boom period earlier—during the years of the Great War and a few months afterward. The markets for wool and beef—the products of Idaho's livestock industry—were in high demand and prices had skyrocketed. Idaho's ranchers enjoyed a unique prosperity that they would never enjoy to the same extent again. The same was true for Idaho farmers. Europe's crop heartlands had been decimated by the war and crops like corn, wheat, and potatoes were in great demand. And, there was a patriotic fever associated with livestock and agricultural production. With encouragement from the government to grow as much as possible, Idaho ranchers and farmers really believed that they were helping the war effort.

In 1920 it all collapsed. War-torn Europe was destitute; there was no money to buy American exports. Within the United States there were growing surpluses of all the agricultural products that resulted in a collapse of prices. Idaho potatoes that sold for $1.51 per hundredweight in 1919 fell to $.31 in 1922. Corn that brought $1.65 a bushel in 1919 sold for 50 cents just two years later. During the Great War many ranchers and farmers had expanded their operations by buying more land, livestock, and machinery. However, during the twenties when prices had declined 300 to 500 percent, they faced mortgage payments that were impossible to meet.[8]

Another segment of the Idaho agricultural industry also fell victim to a major change in American culture and technology. Up through the teens Americans depended upon millions and millions of horses for transportation and for work on the farms. However, during the twenties, Studebakers and Buicks and Model-T Fords were gradually replacing horses for transportation, and companies like J.I. Case, International Harvester, and Allis Chalmers were beginning to produce the machinery that would replace the working horses on the farms. The number of horses in the country fell precipitously as did the demand for oats, which was the grain fed to working horses. With the market for oats collapsing, farmers throughout the country who needed a grain crop in their rotation planted wheat instead. This resulted in a wheat surplus and the Idaho wheat growers saw their market collapse.

So, contrary to what many history books say about the Great Depression starting in 1929, it began much earlier, at least in Idaho. When Will and Marie were married in 1920, they would not enjoy a prosperity even remotely similar to what their children would experience for another twenty years when the buildup for World War II began.

There is another misconception about the hard-times period in Idaho. Will McClure was a lawyer, a professional man who, in addition to being respected in those days just for being a college graduate, was also building a solid reputation in Payette as a man of intelligence and integrity. His practice was growing with his reputation and he was soon elected county prosecutor. And when men and women were working in the local fruit packing plants for 10 cents an hour—$1.00 for a ten-hour day—it was commonly believed that a professional man like Will McClure was one of the "well off" members of the community.

The facts were considerably different. First, as Will McClure said many times to his children, "When times are hard, people have a tendency to settle their own problems. They don't want to have to get involved with a lawyer." Also, even though Will had a law practice that might be described as "flourishing" that did not mean that he was getting paid for his work. His two surviving sons estimate that during this period of his life he did more work for free than work for which he got paid. His daughter, Jean McClure, who was born (and adopted) in 1930, remembers as a little girl walking home with her hand in the pocket of her dad's overcoat and him telling her the story of how in one recent year of his practice in Payette he only made $300.[9]

In 1929, after the stock market crashed, the hard times the McClures were suffering in Payette, Idaho began to spread across the whole nation.

Specifically, the industrial sector of the economy followed agriculture into the doldrums and millions of workers became unemployed. Savings evaporated, banks failed, and the nation's economy fell precipitously. In addition, much of the central and western United States was struck by a severe drought. Before the drought, farmers could at least raise enough food to keep their families from going hungry. But now, in a region known as the "Dust Bowl," which stretched across southern Kansas, Oklahoma, north and western Texas and southeast Colorado, farmers could not even do that. They were forced to abandon their farms and they took to the roads by whatever means they could. Some men left their families with relatives and rode in or on boxcars to California and the Northwest, begging food along the way and doing whatever work they might find.

Payette, Idaho was on the Union Pacific's mainline to the Northwest and was one of those stopping places. Fred Rabinau, a friend and classmate of Jim McClure remembers as a boy how, "Hundreds of men would come to our house and my mother would always seem to find some kind of food for them. And they were not just beggars. I remember my mother once telling one of them after he volunteered to cut the grass, 'Look at that lawn; it's already been cut five times this week, and I've got enough firewood cut to last me all winter.'"[10]

Many of the poverty stricken families tried to stay together during their migration. Ellis Hallman, another friend and classmate, remembers a family who stopped by their farm while his father was putting up his alfalfa hay crop. "They had this old jalopy—I think they were from Nebraska—and dad hired the man for the day. Well, you know in those days, the woman of the house always puts out a big meal during haying and this fellow ate with us in the house. After the dinner, he mentioned that his family was waiting out in the car. My mother said, 'Well, why don't you bring them in; they're surely welcome to eat with us'—of course we had already eaten. He went to get them and they had this girl who had rickets[i]—she was a pitiful looking little thing. And she was so ravenously hungry that she just grabbed food in her hands from the plate and stuffed it in her mouth. . .it was a pitiful sight."

Numerous individuals have described their experiences growing up in Payette, Idaho during the Great Depression, but most of them never experienced hunger themselves, or knew of others in the town who had. Said Ila "Ike" Frazier who had immigrated to Payette from Nebraska and whose father was a semi-invalid because of trauma suffered in France during World War I, "People like us didn't have a lot to eat and we didn't always have what we wanted—I never owned a bicycle in my whole life—but we never went hungry. Most people had a garden and sometimes a cow and chickens and there was a lot of barter. People would trade work for food—and also people would look out for each other. If a family was in trouble, other folks would help them out." Her husband, Ken, added, "When I talk about those days with my friends, they talk about having nothing to wear but overalls. I tell them that they were lucky. At least they had factory-made overalls. The overalls I wore were made by my mother."[11]

Money was the problem; there was very little of it around. Fred Rabinau, and, later, several other of Jim McClure's contemporaries, speculated that out of perhaps 600 families in the town, at least 100 of them, at any given time during the middle 1930s, would not have been able to come up with $1.00 in cash. After Warren McCain, a retired CEO of Albertsons who was another McClure contemporary, heard about that speculation he said, "I think they were too conservative. I would bet there would have been maybe two or three hundred families that wouldn't have had a dollar to spend on anything they wanted."

McCain also disputed the claim that no one went hungry in the town. "I know that this one friend of mine, who came from a family of eight or nine children, did go hungry at times. They just didn't have enough food for all of them and he used to talk about it. And there were other families like that. I was lucky that my mother was always able to scavenge enough to keep us (from being hungry). One thing that saved us was the local creamery. I remember that we used to take this gallon jug down there where we could buy skim milk for five cents a gallon. Later, when some of my friends would get together and talk about those times, we would refer to ourselves as the people who wore the same brand of cardboard in our shoes. We all went to school with holes in our socks and holes in our shoes."[12]

Another Jim McClure contemporary, Lucie Cobb Lengel, whose father abandoned her twin sister and her when they were babies, said, "I suppose we had *enough* to eat—at least I don't remember going to bed hungry—but, I'll tell you this: I never tasted meat until after I was married, which was three months after I graduated from high school. My mother worked all day, then came home and at night and sewed, by hand—she never had a sewing machine—all of the clothes we wore. Needless to say, today I like nice clothes and I'll tell you, I rarely have a meal without meat today—and I still only weigh 98 pounds!"[13]

Things got worse as the depression continued. Tools wore out and there was no money to replace them. It became harder and harder to plant gardens because there was not enough money to buy new seed. It also became harder to keep clean. Brooms were expensive and a new broom was considered a luxury. According to Fred Rabinau some families used homemade brooms. Soap was also expensive and many children grew up taking their Saturday night bath with harsh, homemade soap made out of lye and animal fat.

Many who survived the hard times of the '20s and '30s tend to look back upon those years with nostalgia, remembering with fondness the ways people helped each other and looked out for each other. It is probably true, as human behaviorists postulate, that amity in a community increases as

Courtesy McClure family

Jamie, Bobbie and Raymond with their grandfather, A. R. McClure.

the threat to the community increases. However, it is also true that the town of Payette also had its share of enmity among its peoples. Mary Meechan Davis, who was the valedictorian of Jim McClure's high school graduating class, said, "As a little girl I remember standing by my mother one night, holding on to her legs as a group of men shrouded in white sheets gathered on our front lawn. If my memory is correct, they burned a cross on the lawn that night."[14] [ii] Another contemporary, Bob Hanigan, a retired Payette Chevrolet dealer, also remembered his father telling him how the Ku Klux Klan burned a cross on his father's lawn after he was elected as Payette County's first sheriff.[iii]

What was there to hate about the Meechan and Hanigan families, and perhaps others in the town of Payette? They were not Negroes or Jews—the typical targets of Klan hatred. They were Catholics, and in those years, there were bigoted people who truly believed that the Pope and his "mackerel-snapping" followers who worshiped "idols and graven images" were as inferior and detestable as Negroes and Jews.

Of course, Negroes did not fare any better when they showed up in Payette. Numerous McClure contemporaries told of how Negroes were met on the outskirts of town by a law enforcement officer and escorted to the city limits on the other side of town, reportedly after they were fed. They also tell of the lone Negro who lived just a few miles away in New Plymouth, a man named Abe Venable. Abe himself had a secure niche; however, according to those who knew and liked him, he was hard on other Negroes who tried to move into the area. "He would run them out," said Ila "Ike" Frazier. "I think he would physically intimidate them. But he was very respected. Everybody liked old Abe."[15]

Everybody also liked Marie and Bill McClure[iv], and in interviews throughout the community, people who remembered them spoke of them with affection and respect. When asked the question: If I had walked down Main Street in Payette in the thirties and asked people what they thought of Bill and Marie McClure, what would they have said? The author heard several comments about Bill, the gist of which was, "I would say, if you want a lawyer with honesty and integrity, go see Bill McClure—he'll never be rich—he's too honest—but you can trust him."

The same question elicited a variety of responses about Marie McClure. Several spoke of her generosity in the community and how, in a quiet, unobtrusive way, she helped people who were having trouble. They also spoke of her Christian values: how she lived by them and how she tried to impart them to others as a Sunday school teacher at the First Methodist Church. Some made it a point to emphasize her strong feelings against the use of alcohol and tobacco, remembering that during the Apple Blossom Festival held each spring, Marie would march in the parade with the members of the Women's Christian Temperance Union (WCTU).

Sometimes there would be a chuckle or two when Marie's stalwart opposition to alcohol and tobacco was mentioned. One of Jim McClure's classmates, who asked for her name not to be associated with her comments, said, "Just after I graduated from high school, I was hired to do part time work in his (Bill McClure's) office. One afternoon his door was closed and not knowing any better, I walked in on him and found him sitting on the floor, smoking a cigarette. He looked at me and smiled and I smiled back at him, then left his office. He never mentioned it again and neither did I."

Bill and Marie's daughter, Jean, laughed when she was told that story. "I don't doubt it a bit, although I wonder why he was sitting on the floor. It was obvious that he smoked because his fingers were stained yellow. I remember asking him about it but don't remember what he told me. I never actually saw him smoke at home, but I can remember looking out in the backyard at night and seeing this red arc moving that had to be the light of his cigarette. As far as drinking—I don't think he drank much—although I remember one time I was home from school and went to his office to pick him up for lunch—it might have been during the Christmas holidays--and I could smell alcohol on his breath. I told him, 'Dad, you better get some Sen Sens[v] because you can't go home smelling like that."

Jean was also impressed with her dad's athletic prowess. "One day I was watching dad and my brothers coming home through the pasture behind our house and they challenged him to a foot race. This was when they were in high school and he beat them to the barn. He could run like the wind when he wanted to. Another time we were out in the backyard and the woman next door came out of the house screaming. She was holding a frying pan that was on fire. Instantly, he jumped over two fences and knocked the pan out of her hands. . .I was so impressed with his athletic ability. . ."

She was also impressed the first time she saw him in the courtroom. "It was hard to believe that this man in court was the same man who was my father. He actually talked! And he was aggressive. He was never like that at home. He was very quiet and rarely said anything."[16] Her brother Raymond said that he had the same reaction and that others in the community did, too. "I remember my mother-in-law telling about a couple of trials she observed. She said, 'I can't believe that man. . .He gets after them. He's very, very aggressive. He's nothing like he is at home."[17]

According to his three surviving children, Will McClure, by all accounts, was a very private person. At home he was quiet, even a bit withdrawn at times, and when they went on family picnics in the mountains, he sometimes left the family and went off hiking by himself. Marie made up for his silence and his tendency to be reclusive. She eagerly sought and enjoyed a good conversation; she was naturally ebullient and outgoing in the company of people; and at the picnics she enjoyed so much, she often sang in her beautiful soprano voice. She was also the family disciplinarian and displayed no reluctance or favoritism when she felt the need to apply her hand to the bottom of one of her miscreants.

None of the surviving children of that marriage can remember ever hearing a harsh word spoken between their parents, nor can they remember observing any other manifestation of anger between them. It seems reasonable to conclude that Will and Marie—childhood sweethearts who never experienced another romance--came very close to enjoying an ideal, mutually fulfilling marriage, and one that would last for fifty-four years.

Chapter 3 notes

i A Vitamin D deficiency disease that affects the bones.

ii Mary Meechan Davis later confirmed with her older sister that her memory was correct.

iii Payette County was carved out of Canyon County in 1917.

iv In Payette the name "Will" continued to be used by his family, but the rest of the people knew him as "Bill".

v Tiny pills that many people chewed in those days to mask the smell of alcohol on their breath.

Chapter 4

Jamie

James Albertus McClure, the third son born to Will and Marie, would never be known by his given name. Through his childhood and teen years he was known to his family, friends, and teachers as "Jamie."[i] After he graduated from high school and left home for college and service during World War II, he was usually known as "Mac". It was not until after the war when he returned to college that he acquired the name, "Jim", by which he is known today.

Nor would Jamie McClure know the kind of childhood that all his friends and contemporaries would experience while growing up in Payette, Idaho. During the summers the kids of Payette swam and searched for pearls in the mussels living in the waters of the Payette River that ran along the western edge of the town. Or they splashed and frolicked in the "big ditch", an irrigation canal from the Payette River that ran at the base of the hill where the "eastsiders" lived. Or, as Bob Hanigan, one of Jamie's friends said, "A lot of us would just walk to the highway and wave our swimming suits to a passing car and it would stop and give us a ride to Wilcox's Pool that was at the Gayway Junction about three miles away."

Jamie and his two older brothers had drastically different summer experiences. In May after school was out, the three boys —Jamie when he was five or six years old—would ride in their father's 1926 Buick or his 1936 Chrysler to their Grandfather McClure's Hornet Creek Ranch[ii] just outside of Council. There they would spend the entire summer working on the ranch, milking cows, cutting cockle burs, shocking and putting up hay, fixing fence, and performing a myriad other chores that were required on a self-sustaining enterprise which small ranches were in those days.

Grandfather Rob McClure, whose own father died after being wounded in the Civil War, was a big, friendly, gregarious man, formally schooled only to the third grade, but an avid reader who owned, among other books, a twenty-eight-volume collection of Mark Twain's works. To the sons of Will McClure, who was absent from the home while working in his office during the day and almost every evening after supper, Grandfather McClure also had a dominant fatherly role in the raising of the three boys. Both surviving grandsons clearly remember how he imprinted them and can readily recite his admonitions. Said grandson, Ray, "I can remember him over and over again saying, 'Don't wait for me to tell you what to do or how to do something. You know what to do. Use your own initiative. Use your own ingenuity. You know how to do it; you don't need me to tell you.' I also remember his independent streak and his dislike of government interference. One day while we were there a government official came out to the ranch and talked to him about one of the agricultural programs—I think it was the AA—the Agricultural Adjustment Program—a '30s New Deal program—and my grandfather listened a while, then told the man to get off his property—that nobody was going to tell him what he could grow and what he couldn't grow—'You found the gate to get in here so now you can find the gate to get out of here,' he told him."[1]

Jim McClure said, "I spent more time interacting with him than with my dad. . .I remember vividly that he had an influence on me. He was always saying, 'Figure it out for yourself.' And it wasn't an impatient kind of thing with us—he wanted us to learn while we were doing things. 'Learn while you are doing it. Use your brain.' I can still hear him saying that. Also, I remember him telling us, 'I can hire almost anybody to do what they're told, but it's hard to hire people who will look around and see what needs to be done.' I remember there was a man who came to work on the hay crew one year, and if he spoke thirteen words, five of them would be profane. My grandfather never swore nor would he put up with those who did. Well, when that man came on the job, one of us asked my grandfather why he put up with this man and he replied, 'He may cuss a lot, but he's a good man and I'll put up with him because he's not afraid to do more than his share of the work.

"My grandfather was as independent as anyone who ever lived. And his word was his bond. We were taught that. He'd tell us that an agreement didn't have to be concluded with a handshake, but if there was one, that just underscored the agreement. Also, he didn't believe you should buy anything until you could pay for it. He never had much but he never owed anyone a dime. He had an impeccable reputation in the community. He worked hard and expected others to do the same. I know this had a direct influence on how I conducted myself later in public office. When I first started serving, I consciously decided that nobody in my office was going to work harder than I, and that I was always going to be there when my people arrived and I was going to be there when they left. I have a bit of a guilty conscience about that now because of the price my family paid, but it was something that was instilled in me by my grandfather when I was just a boy."[2]

Jim McClure also vividly remembers some nonverbal lessons he acquired at the Hornet Creek Ranch. "When I was a little guy, I had to stay at the house to help grandmother with the dinner, haul wood, keep the fire going, haul the slop out, etc. when my brothers were out in the field. Of course, I wanted to be out in the field, too, and even though I was too little,

Courtesy McClure family
Jamie McClure.

I kept pestering my grandfather to let me go out there and work. He had a policy that whenever he brought in hired help to put up the hay, he would also pay my brothers the same wage, and I wanted to earn money like they did even though I was too little to keep up with them. On the ranch there was an old channel of Hornet Creek and a new channel, and in a field between the two branches there was a patch of native hay—not alfalfa—and one day, after pestering my grandfather, he said, 'Okay, I'll give you a quarter to shock all the hay in that field.[iii]

"Well, the hay was too heavy for me and I got frustrated, then angry, then I got upset and cried. Also, I remember the water bucket I carried out there—the others carried a water bag—it was a five-gallon lard bucket and I stuck it under a shock of hay. Then, I got so frustrated I threw the pitchfork into the shock, hit the bucket, and punched a hole in it. But, I got the field shocked and got my quarter, but the main thing I got was a lesson that would stay with me. At no time did I get any sympathy or instructions or encouragement from my grandfather. And, I got no praise when I finished. The lesson he taught me was that if you make a bargain, you stick with it until you have done what you have agreed to do no matter how difficult it may be. My grandfather had a great influence on me and I loved him dearly."[3]

Almost every weekend during the summer, Will and Marie with daughter, Jean, would make the two-hour and ten-minute drive on the narrow gravel road that linked Payette and Council. They would usually arrive on Saturday morning, but sometimes would come in on Friday evening. Almost without fail, every Sunday would be devoted to a picnic, often on Cuddy Mountain where Marie's Uncle Will Freehafer had a mine, but at a variety of locations in the mountains and hills around Council and the next town to the north, New Meadows. In hearing about those excursions, one is struck by the vast difference that six decades has made in that area. At a point along the Little Salmon River, which is on U.S. Highway 95 and the main route linking north and south Idaho, the family would park along the gravel road and during the four or five hours they would be there, only three or four cars would pass by on the road.[4]

Both surviving sons of Will and Marie have pleasant memories of those summer outings. Ray remembers that his father often went off hiking by himself while the rest of them, including their Aunt Mamie, would pick huckleberries, each with the bail of a five-pound lard bucket under their

Courtesy McClure family

Bobbie, Raymond and Jamie take a cruise on the lake during a family outing.

belt, or they would take binoculars and nature guide books on hikes with the goal of identifying as much of the local flora and fauna as possible.[5] And Jim remembers that "Auntie Mamie was especially interested in birds and wild flowers and I suspect that influenced me. I still keep a set of binoculars. We have bird books. We try to identify new species. I'm constantly finding something new around me."[6]

On special occasions the family would stay at the ranch on Sunday and the boys, for their contribution to the family dinner, would go to the little house where ice was stored in sawdust—ice that had been cut from the Weiser River the previous winter—remove some of it, shave it into small pieces with a five-pronged ice pick, and use it in an ice cream maker with a crank that they would turn by hand.

The Sunday outings for the McClure family were not just summer events staged out of the Hornet Creek Ranch. In Payette, especially in the springtime, the family would motor across the Snake River, then on one of the many trails out into the uninhabited Eastern Oregon desert where they would picnic amid constellations of color created by the blooming balsam root, yellow bells, hyacinth, death camas, phlox, wild onions, Oregon grape, sego lilies, pansies, and wild iris.

The boys also learned how to handle guns at an early age. On the ranch they used a .22 rifle to shoot ground squirrels that were depredating their fields. As they got older their Grandfather Freehafer taught them to shoot grouse and pheasants on the wing with his 12-gauge Winchester Model 97. And, while they were still in high school, Jim hunted deer and elk with the 30-40 Craig rifle that his father was issued during World War I and which he was allowed to purchase when he was discharged.

Another influence in their young lives was their uncle, Paul Freehafer, who was born in 1914, sixteen years after their mother. Unfortunately, Paul contracted scarlet fever when he was an infant and the disease damaged his heart and left him a semi-invalid. However, this had no effect upon his brain; those who have described him consistently used such terms as "exceptionally intelligent" and "brilliant." What nephews Ray and Jim remember most was his enthusiasm for science fiction and his prescience in predicting future space accomplishments that were pure fantasy in the Buck Rogers comic strips of their childhood and youth. Paul was also a serious student of classical music and, over the years, accumulated a large collection of 78 rpm recordings. Fred Rabinau, one of Ray and Jim's neighborhood friends, especially remembered sitting on the floor in the McClure living room with Jamie, listening for hours to some of the recordings borrowed from that collection. "I developed a love for classical music that stayed with me all my life," said Rabinau.[7] Apparently the young Jamie also developed a similar fondness for it is unusual, even today, to enter his home and not hear classical music in the background.

PAUL FREEHAFER

After graduating from Payette High School in 1932, Paul went to the College of Idaho in Caldwell for awhile (his schooling was interrupted several times by illness), then to The California Institute of Technology (Caltech) where, in 1940, he graduated with a degree in chemical engineering. He then helped found a dynamic new company called the Filtrol Corporation, which later became Aerojet-General, a major defense and aerospace contractor. In March, 1944, so exhausted from his work that he was near collapsing, he rode a passenger train from Los Angeles to Payette for a recuperative leave in the McClure home. However, because of the wartime shortage of Pullman coaches—these were being used on troop trains—he had to sit up all the way and arrived so exhausted he died a few hours later. He was 30 years old.

The McClure boys were also the recipients of a more direct kind of musical influence from the Freehafer family. Said Ray, "I can remember going down the road with Grandfather Freehafer driving maybe 70 miles an hour and all the time he and my mother and grandmother would be clapping and singing and having a great time. My dad dreaded for us to ride with him because he was so carefree when he was behind the wheel. But, it was my Grandmother Freehafer who had the greatest musical influence on us. A musician herself—she played the piano and probably the coronet—at least we saw one at the house—she wanted each of us to learn to play a musical instrument and she agreed to pay for it when we started. Bob, my older brother, started on the trumpet, probably when he was in the fifth or sixth grade. My mother then decided that I would learn to play the piano and I started the lessons. But, I hated it and she finally let me change over to the clarinet."[8]

When it was Jamie's turn to take up a musical instrument, his Grandmother Freehafer had passed away[iv] and the decision on which instrument he should play was made outside the family. Jim McClure explains:

> *Our band director was a man named Jay Stoner. He had taught in Council and had played the trumpet in John Phillip Sousa's band before he moved to Payette. He was a wonderful man and a friend of our family who fished and hunted with us. When he decided that he needed a flute and piccolo[v] player coming up for his high school band, I was nominated when I was in the fifth or sixth grade to be the one who would start training for that position. I didn't mind too much—it was easy to carry around, especially the piccolo—but I would rather have learned to play something like the sousaphone.* [9]

All of the McClure boys were given an allowance of 25 cents a week, but the disbursement of those funds was rigidly controlled by their parents. Jim McClure laughed as he recalled the disposition. "We got the 25 cents but five cents had to go to our church, five cents had to go to savings, five cents was put back for Christmas presents, and we were allowed to spend five cents. I don't remember now where the other five cents went but it was not for us to spend."[10]

The boys' real spending money came from part time jobs and, because their parents would only pay half the money when they got big enough to purchase a bicycle, they had at least one strong incentive to find paying jobs. Ray remembers one of the jobs he had while he was in high school. "New cars used to be shipped in boxcars—four cars per boxcar—and one of my jobs was to unload them and drive them to the dealer when they arrived on the Union Pacific siding. For some reason they always shipped them without water in the radiators, so when I started them, I couldn't waste any time getting them to the dealer or they would overheat. I was really proud that they trusted me to do that."[11]

Jim remembers several ways he earned money. "One of the first things I did was to go around to different houses and try to sell White Cloverine Salve. I don't think I was too good at that. I did better when I started selling the *Saturday Evening Post* which was a weekly magazine. I also remember digging onions out of our garden and selling them at one of the grocery stores. My best job—best paying job—was the one I had during the last two years in high school when I would get up at five o'clock and deliver milk for a dairy. I remember several times when I would finish my deliveries, come home and grab a quick breakfast, then go down to the river and sloughs behind our house and shoot ducks. I remember one season when I got 42 ducks with 45 shells. Then I would walk a mile to the high school."[12]

Courtesy McClure family

Jamie the country boy.

But, the boys also had lots of fun. Ray still has the scooter that he rode on the sidewalks in his neighborhood. Both brothers remember riding their bicycles up to the cider mill in the center of town where, in the fall, they took turns gulping free apple juice from the community tin cup that hung by the spigot on one of the barrels. Like all boys of that era, they played a lot of marbles despite a disapproving mother who believed playing "for keeps" was a form of gambling. They also rolled hoops and tires (until all old tires were taken for recycling when World War II started), and even turned old tires inside out so they could more easily curl up inside and be rolled down the slope of their neighbor's earth-covered cellar.

All of the rough and tumble play was hard on clothes and, because families at that time passed clothes along from the oldest to the youngest, the clothes Jamie inherited from his two older brothers—especially the overalls—were always well patched. But, even after repeated patching, there were always tears in his overalls because of the rough-house play with Old Pete, the family dog. Anytime there was a running game, Old Pete felt that in order to be included in the game he had to grab one of Jamie's pant legs and tug.

And what kind of a kid was Jamie? The mature man, in the eighth decade of his life, said that he was an ornery kid. His brother, sister, and classmates never described him that way, although one or two smiled and used the word "mischievous." Most remember him as a rather quiet kid, a bit shy, but clean cut and always friendly. His sister and one of his classmates were the most vociferous in describing a unique kind of behavior for him.

"He was a lawyer in training even when he was a kid," said sister, Jean. "We would get into an argument—I'd have my side and he would have his—and he would argue and argue and finally I would get upset and agree with him. But, then he would turn around and argue the other side. He used to drive me nuts doing that."[13]

His classmate, Harold Preston, related a similar remembrance of Jamie: "In high school we always relied on him to save us if we came to class unprepared. I remember one such time—it was in Mr Frazier's government class—he was the high school principal—and we told Jamie to get into an argument with Mr. Frazier and burn up some time so he wouldn't call on us. He had that poor principal pulling his hair out. He would start some discussion and then he would turn it around till the principal was arguing against himself. But, he burned up the time and we loved that. He loved an argument." His old classmate also felt that his friend was "going to go someplace." Said Preston, "He always struck me as one who knew where he was going and he knew how he was going to get there." [14]

Jamie was usually a good student—he graduated fourth in his class of 63—but, by his own admission he got by without ever having to really apply himself. With diligence, but only mild enthusiasm, he played the flute and piccolo in the high school band and in the county band when concerts were held at times other than during the summer. Dave Bivens, who was in the county band with him, said that "Jamie really did himself proud when the band played *Stars and Stripes Forever.* He did an outstanding job."[15]

Later, Jim remembered some of his good teachers in high school. "Jay Stoner, of course, was an outstanding band director and a good friend. One of our math teachers, Sherman J. Millbrook, was probably the best academic teacher I had. He was a strict disciplinarian but a very respected guy. He was nobody's buddy. He was the teacher. We were the students. There wasn't any doubt about that. During my senior year, he thought some of us should be taking advanced math so he took six of us in a special period and taught us a course in solid geometry. He was one of those teachers who could inspire you to want to learn. And we did. He was outstanding. Another outstanding teacher was Mrs. (Herbert) Davis. She was a character. She wrote poetry on the side, some of which was very interesting. She became a good friend and stayed a friend all the rest of her life.[vi] We also had an eighth grade teacher who sponsored a photography club and got twelve or fifteen of us interested—an interest that extended on into high school. We made cameras, and we took pages out of *National Geographic* and made filmstrips that they used in the school. We did a lot of things like that and it stimulated an interest in photography for a handful of us." [16]

While discussing his teachers, the author also heard a confession from the "ornery" Jamie. "When I was in the eighth grade, we had a beginning teacher and she lasted until Christmas. We were segregated into a class of all boys at that time and eighth grade boys have a tendency to be unruly and disruptive—and we were no exception. I remember one boy who built a fire on the windowsill—he used a magnifying glass to concentrate the sunlight on a piece of paper. I'm afraid I would have to say we drove her out. Unfortunately, that was an example of how cruel kids can be. She was a nice person I'm certain, but she was never in charge. We got a minister's wife who taught the rest of the year. She was strict. There was no nonsense with her."[17]

Courtesy McClure family

Jamie the fisherman.

The one thing Jamie McClure never experienced during his growing-up years was the thrill of participating in team sports. For many years Payette has been a "baseball crazy" town, an interest undoubtedly stimulated by big-league players like Walter "Big Train" Johnson, a Hall-of-Fame pitcher who got his start a few miles away in Weiser, and Harmon Killebrew, the Hall-of-Fame slugger, who grew up and began his baseball career in Payette. But, baseball is a summer sport, and even though Bob McClure was able to buy a good baseball glove, neither he nor his brothers ever had the chance to use it much because their entire summer was spent on the Hornet Creek Ranch with their grandfather.

Jamie also had a problem when it came to team sports like football. "When I was a senior," he said, "I tried out for football—I had played some in the eighth grade—but I was too small and the coach wasn't interested in me. I had quit growing in the eighth grade and at the beginning of my senior year I was still five-foot, four inches tall and I only weighed 128 pounds. The coach had freshman bigger than me. I started growing later in my senior year—in January or February of that year I grew three-quarters of an inch in one week. Still, I was only five-eight and weighed 140 when I graduated. Later, when I was in service I was close to six feet tall and weighed over 160 pounds.

Jamie never did win an athletic letter and gain entrance into the P-Club—the most prestigious club in Payette High School. Nor was he even remotely close to being the "big man on campus" with the girls in his school. Part of the problem, aside from his natural shyness, was that the First Methodist Church, to which his family belonged, prohibited dancing. During his time as a student it was only at school dances when most boys had the opportunity to hold a girl closely and carry on a private conversation. Jamie never learned to dance and, consequently, never had that opportunity. "I was very interested in girls and liked them," he confessed later, "but the truth is that, aside from teasing them, I didn't know what to do with them. That's why I never dated in high school."[18]

In September, 1939, at the beginning of Jamie's sophomore year in high school, Nazi Germany's storm troopers had already occupied Austria, forcibly moved into Czechoslovakia and the Rhineland held by France, and now Adolph Hitler's panzer divisions, supported by Stuka dive bombers, were storming into Poland—a cataclysmic event that caused Great Britain and France to enter the conflict and formally initiate World War II. Clearly, war clouds were on the horizon in Payette, Idaho, but, aside from some enlistments in the National Guard by some of the older boys, sometimes for patriotic motives, sometimes for economic motives, the war now raging in Europe was not affecting the carefree life of Jamie and his classmates. He and friends, Leo Ballinger[vii] and Cliff Colton, bought the 1926 Ford Model T Touring Sedan that the Gissel family had traded to a dealer. They paid $15.00—five dollars each—but had to park it in a vacant lot near Leo's house because Jamie did not dare let his mother know what he had done. But, he did know how to drive; he had learned, sitting on his Aunt Mamie's lap during her lunch hour when she arrived with her car at the ranch gate, and when she left the ranch to return to work. And besides the Model T owned by Jamie and his two friends, Harold Preston remembered that there was another student-owned Model T in town—a pink one with slogans painted in white lettering, one of which said, "You girls that smoke, throw your butts in here."[19]

Courtesy McClure family

Jamie at the center of a family celebration, Grandfather A. R. McClure in background.

In 1940, as Jamie started his junior year in high school, German forces had added to their conquests France, Belgium, Holland, Denmark, and Norway, and a fierce air battle—later called the Battle of Britain—was raging over the skies of England. That battle, if lost, would open up the British Isles to invasion by German troops. In addition, in Asia where the Japanese Imperial Army was on the move, much of China seemed on the verge of collapse as Japanese forces pounded at some of their major cities. However, despite the ominous threat hanging over the teenagers who would have to fight any war America might get into, their mood remained relaxed and upbeat. Bob Hanigan and a carload of his friends—all well underage--were now in the habit of sneaking out to the Gayway Dance Hall where they danced into the night to the swing and jitterbug jazz of George Shurtleff, and where they were able to imbibe with relative immunity. And among the elders there was a quickening of the spirit that accompanied the acceleration of defense spending which was creating a surge in the economy. In general, most people sensed that there were better times ahead, even though there were war clouds on the horizon.

And what was Jamie McClure thinking? By this time he was almost certain that he wanted to follow in his father's footsteps and become an attorney. However, with the war clouds turning darker, he was also thinking about some of his father's other footsteps. He had already built model airplanes. Now, he was reading a book that thousands of young men across the country were also reading. *I Wanted Wings* by Beirne Lay, Jr. was influencing a new generation of idealistic, young Americans not to think just about fighting on the land and seas should they have to go to war. There was another niche now open for those who would have to fight America's wars. Now, there was the wild, blue yonder which unlike the land and the sea, had limitless boundaries for those with the courage and daring to fight in that realm. Jamie's father had tasted the thrill of freedom in the third-dimension before the First World War ended. Now, if war really was to come again, Jamie knew that he would also try to follow in those footsteps.

Chapter 4 notes

i. Former classmates interviewed for this book still called him by that name.

ii. Technically, it was a farm, but they all called it the "ranch."

iii. To "shock" was to take a pitchfork and make small individual stacks from the hay that had been laid out in rows to dry. The shocks were then loaded on a wagon and hauled to the barn.

iv. Olive Freehafer died in 1934 after thyroid surgery.

v. A piccolo is a small flute pitched an octave higher than a regular flute.

vi. Warren McCain, retired CEO of Albertson's, felt so indebted to Millbrook, Davis and a teacher named Pauline Howarton, that he established permanent scholarships for Payette High School graduates in their names. Of the three, Millbrook lived to enjoy the honor of this award.

vii. Later killed in a Kamikaze attack during World War II.

Chapter 5

Mac

Jamie McClure graduated from Payette High School on May 15, 1942. After graduation he went to his grandfather's Hornet Creek Ranch, but that is not where he wanted to be. He wanted to be in northern Idaho working on the White Pine Blister Rust Control Program. He had written to the St. Joe National Forest several weeks earlier requesting a job, but he had not heard from them.

His classmate and friend, Harold Preston, had also applied for a job controlling blister rust but he had not heard from them, either. After Harold graduated, he went to work in the Farmers Coop Creamery in Payette where his father was office manager. However, he hated the work. He had to report at two o'clock in the morning and clean the powdered milk machine so it would be ready to go when the morning shift of workers arrived. After that, if his help was needed, he "dumped milk" that was brought in from the farms and dairies. A few days after he had gone to work in the creamery, his mother phoned. She informed him that he had received a letter from the Forest Service and that he was to report to work. "I threw my oilskin apron clear across the creamery after I got that phone call," Harold said. "Then I borrowed my father's car, drove home, and read the letter."[1]

He did, indeed, have a job in blister rust control, but there was a major problem. He had to show up in Clarkia, Idaho, a small logging settlement in the Clearwater Mountains over 200 miles away, and he had to be there by 4 p.m. the next afternoon. While Harold started packing, his mother phoned Mrs. McClure to see if Jamie had also received a letter. He had not, but Mrs. McClure said she would have her husband call Jamie at the ranch, and if he wanted to go with Harold and take a chance on getting hired, he would be waiting at the bus stop in Council.

"The bus to northern Idaho had already left Payette by the time I was ready," said Preston. "So, driving as fast as I dared with my mother in the car, I headed for Weiser, passed the bus, and was waiting to board it when it arrived. Later, when I got to Council, Mac—I had been calling him that for some time—was waiting at the bus stop, suitcase in one hand and battery-powered radio in the other." [2]

Mac McClure's mother would not have liked the expression, but the truth was that her son had decided to gamble—in two ways. First, he was going to gamble that he would be hired even though he had no letter of acceptance, and, second, he was going to gamble with Harold that they could make it to Clarkia by four o'clock the next afternoon. The latter was a daunting challenge because they had no idea how they were going to get to Clarkia from where they would have to leave the bus in Moscow.

"We got in that evening," said Harold, "and we were met by Mac's two brothers (who were at the University of Idaho in Moscow). We stayed in a hotel that night and his brothers tried to talk us out of going on blister rust control. They said that the Navy was building Farragut, a basic training base near Sandpoint, and that they were hiring people to clear brush. They said we could make more money doing that, but we decided to stick with the Forest Service. Early the next morning we caught the bus to Bovill, which was the end of the bus line. We were still fifteen miles from Clarkia so we went down to the train station. There was an engine with a passenger car on the tracks, but when we asked when they were going to leave for Clarkia, they said it might be in an hour and it might not be until evening. We couldn't take a chance so we started walking."[3]

They walked on the dirt road that paralleled the West Fork of the St. Maries River, both carrying a suitcase and Mac carrying his big portable radio, ". . .that must have had a ten-pound battery," he said later.[4] They trudged along, hour after hour, stopping to soak their overheated feet in the river from time to time, and passed a work crew replacing a culvert in the road. After they passed them, the crew came along in their truck and gave them a ride for a few miles, until they had to stop and work on another culvert. "We continued walking," Harold said, "and finally we came over a hill, looked down, saw Clarkia and that there were kids on the school play-ground. For reasons I can't remember now we thought that since kids were on the playground, we were too late—neither of us had a watch—that was a luxury in those days. But, we found the Forest Service office and discovered that we had made it in time. And there was good news for Mac. They said they were losing lots of men to the services and that they were going to take both of us up to the work camp where there probably would be a job for him."

But, the two young men still had a problem. They were informed that they could not go to the work camp without a pair of calked logging boots—boots with metal studs in the soles to provide traction on logs and steep mountainsides. To purchase their boots they were sent to a small general store owned by a Korean named Frank Tom. There they were shocked to discover that the cheapest boots, the "Bone Dry" brand, would cost them $14.95 and take practically all their money. "This blew our minds," said Harold, "because we were wearing shoes that cost us ninety-eight cents a pair."[5] McClure remembers that it was an even bigger shock to learn that White brand logger boots, ". . .the *creme de la creme* of the logger boots" cost the astronomic sum of twenty dollars.

Harold and Mac left Clarkia in a Forest Service truck a little after four o'clock that day. They followed the Main Fork of the St. Maries River to Fernwood, then to the village of Santa where they turned off the main road and started up Renfro Creek, which was one of the streams on the west side of Beaver Mountain and Renfro Peak. About five miles up the creek, they came into Blister Rust Control Camp Number 259, a camp of pitched tents. One of those tents would be their home for the next three months.[6]

The next day they got acquainted with a tool called a "hoedag". On an axe handle a steel head was mounted with a narrow axe blade on one end and a forked, hoe-like digging instrument on the other. The *Ribes* plants that they were to grub out of the ground were usually small bushes 18 to 24 inches tall. The usual technique was to dig the forked end of the hoedag into the ground, striking so as to get the main stem of the plant into the fork, then to push forward using the leverage of the handle to pull the plant out by its roots. The technique was the same as one uses to pull a nail with the fork on a claw hammer. Occasionally the bushes were so big or deeply rooted that it required two men on the handle to uproot a plant.

Soon they fell into the work routine. Their day would start around six when they woke up. For the most part the mountain air was clear and cold and rather than jumping right out of bed, one of them (there were five cots in each tent) would use a match to light a twisted length of toilet paper, one end of which had been placed under a bed of paper and wood in their sheet metal stove, the other end near one of the cots. Like a fuse on a firecracker, the flame would travel down the twisted toilet paper and into the stove. Within a few minutes, when their tent was toasty warm, they could get out of bed and dress in comfort.

They ate morning breakfast and evening supper in the camp mess hall which was run by a tyrant with one ironclad rule. Said Jim McClure, chuckling, "We had this fellow, maybe six feet tall, pale blue eyes, sparse grey hair—and not much of it—and he believed that when you came to the mess hall, you came to eat and get out of there, not talk. So he had a rule: no talking while eating. Well, we had some wise kids from the east who thought they were tough and one day they decided to test him. They started talking and he came out of the kitchen and told them to stop. They continued and then he came out with a big meat cleaver in his hand and he looked like he was going to come across the table after them. They shut up, and the rest of us were awfully quiet, too."[7]

After breakfast, they stayed in the mess hall long enough to pack their lunch. They made sandwiches from meat and bread laid out on a table and put them in a five-pound flour sack. They also put in a small can of fruit that they held in the top of the sack so they could carry the sack under their belt and the can would keep the sack from falling out. They were being paid 70 cents an hour, with $1.20 a day held out for meals. And the work was arduous. Some days they had to walk and climb for an hour just to begin their work, and in some locations such as stream bottoms where huge skunk currant bushes *(Ribes alterium)* had to be uprooted, they felt they needed a bulldozer rather than a hoedag.

Eventually, Mac McClure got into trouble. The procedure was for a string crew to lay out long, parallel lines of string anywhere from 30 to 50 feet apart, depending upon the terrain and density of the plant growth. Then a crew of "ribe pickers"—three men and a crew leader—would each take about twelve to fifteen feet and zig-zag within the string boundary, trying to make sure that they completely eliminated all of the *Ribes*. "Well, we had a straw boss (the man in charge of three crews) who took an immediate disliking of Mac," said Harold, "and he was on Mac all of the time, claiming that he wasn't doing a good job. Mac didn't like him either and didn't bother hiding his feelings. Finally, it got so bad that this straw boss went to the camp boss to get Mac fired. Luckily, the camp boss respected me and called me in for advice. I argued that Mac was being picked on unfairly and that he should not be fired. The camp boss agreed and it wasn't long until both of us were given more responsibility. Mac was put on a rework crew—this was the crew that went behind the regular crews to make sure that all the *Ribes* in the marked area had been cleaned out. I was made a crew leader. Both of us were paid an additional five cents an hour which to us seemed like a big raise."[8]

The two friends also had a lot of fun that summer. After work they would often go fishing and one of the cooks would prepare the fish. On weekends after they had treated their boots with Hubbard's Shoe Grease and done their laundry with a washboard and tub, they would go into Santa and hang out at the bar. The barmaid was a character. Sometime earlier in her life a man had tried to cut her throat but she had ducked her head in time for the scar to be under her left ear and jaw. She liked the ribe pickers, but she kept a baseball bat ready under the bar in case one of them or one of the loggers in the area became troublesome. One Saturday night Harold, Mac, and two friends from Weiser tried to go to the local Grange Hall for a dance, but were kicked out. They had worn their calked boots and the locals did not appreciate what the metal studs would have done to their dance floor. Neither of them can remember if it was this same night that one of their Weiser friends drank, as McClure remembers, ". . .about sixty beers and got wildly drunk. We walked him back and threw him in the creek to sober him up, but he almost drowned. It's a wonder he didn't die of alcohol poisoning."[9]

On one other weekend they came into town and the hotel owner pleaded that help was getting so hard to find because of the war that he had nobody to get in his hay crop, which was in a field across from the hotel. Harold and Mac agreed to do it for $1.50 an hour and the next weekend they brought the hay—it was already cut and windrowed—into his barn, where they also slept. When they finished, the man's sister, who ran the café in the hotel, fixed them the biggest fried chicken dinner they had ever seen. Said Harold, "I have never eaten so much fried chicken in my whole life."[10]

About this time they also significantly improved their living quarters. On their original trip up Renfro Creek they had observed the collapsed roofs and walls of cabins that had been a Civilian Conservation Corps (CCC) camp. "Somehow we learned that the floors were still intact," said Harold, "and a bunch of us took a cross-cut saw to the camp and sawed out floor sections that would fit in our tents. We hauled those to our camp and after that, we no longer had to live on a dirt floor."[11]

In the hot months of July and August, the Idaho mountains are famous for their "dry thunderstorms." Typically during the afternoons, a few large thunder heads will build and in the late afternoon or evening they will start discharging lightning to the ground. This lightning is followed by visible, dark tendrils of rain, termed "virga", which, because of the dryness of the air, evaporates before it hits the ground. Forest supervisors dread the season of dry thunderstorms because the lightning from just one of them can ignite several fires that have no chance of being extinguished by rainfall. On the other hand, the forest workers—in those days often hungry for money so they could go back to college—looked forward to them because they would be recruited for fire-fighting duty, make lots of overtime pay, and have the cost of their meals defrayed.

Harold and Mac were two of those hungry workers and they were delighted when they were called out to fight the first fires that were ignited in their area. On one of them Mac went out with a "camp flunky" named Slim to fall a burning snag[i] and discovered, painfully, that firefighting was not quite as romantic as he imagined. When they started to fall the snag with their axes, he found that every time he struck the snag with his axe, the vibration would bring showers of sparks down upon him.[12]

As the fire season progressed, both young men were drafted from their duties as ribe pickers and assigned to major fires that were in the St. Joe Forest. Harold was assigned to duty building fire lines with shovel and Pulaski[ii] while Mac became a water boy. Mac's was a grueling job requiring lots of stamina for he had to carry a five-gallon water bag on his back from whatever creek he was near, up the mountain to the fire line where he dispensed water to the workers from a spigot in the bag. Somewhat joking he said later, "I used to get mad at some of those guys who would take a drink and spit the water out. I didn't want them wasting it."[13]

As the summer waned and the days grew shorter, the two friends talked more and more about their future. Both were 17 years old and knew well that they were only in control of their immediate future. War was raging all over the world and millions of young men their age were destined for a maelstrom from which there was little chance of escape. The war news at the time was especially grim. Hundreds of United States merchant ships were being sunk right off our eastern shoreline. In the South Pacific the Philippines had fallen—the greatest military disaster in American history—and the Japanese were storming over all of Southeast Asia. In Europe the continent was almost totally occupied by Germany and it appeared that German forces, knocking on the door of Stalingrad, were to finish their conquest of the Soviet Union. In late August when the two friends were discussing their future, they were well aware that their country and its allies were losing the war. They were not pessimistic; few Americans were. Deep down they knew that America would win, eventually. But, they were realistic. They knew that any victory would be bought with a lot of blood sacrificed from young men like themselves.

Mac McClure had his immediate, post-summer plans firmly in mind. His father and mother had graduated from the University of Idaho and his two brothers were in attendance there. There were no other options to consider; he, too, would enroll there and join his brothers. For Harold Preston, college was another matter. First, he was not sure that he really wanted to go to college. Also, he would be turning 18 later in September and he had a strong desire to go right into the Army Air Force and learn to fly. Throughout the summer his friend Mac worked on him, telling him that he should, at least, try to get one year of college out of the way before going into service. Eventually, the idea took root. Maybe it was not such a bad idea to get a year of college before taking flight training.

Then the weather caused them to accelerate their plans. In the first days of September, low clouds, drizzle, and fog settled over northern Idaho for an extended period and both friends agreed that, since they were going to leave anyhow, they might as well head home to sun-drenched southern Idaho and enjoy a few days of freedom with their friends before heading back north to the University. "We were glad to get the heck out of that miserable weather," Harold said.

Both of them enrolled for the fall semester at the University of Idaho, and both of them became roommates in the Campus Club where Mac's brothers were living. This was a co-op dormitory. To cover their $126 per semester room and board fee, they were required to work in the kitchen or do janitorial work for one out of every six weeks.

Jim McClure later remembered the school year of 1942-43 as "absolute turmoil" because of the male students who were leaving for the armed forces. As an example, by the end of the first semester his Campus Club had to close because there were not enough men still living there to justify keeping it open.

He also remembers his dismal academic performance during that school year. "I managed to be a good student in high school, but I never really learned to study. Consequently, by the end of the first nine weeks I was in trouble and it got more difficult after that. It was hard to concentrate—I can't overstate the turmoil that was created by the wartime conditions. Most of us felt that it wouldn't be long before we could be dead. When you enlisted in those days, it was for the 'duration' which meant that you would be in there as long as the war lasted. And from our perspective, it looked like we would be at war for a long time. We really thought: What is the point of this today because in short order we'll be dead. That's also when I started partying and drinking—not much drinking; I really didn't care much for whiskey and beer. But, there were lots of parties. I remember when the Beta House had to close down—they had some money left and they had a big party with kegs of beer which everybody drank until it was gone."[14]

He also learned a new skill about this time. A housemate from Wisconsin who happened to be that state's archery champion taught him to shoot a bow and arrow "well enough to hit the target but not good enough to go bow hunting." (This same friend and another fellow from Wisconsin had an old Buick that "died" so they parked it on campus, painted the windows black, and sold time in it to couples who needed a place for romantic "conversations".)

Mac McClure was certainly not one who rented time in his friends' dead Buick. At age 17 he was still very immature, especially around girls. He claims to have had a definite interest in them, but he was painfully shy and, because he had been raised as a strict Methodist and the church forbid dancing, he did not know how to dance. In those days, holding a girl during a public dance was about the only way a young man, especially a shy one, could get close enough to initiate a private conversation with one. Nearly sixty years later it was still painful for him when he related a tale of a friend at the university who tried to cure him of his shyness with girls:

> *One of the freshmen that year was a girl, Marie Cobb, who graduated with me from Payette High School. She was a beautiful girl and intelligent—she and her twin sister tied for third in our graduating class. Well, I had this friend from Cambridge* [Idaho] *who also lived in the Campus Club the first semester and he kept after me to get him a date with Marie. We had this dance coming up and he wanted me to ask her to the dance. The plan was for me to take her there, then admit that I had really brought her to the dance to meet him. Except, it didn't work out that way. He didn't show up and there I was, stuck with this girl, not knowing how to dance and very embarrassed. I probably did get her out on the dance floor, but I'm sure I also encouraged a lot of the other guys to dance with her—which was no problem because she was so good looking. I never forgave that fellow. He thought it was funny.*[15]

A lot more than girls and the tribulations of first-semester-of-college-classes were on Mac McClure's mind that fall. Like all the other young men who were about to turn 18, he had to make up his mind how he was going to fight in the war that was in his immediate future. His brother, Raymond, left the university that fall, enlisted in the Navy, and by a unique coincidence, was sent to a Navy technical school that was housed in the old Intermountain Institute in Weiser where his mother had attended high school. His oldest brother, Bob, was still at the university—a senior majoring in electrical engineering who had plans to go into the Navy as an officer after his graduation the next spring. Mac was also thinking Navy, but his ambitions differed from his brothers. He had long dreamed of being a pilot, and his focus was on the Navy V-5 program he had learned about where college students could finish the current school year before going into a flight training program. This was the program that he had in mind when he went back to Payette for his Christmas vacation. And, at that time, he did not have many options. Unless a young man enlisted in his preferred branch of service before his 18th birthday, he lost all of his options and he would be drafted and sent to the armed service that best suited the "needs of the country."

When he got home, he had a long talk with his parents—who had to give their permission for him to enlist at age 17—and with an insurance agent in the town who happened to be an outspoken advocate for the Navy. Then, on December 26, the day before his 18th birthday, he borrowed his parents' 1941 Chrysler, drove to Boise with a letter of permission signed by his parents. At five minutes till five o'clock that afternoon, he was sworn into the United States Navy with the assurance from the recruiter that he could finish the current school year and would then enter the V-5 flight training program.

When Mac returned to the university, his days were numbered with his roommate, Harold. The Campus Club was about to close and the two friends were to go separate ways. Harold went to the co-op dormitory next door, the Idaho Club, while Mac, after receiving a pep talk from an older student from Payette who was the house manager of the Sigma Nu Fraternity, decided to pledge there. Harold, who had always been a pretty good playground wrestler back in Payette, had gone out for the freshman wrestling team, made it and won a freshman numeral, but suffered a hernia that unfortunately from his standpoint, disqualified him physically for his dream, which was to fly in the Army Air Force.[iii] Later, Mac also became an athlete, but in another sport. He loved to run, and when he was growing up in Payette, he often ran places just for the sheer joy of it. During one of his physical education classes that winter, the track coach happened to see him running in the gym and invited him to try out for the freshman track team. He did and was surprised to find himself a half-miler in enough field events to win a freshman numeral. "I wasn't that great," he joked later. "I never did run a two-minute half mile."[16]

After Mac joined the fraternity, his academic performance became more dismal. "That's when I learned to play bridge," he said, "and there was always a game going on with people standing around waiting their chance at the table. We just didn't care at that time. Most were living day-to-day, just waiting for the mail or a telegram that would be the call into service."[17]

But now, Mac McClure was Navy property and that became clear to him in the spring when he was ordered to take a train to Seattle for a flight physical. He went, along with others who had signed up for the V-5 program, and while initially confident of his physical condition, was soon to doubt himself when the star halfback on the Idaho football team, a rugged physical specimen, flunked the physical before him. He did pass; however, it was a conditional pass based upon a bizarre deficiency that he would have to correct. For reasons never explained, a pilot candidate had to be able to focus his eyes on his index finger as he moved it from in front of his face to his nose. Mac McClure could not do that at the time of his physical, but he was assured that he could learn to do it with practice. When he did and was able to demonstrate same, he would be fully qualified physically for pilot training. In the weeks that followed, the intrepid candidate religiously practiced the art of looking cross-eyed at his finger on his nose, succeeded with a demonstration to a Navy doctor, and when the school year was over, the U.S. Navy had one more pilot candidate eager to start his training.

Chapter 5 notes

i. An old dead tree still standing.

ii. A combination axe and mattock—a sharp digging tool.

iii. He volunteered for 12 physicals during the war but flunked them all. Then, in 1946, when he had a wife and no longer wanted to go into the service, he passed the 13th physical and was drafted.

Chapter 6

Aviation Cadet

By the end of May, 1943, when Mac McClure had completed his first year at the University of Idaho and was home waiting for orders to report to one of the Navy's flight prep schools, the tide of the war was changing. In the Pacific, U.S. Army and Marine Corps troops had driven the Japanese off Guadalcanal, the first of a series of bloody island victories that would eventually drive them back to their homeland. In Europe, the German Sixth Army that, in December was knocking on the door of Stalingrad and threatening the Soviet Union's collapse, had been surrounded and captured, and by May a Soviet counterattack was beginning that would eventually drive the Germans back to Berlin.

However, these ultimate victories were two years in the future and the 18-year-old Mac McClure was sure that, as he spent his days in his father's law office waiting for orders, he would be in the cockpit of a Navy fighter doing his share of the fighting. In June his orders arrived, and he learned a lesson about assurances from Navy recruiters. He was not to report to a flight preparatory school as he had expected. Instead, his orders told him to report to a deck-officers preparatory school at the University of Idaho Southern Branch at Pocatello, Idaho. He was to participate in the Navy V-12 Program, not the V-5 flight preparatory school that he had been promised.

When he received his orders, he had to remind himself that he had officially been inducted into the Navy almost six months earlier and that orders were orders, even if he did not like them. So, in his civilian clothes, including "Joe College" white and brown saddle shoes, he boarded a train in Payette and departed for his first official assignment.

When he arrived at the college, there was good news and bad news. The good news was that he received assurance from the commander of the detachment that once there was an opening in the V-5 program, he would be sent to one of the flight preparatory schools. Instead of a future as a deck officer on a destroyer or mine sweeper, he could again look forward to the cockpit of a fighter. The bad news was that the program at the college was just getting started and they were not ready for them. They did get a uniform—that of a second-class seaman—but no shoes. So, for awhile, the hopeful Navy fighter jock paraded around the campus in a blue uniform accented with white and tan saddle shoes. Nor did they have sheets or blankets

Courtesy McClure family

Navy recruit McClure.

for their bunk beds in Gravely Hall, a girls' dormitory. At night, because it was a cold June in Pocatello, they slept in their clothes in a mattress sandwich—with a mattress under them and a mattress over them.

The V-12 Program was essentially a college program—McClure signed up for geology, meteorology, chemistry, calculus, and English—with an additional heavy emphasis on physical conditioning. "It seemed like everybody there had some background in coaching or athletics," he said later. "I remember that the Executive Officer, Dutch Conlon, had been a Rose Bowl referee, and the big talk was of the former Oregon State halfback, Don Samuels, who did 1,300 situps and was still going when they stopped him."[1]

The program called for them to finish the equivalent of two semesters by February so all the courses were accelerated. This proved to be a problem for Seaman McClure. Said he, later, "We had this UCLA professor for calculus who believed that he had to grade strictly on the curve. That meant that in our small class—there were twelve of us—there had to be one "A" and one "F". Well, I wasn't in that class very long before I realized that I was the one destined to get the "F". We had several tests and luckily he posted our points. As the final approached, I knew I had to get a decent grade in order to pass so I worked very hard and just managed to squeak by with a "D-".[2]

In January, near the end of the second term, Seaman McClure became ill and the unit's old doctor, who had retired after World War I but who had been recalled "and hadn't opened a medical book for years," prescribed the new wonder drug that had just been developed called "sulfa." "Two or three days later," said McClure, "feeling nauseous and needing to vomit, I went to the head [bathroom] and passed out on the floor. They found me there, unconscious, and when the medics arrived, they gave me a coffee enema—I suppose to get caffeine into my system quickly, then took me to the Bannock County Hospital.[i] I don't remember anything about the first two or three days there, but know they were so worried about me that they notified my parents. I ended up staying in the hospital two or three weeks and missed the second-term final exams. I was told that this old doctor had diagnosed me as having mononucleosis, but the symptoms don't fit. I've always believed the sulfa gave me some kind of poisoning."[3]

Shortly before his illness, McClure saw a notice on the bulletin board that there were five openings for the V-5 program, but before he could get to the office to sign up, there were already five volunteers. When he heard that, he protested, pointing out that he had long ago signed up for the program and had already passed the flight physical. He must have been persuasive. They bumped one of the other volunteers, who happened to be one of his friends,[ii] and before he got out of the hospital, he had orders to report to Sandpoint Naval Air Station in Seattle. What he did not know was that he was being placed in a special program called "Elimination".[4]

When he got to Sandpoint, he was assigned to VR-5, a transport squadron flying the Douglas four-engine R5-D[iii] to Alaska and the Aleutians. Soon they had him working as an orderly on the flight line doing such things as cleaning the "honey pots" of the airplanes that had just arrived from Alaska or the Aleutians ("great for learning humility") or draining and refilling the deicer tanks with alcohol. There was also a lot of drill where he learned that the Puget Sound seagulls were especially accurate in their bombing of any platoon that happened to be in formation. At nights he witnessed the air defense system of Seattle in action, when searchlights all along Puget Sound would coordinate with antiaircraft batteries in practice exercises against incoming aircraft. He also completed training as an aerial gunner, learning how to field strip a .50 caliber machine gun while blindfolded, watched a USO show with radio stars George Burns and Gracie Allen, and as a special favor, while wearing his orderly hat, was allowed to simonize the Whidby Island Naval Station commanding officer's staggerwing Beechcraft whenever it was flown into the base. Clearly, the three months at Sandpoint highly motivated him to continue his pursuit of a naval officer's rank and duties.

> ELIMINATION
>
> According to Ken Snyder at the National Museum of Naval Aviation (who went through the same program during WWII) the Navy had an official program called "Elimination" that put wannabe pilots through a three-month program "where they were treated like dirt." Partly, the program was designed to separate those with determination from those looking upon aviation just as a glamorous alternative to chipping paint as a seaman. In addition, those in the program were to learn military basics ordinarily taught in boot camp, and to learn a skill that could be transferred directly to naval operations.

In early June, 1944, about the time of D-Day when U.S. troops were landing on the beaches of Normandy, he finally became Naval Aviation Cadet McClure and reported to St. Olaf's College in Northfield, Minnesota for the first phase of preflight training. Soon he was engrossed in basic aviation officer training which included aircraft recognition, officer protocol, formal etiquette, and formal traditions. The aircraft recognition class was especially challenging. The instructor had a slide projector with a photographic shutter on it and photos of aircraft, enemy and friendly, were flashed on a screen, first at a shutter speed of 1/10th of a second, then, eventually, at 1/50th of a second.

For a Payette, Idaho boy, Northfield, Minnesota itself was a shock. "I had never experienced humidity before," McClure said. "We had extremely good weather in Seattle—not the usual rain and humidity—and in Northfield it was both hot and humid—so humid, that after taking a shower I was wet before I could get dressed again. That was real trauma. I also got acquainted with some new fauna. I found out the hard way that anytime you sat in the grass you'd end up with bites from bugs called chiggers. And at night I was amazed to see flashes of light in the air all around me caused, as I discovered, by flying beetles that the locals called "lightning bugs." Also, this was the first time I ever saw mold growing on the inside walls of a room. It was all over the basement rooms where we had our classes."[5]

Aviation Cadet McClure also had fun in Northfield. Carleton College was across town and the population of girls there considerably outnumbered the boys. Cadet McClure admits that by this time he had finally figured out what to do with girls and he enjoyed a number of relationships. And, he said later, smiling, that he might have made a spectacular catch if he had been a little quicker witted. "One Sunday I had gotten liberty to go downtown to attend service at the Methodist Church. I was fairly blond in those days and, after the service, an old Norwegian farmer who had his beautiful daughter with him asked me if I was Norwegian. I said, no, but too quickly because I could have told him, yes, that my name went back to Olaf the Black who established a castle on the coast of Scotland in the 700s. I've often imagined that had I said, yes, he might have invited me home to meet his beautiful daughter."[6]

On one long summer weekend, McClure and a friend took liberty and went to a lake resort near Brainerd, north of Minneapolis. "The owner treated us like royalty," he said, "but I got a surprise when I dived off a platform out in the middle of the lake. When I hit bottom my hands went into deep, soft mud—I had never seen that kind of a lake bottom before. Also, the owner, trying to be polite, took us up to the end of the lake where he said we could see their mountain. It turned out to be a little hill."[7]

In September, after three months at St. Olaf's, Cadet McClure went back home on leave. "I'm sure I went to the Gayway Dance Hall and to the Athena Club in Weiser—the Athena was a hangout where all the GIs went—even those from Boise. Like the others, I was smoking and drinking at the time, but never dared do any of that in front of my parents, or even let them know that I was doing it. But, there was an urgency to life back then. Every minute counted. You wanted to live life to the fullest because you didn't know how long it was going to last."[8]

For the next phase of his preflight training, Cadet McClure moved south about 180 miles to the Tall Corn State and the University of Iowa. There he spent about half the time in practical subjects such as navigation and half the time in physical conditioning activities. This is where he learned to play

Courtesy McClure family

Mac, right, and Chuck Couper, strike a pose.

water polo—an activity deemed to be good training for water survival—and where he became familiar with the infamous Dilbert Dunker. The latter is a steel cage meant to simulate the cockpit of a single-seat airplane. The occupant rides this cage down a chute with rails and it hits the water in an attitude of an airplane that is ditching. Immediately on impact the cage tumbles inverted and sinks (the way a ditched airplane might), and the occupant has to unstrap from the shoulder harness, get the door open, and swim to the surface, remembering to part the water at the surface with the hands to simulate dispersing burning oil. After the first ride or two in the Dunker ("I was scared to death during that first ride"), aviation cadets usually learn to enjoy practicing underwater escapes. The same cannot be said of their 90-foot jumps.

To simulate jumping from the deck of an aircraft carrier, the cadets had to jump through a hole in the roof of the university field house into a swimming pool 90 feet below. ("It looked like a postage stamp and you wonder if you are going to hit it.") That was truly frightening for most cadets and the author has not heard of anyone who claims to have enjoyed the experience.

The cadets got a break from their classes at Christmas, and while some of their fellow GI's were battling in freezing temperatures against a major German offensive in the French Ardennes known as "The Battle of the Bulge", Cadet McClure and his friends were confined to quarters and were engaged in a twenty-four-hour-a-day, five-day poker game that ended when authorities finally gave the cadets liberty. And while his teetotaling mother back in Payette might have been shocked to learn that her fair-haired son had discovered smoking, drinking, girls, and poker, she would have been proud to have seen him as he performed faithfully in the chaplain's choir every Sunday in the field house, and she would have been touched to see the tears in his eyes every time they sang the *Navy Hymn*. When Cadet McClure reached his 20th birthday on December 27, 1944, he was like the millions of other young men of his generation whose aging and maturation was being accelerated by the unique events of their times.

Sixteen days later, Cadet McClure was to suffer an experience that would further accelerate his maturity. In January, 1945, he was back in Payette, home on leave after completing the preflight portion of his training. Living next door were his Grandfather and Grandmother McClure who, the previous year, had retired and sold their Hornet Creek Ranch outside Council. About mid-morning on the 12th, Cadet McClure was backing out of the garage in the backyard of his grandparents' house. He was in the 1939 Plymouth coupe that had belonged to his grandfather Freehafer (who died in 1940) and then to his Uncle Paul Freehafer who had also passed away. The driveway was typical of driveways of that time; it consisted of two narrow strips of concrete. To stay on those strips, he had the driver's door open and was leaning out, steering the car so as to remain on the strips and out of the snow in the yard. Then he saw something that he would remember for the rest of his life. His beloved Grandfather McClure was lying on the ground, motionless. He turned off the engine and rushed to the prostrate form, finding him semiconscious. With strength he could not explain, he lifted the 185-pound man in his arms and carried him to the back door, which his grandfather was conscious enough to help hold open, then placed him in the living room on the sofa. "My grandmother sat with him," McClure said, "while I ran next door and told my mother. She called Doctor Woodward, Auntie (Mamie McClure), who was working in the courthouse, and my dad, who started walking home. I knew his walking route and drove up to meet him."[9]

Two hours later Rob McClure, whose own father had died in a Civil War hospital and who had been a greater influence on young Jamie McClure than any other person, was pronounced dead. He never regained consciousness. The doctor diagnosed that he had suffered a fatal stroke. He would have been 80 years old in May.

Cadet McClure returned to the University of Iowa to mark time until he would be called to flight training in the Class of 3-A-45. This was a time when the Navy was not sure of the number of pilots that would be required to complete the war. In the words of one naval aviation historian, "The pilot pipeline was full at that time and there weren't enough cockpits out there so they were dragging out the training schedule."[10]

Finally, in March 1945, while 6,281 Marines were dying on a barren, eight square mile island in the Pacific called Iwo Jima, and while Germany, desperately fighting on their own soil, began drafting boys born in 1929—even if they had not reached their 16th birthday—Cadet McClure began his primary flight training at what was then known as "North Base" outside Norman, Oklahoma.[11] There, he was to enjoy 207 hours of flying in the "Yellow Peril".

The Yellow Peril was the nickname for the Navy N3N-3 primary trainer in use at that time. It was a two seat, tandem biplane powered by a 235-hp Wright Whirlwind 7-cylinder radial engine and it was extremely rugged—"overbuilt" in the terms of an aeronautical engineer in regard to the g-forces it could withstand without breaking up—a factor that probably saved Cadet McClure's life. It was painted a sunshine yellow, of course, and, because it's landing gear was narrow, it was easy for a novice or careless pilot to overcorrect with the rudder on landing and set up a series of oscillations that resulted in the tail swirling the airplane around in a maneuver called a "ground loop." Although such accidents rarely resulted in severe damage or injury, this ground-looping tendency of the N3N was perilous to a pilot's reputation and ego, hence the source of its nickname. At the time Cadet McClure was going through his training, a common expression about the Yellow Peril was that there were those who have ground looped the airplane and those who *will* ground loop it.

NORTH BASE

Early in the war, an editor for the University of Oklahoma Press happened to be on a train with a Navy official who lamented that they needed training bases for all the pilots that would be needed. When the editor returned to the university, he met with the university president and he agreed that land owned by the university could be used to the benefit of the nation and the university. Two fields were soon in operation, North Base and South Base, both primary training fields. Tinker Field, an Army Air Force Base, was ten or twelve miles northeast of North Base, but there was no conflict. University buildings and Westheimer Airport are now on that land.

McClure, today, clearly remembers his first flight in the Yellow Peril. "We went into the ready room and came swaggering out with our helmet, goggles, and seat-pack parachute. I really felt macho. Then, when it was my turn to fly, the instructor got into the front seat and I turned the prop by hand several times. If you didn't, oil would pool in the lower cylinders and since oil isn't compressible, the pressure when the engine started would blow out the cylinders—turning the prop caused the oil to disperse through the valves. After that, I went to the side of the engine cowling and began to turn a crank which was connected to a flywheel. It was not unlike turning a cream separator on my grandfather's ranch—it started slowly with a lot of effort, and slowly built up speed. The procedure was to turn it as fast as you could, then stow the crank in the cowling, run get into the back seat, buckle your parachute and harness, prime the engine with a manual primer, then pull a T-handle that engages a clutch that allows the inertia of the spinning flywheel to turn the prop. If you didn't get the flywheel going fast enough, the engine might not start and you would have to get out and go through the procedure again."[12]

Cadet McClure was introduced to the basic flying maneuvers—steep turns, stalls, and spins, as well as a number of full-stop and touch-and-go landings—all with his instructor in the front seat watching him in a mirror and communicating with him through one-way "gosport tubes" that connected to the student pilot's helmet. (There was no way for the student pilot to communicate with the instructor except by hand and lip signals.) When he first started flying, McClure was apprehensive because as a youngster, riding in a car on the winding roads to and from Council, he had experienced chronic motion sickness. "I started to feel a bit that way on my first flight, but my instructor, looking in the mirror, must have detected it for he immediately gave me the controls. When I started flying the airplane myself, the nausea ended and I never got airsick after that."

It was the Navy's philosophy to give students a lot of flying experience before they were allowed to fly solo. Consequently, the actual solo first flight was an anticlimax, at least for Cadet McClure. After that, he vividly remembers his training in formation flying. Most student pilots are shy about formation flying—as a wingman they have to be urged to tuck their wing in close to the lead and the expression "tuck it in" is usually often repeated. (In McClure's case, when there were no radios in the airplanes, hand motions were used to convey the same message.) "That was not a problem for me," McClure remembered. "In fact, I loved formation flying and enjoyed the challenge. I always had my wings right in where they belonged—or a little closer. One instructor, after landing, told me that I had gotten too tight. One of the guys actually got so close he scraped the fabric off the end of a wing. But, we were cocky about how good we were and we especially believed that we were much better than Army pilots. I remember one saying at the time: that an Army formation was two or more airplanes flying in the same direction at approximately the same time."[13]

McClure also remembered his first loop. "My instructor demonstrated one; then he gave me the controls and it was my turn. I went down and over the top, then pulled out and, in a little while, the instructor said, 'It must have been a good one; I blacked out.' I probably pulled a little hard, or maybe he had just been out on the town the night before."[14]

It was important to be able to handle the airplane in all attitudes so aerobatic flight was an important part of primary flight training. So, day after day, they went aloft, initially with an instructor when learning a new maneuver, but then by themselves to practice aileron rolls, slow rolls, snap rolls, barrel rolls, chandelles, loops, Immelmanns, falling leaf, and spins. McClure loved them all, but in particular he loved the Immelmann, a maneuver invented by the German Ace, Max Immelmann during World War I, where you dive the airplane, pull up and over into half a loop, then roll the airplane level and in the opposite direction. Springtime in Oklahoma is a season when heat causes cumulus clouds to build up into towering forms and to be alone in an aerobatic airplane amid the pillars and palisades of the towering, brilliant white cumuli, rolling, diving, looping, and spinning is one of the most exhilarating and ethereal experiences one can ever know. It is also a humbling experience to see yourself as such a tiny flyspeck against the massive size and power of those towering monsters. And, even though it was strictly forbidden, did Cadet McClure succumb to the almost seductive pull of those puffy mountains as he soared through the billowing canyons between them? Of course; they were irresistible; there has probably never been a naval cadet flying an open-cockpit trainer anywhere, anytime, who was not seduced into poking the nose of his airplane into one of the white pillars and experiencing the sudden darkness and splat of water against windscreen and goggles.

Courtesy McClure family

Cadet McClure.

Springtime in Oklahoma is also the time when continental polar cold air masses bulge down from Canada and collide with moist warm air masses flowing north from the Gulf of Mexico. The leading edge of the cold air mass, the cold front, moves rapidly and its wedge-shaped face forces the warm air upward in violent updrafts, and as the air rises and moisture condenses, the heat given off during the condensation adds further energy to the system which accelerates the upward flow. The result is a squall line of huge, towering thunderheads, six to eight miles high, that spawn severe thunderstorms and tornadoes; hence the region's name: Tornado Alley. But, it was the cadets' duty to fly whenever the ceiling and visibility would allow it. McClure remembers flying one afternoon when he observed a tornado funnel that struck twenty miles away, and on one other day when the thunderheads were building (*they were miles high and evil looking, greenish in color*), there was a break in the overcast. "Over the loud speaker we heard 'Brinovc! (pronounced brin-o-vic) Everybody out!' That was the abbreviation for 'break in the overcast' and we were ordered out to fly. Another day the winds were so strong that a cadet couldn't land—the wind was at a higher velocity than the stall speed of the airplane. A bunch of cadets went out and grabbed the wings, pulled it on the ground, and walked it to the ramp. I watched them do it. The wind there was so bad that when we parked the airplanes, we tied spoilers—one by four boards painted red and with ribbons on them—to the outer struts so the winds wouldn't cause the airplanes to take off by themselves."[15]

On Saturday night, May 12, 1945 while soldiers and Marines were fighting desperately on the island of Okinawa, and while Raymond McClure, who had joined the Navy so he wouldn't have to live in foxholes, was dodging deadly artillery fire, bombs and kamikaze suicide planes on the beach of that island while maintaining shore-to-ship radios, Cadet McClure and his buddies went into Oklahoma City and partied, undoubtedly celebrating VE Day (victory in Europe day), which had been declared on May 8. The cadets were living the good life—lots of flying with frequent liberties into the adjacent cities. However, the next morning the good life turned bitter. Cadet McClure woke early, hearing an announcement on the loud speaker that he was to report to the watch office. "Somehow, I knew what it was when I heard the message," he said later. "There was a telegram there from my father. My brother, Bob, had been killed.

"I went to the phone office[iv], placed a call home, but had to wait around all day before I got through—I didn't learn until later that I could have gotten through immediately if I had told them it was an emergency. I was just numb. We had been close growing up and Bob was always the leader and the arbitrator. Ray and I used to fight a lot as kids and it was always Bob who broke it up and got us to settle down. I took a train home and waited until the casket came in on another train. Several had been killed from Payette, but it was rare for any of the bodies to be brought home. Bob's remains were accompanied by a Navy escort officer and from him we learned what happened. Bob was an Ensign and had been with the Atlantic Fleet stationed at Banana River, Florida. As an electrical engineer he had some kind of responsibility with radar and had gone on a flight in a twin-engine Martin Mariner patrol bomber. On takeoff it lost an engine and the pilot lost control and put it in the bay. There were six or eight on board and all but Bob survived. Apparently he was sitting on the radar keeping warm, was knocked unconscious, and drowned. Rumors that he died because he couldn't swim were false. One summer he swam clear across Payette Lake at its widest point."[16]

The loss of their oldest son was a deep, emotional trauma for Will and Marie. When Jim McClure now thinks back upon that tragic event, he regrets that with his only other brother Raymond, fighting for his life on Okinawa and unable to help them, that he, himself, did not give better emotional support to his parents during and after the ordeal. On the other hand, the tragedy deepened the youngest son's resolve to make his parents proud of him. After his emergency leave, he returned to Norman, Oklahoma with his brother's ensign bars and braid, determined that he would wear them proudly when he earned his wings.

And that turned out to be the source of a mental conflict. Jim McClure tells the story:

> *"Sometime after I returned to Norman, a F7F Grumman Tigercat landed at the base. This was the hottest new fighter—it had two engines with a total of more than 4,000 horsepower and the Marine who flew it in was, as I recall, a double or triple ace in the Pacific. For some time a red-nosed P-38 from Tinker Field—it wasn't far from us—we could see their beacon at night—had been flying low near our field, rocking us good with his propwash—we learned to hate that guy. We mentioned that to the Marine and he said, 'I'll take care of that.' The next day, when the P-38 buzzed us, he got in the Tigercat and just made a monkey out of that airplane—we watched part of it. That P-38 didn't come around any more after that. While he was there, he decided to give us a demonstration of the airplane's capabilities. He came low across the field and was doing about 300 knots with one of his engines feathered. Another time he came low across the field, pulled straight up and did about ten slow rolls. Of course, all of this impressed me. I had already bought a fighter pilot's scarf, anticipating that I would be wearing it in a fighter cockpit someday. I didn't want to fly anything else. Now I had my airplane. The Tigercat was it. That is what I wanted to fly. However, there was a problem. It was a new fighter and the word was that the Navy was giving it exclusively to the Marine Corps. As cadets we would have our choice when we graduated; we could fly Navy or with the Marines. But, I had already committed myself to wearing Bob's bars and braid. I had to go Navy, so I had to give up thinking about the F7F. It was probably just as well. They were turning the airplane into a night fighter and, at the time, I didn't think I was that good flying instruments."*[17]

But, like most of his peers, 20-year-old Cadet McClure had more than his share of cockiness—and that almost got him killed.

In the primary flying syllabus there were mandatory flight training steps that had to be completed and evaluated by a series of check rides. But, also built into the program was a generous amount of "bonus time"—time that the cadets could use just to go out and practice whatever they felt they needed to do. Nobody called those bonus-time flights "joy rides", but, in fact, that was what they were—and no one quibbled about that—cadets learned to fly by flying and every hour's experience made them better pilots. Cadet McClure looked forward to those bonus-time flights and in his cocky frame of mind, decided to use one of his two-hour flights for an experiment. With his plan in mind, he took off and climbed to 10,000 feet, which, in the heavy, slow-climbing N3N, took him almost the whole two hours. Then, while holding the airplane level with the stick, he put in full forward trim—trim tabs[v] were on the elevator and with full forward trim, if he had let go of the stick, the nose would have headed straight down. What he was planning to do was an outside loop, notwithstanding the fact that he had never heard of one being successfully done in that airplane. Ready now, and with downward trim as far as it would go, he nosed over into a dive, hoping that the forward stick pressure plus the down trim would tuck the nose under, invert the airplane, and then allow him to climb up outside an imaginary circle and leave him upright on the top of the loop. It did not work out as planned. As he dived, the increased airspeed over the wings increased the lift, and when he pushed harder on the stick, trying to get the airplane to tuck under, he just accelerated the velocity of the dive. He was losing thousands of feet, very rapidly, but he was in more danger than he realized because the airspeed quickly went past the "red line"—the never-exceed-speed of 180 knots—the speed beyond which the airplane could disintegrate. With the ground coming up fast and the wind screaming through the wires and struts, he discovered that he was way past the red line. Losing his nerve (*a good thing*), he began pulling out of the dive. Fortunately for him, the engineers who "overbuilt" the airplane, had anticipated that there would be Cadet McClures in the airplane's future. He pulled out (*too close to the ground*), and after telling the story for the first time to anybody, he said, "That was the most foolish thing I ever did, for sure."[18]

One more event in Norman would leave lasting memory traces in Cadet McClure's mind. He was in the base theater one evening and watching the newsreel that preceeded the movie—in those days the newsreel was the only "video" news available to the nation. Surprisingly, between scenes of fighting on Okinawa and Kamakazee planes diving on ships offshore, a hick-looking cowboy came on the screen, standing on the steps of the U.S. Capitol building, twanging on a guitar, and singing:

Oh, give us a home
Near the Capitol Dome
With a yard where the children can play—

Then the theater erupted with hoots and catcalls. "McClure, is he one of yours?" they yelled. Much to McClure's embarrassment, the hick-looking cowboy twanging on the guitar was Senator Glen Taylor from Idaho who had won an upset election by going around the state, stopping on the outskirts of town, then riding in on his horse and, later, putting on a musical show with his wife, Dora, and his son, Arod (Dora spelled backwards). Now Senator Taylor, always a populist neo-socialist, was campaigning in his folksy offbeat way for the Congress to pass legislation for affordable housing and he had succeeded in getting the coverage he desired.[vi] After the catcalls subsided and had made their impression on the young man from Idaho, he undoubtedly slumped in his seat and tried to concentrate on the other news and the movie that followed. What did not cross his mind then, or for the next two decades of his life, was any thought whatsoever that he, too, might someday be standing on the steps of the Capitol making national news.

In June, as Cadet McClure was finishing his primary training—he lost two weeks by attending his brother's funeral and had to move into another squadron—the war in the Pacific was reaching its first climax. In the Philippines and on Okinawa, American troops were fighting desperately to clean out remaining pockets of fanatical Japanese who would commit suicide rather than be dishonored by surrendering. The second climax, the actual invasion of Japan itself, was scheduled for November 1, with Operation Olympia, the invasion of Kyushu, the southernmost island of Japan. Already, American battleships and cruisers were pounding the coast of Japan with their heavy guns, and hundreds of B-29s continued their almost daily raids on Japanese cities and military installations. There were hopeful souls in Washington who believed that the relentless bombing of Japan itself would persuade Japanese leaders that there was no hope for victory and that it was time to surrender rather than see their homeland destroyed. If these optimistic souls had spent a few minutes talking to the soldiers and Marines who were engaged with the Japanese fanatics fighting *away* from their homeland and who were committing suicide rather than surrendering, they would have understood that it was absurd to expect the people on their home soil to even think of surrendering. Later, after the war, it was discovered that men, women, and children were aggressively preparing to die in the last ditch fight they knew was coming. Like high school drill teams of today, women and children were choreographed to make coordinated attacks with sharpened bamboo sticks and spears.[19] And besides the kamikaze suicide pilots who had been killing themselves on suicide dives into our ships for over a year, there were "kaiten"—human guided torpedoes waiting to be launched, and a new suicide cadre now being trained to stop the invasion they knew was coming. These were the "fukuryu"—crouching dragons—whose task was to swim out to the invading landing craft and supply ships and place mines on their hulls which they would then detonate, killing themselves in the process.[20] That the Japanese would surrender without an invasion was a fantasy that had no basis in fact or evidence.

While the final stages of the Okinawa battle were raging and the mass bombing of Japan by B-29s was approaching a crescendo, Cadet McClure completed the primary phase of his training and, with his fellow cadets, was shipped to Whiting Field outside Pensacola, Florida, for the intermediate phase of his flight training. (One of his classmates, obviously wealthy, chartered a club car while the rest traveled by troop train and he got tagged with the sobriquet, "Pullman E. Club Car".) When they arrived, they had to wait a day to get in their barracks because it had just been disinfected for bed bugs, and their first days were spent with the lingering odor of the creosote

Courtesy McClure family

Mac McClure. May 21, 1945.

spray that had been used on walls, floor, ceiling, and mattresses. Then came the bad news. The Navy did not know what to do with them. Officials in Pensacola had been ordered to stop further pilot training—a surplus of pilots had been trained and, even with the scheduled invasion of Japan in the final planning stages, there was doubt that McClure's class would be needed. So, while the war against Japan continued to rage, and while America's new president, Harry Truman, was in Potsdam, Germany, telling Churchill and Stalin that an atomic bomb test had been successful in the New Mexico desert, Cadet McClure and his fellow trainees did "absolutely nothing"—at least of a nature that would further the war effort.

Of course, they had at least one regular military formation to meet each day, and their quarters were inspected in the interest of maintaining good order and discipline. But, mostly they tried to have fun. Cadet McClure, while still in high school, had spent two weeks with his friend, Randall Imler, on Lost Valley Reservoir north of Council, and while there had learned to skipper his friend's small sailboat. Now, with liberties available for the asking, and free recreational sailboats available at the docks of the Pensacola Naval Air Station, Cadet McClure was suddenly in high demand because he had proven to the authorities that he was, indeed, a true sailor, and was given a skipper certificate that allowed him to take one of their vessels into the Gulf waters anytime he desired. This was a neat arrangement for him; everybody else paid for the beer; all he had to do was sail the boat.

Then there was the WAVE[vii] barracks sixty yards away from where the cadets were housed. Healthy young women housed near healthy young men, and both with lots of spare time and energy, was a formula for high jinks and escapades that were bound to leave indelible memories. In an interview, after a bit of prodding, McClure said:

> *In those days seamen wore a tailor-made kerchief, an inch or inch-and-a-half wide, that was easier to tie than the issue type. One day one of the WAVES came out wearing only one of those kerchiefs around her chest. That caused quite a furor.*[21]

After that, there was a pause, but no further comments were made.

Then, on August 6 and again on August 9, atomic bombs were dropped on Hiroshima and Nagasaki. The devastation was incredible, but still, at a secret meeting in Tokyo the vote for surrender by the six war leaders was a three-three tie. The war would go on and the bombs (conventional) would keep falling and Japanese and Americans would still die. But then, the Japanese leaders held a meeting with Emperor Hirohito and he broke the tie. ". . .the time has come," the Emperor said, "when we must bear the unbearable. It cannot be helped." After the Emperor spoke, there was two weeks of bitter infighting, plots and thwarted coups by defiant military leaders who were determined to fight until every last person in Japan was dead, then capitulations and suicides after the Emperor's first-ever radio speech finally silenced the opposition. Japan formally agreed to surrender.

Cadet McClure was on liberty in Mobile, Alabama on September 2 to celebrate the formal day of surrender known as VJ Day (victory over Japan day). And while he and many of his comrades were concerned over the tragic loss of life caused by the atomic bombs dropped on Hiroshima and Nagasaki, and also a bit uneasy over a future where weapons of such mass destruction would forever be in any war equation, there was also a euphoria and a mental release from the foreboding thoughts of impending death that had hung over them for the past few years. *Maybe I am not going to die young; maybe I will live to be an old man; maybe there is a future for me, after all.*

What is going to happen to us now? That question was foremost in the minds of the cadets stranded in the middle of Navy flight training at Pensacola after VJ Day. An answer was not long in coming. "You have five options," they were told, but only two of the options interested Cadet McClure. One was to agree to stay in the Navy five more years, an option that would allow them to complete their flight training. The other was to get out of the Navy immediately. Cadet McClure pondered both of those. He loved flying; he had his fighter pilot's scarf; he had his brother's bars and braid; and he really wanted to win his wings and become an officer in the U.S. Navy. But, five years seemed an inordinately long time for a young man of 21 years—that was about one-fourth of his whole lifetime. After some time contemplating his options, and after learning that he would be exempt from the draft if he got out (he did not have near enough service points which other servicemen needed for discharge), he decided to get out and start his real life—the same decision under the same circumstances his father had made twenty-seven years earlier.

He was sent to Bremerton, Washington, the Navy installation closest to his home, and was discharged from there on Monday, October 4. His travel expenses were paid to Payette, and he was entitled to wear the "ruptured duck," the pin that identified him as a World War II veteran. He was also given $300 separation pay, which he put in the bank when he got home. Four years later he would find a very good use for that money.

Chapter 6 notes

i. A modern internal medicine specialist speculated that the problem was vasovagal syncopy, a dramatic lowering of the blood pressure that could have been ameliorated by the infusion of caffeine.

ii. The friend was Rulon Jensen from Idaho Falls and his brother, Berne, a prominent Boise attorney who was not aware of this incident, would later assist in all of McClure's congressional and senatorial campaigns. When Berne finally heard the story, he scoffed, "Rulon wouldn't have made it anyhow; he had diabetes."

iii. The Army version was the C-54. After the war it became the DC-4, a workhorse of the airlines.

iv. Every military installation had a "telephone central", an office with a switchboard and numerous phone booths where service personnel could place long-distance calls at a reduced rate.

v. Small, movable control surfaces.

vi. That's all he succeeded doing in politics. After his first term he was defeated and even though he was a persistent candidate he never won another office. For his next career he moved to California and became a successful marketer of wigs for men called "Taylor Toppers".

vii. *W*omen *A*ccepted for *V*olunteer *E*mergency Service—women serving in the Navy.

Chapter 7

LAW STUDENT

The young man, who returned to Payette in October, 1945 was a far different young man from the one who left home for the first time in May of 1942. This one was six feet tall, a lean, muscular 155 pounds hardened by two years of intense physical training, and with a supreme attitude of self-confidence who thought that he "could conquer anything." Except to his mother and a few of his old school classmates, he was no longer the little "Jamie" of yesteryear, the smallest or next-to-smallest boy in his graduating class, and whose only achievement of note was to have been a mediocre performer with the piccolo and flute. Had he been like most of the other boys of his age and reached his physical maturity while still in high school, he undoubtedly would have played football and basketball and been initiated into the elite "P Club" and worn the prestigious athletic letter sweater for which he yearned, but which he had had absolutely no chance to earn.

Now he was the adult, Jim, a "returning GI," eager to meet others from his hometown who were starting to dribble back home. Not having combat or POW tales to share with these buddies was not a social handicap in those days; veterans of combat and POW camps rarely, if ever, discussed their experiences, wanting instead to bury those nightmares into their deep subconscious and never let them surface. It was not uncommon for wives and mothers to hear screams in the night and to see their young men walking the floor in sweat-drenched night clothes, but at the bars and the pool halls where veterans, before they started school or work, hung out and talked, the conversation was more likely to be the usual male fare—girls and sex and girls. That there was a pent-up demand for both is documented in the demographic tables and by a term from that era added to our lexicon: "baby boom."

Jim McClure was in no hurry to do anything when he got home. He lounged around the house, enjoyed his mother's home cooking, went pheasant, duck, and goose hunting with his friend, Johnny Goldsmith, spent some time hanging out in his father's law office, and, in evenings, hung out in places where the other veterans congregated. There was no doubt in his mind about his ultimate goal. In January, in time for the second semester, he would return to the University of Idaho, complete his prelaw studies, then enroll in law school, graduate, and join his father's practice. He had planned to do that since the seventh or eighth grade, and nothing that he had experienced since had tempted him to change his mind.

He did have one secret goal for the immediate future. It had always bothered him that he could not dance. This was particularly bothersome on the Idaho campus where fraternity and sorority dances were the main social events. He liked girls and wanted to meet girls, and he knew that the dance floor was the best place for that to happen. In addition, if he did meet a girl he liked, there was an excellent probability that, for it to be a successful romance, she would expect him to escort her to all the dances. So, in his mind, whether he liked it or not—and he did not—he would say later: "When I woke up from a nightmare, I realized that I was at a dance"—he was determined that learning to dance was something he had to do. And how does one learn to dance as a 21-year old young man in Payette, Idaho? The best way was to go out to the Gayway Dance Hall at the Gayway Junction south of town and simply get out there on the floor and start dancing to George Shurtleff and his music. Girls did not mind if you were a learner. They were used to having their toes stepped on and they were tolerant of men who horsed them around in offbeat rhythm. And Jim did do a little of that after he got home. But, secretly, he used another method. At his home, undoubtedly with his mother out of the house, he put dance records on the Victrola, then, sans partner, and with an Arthur Murray instruction book on dancing in one hand—the book had probably been purchased by his late Uncle Paul Freehafer—he stepped and glided his way through the series of lessons. And was it effective? While not particularly proud to be admitting all of this, he said later, a bit grumpily, "I managed to get around the dance floor after that."

Jim also dated some of the local girls, one of whom would occupy a lasting place in his life. Betty Miller, a pretty southern girl from Mississippi, had come to Payette in 1944 with her family and had finished high school there. The pair went to the movies and to ball games together, and while the relationship was not destined to blossom into a romance, their family names must have left some kind of subconscious attraction for both of them. The following spring, after Jim's brother, Raymond, had returned to Payette, a group of the young people from town went to McCall for a ski meet and to observe the ski jumping contests. Raymond McClure met Betty Miller that day and three months later they were married. And three months after that, Jim McClure would meet another Miller girl—this one a purebred Idahoan—but that is another story.

As autumn waned and the months of winter were pending, Jim McClure was far more optimistic than the business and political leaders of his nation. Jim McClure knew his future, and after he drove to Pocatello to see what the University of Idaho Southern Branch would do with the credits he earned there in the V-12 program, he learned that the last courses he took, for which he did not take the finals because of illness, were to be credited to him because he had been ordered to leave before he could take the finals. Altogether then, including the first year credits that he had earned as a freshman at the University in 1942-1943, and further credit for some of his V-5 courses, he would return to the university with the status of a mid-term junior and needing only one semester of course work to complete the three-year prelaw requirements. That was good news. By next summer he could start his studies in law school.

Courtesy McClure family
Mac and his mother in 1945.

Things were a lot less hopeful on the national scene. Millions of young men were returning to civilian life just as the massive war industry was shutting down. Where were all these young men going to work? That problem was frightful, and it was exacerbated by the fact that millions of women, whose life before the war was confined to house and hearth, but who filled in for the men during the war and built munitions, guns, tanks, airplanes, and ships, did not necessarily wish to return to their prior status as homebodies. One of the worst depressions in United States history had occurred just before the war, and many believed at the time that the only reason the country emerged from the Great Depression was because of the economic stimulus of war production. With the specter of massive unemployment, was the country destined to return to the doldrums of the thirties? Of course, with hindsight, we know that pent-up demand for consumer goods and housing, among other factors, initiated the opposite of what many feared; a postwar business boom, albeit with a few minor cyclic interruptions, followed the war and persisted for the remainder of the century.

However, Jim McClure and his fellow veterans—and ultimately the country—benefited from the pessimism of our leaders at the time. Even before the war was over, leaders like newspaper magnate William Randolph Hearst remembered the problems that followed the end of World War I—problems with unemployment and a stagnant economy while shifting from wartime to peacetime production. Because of the massive war industry that had virtually exploded during World War II, they predicted that the problem would be far worse this time around, and Hearst, especially, through campaigns in his chain of newspapers, lobbied the public and Congress for legislation that would already be on the books, ready to confront the problem as soon as the war was over and demobilization began. The lobbying was effective, and in the spring of 1944 a bill titled *The Servicemen's Readjustment Act of 1944* passed unanimously in both houses of Congress, and President Roosevelt signed it on June 22 of that year. The resultant legislation, later called the "GI Bill of Rights," is now, because of its long-range impact, considered one of the most profound pieces of legislation ever passed by Congress.

The feature of the GI Bill that was most significant to Jim McClure and, ultimately, 2.2 million other World War II veterans, was the educational provisions. For those who wished to attend a college or university, the government would pay up to $500 a year for tuition and books plus a living allowance of $50 a month. (The latter was increased to $60 in 1946 and $75 in 1948.) Married veterans were paid slightly more. Those figures might seem minuscule to later generations, but in the economy of that day, the $500 covered tuition and books at most institutions and the monthly stipend was not much less than what many of them had been earning as servicemen. In other words, the money from the GI Bill was adequate if the veteran was careful, and if the summer vacations were used for work that would supplement the income.

In January 1946 Jim McClure returned to the University of Idaho campus, took residence again in the Sigma Nu house and enrolled in a full load of classes. More serious now, as were most of the other veterans who had enrolled, he dramatically improved his academic performance over the dismal record he had established for the spring semester of 1943. He earned "A's" in all of his courses but one, and he explained what happened. "In that course, which was Comparative Government taught by Dr. Robert Hosack—a fine professor, greatly admired, I got a "B" and when I went in afterwards and asked him why—I thought I had done "A" work—he agreed that I had done "A" work, but he said he gave me a "B" because he felt that I could have done better."[1]

McClure, after a perfunctory interview with the dean, enrolled in the law school at the end of the spring semester. Academically, it was a unique experience, and one that would trouble him for the next three years. In regular undergraduate classes it was the normal procedure for the professor to give a number of interim examinations just to keep tabs on the progress of the students. They might be weekly quizzes; they might be three-week exams; for sure there would be a major mid-term test. However, the law professors did not do that. Material was assigned regularly, and although students might be called on for recitations in some of the classes, there were no exams other than the final. "That was hard for me," said McClure later, "because I didn't have the discipline to keep up the way I should have. I have never been a well-organized person and without the incentive of the interim exams to prod me into studying, I was not one of the all-star law students."

When the summer term was over, McClure returned to Payette and ran into Jack Bowman, one of his high school friends. Jack had been a P-38 fighter pilot in the Far East during the war and now, in an attempt to make a living flying as a civilian, he had teamed up with one of Idaho's all-time characters, Ferris Lind. Lind had been a Navy pilot, and after the war, he started a chain of discount gas stations[i] and an aerial application business for agriculture. Jack was hired to be a pilot and to run the aviation business using war surplus Stearmans (a biplane trainer similar to the N3N McClure had flown in primary training) modified with more powerful 450 hp Pratt & Whitney engines. "You need to make money and I need some help," was the gist of the conversation between the two old friends, and McClure went to work immediately, flagging and doing other odd jobs for Bowman's spraying/dusting operations. In addition to the Stearmans, the operation also owned a Piper Cub that had limited use for dusting operations. Eager to get into the air again, McClure flew the Cub a few times even though, technically, he was not qualified because he did not possess a civilian pilot license.

McClure returned to a drastically different University of Idaho campus in the fall of 1946. Most of the war veterans were home now and those who were starting college would make up a student body very different from what was found on campuses before the war. All of the veterans had lost two, three, or four years from their lives because of their military service; many had wound scars, or carried shrapnel still embedded in their bodies, or wore metal plates in their heads, or limped with injured joints that would never heal properly. For the most part these veterans were a determined lot, anxious to make up for all that lost time and get on with their lives. And their mood, as they registered for their classes and settled down into campus routine, was far from typical of the 17-year-old naive freshmen right out of high school. These veterans brooked little nonsense. At a fraternity initiation one could easily hear, as an 18-year-old sophomore came at a veteran with a paddle, "Don't come at me with that paddle or I'll shove it up your [bleep]." And the same kind of defiance could be heard in the classroom as a veteran, listening to some mealy-mouth professor trying to make a point would, disgusted and ill-tempered, stand up and say, "I'm tired of listening to all your [bleep]; why don't you just say what you mean." Arrogant professors, who, during their previous years of teaching, had been used to playing God with their students, were now often intimidated, even frightened by these new men on campus, many of whom were practiced killers and had only recently been roasting their fellow human beings with flame throwers and napalm.

Veterans were just beginning to flood college campuses in the fall of 1946; by the fall of 1947 their numbers increased to the point where veterans on the GI Bill made up half of all the students attending college in the United States.[2] Their presence on college campuses was much more significant than their numbers. For example, they were used to drinking and hard living and what they deemed the sissy-like attitude of some college administrators regarding such activities was an attitude they delighted in exploding. In addition, there was a subset of veterans on every campus who really did not know why they were there except that the government was going to pay for all their tuition and books and give them a monthly allowance. "I'd be stupid not to take that" was the attitude of this minority who used the college campus primarily as a place to party and chase the pretty little coeds who were much more attracted to the mature males than the fuzzy-cheeked boys right out of high school.

Another subset on the campuses in those years was the married veterans, typified by McClure law school classmate, Idaho Senate colleague (later), and friend, the now prominent Rexburg attorney, Ray Rigby. He said:

> *"Some of us, despite our desire not to leave widows and children, let our passions overrule our brains during the war and we got married. After the war, the GI Bill offered us the chance to do something with our lives and, despite our extreme poverty, we headed off to college. In my case, I had a wife and one child and we headed off to the University of Idaho in a 1937 Chevrolet Coupe—three of us in the front seat—and before I finished, we had the second child and we all had to share that same seat. When we first got there, they put us in Lindley Hall, a boy's dorm, each room with two bunk beds—you can imagine the creative ways those were arranged after we took over—and the next year they threw up some Quonset huts that became veterans' family housing. We were like a big family there—we looked after the neighborhood kids and they looked after ours. Our food was rice, beans, and macaroni for our main meals, Germade—a mush cereal—for breakfast, and recreation was a movie and the sharing of a ten-cent bag of popcorn."*[3]

There was also a significant difference in the University campus after World War II and the campuses of recent years. Music, which has always been an integral component of American culture, was probably embraced most intensely by veterans and college-age young people in those post-war years. And in the late 1940s, unlike current popular music, the songs of that era had words and melodies that were easy to understand and replicate, either by humming or whistling by individuals as they performed their daily activities, or by singing, especially when high-spirited young people would get together for a party, and in the fraternities, sororities,[ii] and other living groups, each of whom sponsored a chorus that competed each spring in the annual campus songfest. In short, musical expression, especially singing, was not only a dominant activity of young people when they gathered, it was an outlet for their youthful exuberance and, simply, just great fun.

Jim McClure was definitely one of those high-spirited young persons who sang out of exuberance and to have fun. He had done that as a youth;

he had done it more formally in choirs while in the Navy; and now that he was back at the university, he tried out and was selected as a member of what was, and probably still is, the best known choral group in Idaho: the University of Idaho Vandaleers. For a reason that he could not foresee, the decision to try out for the Vandaleers would be the most fateful of his life.

Like everything else on the campus, the Vandaleers changed drastically as the veterans came to the campus in the fall of 1946. Male voices, which are much more slow to mature than female voices, give any chorus a distinct sound, and when the males in the chorus are typical college age of 17 to 21, the sound is immature when compared to more adult choruses. Literally, the Vandaleer sound changed when the older veterans joined the group, starting the fall of 1946, but especially in the next three or four years as the influx of veterans peaked. Roger Vincent, who was one of those veterans and who later went on to sing professionally in a traveling opera company, declared ". . .that because of the mature male voices, the Vandaleers during that period was the greatest choral group the university ever had."[4] Glen Lockery, who had sung professionally for the Robert Shaw Chorale in New York City before coming to direct the Vandaleers for thirty-four years, agreed that, because of the mature sound of the veterans, the group during the late forties "had a more mature quality, and certainly a beautiful quality."[5]

Another who auditioned and who was accepted into the Vandaleers that fall of 1946 was a freshman girl from Nezperce, a small farm town and the county seat of Lewis County. Louise Marilyn Miller—her friends and classmates called her "Lou"—had graduated that spring as the valedictorian of her class of eighteen, and had already spent practically her whole lifetime engaged in musical pursuits. At the age of three, dressed in a Shirley Temple dress made for her by her mother, she was belting out the refrain of *The Little Brown Jug* and other Shirley Temple songs to receptive audiences in their Christian Church, elementary school, and at a variety of social gatherings. And, under the guidance of her mother, who was an accomplished singer and musician, she started sporadic study of the piano at age five. Soon she was playing both harmony and melody by ear, without reading the music, and when she was in the fifth grade she began playing the E-flat clarinet. Later, she and her mother sang duet at funerals and other functions in the county, and she played the clarinet in the high school band that, despite the small size of the school, always placed high in the competition held each year in Lewiston, the regional capitol for the central panhandle of Idaho.

Louise Miller, who came to the university to study voice and major in music (with a minor in education so she could teach music), was an immediate popular success on the campus. She pledged Delta Delta Delta Sorority, plunged into the party life on the campus, and dated a number of boys including a handsome, dynamic member of the Kappa Sigma Fraternity named Bill Sweet. This relationship bloomed almost immediately into a romance, and before the first semester was over, Louise accepted his fraternity pin in a formal pinning ceremony. After that, they were more than just a couple going steady; by accepting Bill Sweet's fraternity pin, she was, by the unwritten standards of the time, accepting the relationship as a kind of pre-engagement, meaning that they were serious about each other and that the relationship might get even more serious in the future.

Courtesy McClure family
Louise Marilyn Miller.

Bill Sweet was a baseball player and on an athletic scholarship. He was also very active on the campus and heavily involved in his fraternity. Louise liked that; she was a dynamic young woman herself and she admired Bill for his growing reputation on the campus. But, she was also intrigued by one of the older men in the Vandaleers. Said she: "The first time I really noticed Jim McClure was one day when he was pestering the girl who was our piano accompanist. He was giving her a bad time. It was a repartee as they traded barbs and they were laughing and joking. Later, the new [Vandaleer] director, Glen Lockery, got us a regular period at the end of the day that we used for practice—before that we just had to work practices in at various times during the school day. Since we were all together at the end of every day, some of us got in the habit of stopping in at the Bucket or the Nest[iii] for a cup of coffee. There was a bond between the students who were interested in music and we enjoyed being together. I was always in that bunch and so was Jim, and so I got to know him a whole lot better. Gradually, I began to develop a lot of respect for him. I appreciated his maturity and his brain—he was very intelligent and I liked that. I remember that we talked about a lot of things that college freshmen and sophomores didn't usually discuss. He contributed to my intellectual development and I appreciated that."[6]

Then there were the Vandaleer tours. During spring break and at certain other times of the year, two busloads of Vandaleers would leave the campus and do a series of performances in various communities around the state. These tours had a way of strengthening the bond between the members of the group, and it gave them many hours of togetherness that they would never have experienced just as students on the campus. Of course, the Vandaleers of the late '40s was not the typical college group because about half of them were veterans. Said one of them years later: "We had a great time on those tours and, after the performance and before we would go to the people's homes where we were staying, we would often find a bar in the town and proceed to continue the performance there. A lot of the girls were too young to be in the bar, but I can't remember any bar owner who objected—it was good business for him. We would have a great songfest, and I remember Henry Sijohn, who was an American Indian with a beautiful baritone voice. When the night was over, he would always lead us in the singing, *Here We Have Idaho.* This was probably a problem for Hal Macklin, the head of the department, and Glen Lockery, our conductor. We expected there would be fireworks if the administration found out about these [extracurricular activities] but they never ever said a word to us. I don't know how they pulled that off."[7]

Another member of that group, who later became a music teacher in Idaho, laughed when he was asked about the after-concert sessions. "Things were relaxed in those days, and we could go into a place like the Buffalo Club in Boise and have a really good time. There was always a lot of laughter and good fun and I can confirm that it was a tradition to close the place down with *Here We Have Idaho.* We also had a lot of fun on the bus. Glen Lockery knew more verses of *A Rovin*[iv] than anybody—he could sing them all day long."[v] [8]

Like all the other veterans on the GI Bill, Jim McClure was paid a monthly stipend during the months that he was in school. However, when classes ended in May, so did the stipend. This meant that every veteran had to scrounge for some kind of employment during the summer months, and this was not easy in the postwar economy. In the summer of 1947 Jim McClure got lucky. After a few weeks of running a spray rig for Ferris Lind, for whom he had worked the previous summer, he discovered that his old school chum from Payette, Ellis Hallman, was in charge of the body shop at Francisco Motors, the Nash automobile dealer in Moscow, and that he needed some help. So Jim McClure went back to Moscow, moved back into the Sigma Nu house, boarded with Ellis and his wife, and went to work for Francisco Motors in the body shop where he learned how to hammer out fenders, stretch and shrink metal, fill dents with molten lead, and to file, sand, and paint cars. "I never did any of the work that required real skill," he said later, "but, under Ellis' supervision, I got reasonably good at what you could call the body and fender grunt work."[9]

By this time Jim McClure had gotten a little more interested in Louise Miller, and from comments from those who knew her then, he had good reasons to be interested. She had already been elected the Kappa Sigma Fraternity's first "sweetheart," and the following year she would be the runner up for the Athletic Association's "I Queen." And by all accounts, she was a charming, talented, and intelligent young woman. The sticking point for McClure, of course, was the fact that she was pinned, and therefore committed to the popular Bill Sweet. By the summer of 1947, he was definitely not nourishing any hopes of a romantic relationship with her, and while he might have thought of her occasionally as he hammered and sanded away fender dents, she was not the only girl who would occupy his mind.

> **THE BATTERED CAR**
>
> A fraternity brother from Coeur d' Alene had a girlfriend in Baker City, Oregon, and when Jim McClure went home for spring break, he dropped his friend off to see his girl, then picked him up on the way back to Moscow. Jim was tired and the friend was driving, and as Jim dozed, he heard his friend yell as the car went off the road and rolled. Luckily they stayed in the car, but, upside down and dazed, they heard gasoline gurgling and managed to get out by breaking one of the windows. Neither was hurt seriously, but they had scratches because the car had landed in blackberry brambles, and Jim had "a beautiful shiner" resulting from his head slamming into the dash. The top was caved in, the frame was bent, and the doors were sprung, but he had his car towed from south of Walla Walla to Moscow and after some primitive body work, was able to continue driving it. Ever after the "battered car" would be a part of the McClure image that would be remembered by his friends.

However, during the next school year, with the daily Vandaleer practices and the after-practice coffee klatches a part of the routine, the McClure-Miller friendship began to grow. Louise still continued to date Bill Sweet and to consider herself as his steady girlfriend, and Jim occasionally dated other girls. But, the two of them got to know each other better and they discovered that there was a mutual attraction. She liked and respected his intelligence and maturity; he admired her beauty, her intelligence, her sense of humor, and her penchant for good conversation. And it was probably his own sense of humor and his tendency to be self deprecating that kept him from being more aggressive and playing the role of the impetuous suitor. So, as their friendship grew and they became more comfortable with each other, they were able to enjoy a relaxed, platonic friendship. And, of course, both of them were extremely busy. He was buried in his law studies, and while he would never be known as a law scholar, he worked hard because he wanted to do well. She was also taking her studies seriously; music had been a dominant force in her life, and even though she had no idea what she was going to do with a major in voice and a degree in music (except teach), she was determined to be the best that she could be.

By both of their accounts, the relationship between the two of them experienced steady growth during the school year 1947-48. Bill Sweet could see that, too, and later he was to comment: "I could see it happening between Jim and Louise because they had so much in common. They shared this great love of music and I couldn't compete with that. I think there was another factor, too. About that time, I switched majors—from education to agriculture—I had my uncle's farm waiting for me and that seemed like a practical choice. I don't think Louise wanted to go back to a farm. I don't think she wanted that kind of life."[10] When Louise was asked to comment on her former boyfriend's remarks, she replied, "I think Bill was 100 percent correct. I think we both liked and respected each other, but we grew apart as Jim and I grew closer."[11] The romantic relationship ended sometime in the spring of 1948 when she returned Bill Sweet's Kappa Sigma pin.

The courtship was on now. Daily, Jim watched for Louise to go by his Sigma Nu House as she walked from the Tri-Delt House to classes, or from her classes to the House, and he would often join her. Of course, they also had their daily meetings during and after Vandaleer practice. In addition, Norman Logan, one of the instructors in the music department, asked for volunteers to sing in a male quartet that he was organizing. Jim auditioned and was accepted as the bass voice, because, said Logan, "It wasn't excellent singers that I necessarily picked for such an ensemble; I picked guys who had fun singing and who liked to sing—that was Jim McClure."[12] A piano accompanist was also needed for the quartet and the tryout for that position was won by Louise Miller who, added Logan, "was very good." Thus, during the daily practices of the quartet, there was one more reason for the two to share time together.

The following summer Jim worked for Ellis Hallman again, both in the Francisco Motors body shop, and in the evenings and weekends when Ellis, who also had an aircraft and engine mechanic's license, moonlighted at the airport on the south edge of Moscow. Their first moonlighting job was for Pete Fountain, the airport manager, who had bought a war surplus Stearman that needed recovering. So, Jim McClure began learning the craft of aircraft fabric stitching.

However, his mind continued to wander that summer. There was this girl, now special, who lived in Nezperce, and she was home with all the old boy friends who had courted her ardently when she had been in high school. He did not like that situation and later he said, "trust was one thing, but being foolish was another."[13] So, on several weekends he would leave the moonlighting to Ellis and drive to Nezperce and spend two days with Louise, sleeping in the basement under the watchful eyes of her parents, of course; and late Sunday night he would head back to Moscow, stopping from time to time to nap, and arrive Monday morning in time to start his day at Francisco Motors.

Then it happened, as it happens to many young men at some time in early adulthood. He got stars in his eyes over an automobile. And what a spectacular automobile it was. A businessman from Moscow had traded in his 1942 Chrysler Highlander convertible to Francisco Motors for a new Nash. It was a beautiful sage green, with red plaid upholstery—hence the "Highlander" designation, and looked like a new car. And despite the astronomical—for that time—$1,500 they were asking for the car, the stars in Jim McClure's eyes short-circuited his good sense, and after a telephone

Courtesy McClure family

Jim and Louise and the 1942 Chrysler Highlander convertible..

call to his father who, perhaps reluctantly—we will never know— agreed to loan the money to his son, he drove away, probably with the top down, and his image on campus as "the battered car driver" would change; now he was the "Payette dandy" who bought a spectacular car to impress the pert and beautiful Miss Louise Miller who was now unpinned and fair game for all the ardent, unmarried young men on the campus. Whether or not young Jim McClure was also attempting to send a message to Louise's parents that, someday he would support their daughter in high style, is speculation that has never been acknowledged.

In the fall of 1948, as Jim McClure was starting his final year in law school, the national and international news was frightening. Day after day there was news about the unrest of our industrial labor forces, with walkouts, strikes, and threatened shutdowns, with the United Mine Workers under their militant head John L. Lewis being the most aggressive. But far worse were the events in Europe that could easily have triggered World War III. The Soviets, under dictator Josef Stalin, were not only flexing their new postwar strength, they were shoving the collective noses of Britain, France and the United States into the dirt and literally daring these former allies into doing anything about it. Throughout September, October, and November, the newspaper headlines screamed about the outrage of the Soviet military blocking off all access to Berlin for their former allies—this after the Potsdam agreement by all the allies to share access to the four zones of occupation. The goal of the Soviets was to starve the Berlin people, and at the same time cause the collapse of their former allies, making it inevitable that all of Berlin would join Communist East Germany.

President Truman, who was considered an accidental president because of his ascendancy after Franklin Roosevelt's death and who was considered to be the underdog to Thomas Dewey in the upcoming November election, had refused to send troops and tanks against the Soviets who were blocking highway and rail access—an action that could have triggered a war. Instead, he ordered Air Force transport aircraft to overfly the Soviet zone and thwart the blockade by carrying supplies in by air. This unprecedented use of air power that came to be called the "Berlin Airlift" was in full operation as the fall semester got underway, and with the winter season pending and thousands of tons of coal and food needed to keep the Berliners from freezing and starving, the tension in the nation was palpable nearly everywhere. Could we save the Berlin people with just the airlift? Or, would we have to go to war with the Soviets? That we would just let the Berliners freeze and starve was an option that no responsible American seriously considered.

These were the weighty matters discussed on the front pages of every daily newspaper in the country that fall. But, then as now, college and university campuses are notorious for being islands isolated from the real world. Certainly, Jim McClure and his law school classmates, if their memories are correct, were not experiencing tension over the momentous national and international events of the time. They were in their own little world, trying to pay their food and room bills with their meager stipend or allowance, and they were in a very demanding professional curriculum that, unlike education, for example, where a professional license was guaranteed after graduation, there was no guarantee. Graduation from law school meant only that you *might* be able to go out and practice law and earn a living. There was the all-important bar exam that had to be passed, and as Jim McClure and his fellow classmates started their last year of professional training, the height of that future hurdle loomed higher and higher.

Jim McClure and his close law school friend, J. T. Peterson, decided that they had to make some changes in their life if they were to get the maximum benefit of their law school studies. Both had been living in their fraternity houses but, so they could get away from the younger students and the inevitable turmoil of fraternity life, they decided to move off campus to a quiet environment where they could study together. Thus, they both spent the school year on West Third Street in the two front rooms of a house owned by Mrs. King, an elderly widow. However, they continued to take their meals at their respective fraternity houses, and it was probably after one of those meals when they had stopped in at the Perch, a little hamburger joint on campus, and got in a fateful conversation with some girls from the Gamma Phi Sorority.

J. T. Peterson was into drama and theatrics, even in his later life, and he must have used some of his natural charisma to hatch a plot and secure perpetrators for a scam that would end up putting Jim McClure into his first publicly elected office. Here was the plot:

Either he or McClure had noted in the local newspaper that, for the general election that would be held November 2, no candidates had filed for the positions of justice of the peace or constable. During their conversation, J. T. announced that there was an economic opportunity available to his friend and himself if they could get some voters to write in their names for the two uncontested offices. It seems that there was a notorious stop sign down the hill from the Administration Building that was hidden by a tree, but staked out regularly by the city cops who made frequent arrests of drivers who inadvertently ran the stop sign. That it was notorious was confirmed by Bob Yost, a classmate of McClure's who went on to become Canyon County prosecutor for many years. Said Yost, "The situation was so bad, I felt it was my duty as a citizen to approach the police and urge them to cut down the tree and eliminate a potential hazard. When I did so, I was shocked at the policeman's reply. He said, 'We can't do that. How could we make any arrests if that tree wasn't there?'"[14] So J. T.'s plot was to get McClure elected as justice of the peace and himself elected as constable. With the constable's law enforcement powers, he could then stake out the stop sign, arrest drivers who ran it, give them a ticket that they would have to take to McClure as justice of the peace, who would then fine them and split the proceeds with J. T. "Good thinking, J. T." McClure must have replied when the plot was laid out, for with enthusiasm, he acceded to doing his share of the enterprise—if they could get elected, of course.

They now had to have perpetrators—citizens who, in good conscience, could write in the names of McClure and Peterson on the ballots and trust that law enforcement and justice would be duly and fairly administered in their environs. Again, J. T.'s flair for dramatics must have been persuasive, because the Gamma Phi girls—those who were listening to the conversation and perhaps some of their sisters who heard about it later, pledged their support for the two stellar candidates, and they agreed to campaign in their house for more votes. The record of this important electoral decision has long since disappeared—at least it is not in the county clerk's archives nor in *The Daily Idahonian* of that week—but McClure is adamant that both he and J. T. Peterson were duly elected by write-in votes. However, there was a slight problem. The Gamma Phi girls got confused. They elected J. T. Peterson as justice of the peace, and Jim McClure as constable. "That wasn't the way it was supposed to have worked," said McClure chuckling. "But, I went to the courthouse, got my star and certificate, but they wouldn't give me a firearm. When I walked out of there, I said to myself, 'Maybe I could have fined those brought to me as justice of the peace, but there was no way

I could go down there [to the stop sign] and arrest fellow students. So I gave up the whole idea, and never qualified.'"[15]

Besides that, he was a lot more interested in pursuing the little voice major from Nezperce than roaming around Moscow wearing a star on his shirt. Louise Miller had given up her Kappa Sigma pin but she was not wearing McClure's Sigma Nu pin either. By her memory she was just having fun, socially, and with her classes. She truly loved music, even the difficult courses like music theory that most other music students found difficult or even hated. But, she enjoyed the singing most of all, and she got to do that every day while the ordinary students on the campus listened to lectures, pounded their texts, and sweated the essays they had to write in little blue books. Of course, her suitor was not exactly having an easy time of it. This was his last year of law school—at least, that was what he expected it to be. So this was the last go-around, the last chance to load the brain cells with all of the legal minutiae that would be needed to pass the bar exam and go on with his career. He, too, was pounding the books but with the knowledge that something more than the first two letters of the alphabet were at stake. The blue books that he was destined to fill would determine the whole future of his life.

Then his fine mind won him an interim prize. Louise Miller liked him for a variety of reasons: he was tall and handsome, he was gentle and kind, he had a great sense of humor, he loved music, and his morality was impeccable. But most of all he was alert, inquisitive, and very intelligent, and that appealed to her very much. She had gotten to know a lot of boys and young men, both in high school and college, and she knew herself well enough to realize that she could never be happy with anyone with less intelligence than her own. Jim McClure was an equal, or better than an equal, and the weeks and months that had germinated a friendship and deep respect for him were now nurturing the ultimate emotional response: love. Sometime in the spring of 1949—neither can remember when it happened because it was just such an intense and gradual thing—both declared their mutual caring for each other and she happily accepted his fraternity pin. She became his special girl, and quite likely other things would follow.

But he did not graduate with his class in May; he had procrastinated and a major paper that was due before graduation did not get done. Darn it, he was not going to be able to leave Moscow; he was going to have to come back the next fall and complete the paper. Of course, there was a rosy lining to this scenario. His girlfriend had just one more year and if he came back in the fall, he would get to be with her. And also keep an eye on her. And be there so her heart would not grow fonder for someone else. So, was the procrastination and unfinished law-school paper a deliberate, or even subconscious act designed to prevent the quarry from escaping? When asked,

McClure never answered the question directly. He just smiled and said, "I wasn't too anxious to leave."

"It's one thing to trust; it's another thing to be stupid." That statement was repeated, however, and it was justification for how Jim McClure spent the latter part of the summer of 1949. (He cannot remember how he spent the early part of the summer but speculated that he went back to the Francisco Motors Body Shop.) He spent it on a 1,500-acre farm on Nezperce Prairie working 12-hour days and seven-day weeks for Louise Miller's father and brother. He stood exposed on the platform of the combine as it was towed by a Caterpillar crawler, a large wheel in front of him that he used to raise and lower the header and thereby adjusting the level of the cutter bar as it went through the wheat and barley. It was a manly job, requiring strength and stamina, and a tolerance for the furiously itchy beards from the grain heads, especially barley. Little Louise Miller had done this same job when she had been a high school student and when the men were gone during the war. And there was the plowing, the Caterpillar crawler pulling two, four-bottom plows through tall stubble that persistently fouled the plow blades and required the operator to get off and dig the tangled mess away—a chore described by Duane Miller, Louise's brother, as "very exasperating." Even more wearisome was the plowing of rocky ground where the plows, after hitting a rock, would trip the hitch that held them to the Caterpillar. This necessitated a stop, a precise reverse movement, then a heave on the heavy tongue to set it back upon the ring that attached it. Duane Miller, who spent his entire life on that farm and who was accustomed to hard manual work of every kind, said, "It was heavy, hard work and it made you sweat. I remember taking turns with Jim and it still took us ten days to plow just 200 acres."[16]

The summer also initiated Jim McClure into another family, both alike and dissimilar from his own. Mrs. Dorothy Miller, like Marie McClure, was an intelligent, vivacious woman, talented in music, and would probably have been a member of the Womens' Christian Temperance Union if there had been a chapter in Nezperce. But, unlike Marie, whose father, A. L. Freehafer, was an ardent Democrat and, before he died, a strong believer in Franklin D. Roosevelt and the New Deal, Dorothy Miller's parents, sister, and brother were strong Republicans. But, Louise's father, Claude, was another story. His side of the family was like the Freehafers; they were ardent Democrats. As Louise remembers, ". . .there was no problem when it was just my immediate family in the house—we didn't hear much about politics—but when the whole family got together, there were strong discussions, even heated arguments, and usually at the dinner table. My [paternal] grandfather thought FDR was God and mother's sisters and brother felt that FDR was ruining the nation. Even while I was in high school, I decided that

I never wanted anything to do with politics, ever, because I didn't like the arguments."[17]

Louise cannot recall any adverse reaction of her father to her boyfriend's political views even though Jim was never reticent about expressing support for Republican principles and actions. However, her brother, Duane, remembers his dad, Claude Miller, joking numerous times that, ". . .a blue-eyed Republican is going to run off with my daughter and he'll be the first blue-eyed Republican in the family."[18]

Courtesy McClure family

Jim and Louise. Holly Dance, December 8, 1948.

What Claude Miller did object to about Jim McClure was the way he treated his daughter. Said Louise, "Jim was very competitive and it was natural in his family to put each other down in a jovial way. Jim would put me down the same way, but he didn't know what it sounded like from my family's point of view. He would put me down in a negative way, which was flippant to him, but perhaps acerbic to them, and even me. It took them awhile to adjust to that. It took me a long time to adjust to it, except that I understood [that was his nature]. Dad never came right out and said, 'Why doesn't he treat my sweet little daughter with more respect?', but I saw his reaction and knew he was thinking that. *(McClure: We grew up teasing, and we took it for granted that if there was someway to get at somebody else, do it.)*[19] They also had some trouble adjusting to his strict observance of the rules when we played cards. Dad and my brother would occasionally cheat just as a joke—they thought it was fun to see if they could get away with it. But Jim had to go by the book; if a card was played wrong, he would not let it go by. That took some getting used to on their part."[20]

When they went back to Moscow, Louise began to seriously prepare for her senior recital, a formal presentation in the campus auditorium of eight to ten vocal pieces specified by her major professor, including at least one aria sung in a foreign language. During practice she was sometimes accompanied by her close friend Ellomae Holden. Both young women would practice several hours a day in the little white, clapboard bungalow that housed the music department in those days, and, even though they belonged to different sororities, their friendship would grow and deepen—Louise, an excellent seamstress would make Ellomae's wedding dress—and the close friendship would be maintained the rest of their lives.

Throughout that autumn the McClure-Miller romance continued to grow; however, by the time the Christmas vacation came, McClure had satisfied all of the requirements for his law school degree and was heading home, not to return for anything official until the May graduation of the 1950 law school class of which he was now considered a part. This left a pinned, but otherwise non-committed Louise Miller still on the campus and surrounded by hundreds of young men ready and eager to provide companionship to such a lovely and talented young woman. Thus, while Jim McClure was establishing an office with this father above the Ritz Theater in downtown Payette and trying to bear down in his studies for the upcoming bar examination in April, Louise was savoring the last months of what she would later consider to be some of the happiest months of her life. And to make life uneasy for her boyfriend, she and Ellomae began to pal around with two unattached male friends, both veterans, both singers in the Vandaleers, and both intelligent and attractive. One of them, Cal Long, who would later be the head of the math department at Washington State University, had just broken up with his girlfriend, and the other, Ben Strohbehn, who would become a social worker and a minister, was especially lonely after the tragic death of his young wife. Said Ellomae, "Louise and I were lonesome . . .and those two fellows helped us pass a lot of lonely hours. [After Vandaleer practice] we'd go out and have coffee, coke, or sometimes a movie, or go up to the library and study. . .there was a chemistry between us, and in another time and another place there might have been something more to it. . .but it was a simple time when one could have a platonic relationship. I'm sure Jim was very concerned about leaving Louise there."[21]

The anxiety, or the loneliness or, perhaps more fundamentally, the desire, finally got to Jim McClure in February at which time he went in to visit his friendly jeweler, Emil Fruechtenicht. He had his $300 Navy separation bonus plus four and one-half years of interest and he wanted the best quality diamond he could buy for that money. (*"I wanted good quality much more than size—Louise wasn't very big, either, but she had high quality.*")[22] Then, on Valentine's day, on the hill by the University I-Tank, and while looking out over the lights of Moscow, he pulled the ring box out of his pocket and asked the question men dread and women cherish. The answer was, "yes," and now the lawyer-to-be had both parties ready for the contract. How and when that would be consummated was the next item to negotiate.

The big question in his mind was whether or not he would be able to pass the bar exam in April. They agreed that if he did not *("I had this old fashioned idea that I should be able to support a wife before I got married"),*[23] she would get a job teaching music someplace and that they would wait until he had another go at it six months later. However, even if he did pass the exam the first time, it was doubtful that a late spring or summer wedding was possible. Life on the Nezperce Prairie at that time of year left few options for frivolous events like weddings. In an area called "hail alley" where the Miller farm was located, it was all-day, everyday work, with a fearful eye out every afternoon for the dreaded, dark thunderheads that could, in a crescendo of furious wind and precipitation, devastate the fruits of that labor and wipe out a year's annual income. If there was going to be a wedding when the Miller family could totally relax and enjoy the festivities, it would have to wait until September, after the crops were harvested and safely off to market.

Courtesy McClure family

Wedding photo. September 23, 1950.

In Boise in mid-April, while he was staying with his brother, Raymond, and while Raymond's wife, Betty, was giving birth to their first child, Jim McClure took and passed the bar examination. So, while the new lawyer began his fledgling practice in downtown Payette and dreamed what life was going to be like with the woman he loved, Louise and her friend, Ellomae, who was, herself, now engaged, ". . .poured over bride's magazines [and] spent lots of hours dreaming about what we were going to do. . .in Spokane we went shopping for wedding dresses and for what we were going to give our bridesmaids. . ."[24]

And during the summer, the more practical husband-to-be did something highly unusual for an unmarried man: he went shopping and bought a house—after the bride-to-be visited and approved it, of course. The one he purchased was at 634 Hughes Drive, a fashionable east-side address with a magnificent view of the city and the Oregon desert to the west. It was a small but comfortable frame house—840 square feet with two bedrooms and one bath, and with a two-car garage in a daylight partial basement. He paid $11,000 for the house with all its furnishings, which he financed with a 30-year, 4-percent G.I. loan with payments of $65 per month.

Then, on a lovely Saturday evening on September 23, 1950, the two were married in a candlelight ceremony in the Nezperce Christian Church. The bride was attended by three close friends, including Ellomae Holden who was now teaching music in Boise, and at the side of the groom was his older brother, Raymond. Ben Strohbehn, Louise and Ellomae's close friend from the University, sang *The Lord's Prayer* and Edvard Grieg's *I Love Thee*, and a simple reception with cake, non-alcoholic punch, nuts, and mints was held in the church reception hall. Relatives and friends were in attendance, but significant was the added presence of most of the music faculty from the University, which was an indication of the bonds of friendship forged in that department—bonds that would persist for the next fifty-plus years.

The new couple's Chrysler convertible did not get decorated with suggestive slogans or other paraphernalia, which were typical pranks of the time; however, even after it had been hidden in a great aunt's garage, a supposed secret location, it ended up missing and it was not until after midnight when Louise's brother, Duane, finally felt sorry for the exasperated couple and led them to the middle of a wheat field where the car had been taken. Then, with straw from the wheat stubble sticking out of the doors, they headed to Lake Louise in Alberta, then to Vancouver and Victoria in British Columbia for their honeymoon. And practically everyone who knew Jim McClure then or later, and who has spoken to this author on the subject, has made it a point to declare that this was, by far, Jim McClure's greatest victory.

Chapter 7 notes

i. Lind capitalized on the fact that the "big boys"—the regular gasoline retailers—did not like him undercutting their prices, saying that, "They call me a stinker," and he parlayed that image into the skunk logo for his highly successful "Stinker Stations." He also achieved national fame for posting humorous advertising signs along U.S. Highway 30; for example, near a bed of rounded lava rocks a sign announced: PETRIFIED WATERMELONS. TAKE ONE HOME TO YOUR MOTHER-IN-LAW. Sadly, this dynamic young man got vaccinated with a bad batch of polio vaccine in the 50's and spent the rest of his life in an iron lung.

ii. In at least two, and probably all sororities at the time, grace was sung before seating at the formal evening meal, then there was singing between the salad course and the entrée, between the entree and the dessert, and quite often one or two songs after dinner.

iii. The Blue Bucket was in the Student Union; the Nest was a little "greasy spoon" near the administration building where students often had coffee between classes.

iv. A sea chanty (pronounced "shanty"), a song originally sung by seamen to keep time when they used oars to propel their boat.

v. Lockery, when queried about this replied, "Actually, I only knew a few that were printable."

Chapter 8

The Lawyer

The Census Bureau counted 4,032 residents in the city of Payette, Idaho in 1950. We will never know if that count included Jim McClure's new bride that he brought there in early October. We do know that in the rest of the county, which, geographically, is the smallest in Idaho, there were an additional 7,889 people who looked at Payette as "their" city when it came time to shop or look for professional services. Also, because of the quantity and quality of businesses in the city—for example, there were three large department stores, including a J.C. Pennys and seven thriving automobile dealers—people from Washington, Adams, Valley, and Gem Counties in Idaho, and Malheur County in Oregon came to Payette at least for some of their shopping and services. In addition, there were fourteen fruit-packing firms, a canning factory, a manufacturer of high-quality church furniture, and an architectural firm that specialized in designing schools and school facilities. In short, when Jim and Louise McClure moved into their new home at 634 Hughes Drive, they were taking residence in a community that was a thriving commercial center for thousands of people in Southwestern Idaho.

Payette was also a beautiful small city. The streets were wide and were lined with tall trees. There was a hospital, a good library, clean parks, and no rundown residential areas that might be called "trashy." There was a bandstand where frequent concerts were conducted by the county band, and a baseball field that was a spawning ground for several talented players including Hall-of-Fame slugger Harmon Killebrew who, right out of high school, was signed by the Washington Senators, an American League baseball team at the time.[1]

In the autumn of 1950, the city itself was a lot more prosperous than the young attorney-at-law, Jim McClure. Ninety percent of his father's business involved real estate, wills, contracts, and estates—services that were billed, not on the per-hour fee now used by attorneys, but on the per-job basis. For example, clients needing an ordinary will without complications were charged a flat fee of $5.00, which included storage in a big safe "that was full of them." However, said McClure, "If we consulted with a person and felt a will was not needed, there would be no charge."[2] Contracts, because of their specific nature, cost more—usually $25.00—and quite often, if payments were to be made under terms of the contract, the law office would collect the payments and charge a small fee for that service.

Their real estate services included sale contracts and, more important, the close examination of real estate abstracts. The latter were compilations of all documents that had been recorded on a piece of property—documents like deeds, mortgages and mortgage releases, liens and lien releases, easements, etc. Traditionally, these abstracts were compiled in a folder by an abstractor who, before the days of copying machines, kept a typewriter at the courthouse in the county recorder's office and laboriously typed duplicates of most of the documents and, with the help of a second person, proofed the copies to be sure they were the same as the originals. After that, the attorney took over, studied the documents carefully, then weighed in with a written opinion for the real estate buyer and, usually, the buyer's bank or other mortgage lender. The McClures were about to lose this business, however. In the 1950s, throughout Idaho, the title insurance companies began compiling and studying abstracts for real estate buyers and offered something more than just an attorney's opinion to buyers and their lending agencies; they offered the guarantee of a clear title and insurance to back up that guarantee. This irritated attorneys, particularly those who depended on this business for a substantial portion of their income because lending agencies began demanding title insurance rather than an attorney's opinion for sales that were financed. Said Buhl attorney, Mike Felton, whose father practiced law in Moscow, "My father howled when that happened and accused the title companies of practicing law without a license. But, the transition occurred and it would be rare to find a young attorney today who has ever looked at an abstract." [3]

The McClures also did a lot of estate work, and even though fees for this work had been established by statute, they felt them to be excessive and charged less for their work. In addition, the attorneys in Oregon based their

HARMON KILLEBREW

Payette, Idaho's most famous citizen graduated from Payette High School in 1954 with sixteen athletic letters, four each in football, basketball, track, and baseball, and according to one of his teammates "was a better football quarterback than he was a baseball player."

Senator Herman Welker, who had been an attorney in Payette before going to the United States Senate, went directly to the Washington Senators management and told them that they should take a close look at the boy. A scout came to town and watched a night game where Killebrew hit a home run over the 400-foot left field fence. When told the distance, the scout could not believe it and asked that the lights remain on after the game so he could measure for himself. The distance proved accurate and the enthusiastic scout's report resulted in an unheard of bonus offer of $30,000. Thus, at the tender age of 17, Killebrew became baseball's first "bonus baby."

fees for a contract upon a percentage of the value of the real estate estate, which the McClures felt was excessive. Consequently, they also attracted estate clients from nearby Ontario and elsewhere in eastern Oregon.

Typically, the clients of lawyers were of middle age or older—except for law breakers, young people in those days had little need for legal services. And the mature clients were much more likely to want to deal with an older, experienced lawyer—particularly one like Will McClure who had established an impeccable reputation for honesty, integrity, and reasonable pricing for his services. So, how was the young McClure able to attract clients and establish a practice? The short answer to that question was: slowly. He began by taking work that his father gave him. Then one day the secretary came into his office and said that there was a couple who had come into the office and wanted to see him. Jim McClure cannot remember the names of the people or what they wanted, but he clearly remembers what went through his mind when he heard that: *"Gosh, those people really want to see me?"*[4]

Also at that time the County Prosecutor, Gilbert Norris, declined to run for reelection; "I had had all I wanted of that job," he said later.[5] Besides young McClure, there were only four other attorneys in the county at that time: Norris's father; Herman Welker, who was running for the United States Senate (and would win his election in November); Vernon Daniel, who was Welker's partner; and Will McClure. None of these were even remotely interested in the job, partly because of the salary, which was $1,800 per year, so Jim McClure filed for the position and was elected without opposition. Then, at the next meeting of the county commissioners, he asked if they could "bump up" the salary a bit and they voted to raise it to $2,000 per year. He had already made an agreement with his father that whatever fees either of them earned would be put into a pool and he would draw $200 a month for his living expenses. The new county job did not pay all that much, but at least he could contribute $175 a month to the partnership pool and he felt good about that.

Both Jim and Louise immediately immersed themselves in the activities of the community. Jim was an active member of the Masonic Lodge, the American Legion, the Kiwanis, and the Chamber of Commerce. Louise was a member of the Order of Eastern Star and was invited to join PEO, an exclusive womens' organization. Also, she was immediately elected as director of the Methodist Church choir and, soon afterward, as her singing ability began to be recognized in the community, she began receiving invitations to sing at weddings, funerals, and service clubs, and she helped form the Friday Musicale, a group of women who shared their love of music. This activity, in turn, caused a number of people to ask her if she would give their children voice lessons, which she started doing in her home. In these pre-television years (It was not until 1954 that a significant number of people started buying television sets and watching the two Boise stations; however, families like the McClures on the east side of Payette got bad reception, even with 50-foot antennas.) there were a lot more evening activities in communities like Payette. Besides the fraternal and social clubs, which met on weekday evenings, there was the weekly choir practice, Parent Teacher Association meetings, book clubs and discussion groups, and at least four bridge clubs. The McClures were invited to join one of the established bridge clubs and in their club, which met once a month in one of the couple's homes, the hosts provided the dinner entrée while the others brought the balance of the dishes for the dinner that was served before the card-playing began. Dessert and coffee closed the evening; however, one of the participants at the time, Jean Peterson, remembers alcoholic drinks being served before and during some of the dinners.

Now, more than fifty years after Jim and Louise McClure settled in Payette, the consumption of alcoholic drinks at social gatherings and in the home—cocktails before dinner and wine with dinner—is, in most Idaho communities (Mormon communities excepted), considered normal civilized behavior and no community stigma is attached to such behavior. Even a high school teacher, for example, could have a six-pack of Budweiser in his grocery cart and he would not elicit a second glance by a fellow shopper or by the checkout clerk. However, the Payette of the 1950s and early '60s was a drastically different place where alcohol was concerned. Ardent prohibitionists who had fought the good battle in the twenties and early '30s were still alive and influential, and the frontline fighters of the time, the ladies of the Women's Christian Temperance Union (WCTU), including Jim McClure's mother, and their allies in the Ladies Aid Society of the Methodist Church (the church that also prohibited dancing), maintained an information exchange network (the medium was called "gossip") that identified and verbally chastised transgressors who dared to be seen buying or consuming alcoholic beverages.

A close friend of Louise McClure verified that such a danger existed. When she was asked this question: If there had been two optometrists in the town in the '50s and one was seen carrying a case of beer into his house, would his business have been affected? She replied that she was reasonably sure that word of that flagrant act would have spread throughout the town and, providing the other optometrist was equally respected, the man who was seen carrying beer into his house would, indeed, have been shunned by some members of the community. Said she, "There was a strict code in Payette in what you could do and couldn't do. . .If you were in the business community, or owner of a store, or a professional, there were things, if they were not approved of by the older people in town, you either sneaked around (and did), or you just didn't dare do them."[6] When asked to agree or disagree with her friend's comment, Louise replied, "I definitely agree."[7]

This same friend also stumbled over another form of prohibition in the city. She said, "My brother-in-law, who was one-eighth (American) Indian and an electrical engineer, came to town for a visit and while there went downtown to get a haircut. When he got into the barbershop, they told him they were sorry but they didn't cut the hair of Mexicans—his skin wasn't any darker than mine, but he had darker hair. I was so mad I was ready to go down to that barber shop, but I called my husband first and he wouldn't let me do it. He said that if it became known that I did that, it would hurt business at the store—he was a pharmacist at Wilson's Drug Store."[8] When Jim McClure was asked if that sounded plausible, he replied, "I don't doubt it, because I remember signs in the windows of some businesses that said 'No Mexicans allowed.'"[9]

It was no great sacrifice for Jim and Louise McClure to conform to the unwritten codes of behavior imposed by the community. Neither of them were drinkers; they went to church because they wanted to do that; and they felt that most of the "thou shall nots" were insignificant in comparison to the benefits that were derived from living in such a community. There was virtually no crime; people rarely locked their doors; and, perhaps best of all, it was a great place to raise kids because there was little chance that young people could get into real trouble: Because of the "fishbowl effect" any strange or aberrant behavior would likely be observed by an adult who would report same to the parents of the juveniles.[i] [10]

McClure strongly believed in the efficacy of the fishbowl effect and, as a part of his ongoing concern about the juveniles of the community, formalized the effect with an organization he called the "Community Council." This was a loose coalition made up of the ministerial association, school officials, police chief, and the district head of the State Department of Public Assistance (welfare) whose office was in Payette. His idea was to catch juvenile problems early and take actions that would keep these problems from getting serious. For example, one of the first indicators of a problem is when a juvenile's school work suddenly deteriorates. When that happened, McClure wanted to hear about it from the school representative, then convene members of the council to see if any of them were aware of other signs of trouble; for example, had the police happened to observe that the individual was on the street late at night, or had a welfare worker noted a possible problem in the home.

As Payette County's chief law enforcement officer, McClure had to prosecute some high-profile crime cases, including several murders, and he frustrated himself numerous times bringing "driving under the influence" offenders into the courtroom only to lose every case because "there was always at least one on the jury who felt sorry for good old Joe because he might lose his driving privileges." [11] But, the juvenile cases often brought real heartache because of the limited means for handling them at the time.

The state had no programs for handling juvenile problems—no foster homes, no juvenile detention centers, no real alternatives for placing a juvenile except back in the parental home or the "reform school" at St. Anthony where juvenile criminals were incarcerated. McClure recalls the agony of one of the cases he had to handle:

> *"There was this 14-year old boy who someone discovered sleeping in a woodshed. It was in the winter and all he had was one dirty, old quilt. After investigating, we found that his stepfather had locked him out of the house and that (the woodshed) was the only place he had to go. This was a tough one. For his own protection we didn't dare try to put him back into the home. The only other choice, strictly for his protection, was to send him to the reform school. That haunts me yet."*[12]

> FRUSTRATION
>
> "We had this old German immigrant, a bachelor, who had been downtown drinking and then got into his car. It was parallel parked, and in the process of getting out of the spot, he banged the car in front of him, then the car in back, and when he started down the street, he swerved from curb to curb. When the police stopped him, he got out, staggered when he tried to walk, and he had slurred speech.
>
> I prosecuted the case and his defense attorney, Vernon Daniel, said that the reason he staggered was because he had a trick knee, and that he had slurred speech because of his German accent. All it takes is to convince one on a jury and he [Daniel] did that. I lost the case and got to feeling real bad. I wondered if there was something wrong with me, but realized that my predecessor had the same problem."

In the city election in the fall of 1953 a new mayor, Ursus Dalton, was elected and he promptly appointed Jim McClure as city attorney. The new city attorney had already learned that the best way to keep the county commissioners out of trouble was to attend their meetings and shortstop any problems before they got out of hand. When he became city attorney, he carried that approach over to the city council and for the next three years, when he served in both public positions, he became heavily involved in events both in the city and in the county. This activity, in turn, led him to get involved in the Idaho Municipal League and to begin reading journals that applied to city and county government, for example, the journal from The National Institute of Municipal Law Offices. This was not just duty-reading; he did this out of a keen interest he was developing in all forms of government. To say that he had politics in his blood would not be far from the truth—his maternal grandfather, A. L. Freehafer, had served six terms in the state legislature—three from Washington County (when Adams County was a part of it) and three after he moved to Payette, and, in addition, had served a term as a public utilities commissioner (a commission he helped create when he was a state senator), as a high-level regional bureaucrat during the Roosevelt administration, and twelve years on the Payette School Board. Will McClure, although considered by contemporaries as a shy, very reserved man, had also done his stint at public service by serving on the Payette School Board for thirteen years. So, if politics was not in his blood, it at least had been in his environment all through his growing up years, and, when he took his first political science course at the University of Idaho, his appetite for all things political began to develop. And now, in the mid-'50s, he was no longer getting his political science from a textbook and a professor; as county prosecutor and city attorney he was immersed in Practical Politics 101 and 102 and the immersion would not be in semesters, but in years.

It was said earlier that Payette was a thriving commercial center and the central shopping area for thousands of residents in Southwestern Idaho. However, if one looked closely—and Jim McClure was looking closely—there were ominous signs that senescence was creeping into the fabric of the community. For example, the owners of the commercial buildings on Main Street and Center Street in the heart of the city, most of whom were nonresidents, were not investing in the upkeep of the buildings because there was nothing they could do to raise the return on their investment. Also, the established leaders of the community, whom current residents in McClure's age range often called the "old guard" were, by all accounts, opposed to change. This old guard is reported to have had the general attitude that "things are going just fine, thank you, and we don't see any need for changing anything." Several examples of this attitude in action have been reported (but not verified) by old-time residents. In the late 1940s, after the impounded water from the Owyhee Reservoir became available for agriculture in Malheur County, Oregon—just across the Snake River from Payette—a sugar company wanted to put a processing plant in Payette. Ontario, now a thriving city more than twice the size of Payette, might, to the modern reader, seem a more logical site. However, in the late '40s Ontario was just a wide place in the road, reportedly with just one paved street—4th Avenue that went through the town. Payette had the workers, it was on the Union Pacific Railroad, and it was a beautiful, well-maintained small city—an ideal place, in other words, to establish a new business. But, the proposal was strongly opposed, reportedly, by the old guard and, in particular by the owner of the Idaho Canning Company who is alleged to have declared, "They'll steal all my workers and I'll have to pay higher wages to get replacements." (One fruit packing house is alleged to have placed ads in newspapers for workers even though they did not need them—the reason: they wanted a lot of extra workers around so the demand for jobs would be greater than the supply of jobs, which would enable him to keep wages low.)

A similar outcome reportedly resulted a few years later when Nephi Grigg, the head of the Ore-Ida Food Company, wanted to put a potato processing plant in Payette. Allegedly, it went to Ontario instead when Payette leaders again voiced strong opposition.

Another reactionary force in the community was centered in its only bank, the Payette Branch of The First Security Bank. Stories abound of its tight-fisted manager, Pat Murphy, who is blamed for the lack of the availability of capital for development or improvements in the community. Said Ron Manser, who, with his dad before him, owned the Ford dealership in Payette:

> *For several years my dad had been putting $375 in a war bond every month, some for them and some for the kids, and after several years, he happened to be in McCall and found a cabin that he wanted to buy. I remember, it was $14,750 and he wrote a check on the spot. When he got back to town, he went in to see Pat Murphy and explained that he wanted the bank to cover his check and that he wanted to pay the $375 a month on the loan rather than on bonds. Pat Murphy looked at him and said, 'You and Dorothy don't have any business owning a cabin in McCall,' and he refused the loan. So dad just cashed in some of the bonds and paid for the cabin that way. Later, almost the same thing happened to me. Right after I was married I wanted to take my wife on a vacation so I went to Pat to borrow $125—I know that doesn't sound like much today, but then you could get a good motel room for $5.00—anyhow, he looked at me and said, 'Why don't you borrow it from your father?' I replied, 'My dad taught me that we run a car store and that's where you buy cars; go to a money store if you want to buy money. I'm coming to you because this is a money store.' But, he refused to loan me the money.*[13]

Jim McClure also had a Pat Murphy story. "We had a fellow who retired back east and bought a small retirement acreage on the Oregon Slope, just across the river. He opened an account at our bank, and figured that the best way he could develop credit in the area was to borrow some money. So, he went in and asked to borrow $10,000—he had more than that on deposit—and Pat Murphy wouldn't give him the money, saying 'I'm not going to give it to you because you don't need it.'[14]

Eventually, Jim McClure, himself, was to run afoul of the old guard. As a young professional in the community, he took a keen interest in what was going on, and he was willing to spend the extra time that it takes to become a community leader. He became president of the Chamber of Commerce and the Kiwanis, and he became an advocate for changes that would make Payette a more progressive city. For example, after considerable study of journals on municipal government, he concluded that the part-time mayoral system was not working—that too many things were not getting done because the mayor was not spending enough time supervising public works and other city agencies. He believed that Payette needed a full time city manager, and he sold that concept to the city council, which, in turn, hired Dirik Nedry to fulfill that job. In addition, along with other community leaders, including his friend and city councilman, Cliff Masingill, McClure urged the city council to obtain revenue bonds for a Local Improvement District (LID) that would finance curbs, gutters, and sidewalks along many of the city streets. With some exceptions—some residents would not agree to pay their share of the street improvements—the LID was a success. However, the city manager, who, by all reported accounts did an excellent job in the three or four years he was on the job, was a thorn in the side of the old guard. So, they got even. On the legality of even hiring a city manager, McClure argued that the city had the right to do so because it was not specifically prohibited by state statute or the Constitution. However, a group of disgruntled citizens hired a young attorney from Weiser, James Donart, to challenge the action in court and they won. After that, the "progressive" council—or most of them—was voted out at the next election, and Jim McClure was not reappointed as city attorney. Later, McClure was to admit that this was a "mild" blow to both his income and his ego.

It was a "mild" blow because his income was growing from his expanding law practice and because his ego was anchored in the knowledge that he had done the right thing. But, there was more. His profession was not his life. His family was his life, and it was growing. On Father's Day in 1952 he was honored with the birth of daughter, Marilyn Leigh McClure. Two and one-half years later Kenneth Robertson joined the family, and almost two and one-half years after that, another boy, David Kevin, joined the household at 634 Hughes Drive. There were three generations of the McClure family now in Payette, and the oldest generation, particularly Jim's mother, Marie, and his Aunt Mamie, were eager to share Louise's care-giving chores. Of course, the family always met on Sundays after church for dinner or, on the nice Sundays of summer, in the surrounding area or the mountains for picnics. But, throughout the week, when Louise needed to be at the sewing machine making clothes for herself and the children, or canning fruits and vegetables from her yard and garden, both grandmother Marie and "Auntie" Mamie were always available for baby sitting. "I can't say enough good about them," Louise said later. "They were a tremendous help to me during those years."

In the days when Louise and Jim McClure were nursing babies and his career, there was an aphorism often heard among common folks when the duties of men and women were discussed: *A man works from sun to sun, but a woman's work is never done.* In the house at 634 Hughes Drive that was only a half-truth. Louise's work was never done, but in the fifteen-plus years they lived in that house, Jim McClure's work in remodeling it was never done, either. Even today, former neighbors and friends smile when they describe the "work-in-progress" where the McClures lived and, Marilyn, their daughter, laughed when the work-in-progress was mentioned. "In all my growing up years in Payette I never lived in a completed house," she said.[15]

Before the author embarked on this project, several intimate McClure friends and associates felt that they needed to enlighten this subject about an apparent idiosyncracy of the distinguished United States senator. The gist of their revelation:

> *You need to know that Jim McClure fancies himself as the consummate do-it-yourselfer. He did all the wiring and plumbing and heating installations in his Payette house during the years when it was undergoing remodeling, and he did the same thing in his cabin on Payette Lake outside of McCall. There isn't anything around a house that he thinks he can't install or repair.*[ii]

The intrepid repairman, along with his friend, Vern Swanson, began by tearing out the front door and entryway that they never used and contributing that space to the main dining room. Then a fireplace was built, steps to the partial basement were reworked, and their fuel oil tank was buried. After that, he added a bedroom, bathroom, and utility room to the south side of the house, and while that was going on, he bought a front-end loader from his father-in-law in Nezperce, hauled it to Payette, excavated the remainder of the basement and used the dirt to build terraces in his back yard, built retaining walls, and then sold the loader to Vern Swanson who was now doing all of the actual building.

Sometime during the 1950s after reading one of his do-it-yourself magazines—probably *Mechanix Illustrated*—he discovered that some company was making a unique refrigerator—one where the cabinet of the refrigerator hung on the wall while the motor and condenser element could be plumbed and wired into a remote location where the heat exchange would take place more efficiently. That discovery triggered a remodeling of the complete kitchen and, of course, the installation of his pride and joy: probably the only refrigerator in southwest Idaho (or even the whole state) that hung from the wall and operated silently because the cooling element was in the basement.

But, that was just one of his innovations. Have you ever wondered why the faucet for a bathtub is always over the low end of the tub where, if you want to rinse out the whole tub, you have to swish water uphill to do the job? That did not make sense to the logical mind of McClure the plumber and he did something about it: when he added the new bathroom, he put the plumbing for the faucet in the wall at the rear of the tub—an innovation that one of his neighbors claimed he showed off with great pride. The same neighbor also remembers the pride with which he showed off the louvered screens that he installed on the west side of his house—screens that he read about in one of his magazines, and which he claimed were a useful innovation because they could be set to block out the hot, late-afternoon sun.[16]

The final project, which was still not completely finished when the McClures left for Washington D. C., was the addition of a combination living room and dining room on the northwest side of the house along with a small half-bath off the kitchen and an outside deck.

As a young professional in Payette, three Jim McClures have been described. First, there was the lawyer successfully building his reputation for honesty, integrity, and competence, and with a law practice growing with his reputation. Second, there was the community leader—the president of Kiwanis, the president of the Chamber of Commerce, and the young man who, if he was not spearheading progressive projects in the community, was operating quietly behind the scenes giving advice and encouragement to those who were at the forefront. Third, there was the Jim McClure who was the devout family man, who spent every Sunday with his extended family, and who, on the nights of the week when he was not involved in community affairs, worked long into the hours of the night trying, on his modest income, to provide the best possible living quarters for his wife and children. But, there was also a fourth Jim McClure.

There was the Jim McClure who craved the outdoors and, in particular, the beauty and solitude of the high mountain lakes of Idaho. After talking with several friends who were his hiking partners in those years and learning, for example, that he was, far and away, the strongest hiker among them and a near-expert with a fly rod, he was asked to describe some of the trips and the lakes he visited. Without a second's hesitation for thinking, he started reeling off names: ". . .Sheep Head's Lake, then on the northwest side of the Seven Devils go past Seven Devil's Lake across the ridge down to Baldy Lake, then the two East Kennally Creek Lakes, then to Black Lake, Emerald Lake, and a little farther down, Pearl Lake, then farther to the west, Six-Lake Basin. . .then to Twin Lakes on the north side of Smith Mountain. . .and around McCall, Loon Lake, Rainbow Lake, Snowslide Lake, Thirty-three Lake, Brush Lake, Hum Lake, the three Hazard Lakes—upper, main, and lower—Eastern Brook Lake, Coffee Cup Lake, Serene Lake, then the Twenty-mile Lakes, and east of Marshall Mountain, Cook Lake, No Name Lake, Marshall Lake, Bear PeteLake. . .and you know the story of the bomber that landed on frozen Loon Lake and is still in the trees. . ."[17]etc. etc. etc.

The recitation of lake names was a torrent, like it was coming from a sixth grader who has memorized a passage and who seems on the verge of a verbal explosion when it finally comes time to recite. Clearly, the fourth Jim McClure had a deep passion for the mountain wilderness and it is fair to speculate that, as he laid on his pillow searching for sleep at the end of his long days, visions of casting a size 22 Gray Hackle on Black Lake toward a rising fish from a wired-together log raft powered by his Martin-20, 1.5 horsepower "kicker" that he had carried while it was strapped to his back pack, was the mental tonic that eased him into sleep and provided the dreams that he would fulfill summer after summer, first with his old friends, and later with his own children.

Then, in the fall of 1960, a fifth Jim McClure arrived on the scene.

Chapter 8 notes

i. Jim McClure commented on this aspect of life in Payette-size communities: "One day in the 60s I was walking down a street in Bonners Ferry with classmate, Pete Wilson, when he nudged me and indicated that the boy walking toward us was his son. When the boy reached us, Pete said, 'Why did you get stopped by the police this morning?' The boy's face dropped; Pete had already heard that his son had run a stop sign that morning. This was a clear example of the advantage parents have of raising kids in smaller communities."

ii. In the spring of 2001 McClure's ladder slipped while he was doing a maintenance chore on his cabin and he broke an arm and a leg.

Chapter 9

The Legislator

In the spring of 1960 much of the political talk around the nation was about the young, handsome senator from the Commonwealth of Massachusetts who, despite the serious burden of his Catholic religion, was aggressively campaigning in state primaries across the country for the Democratic nomination for president. No Catholic had ever been elected to that high office in America and there were many who thought that John F. Kennedy, despite his intelligence, wit, and good looks, would have little chance to win the nomination, let alone the Presidency.

But national politics was not what the good old boys in Payette, Idaho were talking about that spring when they gathered for their ritual, mid-morning coffee klatch at Maudies Cafe. They were discussing another political figure, their local Payette County State Senator, Vernon "Crabby"[i] Daniel.

In the early fifties Daniel had been the law partner of Herman Welker who had been elected to the U. S. Senate, but Welker had been defeated by Frank Church in the 1956 election. Welker died of a brain tumor shortly after that and Crabby Daniel, now on his own, ran for and was elected twice to the Idaho Senate where Welker had also served. In 1960 he was running for his third term in the state Senate, but this was troubling some of Payette County's leading citizens. Jim McClure explains:

> *In many respects he* [Daniel] *was an embarrassment because of his loud, boisterous—some would say uncouth—behavior, and his heavy drinking. He had also spread the word that the legislature was a terrible place, that broads were knocking on his door every night, and that they* [lobbyists] *were passing out fifths of whiskey. We had several discussions about this around the table at Maudies—I can remember that several were involved, including the Massingill brothers as well as the Mansers and Hanigans* [fathers and sons]*—and it was the consensus that we should find somebody to run against him in the May primary. When we started considering who could do this—who could leave their work or business and go off to the legislature for sixty days every two years—it was soon apparent to me that I was in a better position than other potential candidates because I had a father who could cover for me. Also about this same*

> *time, Ben Wherry, the Payette County Republican chairman, came to my office with some other fellows and asked me if I would consider running against Daniel in the primary. After that, I talked it over with Louise and my parents and a few others in town, and with their encouragement I decided to give it a try. In no way did I imagine this to be the first step in establishing a political career. That thought never entered my mind. I thought of it as just something I should do. There was a job that needed to be done in Boise and I was in a better position than most to get away and do it.*[1]

McClure did not campaign for the primary election, (*I had been in the county all of my life and there wasn't anything that I could tell them about me that they didn't already know.*[2]) at least in the traditional sense of knocking on doors and standing on street corners shaking hands. However, both he and Daniel invested in display advertisements for two consecutive weeks in the local weekly. We shall never know whether it was dissatisfaction with Daniel's behavior or McClure's attractiveness that swayed the Republican voters of the county; those who could best comment are no longer around. What we do know is that McClure defeated the incumbent in the primary, garnering 55 percent (723 to 586) of the vote. After that, his election to the Senate was assured in the general election because no Democrat even filed for the office. Payette County was a Republican stronghold.

So was the nation—at least it had been during the last two presidential elections when Dwight D. Eisenhower was elected for consecutive four-year terms. But the nation got a surprise the morning of November 2, the day after the general election, when the Catholic from Massachusetts was declared the winner (barely), initiating a Democratic reign that would change the country forever, and, ultimately, be a major factor in drawing Jim McClure beyond the borders of his native state. But, that was in the future.

Most people in the nation were watching the Rose Bowl the evening of January 1, 1961 when the University of Washington upset the favored Golden Gophers from the University of Minnesota, 17-7. But, not Jim McClure, nor the rest of the legislators gathered in Boise for the 36th biennial session; they were in party caucuses voting for their leaders. McClure was in the Senate Republican Caucus, and since that party held a 23-21 majority, their first order of business was to decide who would preside over the senate as president pro tem. That office went to the veteran senator from Bonneville County, A. W. Naegle, an automobile dealer from Idaho Falls. Following that decision, Jack Murphy, an attorney from Lincoln County (Shoshone) was voted majority leader, and William "Bill" Roden from Ada County (Boise), another attorney and former Ada County prosecutor, was elected as assistant majority leader.

After the caucus, McClure and another freshman, Senator Don Samuelson[ii] from Bonner County (Sandpoint), shared a room at the Sands Motel on State Street, two and one-half blocks from the Capitol. Their need to share a room was practical; they were being paid $15.00 per day for room and meal expenses, but they would not even be eligible for those meager funds until the next day when the session began. Louise and the three children were still in Payette; however, like many legislators' wives at the time, she would soon pack up, withdraw the children from school, enroll them in a Boise school (in this case, Koelsch Elementary School), and settle the family in a rented, furnished house for the two months the legislature would be in session. Also, both she and Jim felt lucky that her parents, Claude and Dorothy Miller, thought it would be wonderful to get off of the bleak Nez Perce Prairie for two winter months and move in with the daughter and son-in-law to help care for the children. This gave Louise the time and freedom to observe a lot of the legislative events and to fulfill occasional requests for singing performances.

The 36th legislative session began at noon, January 2, with a joint session in the house chamber where all the legislators were sworn in by Chief Justice Clarence J. Taylor. This ceremony was followed with a performance by the Elks Glee Club singing *Here We Have Idaho*, followed by *This is My Country*, and, finally, *The Lord's Prayer*. John Corlett, political writer for *The Idaho Statesman* speculated that all would not be sweetness and light in this session because of the close split of the two parties, with the Republicans barely in the majority in the senate and nearly tied (30-29) in the house. The Democrats, a minority in the state after the years of the Great Depression, were feeling buoyant and flexing their muscles as the new administration in Washington would be replacing thousands of Republican appointees with Democrats, several of them Idahoans.[3]

The major issue facing the Legislature, however, was not one that would pit one party against the other. It was an issue that would split both parties, with Republicans and Democrats as both passionate advocates and strong opponents."[iii] The issue that would trigger such bipartisan passion was a potential new tax: the sales tax.

Actually the sales tax was not a new issue for the 1935 Legislature had enacted a one-cent sales tax that was shortly afterward killed by a referendum vote of the people. But, the issue would not die. After slot machines were banned (by the 1953 Legislature) and that revenue was lost to cities and counties (see text box), the Idaho tax program was described as a two-legged stool, meaning that it was unstable and inadequate because it relied on revenues from property and income taxes only, and not a sales tax that all the people would pay. Governor Robert Smylie, who addressed a joint-session of the Legislature during its second day referred to this two-legged stool and described any effort to raise additional revenue, which practically all the legislators agreed had to be done to deal with crumbling public buildings and inadequately funded schools, without an overhaul of the whole tax structure would be merely a "patch and scratch" effort. As a part of that patch and scratch effort, the previous Legislature had passed an unpopular $10.00 head tax, a tax that every adult citizen was obliged to pay. As a part of Smylie's address to the legislature, he recommended the abolishment of the head tax and the need to take a whole new look at the tax structure.

With his home county so paranoid over the potential passage of a sales tax, McClure went to this 36th session looking for allies should there be an attempt to push a sales tax bill through the Senate. However, what he found was a much hotter issue—one that also had passionate supporters and opponents in both parties. The issue was Sperry and Hutchinson (S&H) trading stamps[iv], known, because of their color, as "green stamps."

For the reader too young to know about Green Stamps, an explanation is in order. Some merchants paid Sperry and Hutchinson a fee for the stamps, which they then passed on to consumers as a percentage of merchandise purchased; buy x amount of merchandise and you were awarded y number of Green Stamps that were then pasted into little books. As consumers accumulated filled stamp books, they would

THE PAYETTE PROBLEM

Oregon did not (and still does not) have a sales tax, and since Ontario was only five miles from Payette, the merchants of that city literally lived in deathly fear of the enactment of an Idaho sales tax, sure that shoppers would go to Oregon. That this fear was serious is evident from an article in the Payette *Independent-Enterprise* of December 6, 1949—twelve years before McClure's first session in the state legislator:

Payette businessmen, realizing the threat a proposed sales tax would have on local business. . . [expressed] *a unanimous opposition to the enactment of such a law. . .Businessmen expressed the belief that the enactment of a sales tax. . .would discriminate against Payette county business interest almost to the point of extinction. . .Local businessmen also expressed the belief that if the slot machine law become* [sic] *invalid through legislative action that the sales tax would be the only alternative. This conviction was based on the fact that if the slot machine law were repealed with its accompanying loss of revenue to the state, county and municipality that a sales tax would then follow. . .should the Chamber. . .take a stand on the proposal to outlaw slot machines? . . .realizing this to be a most controversial question it was decided to* [take] *a poll. . .Chamber secretary. . .posed the question "Which would you prefer a sales tax or legalization of slot machines?" Fifty-two businessmen, city and county officers were interviewed and . . .forty-eight expressed themselves as being opposed to the repeal of the slot machines . . .if it meant the enactment of a sales tax.*

And this was in a city with strong anti-drinking, anti-gambling sentiments and where the Methodists were still very much opposed even to dancing.

look wistfully through the S&H catalog full of four-color photos of toasters, waffle irons, golf clubs, radios, and a host of other prizes that could be redeemed with varying number of books at the regional S&H redemption center. Some households loved them and made certain wherever they shopped for anything from groceries to gasoline, they patronized a merchant who gave green stamps with their purchase. (Some merchants sometimes went overboard and offered double, even triple stamps on occasion.) Other households avoided merchants that gave Green Stamps because they knew that the merchant's markup had to include the cost of the stamps and that merchants who did not give stamps could (but not necessarily did) charge lower prices. So, consumers were split on the issue; some loved them and some hated them.

There was also a split among the merchants themselves; some thought that they should have the right to give Green Stamps if that is what they wanted to do as a part of their marketing effort. Such merchants resented legislators, such as many in the 36th Legislature, who were proposing a law banning the use of trading stamps. Other merchants, particularly some of the smaller ones who had trouble competing with the big chains, felt that they were being discriminated against—that the muscle of the big chains, especially when they offered double stamps, was hurting them. The opponents also argued that the stamps caused prices to remain artificially higher than they should be and that the glittering merchandise prizes in the redemption centers were overpriced in comparison to what they could be bought for on the open market with the savings that should result if trading stamps were banned.

The lobbying on both sides of the issue was intense and one lobbyist for S&H, Hope Kading, a former Mississippi beauty queen married to Boise attorney, Dick Kading, became well known to all the legislators and their ladies for the lavish luncheons and dinners she hosted to win favor for her company. These were also the days when telegrams from constituents were solicited by lobbyists; telegrams reportedly got more attention among legislators than more prosaic letters and postcards. Jim McClure was inundated with all kinds of letters, but, in addition he received 108 telegrams, the wording of one of which he still remembers. Laughing, he repeated the words of a telegram from a young woman in Payette County, which the author later found in the archives:

James McClure
State House
Boise, Idaho

I just got married & boy Green Stamps are wonderful.

Mrs L L Wells"[4]

The first Senate vote on trading stamps would be three weeks in the future and McClure would have plenty to do before he would enter the trading stamp debate. The leaders of this particular session decided that with twenty-three Republican senators, there should be twenty-three committees to examine the nearly 500 bills that were ready for consideration. Since McClure was a city attorney and had been active with the Idaho Municipal League (the organization that later became the Association of Idaho Cities), he asked for and was given the chairmanship of the Counties and Municipalities Committee. In addition, he was appointed a member of committees on judiciary and rules, public health and welfare, banks and utilities, and elections.

But, that was not all. Majority Leader Jack Murphy had another chore in mind for the freshman. (*"He probably felt that young energetic guys need work that will take up their energy; the devil always finds work for idle hands."*[5]) He wanted McClure to take a close look at the senate rules and suggest revisions that should be made to modernize them. This might have been an onerous chore to many legislators, but it turned out to be not only an interesting job for McClure, but one that turned out to be very helpful to him, then and later. Prior to this time, his only experience with procedures and rules was in organizations where *Roberts Rules of Order* were the guidelines. However, in parliamentary assemblies, both national and state, *Cannon's Precedents* prescribed the way a legislative body should function. These procedures were new to the freshman senator, but he dug into the task with enthusiasm and spent many hours in the law library (then on the second floor of the Capitol) reading, rereading, and revising the current senate rules—rules that were later accepted almost verbatim by the leadership, then the senate itself.

McClure's other work in the senate reminds the author of a fictional character named Jake Holman, created by the author of *Sand Pebbles,* a book published the year after McClure went to the state senate.[6] Jake was a career sailor, but he hated the bureaucracy and the regimentation of the military so he developed a system to beat it—a system that gave him autonomy and freedom even when the most tyrannical captains and chiefs could have court martialed him. No matter, Jake always won out. The author said:

> *"By the time they realized they were in a struggle, Jake Holman would already have made for himself the place he wanted on their ship and they could never dislodge him, or wish to."*

One would have to read the novel to fully appreciate Holman's method, but the following passage, describing how Holman, when he took over the supervision of the engine compartment and propulsion system, went about preparing himself for the job, sets the story:

Courtesy McClure family

A McClure family portrait, 1961. From left, Kenneth Robertson, Louise, Jim, David Kevin and Marilyn Leigh.

> *The piping had hundreds of valves and fittings and it branched and snaked behind things and through bulkheads and in and out of bilges until a man's eyes became lost and dizzy trying to trace and remember. . .on an old ship there would always be hidden cross connections and plugs and blanks and drain valves, put in for some forgotten purposes by men long since dead or transferred, and no one would even know they were there. No one but Jake Holman. It was a part of his secret to take all of the piping, clear and sharp in detail, inside his head. . .*

McClure's long hours studying and revising the arcane rules from *Cannon's Precedents* were his first efforts to understand the hundreds of valves and fittings in the bulkheads and bilges in the Senate, and perhaps, in the late hours of the evening his eyes may have become lost and dizzy in their study. But, he had just gotten started. If he was going to master the whole system, he would also have to confront the 500-odd bills that *all* the committees would be considering. Some were trite, some were nonsense, and there were probably some written by men long since dead or transferred, and no one in the Senate would even know what was in them all. No one but Jim McClure. It was a part of his secret to read, study and understand the content of all the bills until the details were clear and sharp inside his head. Jake Holman would have appreciated Jim McClure (who after all, had already mastered the intricate details of running wires, plumbing, and heating pipes in the many remodelings of his house) and Jim McClure would have admired Jake Holman, if he could have known him at the time.

Of course, it is a stretch to say that Jim McClure had the details of 500-odd legislative bills clear and sharp inside his head. But, when asked the question by the skeptical author: "Wait a minute—there is no way you could know what was in those 500 bills—how could you have found time to do that?" McClure answered defensively, but with assurance: "Well, I did try to understand what was in those bills and as far as time was concerned, the senate was not always in session. We had a lot of recesses, especially in the early weeks. It was not an impossible task."[7]

Jim Goller, who at that time was publishing *The Idaho Legislative Report* which summarized all the bills and notified clients of those that might impact them, said, when asked if McClure was exaggerating when he claimed to have read the 500-odd bills: "No, I don't think he was exaggerating because he quickly built a reputation in the Legislature for knowing what was in those bills. I knew him, and I think most legislators knew him as what I'd call a "go-to guy"—a legislator you could go to when you hadn't read, or maybe not studied a bill, and quickly find out what was in it. In my opinion that was Jim McClure's hallmark, or trademark, or whatever you want to call it. . .his reputation. . .that was his reputation and it stayed with him all while he was in the legislature."[8]

Perry Swisher who, during McClure's first session was a lobbyist and who, during McClure's later service in the state senate was a Senate colleague and occasional strong antagonist—especially on the sales tax—said, when asked to assess McClure's ability to analyze and retain legislative detail:

> [when I started as a lobbyist] *I became quite well acquainted with new members, including Jim, and one of the first things I noticed was when legislation was under consideration, Jim could look at it phrase by phrase, syllable by syllable, diagnose it, keep his mind focused on the language. . .I'd never seen anybody quite that focused. I don't think it is a personality quality—it is a mental quality. . .I think the entire state code was just a Rolodex* [for him]. . .*he could bring it up at will . . .any page in his head while talking to you. If he was thinking of a given page he had seen in the last twenty-four hours, it was all there. . .Jim was very important* [in the Senate] *because he made sure the seams* [of legislative bills] *matched up. He was the best I ever saw in that regard.* [9]

Eventually, McClure began to take the floor in debates on various bills that were under consideration. And when he spoke, his fellow senators quit shuffling their papers and talking to those at their neighboring desks. As Watt Prather, a former law school classmate and fellow freshman from Boundary County put it, "When he (McClure) spoke on a subject, people listened to him because he always knew what he was talking about. He became a very skillful debater just for that reason, because he was informed while some of the others were just bullshit artists. Also, he never made any personal attacks or belittled anybody. He was good with people on both sides of the aisle. He listened to their [Democrats] ideas and even if he didn't agree, he listened with respect."[10]

As the weeks went by, McClure began to feel more and more comfortable in this new role as a legislator, and several times, as he paused in the marbled halls to study the photos of previous senators who had served the state, he could not help but feel pride in seeing his grandfather Freehafer in so many of them.[v] And while he sat on the other side of the aisle from where his grandfather had been, he took further pride in knowing that his grandfather had been fiercely independent in his thinking, and that he, too, tended to think more independently than many of the partisans with whom he was serving.

When asked how he as able to take stands different from the majority of his own party, McClure replied,

> *I don't recall it ever being a problem. What I learned, or maybe I already knew it, was never to blind-side the leaders of my party. In caucus I always made it a point to alert the leadership when I was leaning the other way on an issue so they would know ahead of time not to count on my vote. They didn't have trouble with that—oh, they may not have liked it sometimes, but they always knew I had good reasons for why I would take a stand on an issue and I think they respected that. I often sided with the Democrats—the Democratic leadership was conservative in those days—often more conservative than Governor Smylie. I was much inclined to follow my own views and not be led just because it was my party's position.*[11]

McClure, who has a dry sense of humor, also enjoyed the good-natured kidding that went on between several of the senators on both sides of the aisle. Bob Wetherell, a veteran Democrat senator from Mountain Home, who was the most notorious of the senate pranksters, had somehow come into possession of a stuffed crow, which was passed around the chamber to the member who, because of some action, needed to "eat crow." McClure cannot remember how or why he ended up with the crow on his desk, but he can remember the difficult time he had getting rid of it. Then one day he looked in the back of the senate chamber where the *The Idaho Statesman* political writer, John Corlett, had been given a special seat—all other newsmen were required to sit in the press gallery. There was Corlett, sound asleep with his mouth open and snoring. McClure waited until Corlett woke up then presented him with the crow. "He didn't think that was a bit funny," McClure said later, laughing and with a mischievous gleam in his eye. "He [Corlett] had been such an important fixture for so long and was so close to Bob Smylie that he had lost his humility. I pricked his pride and he didn't like it."[12]

WATT PRATHER ON BOB WETHERELL

Bob Wetherell was always doing something to shake up the somber atmosphere of the Senate. I remember the crow being passed around. I also remember that he had a set of false teeth hooked up to some kind of motor. He sat just across the aisle from me and whenever some long-winded orator had been on the floor too long for Wetherell, I'd see him get into his briefcase and bring out those false teeth. Then he would turn on the motor and the teeth would start clattering. I laughed and laughed. . .and it didn't matter who was up there, Democrat or Republican; it didn't make any difference to him.

McClure also learned a lesson about lobbyists. At that time in Idaho there was a state law that regulated the hours that banks could remain open. These "bankers' hours" were remarkably truncated when compared to other businesses—they were only open from mid-morning to mid-afternoon, and not open at all on Saturdays. This was an inconvenience for everybody who needed banking services, and the banks, whenever anyone complained, always came back with the excuse: "Yes, we understand that it is a problem, but there isn't anything we can do about it; the state governs our hours by statute." For many years this was a problem with which Idaho residents just learned to live. Except those who lived near enough to Ontario, Oregon to do business in their banks—like the residents of Jim McClure's home county of Payette. There was no such law in Oregon, and the banks in Ontario stayed open the same hours as other businesses, and they were open on Saturdays. Of course, this created problems for the Payette banks—there were now two of them, and freshman senator McClure decided that he was going to do something to help them.

At that time the Idaho Banking Association had a representative—they did not call them lobbyists in those days—named Lloyd Adams. McClure went to Adams and gave him his view, which was that he could see no reason whatsoever why the state of Idaho should be concerned about the hours that banks stayed open to the public—that it was really none of the state government's business and, hearing no objections or reasoning on the part of the banking industry, he was going to try and repeal the law. Adams got back to McClure and assured him that the banking industry really didn't care if he did introduce such a bill and that they would keep hands off. However, when McClure's bill started attracting supporters, Adams began rallying his forces against it and it was defeated. The lesson for McClure: so much for the word of lobbyists. The lesson for the bankers: beware when tangling with a determined foe; the "bankers' hours" statute was repealed in a later session with Jim McClure as one of its leading proponents.

It was a busy session and out of McClure's committee came, first, a bill to change the date of municipal elections from April to November to coincide with general elections, then a Civil Rights bill that would end the kinds of discrimination McClure had seen in Payette where Mexicans were blatantly refused service in some local businesses. Both bills passed the senate, then the house, and were signed by the governor. McClure did not fare as well with the green stamp issue. He did not want them banned, not because he liked Green Stamps (although Louise liked them and saved them), but because he believed that merchants should have the right to use whatever marketing techniques they desired without interference from the state. When the vote came in the senate, it was overwhelmingly in favor of banning the stamps. He was one of only four Republicans who voted against the ban. (The ban was later overturned by a court, but the stamps gradually faded away without further legislative interference.)

On another issue, McClure picked up a divisive label that would haunt the legislators in the next two sessions. Since the Senate was made up of forty-four members, one from each county, the senators from sparsely populated counties like Clark (Dubois), Camas (Fairfield), Owyhee (Murphy), Custer (Challis), and Lemhi (Salmon), had equal power with the senators from the populous counties of Ada (Boise), Bonneville (Idaho Falls), Nez Perce (Lewiston), and Bannock (Pocatello). And, whereas the former counties were more interested in ranch and range issues and the latter counties were more interested in urban issues, there had developed two factions in the Senate, one labeled "cowboys" and one labeled "city slickers." McClure was not placed in either category until the driver's license issue arose. One faction, mostly made up of the "city slickers," wanted the minimum age for drivers raised from age 14 to age 16. Proponents of this bill argued that it was a safety issue and that forty-eight states in the nation required drivers to be 16 before they could be licensed. The "cowboys" objected, citing the need for family farms and ranches to utilize young drivers for essential chores and to allow rural young people the freedom to participate in after-hours extra-curricular activities in their schools. McClure came down on the side of the "cowboys" on that issue, no doubt influenced by his early years on his grandfather's ranch near Council. According to Jim Goller, whose job was to be a close observer of the Legislature, this was probably one of the key issues that caused McClure to be labeled as a "cowboy." For the record, however, McClure proposed a compromise that would raise the age to 15, but it was not accepted; in that session the driving age was raised to 16, however a driver training program was initiated in the high schools of

Idaho and those who completed it could earn a daylight-only license before they reached that age.

Near the end of the session the Democrats grew more and more discontented with what they considered ill treatment by the Republican leadership. They expressed this discontent with parliamentary techniques designed to slow down senate proceedings, which would ultimately keep the senate from adjourning on schedule—on the sixtieth day. However, after considerable negotiations (and probably some unrecorded promises), the Senate got back on track, tackled some last minute hot potatoes—Smylie insisted that the $10.00 head tax be repealed; the legislators kept it but earmarked the revenue for the building fund—and the Senate adjourned *sine die* at 4:41 a.m. on March 2. Jim McClure was now free to return to Payette.

His daughter, Marilyn, a third-grader, could not have been happier. Always a little shy, the move to Boise had been traumatic for her. Forty years later she said, "Those times were miserable for me—that first year all three of us [with brothers David and Kenneth] were in one room, and I was homesick so badly. I remember that mom took me home for a Valentine party and that was nice, but I was a shy little kid and two months wasn't enough time for me to establish myself. I was always hiding behind mom's skirts; I was so shy I didn't even go to kindergarten; I was content just to stay home with my books, records, Lincoln logs, and paper and crayons. . .I don't think I ever tried to adapt—it just shut me down for two months."[13]

It also about shut down McClure's law practice even though his father tried to handle some of the routine work. Invariably, over the two-month period there would be clients with conflicts and problems that his father felt he should leave for Jim to handle. This was particularly true on public land and water issues with which Jim McClure had become progressively more involved, and with which he was keenly interested—so much so that, inwardly, he wished that he could specialize in such issues and leave the divorces and contract writing and criminal defense to someone else. The city of Payette had also been without an attorney for two months and much of this backlog of work had also mounted on his desk.

But, despite the effect upon his law practice, McClure felt good about his first term in the Senate and he had firm plans to run again for the same position. It had been an enlightening experience. Before he went to Boise he had been active in the Idaho Municipal League and had gained a somewhat broader perspective on issues that faced Idaho's cities. However, the two months in the state senate had widened his perspective on a great variety of issues and problems that affected Idaho. In short, it had been an intensive and demanding two-month educational experience and he liked that. Many years later his wife, Louise, said that he had been very stimulated by the experience, and she admitted that it had also been a stimulating experience for her.

Back home again, the McClures resumed their routine. Louise continued to give voice lessons, sing at funerals, weddings and miscellaneous social events, and direct the Methodist Church choir. Jim remained active in Kiwanis, the Payette Chamber of Commerce, and served on the church board. Both enjoyed their Sunday family dinners, especially when their nephews and nieces visited from out-of-town, and they especially enjoyed socializing with their friends at the monthly bridge club meetings. And, during the summer there were a lot of family picnics on weekends, and while Jim, himself, continued his habit of taking rigorous back packing trips into remote mountain lakes with his friends, he also began introducing his children to shorter, more benign wilderness trips. Daughter, Marilyn, when asked about those expeditions, said, laughing, "I remember my first trip when he just kept repeating, 'It's just over there [the lake],' but it wasn't and we slept that [first] night in a dry stream bed."[14]

Like many Americans, Jim McClure also had some serious concerns about his country and the wonderful life of freedom that he and his parents and grandparents had enjoyed. Would his children and his grandchildren also be able to enjoy that kind of life? If the times in which he was living were not frightening, they were, at least, worrisome. The Soviet Union and its satellite nations in Eastern Europe, had, for over a decade, been flexing their muscles on the world scene, stirring up trouble and fomenting revolution wherever there was a weak government that was vulnerable to their agents. In addition, the Communists in China, though only tentative allies of the Soviet Union, were also trying to encourage wars of liberation in countries outside their borders, particularly among the unstable post-colonialism regimes in Africa. Backing these subversive movements was a nuclear arsenal and delivery technology that took away America's historic sanctuary between the two wide oceans; now Payette, Idaho and every other city and town in America was a potential target for mass destructive weapons.

And the tentacles of Communism were not just threatening poor countries like Angola and the Congo, and spawning terrorist organizations like the Red Guards in Italy and Germany, and the Shining Path in Peru. In quieter, more benign ways, Communist agents were infiltrating organizations in the democratic countries where class conflict was natural and almost inevitable. For example, they were active in organizations such as labor unions where there has always been a built-in antagonism between workers and capitalists. The International Longshoreman's Union was one such organization; Communist agents were active in that union even in the '40s. But, there was another union riddled with Communists, and it was much closer to home. It was, in fact, in Idaho, in Shoshone County where the workers in the lead and silver mines near Kellogg, Wallace, and Mullan were controlled by the International Brotherhood of Mine, Mill, and Smelter Workers Union whose president had openly declared himself to be a Communist.[15]

A group of alarmed citizens in Shoshone County formed an organization called the Shoshone Anti-Communist League with the mission to educate the people of the region to the ways Communists used front organizations to recruit members and to further their objectives. Bob Robson, Kellogg attorney and later an Idaho attorney general, one of the leaders of that organization, said, "We were damned scared of that union and I started contacting the workers and letting them know the facts. They didn't like it, either, and when I finally was able to get a vote, we beat them at their own game. We formed our own union, The Northwest Metal Workers Union, and we took the bargaining rights away from Mine, Mill. They only had two outfits they were representing, [the Shoshone County workers and one in Canada] and when they lost our workers, they went broke. We didn't have any Birchers [John Birch Society members] in our organization—some of them were kooks. We were just ordinary citizens who didn't want to see Communists in power. "

Jim McClure had been one year behind Bob Robson in law school and they had both been county prosecutors. So, when McClure heard of the formation of the Shoshone Anti-Communist League, he contacted Robson and soon was getting literature from the organization. Alarmed at the inroads the Communist Party was making, or seemed to be making, McClure began using the league materials at informal study groups that he organized in Payette County. Shirley Massingill, wife of Payette businessman, Cliff Massingill, remembers some of those sessions and said, "Jim and some other conservatives in the town held meetings warning us of the dangers of creeping Communism and socialism and I can remember my husband having an anxiety attack over that so bad he had to go to the doctor and get tranquilizers."[16]

Cliff Massingill was not the only American who had a need for tranquilizers, especially in the years 1961-62. In 1961, under Nikita Khrushchev, it was reported that the Soviets were accelerating their production of intercontinental ballistic missiles (ICBMs). And, they were literally daring the United States to do anything about it. For example, in June of 1961, just after McClure completed his first term in the state senate, President Kennedy went to Vienna to meet with Khrushchev and was humiliated by Khrushchev's flat ultimatum that a peace treaty with East and West Germany had to be in place by the following December or the Soviets would proceed with unilateral action. Shortly afterward, in August, the Soviets erected the infamous Berlin Wall, which was to precipitate a period of extreme tension known as the "Berlin crisis." Boasting of their great military power, the Soviets and their satellite Communist nations crowed to the world with their "What are you going to do about that, America?" propaganda.

Of course, we did nothing, although documents since released[17] reveal that President Kennedy and his military advisors were seriously considering a preemptive first strike with nuclear weapons—an attack into Soviet territory designed to take out the ICBMs that could reach us.

Then, about a year later in October, 1962, America faced what arguably may have been the most potentially dangerous thirteen days of the twentieth century. Now known as the Cuban Missile Crisis, this event, triggered by the Soviet installation of missiles in Cuba, resulted in a standoff between Khrushchev and Kennedy that could easily have escalated into a nuclear holocaust for both countries.

Ordinary citizens in America were, to various degrees, shaken by the tension during the Cuban Missile Crisis, and it is quite logical that during the election the following month, the citizens of Payette County, who elected Jim McClure for a second term in the state senate by a 2-1 majority[vi], were, to some degree, influenced by his known vigorous stand against the many subtle ways the Communists were trying to subvert key institutions within our country. And certainly, when the 37th Legislature convened in January and McClure took one of the coveted back seats in the Senate chamber—seats reserved for senior senators—the Communist threat was one of the issues that was on his mind.

And he now had a friend and ally serving with him. His law school classmate, close friend, and fellow prosecutor from adjacent Washington County, Hal Ryan, was a freshman senator, and the two of them colluded on a bill that they pushed during the session. The bill, for which McClure would be the floor sponsor, was known as the "Loyalty Oath Bill," and he was quoted in *The Idaho Statesman* as saying, ". . .this bill merely requires that public employees in Idaho sign an oath [saying] he is not a member, nor been a member for the past five years, of an organization advocating the violent overthrow of our government."[18]

The Loyalty Oath Bill aroused strong emotions, both in the Senate and the House, and even though it did pass and was later overturned by the courts, McClure's opponents in later years would use the issue to try and taint him as an anti-Communist extremist.

McClure also became tainted as an anti-government extremist during this session because of his support for a Senate memorial that his friend, Hal Ryan, sponsored. Known as the "Liberty Amendment," it was designed, said McClure later, ". . .to limit the federal government to activities that were expressly authorized by the Constitution. It would have wiped out all of the court interpretations which had greatly expanded the reach and scope of the federal government. [Scholars] have said our form of government is the best ever created by the human mind. However, it was designed by people who distrusted the power of government and they erected a lot of checks and balances. One very important check and balance was the limitation of the power of the central government by vesting all other powers in the states. That has virtually been eliminated by the courts, especially since the days when I was supporting the Liberty Amendment."[19]

In addition to wiping out the court interpretations that took power from the states, the memorial urged the United States Congress to vote for a constitutional amendment that would abolish the income tax, prohibit the federal government from engaging in business activities in competition with private enterprise, and, especially significant in Idaho where about 70 percent of the state's land is controlled by the federal government, return all public lands to the states.

At the time Hal Ryan introduced the Liberty Amendment memorial in the Idaho senate it had already passed in six states: Georgia, Louisiana, Nebraska, South Carolina, Texas, and Wyoming. However, the introduction of the bill in the Idaho Senate triggered strong emotions in those who would testify against it. Opponents offered many strong arguments against the memorial, but they especially targeted one feature: the elimination of the federal income tax. They claimed that this was completely unrealistic and those who would vote for it were irresponsible citizens. When it came time for a vote, the opposition had rallied a majority of senators against it and it was defeated. And even though McClure, who voted for it, was branded by future opponents as an irresponsible conservative for supporting the Liberty Amendment, he claimed, thirty-eight years later, "If I had been in the [U.S.] Senate and my single vote would have passed that amendment, I probably would not have voted for it. But, at that time in the Legislature, I felt it was important to send a message to Washington that the states strongly opposed the rapid growth of the federal government and that that trend should be stopped or reversed."[20]

The Idaho Senate, itself, was considerably different in this 37th Legislature. Even though the parties were closely split (23-21 in favor of the Republicans), there were only six of the senators who had more than one term of experience. (That is why McClure got one of the coveted back-row seats reserved for senior senators.). The new leadership trimmed the number of committees from twenty-three in the previous session to a more manageable fifteen, and McClure became chairman of the Judiciary and Rules Committee. His first task was to prepare the permanent rules for the session and when he produced them in a record four days, he received compliments from both sides of the aisle.

Despite contentious issues that loomed over this session of the Legislature, e.g. the sales tax issue, the first weeks of the session were marked by the collegiality of the two parties. John Corlett, *The Idaho Statesman* political writer, remarked in wonderment that all seemed to be "sweetness and light" in the Legislature[21], and Art Murphy, Democrat-Shoshone, who had served in the Senate since 1937, asked rhetorically, "Am I in the right chamber?"[22]

Surprisingly, the good will continued through debates and votes on the Liberty Amendment Memorial and the Loyalty Oath Bill. However, according to John Corlett, it was all to end in early February when a sales tax bill was introduced along with one that would legalize pari-mutuel betting at county race tracks. McClure's constituents were strongly opposed to both issues, as were those of his friend, Hal Ryan. Together, they began looking for supporters on both sides of the aisle and they ended up with two Democratic leaders, Bill Dee (Idaho County) and Cy Chase (Benewah County). Together, the four of them recruited other senators who could be counted on to support conservative issues, and the group came to be known as the "economy block."

McClure, himself, had always abhorred any waste of taxpayers' money, and now he was more vigilant than ever. He believed, as his supporters in the economy block also believed, that those who supported the sales tax wanted to increase state spending so much that their opponents would cave in and realize that there was no other politically acceptable way to generate the needed additional revenues. Therefore, their best strategy for defeating a sales tax was to fight excess spending.

McClure and his fellow conservatives were successful with the main issue. Despite the fact that the House passed a sales tax bill 31-29, it was defeated in the Senate by an over-whelming majority: 12-23. They were not so successful with the pari-mutuel betting issue. It passed both houses, and after Governor Smylie vetoed the bill, both the house and the senate overrode the veto. McClure, whose constituents were strongly opposed to pari-mutuel betting, steadfastly opposed the bill in both votes.

In this session of the Legislature there were also some issues that McClure could enthusiastically support. He was a sponsor and leading floor debater in support of the establishment of a permanent legislative council—a legislative housekeeping organization that would provide research and continuity during the interim twenty-two months when the Legislature was not in session. On the Senate floor he was quoted as saying, "This [establishment of a legislative council] is a step in efficient government that, in the long run, will save us money."[23]

McClure was also one of the supporters for conferring university status to Idaho State College and the name change was formally approved by this Legislature. However, when it was proposed to reopen the old Lewiston Normal School[vii] under the new name of Lewis and Clark College and to give it a broader educational mandate, he and other members of the economy block saw it as a budget-busting maneuver. "We cannot afford all of these institutions in the state of Idaho," he declared on the senate floor. "This is not good economy. This is not good government."[24]

In the closing days of the session, arguments for and against an increased budget, especially for education, created rancor among senators of both parties. Young Cecil Andrus, Democrat and former logger from Clearwater County, would cement his reputation with the educational establishment for his vigorous support for increased funding. Perry Swisher, former lobbyist and now a senator from Bannock County, and George Blick, a veteran senator from Twin Falls County, were two of the key Republicans who joined Andrus in the fight for more educational funding. When the time for adjournment came, neither side was winning and the session lingered on for another two contentious weeks. Finally, on the morning of March 15, the headline in *The Idaho Statesman* declared, SENATE ECONOMY FORCES ROUTED. A compromise was reached. Funding and "patch and scratch" taxes were raised about 10 percent without the imposition of a sales tax. McClure and Ryan's constituents in Payette and Washington Counties had ducked another bullet. But, both men knew their victory was likely to be temporary. Idaho schools were still under funded—both men admitted that fact and lamented the truth of it.

Eight months after the adjournment of the 37th Legislature, President Kennedy was assassinated in Dallas and his vice president, Lyndon B. Johnson, replaced him. The new president was a protege and ardent fan of Franklin D. Roosevelt who, with his New Deal, had initiated federal programs that had aroused bitter resentment among American conservatives. However, Johnson could have cared less about conservative opinion; with the nation mourning their slain president this astute politician realized that he had a unique window of opportunity to push through New Deal-type social legislation that Kennedy, himself, could never have gotten through Congress. He proceeded boldly, and successfully, and during the next two years his "Great Society" legislation made the 1930s social legislation pale in its wake.

All of this helped polarize American political thought. At one pole were the new idealists spawned when John F. Kennedy became president and who, in his stirring inaugural speech, declared that Americans should, ". . .ask not what your country can do for you, but what you can do for your country." His followers, especially the young ones, took him literally and, in a variety of ways, tried to do what they could for their country. They volunteered by the thousands when the Peace Corps was established and they served unselfishly in hundreds of primitive locations around the world. Many others decided that they could best make a contribution in the realm of politics and they became highly motivated and, in many cases, successful political candidates at all levels.[viii]

At the other pole were those who rallied around a man whom many would argue was just as handsome and charismatic as Kennedy. Coming from the then small state of Arizona, Barry Goldwater epitomized everything that was legendary about the West. He was blunt speaking, modest and self-deprecating, independent minded, and an unabashed sentimental patriot. And what Kennedy was able to do with his inaugural speech, Goldwater did with the publication, in 1960, of a book titled *Conscience of a Conservative*. Prior to this it was common for conservatives to be portrayed as hard-hearted and unfeeling toward the unfortunates in the country who were poor. The result was that many conservatives hid their feelings and were hesitant to express their opinions for fear that they would get beat up by those undesirable labels. Goldwater's book helped conservatives see that they should be proud of their beliefs. In terms of helping the poor, Goldwater helped them see that they were being compassionate when they argued against the outright giving of money and food to poor people. In fact, or in principle, conservatives believed in the Chinese proverb: *Give a man a fish and he will eat for a day; teach a man to fish and he will eat for the rest of his life.* The term "welfare dependent" had not been invented at that time, but Goldwater anticipated it by preaching that without individual responsibility and freedom, all unrestricted welfare giving was essentially inhumane because it would create a class of people incapable of anything but standing in a welfare line. As McClure put it, "Goldwater was articulating what a lot of people were thinking and his book helped people realize that the public perception created by the liberals was wrong—that the opposite was true: you could be a conservative and have a heart and have compassion for people, and conservatives did have a social conscience."[25]

Goldwater found a home in the hearts of Idaho conservatives. In northern Idaho, decorated World War II hero, John Mattmiller, who had never before been involved in politics, became inspired by the Goldwater message and decided that the best way he could save his country from the LBJ onslaught was to run for the First District congressional seat that was held by Compton White, Jr., an avowed fan of the president. Mattmiller ran in 1964, and while the Republican Party more or less considered him a sacrificial lamb and the media gave him no chance at all in a district that, with one exception, had sent Democrats back to Congress since the 1930s, he surprised everybody by coming within about 3,500 votes of defeating the incumbent.

The Goldwater bandwagon also ran through the middle of the Idaho GOP and destroyed the left wing of the party. Robert Smylie, who in 1964 was midway through his third term as Idaho governor, was a friend of New York Governor Nelson Rockefeller who was competing against Goldwater for the Republican nomination for president that year. At the national level, Smylie, as chairman of the National Governor's Association, looked extremely attractive, at least to the media, and was considered to be a vice-presidential possibility on a Rockefeller ticket; after all, few governors of any state had ever been elected to three terms. But, Smylie was vulnerable at home. A native of Iowa, he was an outsider. And, during his second and third elections he was opposed by candidates who had no chance of beating him because of the single issue on which their campaigns were based. In 1958 it was Allen Derr who opposed him touting a solution for Idaho's poorly funded schools: statewide legalized gambling. That did not play well, especially with the

Mormons in eastern Idaho, and Derr was soundly defeated. Then, in 1962, Vernon K. Smith, tried it again, same issue, and with the same results, only he came closer to defeating Smylie. So, while Smylie looked like the white knight of the potato state to the national media, many of the folks at home looked upon him as an arrogant, too-big-for-his-britches governor who was, in their minds, governor by default.

Smylie made his first enemies in the conservative wing of the party during the late summer of 1962. Henry Dworshak, Idaho's much admired senior senator died unexpectedly in Washington and it was Smylie's responsibility to appoint a successor who would fill out the last few months of his term—a new senator would be elected in November. Smylie, himself, wanted the position but he did not dare appoint himself because Lieutenant Governor Bill Drevlow, who would replace him, was a Democrat[ix] and could have helped Vernon K. Smith who would be running against a replacement candidate for Smylie. Instead, he agreed to appoint whomever was nominated by a party convention to be held in Pocatello (where McClure served as temporary chairman—an indication of the respect the young state senator had already gained in the party). At this convention Smylie backed a personal friend, Dr. Raymond White, originally of New Plymouth, who conservative Republicans insisted had cut a deal with Smylie: appoint me to fill out the Dworshak term so I can say I have been a U.S. senator, then, in January I will resign and you can appoint yourself for the four remaining years of Dworshak's the six-year term.[26]

There was a bitter fight at the convention. The anti-Smylie forces led by two conservative stalwarts, Gwen Barnett and Roland Wilbur, effectively seized control of the party at that convention, nominated Smylie's opponent, former governor, Len Jordan, for Dworshak's seat in the U.S. Senate (which Jordan would win on his own by a big margin the following November), and in the next two years their anti-Smylie actions continued to create a wide rift in the party.[27]

The animosity between the two factions reached a peak in the summer of 1964 when delegates to the Republican Presidential Convention in San Francisco were being selected. The Idaho conservative delegates, including McClure, were enthusiastic supporters of Barry Goldwater while the delegates loyal to Smylie were expected to support Nelson Rockefeller. McClure winces when he is reminded of those contentious days and remembers that at the state convention where delegates were picked, he acted as a peacemaker when Barnett and Wilbur tried to keep Smylie, himself, from being a delegate. "I argued that even if they didn't like Smylie, they had to make him a delegate because he was the governor of Idaho. They were really serious and they had the votes [to keep him out]."[28]

The City of Los Angeles was at least partly responsible for initiating the healing process in the party. Thirsty as always for someone else's water, they began casting covetous eyes toward Idaho's Snake River water, which, they claimed, was flowing into the Columbia River and out into the Pacific Ocean without being put to good use. By the summer of 1964 they had already initiated actions that could lead to the surplus Snake River water being diverted southward to Lake Mead, which could be added to the flow in the lower Colorado River. This triggered a "circle the wagons" reaction among Idahoans and Governor Smylie, responding to the threat, called a special session of the Legislature July 29 that was charged with preparing a constitutional amendment that would solve the problem. The concept was to make it legal for the state, through a newly created water agency, to regulate the use of all the state's water and to issue bonds for water development projects—projects that would allow the state to preempt the use of surplus water and keep out-of-staters from stealing it. The session was harmonious and in four days the amendment, with McClure as one of the principle authors, was ready for the November ballot.

After the special session, Governor Smylie and the Republican leadership in the Legislature took a giant stride to bridge the rift in the party. In an unprecedented move, the governor left his statehouse office, away from the prying eyes of the media, and flew in a National Guard Beaver aircraft to the rough, unpaved field outside the town of Shoshone, which was the hometown of Jack Murphy, president pro-tem of the state Senate. There he and his pilot, Brig. Gen. George Bennett, commander of the Idaho National Guard, were picked up by Murphy and taken to his home where other legislative leaders were assembled: Speaker of the House, Pete Cenarrusa, Carey, House Majority Leader, Bill Lanting, Hollister, Senate Majority Leader, George Blick, Castleford, Senator Dick Smith, Rexburg, and Senator Lloyd Barron, Corral. Over drinks and, later, during a luncheon prepared by Murphy's wife, Cleora, and her daughters, they hammered out what was to be a secret mutual commitment that Pete Cenarrusa later called a "gentleman's agreement."[29] [30] Smylie, who in two previous legislative sessions had called for an overhaul of the state's tax structure, had never gone on record as favoring a sales tax. Although he had hinted at the need for the tax by referring to the existing tax structure as a "two-legged stool", he had never come right out and suggested that the sales tax should be the third leg. His political strategy had always been to let the legislators, themselves, become the lightning rods should they pass a sales tax and trigger a public outcry against it—as had happened years before when a sales tax was passed and later repealed by referendum. But, now, at this meeting, Smylie was ready to be one of the lightning rods. According to Cenarrusa he basically said, "Okay, gentlemen, we all know that we must have more revenue—our schools are suffering and we have numerous other programs that are under funded. So, what I am proposing is that I go on record in my speech to the legislature in January and specifically ask the legislature to pass a sales tax. I will do this providing you make a commitment to me today that you will use all of your power to get it enacted."

Cenarrusa said the Republican legislative leaders pledged their total support that day, and also agreed that they would keep Smylie's position confidential until he could announce his intentions to the Legislature. However, word of the agreement did leak. Former Senator Perry Swisher said that he was made aware of the agreement by Jack Murphy, although this may have been after Smylie announced his position to the legislature.[31] But, former governor, Phil Batt, who was a representative at that time, said that he was not privy to any agreement, but "I wasn't one of the cowboys," —implying that Murphy, Cenarrusa, Blick, and Lanting were in that category.[32] And when McClure was asked if he knew anything about the secret meeting or the results thereof, said, "We [who were opposed to the tax] always felt that there had been a deal cut, but we never found out any specifics. To the best of my knowledge, this is the first time I have ever heard this story."[33]

On election day, November 3, 1964, Goldwater was defeated in Idaho, but the vote was close enough to encourage the conservatives in the Republican Party. And in Payette County the vote for their state senator was almost a replay of the 1962 election: McClure again beat his Democratic challenger, Charles Anderson, by a two-to-one vote. Idaho voters also approved the constitutional amendment that would allow the Legislature to set up a water agency to protect Idaho's waters from out-of-state interests.

The 38th Legislature convened January 3, 1965 and after the opening ceremonies, the House and Senate, both with Republican majorities, met to select their leaders. As predicted, Pete Cenarrusa was reelected by a unanimous vote to be speaker of the house and Bill Lanting was selected as majority leader. In the senate, Jack Murphy was reelected as president pro tem and George Blick as majority leader. However, there was a new face in a leadership position in the senate. In the words of *The Idaho Statesman,* Jim McClure "beat out" last session's assistant majority leader, Bill Roden.[34] In a letter to his constituents in Payette County, McClure explained his motive for running:

> *As most of you know, I sought and was elected to the position of Assistant Majority Leader in the Senate. I knew at the time I took this job that I would have added responsibility and that upon occasion I would have to cast my vote or take other action against my wishes and, perhaps, against my better judgment. However I felt that any loss in independence is more than made up by the opportunity to be of greater influence where and when it really counts.*[35]

McClure's constituents in Payette County knew exactly what he meant when he said he wanted greater influence where and when it *really* counts. He knew that the sales tax issue had gained momentum since the last legislative session when it was passed in the house, but defeated in the senate. Addressing that issue with his constituents, he said, "The sales tax is still the measure most likely to pass, but I am hopeful that we can [again] round up enough votes to stop it."[36]

On January 5, Governor Smylie addressed the legislators and, after listing an unprecedented number of proposals that would require significant increases in revenue, he kept his part of the bargain with the leadership and went on record asking the legislators to pass a retail sales tax. It was a speech that even McClure admired, for at a meeting he attended at Maudies Café the next day he admitted, "However you feel [about the speech], he did sound like a governor and very forceful."[37]

From that time on, McClure and his allies were in a desperate fight. Citizen lobbyists from the border counties flocked to the capitol to aid their legislators and by the Legislature's midterm, Tobe Massingill, the leader of the anti-sales tax forces, was calling for more of his fellow citizens to join them in Boise.[38] They were heartened by the first vote in the senate when the opponents engineered enough support to defeat it by a 20-24 vote. However, to the insiders, including McClure, this first vote was a tactic to convince the house, which was overwhelmingly in favor of the sales tax, to support an amendment that would approve a public referendum on the issue at the next general election. However, the governor was adamantly opposed to that idea, a stance that deeply frustrated McClure. In a statement to his constituents published in the *Independent-Enterprise*, he implied that the governor was less than honest when he claimed that the majority of the people wanted a sales tax to help their schools, but, at the same time, opposed a referendum that let them confirm their feelings.[39]

Of course, a three percent sales tax did, eventually, pass the Senate without the referendum amendment, a dramatic conclusion to a legislative

THE 38TH LEGISLATURE

It is ironic that the 38th Legislature, which has been so highly praised over the years, was the last one not apportioned on the one-man, one-vote principle, and the last biennial legislature—a 1966 constitutional amendment authorized yearly sessions. The major accomplishments of this legislature, in addition to the sales tax, include the establishment of:

- The Idaho Water Resources Board and Agency
- The Urban Renewal Agency
- The State Personnel Commission and Department with a merit system
- A statute for establishing condominiums
- The Public Employees Retirement Act
- A professional Parks Department
- An Idaho Outfitters and Guides Board
- Licensing procedure for private contractors
- The Idaho Pea and Lentil Commission.
- An Executive Director for Higher Education
- Community Mental Health Centers

session that was probably the most productive and forward-thinking of any session in Idaho's history. At a 20-year reunion of the 38th legislators, an Associated Press reporter in attendance quoted former Governor Smylie as saying, "I think it was the best legislature that ever sat in Idaho," then added his own comment that, "Smylie spoke for many when he said [that]."[40] And even McClure, who attended the reunion and who had, by this time, seen his hometown business district collapse when retail trade moved across the border to Oregon, said, "It [the 38th Legislature] was certainly, by all commentary, a very good session. We addressed the problems confronting the state and it was an outstanding group of people."[41]

Besides the sales tax, there was one more bitterly contentious issue hanging over the 38th Legislature. Neither the two congressional districts, nor any of the legislative districts were apportioned according to the one-man, one-vote principle that recently had been decreed by the U.S. Supreme Court. In the regular session the house passed a reapportionment plan for themselves and hoped it would be accepted by the courts. But the Senate backed off from the onerous chore—they knew that the least populous of the forty-four counties would lose their senators. Instead, they bargained for time by passing a memorial in support of the "Dirksen Amendment,"[x] which would allow the senate to maintain the status quo.[42]

The other problem, the need to realign Idaho's two congressional districts in such a way to balance their populations, was addressed in a special session of the legislature that Smylie called immediately after the adjournment of the 38th Legislature. Anxious to get home, Jim McClure did not want to see a long drawn-out session so he and his friend, Hal Ryan, decided to try and accelerate the process. McClure explains:

> *Hal Ryan and I decided to get some statistics together and see what we could do with an initial plan. . .we went down to the Secretary of State's office and got all the election returns for several years and sat up all one night with one of the senate clerks, Jane Millner, going through a whole bunch of different alignments to see the political effect. . .and still keep it contiguous. . .we decided to come south* [and make it an east-west alignment rather than a north-south alignment] *so we took in* [the First District] *Ada, Elmore, and Owyhee counties* [and put Custer and Lemhi into the Second District].[43]

That all-night session was successful in saving a lot of legislative time, for the McClure-Ryan proposal was immediately adopted by both houses, with a possible mitigating factor being that the other legislators were equally eager to get home. However, their work was successful; the new alignment of the two congressional districts was later sustained by a federal court.

With both the regular session and the special session out of the way, it was time for Jim McClure to pack up the family and move back to Payette—back to a law practice that was in disarray, back to finding ways to make up the money lost so the bills could be paid, and back to relieve the impossible burden that he had left on his father. The latter weighed heavily upon his mind at the time, and although he made no public announcements to his friends or supporters, he had confided to his wife that he had made an irrevocable decision. He declared that he was through with the legislature. He was not going to run again. And when he was asked thirty-six years later how final that decision was, he replied, in the presence of his wife, Louise, "I was absolutely sure that I would not have run again no matter what the Payette people said." Louise agreed: "I was sure he would not have run again."[44]

Why? There were several reasons besides the problem he was creating for his never complaining, but aging and overworked father. He wanted to get on with his life and do some other things. He had recently worked with a Vale, Oregon attorney named Bill Schroeder on a Bureau of Land Management conflict. This was a land and water issue—the type of legal challenge in which he was keenly interested. The two got along well during their joint venture and had talked tentatively about setting up a practice together that would deal strictly with such issues.[45] Also, money was a problem. It was costly to leave a practice for two—even three months including the special sessions—and there was no way to make up that loss; if you were not there to help your clients, there were no fees to collect. In addition, he calculated that it cost him $1,000 dollars more than he was paid just to attend the sessions. "We hadn't had a family vacation for a long time and, with the legislature probably going to annual sessions,[xi] I thought we could take that thousand dollars and have a yearly vacation," he said later.[46]

So, in the spring of 1965, Jim McClure was not only through with politics, he was a man determined to get his life going in new directions.

Chapter 9 notes

i. The nickname, probably given while he was in high school, was a misnomer for his personality was just the opposite; he was always cheerful, had a ready smile, and, according to his contemporaries, had the stereotypical hail-fellow, well-met type of personality.

ii. Senator Don Samuelson would be Idaho Governor six years later.

iii. Senator Cy Chase, Democrat from Benewah County, an automobile dealer, was quoted in an interview in *The Idaho Statesman* as being "violently opposed" to the sales tax; however, in this and subsequent sessions no violence ensued from this legislator.

iv. There were other kinds of trading stamps but the S&H green stamps were in widest use.

v. A.L. Freehafer served one term as a representative and five terms as a senator from three counties: Washington, Adams and Payette.

vi. R-Jim McClure 3,099, D-Charles Anderson 1, 525.

vii. Closed in 1953 along with Albion Normal School.

viii. According to Chris Carlson, press secretary for former Governor Cecil Andrus, it was a speech by JFK in Lewiston in early 1960 that inspired Andrus to seek political office.

ix. According to a Smylie statement quoted in Paradox Politics by Randy Stapilus, he did not dare attend Dworshak's funeral in Washington because Drevlow had warned him that, in his absence, he would not be able to resist the temptation of appointing Dworshak's successor.

x. Everett Dirksen, U.S. Senator and Majority Leader from Illinois, was pushing a constitutional amendment that would allow state legislatures to retain one house that did not meet the one-man, one-vote decree. It never passed.

xi The 38th Session approved a constitutional amendment for the ballot that would allow for annual sessions—an amendment that passed.

Chapter 10

Fate Opens a Door

When the McClure family returned to Payette in the spring of 1965, they found a community developing a siege mentality as a result of the impending sales tax. Some were erecting a defense; for example, in the March 18 issue of the *Independent-Enterprise* there was a feature titled "We'll Shop at Home" that included a series of quotes from prominent citizens who swore that just a few pennies of added sales tax would never cause them to abandon the local merchants who had served them so well over the years.[1]

But, there were others who were more skeptical and felt that the only way to save the community was to go on the offensive. Specifically, Tobe Massingill, a partner with his brother Cliff in Massingill Furniture, formed and became the chairman of the Anti-Sales Tax Referendum Committee, which, after word spread of its existence, included members from all of Idaho's forty-four counties. The goal of the committee was to obtain 25,545 signatures on petitions calling for a statewide referendum on the sales tax to be held at the next general election in November, 1966. Their slogan—"We took pennies away from Benny and we don't intend to give the bucks to Bob"[i]—was enthusiastically adopted by the workers carrying the petitions and by the middle of May they had collected nearly 60,000 valid signatures, thus guaranteeing that Idaho citizens would finally get to express their own opinion on the sales tax.

Jim McClure was not an active member of the Anti-Sales Tax Referendum Committee. In the months committee members were out collecting signatures, he was buried in work that had accumulated in the three months he had been out of town. "I strongly supported them and wished them well," he said later, "but, I had all I could do just trying to put my law practice back together."[2]

Occasionally during 1965, McClure would bump into a Republican somewhere who would suggest that he should consider running for Congress. To each of these supporters he maintains that his answer was essentially the same as a statement he made to the local newspaper: "I did not seriously consider it because John Mattmiller [who ran in 1964] had not only earned the right to represent the Republican Party in this race, but I felt he was the best candidate."[3]

At this time in his life Jim McClure was also having problems in his law practice. Several sources who wish to be unnamed confided to the author that the McClure law office always seemed to be behind in getting work out. "It was like pulling teeth to get something out of there," lamented a sympathetic friend. "Jim had an excellent legal mind and always did good work, but he always seemed to have too much work piled up. I know that it bothered him." When McClure himself was later confronted with a similar comment from a fellow attorney, he immediately threw up his hands and pleaded guilty. "I'm afraid that was true; there were several people who could have said that," he admitted. "We were postponing a decision that we should have made earlier, and that was to either bring in more help or cut back on the clients that we would accept. I did turn some people away, but probably not soon enough."[4]

At the time of this conversation the author was well aware that his subject much preferred the challenges of land and water law over the hum-drum, bread-and-butter issues that small town attorneys deal with in an office practice every day: contracts, divorces, criminal defense, and estate issues. Suspecting that there was more to the slowness in getting work out than a simple backlog, the author asked the subject in the presence of his wife Louise: "Were you bored with your law practice?"

After some hesitation, he said, lamely, "I enjoyed the law practice." However, Louise spoke up immediately. "I think he was bored with just practicing law," she said. He looked at her, not critically, but as though he was really wondering if what she said was true. Then, in a subdued voice he said, "Well, it was not a relief to get out of practicing law [when he left Payette], but I didn't miss getting called on nights and weekends."

This sounded evasive to the author who then asked the question in another way: "Did you really enjoy the practice of law?" Before he could answer, Louise repeated what she had said earlier, but with more force: "I think he was bored."

After observing the firm expression on his wife's face, and after some hesitation for more self-examination, McClure then admitted that what he had really enjoyed about being a small-town lawyer was the community activities associated with that life and not necessarily the practice of law.[5]

Even though McClure had turned his back on any further involvement in the Idaho Legislature, he still had one more chore to do. In Washington the Dirksen Amendment was defeated in the senate which meant that the Supreme Court's one man-one vote mandate now applied to the reapportionment of the Idaho Senate. The hope that one of the houses of the Legislature could be selected by a means other than by population was now down the drain. Governor Smylie had been informed that the Idaho Senate had to be reapportioned according to the one man-one vote dictum or the court would demand an at-large election for the whole state. With that threat, Smylie had no choice but to call a special session to resolve the onerous problem. Everybody knew that a reapportionment that would satisfy the courts would also cause senators from the least populous counties to lose their seats.

So, despite his desire to stay home and continue trying to unburden himself from his backlog of attorney work, Jim McClure was scheduled to return to Boise on February 14, 1966 to complete his last task as a legislator.

Then came the event that changed his whole life. Twelve days before the special session was to convene, the candidate for the First Congressional District, John Mattmiller, killed himself flying his airplane into power lines just east of his hometown of Kellogg. That same day, February 2, McClure received a phone call from the *The Idaho Statesman* political correspondent, John Corlett. His first words were, "Now are you going to run?"

McClure, who earlier had received calls from Corlett asking him to run—Corlett did not like Mattmiller—replied rather petulantly, "I've told you I'm supporting Mattmiller; he is the best man for the job and he is going to win this time."

Corlett cut him off. "Mattmiller was just killed. Now, are you going to run?"[6]

In a *Statesman* news article the next day McClure is quoted as saying, "This is a shock to me. It takes my breath away. We regarded John highly as an individual and as a friend, and expected he would be a further asset to the state when he was elected next fall." In the same issue, in Corlett's "Politically Speaking" column, Corlett said, in reference to McClure as a potential candidate to replace Mattmiller: "He [McClure] gave the job some. . .thought last fall, but decided he could not run against Mattmiller, who he found was 'both acceptable and available.' He said frankly Wednesday that the loss of Mattmiller requires him to '. . .give a serious look at the nomination.' He can be expected to reach his decision within the next few days. . ."[7]

The next few days were truly days of deep soul searching. According to his friend, Bill Schroeder, with whom he was considered a partnership in a joint practice, Jim McClure was at a crossroads in his life even before Mattmiller was killed:

> *We did pretty well in those cases* [natural resource cases where we worked together] *and he always had an interest in public natural resources and that interest intensified in the resolution of these conflicts that we were involved in. That is what led to his conversations with me as to his interest* [in establishing a joint practice]. *He was at what he felt was a junction in the road for him as to whether he wanted to go the legislative route in addressing these kinds of problems or whether he wanted to go to the courtroom or judicial route. We had a number of conversations on that point. . .*[and I felt] *that he had a very significant legislative talent and that was the place for that talent to be applied. I told him so and when that death occurred and*

he had a shot at that [legislative position], *I really urged him to go for it.*

McClure says his mind is hazy about what happened after Corlett's call, but he does remember some of his thoughts. "Prior to Mattmiller's accident, when people suggested I run for Congress, I did not even consider or think about it. . .I always figured I would starve to death being a salesman—going door to door in sales was something that did not appeal to me at all and to go out and do the things necessary in a campaign was something I had no desire to undertake. Also, I think there were many people who knew I would hate to do something like that. They thought,' Jim McClure is all right but he can't do that.' They thought with my personality that I could never get out and shake hands and push myself as a candidate. But, the idea of campaigning came to me as an intellectual challenge. I'm sure I was analyzing what had to be done and was saying to myself, 'You may not like doing that [campaigning and shaking hands], but if you are going to run for that office, that is what you will have to do.' Once you know what you have to do, then it is just a matter of making up your mind that you are going to do it.

"Also, as I was considering running, I remember that my folks came down and the four of us sat around the table and talked about it. We thought it might be interesting; we thought it might be fun to go to Washington for a couple of years. We had friends and relatives who had closed the door on any advancement in their lives. They were people who didn't walk though a door open to them and didn't get another chance. That was a strong motive [in favor of running].[8]

And there was another factor—one that caused McClure to grow eloquent as he explained it:

This is going to sound trite, but it is true. All of my adult life I had spent watching what our federal government was doing to us—and remember my background spending every summer with my grandfather. I was reared to be as independent as a person could be, independent of government, believing one should be responsible for one's actions and those of your family, and not expecting government to do a whole lot for me. And I grew up in a state where public lands were taken for granted, where we recreated and assumed that as a way of life. I could see all of those things changing because of the policies adopted by the federal government and I wanted my kids to have the same kind of life I had grown up enjoying and I knew if something didn't change, they wouldn't. That was worth changing your life to try to effect. . .so the thought of going to Washington and doing something about the trend [that had been going on since

> Roosevelt, and which was steamrolling under Johnson] *was very, very strongly appealing to me.*[9]

Then Louise spoke up. "I said to Jim, 'go for it.'" I was not holding back at all. I thought it would be a fun and interesting challenge. I had worked with politics enough at this point to prepare me for that attitude. I had no regrets about hitting the campaign trail. Life was ahead of us."[10]

In the days after Corlett's call, Jim McClure talked with a number of his friends and supporters. One of the first to hear from him was friend and fellow senator from neighboring Washington County, Hal Ryan.[ii] McClure felt that Ryan was equally qualified as a potential congressman and he was not going to step forward himself if Ryan wanted to run. However, Ryan assured McClure that he was not interested in running, but that he would support him enthusiastically. Although McClure's memory is hazy about other contacts, he is reasonably certain that he contacted the other men whom he felt might be better candidates than himself, including Bill Young, attorney and fellow state senator from Canyon County, Larry Mills, former house speaker and general counsel for Boise Cascade Corporation, and Jack Hawley, a Boise attorney who had run unsuccessfully against Frank Church in the 1962 election. At this time none of these men expressed an interest in running.

Then McClure contacted a man who was destined to occupy an intimate share of his professional life for the next twenty-one years.

Jim Goller was born in 1926 on a farm south of Hansen, Idaho, that his father had purchased after he returned from France where he had served in World War I. Young Jim was one of nine children and one of his earliest memories is riding to school in a covered wagon drawn by horses—the school bus of the times. As a youngster he did all of the kinds of work that farm boys did, including the sawing of ice out of the Low Line Canal—ice that was hauled to storage where it was packed in sawdust insulation that kept it from thawing even into the summer and until it was used in the family's ice box. The family's drinking water was also carried in buckets from a branch in that canal—drinking water wells on the south side of the Snake River had to be deep and few could afford to drill such a well. He never owned a bicycle and he speculated that there were times during the Great Depression when his father and mother never had as much as a dollar in cash between them; the little cash they did earn came primarily from the sale of eggs and chickens. However, Goller can never remember going to bed hungry; those who were lucky enough to live on farms seldom lacked for food.

Like McClure, Jim Goller was in the Navy during World War II where he served as an electrician on a small wooden-hulled minesweeper in the Pacific. He took part in the Okinawa campaign; saw "lots" of Kamikazes diving into and destroying our warships; and felt lucky that his small ship was not a tempting target for those suicide bombers. Even before he returned home he had made up his mind that he was going to take advantage of the GI Bill that had been enacted and go to college. He enrolled in the University of Idaho in the fall of 1946—the same year Louise Miller from Nezperce started there. He remembers Louise—the author has not encountered anyone who was in that class who *did not* remember Louise—but cannot remember meeting Jim McClure. Goller enrolled in electrical engineering, but also took a night job bartending at the veterans club, which was on the third floor of the First National Bank building in downtown Moscow. He also got married soon afterward. Then a child came, and Goller's after-school work became more of a necessity while his homework suffered. While struggling in his third math course, he switched to extractive industries where the math course was not required, but then, not sure that he would enjoy working in any job for which his major field of study would prepare him, he quit school and, on a whim, took a job in Boise that turned into a career—at least until Jim McClure came to visit with him in February, 1966.

One of the waiters at the veterans club was a student named Carl Kitchen whose father, with the same name but who was called "Old Silver," was the classic old-time politician who had been secretary of the Senate for many years and who, on the side, had a little publishing business that did city codes, city ordinance books, and other small jobs. When Goller mentioned to young Kitchen that he was leaving school and did not have a job, the son suggested that Goller go to Boise and work for his father. Goller went to Boise and took the job, but soon discovered that Old Silver was a very heavy drinker. The good news was that sincc all of the work fell on Goller's shoulders, in a short time he had learned the business. The bad news was that even though Goller was essentially running the business, he was paid flunky wages and the old man was a difficult boss. Eventually, Goller quit, got a temporary job teaching and coaching at Homedale Junior High School, but then Old Silver died suddenly and his lawyer persuaded Goller to come back and save the business, which he did. However, when he saw that he was not going to get the business for himself, he quit, started a similar printing service, then when Kitchen's old business was about to fail, Goller bought it and formed the Voter Publishing Company. Soon, he was publishing a number of products used by lawyers, including, when the Legislature was in session, a daily service with the text of all of the bills that had been submitted in the house and senate. Thus, through the late 1940s and 1950s, Goller became an avid student of Idaho political winds and he grew to become one of Idaho's most astute political observers. Then, in 1961, Jim McClure came to the Legislature and Goller immediately recognized his talent in crafting legislative bills. He also found a kindred political soul—one whose political philosophy coincided to a large degree with his own.

Goller came from a family that worshiped Franklin D. Roosevelt for the way he attempted to help farm families during the Great Depression. The

Courtesy Jim Goller

Jim Goller, left, and Dick Beiber confer on the upcoming Mattmiller campaign. Goller, who became McClure's chief of staff, was scheduled to fly with Mattmiller and Beiber to Kellogg but never received a confirmation call.

politics of his parents came naturally to Goller—he had never been exposed to any other kind of thinking—and when he was a freshman at the University of Idaho, he joined the Young Democrats Club. Then, for his new major in extractive industries, he was required to take a course in economics taught by Dr. Erwin Graue, a German immigrant with strong Prussian tendencies, who became a legend at the University for his demanding teaching tactics and his passion for economic conservatism. "He really turned me into a Republican," Goller said later. "I still remember some of his sayings, such as: 'There is no such thing as a free lunch;' and 'You can't remove the fear of failure from everyone."

Goller became active in the Young Republicans when he moved to Boise, and eventually he was elected their Idaho president. In that position he energized the organization and, in 1962, the Young Republicans, through his initiative, were able to bring Barry Goldwater to address their state convention—a coup that leaders of the senior party envied but were never able to pull off. During Mattmiller's first run for Congress in 1964, Goller helped "some," but for his second run, the top executive of the campaign, Don Day of Boise, wanted Goller to become much more active, especially in Ada County where Mattmiller's campaign manager Dick Bieber had no experience. In fact, in the late afternoon of February 1, before the evening meeting Day and some other Republicans were to have with Bieber and Mattmiller, Goller, at Day's request, came to the house to discuss the upcoming campaign. At the end of this meeting, Day suggested that Goller fly up to Kellogg with Bieber and Mattmiller the next morning so they could spend a few days working out campaign details. Goller agreed and said that he would be standing by his telephone the next morning for a call that would let him know when he was to be at the airport. However, after the evening meeting at Day's house, Bieber and Mattmiller had a disagreement and Bieber refused to go with him to Kellogg, claiming that he had too much work to do in Ada County. So Goller never received the expected phone call, and when he went to the Boise Hotel at noon for lunch, he was shocked to learned that Mattmiller's airplane had crashed that morning and that he had been killed.

While recovering from the shock of Mattmiller's death and his own close escape from the same fate, Goller received a visitor in his basement office at 906 ½ Jefferson. It was Jim McClure and, although he and Goller did not, at this time, consider themselves to be close friends, they knew each other well and they respected each other. According to Goller, McClure confessed that he was considering running for the First District seat and wondered what Goller thought about that. Goller immediately thought it was a good idea and they talked about other possible candidates. Both assumed that since Ada County and its large block of Republican voters were now in the First District, that there would be Republican candidates "coming out of the woodwork" eager to run now that a Republican had a much better chance of getting elected. McClure himself cannot remember whether his conversations with some of the potential candidates was before or after this meeting with Goller, but he does remember that Goller urged him to immediately send a letter to all of the precinct committeemen in the First District telling them that he was seriously considering running for the position. "I wanted to get a placeholder out," Goller said later, "to forestall a bunch of others from jumping into the race, and since there was to be an endorsing convention and these [precinct] committeemen would be selecting the delegates, I wanted them to begin thinking about McClure early. I also urged him to issue a press release to all the weekly newspapers in the district at the same time. I remember that McClure was not inclined to do that—he was still very undecided and he had that special session of the legislature coming up—he didn't want to be involved in partisan politics while they were trying to reapportion the State Senate. Finally, I tried to convince him that the letter and press release would only say that he was seriously considering running and that he could always back out after the special session. I remember that I really pushed him on this."[11]

McClure remembers both his reluctance and Goller's strong insistence that they get out a "placeholder." "My reluctance was natural," he said later. "Hardly anybody knew me out of Payette County. I didn't consider myself God's gift to the First District Republicans. I knew there were better qualified people out there."[12]

But McClure finally accepted Goller's logic and agreed to the letter and press release. When questioned about what happened next, Goller believes that he "had a hand" in the writing of the announcement (*McClure*: *There is no doubt in my mind about that.)* and he remembers that he used the Addressograph machine in his office to address the envelopes to the county newspapers, but that he had to prevail on one of his employees to type out the addresses for the precinct committeemen. The result, which appeared on Wednesday, February 16, in the Payette *Independent-Enterprise* began:

> *Fellow Republicans, I am seriously considering running . . .and I ask Republicans to seriously consider my candidacy . . .If it were possible, I would immediately cover the district and make every effort to talk to you. However, the special session of the Idaho Legislature starts Monday and I have responsibilities to the people of Payette County who elected me as their State Senator. . .*

It took about nine days—Mattmiller was killed on the February 2 and the press release had to be mailed sometime on Friday, the twelfth—for Jim McClure to change his whole mental outlook from that of a small-town attorney to that of a candidate for the United States Congress. The magnitude of this turnaround is even more dramatic when one appreciates his strong belief, just days before, that the upcoming special session of the legislature would be his absolute final effort in the political arena. The only real doubt in his mind prior to February 2 was where he and Louise and the three kids would be taking their new Chrysler station wagon on a long-delayed vacation the following summer.

Also, sometime in that nine-day period, possibly after Goller handed McClure drafts of the letter and press release to proof, McClure asked the question that also changed Jim Goller's life: "If I do decide to run, will you manage my campaign?"

Goller doesn't remember the exact words of his reply, but he is sure that he quickly accepted. "Managing a campaign was something I really wanted to do. I was anxious for a candidate, no doubt about it, and McClure was the best choice. I had studied the statistics in Idaho and knew that it was doable. I committed to him immediately and it's interesting, shortly after that Don Samuelson came in and asked me if I would manage his campaign [for governor] and I had to decline."[13]

Thus was initiated one of the most effective political partnerships in Idaho history.

Chapter 10 notes

i. Referring to Governor C. Ben "Bennie" Ross who pushed for a sales tax and saw it rescinded by voters, and the current governor, Robert "Bob" Smylie.

ii. A lobbyist, Bart Brassey, who was urging McClure to run at this time, said that McClure had to drive to Weiser to see Ryan because he spent so much time on the telephone McClure could not get through to him.

Chapter 11

The Candidate

"I couldn't get enthusiastic about something I didn't believe in," said Jim McClure when asked about the 1966 special session of the Legislature that was called by Governor Smylie. "You might make me do it, but you can't make me like it," he added.[1]

That was probably the feeling of many who gathered in the Senate chamber on February 14, 1966. They all knew that unless they increased the size of the Senate dramatically, several of them would lose their seats in the reapportionment that was mandated.

For days the session dragged on, seemingly with each senator carrying his own pet proposal. In the shadows Jim Goller was watching the day-to-day proceedings closely, not only because his business at Voter Publishing Company required it, but because he wanted to keep a close eye on his potential candidate. He did not want McClure getting carried away with any particular reapportionment scheme because he was afraid his candidate would inadvertently antagonize a potential supporter. However, according to McClure, Goller's fear was unfounded. "I didn't have any special preference, and I couldn't have been a leader if I had wanted to. The members and proposals were so fractionated that it would have been impossible to take the lead."[2]

The squabbling continued with the House proposing a 70-35 plan (seventy in the House and thirty-five in the Senate) and the senate balking. Finally, at the end of the twentieth day—the maximum length of a special session—the Legislature adjourned without a working plan. This was on a Saturday. The same day Smylie called for the third special session of the 38th Legislature—the first had been after the regular session in 1965—for the following Monday. Five days later, after much bickering, the two houses agreed on a 70-35 plan and the third special session ended. The tradition where each of Idaho's forty-four counties would be represented by a senator was over.[i]

A day or two after the special session, Jim McClure and his friend from Washington County, Hal Ryan, showed up at Goller's office at 906 1/2 Jefferson. Goller remembers saying something to the effect, "Well, have you decided to do it?"

McClure was still hesitant—he said that he was still not certain that he was the best one to run against Compton White, Jr., the incumbent. Goller, who was probably a little exasperated with McClure's reticence by now, proposed a solution.

> *Why don't you make one more round to see those guys* [potential candidates like Jack Hawley and Larry Mills] *and see if they are going to run. If they haven't made up their mind, tell them that you are going to do it. They left, and while they were gone, I got out a press release that I had already written. I wanted to get it out that day so it would make all the weekly papers. When McClure and Ryan came back, I asked them how it went. 'Nobody has made up his mind,' they said. Then I got out the announcement and they read it. 'Let's get this in the papers,' I said. Reluctantly, McClure agreed, and I vividly remember the three of us stuffing and licking envelopes and stamps. Then we went to the post office and I remember dumping those envelopes in the mail slot. 'Well, McClure, it looks like you are running,' I said.*[3]

Thus, on that day, in Goller's downstairs office, Jim McClure made the decision that would forever change his life—and for that matter, a decision that would forever change Jim Goller's life as well.

Shortly afterwards, two more Republicans joined the race. Robert Purcell, who was head of the Chamber of Commerce in Lewiston and had formerly held that same position in Caldwell, also was a native of Payette County, born to a father who had owned one of the county's newspapers[ii] and who had served in the legislature with and had been a close friend of McClure's Grandfather Freehafer. Purcell announced on March 17, claiming that the nature of his work required that he get people of diverse backgrounds together and this experience would help him unite the Republican Party in the First District. This tactic, which was designed to attract Smylie supporters, helped him get labeled as the "moderate" in the campaign.

About two weeks later, Boise businessman Kenneth Arnold also announced his candidacy. Arnold, who had been defeated in a run for lieutenant governor in the 1962 election, was best known as the first person who claimed to have seen flying saucers. His book, *The Coming of the Flying Saucers*, had given him fame, if not fortune, and he announced that Barry Goldwater's admonition for conservative businessmen to get involved in politics was his inspiration for running for Congress.

McClure and Goller went to work on the campaign immediately. Their first hurdle was the Republican endorsing convention that was to be held in Boise on June 11-12. This convention would have to endorse a minimum of two candidates, and each candidate had to receive at least 25 percent of the delegates' vote before he could be placed on the ballot.

Both McClure and Goller, in a joint interview, vividly remembered their first morning on the campaign trail. They, with Louise, left Payette early that day and stopped in Council for breakfast.

> Goller: *It was a restaurant right off Main Street. We got a little corner booth—it was tucked in a corner and there was a counter nearby. Some cowboys came in and some ranchers and they were sitting at the counter. Louise and I finished our breakfast and got up. I think I probably said, 'Well, Jim, there's your audience; there's your people. Go campaign.' And Louise and I went to the car. Jim sat and finished his coffee. By that time we had a card that said 'Jim McClure For Congress.' I could just imagine Jim with the wheels turning, saying to himself, 'You know, do I really want to bother those guys?' As I recall, the first person kind of looked at it and put it down, but the second person said, 'Oh, you're Jim McClure,' and that livened it up a little. So, by the time Jim got down the counter and out to the car, he was warmed up.*

> McClure: *I remember that and I remember the feelings I had about the necessity of campaigning. Before I decided to run for Congress, I had to face the fact that I'd have to do those things. I don't think anybody who knew me in the Legislature really believed I'd be a good candidate because I was too reserved. I tended to wait for people to come to me instead of going to them. But, I knew what campaigning had to be. So I undertook it. Not joyfully, but I knew I had to do it. And I learned to enjoy it.*[4]

Goller had a clear strategy in mind for this first campaign trip. They would call on all Republican county chairmen[iii], all Republican precinct leaders, and any Republican legislative district chairmen in the district. The immediate goal was to get to those people first, before Purcell and Arnold, and talk them into taking one of McClure's nominating petitions—Goller had printed a stack of them with McClure's name already on them. That was a critical first step, for if those people agreed to take a petition and proceeded to get the twenty-five signatures required to complete it, they were legally bound to support the candidate. Of course, these same people would either be delegates to the endorsing convention, or they would be appointing the delegates. Either way, getting them to take and complete a petition for McClure would essentially guarantee one or more votes for him at the convention in June.

Goller knew several of the people they would call upon because, as a former president of the Young Republicans, he had been an *ex officio* member of the state central committee and was widely acquainted with many other Republicans in the state. McClure also knew many of them because of his work with Republicans during the past fifteen years. So, as they motored up U.S. Highway 95 in McClure's 1965 Chrysler New Yorker station wagon with a McCLURE FOR CONGRESS homemade billboard wired to the top, Louise would call off names from their Republican directory and either Goller or McClure would tell what they knew about each of them while Louise would write in her notebook (which is still in her possession). Then, before they called on any of those persons, she would play the role of the schoolmaster and drill them on what they should know about that person.

All three of them remember the gratification they felt as they began making their calls. Almost without exception they were greeted warmly, and many times the person they would meet would take them through the town and introduce them to other potential supporters.

In Bonners Ferry it was Pete Wilson, a classmate of McClure's, who met them at the Chicken Shop, a restaurant south of town, and escorted them downtown, stopping at the Panhandle Cafe where they shook hands with the local coffee crowd—in those days probably every town in the district had a place where the locals gathered for mid-morning coffee. Said Wilson:

> *Jim was never a reluctant campaigner. He would do what you told him to do as far as campaigning was concerned. If this was a person I said he should meet, he would walk right up and carry on a good conversation. Once he shook your hand, you felt that he was your friend, and you felt that you were his friend—that's the way he came across to people. He was not reserved. In fact, he was very outgoing. I think the main impression he left* [during that first campaign] *was that he was a very sincere guy who would really devote himself to representing the people.*[5]

In Sandpoint it was Jim and Alice Nelson, who had not known McClure before that, but who were highly impressed with his answers to questions as they introduced him around the town. Said Alice:

> *My very first impression of him came after he started answering questions. He always had an answer, and it wasn't just a short answer; one knew that he had put a lot of thought into what he said. He studied everything and he was so honest, he would even tell them things that he knew they didn't want to hear. That really sticks in my mind. A lot of politicians will tell you what they think you want to hear. And, I never thought of him as being reserved or reticent about campaigning, and neither did my husband Jim. We talked about that. He was always very warm and friendly, but never reserved. We were his coordinators for that first campaign, and every campaign afterward. We were always proud to be associated with him.*[6]

In Benewah County (St. Maries) it was Dolly Hartman who said:

> *My very first impression of him was that he was constant. That's maybe not the best word, but it is my word for him. What I mean is that what he is today is what he will be tomorrow. His attitude of today is not going to change and be something else. What you saw was what you got and his demeanor was downright humble at times. That's not negative. That's a good trait—one that I look for in a politician. He had humility and that's what a politician* [who is going to represent you] *needs.*[7]

And in Shoshone County it was Ruthie Johnson, who was president of the Republican Women's Club in Wallace, which was a town with a population of only 2,500 people, but had 106 members—the largest club outside of Ada County (Boise). She was also a precinct committeeman, and when McClure came to Shoshone County to meet with the Central Committee, she attended the meeting. Said Johnson:

> *I knew Jim and Louise—I had met them on the bus ride to the Cow Palace at the 1964 Republican Convention in San Francisco—but I had made up my mind that I was going to be impartial about the whole thing. I was going to be fair; I was not going to get involved until I had met all of the candidates. Then Jim stood up and talked for about five minutes to the Central Committee and when he finished, I said, 'Let me have your petition. I'll fill it out.' In fact, I took two of them and in about two days I sent them back to him, filled out.*[8]

Not all the memories of McClure's first days on the campaign trail were that flattering. Said Berne Jensen of Boise, who was an adviser on all of McClure's campaigns:

> *I introduced him when he gave his first political speech, which was to the Capitol City Kiwanis. To be honest, it was not a good speech. If he had a fault, it was in giving too much detail. If you asked him what time it was, he would tell you how to build a watch.*[9]

By the time Republican delegates gathered in Boise for the endorsing convention, Goller's strategy had more than paid off. By his count, McClure had more than 80 percent of the delegates. However, this was a mixed blessing and Goller knew it. He knew that the convention, by law, had to endorse at least one more candidate and he was worried about how they were going to do that. Some of the delegates who were supporting McClure would have to switch votes. However, if there were several ballots, confusion might result in the delegates putting both Purcell and Arnold on the ballot.

That was his greatest fear. He suspected that Arnold could be a flamboyant campaigner once he got warmed up on the campaign trail. This could be a disaster because Arnold, since he was a conservative, could end up taking more votes away from McClure than from Purcell. Goller was afraid to take that chance. He did not want Arnold on the ballot, period. So he went to work behind the scenes, approaching an old friend, Bob Robson, the head of the Shoshone County delegation, to whom he proposed that Robson pledge all of his delegates to Purcell, giving him enough to get on the ballot, but freezing Arnold out. Robson, who remembers the deal, said, "Goller and I had been good friends for years and I wanted to help him out. I think I had eight votes and I gave them to Purcell. That was enough to get him on the ballot. It was a ploy. The idea was to help McClure, not Purcell."[10]

MARTY PETERSON ON COMPTON I. WHITE, JR.

Marty Peterson worked as an aide to McClure's opponent, Compton I. White, Jr. What follows is a digest of his remarks about the Congressman.

Comp was a big man, had a gregarious personality, and was very good with people. . .but he had a lazy streak in him which did not serve him well politically. Comp was more inclined to sit down in the Hotel Boise in the coffee shop and have coffee. . .than stand out on the street corner and press flesh. He was a good hand-shaker when he got out there and did it, but he was not, at least in the period that I was with him, highly motivated. He did have a strong belief in serving his constituents. He did not have a big ego, and I've got to tell you, in the last thirty-two years I've worked with and for an awfully lot of political types and boy there aren't many out there who don't have big egos. . . .Comp had a lot of old time ties around and it was interesting going around the district with him because, while his father had been out of office for many years, Comp White, Sr. was really a legendary Idaho politician. I mean there were a lot of stories about him. He was a real rascal. I can't tell you the number of times that I went to places and you'd tell them, "Oh, I work for Comp White." They'd reply, "Oh, God! I've been voting for Comp White since the Depression." They had no idea that this was a different Comp White.

Comp was a real entrepreneur. He had a variety of businesses and he loved mining and lumber activities. He had some real estate. He was a Roman Catholic. His middle name was Ignatius, named after St. Ignatius, the patron saint of the Basques—Comp never succeeded in making that connection between the Basques and him, politically. His family did not like politics. They did not like Washington, D.C. In fact, his wife had a nervous breakdown back there. She just wanted to get out of Washington.

Comp had a great relationship with the Labor folks. It was an era when labor really counted in the First District . . . . I'm going to pull a figure out of the air and guess if we raised $50,000, I'll bet you that $35,000 of it came from the unions. We really didn't have much of a volunteer base.

With McClure officially on the primary ballot, Goller's next major tasks were to raise money, establish a campaign headquarters, hire a limited staff, and recruit as many volunteers as possible.

The money was a real problem because those who would be the likely donors did not want to get involved until after the primary. Fortunately for McClure, none of their limited funds had to be used for posters, handouts, and other campaign literature; without thought of compensation, Goller produced all of that material in his print shop.[11]

For an office they used an empty room above Goller's print shop that was owned by Bill Campbell of Boise. "It was back at the end of the building," said Goller, and I'm sure we didn't pay much for it, if we paid anything. When we got that, I hired Patty Wenstrom who had been the secretary to the revenue and taxation committee [when the house was in session]."[12] Said Wenstrom later: "I was the secretary, office manager, telephone answerer, envelope stuffer—you name it, I kept the home fires burning."[13]

The second person hired was Del Klaus, a University of Idaho classmate of McClure's, who had been the public relations director for the Idaho Highway Department. Said Goller, "Del was a good rah-rah guy. . .you could see him in a racoon coat. . .he'd go out on the road and check with our county coordinators and the other county people. He would put up signs and distribute campaign literature. He was the antithesis of Jim McClure. We'd get a brochure out and Del would go around with it. . .he'd go into a coffee shop and before he got out, everybody in that coffee shop would have a Jim McClure brochure."[14]

Wherever McClure went, his message was more or less the same. The federal government, led by Lyndon B. Johnson, was on a rampage, usurping power from the states, building a massive federal bureaucracy, creating a horrendous national debt, and all of these policies, combined with rising taxes, were driving prices upward in a never-ending spiral of inflation. And, in Washington, D.C., the Idaho First Congressional District had an incumbent congressman who was a fawning acolyte of the President—a Democrat who, when criticized for his obsequiousness to the administration, reportedly said, "To get along you have to go along."[15]

The Vietnam War was also rising towards a climax in the summer of 1966, but Jim McClure said little about it. Privately, he had doubts about our involvement in that war, but his main concern was the sending of young Americans to fight without a clear strategy for winning. If they were over there to stop the march of Communism, perhaps that was a worthwhile goal. But, he wanted no part of a policy that sacrificed the lives of young Americans for some tentative holding action that had no victorious end in sight. However, the issue of Vietnam was not, at that time, a burning issue in the First Congressional District.[16]

The biggest issue among the Republicans who would vote in the August primary was the gubernatorial race. Robert Smylie was running for an unprecedented fourth term. But, he had a determined and unlikely challenger, Don Samuelson, a humble businessman from Bonner County (Sandpoint) who, before the endorsing convention, had gone around to numerous Republican leaders asking each of them to please run against Smylie. To each of those he reportedly said, "If you don't, I will have to." None of the potential candidates stepped forward, so Samuelson, very reluctantly, decided to make the challenge himself, and he got enough support from the anti-Smylie delegates at the endorsing convention to get on the primary ballot.

McClure and Smylie were not close, personally or politically.[iv] Purcell, on the other hand, was observed by reporters leaving Smylie's office one day and, afterward, did not deny it when it was claimed in the press that he was "Smylie's candidate."[17] On the other hand, McClure and Samuelson had been friends since early in 1961 when, as freshman state senators, they had shared a room at the Sands Motel in Boise. Both thought the same way on most political issues and both considered themselves to be Goldwater conservatives.

According to Goller, going into the primary there was probably a tendency for Republicans who considered themselves moderate or liberal and who were admirers of Smylie, to also be supporters of Purcell, whereas the anti-Smylie, pro-Samuelson Republicans, most of whom might have called themselves conservatives, tended to support McClure. "I worried a little about that," said Goller later. "I wasn't sure how the Smylie-Samuelson battle was going to turn out and I didn't want my candidate trapped in that fight. I wanted McClure's abilities to stand out on their own and not be tied to the governor fight. Before the primary I can't remember us doing any campaigning with Samuelson."

As it turned out, they would not have been hurt and might have been helped if they had campaigned with Samuelson for, statewide, he upset Smylie by 19,138 votes (61%-39%). However, McClure did well on his own, carrying the First District by 4,441 votes over Purcell. That was on August 2. They had three months until the general election to (1) try and bring the almost 19,000 Republicans who voted for Purcell into the McClure camp, and (2) appeal to the independent and undecided voters in the First District, many of whom had voted for Democrats in past elections.

And while Jim and Louise McClure were going from town to town, often staying with friends and supporters to cut down on expenses,[18] Goller was constantly on the phone with the precinct workers and volunteers, urging them on with what was for the time, a unique strategy.

Goller's problem was that eleven of the twenty counties in the district were traditional Democratic counties and he had no hope that there would be any change in the 1966 general election. But, he also knew that he needed *some* Republican votes from even the staunchest of the Democratic counties to go with the votes from counties he expected to carry. His real problem was the workers in those Democratic counties: how was he to motivate them to work hard in a county they knew their candidate was going to lose?

Goller's strategy was to develop a realistic quota for each of those eleven counties—a quota that even a pessimistic worker could expect to achieve. For example, in Clearwater County (Orofino), which had an overwhelming number of union sawmill and timber workers, he proposed something to the effect that, "I know you can't possibly get out enough votes for McClure to carry the county, but can you get 750 people in the county to vote for him?" He wanted them to think, "Hmm, just 750 votes; that shouldn't be too hard. I can do that."

GOLLER ON MCCLURE AND VIETNAM

We were in St. Maries campaigning—we were at a supper club west of town—and a group of people came to meet Jim. One of them was an Army man just back from Vietnam, the son of a Democratic legislator. McClure took the young man off to the side and talked to him for what seemed like an hour. It was embarrassing because he was ignoring the Republicans who had come to see him—and what was worse was that it was the son of a Democrat. Finally, I had to go over and remind him that there were others who needed some of his time. But, this illustrates how he felt about Vietnam at the time. He wanted to learn everything he could about it, and he especially respected those who could give him first-hand information.

Goller's quota concept was exceptionally important in Nez Perce County, the largest of the Democratic counties with about 10,000 votes. With all the union workers at the Potlatch Forest Industries pulp mill in Lewiston, there was no hope for a win, but it was crucial to get the Republicans out because they were the third largest block in the district. The key was to motivate the workers, which Goller did by giving them a quota of about one-third of the total vote—a goal they exceeded in the general election by more than 300 votes.

> *Goller: We broke this down by precinct—last time this precinct got so many votes, next time can you get x amount. That gets it down to ten or 15 votes more than they got last time and most workers will say, Yeah, I can do that. Most people get overwhelmed when they look at the state as a whole or the county as a whole, but in the precinct it was their neighborhood and that was more realistic.*[19]

The campaign was a steep learning curve for both McClure and Goller, and those who were associated with them clearly observed the changes. Said Jim Harris who was their 19-year-old volunteer driver:

When I first met him [McClure], *I was a little worried because he seemed so shy. Of course, I was just a kid who didn't know anything, but I'm thinking that this guy isn't very aggressive for someone running for a national office. But, I can tell you one thing about McClure: I saw a real difference in him between the time when I first met him and the time of the election in November. He really became a gregarious politician during that period of time. Later in the campaign I remember several times when he would see a farmer standing out somewhere or on his tractor and he'd say, 'Stop; pull over there.' Then he'd go shake the guy's hand and we would be off. He got very good at that and I think he liked it after he started doing it more.*[20]

The same could be said about his speech making. At the beginning he had a tendency to over explain—to give more details than were wanted, but with wife Louise almost always in the audience waving at him when he got too wordy, he soon learned the virtue of brevity. After awhile, even Goller, who was as constant a critic as Louise, remembers:

One of Jim McClure's strengths developed in that first campaign when he learned how to give the right speech to the right crowd. If a ten-minute speech was needed, that is what they got. If a twenty-minute speech was appropriate, he could give it. I watched a lot from the back of the room when he was giving those speeches. I could see that the people were listening. I could see that he was having an impact on them. I always used to say that you never worried about putting Jim McClure in front of an audience—any kind of audience, whether it is a town meeting or a Kiwanis Club or a meeting of business people. And this strength grew as the campaign progressed.[21]

There also were some bumpy stretches in the road as McClure and Goller learned to work with each other. McClure, by nature, was into details; that was his forte in his law practice; that was his forte in the Legislature; and that would be his forte in his later legislative life. But, McClure's quest for details, from Goller's perspective, sometimes approached the level of micromanagement. That was a problem for Goller because he felt he had to have the freedom to get out campaign materials, press releases, and speak for the candidate. This difference in perspective had the potential to create a conflict and the fact that it did not can be explained by the frank way they dealt with each other. Said they:

Goller: *McClure's natural tendency was to tinker.*

McClure: *I just wanted to know what was going on. . .he* [Goller] *had a tendency. . .he tried to run it all himself and be the candidate. I had to cure him of that.*

Courtesy Jim Goller
Jim Goller, left, confers with Bob Purcell during McClure's first Congressional campaign.

Goller: *That's right. That is absolutely right. There's a lot of mistakes made when you're working in a first campaign like we were. When I look back on it now, I can see that the campaign manager wants to be the candidate.*

McClure: *Because you believed in the issues as I did.*

Goller: *And I was a little more impatient than Jim McClure. There were some incidents where Jim McClure, like a good strong father, said, 'Now, Jim,'—he didn't directly say that I was trying to be the candidate, but he let me know that he was the one running. But we meshed well. We tolerated each other well.*

McClure: *We had a lot of confidence in each other.*

The First District, which ran from Nevada to the Canadian border, is about 500 miles long. But, it had only two cities with more than 15,000 people, Nampa and Boise.[v] It was a very rural district, and also a very mountainous district, with no freeways, and traversed by one, long two-lane road with thousands of curves and three long grades with multiple switchbacks. A hard driver could make it from Boise to Bonners Ferry, the county seat of the northernmost county, in one very long day, but few people wanted to endure that kind of punishment.

This adverse geography had never been conducive to political unity in the state. Those in the Panhandle—if you think of Idaho as a frying pan, the skinny northern part would be the handle—have, from the time Idaho became a territory, thought of themselves as the poor northern cousins, neglected, even forsaken, especially by the politicians in Boise. Yes, they were Idahoans and reasonably proud of it, but for commercial purposes they mostly allied themselves to Spokane, Washington, the area around which shrewd marketers promoted as the "Inland Empire."

Many of the original settlers in the Panhandle were from southern states and the thoughts of secession came naturally to the minds of their descendants as they lamented their status as a political backwater. That is one reason why Compton White, Sr. had been such a popular congressman in the 1930s and '40s. He was from Clark Fork, sixty miles from the Canadian border, and one of them. He knew what it was like to pull a green chain. He knew how to blow stumps with dynamite. He knew what it was like to labor all day in a mine. Most of all, he knew what it was like to live almost 400 road miles from the political capitol of his state. Now his son was the incumbent, carrying the same name, and with an identity known and respected in every town and logging camp. He, too, was one of them, and as he traveled around the district he tried to make sure they did not forget that.

So how was McClure, carrying the image of a downstate, city slicker lawyer, going to make inroads in this hostile environment? How was he going to win the votes of these down-home, plain-talking stump-ranch farmers, miners, loggers, and sawmill workers and take them away from the man with the magic name who was one of them?

That was a challenge that McClure accepted with enthusiasm, for he knew in his heart that he really was not a city slicker. He had spent every summer of his young life away from the city, isolated on a small, hard-scrabble ranch, and molded by a grandfather so tough and independent he would never consider owning a tractor, even in the 1940s. And he knew what it was like to toil for the wages of a working stiff. He had pounded out fenders in a body shop in the northern Idaho town of Moscow; he had wrestled the cutter bar on a combine and, sitting on a Caterpillar tractor all day, had dragged two, four-bottom plows through the rocky soil of Camas Prairie; and he had worn caulked boots, dug *Ribes* with a hoedag, and fought forest fires among the white pines in the St. Joe National Forest in the Panhandle. He identified closely with those farmers, miners, loggers, and sawmill workers and he relished the opportunity to visit personally with them so that, by speaking their language, he could establish a new image of himself—one that he felt he deserved.

So where should McClure go in that huge district? Should he be out in places like Bovill, Elk River, Kooskia and Weippe where, one-on one, he could try and sell himself to those who had been Comp White's people? Or, should he be in Boise where the mass of voters was concentrated, working the shopping malls and the coffee circuit, and trying to persuade the more educated, more sophisticated independent voters that a Republican was needed in Congress?

McClure and Goller had a tendency to think differently on this question. McClure felt that Idahoans are different from voters in many other states of the Union. He believed then (and now) that Idahoans, especially rural Idahoans, fully expected candidates to make the effort to come to them; thus he felt strongly that it was his duty to travel to the remote hamlets and villages in the mountains of northern Idaho where he could meet and shake the hand of each voter.

Goller was sympathetic—he came from rural Idaho—but he had deep reservations about the rural strategy. He knew that most of those rural north Idahoans were diehard Comp White people who had been loyal Democratic voters for many years. Sure, McClure, one-on-one, might, and possibly would, turn some of them around, but the effort, for a few hundred votes, would require a huge expenditure of time which they did not have. On the other hand, by stationing his candidate in a few Albertson's parking lots in Nampa, Caldwell, and Boise, McClure could, in two or three days, personally meet and speak with several thousand voters, none of whom were wearing that northern Idaho chip on the shoulder, and few of whom were wedded to the magic of the Comp White name.

The difference of opinion did not lead to an impasse. McClure joyfully weaved the winding trails into the north Idaho villages and was heartened by the warm reception he received by many of the locals. Yes, they were Comp White people; they had been Comp White people for many years. But, nobody likes to be taken for granted, and the fact that Jim McClure made his way to their town, spoke their language, and genuinely seemed to

A CAMPAIGN STORY

Jim Harris, a Boise attorney and former Ada County Prosecutor, was a 19-year old freshman at Boise Junior College when he volunteered to help with the McClure campaign. This is his favorite story of the campaign:

We had a 1965 or 66 Ford Torino that somebody donated and it was a piece of junk—I remember on one occasion the steering went out and I ended up in the middle of a cornfield in Idaho County...it was a terrible car but I was Jim's "wheel man"—I drove him several times from the bottom to the top of the state. . .on one of these major trips, just before the General Election, we were in St. Maries, staying with one of his supporters. We had a couple of hours before dinner and Jim said to me, "Come on, Harris, take me downtown; we'll make some rounds and shake some hands before dinner." So I drove him downtown and in those days St. Maries was a pretty wild town. . .we spotted a group that I identified as being a bunch of lumberjacks on the sidewalk in front of a bar. So we pull up to these lumberjacks and Jim gets out and starts his little routine—there's six or eight guys and as Jim's talking, a bottle of Jack Daniels shows up and these guys start passing the bottle around. Now, neither Jim nor Louise drank in those days, so I'm thinking this is going to be real interesting because they were all taking a heavy swig from the bottle as it was being passed around. Well, I'll be darned if Jim doesn't say, "Thank you," and takes a big swig of that whiskey. And the bottle comes around and he takes a second swig. We then go back to the house and dinner's about ready and when Jim comes in, Louise being Louise, she is aware that Jim has imbibed a little bit. Then, at the table, someone asks Jim a question that he should have remembered and when he couldn't, Louise made the comment, "Well, if Jim was himself this afternoon, he would have remembered." And that's all that was said. Nothing else. Jim said nothing. I said nothing. She never asked me about it and I doubt that she said anything more to Jim. But it was clear that Louise always knew what was going on.

be interested in representing their interests, impressed many of them. Even if they were not going to vote for him, they admired and respected him for his effort. And Goller also got his way. In the Boise Valley, McClure spent days going from supermarket parking lots to shopping malls, and to a host of coffees held at the homes of his supporters, almost always with his attractive and enthusiastic wife at his side, and often accompanied by his three children in the weeks before school started. Of course, McClure much preferred the rural environment, but he understood the importance of the urban campaigning and he went at it with diligence.

And somewhere, when he was on one of those winding trails in northern Idaho, Jim McClure came up with a novel idea. He well knew that the people of the Panhandle were tired of their geographic disadvantage in dealing with government. For example, if a retired person in southern Idaho had a problem with Social Security, that person did not have to write a letter to the congressman in Washington. It was much simpler just to get into the car and drive to the congressman's office in the Boise Post Office. There the problem could be explained to one of the congressman's staffers who, with an understanding of the problem far better than might have been achieved from an explanation in a letter, could immediately pick up the telephone and, perhaps in a short time, resolve the constituent's problem. However, a constituent with a similar problem who lived in Coeur d'Alene or Sandpoint or Plummer did not have that option, unless, of course, he or she felt motivated to drive for two long days on the torturous north-south highway and could afford the expense of meals and lodging along the way. McClure wanted the northern Idaho constituents to have the same option. He wanted to solve their problem of geographic isolation by establishing two congressional offices in the Panhandle—Lewiston and Coeur d' Alene were the logical sites. And, why not? He knew that a congressman was on a budget, but he also knew that, for the hiring of staff and paying rent on office space, he could split the expenses any way he chose.

Goller liked the idea—Goller and McClure had agreed early on that constituent services should always have the highest priority—and it was not long before Goller's press turned out a news release announcing McClure's commitment that, if elected, he would establish congressional offices where northern Idaho constituents could come and deal directly with one of his staffers.

Sometime during the summer they added one more staffer. Her name was Louetta Harper, but probably no one but her mother and father knew that was her first name; since she was a baby, she had been called "Scootch."

Scootch had been a student at the University of Idaho for two years when she was hired as a stringer for a Spokane paper, *The Spokesman Review.* At the time she was dating a fellow who was the northern Idaho reporter for *The Lewiston Morning Tribune*, and when he was drafted for Vietnam, she took his position. Scootch had grown up in a political environment. Her grandfather, Tom Heath from Franklin County (Preston), had been the Republican majority secretary of the Senate. (Her godfather was the most famous Republican in Idaho history: U.S. Senator William Borah.) Because of this background, it was natural for Scootch to lean toward the Republican Party and this later created a problem for her in Lewiston. While working at the *Tribune,* she covered some political event and wrote a report that happened to be favorable to the Republican candidate. According to Scootch, a *Tribune* editor, Bill Hall, well known as a Democrat partisan, called her editor and told him never to let her cover politics again. "She's tainted," he reportedly said.

In the summer of 1966, Scootch's friend was back from Vietnam (due to a family hardship) and had taken over his old position at the *Tribune,* and Scootch was in Boise with her parents, waiting for a United Press International reporter's job to open up the following January. Through her mother, she learned that McClure needed secretarial help, but when she went to apply, she learned that Patty Wenstrom had been hired for the position. However, as she was about to leave, Goller, who was doing the hiring, said that what he really needed was someone who could write press releases. After Scootch explained her journalistic background, Goller showed her to an empty desk. "You're hired. Now, I need you to write a press release on farm subsidies," he said. "We have to get it out immediately."

Scootch complained, "I don't know anything about farm subsidies."

"Neither do I," said Goller. "Here's the Republican Briefing Book. Go to work. I'll look it over."[22]

And so Scootch Harper, before she was old enough to vote[vi], began work as a political staffer—a job that ultimately would take her away from Idaho and keep her immersed in the political cauldron for the next thirty-six years.

As the autumn days passed and election day neared, Goller and McClure wrestled over the schedule—Goller always striving to get the candidate to places with the highest number of potential voters, while McClure, with missionary zeal, stubbornly persisted in going into territory where his opponent was the strongest. In Kellogg and Wallace he was out at the mines, in the dark, at the 6 a.m. shift change, passing out brochures, the litter from which made a visible pathway from where he stood. In town he went to Johnny Posnick's bar, sat on a stool and passed the time of day with the owner, a state representative, and the miners who stopped by. When he introduced himself to the miners as a candidate for Congress, "Some would laugh and some would sneer, but you didn't shy away from that," he said later.[23]

Meeting workers at Lewiston's Potlatch Mill even proved to be a hazardous endeavor. As McClure stood on the center line on the road outside the mill to catch workers coming and going, some of the workers thought it was great sport to see how close they could drive by him without hitting him. "Sure, it bothered me," he admitted later, "but you recognize that some of it is going to be unpleasant. You do it because it has to be done."[24]

The campaigning was definitely more pleasant in Boise where workers like Shelly Alden (McClure*: The best precinct worker I've ever seen.)* arranged a host of neighborhood coffee meetings at various homes around the city. At these events McClure and his wife were greeted warmly, even by former Purcell supporters. Smylie's loss to Samuelson "scared the bejusus out of a lot of Republicans" said one Republican worker,[25] and there was now a circle-the-wagons, let's-pull-together mentality among them, especially as the specter of Lyndon B. Johnson's Great Society was looming more and more ominously from Washington. To the middle-of-the-road Republicans, Jim McClure might be perceived as being far right of center, but he was much better than a Democrat like Comp White who had openly wedded himself to the unions and to the agenda of LBJ.

In the last days of the campaign, Goller made one last sweep of the district to encourage the campaign workers in the Democratic counties. His message was always the same. Do not be discouraged. McClure can never win here. But he can pick up votes. It may be a Democratic county, but there are Republican votes here. You have agreed to a quota of votes. You have said that we can get that number. McClure is counting on you. He cannot win without you.

Many have given flattering descriptions of Jim Goller and he has a lot of admirers in Idaho. Most often he is credited with being the most astute political tactician in the state's history. However, nobody has ever described him as being audacious, but that is the only way to describe his actions the night he stopped in Wallace and went to the Elks Club.

Up on the wall in the bar of the Elks Club was a chalkboard where the members wrote out wagers, and where challengers chalked their acceptances. While perusing the board, Goller noticed that there were a number of wagers proposed on the coming election, all that White would win. Said Goller:

> *It was a $50 bet here and a $100 bet there. Well, I was absolutely confident that we were going to win. I sat down at the bar and decided that I wanted to put a wager up there myself, but one large enough so that nobody would erase it. So, I phoned Janie McClary in Boise—she was the Republican chairman in Ada County. I got Janie and I said, 'I want to put a bet on the board up here.' She said, 'How much?' and I said, 'Five thousand dollars,' and she said, 'Are you going to win this thing?' and I said, 'Yeah, we're going to win this thing, but I can't cover it.' She said, 'Go ahead,' so I put it up on the board: '$5,000 that McClure will be the next representative.' I was told later that nobody had the guts to take the bet, but that shows you how confident I was.* [26]

On election evening Goller maintained this audacity at another Elks Club, this one in Boise, just a block from the capitol. The ballroom floor of the Elks Club was the traditional location for Election Central, where the latest results from the precincts around the state were phoned in and recorded on a big board. The ballroom itself was restricted to the media and the Election Central workers; however, Goller had somehow obtained a UPI press credential that allowed him to be on the floor. Early in the evening, right after the first results were trickling in, Comp White had the lead and Patty Wenstrom, who was in the balcony above the ballroom, remembers her panic. "I was going crazy with worry and, finally, I couldn't stand it any longer. I wrote a note on a piece of yellow paper and dropped it down to Jim [Goller]. It said something to the effect that we are losing; what is going on?"[27]

Goller remembers the note and how he answered. "I wrote on it: 'Oh ye of little faith, why do you doubt me? We are going to win by 5,000 votes.' Then I sent the note upstairs. After awhile, Patty signaled and dropped the note and on it she had replied: 'THANKS, GOD!'"[28]

And how did McClure feel at this time? "Well, I was obviously somewhat nervous, but I still felt good about it, even when Patty was just about to collapse. I wasn't quite as confident as Jim [Goller] was, but we'd done our work and I knew what the figures were. I knew that our workers out there knew what their quotas were. I knew that they had said, yes, we can do that. That to me was the real key of that campaign—being able to motivate workers [when they were in a minority] to go out and get their quotas."[29]

The Comp White lead soon evaporated as the evening wore on, and by eleven o'clock the county-by-county vote was coming through very close to the way Goller had predicted. He had told Patty Wenstrom (and anybody else who would listen) that they were going to win by 5,000 votes. When the official vote was certified by the Secretary of State, out of a total of 135,856 votes cast in the First District, McClure won by a margin of 4,964. Goller missed his prediction by thirty-six votes.

The euphoric McClure team left the Elks Club and walked toward the Hotel Boise where, in the ballroom, microphones of the news media were set up for the McClure victory speech—Comp White had already conceded. Goller remembers that walk. "We were just bouncing—at least I was—and I remember how happy we were until we walked by a little office right on the alley by the Hotel Boise. It was Comp White's little office, his campaign headquarters, and as we walked by the doorway there was this young staff assistant just sobbing his heart out. That was kind of a comedown."[30]

Added McClure, ruefully, but with a slight smile, "I remember that we felt sorry for him, but not very."[31]

Chapter 11 notes

i. The senate seat in Jim McClure's home county was one of the casualties. One senator would be elected from Payette and Washington Counties.

ii. The *Independent* before it was merged with the *Enterprise*.

iii. The author is using the gender specific names as they were used in 1966.

iv. When McClure was Assistant Majority Leader, he was at a strategy meeting where Smylie dictated a detailed strategy of how "we" were going to proceed on a variety of issues. When he finished, McClure said, "Governor that may be how you think we should proceed, but let me tell you, that is not how I think we should proceed." According to McClure, the bad vibes persisted long after that meeting.

v. In the 1960 census Nampa had just over 18,000 people and Boise just over 34,000.

vi. One of the volunteers made her a badge with the inscription: IF I WERE OLD ENOUGH TO VOTE, I WOULD VOTE FOR JIM McCLURE.

Chapter 12

From Payette to Washington, D.C.

In 1966 Jim McClure left his law practice in mid-February for a special session of the Legislature. That session was extended into another special session, and after that, in mid-March, he started campaigning, first for the nomination, then for the congressional office itself. By early November he had won the election and he knew that he would be going to Washington, D.C. as the new congressman for the First Congressional District of Idaho.

By early November he also knew something else—that he was flat broke. In his words, "I didn't have a penny to my name."[1]

The reason, of course, was because he had been doing little or no work in his law office. Yet he had a mortgage on his house, a family of five to feed, and now an expensive move to a city where the cost-of-living was far greater than in Payette, Idaho. In addition, despite his admonition to Jim Goller that the campaign should absolutely not run a deficit (*If you lose, you have to ask people to pay for a dead horse, and if you win, they're going to pay because of that, and that is bad news, too.*[2]), Goller, on his own, went to Louise's parents and got them to back a $5,000 note that Goller signed at the bank—money that was used without McClure's knowledge for last minute radio spots and other campaign expenses that Goller felt were essential. Some of that borrowed money had been covered by late contributions to the campaign, but there was still a debt for which McClure was responsible.

Besides that, he was getting cold feet at the thought of leaving the security of Payette with all his friends and family. His roots were deep there and, yes, in an abstract sense, the challenge of representing Idaho in the Congress was a heady thought—even exhilarating when he allowed himself to envision the process, but there were two daunting practical problems: (1) Where were we going to live back there and (2) How were we going to afford living back there? In addition, there were the children, ages 9, 12 and 14. What was he doing to them? Would the move and the strange schools in a foreign environment—urban was foreign to kids from Payette, Idaho—prove traumatic for them? Would they adapt to the new environment or would they, for the rest of their lives, blame the ambition of their father for wrecking their childhoods?

Father and mother, undoubtedly after much discussion, developed a strategy for dealing with their childrens' anxiety, or what they perceived to be their childrens' anxiety. They decided that they would imprint them with two concepts that would always be foremost in their minds. To their children they would say repeatedly: listen, this is not a permanent move; look at this as just a two-year adventure; people can be fickle; they can change their mind about your father and, at the next election, he could be defeated. Also, you are not leaving Idaho for good. We are keeping our house in Payette. Yes, we will rent it out, but not for the whole year. We will make sure that it is empty every summer so you can come back and spend your summers with your grandparents and your friends.

That strategy, they believed, would ease the minds of their children. But, the two main problems remained. They had to have money and they had to have a place for the family to live back in Washington.

To solve the money problem he went to one of the local banks and, on the strength of his signature, borrowed $10,000 that he used to pay his outstanding bills, finance the trip to Washington, and to sustain them there until he began receiving his monthly congressional salary.

He and Louise solved the second problem when they went to Washington in early December to attend an orientation meeting the National Republican Party held for the new House members elected to the 90th Congress. George Hansen, the congressman from Idaho's Second District, had been back there for two years, and even though they barely knew each other, Hansen and his wife Connie went out of their way to help the McClures. Together, they explored their own neighborhood in the New Dover area of north Arlington (Virginia) where they found a partially furnished house that was available to rent. It was not what the McClures really wanted, but they decided it would solve their immediate problem and serve as a base from which they could search for something more suitable.

And, undoubtedly, there was talk of politics while he was back in Washington, especially in regard to the committee assignments that a minority freshman like Jim McClure might receive in the upcoming 90th Congress. The choice assignments were to the ways and means and appropriations committees. McClure must have suspected and Hansen probably confirmed that there was no chance he would get either of those; minority vacancies on those committees went to representatives with seniority and who were from populous states like Illinois, Michigan, Ohio, New York, or Pennsylvania. Likewise with the next two most desired committees: armed forces and foreign relations. Two other states, Washington and Alaska, tried to control another desirable committee, the commerce committee, because it held jurisdiction over fishing, which was a major industry in both of those states.

What McClure really wanted was an assignment on the Interior and Insular Affairs Committee, but there was a problem: George Hansen was

Courtesy Marilyn Roach

Louise took this photo of the McClure family at Bill McClure's Evergreen Cabin before they left for Washington, D.C. Front: Marilyn, Ken and Dave. Behind: Jim, his father, Bill, Auntie Mamie and his mother, Marie.

already on it. Although representatives from the East normally had little interest in that committee and it was dominated by Westerners, still, convincing the House minority leadership that both congressmen from a small state like Idaho should be on it seemed, to both of them, to be an uphill struggle. Nevertheless, while back at the Republican orientation, McClure buttonholed every Republican leader who had a moment to listen to present his case.[i] And, reportedly, Hansen did the same later when the 90th Congress convened.[3]

Back in Idaho, moving preparations got seriously under way. McClure worked long hours winding down his law practice while Louise and the kids packed and prepared the house so that it could be rented until their return in the summer. This Christmas it was their turn to spend the day with Jim's parents who lived just a few houses up the street—on alternate years they would spend it with Louise's parents in Nezperce. However, none of the family remembers much about the Christmas of 1966; all of their thoughts, especially those of Marilyn and Ken, were on the great adventure that was ahead of them. (Dave, who later joked that "I was not just nine years old but nine and three-quarters and counting myself ten," did not "buy into the exciting adventure scenario" because he was not in favor of leaving Payette and his friends.[4]) Also, in keeping with the two-years-only-in-Washington scenario that they had tried to program into their children's minds, the parents had

Courtesy McClure family

The McClures load their 1965 Chrysler New Yorker station wagon for the journey to Washington, D.C.

gone out of their way to emphasize that the motor trip back to Washington was to be a learning experience and a once-in-a-lifetime adventure. And, to enrich that experience, each of the children were given their very own Rand-McNally 1966 Road Atlas so they could study the geography and make personal notes as they traveled.

The five McClures started their adventure in mid-morning the day after Christmas, their heavily loaded 1965 Chrysler New Yorker station wagon tethered to the largest U-Haul trailer they could rent. In Boise they stopped at Jim Goller's print shop on Jefferson Street to go over last minute administrative details. (Although Goller would be called "district assistant," he was, in fact, going to become the first congressional chief of staff to exercise his duties while remaining in a congressman's home district. Since then the practice has become quite common.) The Boise hiatus did not sit well with the family, especially Ken who later said, "After all the excitement of leaving Payette on this big, exciting adventure—everyone waving goodbye—then we get to Boise and have to sit in the car for what seemed like hours. . .it was a long time and it really annoyed me. . ."[5]

Ken remembers staying in Pocatello that first night; daughter Marilyn believes that they went farther to Soda Springs; while neither Dave nor the parents remember for sure where they stayed. For certain it was a slow trip for there were only short segments of the Interstate freeway completed in

Idaho at that time. They got an early start the next morning, but when they reached Interstate 80 near Little America, Wyoming, one of the tires on the station wagon blew out. As fine snow sifted across the highway, propelled by a bitter, cold north wind, Jim mounted the worn spare; then, with some anxiety, drove cautiously to Green River where he was able to purchase a new tire. After that, they made good time on the freeway; however, as they were nearing Cheyenne, weather reports on the radio warned of a strong winter blizzard over Nebraska and Kansas, so they decided to go around it. They turned south in Cheyenne, and as they approached Denver, they came upon an exciting scene that the three youngsters would remember for the rest of their lives. Said Ken, "It was a clear night and as far as we could see there were lights sparkling...it was a heck of a lot bigger than anything we had seen in Payette or Boise.[6] For Marilyn, ". . .it was my most exciting moment. Actually, coming into Denver itself was the first realization that we were going someplace really different."[7]

But for the kids, this was to be an educational trip as well as an adventure. So, despite the late hour, their tiredness, and the big U-Haul they were dragging behind them, Sergeant Mom insisted that Dad had to drive them through all the traffic into the heart of downtown Denver so they could add the Colorado State Capitol Building to their list of geographic sites visited.

The next morning, after confirming that, indeed, a blizzard was raging in Kansas, they continued south to Colorado Springs (Dave remembers lying in the back of the station wagon and watching them pass Pikes Peak), through Raton Pass into New Mexico, then down to I-40 and Amarillo, Texas where they ran into snow. "That surprised me," said Marilyn, because I had an image of Texas as a hot place."[8] They spent their third night in Shamrock, Texas, near the Oklahoma border, and by noon the following day they were circling the Oklahoma State Capitol, gawking at a scene that surprised them. Said Dave, "I was amazed and a little amused because right there on the statehouse lawn there were oil wells with the pumps actually working." That night they made it to Morrilton, Arkansas just north of Little Rock. Marilyn's cryptic notes from her atlas and from postcards that she wrote but did not send summarize the rest of the journey:

> *Left Morrilton at 6:45, drove around Little Rock, saw capitol, quite impressive, also saw big beautiful mansion, crossed Mississippi River into Memphis, looong bridge, quite unreal. Right through Memphis, lunch at Esso gas station. Pretty country into Nashville by way of Bellemeade, drove to Hermitage* [Andrew Jackson's home], *got there just after closed, drove back, got hotel, ate, water rusty, wonderful beds, though. Up at 6:15, drove around Nashville, saw replica Parthenon, beautiful, saw capitol, breakfast Pancakes International, out to Hermitage, nine to eleven thirty, gorgeous, saw cardinal, seemed artificial. Pretty country. Lunch Knoxville, passed*

> *time zone, soup for lunch, Smoky mountains beautiful. Gatlinburg: hotels, motels all over, good mountains up to 5,000 feet—6:30 Payette time, 9:30 our time—had dinner 45 minutes ago, hamburgers. Staying Maggie Valley Hotel, Maggie Valley, NC on US 19, telephone exchange is in Waynesboro. Still on I-40, turned north at Raleigh on Highway 1, I-95 at Petersburg, then into Washington pretty late, dark, cold, and tired. Found the house in Arlington we were renting, unloaded beds that night, mattresses on floor. Kind of newness and unreality.* [The house was] *kind of on a hill, under traffic pattern for National* [airport], *saw headlights of airplanes* [over us]. . . [9]

Ken picks up the story:

> *"The new house, it was cool. It was a split-entry, tri-level, had a nice yard in a nice neighborhood. We ran in and fought over who was going to get which bedroom—that sort of stuff. The next morning we had a real comical adventure. We all went to the grocery store—Giant Food in Lyon Village. It was right at the top end of Spout Run, one of the side roads that feeds into the George Washington Parkway. In the store we bought everything from sponges to soap to every kind of condiment and spice you could think of. . .and it was unusual because I'd never been grocery shopping with dad before. But, we all went and it cost a bundle of money, something along the order of $200 and I was just flabbergasted that you could spend $200—in 1966 that was a lot of money to spend in a grocery store. We loaded up and the car was absolutely crammed with grocery sacks. . .as we pulled out we made a wrong turn and got on Spout Run and once you get on it you don't get off because it runs down into the George Washington Parkway and across the bridge* [over the Potomac]. *So, even though we had ice cream and all this other refrigerated stuff in the car, dad and mom decided that since we were down there, we might as well make a tour of the Capitol Mall. So, before breakfast we saw the Washington Monument, the Lincoln Memorial, the Capitol Building and the White House. . ."* [10]

Take seven days for the traveling and add one day for getting the home livable—after touring Capitol Mall, and after unpacking the groceries and eating breakfast, they went out again and shopped for more furniture—and Jim McClure's time with his family totaled eight, 24-hour days. That turned out to be the high-water mark for this father; he would never again spend that much exclusive time with his whole family.[ii] The second day after he arrived in Washington he went to work and in the process mounted a treadmill from which he did not escape for twenty-four years.

To be a successful congressman you must be a leader. But how do you lead? McClure said that he first pondered that question when he was installed as president of the Payette Kiwanis Club back in the 1950s. "What was I going to say as a young guy to all those guys older than me? How was I going to be a good leader? I decided that there were two ways to go about it. One was to lead by inspiration. The other was to lead by example. I had no illusions about my ability to inspire, so I decided that I had no choice but to become an example by working harder than anybody else. After that, I took that philosophy to the legislature, and when I was driving toward the Capitol Building in Washington that first time, heading to the Longworth Building, I had already made up my mind that I was going to use the same approach as a congressman. Specifically, I was determined that I was going to be there before eight o'clock in the morning—before anybody else—and that, unless I had a function to attend, I would be the last one to leave in the evening—and that was almost always the case, especially in the evening when I would not get out of there until seven, eight, sometimes even nine o'clock."[11]

McClure was also aware of the limitations of his approach to leadership. His congressional campaign had taught him that he could only do so much on his own—that he could not have won the campaign without the astute leadership of Jim Goller and the team he put together. Now, if he was going to be a successful congressman, he knew he had to put together another team to handle all of the varied demands upon a congressional office. Jim Goller, of course, was still the team leader with the title of district assistant, and with advice from McClure, was selecting personnel who would staff the Boise office as well as the regional offices in Lewiston and Coeur d'Alene that McClure had pledged to establish during his campaign. However, as Jim McClure approached Room 1413 in the Longworth Building that first morning on the job (after a frustrating search for a parking spot in the garage where congressmen did not have reserved spaces), he was well aware that his first and most important task was to find the right personnel to staff his office.

He already had two staffers on the job that first morning. Del Klaus, the former highway department publicity director who had worked as the "ra ra" guy in the campaign, had been sent back to Washington to serve under the title of "administrative assistant." And Scootch Harper, who had been the dedicated, too-young-to-vote, college dropout/reporter who had worked in the campaign, was also sent back. She was given the title of "secretary."

What McClure did not have was a staffer with Washington experience—one who was intimately familiar with the bureaucracy—one who knew everything from how to finagle office supplies and furniture or how to get passes for visitors to the White House and Capitol or how to get resolutions and bills printed and inserted into the *Congressional Record*. So, the first day on the job, McClure started looking. His desk was already loaded with resumes from staffers displaced by the huge turnover in the last election when forty-four House Democrats had been defeated by Republicans. He knew there might be a few good people in that stack of names, and he did interview some of them. But, he was specifically looking for one intelligent, resourceful congressional veteran who had all of the necessary qualifications and who was *also* a conservative who would be philosophically compatible. He lucked out on the second day of his search when a man recommended by Senator Len Jordan's office came to him for an interview. Dick Thompson said:

> *We instantly hit it off, laughing, talking about issues and things, and by the time that meeting was over, I knew he was going to offer me the job and I knew I was going to take it. We had a lot in common. Our political views were virtually the same. And I liked him instantly. I liked him so much that the salary, which wasn't great, didn't matter. I knew I wanted to work for him.*

McClure did, indeed, offer Thompson the job, and on McClure's third day in his office, he went to work as a combination legislative assistant and press secretary.

At roughly the same time he also hired a woman with years of experience on the "Hill" as his executive secretary. She was Ann Woodward, and while Dick Thompson turned out to be the trusted and knowledge-able aide that McClure needed, Ann Woodward became a divisive force in his office whom he probably waited too long to fire.

The office itself befitted a minority congressman from a state that ranked near the bottom in population. In distance it was about as far from the Capitol Building as one could get. In space it was the smallest of all the offices. It had two rooms, one that was about 16 by 30 and served as the staff office. In the back of that room, on the left side, was a door that led into a room about 15 by 15 that was the congressman's office. In front of his office was a very small restroom, and in front of that was a small storeroom. Within a few weeks, after McClure had hired two more staffers for clerical help (Jan Reed and Jane Collins), and after all the necessary desks, chairs and filing cabinets had been moved in, the staff office, with everybody sitting almost on top of each other, talking on the phone and typing, looked much like the old image of the city room for a busy metropolitan newspaper. Eventually, when they got a machine that coded names, even the storeroom had to be used as an office for the machine and the operator.

McClure was concerned about the office, not so much because of its space limitations—he knew what a person of his lowly status could expect in the way of amenities—but because of its ambience. It was just a typical looking office. And he did not want that. He had to come to work there every day. And he knew he was going to get a lot of visitors. For his own morale and to impress those who came to visit, he wanted an *Idaho* ambience. He wanted to see Idaho when he came into the office, and he wanted his visitors to be aware of the greatness of his state.

So he and his staffers went to work. First, they contacted Louise Shadduck, head of the Idaho state tourism office, and requested attractive pictures that could be mounted on the walls. She furnished some and gave them leads to the U.S. Forest Service and Union Pacific Railroad where others were obtained. And, someone managed to get a decal of the Great Seal of Idaho that was affixed to the office front door. Soon the McClure city room had an Idaho ambience.

DICK THOMPSON

Dick Thompson was born and raised in the small southern Indiana town of North Vernon. His family of political activists included a grandfather who ran Republican Headquarters in the state and a father who served three terms in the state Legislature. He graduated from Butler University in 1950 with a degree in journalism, then served on active duty with the Indiana National Guard during the Korean War. When that was over, he worked in the unsuccessful congressional campaign of Ed Whitcomb, a man from his hometown who later was a successful candidate for governor.

After the congressional campaign, Whitcomb asked Thompson what he wanted to do and he replied that he would like to go to Washington, D.C. Whitcomb then called Indiana Senator Bill Jenner, inquired if he knew of any positions available for a good young man, and Jenner said that one of his committees, the Printing Committee, would soon have a vacancy and that Thompson could have that. That got Thompson to Washington and gave him his first job, which was to index the *Congressional Record.* This job required him to read every page of the *Record* every day for four years, which gave him a unique perspective on what was going on in the Congress, and knowledge greater than that of any one senator or representative.

Also at this time, he became a big fan of Senator Barry Goldwater. In 1964, when Gold-water ran for the nomination, then the presidency, Thompson took a year off and worked enthusiastically in those campaigns. After that, he heard about a staff position with the new research center being established in the House, and he was one of five persons selected for that staff. He served there for two years writing speeches and doing research for such House power brokers as Jerry Ford and Melvin Laird. Then he received a call from a friend who was on Idaho Senator Len Jordan's staff. She told him that Jim McClure was coming to Washington as a new representative from Idaho and that his present staffers had never been east of the Mississippi. "You would be the ideal person to serve on his staff," she told him. Thompson was interested. He knew his way around the House, and if McClure was a man with integrity and a true conservative philosophy, he could think of nothing he would rather do than to serve such a man and help make him successful. So, he arranged for an interview.

Then he had to buckle down to the serious work. He was sworn in January 10, which was the official day that his work started. But, he was a congressman in limbo, without an official committee assignment, and his status had not changed a week later. This was an anxious time for him, and on the advice of several whom he consulted, he decided to make one last effort to resolve the matter. In a letter to the members of the Executive Committee of the Committee on Committees of the Republican Party—the group that would make the committee assignments— he admonished them, in a letter dated January 18:

Dear Colleague:

I know that the demands of your office and this particular task are time consuming. I know, too, that you have been button-holed, cajoled, entreated, exhorted and (perhaps, politely) threatened—all at great length. Because I know this, I have not taken your time before now. I am sure that what I say on my behalf has been said by a hundred others.

Each man and woman here is important and has his or her own important problems and considerations. I ask no special consideration for my problems, but only fair evaluation.

I have served the people of my county as Prosecuting Attorney in three successive terms. I was elected to the State Senate in 1960, defeating an incumbent, and was successively elected twice more. I was Chairman of Judiciary and Rules Committee in my second term and was elected by my fellows in the Senate as Assistant Majority Leader in 1965. In that latter position I had the responsibility of making committee assignments, and I sympathize with you in your present problems.

I have served on the Resolution Committee of the Idaho Reclamation Association for ten years and on its Legislative Committee during the last two years. I serve as the Idaho representative on a special study committee of the National Reclamation Association.

The First Congressional District of Idaho has within its boundaries almost every interest of the Interior and Insular Affairs Committee from the great reclamation projects of the southern part of the district, public lands throughout, mining in the northern position, and Indian affairs in both sections. Wilderness areas and wild rivers are among our concerns.

As you know, Hon. Abe McGregor Goff, now of the I.C.C., was once elected, and Dr. John T. Wood was elected to one term in this district. Otherwise, the Democrats have had firm control for well over thirty years. Although re-districting has helped, the Democrats did not expect to lose this year and I am sure they will make a major effort to retake it in 1968. My margin was approximately 5,000 votes

Courtesy McClure family

Idaho's new representative and family stroll in front of the Capitol Building for an official photo for the newspapers back home.

in 138,000 votes cast. I believe we can hold this seat, but I do need whatever assistance I can get. Committee assignment can be a very important factor. The position of Compton White on this committee and the fear of losing this representation if I were elected was a substantial factor in the last election. I lost some Republican support on this account...Already it is being used against me and I can point to a public statement and press release of Senator Frank Church.

For these reasons I have asked that I be assigned to the Interior and Insular Affairs Committee as my 1st choice.

I recognize the difficulty caused by the fact that Congressman George Hansen now serves on that committee. I realize that the appointment of two Members of the same party from the same State is unusual, but it is not without precedent. The best illustration is the Membership of that committee upon which three Democrats and

> *two Republicans from the State of California served during the 89th Congress. I might point out, also, that this would give the possibility of representation on sub-committees of great interest to my State and District not now directly represented except through the full committee. . .*

McClure was one of forty-four Republicans who, nationwide, defeated Democratic incumbents in a mid-term backlash against President Lyndon B. Johnson. There were a variety of reasons for this animosity toward the President—the escalating, but dismal prospects in the Vietnam War, record inflation, massive new bureaucratic programs of Johnson's Great Society, and perhaps most of all, the uneasy feeling across the country that a new, liberal-supported phenomenon called the "Hippie Movement," which was manifesting itself with open abuse of drugs, uninhibited free sex, slovenly personal hygiene, disrespect and mistrust of authority, and uncouth clothing, language and behavior, was somehow related to the policies of the Democrats.[iii] It was about this time in our history when the workers and other middle-class citizens began to have second thoughts about the party that many believed saved the nation during the Great Depression—second thoughts that led Richard Nixon to two huge victories in 1968 and 1972, and coalesced to carry Ronald Reagan to two landslide victories eight years later.

To the Republican leaders in the House, McClure's victory in a Democratic stronghold like Idaho's First District must have been impressive, even dramatic proof that this new congressman had exceptional appeal to the home folks. And that, combined with the solid evidence that President Johnson and the Democrats were losing respect with the voters, probably convinced them that they should do what they could to insure that a Republican would continue to occupy that traditional Democratic seat. So they gave McClure his first choice. They appointed him to the Interior and Insular Affairs Committee.

They also gave him another assignment. They appointed him to the Committee on Post Office and Civil Service.

Now he went to work in earnest.

Chapter 12 notes

i. In a letter to House Minority Leader Gerald Ford written December 22, McClure officially listed his preference for committee assignment with Interior and Insular Affairs as his first choice. His rational was to stake out his position early so, later, the leadership could not say, "Gee, Jim, I'm sorry you didn't get Interior—I wish I had known that it was your first choice." His position was acknowledged by Ford in a letter dated December 29th.

ii. Interestingly, the other times when he spent prolonged hours with his family was later, during some of his busy campaigns, when they all rode the bus together and stayed at the same motels.

iii. By the time of the presidential conventions in 1968, those who led riots and demonstrations were clearly identified with the Democratic Party.

Chapter 13
THE DELUGE

It started quietly enough. There was some holdover correspondence that had been sent to the former First District Congressman, Compton White, Jr., but that was easy for the new staff to handle. And when the letters started coming to McClure, they just came in dribbles. Many of those were congratulatory and from lobbyists who wanted to get their names known. And even those from constituents were relatively easy to handle. An example is the following mailed on January 13 from Pat's Pantries in Payette:

> *Dear Jim:*
>
> *It has been suggested to me. . .to write you and see if you could obtain a name or names of the Food Distributor for the Armed Forces Men. They seem to think that the natural Fresh Fruit flavor of this Frozen Jam would go over real well in the kitchens and other places of the Armed Services. . .I know how busy you must be Jim, but I certainly would appreciate it to have these names and see what I can do.*
>
> *Hope your family are all well. We miss you in Choir & Church & just seeing you around. . .Mrs. Pat DeBord*[1]

After a few days, McClure worked out a set of procedures for handling the correspondence. Top priority must be given to letters from constituents and those from his House colleagues. Del Klaus would open the mail and distribute the letters to the staffer who was designated to handle particular topics. For example, Scootch Harper got everything that had to do with natural resources, health and social security. She, in turn, would draft a proposed response, which, with the original letter would go to McClure for his perusal. Rarely, however, did a proposed response pass muster with the boss. Invariably, he would pen comments and suggestions, and often he would rewrite the letter completely. The staffer would then type a new letter, trying to make the response exactly as he requested. Then it would go on his desk and wait for his signature.

His signature? How could that be? It is well known that every congressman uses a signature machine.

"I showed him a signature machine one day," said Scootch, "and he looked at it like it was a rattlesnake. He was absolutely adamant about one rule. He would read every letter that came into his office, and he would read *and sign* every letter that went out of his office."

Okay, the policy is set and the procedures are in place. And then comes the deluge.

There is a war on. President Lyndon B. Johnson has a half-million soldiers, sailors, Marines, and airmen fighting and dying in Vietnam, and the people don't like it. Those in Idaho are probably more tolerant than folks from other parts of the country, but they are perhaps more outspoken. At least the three thick files of correspondence from McClure's constituents suggest that might have been so. Soon after he set up his office he began receiving letter after letter saying basically the same thing. Examples:

> *Dear Jim,*
>
> *. . .Why is President Johnson pussyfooting around and sending America's boys to die in this slow-dragged out war? We should have whipped the V.C. and any other Communist front by now. Why haven't we done it?. . .You probably explain our not winning as President Johnson does, that we cann't* [sic] *risk a war with Russia. Why would Russia want to start an open war with the U.S. . . .This is not even a reasonable excuse. SO WHY AREN'T WE ABOUT THROUGH WITH VIET NAM?*
>
> *emphatically and respectfully yours. . .*

> *Dear "Jim",*
>
> *I did not vote for you to get us involved in a land war in Asia which presently involves 500,000 people and Westmorland is asking for 250,000 more!?. . .Where are the brains in D.C.?*
>
> *Sincerely. . .*

> *Dear Jim,*
>
> *March 13th our oldest son turns 18. He is a fine young man. Must we sacrifice him to a useless war? There is no sense to this war in Vietnam, we are furnishing war materials, directly or indirectly to both sides. There can be no co-existence with communism, either we are all for or* ***all*** *against it, there must be no middle of the road. Lets* ***win****, then get out with honor and dignity. I have never before written to a congressman. It tears my heart out to think that my three sons could be sacrificed so uselessly. . .*
>
> *Respectfully yours,. . .*

In going through this correspondence and reading McClure's replies it is obvious that another of his admonitions was being obeyed. He loathed

Courtesy xxxxxxxx

McClure's first staff in the House: From left: Jan Reid, Jim Goller, Jane Collins, Del Klaus, Scootch Harper, Ann Woodward. Dick Thompson.

the kind of bureaucratic boilerplate that emanated from most congressional offices—in his mind the gutless, mindless pieties that usually begin: *Thank you for taking the time to express your views. I will give them full consideration as I evaluate my future votes and actions.*" McClure wanted none of that and he made that clear to his staff. He wanted every letter to read like it had been written by himself in a specific reply to the constituent. And, he did not want to sound like a fence-straddling politician. For example, in reply to one of the above letters he/his staff wrote:

> *Thank you for your letter. . .Like you, I am confused—and often dismayed—by our policies in Vietnam. If one were to explain the limitations placed on our Vietnam operations in terms of fear, it would more likely be a fear of China rather than Russia. In either event, I feel that fear itself is an improper motive for restrictions placed on American fighting men. . .*

To another he gave this blunt reply:

> *I realize that the news media attributes our presence in Vietnam to helping those people attain freedom. While that is probably one of the reasons, I have always felt that the main reason was to stop the spread of communism. . .*

And, to a letter signed by three young people who protested the war and declared that they will go to Canada to avoid fighting in it, he was even more blunt:

> *One of the strange inconsistencies of your generation is that you disapprove of nearly every action taken by those in authority, and yet then you turn to the rest of us to justify your positions. . .If I were a young man facing the problems that you face. . .and prior to making a decision, I would consider my obligation to my family, my community, and my country. . .and finally, I would have to face the fact that other young men are in Vietnam fighting and, yes, dying in a strange, filthy war not of their own making. I am not at all certain that I would want to go through life harboring the suspicion that I let them do my fighting for me. . .Perhaps, in the final analysis, those who refuse to face up to the fact that this country is at war are in reality too immature to make a contribution to its eventual outcome . . .*

There was also another type of Vietnam letter that caused McClure and his staff great angst. Dick Thompson explains: "Every so often we used to get a heart-wrenching letter from a mother or wife of somebody killed in Vietnam—an Idaho person. McClure anguished over those letters. He would ask me to put together a suggested reply and then he would work on them, saying, 'I know how much this response will mean to those people.' These were terrible to write. The tone of the letter from the loved one was almost always, 'Why did my son or husband have to die? I don't see any purpose in this war.' I know those letters made him more sensitive to the Vietnam War. . ."[2]

The Vietnam War letters were an example of what the staff called "issue mail"—mail on current issues being reported and discussed by the news media. Another example was the barrage of letters he received about one of his fellow congressmen who was a hot topic for the national media. Adam Clayton Powell, a black man (the term "African-American" was unheard of at that time), was a representative from the Harlem District of New York City. However, as the 90th Congress convened, his colleagues in the House were threatening a vote that would keep him from taking his seat. The problem was his behavior. Investigators were reporting that he had defrauded the government out of thousands of dollars by illegal spending of office and expense-account money, as well as other illegal behavior. Of course, some in the media implied that there were racial overtones to the affair—overtones that implied that congressional red necks were out to get Powell because of his strong stands against discrimination of the types that were still practiced, especially in the South. McClure's mail from Idaho was thunderous. *Don't let that crook get away with those crimes. Run him out of the congress! Throw him in jail!*

At first, McClure wrote cautious replies: *We have to let the investigative process run its course. . .* But, after investigators gave their report to the full House and everyone saw that Powell was clearly guilty, McClure voted with the majority against seating him, and his correspondence reflected his views that such conduct was clearly criminal and that no such person should occupy a seat in the House.

> *. . .I had decided in January that if the committee investigating Powell's activities substantiated the charges brought against him, we would have no alternative but to expel him. To have done otherwise would be like catching the bank teller in the act of filling his pockets, making him put it back, but allowing him to keep his job. . .*

He also reported that a special House ethics committee was being talked about to deal with future problems of this kind, and that he was strongly in support of its formation.

Another issue that generated hundreds of letters (three huge files in 1967), but which came in a steady flow all the years he was in Congress, was gun control. The average Idahoan, particularly in McClure's First District, was adamantly opposed to any type of control and many of the letters were highly emotional, even belligerent—*the only way the government is going to get my guns is to pry them out of my dead hands.* McClure was always completely sympathetic and repeatedly pledged to do everything within his ability and power to stop gun control.

Idahoans were not without humor when they addressed some controversial issues. Early in 1967 a news item appeared in the newspapers and perhaps on television that described a "Little Brother" doll that was being imported from France. The problem, according to many Idahoans, was that little brother came with all of his private parts. *Outlaw them. Send them back to France. How does any business dare stock and sell such immoral objects?* That was the tenor of most letters. But, the occasional writer wanted to chide McClure. *Now I suppose you are going to advocate emasculating little boys. Shame on you. Of course, little brothers shouldn't be equipped that way. It's a disgrace.*

Besides the issue mail that was starting to flood his office, he also began receiving "generated mail," which consists of letters, postcards, and, sometimes, telegrams, often with the same wording, that have been generated by some organization or media personality that has persuaded followers to write their congressman and express a particular view, usually on some kind of proposed legislation. McClure had not been in office but a few weeks when the Women's Christian Temperance Union (WCTU) leadership decided that Oregon's maverick Republican (later, Independent) Senator Wayne Morse, who had introduced a bill to prohibit liquor advertising and alcoholic beverage consumption on domestic airline flights, needed broad national support. As a result, letters poured into McClure's office, especially from his mother's local chapter in Payette County. She, of course, was one of the writers.

So what does the staff do when two- or three-hundred letters arrive within a one-week period, all saying the same thing? One can imagine Dick Thompson and Scootch Harper in McClure's office pleading that boilerplate letters deserve a boilerplate reply. Neither remembers this particular incident, but Scootch does remember McClure's shock when she pulled an unsigned letter from his desk, and while he watched, brilliantly forged his signature. "See, you don't have to waste your time on all these letters," she told him. "Just tell us how you want them answered and we'll crank them out and sign them."

The answer was a sigh and a grumble—and a compromise, which was, essentially, "Okay, I'll agree to a boilerplate response, *but,* I'm going to check every letter and if it is from someone I know, I'll pen something personal on it, *and I will still sign every letter.*" (Scootch admitted that on several occasions later, in order to get certain important letters out of his office in a timely manner, she did forge his signature.[3])

McClure's boilerplate answer to that first barrage of generated mail is also an indication of his desire to shake the image of the political yes-man. To those who pleaded with him to stop the advertisement of liquor and to ban drinking on domestic airline flights, he thanked them for their views but said, basically, that he was in complete disagreement with them—that the Volstead Act (Prohibition) did not stop drinking in the 1920s and early '30s and the American people did not need the federal government trying to regulate their behavior now. Of course, we will never know what personal note he penned on lots of those letters, including the one that went to his mother. Only the tissue-paper carbons remain in the files.

A third kind of mail needs a bit more explanation. Two-thirds of Idaho is owned by the federal government and those lands are managed by various federal agencies. The Forest Service which manages the national forests, the national recreation areas, and various wildernesses, is the dominant agency in the state. Second in importance is the Bureau of Land Management (BLM), which manages much of the sagebrush desert. In addition, the Bureau of Reclamation and the Army Corps of Engineers has a management responsibility over certain rivers and reservoirs, as well as the wetlands, while the Environmental Protection Agency (EPA)[i] and the Fish and Wildlife Service has management responsibilities that overlap the other federal agencies. And then there is the National Park Service, which manages the national monuments, and the Bureau of Indian Affairs that administers the reservations on which Idaho's Native Americans live.

Directly, or indirectly, at least 100,000 Idahoans interact with these federal lands or their managers every working day. And conflicts or misunderstandings are bound to occur. The owner of a mountain cabin in a national forest wants to cut trees and clear a firebreak to protect his cabin during a dry summer. But, he cannot get a permit, or his permit is turned down, or he gets a permit and cuts the wrong trees, or his efforts are stymied because his work might impact the habitat of an endangered species. The list of potential problems goes on and on. And multiply those problems with all of the other activities on the federal lands—grazing, logging, mining, hunting, firewood cutting, boating and rafting, trail-riding, snowmobiling, camping, and just plain walking on the thousands of miles of trails.

In addition, every citizen of the state has occasions to run afoul of other agencies of the great federal bureaucracy. Three of the most notorious are the Social Security Agency, Veterans Affairs, and the Internal Revenue Service. McClure, himself, cited one of his personal conflicts as an example of how one can get oneself ensnared in the federal quicksand:

> *I had never gotten social security since I retired although I'm well over retirement age. I started three years ago to get my social security lined out for when I passed the age of 72, which then was the magic age for me. So, I went to the caseworker and she said I need to get my military service records. But, I couldn't do that because I couldn't remember my military service number. I haven't used it in years. Well, I got the address of personnel records and I wrote to them. I know it takes awhile so I wasn't panicked. I waited two or three months and hadn't gotten an answer. So, I called them; they had a hotline number to call. No answer. So I wrote them another letter and waited another several months. No answer. So I wrote them again, enclosing a copy of the first letter and sent it registered mail. I got the return receipt back, but that's all. I waited several more months and still got no answer.*

So what does the owner of the mountain cabin do? Or the snowmobiler who thinks she is innocent of the charge by a Fish and Wildlife officer that she maliciously disturbed an elk herd when she was trying to take their picture? Or the sick World War II veteran who is destitute but who has been turned away at the veterans hospital? Or the wife of a farmer who has to undergo major heart surgery and her only son, who could milk their eighteen cows and tend the farm, is in the Army and stationed in Heidelberg, Germany? Or the retired senator who finds it impossible to cut through the bureaucracy and get his military service records?

What you do is write your congressman or senator. And you explain your problem the best way you can and ask for help.

For an Idaho congressman issue mail tends to come in spurts, depending upon whether or not a particular issue in the news is burning the hearts of average Idahoans. Generated mail typically comes in cascades—hundreds of letters and postcards within a short period of time. The third type of mail, which is mail from persons ensnared in some agency of the federal government, is named for what it produces in the congressional office: "casework." And the flow of this mail seldom comes in spurts or cascades; it comes in a steady flow, which, analogous to rain that falls day after day, can create a flood in the congressional office.

Certainly, neither Jim McClure nor Jim Goller dreamed that they would be inundated with so many constituent problems, or that it would create such a backbreaking workload for their Washington and Idaho staffs. Together in a joint interview they talked this over, admitted that the magnitude of effort needed to handle all of a congressman's casework was totally unexpected, and, when asked what percentage of a staff's time was devoted to casework, debated among themselves whether they should estimate the percentage at 80 or 90 percent. McClure, using his personal experience, explains what a staffer has to do:

> *I don't mean to beat up on the bureaucracy, because there are a lot of good people out there. But, they are flooded with a lot of paperwork. The stacks grow. And somewhere in the stacks is the constituent's inquiry or complaint and they are ignoring it. They are dealing with other things of a more urgent nature. One thing a congressman* [staffer] *can do is get that paper pulled out of the stack and to the attention of the decision maker. For example, in my own case when I couldn't get my personnel records, I called* [Senator] *Larry Craig's office and I said to Larry, or I said to his staffer, I'm having a problem and they won't answer. I gave them the data, and four days later I had an answer. Now that isn't the way government ought to work, but it is a practical fact that that is the way government does work. Over a period of time I found that there are honest bureaucrats who care about their job and want to do a good job, and then there is the big mass of personalities who are the way the average citizen sees the bureaucracy: impersonal at best and hostile at worst.*[4]

McClure then went on to comment about this phase of his work in Congress:

> *People ask me: What is the most satisfying thing you ever did in Congress? Well, one thing that was relatively early and I remember very well. . .a lady up on the Clearwater River was having trouble getting her social security. Her husband had died and her social security checks had stopped, and she had not one penny to live on.*

> *And they had stalled her and stalled her and she couldn't get an answer and couldn't get it resolved. I* [personally] *took it and it took awhile—it wasn't in two or three days—and it took some effort, but I got her a check for $2,800 and a regular check thereafter. I felt good about helping that lady who had no place else to turn.*[5]

Because of the personal nature of the casework correspondence, and also because some of the correspondents were embarrassed after staff investigations found them guilty when they were pleading innocence, McClure decided that all of this archived casework correspondence should be sealed from public view until 2016 (without written consent of McClure or his designee). Consequently, until that date, any investigator must, of necessity, rely on general comments of staffers and the occasional casework correspondence that escaped McClure's embargo for the single activity that demanded 80 to 90 percent of his staff's time, and which also took an unknown but certainly a huge amount of McClure's personal time as well.

McClure also was surprised at the volume of another type of mail: invitations. When he went to Washington, he had not thought about the number of national meetings that are held in the capitol, nor did he anticipate how many of them would request his presence at their receptions or dinners. In Payette he was anything but a party goer; nightlife was pretty well limited to monthly dinner and bridge with their social club and to choir practice. That is the way it had to be for, since his house was a continual work in progress, he had to spend almost every evening plumbing or wiring or digging some new foundation with a backhoe. So, with this background, McClure would send his regrets to most of the invitations he received to join the Washington social merry-go-round, right?

Wrong. In the words of Dick Thompson:

> *If Jim McClure knew there would be one person from Idaho at one of those receptions, he would break his neck getting there. And if it was a nice event, he always tried to take Louise because she was home alone a lot. I remember very well Louise coming into the office one day, just bubbly and enthusiastic and I commented on that. She said she had a good reason, that they had enjoyed a nice family dinner at home the night before, which, she said, was the first time that had happened in six months. Now, she might have been exaggerating a bit—maybe it had only been two or three months—but the point is that he attended a lot of those things. Why did he do this, especially since he was anything but a party boy—and believe me, in my years on the Hill I saw a bunch of those. He did it because he felt that it was his duty—that people who had come all the way to Washington from Idaho deserved to see him and, also, that he needed to listen to what they had to say. Lots of times he wouldn't stay long; they almost*

always served finger-food and that would be his dinner and then he would head back to the office for more work. [6]

Staffers estimate that McClure's office was soon receiving fifty to seventy-five letters a day, which totals over 1,000 letters a month. And that does not count the generated mail and telegrams—one day in early 1967 he received about 300 telegrams from postal employees, all of whom received a boilerplate reply. Also, it should be pointed out that this was in the days before computers and printers. Each letter, even if boilerplate, had to be typed on a typewriter by some staffer and woe to the staffer who tried to correct a mistake with an eraser. McClure would not let any letter go out when he detected such a correction.

It was not long before the deluge of correspondence began creating problems in his office. In Scootch's words, McClure's insistence upon taking such an active role in reading and answering correspondence "began to drive us nuts."[7] The problem was that a letter might arrive on the eighth day of a month, the reply might be typed and dated the fifteenth of the month, but it would stack up on his desk (sometimes the stacks would also cover the sofa in his office) and not be signed and ready to be sent out until the eighth day of the next month. Of course, that was unacceptable—for two reasons. One, the reply in the letter might be out of date because of some further action on the issue or problem, and, two, because it just did not look good for a constituent to get a letter with a date that is two weeks to a month old—and remember, he did not allow the staffers to erase and change the date on a letter.

So what to do? That question really bothered Dick Thompson. At first he just worried about the problem. Then he took action. He began taking the oldest letters home with him at night and there, with his wife, Jean, typing, he would update the letters that needed new information, and just retype those that needed a newer date. "Many nights we did that while he was in the House, and my good wife, bless her heart, never complained."[8]

Why did McClure create this problem for himself and his staff? McClure, when asked that question, shakes his head, smiles wanly, but sticks to his guns:

> *"I just believed that if people took the time and effort to contact me, I believed it was important to read and sign what went back to them. And part of it was control. I didn't want statements to go out that were not mine and were not what I believed or felt. I ignored some of the mail from pressure groups outside the state—according to my memory we didn't even answer a lot of that mail."*[9]

When his alter ego, Jim Goller, was asked that same question—and, by the way, McClure, himself, used that term to describe Goller[10]—he said:

> *McClure just wanted to stay in close touch with his people from Idaho—he looked upon them as his people—and he just felt that it was his duty to know what they thought and what they felt. And there is another thing. McClure hated phonies. He just didn't care for a politician who, in Washington, D.C. wore the fancy suits and played to the eastern, liberal crowd, but who would, while in his home state dress up in cowboy clothes and try to pretend that he was a cowboy. I think to him a signature machine was like the cowboy clothes; it produced a phony signature and he didn't want any part of it. He wanted people to know, that if they got a letter from him, it was really from him and not from some staffer or a machine.*[11]

Of course, there were good reasons why the outgoing correspondence stacked up on McClure's desk and sofa. At the same time he was trying his best to interact with his Idaho constituents, he was playing the role of Jake Holman again, especially in the meetings and hearings of the Interior and Insular Affairs Committee and subcommittees.

Chapter 13 notes

i. Some legislation such as the Endangered Species Act and that which created the EPA was enacted long after McClure went to Washington.

Chapter 14

THE COMMITTEEMAN

In the 90th Congress there were thirty-two representatives listed on the House Committee on Interior and Insular Affairs, nineteen Democrats and thirteen Republicans. James A. McClure from Idaho was the last name on that long list, which meant that he was the lowest ranking member of the committee—even lower than his freshman colleagues who happened to be Democrats and were members of the majority party that controlled the House.

As McClure took his seat on the raised dias in the committee hearing room, which was at the far corner of the Longworth Office Building, it would have been quite natural for him to be intimidated in that new environment. The chairman, Wayne Aspinall, a Democrat from the western slope of Colorado, was something of a legend in the House for the autocratic way he conducted the affairs of the committee. Gruff, and very formal, he not only controlled the committee as a whole, but also appointed the chairmen and controlled the agendas, budgets, hearings, and meeting times of the six subcommittees: Indian Affairs, Mines and Mining, Public Lands, National Parks and Recreation, Irrigation and Reclamation, and Territorial and Insular Affairs. And whether it was a general discussion of some issue, or comments on a piece of proposed legislation, or in the questioning of witnesses during a hearing, the chairman's strict protocol was always followed. It started with the chairman setting a strict time limit on comments. Then the chairman, himself, spoke. He was followed by the ranking Democrat on the committee, then the ranking Republican on the committee, then back to the second ranking Democrat, the second ranking Republican, and so on until the last person, the lowest ranking Republican was heard. And woe be it to the committee member, Democrat or Republican, who had not finished with his or her comments at the end of the allotted time. If this happened the miscreant would be harshly gaveled to silence, even in mid-sentence, and the next speaker would be told to continue.

When McClure joined the committee, some of the members who had been around awhile were already chaffing at the chairman's autocratic management. Phillip Burton (D-California), an outspoken, chain-smoking, hard-drinking, and, according to minority member, Sam Steiger (R-Arizona), a "genuine, rug-chewing liberal activist,[1]" felt that he was being treated like a kindergartner, and one day, "...arriving late to a committee hearing, Burton burst into the hearing room, talking loudly, slapping spectators on the back as he made his way to the dias...by rudely interrupting the meticulous Aspinall in mid-question and blowing his nose loudly at inopportune moments, he showed his colleagues they did not have to sit like terrified school boys quivering in fear of their stern headmaster."[2]

Another rebellious member was Lloyd Meeds (D-Washington) who, when gaveled to silence while commenting during a committee session, shouted back to Aspinall that he was not finished and deserved more consideration from the chairman, then added that he felt he had received little consideration from him for the past year. Aspinall met this challenge by recognizing the next speaker, then by going back to Meeds to let him conclude his statement. According to the witness who reported this, Aspinall was thus able to maintain control, but he made another enemy who would eventually team with Burton and others in a revolution against him.[3]

However, according to the opinion of witnesses and a statement by McClure, the crusty chairman did not, in any way, intimidate the freshman from Idaho. To the contrary, those who observed McClure as he took his place as the lowest ranking member of the committee felt that a feeling of mutual respect grew between the two men. Actually, they had a lot in common despite their allegiance to different parties. Aspinall was a student of the proposals and bills that came before the committee, and he was a dedicated legislative craftsman who went to great lengths to make sure the wording in a bill was exactly as it should be. In addition, he was what was known at the time as a "multiple-use" advocate in regard to the use of the U.S. public lands. He believed, generally, that controlled logging should be permitted in the national forests; that those with legitimate mining claims should receive patents on public lands; that longtime sheep and cattle grazing permits should continue to be honored; and that where it is feasible to reclaim public lands with irrigation projects that would support agriculture, this was a progressive thing to do, especially if cheap electric power could also be generated by the project. McClure, though holding numerous reservations regarding specific activities on public lands, counted himself as a multiple-use advocate and, as the months went by and he became involved in committee issues, he found that he and Aspinall were often in agreement on such issues.

Ironically, the relationship between McClure and the ranking Republican on the committee was anything but compatible. John P. Saylor (R-Pennsylvania) was what would later be known as an environmentalist, one of the earliest of that breed in Congress, and, generally speaking, an opponent of almost everything that McClure supported. In his view, loggers were destroying the forests, miners were rapists and despoilers, sheepmen and cattlemen were getting wealthy by not paying their fare share while overgrazing the rangelands, and irrigation projects were a boondoggle that exacerbated farm surpluses. Moreover, he was one of the early supporters of the Sierra Club, an emerging powerhouse with the money and clout to become the most aggressive environmental lobby in Washington. Challenged on such issues within the committee, Saylor was fond of reminding its members of his ability to generate publicity and huge volumes of telegrams from irate constituents to congressmen who opposed his views.

Although Saylor was a thorn in McClure's side, the Idahoan could have cared less about the threats from Saylor's environmental friends. With the exception perhaps of Owyhee and Payette counties, there was at least one major sawmill or wood processing plant in all the other twenty-five counties in his district. Mining was also a major industry, with the jobs and wealth of Shoshone County (Kellogg, Wallace, and Mullan) almost totally dependent upon the lead, silver, and zinc extracted from its mined ores. Also, the sheep and cattle industries were much more robust than they are now, and, in the southern part of his district not a potato, sugar beet, or ear of corn could have been grown without the water from irrigation projects that had reclaimed the farm lands salvaged from the Great Basin desert. In short, the livelihoods of the great majority of McClure's constituents

DAVE LEROY ON McCLURE

I graduated from Lewiston High School and even though members of my family were hard-core Democrats—like the majority of the county—I had an American government teacher who tried to instill in all of us that it was our duty to analyze all dimensions of the political spectrum and make up our own minds about the party we would support. I did that and became a Republican.

While at the University of Idaho, I applied for an internship in Congressman McClure's office and was accepted. That was his first year in office. What first impressed me was not the tiny office with everybody working on top of each other—that was expected of a freshman. What impressed me was his mild manner and modesty, but, most of all, his sincerity and work ethic. He was always the first to arrive and the last to leave.

And did I see the Jake Holman in him? Absolutely! My main assignment was to write a 1,000-1,500 word position paper on Idaho anadromous fish. Every time I went in with a draft, some pipe or fitting or some thought or observation was not there. I was amazed at his depth of knowledge—he had somehow memorized every detail and he wanted that paper to be perfect. I rewrote it time after time, but it was never just right. He would not forgive any lack of perfection. I was used to writing something once and that would be it. I must have rewritten that position statement five times a week for I don't know how long. Finally, though, I got it right, and it went into the Congressional Record exactly as I wrote it. That made me very proud, and he was kind enough to send copies of the Record to me when I returned to Moscow. Later, as Idaho Attorney General, I used that same research arguing a case before the Supreme Court involving a conflict between Idaho and Oregon.

depended directly, or indirectly, upon multiple use of public lands or irrigated agriculture.

And they were clamoring for more—desert lands that could be irrigated, that is. When McClure went back to Washington, he was carrying with him the hopes and dreams of many of his constituents in Elmore County. Specifically, the community leaders in the city of Mountain Home, who were constantly living in a state of anxiety, worrying that the economic engine of the city, Mountain Home Air Force Base, might be closed at any time, were determined to acquire a more permanent future. They wanted their community to have a stable agricultural base like most of the other cities in southern Idaho. And their planning for this new future was based upon a massive new reclamation project called the Southwest Idaho Development Project, which called for diverting water from the North Fork of the Payette River to a reservoir behind a dam on the South Fork creating a reservoir in Garden Valley. From there, water would be pumped to the Boise River to replace water that would flow from Anderson Ranch Reservoir through a tunnel to the Mountain Home Desert. Politically, this was an important project for Idaho and McClure learned during the last election that it was a contest between politicians to see who could be most supportive of the plan.

But what McClure learned during his first weeks on the Interior Committee was that the immediate chances of getting a Southwest Idaho Development Project approved—the first step in the process, which had to be followed by approval in the Interior Committee of the Senate, a favorable vote in both the House and Senate, then in a conference to meld the two bills and, finally, approval by the President—were somewhere between nil and naught. To complicate matters the chairman himself had his own pet project, which was a burning priority, but which was encountering much opposition. It was called the Lower Colorado River Basin Project, a combination irrigation and power-generation project that included the Central Arizona Project, which was a major irrigation development also strongly supported by the Arizonan who was secretary of the interior, Stewart Udall, and his brother, Morris Udall (D-Arizona), who was a ranking Democrat on the House Interior Committee. In addition, it had the support of the entire Arizona delegation, which included the 89-year old Arizona Senator Carl Hayden who had tremendous power in the Senate. Moreover, McClure's task of moving an Idaho project through his committee was made enormously more difficult by having the senior Republican, who might have been a helpful ally, a dedicated opponent of western reclamation projects.

And, according to those who observed the committee at work, having another Idaho Republican, George Hansen, on the committee with him was no help at all. To the contrary it may have hurt him. According to one committee staffer, "George Hansen was not highly regarded by anyone as a bright person. He was likeable—nobody disliked him—but he was a John

Wayne kind of person, not taken with seriousness as was McClure. Said another staffer: "He would pop into a committee meeting or hearing, often ask questions that had already been answered and discussed, then pop back out again. But, oh was he uncanny whenever there was a camera around. He always seemed to make it to the right place on time when there was a photo opportunity."[4]

So, with all these hurdles, how does the freshman congressman proceed? The way Jake Holman did on the *Sand Pebbles*, of course. And just the way Jim McClure did in the Idaho state Senate: by a relentless effort to outwork everybody on the committee. Looking back on that experience, here is how McClure himself described his effort:

> *If I had any failing as a lawyer, I over prepared for a lot of my cases. That is how I started as a young lawyer, by over-researching—preparing my opponent's case as well as my own. That way I could anticipate what my opponent was going to do. I approached my service on the Interior Committee the same way. You know what is coming up; you do the studying before you get there. You have the agenda; you know what the legislation being proposed is about; and you know what the discussions will be about. You can do a lot of work before you get to the committee.*
>
> *The second part of it is: you work at it. You go to the committee meetings; you go to the hearings; you listen to all the questions asked by other committee members; and you seek information from the witnesses. A good many times a hearing is just a forum for the expression of the views of the members. I didn't have much time for that—the time should be spent getting information from the people testifying. If you're talking, you only repeat what you already know; if you listen you might learn something—*[chuckling] *my wife, Louise, is always telling me that. The work of the congress takes place in committees. If you're not going to work in the committees, you are not going to do good work. I'm sure I spent more time in hearings than the average congressman. Often I stayed to the end—as a junior member you are the last one to ask questions. . .and if you wanted a second one, you waited until it went around again, and I always had more questions. And, yes, it was not uncommon for me to stay and help staffers* [with the wording of legislation]. *I took it seriously.*

As a freshman, McClure had many more opportunities for his work ethic to be appreciated during sessions of the three subcommittees upon which he served.[i] Each was chaired by a Democrat, of course, but, according to staffers who remembered the freshman from Idaho, McClure's superior knowledge of the issues, often gained by long hours of research and reading before the subcommittee meetings, quickly earned him respect from members of the opposition party. Said Lloyd Meeds (D-Washington), "I had a very high regard for him. He was a bright guy and when he questioned witnesses at a hearing, they knew they had been examined. He was a great cross-examiner—people couldn't avoid his questions—they couldn't slide away [with a vague answer]. He was a very productive member and he took the job seriously."[5]

A staffer for the opposition party felt that McClure was lucky to arrive on the Interior Committee at that time because it was a time in the House when there was little partisan bickering—in contrast to the rancor between opposing parties that arose in the Nixon era of the '70s. He said:

> *It was a time when there was a calm between parties, when people could express their views. . .when you could say what was on your mind and nobody would hold it against you. McClure was a constructive participant, in my opinion, and in the process he was thoughtful. He studied the legislation, knew what he was talking about, and he was the kind of person you would like to have as your congressman regardless of party—he wasn't political is the best way to put it. He had his own point of view as did Aspinall, but people could work things out with him, large or small. You could talk to him, and maybe he would say, 'I don't agree with that; I'm probably going the other way. . .*[or] *he would say, 'I appreciate your point of view but mine is just different.' At the end, after an agreement, his word was good. You didn't worry about counting on him on the floor. He was always mild mannered and not flamboyant* [like some of the others], *and he was always pleasant and friendly to everybody. He was generally well liked as a person and he was never that impressed with himself or that position. The thing I remember most was his enquiring mind and how he would always offer amendments cleaning up the language on a bill. Now, Aspinall, who hired me and who was my boss, was impressed with being a congressman and with being chairman, and Saylor* [who should have been McClure's ally] *was quite pompous at times.*[6]

McClure, himself, found the work on the Interior Committee fascinating, and there were issues before it in which he had a keen interest. In his subcommittee on National Parks and Recreation he would actively participate in hearings and legislative crafting sessions that would create two new national parks: the Redwoods National Park in California and the North Cascades National Park in Washington. In addition he would help establish new legislation for The Wild and Scenic Rivers Act, which, initially, would establish two out of the original eight stretches of protected water in Idaho: the Middle Fork of the Clearwater River and the Middle Fork of the Salmon River.

In his subcommittee on Mines and Mining, McClure's chief interest was in matters that pertained to the silver, lead and zinc industry that generated most of the jobs in Shoshone County. In the year prior to his election to Congress, the U.S. Mint had eliminated most of the silver in coins, an action that was threatening the future livelihood of the thousands of miners living in Kellogg, Osburn, Wallace, and Mullan whose livelihood depended heavily upon the silver that was being produced in their valley. In addition, the importation of lead and zinc, particularly from some of the low-cost sites in newly opened African mines, was another major threat that he was keen to attack. This challenge frustrated him for there was not much he could do in his subcommittee to counter such threats. However, Chairman Aspinall did appoint him as an advisor to the U.S. delegation of the International Lead-Zinc Study Group that was to meet in Geneva, Switzerland. At least that was a start in the right direction.

In McClure's third subcommittee, on Indian Affairs, it would have been natural for him to feel overwhelmed when he learned that he was to share the legislative responsibility for nearly a half-million Native Americans, many of whom were living on or near approximately 52 million acres spread over twenty-nine states, and many of whom belonged to obscure tribes like the Muckleshoots and the Quechans of which he had never heard. But, getting up to speed with all the issues of these tribes and then helping dispense with 169 measures that were brought before forty-one meetings of the subcommittee was an interesting, but daunting challenge.

Although both McClure and his Idaho colleague on the committee, George Hansen, hoped that they could get some action on their pet Southwest Idaho Development Project, Chairman Aspinall had much grander plans. For several years prior to McClure joining the committee, Aspinall had been trying to get a comprehensive development project approved for the Colorado River, the headwaters of which originated in his home district. In order to strengthen support for this project, he had enlisted the powerful Arizona delegation by adding the Central Arizona Project (CAP) to the overall project—a plan that would take Colorado River water through canals to central and southern Arizona. However, there was determined opposition, both to the plan in general, and to specific parts of it. In general, the California delegation was opposed; they were the beneficiaries of the current flow of surplus water and with the exploding growth they were experiencing, they knew that any surplus water would be a critical resource in the future. But, the awakening environmental movement was also targeting Aspinall's pet project. In particular, David Brower, leader of the Sierra Club, was aggressively attacking plans for two proposed dams on tributaries of the lower Colorado: Marble Canyon Dam and Bridge Canyon Dam (also known as the Hualapai Dam). In April, 1967, McClure was one of a group from the committee who received a memo from Morris Udall (D-Arizona), which was an invitation for him and his colleagues to float the Lower Colorado from Lee's Ferry (below Page, Arizona) to Lake Mead. In the memo Udall gave his rationale for the trip:

> *In this Congress we have pending a great number of bills to authorize the Central Arizona Project, The Colorado Basin Project, etc. There are other bills to extend the boundaries of Grand Canyon National Park both below and above the Park boundaries. While many members of the Committee have visited Grand Canyon, Lake Powell, Lake Mead, etc., very few have seen at first hand the Colorado River as it flows. . .I think this is unfortunate, and I believe our Committee would be better prepared to act on all these matters in the future if a representative group could make a river trip to see all or part of the gorge as it goes through Marble Canyon, the national park, the national monument. . .*[7]

McClure accepted with alacrity. Yes, he needed to see first hand the Colorado River as it flowed through the canyon; he needed to know what he was going to vote for and against, both in the committee and on the House floor. But, he also had to look upon the proposed float trip as a surrogate for the wilderness trek that, for the first summer in over a decade, he would not be taking into his own Idaho wilderness. In his first three months on the House Interior Committee he had learned that the duty required very hard work and long hours. Now, he learned that it was also going to have its perks.

That could never be said about his other committee assignment. As a price for getting his first choice of assignments to the Interior Committee, he was relegated for his second assignment to the unheralded, mostly unwanted Committee on Post Office and Civil Service. Yes, his district probably had a hundred or so post offices and a relatively small number of Civil Service workers. But, his goal in going back to Washington was to help Idahoans in general and his First District's constituents in particular. On either of his other preferred committees, the Agricultural Committee or the Armed Services Committee, he would have been in a position to influence legislation that could have profound effects upon Idaho. But, not so on this second committee. The best that he, himself, could say about the assignment was that it was "interesting."[8]

McClure was less enthusiastic when he was asked to describe the chairman of the committee, Thaddeus J. Dulski (D-New York). One suspects that he was trying to be kind by describing him as "very pedestrian" when one of his staffers, with an inference to the chairman's last name, said that he was "not a bright light." [9]

At the time McClure joined the committee, the U.S. Postal Service was probably at a low ebb in terms of its image before the American people. One reason was that postmasters were appointed to their jobs on the basis of their political weight in the community. At least that was the first consideration of the congressman in whose district the post office was based. However, both McClure and his Idaho assistant, Jim Goller, claimed that they always screened their nominees on the basis of merit as well as their party credentials, but both also claimed that this was one of the more onerous tasks of the Congressman because it was a no-win situation: the one person who got the job would be your friend while those who did not get the job would become your enemies.

The U.S. Postal Service was also notorious for poor service and often the brunt of jokes by late-night comedians. It was common to hear horror stories of letters taking three weeks to get from one section of a city to another. Postal workers, themselves, often bore the brunt of the criticism, and, when a politician wanted to beat up on the federal bureaucracy, the postal worker was often the most convenient target. Fortunately, in just a few short years, a drastic overhaul of the Postal Service was initiated by Congress when it created an independent postal service, which would be relatively free of politics, and which, in a relatively short time, would become a much more efficient institution. McClure saw that happen while he was on the committee, and he was an active participant in effecting that change.

He also discovered that he was a target for two large constituencies outside of his home state. Postal workers across the land inundated his office (and presumably the offices of other congressmen on the Postal Committee) with hundreds of letters and telegrams lobbying for higher wages, better hours, and special issues. One of the latter—an effort by Seventh-Day Adventists to be freed of Saturday work—McClure took seriously, and along with Jerome Waldie (D-California), a liberal Democrat on the committee—an unlikely ally—he helped get post office work rules changed so that those workers could practice their religion while still maintaining their jobs.

The other constituency was a fluid one whose members were constantly changing. This constituency was made up of folks with a burning desire to see a commemorative stamp issued by the post office to memorialize some person, place, or cause. McClure got hundreds of letters from all over the country, all extolling the virtues of their favored subject, to which he replied in near-boilerplate that, in Army sergeant's terms, any decision to create commemorative stamps was above his pay grade. He did make one exception, however. In the case of Farragut State Park in northern Idaho (during World War II it was the second largest naval training base in the world), which was going to host a National Boy Scout Jamboree in 1969, he worked very hard and, with some help from other members of the Idaho delegation, was able to get a stamp issued to commemorate the occasion.

In his first year he also went to bat for his one-time roommate, Don Samuelson, who was now governor of Idaho and who was angry over a recent decision by the postal service that required state and county documents to be sent first class instead of third class—a requirement that significantly increased the cost of such mailings. In an effort to exempt states and counties from the new rule, McClure managed to get an appointment with Postmaster General Larry O'Brien—a political heavyweight in both the Kennedy and Johnson administrations. However, he was not successful; they were not about to change the rules for a lowly congressman from Idaho who had the additional handicap of being a Republican.

One good thing about his service on the Postal Committee was that it did not require as much time as the Interior Committee—for three reasons. First, there were significantly fewer meetings of the whole committee, and second, he only served on two subcommittees (Position Classification and Census and Statistics), both of which met far less often than his three Interior subcommittees. In addition, he did not have to spend near as much time researching the issues. Few of them were as complex as the simplest issues before the Interior Committee. His legislative assistant at the time, Dick Thompson, also pointed out that quite often there would be a conflict between the two committees with meetings called at the same time. "McClure almost always felt that his first priority was the Interior Committee because so many issues affected the West in general and Idaho in particular. Also, the Interior Committee was probably the busiest committee in the House at that time. Of course, if he couldn't make a Postal Committee meeting, he would usually send a staffer who later briefed him. If I had to make a wild guess on the proportion of the time he spent on the two committees, I would say he probably spent at least 80 percent of his committee time with the Interior Committee."[10]

DICK THOMPSON ON THE FARRAGUT STAMP

The Farragut stamp was a big deal to McClure—he had a special affection for that part of Idaho, and he had worked very hard to get that sucker approved. Well, one day he came in—we had been waiting and waiting to hear whether it was going to be approved—and he said, "You know what is going to happen don't you—we did most of the work on that stamp and Frank Church's office is going to get all the credit." That bothered me because that stamp meant so much to him. So I got to thinking, then decided to do it. I called Frank Church's office and pretended to be somebody else—who I don't remember now. Anyway, I asked the fellow there, "Hey, have you heard anything about the Farragut commemorative stamp? He replied, "Well, yeah, we just got word that it was approved." I hung up and didn't even bother writing a press release—I phoned it back to Idaho and we beat Frank Church with the news. Of course, it probably didn't work out just the way I planned it—they probably combined our release with Church's, but at least we got equal coverage. The irony is that we were not officially notified until a day or two later. That's the way it is when you are in the minority party.

But there was more in this freshman congressman's life than committee meetings and the endless chore of answering constituent mail.

Chapter 14 notes

i Mines and Mining, National Parks and Recreation, and Indian Affairs.

Chapter 15

Congressional Balancing Act

By the time the cherry blossoms were blooming in April, Jim McClure was beginning to create a semblance of order out of his hectic three lives.

After many hours of labor, often into the night, he was beginning to get a handle on his day job at the Capitol. Constituent mail was getting answered, albeit slowly, and the situation was destined to improve a little after McClure sent Del Klaus, who was ineffective with administrative detail, to the Interior Department and replaced him with Dick Thompson as his chief assistant. In addition, he was working hard on the two committees and five subcommittees, and as one of the committee staffers noted later, he eventually became so valuable in the art of word smithing committee bills that the chairmen grew reluctant to engage in bill—drafting or a markup session without his presence. In short, after three months on the job, he was on a fast learning curve in his office and in the committee rooms.

But, a congressman must, of necessity, try to live a second life among his constituents at home. That is not so difficult for a congressman from Philadelphia or Richmond or Annapolis. Just jump in the car on Friday, or even Thursday, and your regional office is just a short drive away. Even congressmen like Tip O'Neill (who would become House Speaker) from Boston or Dan Rostenkowski from Chicago rarely missed a three-day weekend at home, and McClure's friend and freshman colleague on the Post Office Committee, Fletcher Thompson, usually took off in his Mooney airplane on Thursday evening or Friday morning for his home district in Georgia. But, Boise, Idaho was 2,000 air miles from Washington, D.C., and the round trip was time consuming. The key to getting a long weekend was, on late Thursday afternoon, to fly out of Friendship Airport in Baltimore (now Baltimore-Washington International)—*they looked after our cars better there than they did at Dulles or National*[1]—and get into Chicago before the direct United Airlines flight to Boise left about 8:30 p.m. That flight would get him into Boise around 10:30 where he would often be picked up by a friend like Dick Wilcomb (Louise was his wife's close friend and bridesmaid) or by Jim Goller. Getting to north Idaho was more difficult and often involved getting a flight to Spokane out of Detroit or Minneapolis. Dick Thompson, while reminiscing about those early days, remembers McClure making several "mad dashes" to the Baltimore airport, and also some of the irregular routes McClure had to take in order to get home. Said he, "Sometimes the flights he wanted were not available and we had to send him off on a crazy route like to Texas before we could get him on a direct flight to Boise, or Spokane."[2]

The trips also were expensive. When he was in the 90th Congress, he was allowed four round trips for official congressional business each fiscal year. That fell far short of his needs, for as Jim Goller was to say later, "People in the First District began to look upon McClure as a rising star and they wanted him to speak at their meetings and conventions. And it was tough; we just didn't have the money—we ended the first campaign in debt and we had to pay that off. Some of those people recognized that McClure couldn't afford those trips and they would buy his ticket and pick up his hotel bill—occasionally they would even come up with a small honorarium. But, there were many times when there was no money and we would scrounge to get him places to stay in our friends' homes, like with Pete Wilson in Bonners Ferry, the Nelsons in Sandpoint, or with Ruthie [Johnson—his north Idaho administrative assistant] in Wallace. And, there were a lot of times that the expenses came out of our own pocket and McClure couldn't afford it. I know for sure during that first term, I bought all the gasoline for my car when I traveled for him."[3]

Then there was this third life—his life with the family. During the week that life was strained; he tried to keep to his word that he would get to the office early in the morning before any of his staff, and after working hours, visitors, receptions, meetings, and desk work almost always kept him away from home until after the rest of the family had finished their evening meal. However, the weekends were another story, if he was not back in Idaho, which his staffers at the time estimate was twelve times a year—roughly once a month. Despite signs that support from his constituents and his colleagues was growing, both parents, in conversations within the family, still insisted that his congressional term had to be considered a temporary adventure and that they should not waste any opportunity to get out on weekends and see historical sites and other important eastern attractions.

So on most weekends Jim McClure lived the life of a tourist with his family. In the beginning they toured the prominent Washington sites: The National Art Gallery, The Smithsonian Institute, Library of Congress, and son, Ken, says he cannot remember the number of times he climbed the Washington Monument with family and friends. (That was back when they allowed people to do that.) Then they started reaching out. They visited the Luray Caverns in the Shenandoah Valley of Virginia—beautiful caves with spectacular stalagmites and stalactites and an incredible stalacpipe organ. They toured Monticello, third-president Thomas Jefferson's home, and Ash Lawn, the home of James Monroe, the fifth president. They saw the historical sites in Philadelphia, observed the Amish in rural Pennsylvania, and bought their first serious art piece at a street fair. (It now hangs in their McCall cabin.) They attended church services in the Washington Cathedral and at the chapel of the Naval Academy in Annapolis, and enjoyed two big parties for the children of congressmen and senators—one at the Congressional Country Club and the other an old-time country fair/carnival that Lady Bird Johnson hosted on the White House lawn. (Despite their political differences, daughter Marilyn is still proud of Lady Bird's autograph she collected for her scrapbook.)

The family also engaged in another activity on weekends. All during the spring, Sergeant Mom would scout the Arlington area on weekdays with their realtor and look at the various houses for sale—the six-month lease on the house where they were living would be up in June and, despite the high cost of housing in the region, they wanted to own their own place. Then, on the weekends when the father was not traveling and they were not sight-seeing, the whole family would inspect the list of houses mom felt would fit their budget and tastes. And sometime in May they found the house they wanted—a four-bedroom, one and one-half bath *sort of a ranch house—definitely not a colonial—we didn't want that—with a big daylight basement, sitting on a little knoll, nicely landscaped, with a big back yard walled off by trees.*[4] They paid $55,000, financed through the Riggs National Bank, and they considered the sum so outlandish they never told their Payette friends for fear they would be ridiculed. In the telling of this story Louise now smiles when she relates that the house next door, a comparable value, just sold for $967,000.

Their plan had always been for Louise and the kids to return to Payette and their home there for the summer. This was all part of the *politics is fickle, we could get thrown out of office anytime, we're not going to give up our Idaho roots* family doctrine.

They had planned to rent their Payette house to help cover the mortgage payments but had not yet been successful, so the house was waiting for them as were the two sets of grandparents (both had already been back to Washington for visits—Louise's parents for some time to help with the kids and to free Louise for the many congressional wives' activities she enjoyed) who were eager to have them back in Idaho. However, they did not return immediately when school was out the middle of June. According to Marilyn's scrapbook, they attended the Army's Torchlight Tatoo, with the Army band, fife and drum corps, Army chorus and Army drill team on June 14, and on July 7, attended the famous harness races in Laurel, Maryland. Also, after school was out, they bought much new furniture and moved into the new house where each of the sons and the daughter would have their very own room.

Sometime after that, son Ken remembers that to go home he had to dress up in a coat and tie and take his very first airplane ride. (In the 1960s taking an airline trip was a big adventure for most people and they usually wore dress clothes for the occasion. Daughter Marilyn was so impressed with the trip she saved the printed menus that were handed out by the flight attendants—a practice long since abandoned, at least in coach class—for her scrapbook.) And as eager as they were to be back in Payette, they each experienced a little bit of a let down after they got there. Said Louise, "I came back primed with all this information about Washington, D.C., and the places we had visited. I was eager to share all of this with our friends and I thought they would be just as eager to hear about it. It was a bit of a let down to me when I discovered that they really had no interest in all the neat things I was going to tell them. They just wanted to talk about what was going on in Payette, Idaho—and that was okay—I didn't mind. So I just stopped talking about it. Later, my congressional friends said the same thing happened to them when they went home the first time."[5]

FROM DAUGHTER MARILYN'S DIARY

April 17. Monday is usually a dull beginning of another week. This wasn't. After school Mrs. Snader [the realtor] *took Mama, Panto* [my grandfather], *and me to see a house. It was just what we need with the exception that the kitchen is a little small. . .The lot is 250 ft. deep and covered with trees. It's kind of like a home in a forest. There are four bedrooms with two baths upstairs on the main level and a bath with a possible fifth bedroom in the basement. The rec room has a folding door across it that makes one end a bedroom. There is a laundry, living room, balcony, patio and a screened-in porch besides. We came back home and went back with everyone this time. Mrs. Snader came over tonight and they wrote up a contract for the house. Oh, I hope we get it!*

April 18. School again. When Mama came home around seven, we all clamored to know if the contract had been accepted. She wouldn't tell us till Daddy got home. Then after he teased us for a while, he said that we did. Yay! No more house hunting. It was fun for a while but began to get bothersome. We finally have our own. We will move in around July 1. I can hardly wait.

Marilyn remembers having a similar experience with her friends but that was okay, she was back with them and that was what counted. One good friend had saved her a yearbook and presented it to her, all signed by her classmates. And soon she was back into the social swirl, which for teenagers in Payette meant hanging out at the town's A & W Root Beer Stand or at the Pirate Cove, which had just been opened near the new high school. On Saturday nights the big entertainment was to load up one of her friend's cars—a friend old enough to drive at night—and cruise over to the Ontario hospital and back, and while en route hopefully meet and chat with other friends doing the same thing. Also, Sergeant Mom made sure that she continued her 4-H development program, which, this summer, was scheduled to teach her how to be a judge at the fair. This she enjoyed, and near the end of the summer, at the Payette County Fair, she scored first place in that competition (which meant that her scoring of many different competitive events was closest to the senior judges' scores) and won the opportunity to compete with similar finalists at the regional competition in Portland. But, she did not get to go because school was starting back in Arlington at the same time. "I resented that a little," she said later, "but not too much because my good friend came in second and she got to go in my place."[6] Meanwhile, father McClure was stuck in hot, humid Washington, and in a house that had no air conditioner. "I had experienced heat and humidity the summer I spent in Minnesota when I was in the Navy," he said, "but that was nothing compared to that first summer in Washington. It was very hard to sleep and the humidity was like nothing I had ever experienced. That was the first time I saw mold growing on the soles of shoes that were in the closet. (Daughter Marilyn remembers him complaining about green "whiskers" growing on his shoes.) It was also my first experience with sand fleas. We had acquired two kittens, and when they came in from outside they brought sand fleas with them and left them on the carpet. Then, when I walked on the carpet, they would crawl up under my pants legs and bite. For awhile, I was a mass of bites up to my knees.

It also was a hot summer in other ways. In June, in a remarkable six-day offensive, the Israelis destroyed the entire Egyptian Air Force—200 MIG jets that Nasser, the Egyptian ruler had obtained from his Soviet friends—then in separate battles captured the Sinai Desert and opened the Suez Canal that Egypt had closed to them, routed Jordan's troops and occupied the West Bank, and fought and captured Syria's Golan Heights, which had artillery sites that had harassed Israeli settlements in that area. McClure, like most other of his congressional colleagues watched the events unfold on television and, afterwards, his correspondence from Idaho indicated that his constituents had little or no interest in this Middle East action. McClure himself admits that at the time he had just a "casual interest" in what came to be known as the Six-Day War and an event that would have repercussions well into the next century. This casual interest was destined to change dramatically.

It was also a hot summer much closer to home. In July, first in Newark and later in Detroit, disgruntled Negroes[i] rioted, then burned large areas in the run-down neighborhoods, or ghettos where they lived. Twenty-seven died in Newark, forty-three in Detroit, and thousands were injured. In addition, thousands of small businesses in those neighborhoods were looted and burned. A riot like these had occurred the previous summer in Watts, a suburb of Los Angeles, but prior to that the American people had not seen such domestic violence since the Civil War when New York's Irish minority looted, burned, and hanged Negroes (who competed with them for jobs) while protesting the nation's first draft lottery. And while McClure also watched these events on television, his Idaho constituents were outraged and they inundated his office with scathing letters demanding that he and his colleagues do something to stop such irresponsible behavior. In his replies, he pleaded that there was little he or anyone else in the Federal Government could do, but reading the correspondence leaves one with the feeling that he was as frustrated by the problem as his constituents.

However, the summer was not all heat, humidity, sand fleas, and race riots. The previous April, McClure had accepted Congressman Morris Udall's tentative invitation to float the Colorado River from Lee's Ferry below Page, Arizona to the headwaters of Lake Mead, a distance of 285 miles. As the summer progressed and the scheduled August recess was to materialize, plans for the float trip were finalized and McClure's expense account claims $8.00 for a motel room at the Empire House Motel in Page, Arizona on July 28 and another claim for a room on August 6 for $17.00 at the Riveria Hotel in Las Vegas.

On "one of the greatest trips of my life" he often rode on one of the narrow outrigger tubes like a man on a horse through many of the approximately 160 stretches of white-water rapids, losing one of Louise's favorite shirts in the process. The trip was both an adventure and an education, and ever after the staunchly conservative, fiscally tight-fisted McClure maintained that it was well worth the expenditure of tax dollars to enlighten him and his colleagues to the great value of the Grand Canyon. A bonus was the closer personal relationships that were forged on the trip. Rogers C. B. Morton (R-Maryland), destined to be Secretary of the Interior under President Nixon, became a much closer friend on this trip. Even some of the antagonism between fierce political opponents was softened by the camaraderie. Said McClure, "Bill Ford, a very liberal Democrat from Michigan, was along on that trip with his son—he was on the Education Committee but somehow got an invitation. He and I were about as far apart as could be and I never really liked him, but the great value of such a trip was that we had the opportunity [for discussions] that enabled us to really understand each other and [after that] we were never quite the adversaries we would have been."[7] [ii]

Daughter Marilyn also remembers one of the trip's legacies: "When dad came home all of his clothes were stained pink from the silt that was embedded in them."[8] The daughter's memory triggered the same recollection from Louise: "I was really disappointed that he lost my favorite shirt, and I do remember that his clothes were all pink, but I don't think the silt actually ruined any of his clothes—I'm pretty sure I was able to get them clean in the laundry."[9]

Now the summer is over. The kids are back in the Arlington schools. Louise is busier than ever being a wife and mother, and with her activities with the 90th Club Republican wives, and, most important, with getting the new house converted to the type of home that she wanted for her family. And

Jim McClure? He liked what he was doing. He said that, and the staffers who worked with him said that. And why not? The work was stimulating, as were the people with whom he was associating. Yes, being a politician and depending upon the goodwill of his voter constituents to keep his job was a source of anxiety. But, he had one important thing going for him. He deeply believed that he and most of his constituents were from the same mold, believing in the same things, wanting the same things for themselves and their country. To be sure, he was going to have to go on the campaign trail again next year. However, he did not dread that. Campaigning to him was not asking for votes. Campaigning was getting out and meeting people and convincing them he believed in the same things they did and wanted the same things they wanted. Once his constituents understood that, he believed the voting would take care of itself. That belief was to get a tremendous boost when his staff compiled the results from his first questionnaire.

Chapter 15 notes

i. This is what they were called at the time of the riots. Within days, responding to demands from African-American leaders, the media changed and started calling members of this minority "black Americans" or "blacks."

ii. Ted Kupferman (R-NY) withdrew at one civilized stop saying, when challenged for being a spoil-sport, "If you were touring New York City, I wouldn't make you ride on every elevator in the city."

Chapter 16

The Pace Increases

Bill Hall was a thorn in Jim McClure's side. As the editorial page editor of *The Lewiston Morning Tribune*, and as both an avowed liberal and Frank Church supporter, Hall usually did not miss opportunities when, through his editorials, he could dispatch arrows toward the new conservative congressman now representing Idaho's First District. However, in the fall of 1967, after almost 15,000 questionnaires mailed the previous spring had been returned to McClure's office and the results tabulated and released, Hall wrote an editorial that did, indeed, dispatch the expected arrows, but he was also fair-minded enough to give McClure credit for trying to construct an honest questionnaire. After noting that congressional questionnaires are primarily tools to get the congressman re-elected, he admitted:

> *. . .McClure's is a prime example of one that is largely honest in intent. The questions are not entirely loaded. Some in fact bend over backward to see the other side. He asks, for instance: "Do you favor increased trade with the Communist bloc nations as a means of easing tensions?" Strike the last six words from that question, and you will see what he could have done to produce a higher percentage of reactionary answers. So the questions are, for the most part, as fairly stated as they can be in an undertaking with a biased purpose. And there are indications that the congressman made every attempt to give the questionnaire broad circulation, permitting critics as well as supporters to participate. . .*[1]

The reader today is not likely to get excited over receiving a congressional questionnaire or in seeing the results of such a poll. Such questionnaires are commonplace and most people are cynical when they see the results: *the congressman/senator got just what he was trying to get*—that is the thought that often is associated with congressional questionnaires.

McClure's first questionnaire was much more significant. In the archives there are eight thick files of letters that accompanied the returned questionnaires, and one cannot help being deeply impressed with their tone. This from a man in Wilder:

Dear Sir: It is most gratifying to note that we have some one representing us in Wash. D.C. that cares what the man on the street thinks & is doing. This is the first time in my life, and I am 66 years, that I have ever been poled [sic] *on my opinion and I wish to congratulate you. . .*

And a husband and wife from Cocolalla:

Dear Congressman- We received your questionnaire card today and want you to know how much we appreciate this opportunity to express our opinion. No other Senator or Congressman has ever done this, at least not for us and I hope you get every one of them back all filled out and signed as we have done. . .

And a lady from Lewiston:

Dear Sir,

Your questionnaire came in the mail recently. I am glad that a congressman has taken the time and effort to poll his people and to evaluate their opinions. However, on some issues, I feel more strongly than this small card can indicate. My opinions may not be of much value, but since you asked—here goes. . .

All of these letters were written *in addition* to the completed questionnaires and there has to be well over a thousand of them in the eight thick file folders. Practically all of them have the tone of those above. Clearly, the voters in the First Congressional District of Idaho had never before been asked to express their opinions to a congressman by means of such a questionnaire.

That was satisfying to McClure and his staff. But it was more than that. The results demonstrated that McClure's positions and beliefs almost exactly coincided with his constituents, something McClure strongly suspected, but which was now confirmed. After those results came in, both he and Jim Goller (who was already planning) knew what strategy they would be using for next year's congressional campaign. They would get McClure out there to talk to as many people as possible so he can let them know what he is thinking about government and its problems. McClure had always felt that he was one of them. He was sure of that now, and according to Goller, "The results of that first questionnaire really energized McClure."[2]

However, all of this enthusiasm was being generated under a heavy black cloud. The nation itself was in turmoil. Literally, it was tearing itself apart, spiritually and morally. On New York City's Fifth Avenue 700,000 war protestors marched and screamed obscenities. An estimated 50,000 to 100,000 hippies were massing in San Francisco and promoting a drug culture threatening to grow into a national malaise. Centuries old standards of marriage, then family, were being tossed to the winds. Peace and love became the cry of the new Generation of Aquarius while the benchmarks of past social stability—fidelity, loyalty, trust—were being pilloried, scorned, and cast away. McClure's own generation had tuned in to the world, seen that they were needed, and then responded and sacrificed in order to make the earth safer. Many in the new generation were tuning out and turning inward. Make love, not war was the mantra of the times, and in New York a nude/rock production, *Hair,* which would run on Broadway for almost four years, was glorifying an entirely different kind of morality.

Courtesy Bill Hall

Bill Hall, *Lewiston Morning Tribune* editor, an acknowledged liberal, was a constant thorn in McClure's side, but also was an admirer of McClure's devotion to his constitutents.

Equally depressing to McClure and most of his generation was what Lyndon B. Johnson was doing to the country. Another popular Democrat, Franklin D. Roosevelt had inspired his country to make a choice during World War II. It was guns *or* butter. The people had to choose. He made the country believe that we could not have both.

President Johnson did not believe in giving the country that choice. For LBJ it was guns *and* butter, and while he on one hand as commander-in-chief spending billions fighting the war in Vietnam, he also was using all of his political clout (and that he had inherited from slain President Kennedy) to push major new federal programs of his Great Society. The result was not only massive new government debt, but a Consumer Price Index that had tripled from 1964 to 1967. With this booming rate of inflation threatening the economy, McClure and his fellow conservatives worried that huge new numbers of citizens would be added to the bulging ranks of the poverty stricken.

The trends and events just cited were discouraging to McClure and his staff. Something else under that dark cloud was worse than discouraging. Some of the letters that he was now getting were down right depressing.

As this one from a Nampa mother about her son, Gary:

Sir:

Around Friday, one of our Idaho boys will be brought home from Viet Nam by a military escort. The boys name was Gary, twenty years old and managed to survive three months. Now he'll be returned to us in a casket. Less than a year ago the biggest worry Gary probably had was finding enough gas money for his car. Then the draft took him. . .[and he was sent] *to this nameless hell-hole in Viet Nam to be slaughtered needlessly. . .Gary never once whined or complained except about the attitude of the people for whom he & thousands of American boys have been sent to protect. He was disheartened to find they could care less who kills who, as long as one side feeds & cares for them. . .*

And this from the Canyon County Sheriff about his son, Don:

Dear Mr. McClure:

Yesterday I received word from the Army that our son had been killed in Viet Nam. He had been fighting there about three months. I am not bitter about this, although my wife is heartbroken and he left behind a wife and two small children whom we will have to help raise. . .I cannot help but wonder sometimes where we are going in Asia, if it is not a war worth winning, why don't we get out?. . .During World War #2 I spent two years fighting the Japanese there in Asia and all the time I was fighting I had a feeling that my boy, who was only 5 years old at that time, would never have to fight in Asia. It seems as though I wasted two hard, long years at combat duty. . .

Where, indeed, were we going with this war? To say that McClure was agonizing over this question would probably be an understatement. He had been a consistent supporter of the war for a very simple reason. He truly believed that International Communism was, by far, the greatest threat faced by free peoples all over the world. And there in Southeast Asia was a Communist government at war with and trying to destroy a non-Communist government, all while being openly supported by the two most powerful Communist nations: the Soviet Union and China. The Demilitarized Zone (DMZ) separating North and South Vietnam was McClure's line in the sand. He wholeheartedly believed that if the United States let the Communists cross that line, there was no telling where they would ever be stopped. Would it be after the rest of Southeast Asia fell? Or after Australia and New Zealand were gobbled up? Or after India and Burma and Pakistan were a part of the Red Empire? His worries fit the scenario called the "domino theory" that was authored by President Eisenhower's Secretary of State, John Foster Dulles. That theory has been much maligned over the years, but in regard to that, McClure recently said, "I am no revisionist, and I don't want anybody trying to apologize for the way I was thinking back in 1967 and 1968. I believed in the domino theory back then and I did everything within my power to support the war in Vietnam as long as I believed that it was something that we could win. I had a difficult time with [Senator] Frank

Church back then. I thought he was undermining the men who were fighting and dying over there [by protesting the war]."[3]

But, the deaths of Idaho boys, along with his increasing knowledge of how the war in Vietnam was being micro managed in Washington, was causing him to question his own beliefs. Even in the letters he sent to the bereaved parents of boys killed in Vietnam, he always included two comments that revealed some of his misgivings about the war. One was a simple declarative sentence: *I am convinced that the war could have ended long ago and with a minimum of casualties.* The other was a plaintive admission of his growing skepticism: *Perhaps in time you can help me find the answers, because they are troubling me as well.*[4]

McClure's agony would increase over the next two years, and it would help bring about a complete change in his opinion of the war.

However, at this time there were a few bright spots under the dark clouds. Christmas was coming and the whole family was excited to be spending their first Christmas in their new home—especially since Louise's parents, the Millers from Nezperce, had come to join them for the holidays. And, despite the war that was raging in Vietnam, it was a gala season in Washington and on December 15 the whole family joined President and Mrs. Johnson at the White House for the traditional tree-lighting ceremony. Daughter Marilyn remembers that it was a Vermont tree that was decorated with lights that year, and that the family spent a very cold evening on the dignitaries' stand waiting for the president to switch on the lights. In their own home they decorated a big tree that was in the corner of the living room, and the most memorable event on Christmas day was when son Ken unwrapped his main present, which was a new guitar.

Then McClure left his family in the cold and disappeared for the whole month of January, 1968. He did not desert them, of course. He, along with six other members of the Interior Committee, went on a mission to the Trust Territories in the South Pacific.

In addition to the island of Guam, which at that time was inhabited by almost 80,000 people, the Interior Committee also had oversight responsibility for hundreds of South Pacific islands that were organized into six districts: Truk, Ponape, Marshall Islands, Palau, Marianas, and Yap, most of which had less than a third of the Guam's population. McClure and six others from the committee—Patsy Mink (D-Hawaii), Hugh Carey (D-New York), Tom Foley (D-Washington), Ted Kupferman (R-New York), Lloyd Meeds (D-Washington), and Richard White (D-Texas)—were tasked with the responsibility of visiting Guam and the other six districts on a fact-finding mission. With only written reports and the occasional testimony of someone from one of the Trust Districts, the members of the Interior Committee were ill informed on practically all aspects of the lives and problems of the diverse peoples who populated those far-flung islands. And they were a diverse group of people. A Peace Corps volunteer who was serving in the Yap District at the time of McClure's visit said, "The culture at that time was still very traditionally based, and in my district we had people of three different genetic groups: Polynesian, Micronesian, and Melenesian."[5]

To say that the trip was an adventure is probably an understatement. They left Hawaii on January 4 and flew in an Air Force C-54 to Kwajalein, then island hopped over vast regions of the South Pacific, to such unheard of islands as Ebeye, Majuro, Arno, Ailinglapalap, Kusaie, Pineelap, Ponape, Lukunor, Koror, and Angaur. And that got them halfway around the districts. Then they flew to Truk, Peleliu, Palau, Yap, Saipan, and Guam before they flew back to Hawaii on the January 26.

Lee McElvain, a staffer for the committee, was with the congressmen, and he and McClure also visited several out-of-the-way islands in a Navy seaplane, a small search-and-rescue amphibian which McElvain, a non-pilot, said involved some harrowing lagoon landings that, in the past, had claimed several other seaplanes that had tried the same thing.[6] McClure's assistant, Dick Thompson, remembers that a staffer (probably McElvain) moaned to him after the trip that "McClure wore me out; he wanted to see everything."[7]

According to McElvain and others, the islanders deeply appreciated the efforts of the congressmen to visit them. Tom Foley (D-Washington) remembered that after their first stop, they were ushered to the airport by a large crowd of appreciative citizens. The pilot of the transport, who Foley said was a former fighter pilot, took off in front of the crowd, but when he had climbed to a few thousand feet, he did a wingover, then a dive, and buzzed the runway in front of the crowd—all while Patsy Mink was screaming in terror and the others were holding tight and not understanding what was happening. According to Foley, the group later had a come-to-Jesus meeting with the frustrated fighter pilot and agreed that yes, indeed, the buzz job was worthwhile for the morale of the islanders, but that the passengers would henceforth be advised when such a maneuver was about to begin.[8]

Lloyd Meeds (D-Washington) described the trip as "not easy", but very worthwhile for both the islanders and the congressmen. Although he laughs about it now, the trip did create a bit of a problem for him in his home district. Said Meeds, "When we got back, there was this glowing editorial in the *Spokesman Review* on how Tom Foley and Jim McClure, under hazardous conditions, bravely did their duty in the South Pacific, etc. etc., while the *Everett Herald*, the main newspaper in my district, ran a cartoon with Foley and me on a little atoll, Foley in a grass skirt doing the hula and me lying under a palm tree sipping a mint julep, with the caption saying: *Dear Taxpayer: Wish you were here.* Old Jim and Foley got away with a great editorial and I got skewered."[9]

McClure, himself, looking back upon the trip, described it in a low-key manner. Yes, it was very educational and very worthwhile for him and the other congressmen who got to know and understand many of the problems of the islanders. Daughter Marilyn remembers a father returning who was not so laconic.

> *The trip to the trust territories was very exciting for him and he came back full of enthusiasm and with lots of souvenirs and lots of stories to tell. I remember one story of how he had two kinds of pork at a buffet—one that was real pork and the other that turned out to be dog. I still have a lot of impressions, especially of this kid who was raised in Payette and Council coming home brimming with stories. I remember he brought back a grass skirt and modeled it for us. I remember a little model of an outrigger canoe. He also brought back some bark cloth—bark that was pounded until it melds together into cloth* [tapa cloth]*—he even brought back pictures of how it was made. I still have a couple of wooden dolls he brought back from Yap, and I remember him reciting samples from some of the local languages. I think it was a big experience for him, though it might have been stressful for mom to have him gone for so long, although I don't recall now how or why I think that.*[10]

McClure hit the ground running when he returned from the South Pacific. His staff had done their best with the correspondence, which, according to Dick Thompson, had been post dated to the time when he would be back and could sign the letters. One can imagine him spending many long hours reading, modifying, rejecting, and finally signing the hundreds that would have been prepared while he was gone. And then he had to hit the road again. The Lincoln Day circuit, where he would travel from county to county, meeting Republicans and giving speeches, was an important obligation, especially for a new Republican congressman who is going to have to campaign in the district again the coming fall. (His files have a 30-page speech that he presumably gave to the Elmore County Republicans on February 17.)

In early April he was off again, this time to the northern coast of California where hearings were being held on a proposed new national park. This one was to be a park that would preserve a stand of one of the most unique trees in the world: the Coastal Redwood. Before the Ice Age, redwood trees, which can grow over 300 feet high and live up to 2,000 years, were common worldwide. Now their habitat is restricted to the moist and fog-prone coastal area near Crescent City, California. For years conservationists had mounted efforts to preserve some of the old-growth redwood forests, and at the time of the hearings during the Easter congressional recess of 1968, there were already three California state parks dedicated to preserving groves of these spectacular trees. The hearings McClure attended were for the purpose of deciding whether or not a fourth stand of the trees should be placed under federal protection.

McClure was all for the principal: "Save The Redwoods," which was a slogan on thousands of bumper stickers at the time. But, he went to the hearings with several misgivings. Representative Phil Burton, the radical congressman from San Francisco with whom he served on the Interior Committee, would have put every redwood tree in California under federal protection. McClure disagreed strenuously with Burton. McClure argued that the trees that needed protecting were the old-growth trees—those native giants that would be allowed to live on and be admired by many generations of Americans in the future. He could see no point in permanently locking away those stands of redwoods that were second-, third-, and even fourth-growth descendants of the native trees. The harvesting of those trees provided a valuable industry, which was the main economic base for the region. He did not want to wipe out an industry that supported so many people. With the three state parks and a new national park, he was confident that the region's redwood heritage would survive in perpetuity.

He was also concerned about a matter that few people considering the issue understood. Much of the land that was to be included in the new national park was private land. Companies like the Simpson Timber Company, which was one of four major landowners, had to be compensated for the land and trees that were to be taken from them. However, a legislative bill that authorizes payment of a certain amount in compensation does not necessarily result in the money getting to the claimant. The legislative bill, even after it is signed by the president, merely designates what the government is *authorized* to pay the claimant. What *will* be paid is the amount that is approved in a separate appropriation that also must be approved by Congress and signed by the President. McClure was keenly aware of this discrepancy and was leery of any acquisition that did not also provide for some mechanism that guaranteed just compensation for the private landholders.[i]

According to his biographer, Phil Burton ranted and raved about the redwoods that were not being included, and he was especially distressed with Wayne Aspinall whose autocratic methods as chairman of the Interior Committee he detested passionately. However, on the recommendation of the Sierra Club—an environmental organization that was just beginning to flex it's muscles—that a 55,650 acre park (including 30-odd miles of pristine beach) was about all that was possible at the time, Burton grudgingly[ii] went along with the Interior Committee chairman's recommendation and the Redwood National Park (Public Law 90-545) became a reality just months after the California hearings. [11]

"Nobody said it was going to be easy." That was how McClure responded after the author read him the list of Idaho meetings that he attended from late April (after the Redwood National Park hearings) through June—meetings that he had to sandwich in between his busy schedule in Washington. On April 27 he attended the opening of a potato processing plant in Nampa, then spoke at a noon meeting of the Countryman's Club. On April 29 and 30 he toured the Bruneau Desert and private land developments along the Snake River with the Idaho Water Resource Board. On May 2 he dedicated the Arvin Millwork Company's new plant in Homedale, and the next two days he attended the North Idaho Chamber of Commerce's meeting in Coeur d'Alene. While in Coeur d'Alene, he also spoke at the annual awards banquet of the Elks Lodge. The next day he spoke at the Rotary Club in St. Maries; then rushed back to Washington for an important Women's National Press Club meeting in the Interior Department. A week and one-half later he was in the Apple Blossom Parade in his hometown of Payette, then on a boat trip through Hells Canyon with officials of the Interior Department, Bureau of Land Management, Bureau of Reclamation, and the Army Corps of Engineers. The afternoon he came out of the canyon in Lewiston he drove to Cambridge and gave their high school commencement speech, and a week after that, he was doing the same thing for the Mullan High School graduating class. After that, he flew to Washington, worked there all week, and then flew back to Idaho and marched in the academic procession for the commencement ceremony at the University of Idaho. After another week in Washington, he was back as a dignitary at the Old-Time Fiddlers Contest in Weiser, attended the Republican State Convention

TOM SCHABOT TELLS A STORY

One afternoon I was driving from Nampa to Caldwell on old Highway 30 when the right rear tire on my old car went flat. I managed to get the car off the highway but not by much and when I got out, the cars were zipping by me, missing me by inches it seemed. I got in and got the spare tire, then tried to figure out how I was going to use the jack. I had never changed a tire before. About the time I was trying to figure out what to do, a car pulled off behind me and this man in a suit got out. He greeted me and asked me if I was having trouble. I confessed that I had to learn how to jack the car up then he took off his suit coat, rolled up his sleeves, and told me to stand behind the car so the drivers coming down the road would see me and try to give us some space. Then he loosened the lug nuts, jacked up the car, took off the old tire, put on the spare, replaced the lug nuts, and put the flat tire in the trunk—all while I watched.

As he turned to walk back to his car, I thanked him, then remembered that I didn't get his name. I told him my name and he shook hands and said that he was Jim McClure. I knew the name—he had just been elected to Congress—and to me that was really impressive. It was impressive that he stopped to help me and got himself dirty, but to me it was more impressive that he was going to walk away without telling me his name. I would never have known who he was if I hadn't introduced myself.

in Coeur d'Alene, and was a speaker at the Idaho Prosecuting Attorneys Association in Sun Valley.

It was not easy, but he was doing his job. Actually, it was more than that. He liked his job representing the people of the First District in Congress and he wanted to keep it. This was an election year, and the idea was fixed in his mind that the most significant way he could campaign and keep that job was to get around the district so the people would get to know him better. His opponent had already announced; Compton White, whom he defeated in the 1966 election, was running again and was determined to get the First Congressional seat back for the Democrats. White still believed that the Republican win in his traditional Democratic district was a fluke—an aberration that would be corrected this time around when the Democratic stalwarts realized the severity of their loss. McClure, on the other hand, was reading the results from another poll that he had sent out to his constituents. The people were telling him they wanted less government, fiscal responsibility, and law and order—his bedrock principles. So, whether he was speaking before an audience in the Mullan or Cambridge High School auditorium or at the dedication of new millwork facility, the people of his district were getting to know him better and that is what he wanted.

His visits actually worked two-ways; McClure also was genuinely eager to learn all he could from his constituents, a desire that he sometimes carried to a fault. Said Jim Goller when that subject came up:

> *I sometimes had trouble with McClure. You know, the typical politician goes through a crowd, shaking hands and acting like he is listening when people try to tell him things. McClure was never like that. Sure, he worked the crowds and shook their hands. But, he was always listening. He wanted to hear what people had on their minds. I often had to prod him along, keep him moving, because it was rude for him to get locked up with some guy when there were fifty others who wanted to meet him. And the Vietnam veterans were the worst for me; wherever McClure went, he wanted to hear the accounts of their experiences.*[12]

And there was a lot for McClure to hear. That spring was the most disruptive since the Confederates fired at Fort Sumter and started the Civil War. The Tet Offensive in Vietnam at the end of January and the subsequent occupation of the American Embassy in Saigon triggered violent anti-war protests across the nation. Students had stormed the presidents' offices at Columbia and the University of California at Berkeley and taken hostages. In April, Martin Luther King was assassinated—an event that triggered massive riots in over 100 cities and forty-six deaths. (Louise McClure was almost caught in the Washington D.C., riot but managed to exit a meeting and find a safe route home.) After losing the nominating vote in New Hampshire to anti-war activist Minnesota Senator Eugene McCarthy, President Johnson announced that he would not be a candidate for another term. Other candidates jumped in, including New York Senator Robert Kennedy, the slain president's brother. However, in May, while campaigning in Los Angeles as the front-runner in the race, he, too, was gunned down. In addition, the violent crime rate in the nation had risen 57 percent in just the past eight years.

Of course, McClure's constituents saw none of this first hand, but television was in every home now and the news media was having a heyday with the conflict and the violence. And, because the Democratic National Convention in Chicago that summer was violently disrupted by protest leaders like Abbie Hoffman, Tom Hayden and Bobby Seale, Idahoans sat in their living rooms and began to debate with themselves about the candidates they were going to support. Yes, the miners and timber workers were union men and the backbone of the Democratic Party. But is this kind of violence and protest what they wanted in their future?

Jim Goller felt that many of those hard-core Democrats began to question their allegiance at about this time. He said,

> *They weren't about to admit that they were going to vote for a Republican for congressman or president—they weren't ready for that, for sure—but I think this is when the voter shift began—the shift that eventually led blue-collar workers to be a major factor in Reagan's two huge victories. I also think the same thing was happening with the wheat farmers in the Palouse and on Camas Prairie. They were die-hard Roosevelt Democrats. They believed he saved them during the Depression. But, they were basically conservative and I think all that violence and protesting in 1968 caused them to start rethinking their allegiances. Yeah, Republican was still a dirty word and they weren't going to tell anybody they might vote for one. But, I really think they, too, started questioning where the Democratic Party was leading them.*[13]

McClure was asked to comment on Goller's analysis:

> *I don't want to overstate it; it wasn't a big shift. But, as I stood outside the gates to meet workers, I sensed less animosity than I had experienced two years earlier. Some—not a lot—but some stopped to talk or to ask questions. Of course, I wanted to believe that their shift in attitude was because I had been doing a good job representing them for the past two years. But, now that I think about it, perhaps the violence and the protesting they were seeing on television also may have been a factor in their change of attitude. I suspect that Goller's analysis is accurate.*[14]

The campaign began in earnest in September. And Goller was ready. He already had county coordinators for McClure in every county, and on August 30 he sent the first of a barrage of memos to them. They were advised to work with the local party officers and keep alert for any event that might justify a McClure visit during the campaign, which was officially scheduled to start on September 18 when the fall congressional recess was to begin.

The opposition was ready, too. In June, Frank Church kicked off Comp White's campaign with a big reception for him at the Dupont Plaza Hotel in Washington, D.C. In the invitation he said, "I know you shared with me the disappointment of Comp's hairbreadth defeat in November, 1966, and would like to help return him to Congress. He needs your good wishes and your financial support. . ."[15] The Idaho Democrats were also ready with a strategy. It was unveiled in July when White met with the press during a campaign swing through the Boise Valley where he was quoted as saying, ". . .provincial status quo representation in the U.S. Congress is not what Idaho needs or deserves. A constant 'no' vote, with no suggested alternatives to solving the country's many and complex social and economic problems, simply is not good enough. . ."[16] Soon a handout, FACT SHEET NUMBER 1: THE McCLURE RECORD began circulating in the district with a two-page list of bills, mostly social legislation, that had passed despite McClure's negative votes. It was accompanied with a cover letter explaining "how they can best be used to help Comp win."[17]

Also, the Democrats were laying for him on the "rat issue." McClure's legislative assistant, Dick Thompson, explains:

> *One day I was having lunch in the Longworth cafeteria with a friend who worked for a congressman on the Appropriations Committee. He was really bothered by some legislation that had just been reported out of the committee. "You're not going to believe this," he said, "but there is a bill that is going to put the government into the rat killing business." He went on to explain how big money was going to be spent on the eradication of rats in public housing units. We were both aghast and lamented how the federal government was creeping into every part of our lives. Well, when I got back to the office, I had to come up with a weekly press release and I decided that this would be a good subject. I wrote it and gave it to McClure to read. He frowned and handed it back. "It's a little insensitive, isn't it?" he replied. But, after we talked, he waved a hand, giving me the go ahead. That was a huge mistake on my part—one of the times I really let him down. The press really jumped on that, especially the part where I had McClure saying, "In Idaho we kill our own rats." There were all kinds of negative editorials about McClure's insensitivity, and Bill Hall continued to write about it over and over again.*[18]

Dick Thompson still feels bad about the firestorm of criticism his column generated, but Jim Goller just laughs about it. Said Goller:

> *Neither the publicity on McClure's negative votes nor the editorials on the rat issue bothered me in the slightest. This is Idaho. Idaho people do kill their own rats. We turned that issue around and made it into a positive thing. Sure, McClure sometimes had to defend his negative votes to the press when they asked him about them. But, he was good at explaining every vote. He had studied those bills. He knew there were more bad things in them than good. As far as the people themselves, I can't recall anyone heckling him from an*

DOROTHY HANFORD ON McCLURE

I discovered that he was very honest, but that was his reputation and it did not surprise me. His personality was what surprised me. At first he came off as kind of a fuddy-duddy—I kind of expected him to pull a watch out of his pocket on a chain. He always wore a somber, dark suit, but one day I got a call asking for him to come to some small town—I don't remember now where it was—and the person said, "Do you think you could get that suit off of him—people here would like to see someone dressed more relaxed—he won't go over very well in that formal wear."

I told Jim Goller about that and I said "Maybe we can find him a really nice sweater and he can go in an open shirt." Goller agreed, so I went shopping and bought him a beautiful blue sweater that matched his blue eyes. He was very agreeable [when I presented him with the sweater]*—he had this small smile and chuckle—an embarrassed kind of chuckle but he went along . . .After he got to know you, he was more relaxed. . .*

I never saw him lose his temper, but saw him a little hot under the collar a couple of times. He would kind of screw up his face and plant his two feet firmly on the ground and you thought something was going to happen. This happened one time after he returned from Washington. I don't remember the issue—maybe it was welfare—but he was angry and depressed, and said to me, "This is it; I'm just fed up. I've had it. I'm not going back to Washington. This piece of legislation I have worked and worked on...those people back there don't care about anybody." I guess he just had to let off steam to somebody, because after I talked with him awhile, he smiled and said, "I guess I'll go back, but things like this make me want to give up and quit.". . .

He was quite determined and had quite a lot of drive, too. I never heard him say that he was tired or that he wanted me to get him away from people. He was always gracious and did a good job—although he did make the comment once, "If you would allow me a little time to get to the bathroom, I would appreciate it." I kind of got the hint. Sometimes in the small towns I would only allow 12 minutes in his schedule and he liked to visit with people. Overall, I would say he was kind of grand-fatherly—the kind of person who, if you skinned your knees, he was going to hug you and make it all well.

> *audience about his negative votes. Remember, most of his constituents thought just like he did. They didn't want to see a massive federal government creeping into their lives. The whole Democratic strategy just didn't play in Idaho.*[19]

Goller also pounced upon one of Comp White's own statements. "Somewhere along the line," said Goller, "Comp White was quoted, when defending his close ties to LBJ [Lyndon B. Johnson], that 'when you are in Washington, sometimes you have to go along in order to get along.' We really turned that against him. We had McClure saying, 'When you are in Washington, you don't have to "go along." A congressman's first responsibility is to represent the people who sent him there.' Oh, we used that over and over. We really beat up on Comp with that."[20]

The campaign went into high gear in late September. However, there was a significant change in Goller's strategy compared to the first election. This time he hired a full-time campaign coordinator, Dorothy Hanford, the wife of a Boise dentist. Working out of the Boise regional office, she fielded requests for McClure from throughout the First District and, by scheduling his appearances, she was able to utilize his time more efficiently than Goller had been able to do in the first campaign.

Jim Goller was enthusiastic from the very beginning and he had the complete confidence of McClure. Said McClure:

> *I was definitely more confident in him* [Goller] *during the second campaign. He had the reputation now* [for being a good campaign manager] *and he deserved it. The only differences we ever had were that I wanted to spend more time in small communities and he wanted me in the population centers. It wasn't just that I enjoyed that kind of campaigning more. In a large community you can't see everybody—the* [campaigning] *technique there is to let them know you have been there and that you cared. So much depends upon the press and television to tell them you were there. In a small community you had a chance to reach a good segment of the population. I did spend proportionately more time in small communities because they took it as a mark of respect for them if you were there and I liked that, frankly. I think people in those small communities get taken for granted and are bypassed too much.*[21]

Although McClure ran scared in the campaign—*I used a lot of adrenalin up in that campaign, but if I hadn't done everything I could and lost by a slim margin, I could never have forgiven myself*—but, on election day, November 5, when the voters were going to the polls, there was never a doubt in Goller's mind about the results. And the results were dramatic. McClure lost just five strong Democratic counties—Benewah, Clearwater, Lewis, Nez Perce, and Shoshone—compared to the eleven counties he lost in his first election. This time he carried a total of fifteen counties and won by an overall plurality of 28,868 votes—almost 24,000 votes more than his margin in 1966.

So, on November 6, 1968, Goller was smiling and McClure was relieved. He had a lot more things that he wanted to do in the 91st Congress, and this time he was going to be working with a Republican president in the White House.

Chapter 16 notes

i According to Simpson Timber Company's vice president, Jim Brown, they did, in fact, have to go to court to get paid for the land the government took from them—payment that was authorized in the taking bill.

ii Burton got even in 1977, after much of Aspinall's power had been stripped and he was out of the Congress. Through Burton's leadership the size of the Park was almost doubled.

Chapter 17

An Environmental Challenge

America would inaugurate a new president right after Jim McClure began his second term in Congress: Richard Nixon. Nixon had been defeated nine years earlier by John F. Kennedy, and, in addition, had later suffered a humiliating defeat for governor in his home state of California. His political career—first as a congressman and senator and then as President Eisenhower's vice president for two terms—was supposedly over after that last defeat, but a combination of events, including the lack of a better known conservative Republican contender, enabled him to land the top prize.

McClure, of course, was highly pleased that he would finally be serving under a president who shared many of his views. But many of his fellow congressmen—those on the Democratic side of the aisle that still made up a large majority in the House—were energized by their loss of the White House. Nixon might be President, but he could not accomplish any of his goals through legislation without their cooperation. And for the most part, they were determined to block his entire legislative program. That they largely succeeded, especially in the first session of the 91st Congress, caused McClure and many of his colleagues to refer to the session as the "Ninety-Worst Congress."

Tax reform was one of Nixon's major legislative proposals, and this issue was one of McClure's main interests. In fact, he tried to get on the House Banking Committee at the beginning of this new Congress just so he could become more involved in fiscal matters in general, and the gold and silver policies of the U.S. Treasury Department in particular. And even though he lost that bid, this did not keep him from being an active student and a participant in the important hearings that took place in the spring and summer of 1969. Of greatest concern was the policy of the Treasury Department to sell off the country's silver deposits at unrealistic prices. This practice drove the price of silver down, which, in turn, greatly affected the economy of the silver producers in his home district. Also, the gold price was officially pegged by the Treasury Department at the very unrealistic price of $35.00 an ounce. And since some gold was also produced in the Silver Valley (along with lead and zinc), this further affected the profitability of the mines.

Another issue was emerging about this time—an issue that would become almost as important and as controversial as the Vietnam War.

From the time the country was founded, Americans looked upon the land as a rich and bountiful heritage just waiting to be exploited. The soil was fertile so farm the land and in our wealthy country there would be a never-ending market for the crops. The forests seemed endless so cut the trees and provide the vast supply of lumber needed to house an exploding population. Practically all of the minerals that were needed to feed our booming industrial development were in ore bodies that were easy to recover by mining. Oil, when it became a fuel that would revolutionize our transportation system, seemed to be in endless pools under the earth. Grow, cut, mine, and pump—these four verbs were the action words that drove the progress of the American people.

In the 1960s various writers began to bring another message to the American people. In June, 1962, Rachel Carson's book, *Silent Spring*, revealed startling news about how several wild bird populations—those at the end of a long food chain like the peregrine falcon—were dying because of an accumulation of DDT in their bodies.[i] Up to that time, millions of gallons of this pesticide were routinely sprayed upon bodies of stagnant water to kill mosquito larvae. As a consequence, the World Health Organization estimates that 50 million to 100 million lives were saved by preventing malaria.[ii1] Carson's book was widely read and the reaction among a great many intellectuals was one of great concern, not for the people threatened by malaria, but for the birds. The general impression, especially after the media sensed a great new story in the making, was that we humans were poisoning our planet. What followed was a series of articles and books enumerating doomsday scenarios of how the earth was threatened by rampant pollution and dangerous chemicals, and how an exploding human population was certain to decimate our food supply and other natural resources. All of this, of course, was the beginning of the environmental movement. Said future vice president Al Gore in an introduction written for the 1994 edition of *Silent Spring*: "Without this book, the environmental movement might have been long delayed or never have developed at all. . .it led to environmental legislation at every level of government."[2]

However one feels about the environmental movement today, it is correct to say that, historically, nations rich and poor had paid little attention to the degradation of their environment. In the 1960s rivers were waste receptacles and were being polluted by biological as well as chemical toxins. There was little concern by industrial plants as they released tons of noxious chemicals out their stacks and into the air that people had to breathe. And mining operations of all types were permanently disfiguring thousands of acres—a disfigurement that could never be erased. And this was not just in heavily populated regions of the world. This was occurring in Jim McClure's own pristine First District. One could travel up the Middle Fork of the Boise River through some of the most beautiful mountains in America and be saddened by the miles and miles of historical dredge tailings that would forever blight one's view of the river. One could descend into the beautiful Clearwater Valley and be greeted by a smoky pall hanging over the city of Lewiston—a vile-smelling effluent from a large pulp mill. And, on a visit to what had once been a beautiful Silver Valley, one could see where smelter effluents had poisoned much of the vegetation and where ugly slag and other solid wastes littered the hillsides. It is undoubtedly true that the environmental movement was largely initiated by alarmist zealots who cared little for the human prices that would have to be paid for the changes they advocated. But, is also hard to argue that the movement was untimely and unneeded when it got underway.

Courtesy Jim McClure

Congressman McClure presents President Richard Nixon with a paper mache likeness of Nixon made by "a little old lady" from Emmett, Idaho. The presentation was made in the Oval Office in July 1970.

McClure was in his fourth year in Congress when the environmental movement was considered to have been officially initiated by the first Earth Day, April 22, 1970. For several years prior to this, the American people had grown accustomed to seeing young people with long hair and dirty clothes marching in the streets on their evening television newscasts. For the most part these were protesters against the Vietnam War, and they triggered hundreds and hundreds of letters from McClure's disgusted constituents who felt that both the country and its youth were dragging our culture into a cesspool. And while it is probably true that a segment of the protest movement that was initiated on that first Earth Day in 1970 came from the anti-Vietnam crowd, it is also true that many others who joined the movement were not only well dressed and groomed, but folks who considered themselves true-blue, patriotic Americans. In other words, those who came to be called environmentalists were not all crazies; a great many were conservative citizens who had come to believe that it was time for humans to start learning how to live harmoniously with their environment.

And what was McClure's position when the environmental movement was getting underway? Looking back he says now that he had mixed emotions. And that is understandable considering his background. On the one hand he had a great love for the pristine lands of America. He had communed with nature and the great outdoors throughout his childhood and youth, and even well into his adulthood he continued to cherish the vacations he spent hiking into his favorite alpine lakes. The Seven Devils above Hells Canyon and the mountains and lakes at the headwaters of the South Fork of the Salmon River were precious sanctuaries. On the other hand he was a supreme realist, fully aware that every single product used by humans that was not grown had to be mined, or otherwise extracted from the earth. What bothered him the most was the way the environmental activists who emerged from the movement were hell bent to make mining a dirty word; to continue with mining, in their view, was to desecrate the Earth. To McClure those people were not only misguided, but they were hypocritical as well. For example, these activists blithely drove their automobiles to their rallies against earth desecration—the zealots may even have ridden bicycles—but all the while they ignored the fact that, other than the bit of cotton that may have been in the seat covers, every part of their automobile or bicycle was fabricated from something extracted from the earth.

Prior to 1969 the mining issue had caused little angst for McClure. That all changed when, in that year, the American Smelting and Refining Company (ASARCO) applied to the Challis National Forest for permission to build a 12-mile road into the eastern base of Castle Peak for the purpose of transporting equipment needed to assess the value of the molybdenite ore in their mining claims. News of this proposal came as a surprise to Idahoans and it caused an almost instant polarization. Castle Peak is the highest mountain in the White Cloud Range—a range on the east side of the Sawtooth Valley renowned for its pristine streams, alpine lakes, and meadows. Just the thought of that area being invaded by bulldozers and mining equipment was depressing to a great many Idahoans who had never before thought of themselves as environmentalists. Soon bumper stickers with the message, "SAVE THE WHITE CLOUDS," could be seen on hundreds of cars, and McClure's office (and probably the offices of the other Idaho delegates) was soon inundated with letters from hunters, fishermen, backpackers, and their organizations.[iii]

Of course, there were strong supporters emerging as well, especially in Custer County where Castle Peak was located and where job benefits and tax revenues from the anticipated growth could have a major impact. And then one very important Idahoan added his name in support of the proposed road into Castle Peak. Governor Don Samuelson, McClure's old friend and the unknown from north Idaho who trounced three-term Governor Bob Smylie in the 1966 primary election, announced that such a molybdenite deposit, if it was as large as ASARCO thought it might be, could be a huge benefit for Idaho in general and the folks in Custer County in particular.

That did it. What started as an issue that became emotional now became political as well. Cecil Andrus, the Democrat who lost to Samuelson in the 1966 general election by almost 11,000 votes[iv] and who was waiting in the wings as the strongest candidate to challenge for the governorship the following year, came out strongly in support of those who wanted to save the White Clouds.

The issue also became complicated. For the past two years McClure and the rest of the Idaho delegation had been trying to save Stanley Basin and the Sawtooth Valley[v] from exploitation, particularly by real estate developers who were beginning to plat subdivisions in the area. McClure felt that the scenic value of the area more than justified preservation as a national park ("*In my opinion it had a scenic value greater than some of the other places that were already in National Parks* ."[3]), but, personally, he did not want that and later hearings in Idaho justified his apprehension. Idahoans who testified believed that a national park would draw thousands of visitors to the area and that those tourists would negatively impact the bucolic atmosphere that was the essence of the region. Ranchers, though skeptical of any further governmental control of the area, much preferred that the area be administered by the U.S. Forest Service—a known entity—rather than the much more rigid National Park Service. Hunters were also opposed to a national park because they knew that hunting would be prohibited. What emerged from the hearings was the concept of creating a Sawtooth National Recreation Area (SNRA) that would be administered by the Forest Service. McClure had introduced an SNRA bill in the 90th Congress, but it went nowhere despite the support of all four members of the Idaho delegation. Then in the current 91st Congress, Orval Hansen, in whose district most of the area lies, introduced a similar bill in the House, and in the Senate, Church and Jordan did the same. Since McClure was on the House Interior Committee and Hansen was not, Hansen's bill became McClure's primary responsibility and he supported it enthusiastically.

Then came a curve ball. To the Senate floor came an amendment for which there had been no notice and no committee hearings. This amendment, which passed, added 157,000 acres to the SNRA—essentially all of the White Cloud Range. McClure was appalled at this development. As he said in a statement to his constituents, "No Idahoan had an opportunity to express his views, either pro or con, before its adoption."[4] For two reasons McClure was not ready to support the addition of the White Cloud acres to the SNRA. The first was economic. There were numerous legitimate mining claims in the area and, as he stated in his newsletter, "The holders of these claims have property rights guaranteed under present law. It is not possible to prohibit mining without buying the rights of these claim holders. I think

Senator Church is right in saying that Congress is not likely to appropriate the large sums of money which would be required to accomplish this end."[5]

McClure's second reason for opposing the White Clouds amendment was strictly political: he was keenly aware of the controversy growing in Idaho and he wanted hearings that would allow those on all sides of the argument to express their opinions. Also, timing was a factor. Some of the subdivisions that would forever change the atmosphere of the Sawtooth Valley and Stanley Basin were already starting to advertise. Feeling that time was running out, McClure wrote to his constituents and said, "I have urged the [Interior] Committee to act on H.R. 5999 [Hansen's SNRA Bill] without delay to protect the Sawtooths, one of the most beautiful areas in the world."[6]

The problem was that the chairman of the House Interior Committee, Wayne Aspinall (D-Colorado), would not even consider the bill that had passed the Senate, which included the White Clouds, because no hearings had been held in Idaho. It was his firm policy that local hearings on such issues had to be held before they would be considered by his committee. However, since the White Clouds were an issue and Hansen's bill did not include them, McClure had no chance of getting Aspinall to put it on his agenda. So the Hansen bill died.

Fast forward nine months, to April 1970. The first Earth Day was a major happening, and throughout the nation the environment was becoming a hot-button issue. Everywhere, it seemed, environmental advocates who did not even know what the term meant were calling themselves "ecologists." And in Idaho it was an election year. A new governor would be elected in November. And McClure had to campaign again, this time against Bill Brauner, a Caldwell attorney. In the governor's race, pitting the incumbent Governor Samuelson against Cecil Andrus, the White Clouds were a major issue. Andrus was adamant about saving the White Clouds and he let the voters know it. Samuelson, who defended the proposed mining on economic grounds, was also in trouble with some of the key Idaho Republicans whom he had offended. So that race, normally with the Republican having a built in advantage, was hotly contested, and to nobody's real surprise Andrus won by nearly 11,000 votes.

McClure was seen by some critics as a "fence-straddler"on the White Clouds issue. One of his persistent critics who used that term was the political editor of the *The Lewiston Morning Tribune*, Bill Hall, who also penned a famous line in an editorial saying that, "Today, thanks largely to McClure, a black cloud hangs over the White Clouds."[7] However, even in the face of the upcoming campaign, McClure was sticking to his guns. For example, in a letter to one of his major supporters, Al Teske, executive secretary of the Idaho Mining Association, McClure said, "Simply because this issue is so fundamentally important to Idaho's future, I have not made up my mind and will not do so until I have studied the proposal as fully as I can. . .It isn't enough to be blindly against *preservation* nor is it enough to be automatically against *exploitation*. I haven't yet been able to determine which arguments are factual and which are simply the arbitrary results of inflexible positions—on both sides of the question." [8]

> JIM GOLLER'S NEW ROLE
>
> In the two previous campaigns McClure had the final say on where and with whom he would meet. That all changed in his third campaign. On September 14, 1970, McClure addressed a memo to Goller that said, in part:
>
> "As the campaign accelerates into high gear for the final month and a half, it is now necessary to shift the responsibility and authority for scheduling from the Washington office to the Boise District office. . .I am, therefore, delegating all authority for campaign scheduling in Idaho to you. The line of responsibility shall break down as follows:
>
> (1) All decisions to accept or reject an invitation in Idaho will henceforth be made by you, not me. At this stage of the game, I think you are in a better position to know where it is most beneficial for me to be. . .I no longer want to be bothered with decisions on routine appearances. . . '

Bill Brauner really had little chance to beat McClure. In comments to the author thirty-four years later, in a tone between bitterness and resignation, he said, "The Democratic Party promised me money if I would run, but they didn't come through. I was left high and dry and Andrus got all the support."[9] Even stalwart supporter, Bill Hall, cautioned Brauner in an editorial that he ". . . should not be contemplating the race with too many illusions. There must be some realization that this first effort would be largely for the practice, with the election two years from now as the more realistic target. . .and it is the pattern in Idaho that losers, rather than being destroyed by the experience, do quite well on a second try."[10] [11]

McClure won the election by almost 22,000 votes, losing only four counties, but even in them receiving many more votes than in the two previous elections. He was going back to Washington again, and one of his firm goals was to get an SNRA bill through the House.

And he was in a much better position to do that. While serving on the Interior Committee for the two previous terms he had earned the respect not only of his fellow committee members, but of the crusty old chairman himself. Said the chief Democratic staffer who worked closely with McClure during the 90th, 91st, and 92nd congresses, "McClure was above the norm in intelligence and in being able to articulate things, and he was above the norm in interest in [any] legislation we were working with. He was a constructive participant, in my opinion, and in the process he was thoughtful—he studied the legislation, knew what he was talking about, and he was the kind of person you would like to have as your own congressman regardless of party. He wasn't political—he had his own point of view, as did Aspinall, but people could work things out with him whether the point was large or small."[12]

There was another factor at work that also helped McClure. In the Republican caucus at the beginning of the 92nd Congress a significant rules change was adopted. Heretofore, the ranking Republican on any committee was automatically the Republican with the most seniority. The change that was adopted gave the ranking designation to the Republican who was elected by *secret* [vi] ballot. This was important for McClure and some of the other junior Republicans because John Saylor (R-Pennsylvania), the ranking Republican on the Interior Committee, was an ardent environmentalist with close ties to the Sierra Club, Friends of the Earth, The Wilderness Society, and numerous other environmental lobbyists. In the past Saylor had invoked the threat of bringing "my people" in to fight this or that issue with which he disagreed. According to McClure, that change may have made Saylor a bit less antagonistic when, a year later, the SNRA bill went to the floor of the House for a vote.

A lot had to happen before such a vote could take place. The first hurdle was to convince Chairman Aspinall that hearings by the Subcommittee on National Parks and Recreation should actually be held in Idaho. McClure now shrugs off the difficulty of pulling that off, but Orval Hansen, when asked about his own role in establishing the SNRA, was adamant that McClure's leadership was the key. Said Hansen:

> *My take on it is different than the conventional wisdom that gives Frank Church all the credit for the SNRA. In my view, Jim was the key to it. In the Senate, with Church and Jordan both on the Interior Committee and from opposite parties, such a bill was a slam dunk. It was in the House where it had been stalled in the past and where it* [could have] *languished. But, Jim was a conscientious member of the House Interior Committee, which handled more legislation than any other committee. They handled a great variety—most not all that exciting—and as a dedicated member, he slogged through it all. He showed up and participated—he had a great legislative mind—I saw this in the Idaho Legislature but more so in the congress. Aspinall valued Jim McClure's contribution in that committee, so when Jim said " I'd like the committee to give serious consideration* [to the SNRA hearings], *" he had a friend in Aspinall.*[13]

So Aspinall agreed to the hearings, which would be held in August during the congressional recess. Orval Hansen also had a comment about that:

> *It was one thing to schedule hearings but another to get the members of the subcommittee to commit. The fact that Jim was able to*

> *put the arm on some of those folks is especially remarkable because it was their vacation time—but he did it, although I also worked at it. Some of the people we got were Mo Udall from Arizona, John Camp from Oklahoma, Manuel Lujan from New Mexico, and, most important, Roy Taylor from North Carolina who was chairman of the subcommittee.*[14]

They staged from Boise where a chartered DC-3 picked them up at six o'clock in the morning for a flight to Stanley airport. (Lee McElvain, senior staffer for the Interior Committee, remembers getting chewed out by Roy Taylor who said, "I don't like to get up early in the morning."[15]) From there they were taken by helicopters to view Castle Peak and the White Cloud Range, stopping for lunch at one of the Frog Lakes. After that, they reboarded the helicopters and toured the Sawtooth Range, which as a part of the proposed legislation, was to become a new wilderness area. After that they landed at Toxaway Lake where they spent the rest of the afternoon and evening. Orval Hansen, after enduring a frightening emergency landing at Smiley Creek because of a hydraulic line rupture, hiked into Toxaway Lake, not because of fear, but "because I like to hike." Said he of the evening:

> *We had a great evening—Roy Taylor caught some fish, which made him happy—I commented later that I think the Forest Service sent divers in to put fish on his hook just to make him happy. It was one of those beautiful evenings that you can experience in that country. From the lake we could look between the mountains and could see the White Clouds across the valley, and I remember that we all watched those mountains as the sun was going down. It was a spectacular scene. The conclusion that evening was that this was a unique area of scenic beauty and we had to do it* [preserve it] *and do it soon. Taylor became an enthusiastic supporter and I think that helped with Aspinall—I think he went back and said, "We have to do this."*[16]

The next morning they flew to Sun Valley where they cleaned up, then got ready for a scheduled hearing in the Opera House. Lee McElvain remembers the large crowd that was there, ". . .and it was a problem because with that many—I'm guessing, maybe 400—we couldn't give people enough time to testify. According to my memory, we divided the group by two or three and even then we had to restrict their time. The problem was that some of the folks went from room to room and testified more than once. But, overall, the testimony was strongly in favor of an SNRA and not for a national park. Also, most of the folks who testified were strongly opposed to mining in the White Clouds."[17]

The issue then went to Congress and the Subcommittee on National Parks and Recreation. More hearings were held, and McClure spent long hours crafting and recrafting language that would effect the compromises that would get the bill through the subcommittee, then the full committee. The most contentious issue was the language on how current and future mining was to be controlled. Aspinall was adamant; valid mining claims were private property and the owner either had to be allowed to work the property or should be compensated. No exceptions would be considered. Finally, McClure was able to create language that got the bill through both the subcommittee and the full committee.

There were several provisions. The Sawtooth Range, which had been classified and managed by the Forest Service as a primitive area, was to become a wilderness area and managed as such. The SNRA was to include Stanley Basin and the Sawtooth Valley, the White Cloud Range, and, in addition, the Boulder Mountains including several thousand acres south of Galena Pass. In the SNRA all mining claims (there were several thousand) were to be studied, and evaluated. Assessment work on those claims, which was a yearly requirement until the claim was "proved up," was exempted for five years—the idea being that this would prevent possible future damage to the environment. In addition, there was to be a five-year moratorium on the filing of new claims.

McClure pushed for this provision because he had already written a bill that would replace the antiquated 1872 Mining Law that had been subjected to many abuses. McClure thought that in five years a better law could be enacted. The SNRA bill, though not prohibiting the kind of activity ASARCO was proposing in the White Clouds, did give the Forest Service more authority to control potential damage and to retain the "pastoral, scenic, and recreational" value of the lands. Said Gray Reynolds, who was to become the first superintendent of the SNRA, "We would have preferred language that precluded all mining, but we all breathed a sigh of relief when we saw the language that came out of the committee. We were in a much stronger position, and, in addition, we had the threat to anadromous fish and the new Clean Water Act that we could use in regulating road building and mining activity."[18]

Also, the bill provided money to be used to buy out owners of private property—mostly cabins in new subdivisions—that detracted from the pastoral and scenic values, as well as money for establishing and administering the area. In addition, there was a provision in the bill requiring The Department of the Interior, through the National Park Service, to prepare a report for Congress that would evaluate and recommend whether or not the SNRA should become a National Park. That provision was a spur in the flank of the Forest Service for, as Gray Reynolds said, "We were determined that they [the Park Service] were not going to get their hands on that land."[19] [vii]

The SNRA bill reached the floor of the House on January 26, 1972 where Chairman Aspinall was the first to address its members. Early in his remarks he said:

> *I would be the first one to say to the Members that this has been a controversial piece of legislation, and I would be the first one to say to the members that the legislative process, properly and effectively handled, as in this instance, has brought to the Committee of the Whole what I consider to be one of the finest products that has come out of our committee for a long time. This kind of legislation is most difficult, because there are people sincerely oriented to their positions. . .To take a piece of legislation such as this and to bring into harmony the differing issues which are involved takes real work and dedication. . .*[20]

KIT CAPLES KIMBALL ON McCLURE AND THE SNRA

Kit Caples Kimball, a native of Salmon, Idaho, was McClure's legislative assistant specializing in wilderness and environmental issues. The following comments relate her memory of McClure and the struggle to create the SNRA.

My recollection is that Jim McClure understood extremely well the policy and approach the National Park Service and the Congress used when establishing a national park. A boundary is drawn and no private property is to remain. . . Traditional ranching and hunting, prevalent in the Sawtooth Basin, would not be allowed and, in addition, the creation of a Sawtooth National Park would have been like placing a bull's eye target on the middle of Idaho inviting the world to flood the sensitive high mountain environment. He believed also in private property rights, including water rights, and did not want individuals to lose them or the counties to lose more of their limited tax base. Instead, he knew that part of the beauty and unique quality of the Sawtooth Valley was the picturesque grazing meadows, outlined by jack-and-pole fences, and he wanted to see this traditional western, almost romantic ranching image remain for generations to appreciate. Therefore, his vision of keeping a working landscape in place while still protecting the magnificent backdrop of the Sawtooth mountains and crystalline lakes resulted in the national recreation concept. With this concept the meadow lands would remain in private hands, grazing would continue, but the land could never be sold for development rights. Essentially the SNRA froze the valley in time—about 1950's time compared to the rest of the country. The Senator had a visionary concept and it worked. In fact, it is working so well that the majority of people still don't know it exists, and don't know what a national recreation area means. That is exactly what Jim McClure envisioned—the preservation of one of the most magnificent mountain valleys in the world for all future generations and with its only advertisement a small, wooden welcome sign at its entrance.

Courtesy Jim Goller

Kit Caples Kimball, McClure's environmental aide, briefs an audience on SNRA. Aide Tom Hill is second from left, Hal Ryan, McClure's long-time finance chairman and close friend is to the right of Kit.

Several others, including McClure, spoke in favor of the legislation, but then John Saylor (R-Pennsylvania) took the floor. Only Orval Hansen was aware of Saylor's intent: "Saylor spoke to me just before the debate began. He was apologetic. He said that he would speak in opposition to the bill, noting that 'my people' had asked him to oppose it. . .I was surprised because this was my first indication that there was opposition."[21]

Saylor immediately let the members know how he felt, saying:

> *Mr. Chairman, I rise in opposition to this legislation. My colleagues know that I would be the first on my feet to praise this bill if it were indeed a bill to protect the magnificent Sawtooth-White Clouds area. But this bill is a sham. It provides the form of protection, but not the substance. Instead of designating these areas as a national park, as it should be, this bill provides a confusing, weak, and inherently ineffectual package of provisions, some of which work at direct odds with the goal of protecting the natural character of this area. . .* [22]

Saylor was the only member to voice opposition, and after his statement there was a call for a vote.[viii] The result: yeas-369, nays-9.

Both Hansen and McClure were relieved, mainly because they knew that John Saylor could have been a real threat to the legislation if he had gone all out and urged his lobbyist friends to get a campaign going with letters and telegrams to other congressmen. Looking back, Hansen said, "In retrospect, I am convinced that Saylor knew the bill must pass and that he wanted it to pass. The opponents urged defeat of the bill in the House. Had they prevailed, the bill would surely be dead for the 92nd Congress and it is doubtful that it would ever be considered again. Having suffered a humiliating defeat on a bill he had brought to the floor, Aspinall would probably have taken no further action on the legislation."[23]

McClure's retrospective view was not quite so gloomy, but he does believe that Saylor could have created problems. "If Saylor had gone all out, I think he could have mobilized a lot of opposition—how much I can't say. And maybe I'm a little more cynical but I suspect that our ability to replace him as ranking member [of the committee] by secret ballot could have influenced his decision not to bring in the heavy guns."[24]

The SNRA legislation still was not home free; it was up to a conference committee of the Senate and House to get together and agree on language to bridge the gaps between the two versions. Frank Church and Len Jordan were among the five senators who were "Managers on the Part of the Senate," while McClure, along with Aspinall and Taylor, two stalwart supporters, were among the five "Managers on the Part of the House." The result was a bill that strengthened future management's hand in controlling damage to the lands. For example, in Section 11:

> *The Congress hereby recognizes and declares the need to take action to regulate the use of, and protect the surface values of, the Federal lands in the recreation area, and directs that rules and regulations necessary to carry out this section shall be promulgated. . .Such regulations shall include, when deemed necessary, provisions for control of the use of motorized and mechanical equipment for transportation over, or alteration of, the surface of such Federal land in connection with any authorized activities on such land, including but not limited to* ***mineral prospecting, exploration, or development operations****. (*author's emphasis)[25]

Later, when McClure was asked how that might have affected ASARCO's request for road-building and exploration at the base of Castle Peak, he said: "There was no question in our minds that this provision of the bill would discourage ASARCO."[26]

There were three other significant changes. Instead of a five-year moratorium, "Patents shall not hereafter be issued for locations and claims heretofore made in the recreation area. . ." The House version, where holders of existing claims were excused from their yearly assessment work, did not survive the conference—the feeling being that valid claims should be proven or abandoned. The third change was one championed by McClure.

In the House bill that was passed, management of fishing and hunting was to be the responsibility of the federal government. McClure never did like that idea, and in the conference committee he was able to substitute wording that allowed the Idaho Fish and Game Department to regulate those activities.

On the same day the conference report went to the Senate, the legislation was passed by voice vote. Twelve days later, on August 14, 1972, it passed the House by a roll call vote of 363 to 0. On August 22, 1972 it was signed into law by President Nixon and became Public Law 92-400.

In an essay written much later, Orval Hansen tried to put the passage of the SNRA into perspective:

> *In retrospect, fortune favored those supporting the creation of the SNRA. There was a narrow window of opportunity. The need was clear and becoming more urgent. That helped to mobilize support among the public and close cooperation among the members of Idaho's congressional delegation. Had efforts stalled or the efforts of the last minute opponents prevailed, the window would have closed.*[27]

Chapter 17 notes

i. The DDT weakened the egg shells so when the birds sat upon their eggs during incubation, they were crushed.

ii. In 1943 Venezuela had 8,171,115 cases of malaria; by 1958, after the use of DDT, the number was down to 800. In Italy the number of malaria cases dropped from 411,602 in 1945 to only 37 in 1968.

iii. In the McClure archives there is even a letter from the Boise League of Women Voters pleading with him to save the White Clouds from the miners.

iv. A huge factor in that election was the 53,000 votes gathered by Perry Swisher and Phil Jungert, two independent candidates.

v. There is no precise definition of these regions but the present and former management of the Sawtooth National Forest call the region between Redfish Lake and the headwaters of the Salmon River the Sawtooth Valley, and the rest of the valley north of Redfish Lake, Stanley Basin. There are others who would argue with this delineation.

vi. The Democrats at the same time also voted to elect their ranking members, but by an open ballot. Needless to say, there was no change because the less senior representatives could not afford to antagonize senior members.

vii. Ed Fournier, who was the Sawtooth Forest Supervisor at the time remembers Governor Cecil Andrus at the SNRA dedication challenging the Forest Service to do a good job or otherwise expect the Park Service to take over. When he became Interior Secretary, he read the report and agreed with its conclusion that the area should remain as a recreation area.

viii. This was an historic vote for it was the first time the newly installed electronic voting system was used in the House.

Chapter 18
A New Opportunity

During his third term in the House, McClure felt really good about himself and what he was doing. In the Idaho Legislature he had carved out a niche where he became known as an indefatigable, good-natured workhorse, an exceedingly knowledgeable student of legislative rules and procedures, and, if not the best, certainly one of the most capable legislative craftsmen. By the time he was in his third term in the House, those who served with him on committees as well as those who served in leadership positions, had recognized those same traits, and he was confident that he could, if he kept working at it, carve out the same kind of niche as he had established in the Idaho Legislature.

However, he was refining some of his skills, particularly in the business of wordsmithing new legislation. Two specific challenges in that somewhat arcane endeavor could get his creative juices surging. One resulted from his observations of how government employees would often misinterpret a legislative document while writing regulations for its implementation—the result being regulations that they believed fulfilled "legislative intent," but which McClure believed were not even close to what the lawmakers who voted for the bill intended. Such practices offended him deeply; consequently, he took it as a special challenge to first detect, then persuade his colleagues to revise wording in bills so there would be absolutely no doubt about what the lawmakers had in mind when they passed a bill. And, later, when conflicts arose and were converted into legal challenges in the justice system, he did not want any judge to have to make an educated guess at what the lawmakers had in mind when they wrote the legislation. While superlatives are rightly looked upon as suspect, it is probably not too strong an opinion to suggest that McClure's desire to create clear language that could not be misinterpreted became an obsession.

McClure's obsession with clear language, if it could be called that, involved a lot of tedious, time-consuming work, and he might never see the rewards—in fact, if he did his job right, theoretically there might never be a legal battle where a judge would need to interpret legislative intent. Not so with the other challenge to which he was drawn. On practically every piece of legislation being considered, there were those who were for it and those who were against. A naive way of looking at that is simply to say, "Let the votes come down where they will and let's be done with it." There is a huge problem with that kind of thinking because many (most?) kinds of legislation get to lawmakers because there is a need to solve a problem. In 1971 land speculators and developers were starting to subdivide the Sawtooth Valley and the area was destined to be littered with thousands of cabins, summer homes and C-stores built on the scenic meadows where cattle had grazed for a century. What if lawmakers had held tightly to their positions and an SNRA bill had failed? A precious piece of Western America would have been forever lost.

In his essay on the history of the SNRA, Orval Hansen put this matter succinctly when he said, "We were determined that the perfect should not be the enemy of the good."[1] In a word the SNRA exists today because the lawmakers compromised. For zealots of all persuasions, compromise is a dirty word. For McClure, especially, it was an art. And it was an art that he practiced with his pen. Listening to a discussion in a committee meeting, McClure's antennae were always finely tuned to detect the slightest hint of softness in the positions of antagonists, his mind always groping for language that would shave the sharp edge off a sore point. And when he was one of the antagonists himself, there were undoubtedly occasions when he was torn between some lovely compromise language that one side of his brain created, while the other side of his brain held a position that was dear to his heart. To say that he was a good actor when in these positions might be an exaggeration. But to those who observed him at such work, such as Lee McElvain and Charlie Leppert, majority and minority counsels of the interior committee who watched him work for six years, McClure clearly had an uncanny ability to appear apolitical when he was trying to get two sides together. Today he will only admit to "liking" such challenges, but if truth be known, there was probably an artist's glint in his eye as he penned and tested trial verbiage on warring antagonists.

McClure's talents were also being recognized outside of his committees. In March, 1971, Republican Majority Leader Gerald Ford named McClure as one of three GOP advisers on legislation to be placed on the House Consent Calendar, a job that required him to sift general legislation and decide whether or not a bill was noncontroversial enough to be sent directly to the Floor, or to the rules committee where its merits could be debated. Ford said he chose McClure "because of Jim's demonstrated interest in reforming the rules of the House and his skill as a parliamentarian."[2] That same month he was named chairman of a House Republican conference task force on energy and resources, a prestigious job that recognized his growing reputation as an authority on energy—a reputation that would continue to grow in the next few years. In addition, he was named as captain of one of the three-representative GOP teams that would go out into the nation and explain President Nixon's legislative agenda as outlined in his state of the union address—especially the concept of revenue sharing, a wholly new approach to financing government.

In the summer of 1971, at age 46, it is safe to say that McClure was at the prime of his life, physically and mentally. And, and in his new profession, he was almost unassailable by his colleagues or by the voters of his district. Every year he gained supporters at home. The folks in the First District liked him personally; they liked the way he thought like they did about the tough issues of the time; and they liked the way he was doing his job in Washington. Sometimes career politicians have all that McClure had at that time, but suffered where it counted the most: at home. McClure had no home problems. He had a loving, devoted wife who, despite his long hours and frequent travel, squared her shoulders, and basically said to herself, "Okay, that's the way it is; I'm a big girl with the responsibility of raising three kids and I'm going to make the best of it." And the three kids themselves? Each has said, upon looking back on those years, that they enjoyed their life in Arlington and had no regrets.

Yet, there was talk behind the scenes about a major change in his life, talk between Goller and McClure about Len Jordan. Jordan was 73 years old and his term as U.S. Senator from Idaho would end the next year. Would he run again? He would be almost 80 when the next term expired. Would he want to serve that long? Jordan was not talking and some of his staff got upset when they heard that Jim Goller was speculating that he would not run. "I kind of got in a little trouble with some of Jordan's staff when some of my comments about him not running got back to them," Goller admitted later, "but I was serious; I didn't think he would run again and I wanted McClure thinking about running to replace him. I remember we talked several times about it."[3]

McClure remembers that Goller brought up the subject "at least more than once," but he also remembers not giving it a lot of serious thought. And for good reason. Looking at his travel schedule in 1971, one wonders how *any* correspondence got out of his office—he was still doing his no-phony-signature-machine-for-me number and driving his staff crazy because of the unsigned letters piled high on his desk, sofa, and any other flat surface they could find in his office. Then, on August 21, after the SNRA field trip and hearings, he had just arrived in Alaska with an interior committee delegation that would be evaluating what the proposed Trans-Alaska Pipeline might do to the state when Jim Goller tracked him down and phoned him. Goller told him that Len Jordan had decided to hang it up and that there would undoubtedly be a crowded primary race the next summer. "We need to get a placeholder in as soon as possible," Goller said. "We have to get in this thing and we can't fool around. Smylie is sure to run and a bunch of others are going to jump in. I'm sure of it."[4]

Goller says that McClure hemmed and hawed and was not ready to make a commitment. "I told him, 'You don't have to announce that you are going to run; just let me put out a release saying that you are *thinking* of running—that you are giving it strong consideration. That might discourage some people who are thinking of jumping in.'" McClure, himself, does not remember the exact conversation nor even whether it was Goller or someone on his Washington staff who called him. But Goller is adamant that he was the one, not only who called McClure, but the one who got McClure's permission to release a statement to the press that he was giving it strong consideration. "I wrote the statement and gave it to the press. I remember it well."[5]

The release said, in part:

> *I am surprised! I fully expected Senator Jordan to run for re-election, and if he had, I would have given him my full support . . .His announcement not to run of course creates a 'new ball game.' I would be less than candid with my supporters if I did not say at this time that I am definitely interested. However, it will take careful appraisal. I will talk with party leaders and key people throughout the state in the next few weeks before I begin to arrive at any sort of conclusion. . .*[6]

Three announcements followed closely. F. W. (Bill) Bergeson, a former state senator from Pocatello, announced that he would be a candidate for the Republican nomination next August in the primary. Then former governor Robert Smylie announced that he, too, was a candidate for the nomination. This was followed by an announcement from Washington where former Congressman George Hansen was working. Like McClure, he said that he was strongly considering a run at the nomination. Then from Seattle, where former Governor Don Samuelson was working, came news that he, too, was considering a run at the nomination.

Soon after this news spread, the mail started pouring into McClure's office. Here are snippets of nine out of the hundreds he received, practically all with the same message:

> *Dear Congressman McClure:*
>
> *I think you should re-consider your apparent decision to run for Senator. I am in almost complete agreement with your House votes and political positions and should you run for Senator I will support you both financially and with such influence as I may have. However, I believe your candidacy will split the conservative vote between you and Mr. Hansen, and give the Republican nomination to Bob Smylie. After this, no matter which way the general election comes out, Idaho*

will end up with two liberal senators and lose your considerable influence in the House. . .[7]

Dear Jim:

. . .The one thing bothering me about your entering this race is the number of conservatives running for this seat. If I read the newspapers correctly, it looks like George Hansen, a Mr. Bergeson. . .and possibly Don Samuelson are thinking about running. If you make the decision to run that will make four conservatives running against former Governor Smylie, who is at best known as a moderate, and for all practical purposes can be considered liberal. My concern is that four conservatives making the run will divide the conservative vote four ways and once again we conservatives will...lose out because we cannot get together behind one good candidate like yourself. . .[8]

Dear Sir:

We have been deeply disturbed by rumors we have been hearing that you are considering giving up your seat in the House of Representatives to throw your hat in the ring for the Senate seat to be vacated by Senator Len Jordan. . .we would like to urge you to stay right where you are. You have been doing such a great job for the State of Idaho and we cannot afford to lose you as our representative. . .we feel that your seniority in the House is too important to our State right now to jeopardize in the hope that you can be elected to the Senate position. . .[9]

Dear Jim:

I am concerned about the coming primary election. . .George Hansen is going to run for the Senate. Smylie has already announced and there is a possibility that Samuelson may get into the fray. If you enter this race I can only predict a Smylie primary win. . .With you and George splitting off the conservative vote I can only see Smylie coming down the middle and winning. . .[10]

Dear Congressman:

You have strong support in my neighborhood. . .in your present position. . .don't make the effort for Senator. My opinion is you'll be among the unemployed.[11]

Dear Friend:

Those few I have talked to around Fruitland express the thot [sic] *that you had better stay where you are that you won't make it in a try for the senate. We want you in Washington so don't pull a "Gracie post"* [veteran First District Representative who ran for the Senate and was defeated].[12]

Dear Jim:

As an old follower of the game, my advice to you, whether you want it or not is: If Bob Smylie runs and he is, is for you to stay where you are. You will be elected there but it is a question with the Senate. Nuf said.[13]

Dear Representative McClure:

I have talked to hundreds of people throughout Idaho and I find a strong feeling that you should remain in the Congress...You are assured to be re-elected [but] *you are playing right in to the hands of Robert E. Smylie and Frank Church. If you would give Smylie the nomination, there would be no question that he would be decisively defeated. . .*[14]

Dear Jim:

For the good of your District and more especially for your own future I entreat you not to enter the Senate race. . .The primary contest would split your supporters. You would be through for the House. . .Better be safe and sorry than out *and sorry. . .*[15]

During conversations with Goller he was asked repeatedly, "Didn't letters like that have a dampening effect? And what about their message; didn't it seem feasible that the three conservatives (Samuelson backed out) would split the vote and let Smylie get the nomination?

Goller's memory says that he had little concern. He said:

Yeah, what they were saying seemed to have merit, but listen, I'd thought a lot about McClure's strengths. We had that First District solid—neither Hansen nor Bergeson could touch us there. Then Bergeson got killed in a head-on, a guy coming the wrong way on the freeway here in Boise as I recall. And, yes, Hansen would be strong in eastern Idaho with his Mormon support, but remember, there were a lot of voters in the Magic Valley—Twin Falls County, Jerome County—and even in eastern Idaho there are a lot of non-Mormons in Oneida and Fremont counties. I had the numbers. I had worked on it. I figured the surplus of votes we would get in the First District would more than offset Hansen's vote in the Second [District].

But that doesn't mean that we weren't concerned. I could tell that McClure was skittish—I even think a time or two he thought I was leading him astray. But, we had taken one poll and it showed that McClure was strong. Then we met with Hansen, in the motel annex of the old Bannock Hotel in Pocatello, and we offered him a deal. McClure and I. We explained that we were concerned about tearing the party apart in a tough primary campaign, and we said that we would make a decision based upon a new poll—we offered to use a Mormon pollster—his name was Dick Wirthlin—he was Nixon's pollster and he became the main pollster for the Republican Party—thinking that Hansen would trust that kind of poll. We said, "Our deal is this: whoever has the most strength in the poll stays in, the other drops out. Hansen wouldn't go for it.[i] *He was determined to run, and I think he felt that he was a better campaigner than Jim and thought that he would gain strength during a campaign—strength that a poll at that time wouldn't show. I am speculating about that. He didn't tell us what he was thinking.*[16]

KIRK SULLIVAN COMMENTS

Kirk Sullivan, who worked under Larry Mills (former speaker of the Idaho House of Representatives) at Boise Cascade Corporation, was the youngest member of McClure's official in-state advisory committee—a committee Goller called his "Kitchen Cabinet." Said Sullivan, when asked how he and the other advisors felt about McClure's chances against Smylie and Hansen:

I remember when Len Jordan called Larry Mills and told him that he was not going to run. It was only a matter of seconds later when he came to me and told me to get in touch with McClure and tell him that he has to run. And yes, there were some who felt that McClure should stay in his safe seat and that Smylie might slip in there with conservatives splitting the vote, but none of us in the Kitchen Cabinet felt that way. A lot of it was Goller—he was absolutely positive that this would not happen. As far as George Hansen was concerned, I think he felt that he deserved the nomination since he had run against Church—it was the "I'm the martyr and everybody else should get out of the way" kind of thing. Getting back to Goller, I've since been working around the political scene for the past 35 years and I can truthfully say that he is one of the smartest political strategists I have ever met. It would be very easy to understate his role in McClure's political victories.

At another time, in a conversation with McClure, he was asked to recall that meeting. At first he was not even sure that such a meeting took place, but after hearing what Goller said about it, his memory was jogged and he confirmed that they had, indeed, made such a proposal to Hansen. "What was Hansen's attitude when you met?" McClure was asked. "You two had been good friends during your first two years in Congress?" McClure said that the meeting was cordial, ". . .but they were not lovey-dovey conversations; I was standing in the way of something he wanted to do. . .I don't think anybody could have stopped Hansen. I think he thought that he could beat everybody."[17]

Later, Goller remembered that, at a separate meeting, he had offered the same deal to Bergeson—this was before Bergeson's fatal accident. "He turned me down, too. He felt that as a relative newcomer his lack of name recognition, especially in the First District, would cause him to show up badly in a poll, but that when he started campaigning, he could overcome that handicap." [18]

Then the race became even more complicated. Doctor Glen Wegner, 32, of Kendrick, a medical doctor as well as lawyer, and an aide to White House presidential counselor, Robert Finch, declared his candidacy for the GOP nomination.

McClure announced his interest in running for the Senate in late August. He said nothing else publicly for the next two and one-half months. Then, on November 17, in a Boise press conference he said:

> *. . .It is somewhat early for a formal announcement. . .but I think it is only fair to let others know now who are interested in running for the* First *District House seat. . .I have carefully considered all the alternatives and tested all the arguments. I have used every method of evaluation I know, from professional studies to a family conference. . .the decision has not been an easy one to make, but I have decided that I will be a candidate for the Republican nomination for the United States Senate . . .* [19]

About the same time George Hansen announced that he was resigning his position as deputy administrator of the Agricultural Stabilization and Conservation Service and had also made his decision to run. When a reporter asked him how he felt about competing with all the other candidates, his reply seemed to shrug off the potential conflict. "I guess it makes it all the more interesting when you get a horse race," he said.[20]

What did McClure think at the time?

I wasn't unhappy in the House. I remember when I went in to tell Jerry Ford [Gerald Ford (R-Michigan) Minority Leader] *what I was planning, he was disappointed because he assured me that I was destined to soon move into the House Leadership—he was also a little frustrated, telling me that every time he got someone promising they wanted to run off and leave the House and run for the Senate. I went away feeling a bit chastised, but it was also satisfying to have been told what my future might have been in the House had I stayed there. So it wasn't that I was unhappy in the House or that I was frustrated there. Looking back, I just felt certain that I could be more effective in a smaller body like the Senate—that I could do more to serve Idaho.*

But there was another factor, and both Louise and their daughter-in-law, Sally, brought it up. Said Sally, who was son, Ken's, high school sweetheart when McClure was making his decision, "I can remember that Jim's family was also getting tired of the every-two-year campaigning that they had to do. And even when they weren't involved, he was running off to Idaho every weekend leaving them alone."[21] Louise then admitted, "It was a drag on the family,[ii] and I can remember that when we talked about it [his running for the Senate], he got a very encouraging reaction from the kids who were tired of him being gone all the time."[22]

McClure then faced up to the direct question: Was the thought of having to campaign only once every six years instead of every two years a factor in your decision to run for the Senate? McClure replied: "Yes, I think that not having to run every two years had something to do with it. There was no question in my mind that service in the Senate would be easier on my family. That did influence my decision, no doubt about it."[23]

So it was decided. There would be a campaign fight unlike anything ever seen in Idaho history.

Chapter 18 Notes

i. Dick Worthlin did conduct a poll and, according to Goller, went over the results privately with George Hansen. It showed that McClure was the stronger candidate.

ii. Ken McClure did not feel that way. Said he: "I don't harbor any regrets about dad being gone so much; we still maintained a strong sense of family. I remember that after church on Sunday, we would always go on to dinner when I would rather have gone home and watched football—also that I had to keep a tie on for another two hours. And lots of weekends we traveled; mom was a voracious advocate for making that happen. . .and I worked five summers at the Miller farm and I think Dave also worked there for at least one summer.

Chapter 19

Getting the Nomination

McClure still had over a year to serve in the House when he announced his intention to run for the Senate. And it would be a busy year. Besides the extra duties in the House that the leadership had assigned, as captain of a three-representative team, he had to make numerous forays out into the hinterlands to sell President Nixon's new legislative agenda. And that, by coincidence, led to more extra-curricular activities.

One of the persons on his team, Marvin Esch (R-Michigan), was a former college professor and the kind of person to which McClure was naturally drawn because of their mutual philosophies. One day while they were discussing various matters and trends in the government, they noted that during the last presidential election Richard Nixon carried the Southern states, and by a good margin. This was unprecedented. Since the end of the Civil War those states were solidly Democratic—Republicans were dirty dogs in the South, because of Lincoln and because the party was behind what they felt were the evils of Reconstruction. This breakthrough by Nixon led the two men to a discussion of the current situation in the House of Representatives. Most of the House committees were chaired by Southern Democrats, all with many years of seniority. However, as they well knew, these Democrats really were not Democrats philosophically; they were all conservative and very often voted with the Republicans in the House—especially in recent years as many Democrats under President Lyndon Johnson had moved well left of center. As McClure and Esch discussed this inconsistency, which was well known on Capitol Hill at the time, they began wondering what it might take to cause those committee chairmen to switch parties—to declare themselves to be Republicans rather than Democrats. Of course, this was unlikely; they had their seniority by virtue of their long membership in the Democratic Party. But then McClure and Esch asked themselves another question: How would the ranking Republicans on those committees feel if their chairmen would switch parties; would they agree to let those chairmen remain in the chairman's position, or would they fight that idea and want to claim the positions for themselves? If the former rather than the latter were to occur, McClure and Esch could see that many other Southern Democrats would be motivated to switch parties. And, *voila,* the House would then be controlled by the Republicans!

This was more than an intriguing thought. Feeling that they had little to lose, they began discussing the idea with some of their friends. McClure does not now remember whom or how many, but a small group of them laid out a battle plan and they went to work. McClure and Esch selected the Appropriations Committee, the most powerful committee in the House. Esch went to the chairman, George Mahon of Texas, while McClure met with Frank Bow of Ohio, the ranking Republican. Esch struck out; Mahon wanting nothing to do with such a scheme.[1] McClure was more successful; Bow was interested, although McClure still remembers the bemused expression on his face when he explained the proposition, like "What are these young guys really up to?" But the good news was that several others had success, both with the Democratic chairmen and the Republican ranking members. "We thought we were on to something quite significant," McClure recalls, "but a big problem arose. Nixon, in order to force Southern integration of the public schools, ordered mandatory busing and that ended our pipe dream. No way were the Democratic chairmen going to switch parties after that happened."[2]

However, according to Dick Thompson, McClure's administrative assistant, that really did not end the dream. "That was just an example of the way McClure's mind worked," said Thompson. "I remember that we talked often and at length about those conservative Democrats and how they really belonged with the Republicans. But McClure was like that. His mind was always ranging beyond most of his colleagues; he was constantly thinking of ways to expand the conservative base against the big-government liberals. This project in the House was just a start. This kind of creative thinking was about to pay off."[3]

But before that would happen, and even before he could enter the race for the Republican nomination for Len Jordan's Senate seat, McClure would have to endure a living nightmare. On Tuesday, May 2, 1972, horrific news reached him in Washington. In the Sunshine Mine, located on Big Creek between Kellogg and Wallace in his home district——the largest silver mine in the nation—an estimated 100 miners were trapped by fire and smoke between three and five-thousand feet below the surface. His regional assistant, Ruthie Johnson, who had phoned him in Washington with the news, was now back on the phone pleading with him to do everything in his power to get Bureau of Mines rescue crews to the mine as fast as possible. These were teams of specialists trained to handle such emergencies; however, because fires were so unlikely in the hard-rock mines of the West, all of these teams were in the East where the coal mines were located and where mine fires and other disasters were much more likely.

McClure spent the rest of that Tuesday and the next two days living on the telephone, getting the rescue crews mobilized and arranging authorization for their transportation to Spokane with the Military Air Transport

Service. "Those days are just a blur to me now," McClure said more than thirty years later. "Knowing that those men were trapped down there—that was so horrible to me that I have just blotted most of that from my mind. However, I do remember one incident that made me angry. I was dealing with Rog [Rogers] Morton [Secretary of the Interior] at the time and I remember him saying, 'Well, somebody's to blame for that disaster.' I know I flared back at him and said, 'There is such a thing as an accident, you know.' My nerves were raw and I didn't like him prejudging my people."[4]

When asked what if anything else McClure was doing during that crisis, Dick Thompson replied, "I just remember that McClure had to do most of the phoning and arranging. We would have liked to help him but, at the levels he was dealing, staff just couldn't do it. I also remember that he swore us to secrecy when he left for Idaho."[5]

McClure left for Idaho on Friday. Ruthie Johnson picked him up in Spokane and she clearly remembers McClure's preoccupation with secrecy:

> *He made it very clear to me in his call from Washington that there was to be no press release on his visit and no word to anybody else. I was the only one who was to know that he was coming. That really irked me. Here* [Governor] *Andrus had come into town. . .with everybody knowing that he was concerned and my own boss was not going to get any credit at all for being there. I know when we got to the mine, all of the press had been expelled and were crowded outside the fence—earlier, reporters were sticking microphones in front of grieving widows asking them how it felt to have lost their husbands in the mine. When the manager, Marvin Chase, found out about that, he was really angry, and he ran them all out. They were from everywhere—New York, England, Germany . . .Well, when I was taking McClure to the mine it was getting a little dark and I was worried how I was going to slip him in there without the press seeing him, but I was able to manage that. Coincidentally, the board of directors had been meeting in Spokane when the fire broke out, so while I talked with the president, McClure went into the office and Marvin Chase briefed him with diagrams, outlining the various strategies; then McClure went over where the wives and relatives of the miners still unaccounted for were waiting. His whole attitude was: I want to be sure that the government is doing everything possible to help with this situation. Actually, his presence there was really appreciated and word of it spread mouth-to-mouth throughout the community. I think that helped him in the long run.*[6]

McClure remembers the relatives, a sad experience he said he would remember for the rest of his life. "There was a pall over the whole community because everyone knew everybody. It was unlike anything I ever experienced, seeing those families sitting there, silently waiting. I know I had conflicting feelings about what I should do. If I said something, would they be thinking, 'Here's this politician trying to make himself look good.' If they looked like they wanted to talk, I visited with them. If they didn't, I left them alone."

"Why all the secrecy imposed on your visit?" he was asked. McClure was vehement with his answer. "I have a very strong feeling of revulsion against politicians who exploit tragedies like that to bring attention to themselves; that's why I tried to impose secrecy on the visit. I actually considered not coming at all just for that reason, but I also felt that I needed to be there. It was a real tragedy—there is no other way to describe it."[7]

By the end of the following week all of the miners had been accounted for and ninety-one of them were dead. Investigations and hearings followed, and three years after the tragedy the government report was published. The official conclusion: the exact cause of the fire was unknown.

McClure practically erased his memory of those two horrible weeks, but it seems reasonable to speculate that the event depressed him as much as the deaths of his brother and grandfather back in the '40s. And, if Goller was correct in thinking McClure may have felt that he was being led astray a few times before the Senate race got underway, the aftermath of the Sunshine Mine tragedy would have been a good time for him to have had second thoughts. He was well aware that his support had grown dramatically in the First District, and the tragic experience in Shoshone County undoubtedly made him much more aware of how close he had come to his people in the six years he had served them. Would he at that time have harbored regrets about his decision to leave the House and run for the Senate? Would he have debated with himself, arguing in his mind that had he instead decided to remain in the House he could have been a committee chairman or in the leadership—positions that would have given him much greater power to provide for his constituents?

That is not likely. Perhaps he did have a few second thoughts, but in conversations where past events are measured by those more current, he always proclaimed, "The past is just that; it is the past and there is nothing I can do about it so I have a tendency to blot it out and look to the future." So, while the tragedy in the Sunshine Mine may have depressed him, it was the future he had to face. And Goller's feelings notwithstanding about McClure being mislead into the Senate race, another of McClure's oft-stated declarations is appropriate: "Whenever I agree to do something, it is a point of honor to me to respect that commitment." So, yes, he was undoubtedly feeling remorse and a bit of depression in the weeks following his unhappy trip to Kellogg. But, no, he was not having second thoughts about fighting it out with George Hansen and Bob Smylie and Glen Wegner. If truth be known, he was probably looking forward to the battle.

And that fight would be costly. Goller knew that and McClure knew that, and those who had worked to raise money in McClure's three previous campaigns knew that most of all. Hal Ryan, the Weiser attorney and McClure's closest personal friend, had served as treasurer since the beginning of the first campaign. But Ryan was not a money raiser and neither was McClure—in fact, according to Goller, McClure found it distasteful if the subject of campaign money even came up when he was around any of his supporters. So who was going to get out and raise the 250-300 thousand dollars that Goller estimated they would need just for the primary campaign?

And that was less than half of the problem. An even greater problem for Goller, at least, was: How was McClure going to manage to get a fair share of the votes in the Second District, particularly in Eastern Idaho where George Hansen, as a Mormon, was bound to be a sympathetic favorite among those who were fellow believers.

> **RUTHIE JOHNSON ON MARVIN CHASE**
>
> *Marvin Chase was obsessed with getting his men out, and every night, after leaving the mine, he would visit the families of the miners for two or three hours, go home and get a little sleep; then be back at the mine at six the next morning. Two years later there was a dedication of the memorial to the lost miners. Marvin Chase spoke for the company; then the head of the union spoke for the union members. The widows and families were to have a speaker, and they asked Marvin Chase to speak for them. It was amazing, after such a tragedy, the families would ask the manager of the mine to be their spokesman. They wrote a beautiful letter to him, thanking him for his concern and kindness. Senator McClure was so impressed with the letter that he had it printed in the* Congressional Record.

Goller gets a sly look in his eye when he looks back and thinks of the money-raising problem they faced.

> *We had an advantage that nobody else was really thinking about,* he said with just a hint of smugness. *I knew that Smylie didn't stand a chance. I predicted he would come in last and he did. He was never that well liked around the state. Yeah, he was a three-term governor, but in two of his campaigns he ran against pro-gambling candidates that had no chance in this state. And you remember, in 1964 he was a Rockefeller fan when most of the Republicans in the state were for Goldwater. That didn't go down well. So when he announced* [for the Senate] *there were a lot of Republicans that were worried that he might slip in there if McClure and Hansen split the vote. They didn't want that; they didn't want him going back there and teaming up with Frank Church. The money didn't just come running to us, but to be truthful, I knew there were a lot of donors out there who were scared*

to death of Smylie. Not only that, they weren't all that fond of Hansen either; they didn't trust him the way they did McClure. So, I don't think I was all that worried about money. Yeah, it was a problem; no doubt about it. But I didn't see it as a huge problem.[8]

The Mormons in Eastern Idaho were another problem and Goller had a strategy for them. His greatest asset in breaking into that tight-knit community was his candidate.

McClure had great family values and he had impeccable morals—two attributes that were highly valued in that culture. I never expected that we were going into that territory and come out on top. Hansen was going to beat us in all of those Mormon dominated counties. That was a given. Our strategy was two-fold. One, after compiling a list of all the stake presidents and bishops—names we got from the yellow pages of the phone directories—we were going to get McClure into those communities and with those leaders. We did that—oftentimes I would remain in the car while McClure went into a home or business and met with the individuals one-on-one. Most of the time, of course, he would hear that these leaders were going to support George Hansen, but, most important, he would also hear many say that should Hansen not win the nomination, they would support McClure in the general election. That was our first goal in the strategy: cement that support for down the line when it would really count.

The second element of our strategy was to keep Hansen on the defensive. By us campaigning aggressively in his territory, we wanted Hansen to feel the threat so he would stay in that territory and feel that he dare not leave and campaign in the First District. We wanted him to think that we might be cutting into his margin so he would be afraid to leave and campaign where we were the strongest and he was the weakest.[9]

The Mormon strategy, however, was not quite that simple because George Hansen, even before the campaign started, did a mailing that was an attempt to poison McClure's image with Mormon leaders. Chris Carlson, who was a reporter in Washington, D.C. and whose beat was Capitol Hill, explains how that came about:

One day in November, 1971, I went into McClure's office for an interview on the Prayer Amendment, which was a hot issue at the time and for which McClure had voted favorably, but which his colleague, Orval Hansen, had voted against. I had already interviewed Orval and, because McClure was always an imminently logical person, I was anxious to ask questions to get his reasoning on why he supported the amendment. It was an amicable discussion, as any conversation with McClure always was, and near the end of the interview I asked him if there was somewhere he would draw the line between church and state. He said, "Yes, there is: on release time." Now "release time" is the time that LDS [Mormon] *students in the public schools are allowed to leave school, cross the street and receive religious instruction. This could be a highly controversial opinion so just to be sure that I heard him correctly I made it a point to ask the question again: "Let me make sure I get this straight—you say that release time is a place to draw the line.' He said, "That is correct." I closed my notebook, walked out of his office and turned to Dick Thompson, his administrative assistant and said, "Dick, I have to tell you, your boss just said he was opposed to release time.' Dick said, "What is that?'* [Thompson had never been in Idaho] *I replied as I went out, "Dick, if you don't know, in about three days Jim Goller is going to call you and explain what release time is." Of course, I had gone in for a story on the Prayer Amendment, but I knew that the real story would be in the last paragraph of my column, which I regularly sent to six Idaho newspapers. In that last paragraph I quoted McClure as saying that there, indeed, was a place to draw the line between church and state and that release time was an example for which he was opposed. About a week later Jim Goller called me and said, "Chris, the congressman is going to be sending you a letter." "About what?' I asked. Goller said, "I'm also sending this letter to all the papers who run your column." I asked again, "About what?" He replied, "About your column on release time." I said, "I hope he doesn't say he was misquoted—I made it very clear to him that I wanted to be doubly sure that I was quoting him accurately." "Oh, no, he's not going to say you misquoted him; he is going to say he misunderstood the question." I said, "Fair enough; that's his prerogative." What happened, of course, was that George Hansen, who was about to launch a comeback campaign for the Senate* [he had run against Frank Church in 1968 and was defeated], *circled that paragraph in my column and personally mailed it to every LDS stake and bishop in the state.*[10]

As Goller told Carlson, he immediately tried to limit the damage by sending a letter (that McClure approved) to the newspapers that had run the reporter's column. In part it said:

Apparently I did not make myself clear to the reporter. I was discussing the vote on the Prayer Amendment which I supported, and stated that I did not understand why some people were opposed to voluntary prayer in a public building and yet did not raise an objection to other forms of government recognition of religious practices. I gave examples such as Federal aid to colleges, some of which are church related institutions. . .and release time for religious instruction. . .It was not my intention in giving these examples to indicate any opposition to any of them but to indicate that the amendment for voluntary prayer in public buildings is much less a recognition of religion than many of these practices. The reporter evidently interpreted this as my being in opposition to them. . .[11]

Later, in a series of letters to Mormon leaders McClure himself authored, he alluded to Hansen's backhanded attack:

I am writing you to reaffirm my position on release time. I don't see how my earlier statements could be misunderstood, but the question keeps coming up. This is evidence, I guess, that someone for whatever reason is trying to create a political issue where there should be none. . .I want to make it as plain as I possibly can that I favor religious instruction and am in favor of strengthening church and family influence in our lives . . .Releasing children from school for religious instruction is one way to accomplish that goal. . .[12]

More than thirty years after this controversy McClure was asked how he felt wading into Mormon territory with this kind of cloud hanging over his head. Immediately he grew a bit testy while giving a spirited defense of his feelings about the Mormons. "The Mormon Church is a marvelous social organization," he declared. "It is a model, and the strength of their church is in their organization. If they are going to build a stake house, they get it built and they run it. They have no paid minister or paid janitor, and the church is paid for when it is built because the congregation has paid for it. They have great strength, partly because they started as a persecuted minority. It gave them discipline at the time they had to have it as fledglings. I'm awed by it."[13]

"Then you weren't afraid to charge into George Hansen's territory?" he was asked. "Not a bit," he replied. "I had friends over there and also I had served with many of them in the legislature. I respected them and I think they respected me."[14]

Jim Goller's grand strategy for winning the primary had two other components. Said Goller:

At the time, there was a conservative direct-mail fund raiser in Virginia named Richard Viguerie—he would only help conservative candidates. I knew his services were expensive, but I talked McClure into signing him on to help us in the primary because I wanted to keep George Hansen from tying him up. The way he worked is he sent out a mass mailing all over the country to known conservatives—he had a huge data base—I think his first mailing for us might have been to a million people. Then he might get 200 to 300-thousand back and then he would send out letters to them. Now this was terribly expensive—we could easily spend 350-thousand dollars to get back 375 or 400-thousand dollars. But then, after the second mailing, he would have what he called a "refined list" and presumably the cost-benefit ratio would be much more favorable with the next mailings. Of course, we had to pay the up-front cost for sending out those mailings. After he did two or three for us, we simply cut him off—McClure and I were too conservative to gamble on more mailings. Viguerie got upset over that, saying that he was just getting a refined list that would pay off for us. So, as I recall, we ended up making very little money with Viguerie but we did keep George Hansen from using his services.[15 i]

The plan to let those who feared Smylie make generous donations to McClure; the strategy to keep George Hansen tied down campaigning in his own territory and out of the First District; the plan to go one-on-one with Mormon leaders in Eastern Idaho; and the idea of tying up Richard Viguerie so Hansen couldn't use him—these might be called the strategic elements of Goller's campaign plan. But, Goller also had a tactical campaign plan in mind—a plan that would get individual McClure voters to the polls and the ballot box.

Goller's tactical strategy relied very heavily upon picking good county coordinators, giving them very reasonable goals and quotas, and, especially, relying upon the petition signers in each county as a firm nucleus of supporters who could be used to extend McClure support to a small, but realistic number of other supporters. In addition, these same petition signers could be used as a potential labor supply for what might be called the "grunt" work of the campaign: for distributing bumper stickers, yard signs, hustling people when McClure visited the county, and on Election Day, finding baby sitters, volunteers to man telephones, and drivers to transport people to the polls.

Another component to the tactical plan was to have an enthusiastic motivator out in the field, away from campaign headquarters, who would get to know and who would work closely with the county coordinators. Goller found just such a man. His name was Jack Holley, an Idahoan who had run unsuccessfully for state auditor against an unbeatable Idaho institution, Democrat Joe Williams, two years earlier. Undaunted by that defeat, he joined the McClure campaign in January and for the next four months roamed Idaho getting acquainted with county coordinators and preparing them for Goller's tactical plan when it would be revealed. Probably the highest accolades for his work, both initially and during the campaign, came from McClure himself who said, "Jack Holley was a good motivator, and people really liked him and responded to him."[16]

The major variable in the plan was the candidate, himself. With the Primary scheduled for August 8, it would have been ideal for the campaign to start in early June, especially since McClure was not well known in the Second District. However, his congressional load was heavy, if not crushing at that particular time. He was still fighting to get an SNRA bill passed in the House, and when that occurred, he had to be the key craftsman in the conference committee for the markup session. In addition, he had to honor commitments for his extracurricular duties in the House, and he had hearings and other responsibilities in the aftermath of the Sunshine Mine disaster. "But we got him for a lot of weekends," said Goller, "and in July—I can't remember how many—but there were some recesses and we made good use of them."[17]

Of course, the other candidates knew they were running behind McClure and in their campaigning, for which they had unlimited time, they pounced on every issue they thought might hurt him and help them. For example, Glen Wegner was going around the state criticizing McClure's attendance record in the House, pointing out to his audiences that McClure's attendance for roll-call votes in 1971 was a miserable 58 percent. McClure was continually on the defensive on this issue, always pointing out, when he had a chance, that there were good reasons for this low attendance record, the major one being that the Speaker of the House appointed him to represent Congress at a Lead-Zinc International Conference in Madrid for several days—an appointment he justified because of the importance of lead and zinc production in Shoshone County. In an attempt to rebut such criticism he put out a news release in late July that said, ". . .It just happened that 10 percent of the roll-call votes that year occurred during the time I was gone—a time I felt I was better serving my constituents by being at that Conference. But blaming me for that is a distortion of the facts. I have an over-all average of 82.5 percent for the five and one-half years I have been in Congress. This compares favorably with an average yearly attendance of 81 percent for Senator Church, 89 percent for Senator Jordan, 85 percent for Congressman Orval Hansen and 72 percent for former Congressman George Hansen."[18]

But Wegner was not a threat. Bill Hall, the editorial writer for the *Lewiston Morning Tribune*, said, after attending the Republican State Convention in June, "Wegner, the 33-year-old former White House staff member from Kendrick, is spoken of so highly and treated so kindly by the other three candidates that it probably indicates they don't consider him a threat. Most of the delegates told me they expect Wegner to finish last in the Aug. 8 primary."

In the same report Hall also describes a bizarre speech George Hansen delivered to the delegates:

> *. . .One of the strangest episodes in the convention came when Hansen, who was trounced in 1968 by Democratic Sen. Frank Church, took his turn before the microphone. He began by virtually boasting that he is going to win by writing off north Idaho and concentrating on a heavy sweep of south central and southeastern Idaho. Several north Idaho delegates were offended by what Hansen called his "southern strategy." Hansen also launched into a vague tirade against "political manipulators" in the party, charging that those unnamed manipulators have tried to freeze him out of the Senate race. In one of the greatest distortions of a political episode in my memory, Hansen suggested that, against his better judgment, he was talked into running against Church, "an entrenched incumbent." Church certainly was an entrenched incumbent, but most of the party leaders of that period tried to talk Hansen into staying where he was. . .Against virtually all Republican advice he ignored them, filed for the Senate and was snowed under by Church. . .as he spoke, the former congressman seemed to lose his temper and began blurting out a long, involved dissertation on American and world political history. Toward the end the words were rolling out so fast that he was almost babbling his bitter remarks. . .The convention's modest and slightly embarrassed reception to Hansen's excited remarks seemed to confirm that Hansen's strength does not run very deep with party workers.*[19]

We will never know just how much damage George Hansen inflicted upon himself with that speech to the Republican faithful. What we do know is that, after the tally of the Republican vote in the primary, it was obvious that Hansen's "southern strategy" backfired on him. In Boundary County (Bonners Ferry) he received fifty-five votes while McClure totaled 412; in Kootenai County (Coeur d'Alene) he received 381 votes while McClure totaled 2,516; and in Shoshone County (Kellogg-Wallace-Mullan) Hansen got a whopping forty-eight votes while McClure received 1,042.

And yes, Hansen did beat McClure in southeastern and eastern Idaho, but just as Goller predicted, McClure beat Hansen in the First District by a substantial margin over Hansen's edge in the Second District. Clearly, Hansen's "southern strategy" played right into Goller's hands.

Overall, Robert Smylie came in last in the primary as Goller predicted, receiving 22,497 total votes. Second from last was Glen Wegner with 24,582 votes—again as Goller predicted. George Hansen received 35,412 total votes while Jim McClure's total was 46,522—a 11,110 plurality.

So, on August 9, 1972, McClure was the Republican nominee and one of the biggest fights of his life was behind him. But now an even more difficult battle was on the horizon and it was destined to become the most difficult campaign of McClure's political career.

Chapter 19 notes

i This was about the time that the little, yellow smiley-face logo started being used and Goller also preempted its use by Bob Smylie by attaching it to McClure correspondence.

Chapter 20

The Great Race

William E. "Bud" Davis, ex-Marine, ex-football coach, and ex-English teacher, had become downright popular among the minions of southern and eastern Idaho in the six years that he had been president of Idaho State University in Pocatello. Known widely for his ability to charm an audience with his speeches—it was said that he gave up to 200 per year—and admired for his self-deprecating humor and genuine modesty, he had, by all accounts, carved out a reputation as one of Idaho's most capable college administrators. And a tough one at that. When his office was inundated with campus protestors, he received national recognition when a wire photo showed him calmly puffing on his pipe as he stared down the unwelcome interlopers.

And his politics? Up until late 1971, even reasonably astute political observers could easily have asked: What politics? He seemed to be a non-political creature, and in the halls of the State Capitol where he had to gain favor with legislators for his funding, he had never radiated a hint of political partisanship. Actually, after being chosen in February of the previous year as the master of ceremonies for a Lincoln Day banquet honoring Orval Hansen and Secretary of the Interior Wally Hickel, anyone who would have had to make a guess at his politics most likely would have said he was a Republican.

But he was not a Republican; he was a Democrat. And when he crawled out from behind his apolitical mask and embarked on a campaign to replace Len Jordan as Idaho's junior senator, he brought uncommon talents, Marine Corps drive, self-effacing wit, and immense personal charm to a campaign that would be the toughest in the career of James A. McClure.

According to the same Chris Carlson who had quoted McClure as being opposed to "release time" in one of his columns from Washington, D.C.:

> *Bud* [Davis] *was in D.C. in his capacity as a member of the board of college presidents that have ROTC programs on their campus, and since one of my newspaper clients which took my weekly column was the* Idaho State Journal, *and since Bud recalled my working for the* Journal *while I got my MA at ISU, he knew I was in D.C. So he called*

and we went to lunch as I recall it. I then took him on a tour of the Capitol ending up in the Senate press gallery. . .

The Senate was not in session then but I remember distinctly pointing out Len Jordan's seat to Bud and telling him that could be his seat if he wanted it, that I thought he possessed all the ingredients to make a great U.S. senator. He professed not to be interested and said he'd never really thought that much about it. I asked as we were leaving the Senate chambers whether I could float a little item saying that he was at least giving it some thought. He said sure, why not—that he probably would give it some thought. The Journal *took my little item and bannered it across the front page even before Bud got back to Pocatello, and as he tells it, when he called from Salt Lake one of his daughters informed him he was in big trouble with his wife because that was the first she knew anything about it.*[1]

Davis confirmed Carlson's version of the story but added: "Polly [his wife] was not exactly stoic about the news. 'You could have told me before you announced it to the whole world!' she snipped in her most frigid tone. I tried to tell her that the *Idaho State Journal*'s circulation didn't exactly include the whole world, but it was no time for logic."[2]

That was in November, 1971. Despite inquiries, Davis would admit only that he was thinking about the possibility of running, saying later that, "I still had a college budget to get out of the Legislature and I didn't want to jeopardize that by announcing for a partisan race. I told everybody that I would make up my mind and give a definitive answer when the legislature adjourned."[3]

Meanwhile, three other Democrats had already announced. One, Tony Park, Idaho's attorney general, was considered a favorite as was the second, Byron Johnson, a well-known Boise attorney and Democratic Party leader. The third, Rose Bowman, a Boise woman's advocate, was a political neophyte and not considered a serious contender. However, all three of them had a big advantage over the other neophyte who might join the race, Bud Davis. All of them had several months head start that allowed them to gain name recognition around the state and, more important, comb the state for supporters and financial backers. By the time Davis did get around to declaring his candidacy and visiting party workers around the state in May, he discovered that practically all of the Democratic faithful had committed to one of the other three candidates for party support and money. At that time a Democratic poll showed that Johnson would get 49 percent of the votes, Park 41 percent, Davis 6 percent and Bowman 4 percent. Davis was a long shot, without a job or pay check (the State Board of Education granted him a leave of absence) who was relying on cash borrowed from his retirement accounts and college savings he had established for his five children. Except in his mind he was not a robust candidate.

Then he hit a stroke of luck. At a meeting in Davis' Pocatello home, in walked the Associated Press correspondent for southwest Idaho, Jay Shelledy. Earlier Shelledy had been approached by a Democratic Party operative who suggested that he might get some good experience if he went through a senate campaign working as a press agent. "That sounded good for some reason," Shelledy said later. "I was single, had my bills paid, and I said 'hell yes, I'm ready for a new experience.' So I went to Pocatello to meet Davis and hear what he had to say. Of course, I knew who he was—he had been to Boise several times while he was president of ISU. He came across as a sincere individual, and he was sincere—I found him to be a decent honest person. We talked for awhile and I was sold. I signed on for the campaign, first as a press agent, then the job morphed into where I became sort of a chief of staff." [4]

Shelledy immediately brought discipline[i] and organization to the campaign, and he also laid out a campaign strategy. He thought that with Johnson, Park and Bowman all being in Boise, Davis was better off to write off southwest Idaho and campaign north of McCall and east of Twin Falls. "I believed if we did that we could give the Boise area to those three and we could still win the primary," he said later.[5]

With Shelledy at the wheel, the two of them started an intense campaign to get out in the towns of northern and eastern Idaho where Davis could meet people one-on-one, on the streets and in their homes, campaigning from early morning in local coffee shops till late in the evening at any function where. . . "more than two people would be gathered. It was a grueling schedule, but we always seemed to have enough money for a motel even though Davis jokes about us sometimes having to sleep in his big Ford LTD station wagon. Of course, I didn't dare let him drive because if I did, no matter what direction we were going he would turn the wheel and head toward Pocatello. He really missed his family when we were out on the road."[6]

Davis went down in a silver mine, competed in a log rolling event and fell in twice in front of a big crowd, rode in numerous parades, often with his wife and five-year old twin girls who were always a hit, and through July and up to the primary in August was only able to spend about $25,000—a fraction of what some of the other candidates were spending. But, when the votes were counted, he had a total of 23,953 while his nearest competitor, Tony Park, had 17,636. He had won the nomination by over 6,000 votes.[7] But, Shelledy was worried. During the Democratic State Convention in Sun Valley back in June, Davis had been approached by two or three young Mexican men who explained that Cesar Chavez, while trying to get better conditions for the lettuce pickers in California,[ii] was urging influential people to boycott lettuce by not eating it in salads or on sandwiches. According to

Davis ". . .these were nice young men and I had grown up with Mexican workers near my home in Loveland, Colorado, and I was sympathetic to their needs for better working conditions and a better life. So, I signed the petition, pledging not to eat lettuce until the matter was resolved."[8]

Shelledy picks up the story:

So we're driving from Boise to Pocatello, four of us in the car, and we're somewhere near Burley when Bud says, "You know, I may have done something that might cause us some trouble." I said, "What's that?" Then he told me about signing the Chavez petition at the convention in Sun Valley. As he started telling this my hands were turning white on the steering wheel and when he got it all out, I yelled, "You did what!" and pulled the car off on the shoulder. I could have taken him out of the car and pistol whipped him if I'd had a pistol.

"Well, I feel sorry for those workers; they deserve a better life," he said lamely. I was angry. We were amateurs but we know about the petitions floating around, and we warned him several times that he was likely to get hit by something at the convention and not to sign anything. Nothing. And now he had done it without talking to anyone about it.

When I got a chance, I called the Chavez people and told them that I was afraid his signing their petition might get him in trouble in the campaign. They were nice about it and agreed to deep-six it and deny that he ever signed it if that is what we wanted. I couldn't make that decision; that was up to Bud. So I told him what they said. He just looked incredulous. "But I signed it. How can I deny it when I signed it?" He really didn't understand what I was asking. He was so honest

SHELLEDY ON DAVIS' SENSE OF HUMOR

We were driving into Lewiston one morning when Bud happened to be reading the Morning Tribune *in which Bill Hall had a column saying that Davis would be a much better candidate if he wasn't so shy in meeting people. What he needed to do, Hall said, was to get out there and knock people down if he had to just to get over his shyness—he just needs to become more bold and if he does he would become a much more effective candidate. Well, after Bud read that to me, we happened to be near the* Tribune *building when he spotted a homeless-looking panhandler. He told me to stop the car and he got out and approached the man, offering him ten dollars if he would go into the* Tribune *building, find Bill Hall, and tell him that Bud Davis knocked him down shoving a campaign brochure into his hands. The fellow did that and, in a subsequent column Bill Hall acknowledged that Bud Davis had learned his lesson. I tell this story because it is an example of Bud's sense of humor and his self-deprecating style.*

Courtesy Bud Davis

Democratic senate candidate Bud Davis and family campaign on a rainy day in eastern Idaho.

> *it never really dawned on him that he had the chance to deny it. I actually agreed with him, but I felt that I had to give him the option they offered. Well, after that, I lived in fear and sure enough, Sam Day, who was the editor of* The Intermountain Observer *in Boise, wrote a piece that mentioned Ernie Starr, the mayor of Nampa, Frank Church and Bud Davis signing the Chavez petition in Sun Valley. That was just before the Primary. One shoe had fallen and I just knew the other was going to fall and hurt us.*[9]

Meanwhile, McClure was having his own troubles. Right after the primary, George Hansen released a three-page statement to the press in which he made a lot of accusations against McClure and the "big money and machine politics" that enabled him to win the primary election. According to Hansen all of this, ". . .caused me to take on the dragon of political bossism when it turned its flame thrower at some of us and applied the heat of back-room politics." It was a long, rambling statement full of blatant self pity and an attempt to establish himself as a martyr—a loyal Republican who has thrown himself on his sword in a sacrifice against entrenched Democrats. He also made a claim that has little credence: "In 1966 I worked with leaders in the Idaho Legislature to redraw congressional district lines such that the Boise area fell completely in the First District, making it possible for Jim McClure to be elected to Congress, and cutting my own Republican margin to almost nothing."[10]

Courtesy Jim McClure

On the road during the 1972 statewide McClure for Senate bus tour. From left, Carolyn Keithly (Fancher), Helen Dahl (Timothy), Louise and Jim McClure.

Wherever McClure went, he was dogged by reporters with questions about Hansen's accusations. Mostly he was quoted as saying, generally, "What Hansen was saying was that politics as usual was operating in our state and I don't deny it. People have a right to support whomever they choose, and if a big company chooses to support me, I welcome that support." But the Hansen accusations were bothering McClure because Hansen's supporters in eastern Idaho were critical for his victory in the general election. If Hansen's invective poisoned them against him, he knew that an attractive candidate like Bud Davis could easily gain cross-over votes and that could mean defeat.

He could not allow that to happen. But what was he to do? Jim Goller admits that he did not want anything to do with Hansen and that he probably advised McClure to stay clear of him. McClure himself felt just the opposite. "I knew we had to heal some wounds," he said when asked about Hansen's invective after the Primary. "In politics it is customary for the losers to call the winners and congratulate them. Smylie was the first one to call me. Wegner was the second. Hansen never did. George was very proud and didn't take defeat easily. I knew that if we were going to heal the wounds, I would have to make the initiative. I had learned that one can't carry personal animosities through life—they're just too corrosive. So, even though it was very hard for me to do this, I picked up the telephone and called George. He wasn't bubbling over with friendship, but neither was he antagonistic when

I asked him if he would now endorse me. I'm sure he was reluctant, but he did agree to do it."[11]

Nancy Carlile, who was doing her first stint as a McClure campaign worker in Blackfoot, and who would later become a McClure staffer, picks up the rest of the story:

> *We scheduled one of the biggest events of the campaign with a dinner in the Blackfoot High School gymnasium. George Romney, former auto executive, governor of Michigan and now Nixon's director of HUD* [Dept. Housing and Urban Development] *and a leading Mormon was going to be one of the speakers as was Ernest Wilkinson the well-known president of BYU* [Brigham Young University]. *McClure and Orval Hansen, the two candidates, were to be honored, and George Hansen was there to endorse them both—I'm sure this had all been worked out with McClure. Let me tell you, George Hansen brought the house down with his endorsement. George was a fantastic speaker and he was well liked—he has that charisma that makes everybody love him. It was a full endorsement; it was an enthusiastic endorsement. With hindsight, however, I really think George was performing as much for himself as he was for McClure. After all, there was George Romney and Ernest Wilkinson and 300 or so prominent Republicans from all over eastern Idaho. I think George was just putting on a show to impress them, but I'm sure it was effective for McClure."*[12]

McClure was dogged by another issue during the campaign. Actually, it was the same issue Wegner had pounced upon during the Primary: McClure's roll call record, which was bad in 1971, but which was not that stellar so far in 1972. McClure was frustrated by this issue mainly because, in the short time he had to answer reporter's questions there was not enough time to do what McClure said he needed to do, which was "to educate them." McClure explains:

> *My record took a hit in '72 because I had made a commitment to speak at Rimrock High School in Grand View, a commencement speech that was held on a Monday night. Ordinarily we didn't have many votes on Monday so I stayed over the weekend and gave the speech. It was my luck that there was a big partisan conflict back there and they stayed in session all day and all night Monday and Tuesday. By the time I got back on Tuesday afternoon, my attendance record had gone down by 10 percent in just that one day.*
>
> *But really, those roll-call statistics are relatively meaningless because sometimes it is more important to be somewhere else. For example, suppose I'm working on a tough land use issue and I have*

> *an appointment with the Secretary of the Interior where I can get the problem resolved. And suppose they decide to hold a quorum call. Should I skip the appointment with the secretary when 99 percent of the time the quorum call is meaningless? Most roll-call votes are lop-sided. There is usually no real contest for most of those votes. But when you make the choice not to be there, you give your opponent an issue he can talk about and you never have time when you're replying to questions from reporters to get into all of this. So you're always on the defensive.*[13]

Bud Davis made the most of this issue in his campaign, and he was quoted by reporters numerous times saying, "McClure's attendance is deplorable and all he gives is school-boy excuses." Even one of McClure's backers and closest advisors said in a memo to him:

> *Your opponent had made his best case against you, regardless of the true facts, on the absenteeism issue. This single item could cost thousands of votes. There are other factors, but none contributed quite as much to your situation during the third week of October as the non-voting issue. The best rebuttal was to simply tell the truth in the form of ads. Yet, our action was a classic example of too little. And too late. Too small an ad. Run far too late. . .after the impression had been cemented by the opposition and was almost impossible to erase.*[14]

There was no question that Bud Davis was gaining momentum with his folksy, meet-as-many-people-as-possible, campaign. He was also drawing money and other kinds of support into his campaign. During the third week in August he and his campaign chairman, Lynn Broadhead, went to Washington, D.C., and, with the help of Frank Church in making appointments, met with a number of traditional Democratic supporters: COPE, the political arm of the AFL-CIO, Senator Ernest "Fritz" Hollings (D-South Carolina), the chairman of the Democratic Senatorial Campaign Committee, and a variety of environmental organization representatives, officials of the National Education Association, and several groups concerned about the care and welfare of the nation's elderly. And, according to Chris Carlson who reported this trip in one of his columns, "After the meeting with labor officials, Davis said he felt optimistic about receiving their support," and after his meeting with Hollings, he said that, . . ."Hollings told him that top Democrats are beginning to worry about losing control of the Senate, and hence have picked five key races where they think a Democratic nominee has a good chance of wrestling away a seat previously held by the Republicans. Davis said Hollings considers his race with McClure one of these five key 'winnable' races."[15]

Courtesy Helen Dahl Timothy

Congressional candidate Steve Symms and wife Fran, left, pose beside campaign bus with Louise and Jim during the 1972 campaign.

The money started pouring in, so much near the end of the campaign that Shelledy said it was more than they could use. But, Davis also was carrying an albatross in the campaign. Its name was George McGovern, the Democrat who was running against Richard Nixon for president. Although he had flown twenty-five combat missions in a B-24 during World War II, and even though he was moderate enough in his own views to be re-elected in his home state of South Dakota, his vigorous anti-Vietnam stand and the hundreds of thousands of long-haired youth he had attracted to his campaign gave him the image of a radical—an image that Nixon campaign strategists did everything in their power to enhance. In addition, the liberal Democrats at the national convention had almost unlimited success in infusing the Democratic platform with a host of new and controversial ideas that turned the stomachs of conservatives of all stripes. The net result was that while McClure had to constantly face questions over his attendance record, Davis was bombarded with such questions as: Are you supporting McGovern? and Do you support the Democratic platform? Davis, of course, had to waffle. All polls showed that McGovern was going to get clobbered in Idaho by a huge margin and the Democratic platform played in Idaho about like the Beatles in a church choir.

And on both sides some big names were drawn into the fray. For Davis came Senator Ted Kennedy (D-Massachusetts), Senator Warren Magnuson

Courtesy Helen Dahl Timothy

An unscheduled campaign bus stop. Waiting for a band of sheep to clear the road in Stanley Basin.

(D-Washington), Senator and Majority Leader Mike Mansfield (D-Montana), and Hubert Humphrey, Lyndon Johnson's vice president and the presidential candidate in 1968. McClure also brought in some big guns: Senator Barry Goldwater (R-Arizona), Vice President Spiro Agnew, and Rogers Morton, Secretary of the Interior.

Then a spurious claim entered the campaign. Someone (not Goller) remembered that Timothy Leary had once spoken at Idaho State University. By inference, then, Bud Davis was soft on drugs because that had happened.

But nothing before or since has hit a candidate so hard and sudden as the other shoe that Shelledy predicted was going to drop. The shoe laces came untied just before the primary when *Twin Falls Times News* political reporter, Dave Espo[iii], did a story on his interview with Davis. In it Espo described how Davis admitted signing the Chavez lettuce boycott petition and how Davis tried to sidestep the issue by explaining that he was against "blanket secondary boycotting," which was a concept way over the head of Espo's readers. Then Espo asked Davis if his position on the lettuce boycott could be extended to a boycott on Idaho potatoes. Instead of a flat, adamant denial, Davis was quoted as saying that if facing such a decision, he would have to "look at it on the merits of the potato case."[16]

That equivocation did not surface immediately, although Goller, in an extensive briefing book he had prepared on Davis, made note of it and made sure his campaign workers were aware of the vulnerability of Davis among farmers. Are you for a potato boycott? As a U.S. senator, what kind of merits might make you support a potato boycott? Those questions arose time after time and Davis grew frustrated enough to finally say, "I took a personal vow to abstain from eating lettuce. That's a different matter, and you'd have to be crazy to run for office in Idaho and be for a potato boycott. I'm just plain against it."[17]

McClure had his absentee record to defend, and for awhile he was also attacked for his environmental record, particularly on the White Clouds. However, this latter issue became more or less dead in the water when President Nixon signed the SNRA bill in August.

Courtesy Jim Goller

Jim Goller and the McClure bus during the Senate campaign.

Davis had McGovern and the Democratic platform. Neither were going to go away as the campaign drew to a close. But, just a week or so before the election, the other shoe dropped and created a small explosion.

Goller thinks the impetus came from Vernon Clinton, a Rupert farmer, former New York publicist and one of McClure's advisors. Said Goller, "Clinton was in the office several times demanding that we run a big ad on the lettuce boycott. Our advertising budget and ad campaign was pretty well set and I didn't feel we needed to change it. Clinton said several times that he would go out on his own, raise the money and run the ad. I advised him that it was illegal for the official campaign organization to participate in and have knowledge of independent campaign expenditures. So, without my direct knowledge or approval, Clinton probably approached Louie Lepper, public affairs director for the Idaho Farm Bureau and said something to the effect that, 'This election is too damn close; McClure is liable to get beat and we've got to do something dramatic. I suggest we do a series of big ads and put a copy of the Chavez petition in it then get out the facts that Davis not only signed it but that he said he would have to decide whether he would back a potato boycott on the merits of the case. Why don't you find somebody who will sign on as secretary of an organization that will pay for the ads. Just think up a name that sounds good.'"[18]

Clinton's role is just speculation by Goller, but we do know that Louie Lepper did leap into action, got a devastating advertisement designed, and contacted a beet farmer near Marsing, P. T. Rathbone, to sign on as coordinator for Concerned Agricultural Food Producers and Consumers in Treasure Valley. Said Rathbone, "Louie Lepper came to me and said that McClure was in big trouble—that Davis might win this thing and that would be a disaster for Idaho. I questioned him a bit about how accurate the information was in the ad and he assured me that it was factual—that he had checked it out. I was a little afraid of being sued if I signed on to some false information. So, I agreed to be the head of whatever organization—I can't begin to remember the name. But it was my name that was at the bottom of those ads because I wanted to help McClure."[19]

Jay Shelledy said that the ads were devastating, and when one reads them today, it is easy to imagine how Idaho potato farmers blanched when they saw the petition Davis signed, and read the copy that suggested Davis would be in the hip pocket of Chavez if he started organizing the potato workers in Idaho. Davis tried to counter the ads with an ad of his own that ran the next day across southern Idaho with big copy stating:

Once and
For all...
Bud Davis is
Totally opposed to any
form of a potato boycott.
And he's slowly losing his
good sense of humor over unfounded
stories to the contrary. Innuendos,
rumors and outright lies are being
spread in these last days of the general
election in a calculated campaign of
desperation and they should be recognized
for what they are:
SMEAR TACTICS
"My adamant stand against potato boycotts is a
matter of record. I think it is a sad commentary
on a political campaign when it becomes necessary
to distort the issues in order to win votes. Idaho
voters have a time-honored tradition for rejecting
smear tactics of any nature. I have tried to keep
my campaign on a positive note and will continue
to do so. I plan to drop this matter now and let
the voters determine whether distortions are a
deciding factor in campaigns."
Bud Davis, Idaho Falls, Oct. 27[20]

Other factors may also have influenced voters in this campaign. McClure did a three-week bus tour of Idaho, bringing local candidates along when he was in their area while he campaigned from morning till night in practically every city, town and village. On these visits, with John Phillips Souza music blaring from loudspeakers on the bus, he had volunteers and the "McClure Girls"—comely young women—to pass out literature. And with Jack Holley, who was later joined by a young man from Colorado, Al Timothy, out ahead, distributing thousands of yard signs and generally doing any grunt work that was needed, the McClure armada was bound to impress Idaho citizens in such bucolic places as Moyie Springs, Athol, Fernwood, Green Creek, Ferdinand, Stites, Tendoy, Mud Lake, Moreland and Mink Creek.

Courtesy Dick Thompson

A laid-back McClure laughs with members of his Senate campaign staff as their bus heads for another town.

In Boise he was gifted with a special entourage that further enhanced the ambience of the tour. Blanche Evans, head of a Boise modeling school, recruited tall pretty girls 14-16 years old; dressed them in straw hats, blue blazers, white pleated skirts and white knee socks; taught them to walk "not like they are riding a horse" [21] and carry themselves like models; and had them available at McClure appearances where they would lead him to his campaign position, then pass out McClure literature. Those who remember the campaign have wonderful memories of those McClure girls and the elegance and charm they brought to the scenes.

Davis also had young people helping him—hundreds of them from colleges all over Idaho. Young people had an instinctive feeling about Davis, a feeling of trust, a feeling that Davis was the kind of person who would listen to them and who could understand their aspirations. During the campaign four of these young people, recent graduates of Bishop Kelly High School in Boise who had been students in a journalism class Shelledy had taught there, made headlines and recruited who knows how many hundred voters for Davis as they rode their bicycles and campaigned for Davis all the way from Bonners Ferry in north Idaho to Bear Lake in extreme southeastern Idaho.

And there were the televised debates, about which Bud Davis said when he was first contacted, "And then there was my stupidity thinking I could successfully debate McClure—he with all that knowledge about the laws and issues. Heck, I was just a college administrator; he made me look like a college freshman. He was a pro and I was a rookie."[22] Shelledy takes exception with Davis in respect to the debates. "Yeah, there's no doubt; McClure beat the hell out of Bud in that first debate. We both learned that you can't get by with good-old-boy stuff—you can't glad hand and tell stories on television. But in the other debates—I think there were two more—Bud held his own. I don't think you could say that McClure beat him after that first debate."[23]

On McClure's part the debates were a turning point. "I was feeling pretty nervous and worried[iv] up to that first debate. Davis was a very gregarious, very friendly fellow who I liked then and have liked since—there was nothing personally negative about him. But, as personable and intelligent as he was, it was a surprise that he wasn't better prepared for the debates. The best that could be said of him was that he was very honest and candid and very disarming. I don't remember anything in the debates when either of us was negative or personal. George Hansen was more personally negative than Bud Davis ever was. I do know that I walked away from the first debate feeling a lot better about my chances of winning the election."[24]

Shelledy, who went on to an illustrious career managing several newspapers, including *The Salt Lake Tribune*, believes that Davis was ahead and could have won the election if not for the last minute publicity about the Chavez petition and what he feels were the spurious innuendos about Davis backing a potato boycott. "That just about broke our back," he said, "but you can't ignore the lack of help from the top. McGovern was a liability, no doubt about it." [25]

Goller disagrees. "Look at the numbers. Davis won in eleven counties. McClure carried thirty-three counties. McClure won by 21,000 votes.[v] Yeah, the potato boycott ad may have persuaded some voters, but remember the press had reported this at some length and continued to do so throughout the campaign. To tell you the truth I was never really worried. I felt all along that McClure was going to win. I have a lot of respect for Jay Shelledy and I like him. But I think he is plain wrong to say the potato boycott thing caused Davis to be beat. McClure had solid support. He worked hard and he ran a good campaign. I think it would be distorting history to leave the impression McClure won because of a few negative ads. That kind of thinking makes me a little irritated."[26]

The election was over. McClure was going back to Washington as Idaho's junior senator. Davis went back to his job at Idaho State University, then left Idaho to have a distinguished career as president of the University of New Mexico, chancellor of the Oregon Higher System of Education and, finally, chancellor of Louisiana State University. Idaho would not see another contentious election like this until 1980 when the upstart Steve Symms would challenge and defeat veteran Senator Frank Church.

Just one little bit of trivia can add a postscript to this election story. P. T. Rathbone told the author that he was more than happy to use his name in the boycott ads that ran in the last days of the campaign but after it was over, he said he voiced disappointment to one of the McClure advisors, Logan Lanham of the Idaho Power Company, saying that he had received nothing in the way of thanks for his gesture. According to Rathbone, Lanham asked him what he would like in the way of appreciation. "'I'd like a big

Confederate flag,' I told him. Sure enough, in just a few days here comes my Confederate flag in the mail and I flew that sucker."[27]

McClure's great grandfather died fighting the Confederates. Had he seen their flag flying in celebration of his great grandson's victory, he might have had mixed emotions.

Chapter 20 notes

i. In an unpublished book written after the campaign, *They Don't Call Me Senator*, Davis refers to his campaign chief as Herr Reichmarshall Shelledy.

ii. Actually, Chavez was trying to win the lettuce pickers away from the Teamsters Union to his own union, the United Farm Workers.

iii Dave Espo is now the Associated Press national correspondent covering the House and Senate.

iv Goller said that several of McClure's advisors argued against him debating Davis. "Davis was a famous after-dinner speaker, very polished, and they were afraid Davis would hurt McClure during a televised debate."

v The actual margin was 20,891.

Chapter 21

Freshman Senator

James A. McClure was escorted down the center aisle of the Senate by his Idaho colleague, Frank Church, and was sworn in as Idaho's junior senator. This was on January 3, 1973. Watching from the Senate gallery were his immediate family and his mother who had flown to Washington for the occasion. Afterwards, at a reception honoring the new senators, each of the family members had their photograph taken with Vice President Spiro Agnew. Little did they suspect that the celebrity with whom they posed so proudly would resign in disgrace ten months later.

McClure had many challenges when he became a senator, but one of them evolved from some of the late work he did while he was still in the House. To bring this effort up to date we must turn the calendar back to late 1971. It was about that time when McClure decided to have a chat with Wayne Aspinall, the Democratic chairman of the Interior Committee on which he had served since he had been in the House. McClure was concerned. The economy was not doing well. Inflation had been rampant—so out of control that Nixon had imposed wage and price controls. Unemployment was high and America's heavy industries were floundering, especially the automobile manufacturers that were fighting increasingly strong foreign competition. All of these were factors to worry about, but they were not McClure's primary reason for consulting with Aspinall. What worried McClure was the fuel that kept the whole economy running—the nation's energy in general and the petroleum supply specifically. He had recently acquired an interest in petroleum, especially after he had visited the Alaska North Slope and had been briefed by petroleum experts on many aspects of exploration, recovery, transportation and refinement of the resource. What concerned him on the one hand was the heavy dependence of the economy on the resource, while on the other hand a dramatically increased supply of it was coming from highly unstable Arab countries in the Middle East. He suspected that this supply, which was absolutely critical to the economy, could be cut down, overpriced or withdrawn almost overnight—a result that could be disastrous. After voicing his concerns to Aspinall, who agreed completely with his concerns, McClure suggested that a task force be created to study the problem, and if the nation was, indeed, at the high degree of risk that he feared, by placing the task force report in the hands of congress and the public, this would be

Courtesy Jim Mcclure

Vice President Spiro Agnew, aided by Louise McClure, swears in the new senator. Below, McClure and is House staff celebrate on his return to Washington, D.C. after winning the Senate seat.

Courtesy Alan Timothy

an important first step in mitigating a potential disaster.

Aspinall concurred in the need to set up the task force and appointed McClure as the chairman—a move that did not surprise McClure's administrative assistant, Dick Thompson. He said, "It might seem strange for Aspinall to appoint a Republican to head such a task force, especially since he knew that it would get some publicity; Aspinall was partisan to the core. But McClure had earned his respect for all the hard work he had done, like staying hours after committee meetings working tirelessly with the staff to craft the legislative words that were needed in a bill. Aspinall appreciated that and he would go out of his way to say nice things about McClure.[i] I think he found a Republican who was like a son to him."[1]

> McCLURE'S FIRST SENATE ASSIGNMENTS
>
> Interior and Insular Affairs Committee
> Subcommittees:
> 1. Public Lands (ranking minority member)
> 2. Indian Affairs
> 3. Parks and Recreation
>
> Public Works Committee
> Subcommittees:
> 1. Economic Development (ranking minority member)
> 2. Air and Water Pollution
> 3. Flood Control—Rivers & Harbors
> 4. Public Buildings and Grounds
>
> Veterans Affairs Committee
> Subcommittees:
> 1. Housing and Insurance (ranking minority member)
> 2. Readjustment, Education and Employment (ranking minority member)

Besides giving useful information on energy in general—information that would be helpful to many people when it was compiled—it gave McClure, himself, an education that was unique. And, according to Scootch Harper (Pankonin) who had been on his staff since the beginning, he had the kind of mind that could assimilate all the nuances of the energy problem. Over the next several months experts of all kinds testified before McClure's committee. She remembered:

> *I think where Jim McClure is different is the guy has a memory like an encyclopedia. He is religiously disciplined . . .he never forgets details and he knows them in a context that is not the way the* [general] *population thinks. You either have rote memory. . .or you're associative and he is clearly associative and rote at the same time. And that is very unusual, very rare. None of the details get lost.*
>
> *I remember there would be times when an issue came up that was important—that I'd spend three or four days in the library studying, reading, practically staying up all night the night before thinking that for once I'll be ahead of him. I'll really know this issue* [I told myself]. *We'd sit down before he went over to committee and he would*

leave me in the dust with the amount that he knew seemingly without having made any effort. Now I know that he did. I know he read at home at night. . .but he had a memory bank that was uncanny. And a lot of times somebody like Aspinall would mention something that had to do with history or public power or whatever it might be and Jim would have us request books from the Library of Congress. . .He was constantly requesting things. . .and he studied that stuff. The man just read constantly. He was just a lot smarter than most people—smart with a fantastic memory. And knowing the context in where it fit. Some people are really smart and really well read and they're useless. They don't know what to do with the knowledge. They have trouble getting grounded in committee work. It's unfamiliar to them; it's extremely detailed; it's terribly technical. He just fit right into it. Picked it up as if he'd always been there.[2]

In short, McClure's attendance at the task force hearings was making him an energy expert. Within a few months that knowledge was to take him to another part of the world.

McClure and the Interior Committee staff finished the task force report in December during his last days in the House. When he got to the Senate, he needed more staff and one of his first actions was to give a permanent position to a staffer who had been hired as a temporary assistant for the task force. His name was Mike Hathaway, who prior to his work with McClure, had been an engineer on the Apollo Moon Project. He came on the staff to be McClure's legislative assistant for natural resources, energy and the environment, which meant that he would handle constituent correspondence and problems in those fields and, in addition, would attend committee and subcommittee hearings that McClure could not attend. And as he soon learned, there were to be many of those. Thirteen new senators were sworn in with McClure, but because of his six years in the House, he had seniority over eight of them. Consequently, he was placed on three committees and nine subcommittees, and for three of these he was the ranking minority member. Even the conscientious McClure could not make all of the meetings and he needed an intelligent and knowledgeable person who could. Hathaway turned out to be an exceptionally capable substitute.

McClure also had other staff needs. Dick Thompson explains:

Right at the beginning, while we were getting his new office organized, McClure called me in and said that he wanted to talk to me about a staffing problem. In the course of our discussion he explained that he wanted me to begin looking for two really smart people who could come on the staff and look ahead at some of the problems we were going to face. He wanted thinkers, and even though he didn't admit it, I sensed that he wanted people who were as intelligent as he

Courtesy Alan Timothy

Members of his first Senate staff give the McClures a Christmas gift during a gathering in a committee room in the Russell Senate Office Building.

> *was and who could challenge and stimulate his own thinking. I was a little concerned about how two people like that could fit into the office workings and as I recall he said something like, 'That's okay, I need people in here who think. I don't want people who just respond; I want people to say to me that this would be a good thing for me to do.' I thought about people I knew and came up with two and told McClure, 'I've found the two people you need and I want you to hire them on my say so.' He agreed and we hired Margo Carlisle and Jim Streeter whom I had known back during the Goldwater campaign. Their whole responsibility was just to think. We gave them some other duties, but their main job was to read the papers and make suggestions and to argue with McClure. They were two of the brightest people we ever had. McClure liked to call them in and discuss issues and bounce ideas off them. We wanted them to be idea people and not burdened with letters to answer. That was the best thing I ever did for McClure. I don't know what we would have done without them.*[3]

McClure also lost one of his best staffers. Scootch Harper, who had worked in his first congressional campaign and who had been his workhorse, jack-of-all-trades assistant for the past six years, was given to Steve Symms, the newly elected congressman from Idaho's First District. Both McClure and Thompson hated to lose her, but they agreed that Symms, with absolutely no knowledge of how to run a congressional office, needed her worse than they did.

While poring through the old files from McClure's years of service in Washington, one cannot help being impressed by two of them that are present for each year of service. One is labeled "Invitations Accepted" and the other "Invitations Declined." During the six years he was in the House there are abundant invitations in each file—so many that one's head reels trying to imagine how McClure and his wife could keep up with those that were accepted. But the truly amazing thing, though hardly surprising, is the increase in the number of invitations he received when he moved to the Senate. In an interview McClure and his wife were asked: "How could the two of you possibly keep up with all of the invitations that you accepted during those years?"

"There were a lot of them," McClure replied. "But I just went because Louise wanted to go," he added, joking because she was present. "I enjoyed them," Louise said, not defensively, but firmly. "It was a chance to get out and meet a lot of new people. I liked that and Jim did, too, even if he doesn't want to admit it now."

MARGO CARLISLE ON JOINING THE MCCLURE STAFF

I was immediately comfortable with McClure and, politically, I felt like an Idahoan after I was around him for awhile. I grew very comfortable and loved the way he thought and the way he argued his way through things. You say something; he questions that; then you say something; he questions that; and when you get 28 layers down and he gets to a question you can't answer, you have to say, "I don't know." You had to be completely straight forward with him. It was funny to see how he treated other staff members. He would try to get some of them to argue and they might be terrified, or they might enjoy the challenge. Some of us thought it was fun, and it was fascinating to watch him doing it. I think him asking questions until you came to something you didn't know was just his way of showing his appreciation for what you did know. I was brought up in a highly volatile family where everybody argued so I was quite prepared for McClure.

McClure then became more serious. "I did enjoy it—at least most of the receptions. It was a chance to meet people I would never have met otherwise. For example, as a senator I received invitations to all of the embassy parties—invitations I never received while in the House. When we went to those, and as I recall there were a lot of them, I got a chance to talk to the ambassadors from many different countries. They were usually eager to talk with any senator who would listen to them, and I had a genuine interest in hearing what they had to say—about their country, or the problems they were having with mine. Actually, that's how I ended up going to the Middle East for the first time."[4]

Energy, oil and the Middle East occupied McClure's thoughts more and more after his experience on the energy task force. According to his new aide, Mike Hathaway:

Courtesy Jim McClure

During his last weeks in the House, while serving as chairman of the Task Force on Energy and Resources, McClure started on the road that would make him the leading congressional expert on energy. McClure, left, Roger Zion (Indiana), Bill Archer (Texas) and Hastings Keith, (Massachusetts), listen to testimony.

> *I won't say he was preoccupied with Middle Eastern oil and the potential for it to be cut off, but it was a concern that we discussed many times. I remember in particular that he received an invitation to speak in Dallas to a group of oil men who were having a meeting there; it was in February, 1973, just after he came into the Senate. He asked me to prepare an outline of some of the things he should tell them. When we sat down to go over the ten or so points that I listed that the country should do if the Arabs did embargo our oil, I remember him looking them over. 'Any one of these could get a senator de-elected,' he said, laughing. I had listed things like imposing a 50 mile-per-hour speed limit to save gasoline, burning a lot more coal, and doubling or tripling our use of nuclear energy. Well, McClure went on to give that speech and from the feedback I heard, he made quite an impression on those oil men. It was strange, but here was this new senator from a little western state like Idaho who was quickly building a reputation as an energy expert. I remember that I was so impressed with it that I sent a copy to an old friend of mine, Jim Akins, who was the ambassador to Saudi Arabia.*[5]

What McClure said was that the United States was extremely vulnerable because of our dramatically rising dependency upon Middle Eastern oil. He emphasized that those countries were not friends of the United States, and there was the further problem that they were largely unstable and could suddenly raise the price of oil and send our economy into a tailspin. In addition, he pointed out that because of our strong ties to Israel, should a conflict break out between the Arabs and Israel, there was a strong probability that the Arabs, in retaliation, could cut off our imports—a measure that would drastically hurt our economy. These were strong words coming from a Senator from Idaho with no significant credentials to back them up.

Sometime after that speech McClure convinced Henry "Scoop" Jackson, chairman of the Interior Committee to hold a hearing on the specific problem of America's dependence upon imported oil. Mike Hathaway well remembers the controversy. Said Hathaway:

During the hearing, Scoop Jackson and Secretary of Interior, Rogers Morton, both agreed that our oil imports from the Arabs were minor—I don't remember their exact figures. McClure challenged them and said that they were wrong by half—that we were importing twice what they claimed. This was interesting; Morton was a friend, a Republican who had come to Idaho to campaign for McClure in his senate race. Then Morton's people came in with new data and he had to admit that McClure was right. Jackson's people also acknowledged it. After both had apologized to McClure, he looked at Morton and Jackson and said, 'Here you are—you've got all that staff and all I have is this,'—pointing to me. That broke the place up. After that, people started realizing that he might be a junior Republican from a little state out west, but he knew what he was talking about.[6]

Margo Carlisle tells how McClure also made another believer. "It was sometime about the time of the hearing when Ralph Nader and some of his "Raiders" would conduct interviews, not to learn anything because he thought he knew everything, but so he could evaluate members of Congress. I remember his comment about McClure. Basically, he said that McClure seemed to be a bright and able senator, but that he was overly preoccupied with energy. A few months later we were in long gas lines. What a dunce that guy was. Most senators are on send all the time and McClure was on receive more than send, taking it all in and processing it. The first thing I learned being around him was that he's smart, he works hard and he listens."[7]

McClure, of course, had many other things on his mind other than energy. The mail, for example, had more than doubled, and while there was general agreement among his House staffers that he "drove them crazy" because of his insistence on reading and signing every letter that went out of his office, these same staffers were at a loss for adjectives to describe their frustration with the chaotic mail situation during his first weeks in the Senate. Said Dick Thompson:

He still wanted to do it all, but even he threw up his hands and admitted defeat after a short time. The mail was just too heavy; it was stacked almost to the ceiling in his office. He just couldn't do it and he finally realized it. So we tried a couple of compromises that he suggested. First, he wanted me to read every letter that came in. That didn't work; I was way too busy with everything else that was going on. Then he wanted us to make a list of the names of people who sent letters—a list he could look over each day to see which ones needed his personal attention. He was so afraid that somebody back home would think he was too high and mighty to answer their letters personally.

I've probably said it before, but he hated phonies. He was determined to be the same kind of person the folks in Payette, Idaho knew before he went to Washington. If he had a fault, it was his inability to delegate to his staff. Of course, in the Senate he was forced to do it. Making a list of names and having him check them each day was not practical. We were too busy and he was too busy. Finally, and sadly on his part, he finally allowed me and the staff the full responsibility of getting the correspondence answered. I remember him pointing his finger at me and saying, "I'm holding you personally responsible for the mail going out of here." He also let us use "siggy"—the dreaded signature machine. I eventually solved the problem by putting Al Timothy, who had once been an intern for us, in charge of getting the mail out. That cut me free from that responsibility and Al did a great job for us.[8]

When McClure was confronted with this quote and asked how he pleaded, he said, lamely, "Guilty. *Nolo contendere.*" He also went on to comment on the embassy parties that he and Louise were attending that first year:

I don't know if it was two or three times we were at the Kuwaiti Embassy, but I do know that I got along very well with their ambassador. I think it was because I was so interested in their oil production and he liked to talk about it. Finally—and I don't remember when this occurred—he said to me, "Why don't you come to Kuwait and see for yourself what we are doing? We'll pay for it." Of course, he had a motive. At the time the United States was tilting heavily toward Israel and the Arabs were being largely ignored. I realized his motive; I wasn't naive. . .well, maybe a little—I really didn't know what was going on over there. I should say I wasn't gullible. I knew he wanted to try to influence a senator who might take a more objective view of Israeli-Arab relations. But, I also wanted to find out for myself what was going on over there so I accepted. It is one thing to hear an expert describe what is going on and another thing to go see for yourself.[9]

Mike Hathaway, who was scheduled to go with McClure to the Middle East picks up the story:

We were getting ready to leave the office and head for Kuwait in October 1973 when we got a call from the Kuwaiti Embassy. They said that Ramadan was coming up and this was a bad time to come. The next morning the Syrians and Egyptians attacked Israel and this was the beginning of the Yom Kippur War. I remember that McClure went to a briefing on the war and when he came back, he said that he was told that it would go on for months. I looked at him and said that it would be over in a week. He looked at me and said, "I'm going to make a record of your prediction; I'm going to write in this notebook that Hathaway says it will be over in a week." I was just looking at the progress of the Israelis, especially when they obtained total air superiority. The Arabs initially had superiority because of their anti-tank missiles, but I just knew they would collapse. I knew Israel could not afford a long confrontation because of their economy—a long war would destroy their economy because so many of their soldiers were part time. Later, in a week or so and after the war, we got another call from the Kuwaitis. They said they would like to re-extend their invitation and also they asked us if we would visit Egypt, Lebanon, Jordan and Saudi Arabia. My passport is stamped November 19, when we landed in Cairo.[10]

By the time McClure and Hathaway arrived in Cairo, the Organization of Petroleum Exporting Countries (OPEC) had done exactly what McClure had predicted: they had instituted an oil embargo on the United States and it had been in effect for just over a month. The Arab members were the large majority in OPEC cartel and they were angry at America for shipping arms to Israel during the Yom Kippur war. Also, to retaliate against America's allies in Europe, they raised the price of oil they shipped to them, initially from $3.00 to $5.11 a barrel, but later the following January to $11.65, more than doubling the price. An article on the history of the embargo summarizes its effects:

When OPEC announced the sharp price rise, the shock waves were immediate. Industrial democracies. . .were suddenly at the mercy of Arab nationalism. . .Many of these "new" Arabs were Harvard educated and familiar with the ways of the West, and to many Americans it was impossible to understand how their standard of living was now being held hostage. . .Suddenly President Nixon had to set the nation on a course of voluntary rationing. He called upon homeowners to turn down their thermostats and for companies to trim work hours. Gas stations were asked to hold their sales to a max of ten gallons per customer. . .A severe recession hit much of the Western world, including the U.S., and as gasoline lines snaked their *way around city blocks and tempers flared (the price at the pump had risen from 30 cents a gallon to about $1.20 at the height of the crisis), conspiracy theories abounded. How did Wall Street respond? . . .the market swooned 15 percent between 10/17/73 and the end of November. . .the market would see the Dow go from its1/11/73 high of 1051 to 577 by 12/6/74, a whopping 45 percent decline. . .*[11]

And what was worse, in McClure territory—the wide open space of the west where drivers were used to cruising 70 and 80 mph—a federally imposed "gas saving" speed limit of 55 mph was imposed.

McClure is not sure if he read the outpouring of constituent mail condemning everything about the Arab boycott and its impositions before he went to the Middle East, but he admits that when he arrived there, he was definitely in the listen mode. "I felt that I really had to try and understand the Arab side of the conflict, and I went there determined to keep an open mind."[12]

McClure was the first American of any significance to reach the Middle East after the Arab-Israeli war. And it was a propitious time, especially in Egypt. The strongly pro-Soviet Egyptian leader, Gamal Abdel-Nasser, who had broken diplomatic relations with the United States, was gone, replaced by Anwar Sadat. Sadat reopened diplomatic relations and at the time McClure and Hathaway arrived, Ambassador Herman Eilts and his assistant, April Glaspie, were housed in the Spanish Embassy but working hard to reopen the mothballed American facility. Both McClure and Hathaway met with Egyptian officials who let it be known that Egypt wanted to begin distancing themselves from the Soviets and that they wanted to move closer to the United States, feeling that this would be a much better way to get the peace process moving in the Middle East. Former Ambassador Eilts confirmed this in an interview and said, "McClure did not meet with Sadat at that time, but he was the first senator to come to Egypt after the war and Sadat's people wanted him to take the message home that they were leaning toward the United States. Sadat didn't completely trust us at that time. He wasn't sure how dependable we would be. At that time I was meeting with him every day, and sometimes more than that."[13]

McClure and Hathaway left Cairo on November 21 and flew to Riyadh where they spent Thanksgiving. They were welcomed warmly by the Saudis and because of an earlier event, were treated to the most lavish luncheon either had ever experienced. Hathway explains:

Sometime before we left for the Middle East, we were briefed by the State Department in preparation for the trip—a briefing I might add that had nothing to do with the reality of the situation over there. Shortly afterward the briefer called the senator's office and said that Hisham Nazir, the Saudi minister for central planning was in town and nobody would see him. The briefer wondered if he could meet with McClure for a courtesy call. McClure agreed and suggested that we arrange a luncheon for him in the Capitol—in a dining room right off the floor that the senators used. It wasn't very fancy. We invited some senators and on the day of the luncheon Nasir showed up a little early so McClure and Senator Humphrey took him to the Senate floor and introduced him to some of the senators who were there.

When we got to the dining room, I can remember Mark Hatfield, George Aiken, Chuck Percy and Jesse Helms, and also we were surprised when this fellow from the Treasury Department, Bill Simon, walks in [Deputy Secretary of the Treasury]. *It was a wonderful luncheon, and as a result, when we got to Riyadh, Nasir, in appreciation, hosted a luncheon in honor of the senator at his home. We were shocked when something like 200 people showed up, including Prince Faisal, the son of the king who became minister of petroleum and today is the foreign minister for Saudi Arabia.*[14]

Their key contact, of course, was the United States Ambassador, Jim Akin, who was familiar with McClure because of his Dallas speech on oil Hathaway had sent him the previous February. Akin, a highly respected Arabist, explained to them some of the mistakes the United States had made in dealing with the Saudis. For example, he told them how, earlier, King Faisal had sent his finance minister to Washington with instructions to make a deal with the U.S. The deal was that the king would guarantee the U.S. a supply of oil at a reasonable price regardless of other circumstances in the Middle East if the U.S. would guarantee the security of his country. At the time, according to Akin, the Shah of Iran was coveting Saudi territory and King Faisal was worried about that. What Akin lamented was that King Faisal's representative went to Washington and languished there for three days because nobody of any consequence would bother seeing him. After that, he was ordered to come back home and, according to Akin (as explained by McClure and Hathaway) this caused the Saudis to fall in line with the anti-American Arabs and join the OPEC embargo.

But Akin also had some good news for the visitors. He had shown McClure's speech to the king and he had said he was impressed with McClure's insight and clear thinking. Said Hathaway:

McClure pointed out to the king that he was just one senator acting alone and that he did not represent the United States. He also explained that he came to listen, that he wanted the king to express his concerns and that as just one senator he would do all he could to make sure those concerns were understood by his fellow senators.

This was fairly late in the evening when we met, which I learned is the traditional time the king did his business. I remember that it was a long evening, and what made it more intense was that everything that was said had to be translated. The king explained that he appreciated what McClure had put into his speech and he was appreciative of McClure's warning. He made the point that all his nation had was oil and they didn't want to pump it all out and be left with nothing. He said he was happy pumping four million barrels a day. He also said they didn't want the U.S. to be dependent upon Saudi oil because they were constantly being pressured by radical Arabs to cut off our oil supply. He said that the Saudis wanted to be able to say [to the radical Arabs] *that America was not dependent upon their oil.*

I was impressed with King Faisal. He seemed like an honest man. And he seemed very impressed with McClure. I found out that it was unusual that the king would receive a legislator from the U.S. because in their kingdom, legislators have no respect or standing. A lot of our acceptance had to do with Akin. He explained to me that in checking McClure out he found that he was one of the honest people who did their homework. It was his opinion that for a lot of senators it [the state visit] *would have been one big party.*[15]

From Riyadh they flew to Kuwait and met with their hosts. McClure was impressed with the intelligence and education of the leaders and he quickly gained the impression that they were good businessmen. He was also impressed with their oil resource. Said he:

One of my vivid memories is that Kuwait is a very small and flat country that is completely desolate. There is nothing there except what man has created. There is one bulge that's maybe 400 feet high and they took us there where, in one direction you can see the oil fields where oil is flowing out of the wells by its own pressure. You look in the other direction a half mile or so and you can see the oil going into the tankers. At that time it cost them 14 cents a barrel to put their oil into a tanker—so practically every thing they got out of it was profit. They had the lowest cost of production in the world—lower than the Saudi's.[16]

From Kuwait they visited Lebanon, a beautiful place before violence erupted, then they went to Jordan where both McClure and Hathaway remember a harrowing 90 mph ride with Prince Abdullah at the wheel of his Mercedes with a jeep carrying a .50 caliber machine gun trying to follow and protect him. When they returned home after about three weeks in the Middle East, they vowed that they would never embark on such a lengthy trip again. Said Hathaway, "It's easy to think, 'Well, if we're going that far, we might as well hop over to this country and hop over to its neighbor, etc.' Those countries were so primitive at that time—you had to be so careful what you ate and drank. It was simply too stressful to be traveling over there for any length of time."[17]

In December, after McClure got settled back into his senate routine, he testified as a courtesy to the Foreign Relations Committee on what he had learned in the Middle East. McClure remembers that Chairman J. William Fulbright, (D-Arkansas) was sitting slouched in his chair, apparently bored with the whole affair, when he began his testimony. McClure explained what he had discovered in Egypt, how there was a good chance they would kick out the Soviets and build closer ties with the U.S. if they received any encouragement. "I was watching Fulbright as I was talking," said McClure, "and I noticed that he began to sit up straighter and straighter and that he was giving me penetrating looks."[18] McClure then went on to explain what he had learned from King Faisal in Saudi Arabia, and he told of the mistakes Ambassador Akin had described. Hathaway, who attended the hearing with McClure continues:

> *I wasn't watching Fulbright; I was watching Javits and Church, especially Javits. As McClure started telling about Sadat and the open door we might have in Egypt, Javits started turning purple and I thought he was going to have a heart attack. Finally, he just exploded, gushing forth all kinds of invective on how the Egyptians were just a bunch of liars and terrorists. He really tried to put McClure down. When McClure started talking about the Saudis and how impressed he had been with King Faisal's honesty, Javits exploded again—maybe he even stomped out—I think maybe he did. Church, who also had close ties to Israel, was obviously deeply disturbed by what he was hearing but in his rebuttal to McClure, he was more senatorial in his criticism. I suspected then that McClure was going to become a target by the Israeli lobby and I wasn't wrong.*[19]

McClure may have impressed Chairman Fulbright, but as Hathaway suspected, the testimony would soon land him in hot water with the pro-Israel senators and their backers. Said McClure, "I think it was one statement I made that may have scared the Israeli lobby. I said something to the effect that, 'While there are risks in trying to make peace, I thought Israel ought to assume some of those risks.' It wasn't long after that when the American Jewish Lobby assigned a lobbyist to me—a man from Chicago. At the time they would make the statement that there are no shades of gray for any politician; if you were not completely for them, you had to be on the other side; you had to be anti-Jewish. I think I got that label after my testimony and it stayed with me the rest of the time I was in the Senate."

Fulbright paid the price for being interested in both sides of the Arab-Israeli conflict, at least according to McClure. He believes to this day that the money that poured into Arkansas from the Israel Jewish Lobby during

Fulbright's re-election campaign the following year was a major factor in ending Fulbright's long political career.

The previous January, when he first took his place in the Senate, McClure had reason to wonder if or when he could take his place as a respected member of that body. "It was a bit of a concern," he said when asked about his feelings at the time, "because I can clearly remember the good feeling I had one day when I got out of the elevator with (Senator) Jim Pearson (R-Kansas) and he looked at me and said, 'Jim, you belong.' That meant a lot to me because he was a quiet fellow and not a glad hander, and I knew he meant it."[20] This was in the late spring or summer of 1973 and by then McClure would have drawn some attention from his colleagues for his rise as an energy expert. But, he was soon to give his colleagues several more reasons to respect his worth as a United States senator.

McCLURE AND THE MEDIA

Jim Norell, McClure's first press secretary was not watching Senators Fulbright or Javits; he was watching CBS correspondent, Roger Mudd, and his cameraman who were covering the hearings. Said Norell:

As soon as McClure began to explain how Egypt wanted closer ties to the U.S., Roger Mudd gave the throat-cutting symbol. As soon as he did, the lights went out and the cameraman made a noisy show of shutting down. This made Fulbright angry. He stopped McClure's testimony and told Mudd that he couldn't do that. Later, he said to McClure: 'Your testimony is one of the most courageous things I've heard a senator say.' Also, Fulbright's press secretary came up afterward and made it a point to compliment McClure. Of course, none of his testimony made the evening news.

What I carried away from that meeting was an impression of the profound effect McClure had on Chairman Fulbright. Truly, I think McClure's visit [to the Middle East] *also ended up having a profound effect on U.S. policy.*

Chapter 21 notes

i Said Thompson, "When McClure decided to run for the Senate, we talked about who we might get to endorse him. On my own I went to Aspinall's head man and asked if he could get the Chairman to write an endorsement. Shortly afterward we got a letter saying nice things about McClure that he knew we would use in the campaign. What is amazing about this was that by this time Aspinall was kind of a cranky old man, yet here he was, probably for the first time in his life, writing nice things about a Republican."

Chapter 22

Gold, Clean Air and the Rise to Leadership

Sand Pebbles. Every pipe and fitting and valve and steam conduit and pressure gauge—everything in the bowels of the boat was studied and memorized until the mis-matched, jury-rigged, patched-together ancient propulsion system was mastered. That is what the fictional Jake Holman did when he assumed duty as the engine room chief on the old gun boat, and that sure knowledge, and the extra knots of performance that resulted from his loving ministrations in the engine room, gained this old sailor respect, freedom and independence in a military environment where that ordinarily never existed for an enlisted man. In short, Jake beat the system with his knowledge.

When Jim McClure was first elected to the Idaho Senate, he was compared to Jake Holman. McClure spent many many hours studying all of the arcane rules and procedures by which the Senate operated, and as a result of his mastery of the system, he gained respect and prestige in his very first term when freshmen were largely ignored and when 99 percent of his colleagues, who rarely studied the rules themselves, were content to accede to his known mastery. In the Idaho Senate he gained respect and prestige. Like Jake Holman, he beat the system with his knowledge.

He tried the same thing when he went to the House and had moderate success. However, he was like a Jake Holman on a battleship where there were many others in the engine room with whom to compete. Amid 434 other representatives, mastery of the House rules still meant that he was a long way back in the queue that led to respect, prestige and leadership. And he had a ship's captain, the Speaker, who was probably as close to a dictator as any public servant in government.

Now he was in the U.S. Senate where the queue was less than a fourth as long, and where the rules provided the action parameters rather than a dictator like in the House. It was the perfect milieu for the Jake Holman in Jim McClure and he immediately set about to master this new engine room. He also had an incentive. The majority leader, Mike Mansfield (D-Montana), was supposed to be running the Senate, but he had other priorities and let the Democratic Whip, Robert Byrd (D-West Virginia) have that duty. Said McClure:

> *I watched Bob Byrd—he insisted on being called "Robert"—and I watched the others who were watching Bob Byrd. Because of his knowledge of the rules, he was always invoking them. It seemed to me that there was too much acquiescence* [by the minority party] *to his maneuvering. From my perspective a lot of our members were saying that this is the way it is; there isn't anything we can do about it so we'll hang back and let him do it. I didn't accept that; it didn't make any sense to me that he, alone, should use the rules to accomplish his ends when they were there to protect the rights of all of the members. So, in the context of trying to make things equal—to level the playing field—I decided to do something about that. If he could know the rules, I could know the rules. If he could use the rules for his benefit, I could use the rules for my benefit. So I learned the rules.*
>
> *Every new member is given a small book* [of Senate rules] *about the size of a King James Bible in small print. That is just the outline; there are multiple volumes of precedents—this happened on this date and the presiding officer ruled in this way, then the details of the rules and how they were applied to that precedent is explained. How could I find time to learn all of that? You are going to be working 100 percent of the time anyhow. It's up to the individual senator what you do with that time. Other senators decided not to try to master the rules. They thought it was not worth their time. I made a different decision. If you are going to work in a body, I believed you should learn how that body works. So I used some of my time to study the rules.*[1]

That is not all McClure did. Jim Norell, who was hired shortly after McClure started in the Senate and who was his first press secretary, explains:

> *When McClure first arrived* [in the Senate], *one of the jobs that freshmen senators are given is chair duty, where they have to preside over the Senate. Almost universally new senators hate this job. They find it tedious and basically, when you see new senators in the chair, the parliamentarians are telling them pretty much what to do. McClure did one of the most remarkably smart things when he came in—he took everyone's chair duty, Republicans and Democrats. They thought he was nuts. "Sure Jim," they would say, laughing behind their hands. Jim McClure had the last laugh because sitting in the chair day after day, he learned the rules. The parliamentarians had tremendous respect for him. He, indeed, presided over the Senate and, most important, he spent all that time observing the players. He knew the smart guys; he figured out the dumb guys; he found out who the vain people were; he understood the relationships between senators watching them work. He was able to draw a very clear picture*

Courtesy Alan Timothy

McClure, Senator Frank Church and Representative Orval Hansen.

of alliances, and he learned who the staff movers and shakers were on both sides of the aisle. And he did that for about six months, and when Jim McClure was finished, in name he was a freshman senator; in reality he was a seasoned veteran. And it was brilliant.[2 i]

McClure needed all that knowledge because he did not intend to play the "shut up and listen" role, which as Dick Thompson remembers, ". . .was still a little bit prevalent in the Senate for new members. McClure was definitely not intimidated as a freshman senator. Although "pushy" is not the right word to describe him in those early months, or ever, actually. . .he ran for the Senate because he thought he could accomplish more than he could in the House—that's what he promised the voters in Idaho—so when we got there, he was determined to make good on that promise. Would "aggressive" be a better word? No, that word does not fit McClure. Serious and very determined better describes him."[3]

Evidence of McClure's determination came just twelve days after he was sworn in. On January 15, he introduced a bill that would end the government's prohibition on the private ownership of gold. He had introduced similar bills during his years in the House, but nothing ever came of them; he did not have the seniority to get the attention of the House Banking Committee, which would have to have endorsed such a bill for it to have any chance to be voted on. Besides, the U.S. Treasury Department was staunchly opposed to such a move, fearing, as President Franklin Roosevelt had in 1933 when he successfully pushed through a law banning private ownership of gold, that the accumulation of gold by individuals could destabilize U.S. currency and create monetary chaos. McClure had made numerous speeches before committees and the House itself trying to refute arguments from the Treasury, but to no avail. The whole picture changed in the Senate. Biding his time and watching for opportunities after the introduction of his bill in January, McClure saw an opportunity in early April. A bill was before the Senate that had nothing to do with gold, but with his knowledge of the rules he confidently introduced his gold legalization bill as an amendment to that bill and much to the shock of Treasury officials, it was approved by a vote of sixty-eight to twenty-three. That kind of backing by the Senate got the attention of the House Banking Committee, which sent a similar bill to the floor that lost on a tie vote, but which, after months of maneuver and haggling, later passed. With McClure leading the charge to get Senate approval for a slightly modified new version, it finally passed both Houses and was signed into law. McClure won the first battle he launched in the Senate. On December 31, 1974 it became legal for Americans to own gold again.

McClure was also engaged in another battle about this time. In his Subcommittee on Air and Water Pollution under the Public Works Committee, there was a push to amend the Clean Air Act, which controlled emissions from heavy industry. Chairman Edmund Muskie, who the previous year had failed in his attempt to win the Democratic presidential nomination, was determined to become a hero of the environmentalists by enacting much stricter controls over industry emissions and, more important, bring automobile tailpipe emissions under stricter federal control. McClure was not opposed to reducing air pollutants and as usual when he encountered a new technical issue, he listened carefully to the expert testimony and studied the materials that engineer and Legislative Aide Mike Hathaway and others furnished him. As the hearings on the amendment proceeded, both McClure and Hathaway could see a trend developing that concerned them. Said Hathaway:

> *Each part of the bill had two parts, one that set emission standards and the other that gave the federal government greater regulatory power. It didn't take me long to see that Muskie's staff, especially Leon Billings, his staff director, had a specific goal in mind. I saw that they were sometimes willing to compromise on the standards but never on anything relating to government control. A case in point: A huge issue was how we were going to control automobile tailpipe emissions. GM and Ford were proposing to do it with a catalytic converter; Chrysler had designed a new cleaner burning engine and they wanted to do it that way. The problem was that Billings, who Muskie*

let run things, was determined to set the deadline for emissions controls in the 1975 model cars. Chrysler hadn't even built their new engine yet and, since that was their only alternative, they could not possibly have the new engines ready for that model year. We knew that it would bankrupt them and it eventually did. I remember, when we got that news, I said to Billings, "Congratulations, Leon, you have bankrupted Chrysler; what are you going to do now? He replied, "Take 'em over and turn 'em into a yardstick industry." By that he meant that the government would run the company and, since he believed the government could do it cheaper, the bureaucrats would use their amount of profit as a yardstick to determine if the other two companies were making exorbitant profits. It was a pure socialistic idea and Billings had a precedent in advocating it because that same thing had already been done in England, France and Sweden.[4]

MIKE HATHAWAY ON LEON BILLINGS

During the hearings we invited representatives of power companies to come and give testimony on their emissions and what, if anything, they were planning to do about them. I remember this one meeting, Leon was chairing it for Muskie, and he was sitting up there with this big black cigar. The room was full of smoke. You could barely breathe, and here we were talking about how we were going to protect people's health from air pollution. That day we had this power company executive—I don't remember which company he represented—and before he testified, he handed Leon a piece of paper with the summary of his points. Leon didn't even look at it. Instead he methodically folded it into a paper airplane, threw it back at the executive, then blew out a big cloud of cigar smoke. He thought it was hilarious that these people were thinking of air pollution as an environmental issue.

McClure, himself, has a vivid memory of those proceedings and laments that he was not able to get the deadline extended so Chrysler could develop their clean burning engine and give Americans an opportunity to choose the better of two different systems. As it happened, GM and Ford won, but then they had such a short time to equip the '75 models, which had to be in the showroom in mid-1974, that those cars were notorious trouble makers and the world is still locked into the catalytic converter technology. Also, what still irks McClure is the way the president of GM lied to him during the hearings. "Ed Cole was testifying and talking about fuel efficiency and compression ratios and I knew something about that—I had put a water injector and a new head on my 1942 Chrysler to get more horsepower and efficiency.[ii] So I asked him directly: 'You are saying that there is no relationship between fuel efficiency and compression ratios?' He said that there was no relationship. He flat out lied to the committee."[5]

McClure's woes did not end with the committee hearings. Before the Clean Air Amendment would become law, Hathaway remembers that it had to go through 137 markup sessions in subcommittee, full committee and in joint markup sessions between the House and Senate. "I remember that the members were still in a markup session at 2 a.m one Saturday morning, and that they eventually turned it over to staff. We worked three days continuously, around the clock, going home only to change clothes and shower."[6]

Actually, those markup sessions were only the beginning of McClure's trouble with the Clean Air Amendment. After those sessions, when the members worked diligently to craft language that could not be misconstrued by regulators or judges, it was left to the staff to prepare a committee report which was an expanded explanation of what the bill was about. This is the legislative explanation for the people who will implement the legislation. It is the legislative history that will guide the bureaucracy. That is why McClure went into shock when he saw the committee report. He said:

> *When I read that report, I saw the most bare-faced subversion of a committee's work I have ever seen. I was appalled; there were things in that report that were the opposite of what the committee decided. I went to Ed Muskie and he brushed me aside. In effect he refused to do anything about it. I then went to* [Senator] *Jennings Randolph* [D-West Virginia] *who was chairman of the full committee* [Environment and Public Works]. *He was a perfect gentleman. Saying he was a gentle person doesn't quite do justice to him; he was an absolute gentleman. You could talk to him regardless of party. He had just exactly the right kind of temperament to be a senator and work with people with diverse views. He was the opposite of Muskie who had his own agenda and who was going to force it through. I talked to Randolph, gave him some examples of how the report differed from the legislation, and told him I didn't believe Leon Billings and the staff should get by with such devious maneuvering. I asked Randolph if he would bring the committee report before the full committee for discussion so I could point out errors. He agreed, and this is the first and only time I have ever seen this done. The figures I remember are that I pointed out 126 places where the staff had changed legislative intent and that they agreed with me on 123 of them. As a result the report got rewritten and what came out was an accurate report of what the committee had done—not all that I personally approved of by any means—but what the law intended. This was not the first or last time I saw examples of staff abuse, but this experience with Billings and his staff was the worst I ever observed."*[7]

By the end of McClure's first year in the Senate, everyone who was observing him and with whom the author has spoken believes that McClure had earned the respect of his colleagues for his keen mind, determination, poise on the Senate floor, his humility, and for his dry, almost puckish sense of humor. "He was congenitally incapable of holding a grudge against his adversaries," said one of his staffers. "He admired and respected Bobby Byrd, for example. Byrd had come out of an orphanage in West Virginia and had risen from poverty. McClure admired him for that. Hubert Humphrey was another opponent he genuinely liked even though he hated his politics. And Humphrey liked McClure—I remember one day I was near the floor when Humphrey came up to me and said, 'You'd better go get your boss, a bill of mine is coming up on the floor and I know he'll want to attack it. Can you imagine someone doing that? But that's the way people reacted to McClure. In an amazingly short time he had earned a lot of respect."[8]

Then came a chance conversation between McClure and another conservative Senator. Dick Thompson explains:

> *One day—I would guess that it was maybe in April '74—Teddy Kennedy was speaking and McClure heard Carl Curtis* [R-Nebraska] *say, "I know he's lying, but I don't have the staff to do the research to prove otherwise." McClure replied, saying something to the effect, "You know, there is a way we could do something.* [Senator] *Bill Brock* [R-Tennessee] *has made it possible to pool staff. We could get the conservative senators together and form a steering committee with a staff paid for by contributions from each of the members." That is sort of how it started. I know McClure came back and told me about it. I thought it was a great idea. I checked with Paul Weyrich, who was a special assistant to Curtis, and he had talked it over with his boss and thought it was a super idea. So, with the two senator's blessings, Paul and I divided up the conservative senators between us and began making calls on them. Sometimes I talked to their AA's* [administrative assistants] *and sometimes to the senators themselves. We got really enthusiastic results until we got to Bill Brock. He thought we should include a couple of moderate/liberal senators: Ed Brooke and Chuck Percy, but that would have defeated the purpose of conservatives working together. When we took that information to Curtis and McClure, they balked at that. Then the project stalled. Both of our senators backed off a little. I think maybe two months went by—Paul thinks it was three. But Paul and I kept talking about it and finally, Paul said, "Let's get the two together for a lunch. I'll even pay for it. Let's both brief them on what we think they should do."*[9]

Paul Weyrich, who at the time was a part time staffer for Senator Curtis, but who was working full time on the side getting the Heritage Foundation started, picks up the story from there:

> *Thompson's version is quite accurate and I'll add what I remember. After I proposed paying for the lunch, we briefed our senators saying that it was very important to come out of that meeting with firm plans to get the steering committee started. Okay, we get them together in the dining room and it was one of the most amusing events of my life. Right away Curtis, a no-nonsense, let's-get-down-to-business, no-idle-chit-chat-guy, says, "Okay, Paul here thinks we ought to have a senate steering committee," and before he could say anymore, McClure pipes right up and says, "I completely agree, and you should be the chairman," and Curtis doesn't let him say more when he says, "And you should be the vice-chairman and send out the invitations," and McClure interrupts him and says, "I absolutely want it if you agree"—I mean they were so well briefed going in there that they were answering each other's questions before they were asked.*
>
> *Curtis turned to me and asked how much money we should try to raise from members and I said $25,000. He gulped and said, "All right." Then he explained that if he was re-elected the coming fall, he was going to run for conference chairman*[iii] *and that if he won, McClure should agree to take over. McClure agreed. It was the most perfect meeting I have ever attended and Dick Thompson and I laughed about it years afterward. That was the start. At our initial meeting, as I recall, we had fourteen senators. That was in the summer of 1974—July, I think. Everyone agreed to chip in to hire a staff and to begin immediately. From my viewpoint that was one of the most momentous events in the history of the Senate. Now the Senate Steering Committee includes most of the Republican senators and it has been a major force since its beginning.*[10]

McCLURE ON THE CHRYSLER BANKRUPTCY

At the time we were considering the Clean Air Amendment, Mike Hathaway and I visited all three of the major producers. At GM it was obvious that they were very successful. They had this beautiful campus of buildings and lots of money. Ford was also impressive, with good clean modern buildings. Chrysler was a drastic change. They were operating in a dingy, old multi-story building, and in the executive parking lot behind the building, we could see that the executives were driving Mercedes and various other foreign cars. It was easy to see that there was a vast cultural difference between Chrysler and the other two manufacturers. It was obvious that the Clean Air Amendment and the catalytic converter requirement was not the sole cause of their bankruptcy.

Senator Carl Curtis was re-elected the following autumn, and when he ran for Conference Chairman, he beat out Senator Jacob Javits from New York. McClure immediately began a quiet campaign among his conservative colleagues and by unanimous consent he was elected to be the new chairman of the Senate Steering Committee—a position he would hold for the next six years. By the beginning of the New Year, 1975—just two years after he had been sworn into the Senate—he had risen to become a recognized leader in the world's most powerful body of legislators. It was a proud moment, but there were more to come.

Chapter 22 notes

i. McClure said, after hearing Norell's comment: "It sounds like I had a calculated plan in mind to learn how the Senate works. I don't think that is true. Actually, I spent all that extra time observing the Senate because I was curious and, yes, a bit fascinated by all of the different individuals from all over the country."

ii. Mike Hathaway says that he also noticed Cole's error and showed McClure thermodynamics tables from a textbook that proved him wrong—tables that Hathaway said McClure was already familiar with and easily understood.

iii. The "Conference" is the body made up of all Republican Senators—the Democrats in the Senate call their body the "Caucus." The Conference Chairman is the third ranking Republican leader behind the Majority Leader and the Assistant Majority Leader, or Whip.

Chapter 23

Embattled Minority

Ernest Hemingway was fond of saying, "There always comes a time when a writer has to kill off his little darlings."[1] That is what has to be done now. The fictional Jake Holman on the *Sand Pebbles* served a purpose in this narrative, but it is now time for him to retire to his engine room, happy to be the king of his domain and to be where he can completely ignore where his captain is steering the boat. Jim McClure could not do that. After two years in the Senate he had mastered the rules and he understood how the institution worked, but he did not like the direction it was moving. He had not liked the course it was steering when he arrived in January of 1973. But now it was the late autumn of 1974 and three events had occurred, the results of which caused him to believe that the Senate and his country were on a heading for disaster.

The first of these events occurred in August, 1973 when his friend, Vice President Ted Agnew,[i] landed in hot water. This bothered McClure who said, "I liked his spirit and the way he conducted himself. He made his fame by taking on the press and he did it joyfully, describing them with phrases like, 'nattering nabobs of negativism' and 'an effete corps of impudent snobs.' He took them on with good humor, and those of us who wanted them taken on, cheered."[2]

Agnew had toned down his rhetoric after winning a second term with Nixon in 1972, but the folks who had been called nattering nabobs and impudent snobs were not about to forget his insults and they were laying for him, ready to pounce when he made a misstep. And he had made a big one. Investigators in the U.S. Attorney's office in Maryland alleged that, while governor of Maryland, he had accepted a kickback from a bridge contractor in the amount of $29,500. Even though this was an allegation, the nabobs got their revenge. Shortly after the accusation emerged in August, the media made sure the story was widely reported. A contrite Agnew finally mumbled in his defense that, if he had taken a "contribution" from a contractor, it was strictly for his entertainment fund at the governor's mansion and that none of the money went into his pocket to enrich himself. But this was a pitifully lame admission, and when he was confronted with a further charge that he had not paid income tax on the "contribution," he had no choice but to plead *nolo contendere* and resign from the Nixon administration. He was later fined $10,000, disbarred and put on three years' probation.[ii]

Agnew's resignation hurt President Nixon's image before the American people but he, himself, was already in hot water. The previous year the Committee to Re-elect the President had paid five men to break into and bug a Democratic campaign office in the Watergate Hotel. They were caught, and while Nixon claimed that he had had no prior knowledge of the attempted burglary—an explanation the public believed enough to send him back to the White House with a landslide victory—more and more evidence was accumulating to show that he had engaged in an elaborate coverup to keep the blame from landing in his office. But then it was discovered that Nixon had a secret taping system in his office, and that these tapes would tell the real story if they could be obtained. Finally, through court orders, the tapes were released and some of the damaging conversations were transcribed and released to the public. Jim Norell, McClure's press secretary, remembers what happened next:

> *I remember this big flat dolly coming down the hall stacked high with copies of the tape transcriptions. McClure got his copies and retreated to his office to read them. Then, after awhile, he called us all in and said, "Listen to this." He would read excerpts, then shake his head and say, "Can you really believe the President would talk like this in the White House?" That's when I realized for the first time that I had never heard McClure cuss—so I understood why the language bothered him. Then we would leave and he would call us back again—he wanted to share with us what he was reading.*[3]

McClure has his own memory of those days. He says:

> *I thought then and still feel that the break in was a sophomoric trick but not a major crime. Of course, I have to put that against the backdrop of another event. When Nixon was running for president in 1960, his campaign head-quarters were on the top floor of the Mayflower Hotel and these offices were bugged by the Democrats—I got that from a fellow who knew the facts. Nixon lost, of course, and he was bitter about it and he remembered the bugging when nobody made any big deal out of it.*
>
> *The Watergate break in was really stupid; Nixon was so far ahead in the polls; there was no doubt that he was going to win. I was thinking at the time that if it had been Harry Truman, he would have just said, "So they broke in, what the hell," and he would have gone on and the people would have forgotten about it. But Nixon, with his personality, could not find it possible to trust anyone so he hunkered down and used every tool he had to obstruct the investigation.*

> *In regard to the tape transcriptions, I read some of them; I didn't read them all. I remember the disgust I felt toward the way the people talked. I'm not lily white; I used bad language on occasion, but never like it was used in the White House at that time. You had to feel disgust for Nixon because he was the player. However, it did not then or since detract from my judgment that he was a brilliant man whose grasp of geopolitical affairs was greater than any president in my immediate knowledge.*
>
> *I'm still not sure how it would have affected me on a vote for impeachment. You don't vote to impeach because of bad judgment or bad language or because you want a political change. You never allow it to be an ordinary political battle—that is a very slippery slope indeed. I would have voted for impeachment for Bill Clinton—not for the sexual affair or the trampling of women's rights, but because he lied under oath to a grand jury—nobody should be above the law. I did not see that Watergate was rising to that level. But Nixon had lost his capacity to lead the country at this point and it was a great feeling of relief when he resigned. My emotions had been building for so long and my feelings were so intense. That brought an end to that crisis, but at the same time I had a great feeling of defeat. What was so sad was that he didn't trust the American people enough to tell them the truth.*[4]

Agnew resigned in October, 1973 and Nixon resigned in August, 1974. These two events were devastating to the morale of Republicans all across the country and this was reflected by those in Congress who were trying to cope with already overwhelming majorities of Democrats in both houses. Then came the huge disaster, at least for Republicans. The odor from the Agnew-Nixon debacles[iii] had spread across the land, poisoning the districts of seventy-five House Republicans who were defeated in the November election. They were replaced by seventy-five Democrats, which would tilt the numbers to where the Republicans would occupy less than one-third of the seats. (The Republicans also lost four seats in the Senate.) In addition, many of the new Democrats were young and passionate, not content to "go along and get along" like freshmen were expected to do. These new Democrats came in ready to fight and win for issues that McClure and most of his fellow Idahoans loathed.

Like gun control.

Jim McClure believed (and still believes) that the issue of gun control has polarized Americans into one of two camps. First, there are the liberals who believe that guns cause crime and violence, and the simplest way to stop these evils is to take guns out of the hands of everybody but military and law enforcement personnel. Those in the other camp, the conservatives, believe that criminals cause crime and violence, and the way to stop this

Courtesy McClure family

McClure shares a moment in the Oval Office with President Gerald Ford in February 1975. Ford and McClure had served together in the House of Representatives.

activity is to take the criminal out of society. In addition, the conservatives claim to have a powerful law on their side: the Second Amendment to the Constitution which states:

> *A well regulated militia, being necessary to the security of a free state, the right of the people to keep and bear arms, shall not be infringed.*

That amendment has been debated endlessly, with liberals taking the position that John Doe does not have the right to own a gun if he is not part of a militia, while conservatives argue that the authors of the amendment meant that John Doe should always have the right of self-protection and that nobody can take away that right unless the amendment is repealed.

When McClure went to the Senate, conservatives had little hope of stopping the momentum of the gun control advocates who far outnumbered them. Before that, in 1968 after the assassinations of Robert Kennedy and Martin Luther King, he and his fellow conservatives watched helplessly as the House, by an overwhelming vote, passed a gun control bill that was onerous to the conservatives. So for McClure the situation was grim after the 1974 election debacle with the new gun control advocates even more thirsty for action and the conservatives with even less power. Legislative Assistant Margo Carlisle laughed when she was asked what chance conservatives had in stopping the liberal agenda and especially the gun control juggernaut. Said she, "In the Senate at that time, and especially after the 1974 elections, conservatives like McClure were considered lesser human beings. They were thought of as a lesser breed, like dogs, not people."[5]

Then an amazing thing happened. Jim Norell explains:

> *There was an effort by the Consumer Products Safety Commission* [CPSC] *to ban handgun ammunition as a hazardous product in the home. They asked for public comments on the proposed ban, and the record would be open for sixty days. After talking it over with McClure, I wrote a press release with fairly bombastic language explaining how dangerous this would be to gun owners—that it was back door gun control. Well, the* New York Times *and the* Washington Post—*all sorts of newspapers wrote editorials about this bumpkin from Idaho and how absurd it was that he should be attacking this reasonable proposal—they just ridiculed our press release. But they also went farther. They printed the address of the Consumer Products Safety Commission and urged the readers to once and for all show how the public really feels about safety in the home. They said that if enough people write, this could be like a national plebiscite that would settle the issue. When we read these editorials, we had no idea what would happen. But it was amazing. The responses were like 400,000 against and 400 for—it was just spontaneous combustion. This was the biggest single mass of comments to ever come into a Federal Agency. It was stunning.*
>
> *Then the NRA* [National Rifle Association] *got into the act with mailings across the country and, before the comment period ended, opposition ran 20,000 to one against the CPSC action. Then McClure got into the act by writing a succinct amendment that prohibited such action by the CPSC. On the floor of the Senate it passed by a voice vote. Then* [Senator]*Teddy Kennedy offered an amendment that would permit the CPSC to use any kind of regulation if ". . .the use of either the ammunition or the weapon can result in unreasonable risk or injury to the user." He called for a voice vote and it was defeated overwhelmingly. Then I saw this little creep who worked for Kennedy whispering in his ear. Kennedy immediately got up and asked for a roll call vote. You could read the expressions on the faces of the other senators: Why are you making me go on record on this? So they had a roll call vote and it was defeated 75-11. It was just stunning. The*

whole gun control debate was turned on its ear and was never to be the same since. Prior to this, conservatives had no chance of stopping gun control, nor had any senator been recognized as a leader in that fight. After that CPSC battle, McClure became the leader on anything that had to do with guns.[6]

Idahoans in particular were angry over the effort of the liberals to control the purchase of ammunition. McClure was quoted as saying, "I have personally handed over to the CPSC mail and petitions with now well over 30,000 signatures of citizens—mostly from my state—who wrote in total opposition to a government agency 'protecting' them by banning a product they use. . .The ratio of mail on the issue to my office was 20,000-plus against the ban to none for it."[7]

McClure could take pride in getting his amendment passed, but in a way he was lucky because the gun control issue affected so many Americans in a way that aroused their passions. Unfortunately, many other forms of legislation did not touch off such spontaneous combustion and McClure and his like-minded colleagues deeply felt their inadequacy. But they fought on, McClure lamenting that he constantly had to be "negative" and "against" legislation rather than being pro-active. Margo Carlisle, who had moved from her position as McClure's legislative assistant to staff director of the Senate Steering Committee, said that McClure repeatedly reminded his colleagues, "At least, if we can't pass positive legislation, we can continue to fight and try to stop legislation that will damage our country."[8]

And this they were sometimes able to do. Carlisle describes one such battle:

Sometime in the spring or summer of 1975 the Democrats and Javits Republicans came up with this labor bill that would allow Common Situs *picketing. What this means is that if a one-block construction site has four or five unions representing the different workers on the site, if one union went out on strike, all of the other unions would have to go out. It was a monster that could paralyze the construction industry. Well, McClure believed, even though they were a small minority, that the Senate Steering Committee should take on that bill using Rule 22, the filibuster. So that is what they did. He got guys like Paul Laxalt* [R-Nevada] *to help him and they talked and talked. This stopped everything, which became news. Once the press got involved, they began to dig into the issue. More important, editors of the newspapers like the* Washington Post *got involved. Not only did the* Post *get involved, they wrote an editorial saying this whole piece of legislation was not a good idea and they editorialized against it. Of course, the legislation passed both the Senate and the*

> *House because labor had these huge majorities, but when the bill went to* [President] *Ford, he vetoed it. McClure and several members of the steering committee had met with Ford and I'm sure they helped persuade him.*[9 iv]

McClure had two more big victories before the close of the year 1975. For several years he had been working to get money appropriated for reconstruction of the American Falls Dam. On a national scale the priority for this project did not register on any congressional screen, and every year it had failed. Would this year be any different? Orval Hansen and Jim McClure were determined to give it their best shot, but the biggest hang-up was in the Senate. However, McClure changed tactics. He engineered a mechanism by which the dam reconstruction appropriation would be attached to three

JEFF CILEK DESCRIBES A McCLURE-BYRD CLASH ON THE SENATE FLOOR

Jeff Cilek, who rose from mail clerk to be McClure's legislative director, tells the story of an angry Robert Byrd attacking the Senate Steering Committee. Cilek said:

One day while Senator McClure was in a committee meeting, he received a notice to report to the Senate floor immediately. Before he got there Senator Byrd had been on the floor railing against the Senate Steering Committee:

"So, as to a 'Senate Steering Committee,' let it be known by my colleagues on this side of the aisle, let it be known by my colleagues on the other side of the aisle, let it be known by the press and the public, by all Senate offices, staffs and staffs of committees, that so far as I am concerned that there is no 'Senate Steering Committee.' None."

Then he started attacking Margo Carlisle:

"I hold in my hand a calling card, a beautifully embossed calling card. . . [and there] *appears the name, 'Margo Carlisle.' Who is Margo Carlisle? Would somebody tell me, who is Margo Carlisle?. . .Who pays Margo Carlisle. . .of the so-called Senate Steering Committee. . .I am waiting. I shall yield my time to any senator who will tell me about this so-called Senate Steering Committee."*

Then McClure arrived, asked for the floor, and Byrd said:

"I wait with real interest to hear further from Senator McClure's lips in stentorian tones the explanation of this mysterious 'Senate Steering Committee.'"

McClure rose and told Byrd he knew full well what the Senate Steering Committee was and that, together, they had discussed it. This angered Byrd and they had a heated exchange on who had the right to talk. Byrd was flustered and McClure was enjoying himself as they argued over whether McClure had the right to use the name "Senate" in the committee title. McClure then claimed that the word "Senate" was not copyrighted and went on to read from the telephone directory the names of the Senate Inn, Senate Motors, etc. Finally, McClure needled Byrd by thanking him for all the good publicity he had given his committee.

Courtesy Miles Carlisle

Paul Weyrich shows off to Margo Carlisle and McClure. The T-shirt was created after Robert Byrd's tirade about Carlisle on the Senate floor..

different bills that had to be passed by the Senate: (1) a Social Security bill, (2) a Medicare bill, and (3) a bill to extend an income tax credit for six months. Surprisingly, all three passed the Senate, but the last one was the one that passed both houses of Congress. Said McClure in a tongue-in-cheek announcement to Idaho weeklies, ". . .when President Ford makes the headlines by signing the income tax extension, few people will know that he is really signing the American Falls Dam bill, with the income tax extension attached to it."[10]

His second victory was on an issue with which he had been involved since he was a member of the chamber of commerce in Payette.

The issue was Hells Canyon, the deepest gorge in the world where the Snake River forms the border between Idaho and Oregon. For many years both public and private power advocates coveted the raging waters flowing through that gorge as a great untapped source of water power for generating electricity. Various proposals had come and gone, and during the years when advocates and opponents fought each other over the territory, McClure had not taken any firm stand. However, he did voice opinions. For example, he always declared that Idaho should never lose the right to that water—this when California loomed as a threat to divert water to their massively growing urban population centers. Also, if one or more dams were to be constructed, he declared that he would always fight for private power because private companies would pay taxes that would benefit Idaho.

Despite his lack of a firm stand on the issue, he was privately sympathetic to a solution that would protect and preserve the uniqueness of Hells Canyon. He remembered his father telling how, when he lived in Council, he had hiked into the gorge to meet with one of his law clients. And McClure, himself, had poignant memories of his childhood when he was driven down the precipitous, winding Kleinschmidt Grade into the gorge in his family's 1926 Buick. Hells Canyon had a special place in his heart, and when his questionnaires came back showing that his Idaho constituents strongly favored protecting the canyon and its waters, this was all he needed to hook his private feelings to the sentiment of his constituents and begin a campaign to preserve it. There were several possibilities, including turning it into a new wilderness. However, both McClure and a majority of those who spoke at various hearings held on the matter, felt that the National Recreation Area concept, such as had just been implemented with the SNRA, was more appropriate.

In the past McClure had his critics, many of whom lambasted him in correspondence and at hearings because he did not aggressively stand for preservation—criticism that hurt him because of his inner feelings about the area. However, at the end of 1975, as the Senate was racing to finish its business for the Christmas recess, it was primarily McClure's leadership efforts that got the Hells Canyon Recreation Area bill through the Senate. This, in addition to his efforts to overcome House opposition to the bill, caused the *The Lewiston Morning Tribune,* one of McClure's most persistent and steadfast critics, to opine:

> *Twenty years in the making, the Hells Canyon Recreation Area will become a reality upon the signature of President Ford. Approved by Congress Friday, the bill essentially preserves the free-flowing status of the Middle Snake River south of Lewiston. . .Credits for establishing a recreation area for Hells Canyon must go, of course, to early-day environmentalists whose foresight delayed further power company designs on the already concrete-choked Snake River. Back pats must also be given to members of Congress from the Northwest, like Rep. Al Ullman, Sen. Robert Packwood, and Sen. Frank Church, who were behind the legislation from the start.*
>
> *But the highest tribute should be reserved for Idaho Sen. James McClure, whose pro-recreation area stand placed him at odds with many of his fellow conservatives and those segments of industry from whom he receives much of his campaign support. McClure led the Senate passage and helped to overcome House opposition, championed mainly by his fellow Republican from Idaho, Rep. Steve Symms. McClure steadfastly held out, however uncomfortable, against pressure from political allies to soften his stance.*

McClure placed the welfare of future generations over political expediency. For that, he deserves recognition. A gold star for Jim McClure.[11]

Chapter 23 notes

i Agnew's first name "Spiro" was never used on a personal basis; he was known to his friends by the shortened version of his middle name, Theodore.

ii Eight years later he was ordered by a Maryland court to repay more than $248,000 to cover bribes he took while in state office.

iii Many analysts at the time also placed some of the blame for anti-Republican voting on new President, Gerald Ford, who pardoned Nixon right after he resigned.

iv Secretary of Labor at that time, John T. Dunlop, claims in a 1988 interview that President Ford vetoed it because he was afraid Ronald Reagan would use it against him in the upcoming race for the Presidential nomination. Dunlop, who favored the bill, resigned after that, claiming the veto destroyed his capacity for performing the duties of his office.

Chapter 24

Another Tragedy

His correspondence had more than doubled. He was on three times the number of committees and subcommittees than when he was in the House. His leadership responsibilities had greatly increased after he became chairman of the Senate Steering Committee. He had far more visitors from Idaho who would feel neglected if he did not meet with them personally. Then there were the fund raisers and receptions: industry receptions, embassy receptions, convention receptions, many of which he felt obligated to attend either for his own enlightenment or because Idaho people would be there expecting to see him.

Then there were the speeches. After he became the recognized leader of the anti-gun control movement, every major gathering of gun owners wanted to hear from him. The same for those who, after many years of fighting the U.S. Treasury Department, were now able to buy and sell gold. In addition, more than anybody else in the Congress, Jim McClure was becoming recognized as the Congressional energy expert, and after the Arab Embargo of 1973 and the recession it triggered, he was in demand as a speaker who could specify solutions to the problem.

And there were the foreign trips. He traveled to Japan with a delegation. He spent the Christmas holidays with another delegation in Antarctica and celebrated the New Year at the South Pole. He made another investigative trip back to the Middle East, visiting leaders in Israel, Egypt, Iraq, Saudi Arabia and Algeria. And, with a group of fourteen senators, he visited the Soviet Union.

All of the foregoing makes it seem like Senator Jim McClure had a full plate. Actually, that was not true. The activities thus described made up what might be called the potatoes and vegetables on his plate. The main course, the meat on his plate, had nothing to do with his work in Washington or the lecture circuit or a foreign country. His overriding concern day after day after day was spelled I-D-A-H-O.

A major share of his concern resulted from observations of some of his Senate colleagues. He had observed that many of those who were getting national attention by the media had a tendency to try to live up to their reputations. In other words, big names tended to develop big egos. He saw this as a danger because those same individuals tended to drift farther and farther away from their constituents, physically as well as philosophically. And even though, despite their philosophical differences, he got along with his senior colleague, Frank Church, McClure felt that this was also happening to him, especially since he had become actively involved in the race for the Democratic nomination for President.[i] To McClure, losing touch with your constituents was one of the most abhorrent things a U.S. senator could do, and he was obsessed with the desire not to let that happen to him.

And he had an action plan to prevent it. When he was a First District congressman, he had done what no other Idaho congressman before him had done: he opened congressional offices in Coeur d' Alene and Lewiston—in addition to the traditional Boise office. When he became senator, he did what no other Idaho senator had done: he kept the three offices in Coeur d' Alene, Lewiston and Boise, and he opened new offices in Twin Falls, Pocatello

RUTHIE JOHNSON

The most famous of the regional assistants, Ruthie Johnson, served McClure in his Coeur d' Alene office from the beginning to the end of his congressional career. She was so well known for her heroic efforts to help people in need, Bill Hall from *The Lewiston Morning Tribune* labeled her the "Mother Hen of North Idaho." Here is one of her favorite stories about McClure:

I got this call from his office telling me that he was flying into Spokane and that I needed to meet him and transport him to some meetings in my region. I met the airplane, picked him up and drove him to meetings in Coeur d' Alene, then down to St. Maries, Orofino and over to Lewiston. There we both boarded a flight for Boise where we attended a Republican meeting.

I paid my own way, by the way. Never did I claim any expenses for a political meeting. After the meeting, I flew to Spokane, but in the meantime Wayne, my husband, bummed a ride to Lewiston to pick up my car and, of course, he met me in Spokane. The next day I submitted an expense account for car mileage from Coeur d' Alene to Spokane and back, then to St. Maries, Orofino, Lewiston and back to Coeur d' Alene. A few days later I got a call: "Ruthie, we can't approve your mileage expense because you weren't in the car going from Lewiston to Coeur d' Alene. I said, "That's ridiculous; I drove the senator to Lewiston. How was I to get the car back to Coeur d' Alene?" The secretary said, "Well, that is the rule." I said, "Who made that decision?" She said, "The Senator." "Well, put him on if he's available," I said. McClure came on and I pleaded my case. He said, "I'm sorry, Ruthie, I understand completely, but the rules are the rules and I can't change them." I was irritated and I said, "That's the chintziest thing I've ever heard of, but thank you for listening." In a few days I received my expense check, minus the mileage from Lewiston to Coeur d' Alene. But, I also got another letter and I recognized McClure's handwriting. Inside the envelope was a personal check on his private account for $11.00—the mileage I didn't get from the government. I wish I had kept that check and framed it.

Courtesy Ruthie Johnson

Ruthie Johnson, McClure's regional assistant in Coeur d' Alene was known as "The Mother Hen of North Idaho."

and Idaho Falls. Thus, he had six offices, one in each region of Idaho, with each one staffed with a regional assistant who could deal with constituents directly on a walk-in, face-to-face, personal basis.

That was not all. He was also obsessed with knowing what his Idaho constituents were thinking. As a representative he had mailed out a questionnaire every year and he had carefully studied the results. As a senator he continued that process but, in addition, he asked Jim Goller to work with the regional assistants and schedule town meetings where he could personally meet with constituents and listen to their concerns. According to Goller,

"If I had to guess, I would say we had McClure out here about every other weekend, and perhaps more than that. He'd fly in Thursday night to say, Pocatello, and we'd schedule a meeting maybe in the courthouse in Soda Springs for Friday morning, then in the afternoon the school gym or cafeteria in Bancroft. On Saturday morning we might have a meeting in the American Legion Hall in Preston and in the afternoon, the Chat 'n Chew Restaurant in Malad. And these were good meetings; lots of times we'd have fifty or more people show up. Usually he would get up and give a short briefing on things going on in Washington; then he would always open it up for discussion. McClure was a listener; he could tell you what almost everyone said two days after each meeting. He would always have his regional assistant with him and usually his press secretary—they would take notes and identify the people who needed help with their problems. I'd say we had at least fifty of these town meetings every year, and maybe more than that."[1]

DICK THOMPSON ON RUTHIE JOHNSON

We have talked about Ruthie Johnson, but I wanted you to know how valuable she really was. Ruthie couldn't have been more partisan if she tried, and yet she served all the people of North Idaho with enthusiasm and determination regardless of their political affiliation. To her, the enemy was the Federal bureaucracy, and if, say, a little old lady lost her Social Security check, Ruthie raised unshirted hell with the authorities in Washington until it was replaced. Shy, she was not. And her reputation spread beyond the borders of Idaho. Ruthie attended Republican meetings all over the West. I remember Senator Paul Laxalt [R-Nevada] *coming up to me and saying, "I saw Ruthie this weekend. Boy! I wish I had someone like her working for me!"*

It is easy to wonder how any human could keep such a pace. After a chance comment by the author, McClure's first press secretary supplied an answer.

When Jim Norell was first contacted by telephone, the first questions were a part of the normal routine. How did you get hired? What did you do before that? How long did you work? Only this time the questions did not get answered in a neat, orderly fashion. When asked the first question, Norell blurted, "Let me tell you that McClure was the most intelligent person to ever serve in the Senate." Then the dialogue went something like this:

Author: Okay, but how did you get hired?

Norell: And let me tell you something else. He knew more about the rules and the way the Senate worked than anybody I saw there.

Author: Okay, I've heard that before. Now about. . .

Norell: He was a fantastic debater—you could watch him and see that he was thinking way ahead of whoever was debating him. It was uncanny just to watch him. . .

Author: Okay, okay, I'm not trying to write a book about a saint. You can tell all these good things but the man was human. You traveled with him and you obviously have a good memory. Give me the other side. Tell me something negative about him.

Norell: Negative! You bet I can tell you something negative! I can sum it up in one word: stamina. That guy was incredible. We'd catch a plane in Washington after working most of a day, fly to Boise, get in about ten o'clock, which is midnight our time, and they'd meet us and want to have a beer and talk, and we'd go on and on that night, then get up at the crack of dawn the next morning and drive to wherever, have a town meeting, rush to the next place, have another town meeting, then we'd drive someplace and have a dinner where he'd speak. We'd get to bed at midnight, get up the next morning and go through the same routine. We'd do that the whole weekend, fly back to Washington and I'm just drug out and beat, and there he is, the first one in the office the next morning, ready to slay the tigers and I'm still trying to recover. He'd go to three committee meetings, have a luncheon meeting, work till six or so, go off and attend a reception, then be back in the office working till late. It was just incredible. He would almost kill off staffers who tried to keep up with him.

Author: I've heard. . .

Norell: Let me tell you a story. McClure reads somewhere a piece by this reporter who says basically that senators are lazy—that they live the gilded life—something like this. He has me call this guy. I'm to challenge him to come follow the Senator for a week. I get the guy and he agrees to come on a Monday—I don't remember, say at six-thirty in the morning. Well, he shows up and McClure tells him, "Now you stick to me just like glue; you're going to go every place I go." Guess what? The guy makes it for two days, then disappears. No piece ever appears anywhere. Nothing. The guy just disappears. So you want something negative? That's it. The stamina of that guy made him a staff killer.[2]

The author never heard of any staffer who suffered more than fatigue working with McClure. But in June, 1976 a tragedy in eastern Idaho challenged the stamina of several staffers and even the indefatigable McClure.

Just before the 1972 general election, Nancy Carlile, who was then McClure's Bingham County coordinator, arranged a huge banquet in Blackfoot for regional Republicans, the banquet where George Hansen gave a rousing endorsement of Jim McClure's candidacy. Partly because of her demonstrated organizational skills, but predominantly because of her intelligence and her ability to work with people, Jim Goller recommended to McClure that Nancy should head up his new Idaho Falls regional office. McClure concurred, and it was in her capacity as regional assistant that she happened to be standing on the newly constructed Teton Dam on June 2, 1976, where Governor Cecil Andrus and other dignitaries had gathered to dedicate the new structure. Said Carlile,

> *The water had been flowing into the reservoir behind the dam for several weeks and it was almost full when we arrived that day.*

However, I saw something that bothered me. Every so often big chunks of dirt would break off from the bank and slide into the water. In my lay mind that didn't seem right to me and when I got back to the office, I called Mike Hathaway [engineer and LA to McClure] *and asked him about that. He assured me that was normal for a new impoundment and since my husband was an engineer, I felt the engineers who designed the dam had done a good job. Yet, during all the dedication speeches those huge chunks of dirt kept sliding off the banks and plopping in the water. That stuck in my mind and bothered me, but I let it go.*

That was on a Wednesday. The following Friday, after work, I decided to take my girls and drive to Salt Lake to do some shopping. The next morning we were driving in the downtown area—it was just before noon—and I was tuned to the news as I always was and there was a flash bulletin saying that the Teton Dam had developed a leak and the Madison County sheriff was evacuating Rexburg and the vicinity. I stopped the car, found a phone and called the Washington office. Tod Neuenschwander [new press secretary] *was there and I told him what was happening. He broke out laughing and said, "Nancy that's the funniest thing you've ever said and you've said a lot of funny things. I said, "Tod, I'm heading home; you should call your old station* [Neuenschwander had been a newscaster at KIFI in Idaho Falls] *and find out what is going on. We need to find the Senator and get him over there as soon as possible." Tod got serious immediately and said he would try to locate McClure. I then called Jim Goller who I knew was leaving for vacation. He also thought I was kidding and said, "What do you want me to do, Nancy, go over there and stick my finger in the hole?" I quickly convinced him that I was serious. He ordered me to get back to Idaho Falls as fast as I could and be ready to go to Rexburg* [the largest town in the path of the flood water] *and be ready to coordinate disaster assistance. He said he, too, would try to contact McClure.*[3]

McClure had just landed in Ruthie Johnson's territory in northern Idaho when he got the word—he cannot remember whose call got through to him—that the dam had failed. Goller remembers that McClure called and told him to pack and get to the site as soon as possible to help coordinate emergency teams, and that McClure, himself, was heading back to Boise so he could catch a flight to Washington. McClure picks up the story:

In order to get to Boise I caught a plane that was routed first to Great Falls, then to Boise. The flight took us close to the Teton Dam and the pilot diverted, then banked and circled the site. Water was just pouring through the dam. When I got to Boise, I immediately

Courtesy Jim Goller

Jim Goller and Nancy Carlile confer with an INEL official after the Teton Dam Disaster.

> *started working the phones, then I caught a flight to Washington and on Monday I met with President Ford. He was extremely responsive and I remember then that I insisted that the victims of the disaster had to be fully compensated for the damage at replacement value, not just partial compensation such as the government provided after natural disasters. Ford agreed and said, "We'll make it right and do what we have to do."*

When Goller arrived in Idaho Falls, the Federal Disaster Assistance Administration (FDAA)[ii] was already on the scene and working to bring some order to the chaos. And their officials were in shock. Goller explains: "When they first arrived in the area, they ordered community leaders to do A, which was priority one and they responded saying that A was already accomplished. Then they said for them to do B, and B was already done. As I recall there were three things FEMA [FDAA] wanted and all three of them had already been accomplished. What they didn't realize was that this was a Mormon community and Mormons are organized and prepared for disasters. And their leaders are positioned to take charge whenever something like this happens. And this was just the beginning. By the next day busloads of Mormons from Utah and other places were coming in to help."[4]

Goller set up his headquarters in Rexburg in the National Guard Armory where the FDAA was also headquartered. That started a string of 16 to 18-hour days where he helped solve a multitude of problems. A top priority was to get fifty dollars cash and some food stamps in the hands of the people who had lost everything in the flooding. Once he received authorization for that, he ran into another problem: people were not showing up. The problem was that food stamps were considered welfare and the church was against members taking welfare. Patiently, Goller worked with the Stake president and got him to organize for each Ward to come in and collect both

NANCY CARLILE ON THE DISASTER

The devastation was incredible but, because of the sheriff's department warning the people, thousands of lives were saved. Eleven people died, six from drowning, and the others from heart attacks and related causes. We were working 24/7 for so long—the FEMA [FDAA] *meetings didn't begin until the night and they went on to midnight or two a.m..*

There was tremendous support from outside, but we also had some crimes. I remember Bowen's Music Store in downtown Rexburg. Because of the college there [Ricks College], *they had a number of fine pianos—baby grands, etc. Well, on Sunday or Monday—right after the water went down—this big semi pulls up and the guys go in and tell the owners, "We're here to help you; we're going to haul these pianos away and clean them up for you." They loaded all of the pianos and that is the last they ever saw of them. These were scammers, who were professional thieves that lay and wait for such a disaster. There were others and they got away with it until everybody was warned.*

Somehow the water backed up and pooled in the small town of Roberts. We got a call asking if we had forgotten about them. I remembered that the INEL [Idaho National Engineering Laboratory where her husband worked as an engineer] *had several pumper trucks so I called them and three came and went to work. Mike Field* [McClure's LA for agriculture] *and I went out there. We were wading up to our neck in muck and we ran into this elderly lady who wanted to get back to her house and check on her cat. She was beside herself, wailing, "I don't know what has happened to her—she is about to have babies." We got to her house and they had pumped the water, but it was horrible with mud and muck. She called and called, then she heard a meow. Her cat was up in a tree with her babies—the animal sense is so keen. We called the fire department and they got the cat and kittens down and took them back to the center.*

Lots of people came in to help but I especially remember the Mennonites. They would go up to a farmer and offer to rebuild his barn and fences if he would feed them and give them a place to camp. You can drive through that country today and, if you know what you are looking for, you can pick out the barns they built.

Courtesy Tod Neuenschwander

Tod Neuenschwander, left, McClure and Mike Field visit the destroyed Teton Dam in southeastern Idaho, two years after the dam failed. Field played a critical role in helping area Teton Dam victims get compensation for their losses.

money and food stamps—the latter being declared government compensation for the failure of a Federal dam, not welfare.

Meanwhile, McClure managed to track down Senator Frank Church, who was campaigning for the presidential nomination in Pennsylvania, and get him to co-sponsor a bill that he was going to try and rush through Congress. Church did sign on, but the bill ran into opposition from the Justice Department. The McClure-Church bill called for the victims of the disaster to be compensated at "full replacement cost," which was unprecedented, but which was justified in McClure's judgment because the federal government was at fault for one of their dams failing. The Justice Department balked because, if the government was deemed to be at fault, it would be liable for a string of lawsuits that would be never ending. McClure got around this by adding a provision saying that no liability would be assessed. The other problem was to determine how much money should be authorized in the bill. Jim Goller solved that problem. He said:

> *One day while I was out in the area, the State Police came with their lights flashing and they were looking for me. McClure needed to talk to me and he had sent them to find me. I got to a telephone*

booth and called him. He said, "I've got this bill about to be passed but I need to know how much money to put in it." I had been at several meetings where ag people and others were estimating the loss and I said, "It looks to me like it is going to be $500,000,000." He put that in the bill and it came out that direct claims totaled about 400 million and the rest was used for reconstruction.[5]

Debbie Beattie, who had just graduated from Ricks College, volunteered to help in the communication center where she was known by her call sign, "Goldilocks." She remembers when Idaho's two senators came in to inspect the damage:

I remember them calling in on the radio saying that Senator Frank Church was on his way to inspect the damage. He came into the center looking very much like a dignified senator. He promised the leaders that he would do everything possible to make sure they were fully compensated for the damage. But when he came in, it was a production. Then we heard that the junior Senator was coming. I saw him when he walked in. He was literally wearing jeans and a Levi jacket and he walked up to Keith Walker [a local leader] *and said, "Where can you put me to work?" That was the first time I ever saw Jim McClure and that was a first impression that lasted. From there he went out and worked in the muck with everybody else until a helicopter arrived to take him on an inspection. I remember telling Mike Field, "I am so impressed with your boss; I'd like to work for him some day. Four months later I got a job offer and accepted.*[iii 6]

AFTER THE TRAGEDY
by
Kit Caples Kimball

After the Teton Dam failed, there were about fifteen farmers whose land immediately downstream from the toe of the dam was destroyed beyond restoration—the force of the water had scoured out so much soil that productivity of the land was gone. Even with full compensation, there was no land to buy near their communities. While others got to pick up their lives, albeit with much hard work, and remain on their land and in their neighborhoods, these fifteen or so families didn't have that choice and there was little political momentum left to help them. McClure did not forget them however, and I spent two years working with the families, the Department of Energy and the White House to try and get approximately 3,000 acres of Idaho National Engineering Laboratory land that was near Mud Lake in West Jefferson County. It was a battle even though the land was of no use to the INEL. Mike Field picked up the sword when I left in 1979 and eventually the farmers were given the land. Those people never lost faith in Jim McClure and almost five years after the Teton Dam broke, he was able to fulfill the government's last responsibility to the citizens most affected by the tragedy.

Nancy Carlile also went on the helicopter tour with both Goller and McClure and her memory is that "McClure was as sick looking as I've ever seen him—not physically sick, but emotionally sick. It was just devastating, bodies of cattle piled up, cars like tinker toys."[7]

McClure admitted years later: "I was an emotional wreck after that tour and after being on the ground. But, I have to admit, watching FEMA [FDAA] at work was one of the most heart-moving experiences I've ever had. These were federal officials [much maligned as bureaucrats] but they got into the spirit of the community and there was total cooperation. There was no red tape. They were just determined to get things done to help those people.[8]

Tod Neuenschwander, McClure's new press secretary and who was later to become his chief Washington assistant, said:

> *"I really believe that disaster caused Jim McClure to rise to a new level. He was totally focused on that one issue. He brought the whole staff together. He said, 'Look, we have a job to do to make those people whole again. This was a federal dam. There is federal responsibility here.' He made assignments to the staff. He set up a task force in the office. He really concentrated on the recovery—getting the money rolling. During the rest of his time in the Senate I never saw him jump so decisively into a problem. I never saw him work so hard on an issue. He was determined to make those people who suffered as whole as possible and he worked tirelessly at it.*[9]

Goller, Carlile and Field continued to work in the area for several months, generally tending to emergency problems. However, the bulk of the staff work after that time was in handling problems due to the claim process. As Goller pointed out, "How do you deal with a drug store that has had eight or nine feet of water moving through it? How much do you compensate the owner? Fortunately, I knew several appraisers and I was able to get them working there, but it was a tedious process. We felt sure that most of those people were honest [iv] and would not make false claims, but we had to go through the formal process. Frankly, I was amazed at how patient some of those people were. I mean what do you do when you have an heirloom that Great Aunt Lillie brought to Idaho on a wagon train? What was it worth? How do you separate the actual value from the emotional value? Or do you? Those were the hard questions. Nancy Carlile said one time that we were all social workers even if we weren't trained as such. She was right, but we had to do it."[10]

Goller eventually went back to Boise, but continued to make trips to the Idaho Falls area for several years. Nancy Carlile went back to McClure's Idaho Falls senatorial office, but was replaced at disaster headquarters by Karmen Larsen, who had been McClure's regional assistant in Lewiston.

Mike Field stayed on, and for much of the next three years worked primarily in helping the victims with their disaster claims. Jim McClure came back to the area many times and developed an enduring admiration for the indomitable spirit of the people. That the feeling proved to be mutual was born out in the general election two years later. Jim McClure received 89 percent of the vote in Madison County—the highest percentage of votes in the forty-four counties of Idaho.

Chapter 24 notes

i According to senior staffer, Mike Wetherell, as quoted in Church's biography, *Fighting the Odds*, the Church staff also worried about his absence from the state. Wetherell said he begged his boss to make more trips to Idaho and felt the staff sensed Church disliked "any proposal that entails a trip to the state."

ii All of those interviewed described the disaster team as "FEMA" but this organization was created as a successor to FDAA in 1979, three years after the disaster.

iii She also married Mike Field, worked for McClure for several years and served in the Idaho Legislature as a Representative from Boise.

iv Goller said that he talked to the FBI agent who was the watchdog for fraud and he said he had never seen such a limited amount of fraud in that kind of operation.

Chapter 25

The Carter Years

In the summer of 1976 Senator Jim McClure was in a bind. Ronald Reagan was running for the Republican nomination for president. And Gerald Ford was running for the Republican nomination for president. Which candidate was he going to support?

McClure had mixed feelings. He liked Ronald Reagan's conservative philosophy. He believed strongly that what Reagan had been saying about building our national defense and stopping every attempt by the Soviet Union to spread Communism around the world. But, he also had doubts. In private conversations with the staff director of his Senate Steering Committee, Margo Carlisle, he would say things like, "Do you think Reagan is really for real?" and "Sometimes I worry that Reagan is just a bunch of fluff."[1]

He also had reservations about Gerald Ford. Ford came into the presidency under the Nixon/Agnew cloud and with a Congress heavily dominated by Democrats. Conservatives like McClure shuddered when Ford confided to fellow Republicans that he was going to have to move toward the "middle." To McClure's way of thinking, moving to the middle of the crowd in Congress was a move that would take him well left of center and into the liberal camp. He remembered his angst over the *common situs* picketing bill—a bill that would force all of the unions on a job to go out on strike if just one union struck. It passed the Congress despite the best efforts of conservatives to stop it. McClure worried for days whether or not Ford would veto it. He did, finally, but his hesitation meant that he was undecided for awhile and could just as easily have gone the other way. There was no doubt in his mind that Reagan would have slapped a veto stamp on such a bill the minute it arrived in the White House.

Then one day McClure's friend and colleague from Nevada, Paul Laxalt came into his office with Ronald Reagan. This was the first time McClure had had a chance to sit down and visit with Reagan on a personal basis. And he was impressed. The "Was Reagan fluff?" question undoubtedly ran through his mind, but the man he met seemed very solid, indeed. There was nothing superficial about him. He seemed sincere, determined and intelligent. In short, McClure was impressed. But would he support Reagan in his quest for the nomination?

McClure is not sure he had made a decision until that moment. And it was not easy doing so. He valued Laxalt's friendship, and everything he had learned about Reagan was positive. Deep inside he felt he could even become enthusiastic about having a president with Reagan's philosophy and charm. But another factor weighed in. Loyalty. He had known and worked with Gerald Ford from the time he first sought assignment on the Interior Committee of the House. He knew that Ford did not make the sole decision on getting him that plumb. But he also knew that Ford had to have had a lot to do with that, and he was appreciative. His three-term tenure on that committee and his experience with the Chairman Wayne Aspinall gave him much of the knowledge and experience that was now allowing him to be an effective leader in the Senate. At this moment it is almost certain that it never entered his mind to ask himself: What would Grandfather McClure have done if he were in my shoes? But it seems equally certain that the principles of honesty, loyalty and duty that were inculcated in him throughout his boyhood and teen years under his grandfather's nurturing must have answered the difficult question for him. Without hesitation he looked at Reagan and Laxalt and said something to the effect: "Governor Reagan, I am an enthusiastic supporter of the things you stand for and I believe you would be a fine president. But Jerry Ford and I go back almost ten years. He has been loyal to me and I feel I have to remain loyal to him. My conscience will not let me support you. I have to support Gerald Ford."

McClure was asked, "Did you see any animosity from either of those men when you said that?" He replied, "None. They took it very graciously. I think both of them were the kind of men who could appreciate why I made that decision." [2]

McClure was not alone. Republican delegates from across the country joined McClure in supporting Ford for the 1976 nomination. On the other side, Frank Church and Representative Morris "Mo" Udall (D-Arizona) and California Governor Jerry Brown were battling a political outsider from Georgia for the Democratic nomination. Running on the theme that only a political outsider could bring a fresh approach to governing America, former Georgia Governor Jimmy Carter won the nomination. It then became a race between Gerald Ford and Jimmy Carter. Ford was not perceived as a strong leader, and many still remembered the Agnew/Nixon/Watergate mess that had caused Ford to be an unelected president. That, and the fact that he had pardoned Nixon, probably swayed enough of the independent vote to bring the "fresh voice" to the White House. By a narrow margin, Jimmy Carter became the 39th President of the United States.

On the surface it seemed like McClure and his conservative colleagues were in even more trouble than they had been. The problem was not in the Senate; there were fourteen new faces but the balance remained about the same. What boded ill for the Republicans was the capture of the White

House by the Democrats. With huge Democratic majorities in both houses of Congress and a Democrat in the White House, it seemed that the Democratic steamroller was about to charge ahead.

Fortunately, or unfortunately, depending upon one's political outlook, Carter got off to a rocky start in his dealings with Congress. His campaign message that he would bring a fresh, non-Washington approach to governing did not go down well with entrenched political pros like Speaker of the House Tip O'Neill. Also, his personal staff was loaded with outsiders from Georgia who knew little about what it would take to move a presidential agenda through the Congress. In addition, Carter was much more conservative than many of the Democrats in Congress—a fact that hurt him with the block of liberals eager to advance their agenda. In short, the Democratic president and the huge majority of Democrats in the Congress was not the steamroller many feared. McClure and his colleagues were in for a hard time, but not for a very, very hard time.

DEBBIE FIELD ON McCLURE

When I first got to Washington, I was amazed at how hard that man worked. He worked day and night.

Right after I got there, he had me drive him to the National [Ronald Reagan] *Airport. He had this old turquoise and white Mustang convertible, a stick shift, but it had a screw driver instead of a stick. He was so relaxed—he would laugh and joke. Here I am, a small town girl from Rexburg, Idaho, and I'm driving this United States Senator in all that traffic.*

And almost every time I was with him and there was just two of us, he would challenge me on some issue and he would take the opposite side. After I would get frustrated trying to argue with him, he would start laughing and say, "I agree with you—when two people are in a room and they are agreeing, then one of them is not thinking. That was his favorite thing to do. He would always play the other side and challenge your thinking. This had an influence on me, and now that I'm in the [Idaho] *Legislature, I think about that when I'm debating issues. I learned how important it is to know the other side of an issue so you can defend yourself.*

For the past four years, McClure and his Steering Committee had fought hard against the notion he inherited when he came to the Senate—the notion that Republicans are in such a minority they might as well sit back, work for re-election, and take whatever crumbs the Democrats handed out occasionally. Preaching to his choir, but in a low-key way, he continuously urged his colleagues to use every Senate tactic available to them to defeat, and if not defeat, stall, the legislation he felt would harm the country—mainly the big-spending, big-government, big-regulatory, big-Labor, and anti-defense bills. Then, in the Carter years he both refined his tactics, and with the help of some brilliant staffers, brought creative new tactics to the Senate floor.

The Inside/Outside Tactic. McClure sincerely liked and enjoyed the company of lobbyists. On the surface this does not make much sense. How could a senator with McClure's conservative views enjoy a 30-minute session listening to a lobbyist arguing the merits of bailing New York City out of its self-induced indebtedness, or a Sierra Club lobbyist arguing for the need to cut the Forest Service timber quotas in northern Idaho, or a California lobbyist arguing that Idaho and the Northwest should give up some of its water to the parched Los Angeles basin? Superficially, it would seem that folks like that would be shown the door as soon as they identified their mission.

But McClure had two good reasons for not only listening to such lobbyists, but for picking their brains for every minute fact and bit of logic they could use to argue their side of the issue. And one of the reasons he did that goes back to his prosecuting attorney days in Payette, Idaho. As a young attorney, with little experience in the courtroom, he felt he could overcome this handicap by "knowing the other fellow's case better than he knew it himself." So, no matter what kind of a case he was trying, his very first step in preparation was to prepare the opposing attorney's case better than he could prepare it himself. With that knowledge, he could then prepare his own case in such a way that he could overcome whatever strategy his opponent could throw at him. That same strategy carried over to his House and Senate work. Lobbyists on issues to which he was opposed could save him the hours of preparation he had to do as a lawyer. By getting them to go into all of the details of their side of an issue, all he had to do was assimilate their information—information he could use against them when, in committee or on the floor or while testifying as a witness, he could launch an intelligent, effective counter attack.

His other reason for liking/enjoying lobbyists had to do with what staffers call the inside/outside technique of influencing legislation. Suppose a bill that McClure strongly detests is scheduled to come to the floor for a vote next week. Actually, McClure, himself, probably would not know such a bill was coming; that knowledge would be the responsibility of the legislative aide who covers the field. For example, if it is an agricultural bill or a veterans affairs bill, the ag LA or the vet affairs LA would be expected to not only know that the bill is coming up for a vote, but would be expected to have studied and analyzed the bill and be aware of the parts of it that McClure would support or oppose.

Let's suppose it is a bill that McClure would want to oppose. Typically, if he does not know about it, the LA will get that information to him. Then the fun starts. The staffer has to use every ounce of stealth and guile, every friendship and personal connection with other staffers, to get a head count—to find out how each senator is going to vote. And with McClure having a steering committee staff in addition to his personal staff, he had a force multiplier—he had additional staff people with their own friendships and connections to assist with the head count. As Margo Carlisle, staff director of the Steering Committee, said, "You always knew how Teddy Kennedy and Jesse Helms were going to vote. But, you usually had to work at it to find out how the other senators were going to go, especially the Republican senators. The Democrats were much better disciplined; they almost had to vote the party line or they would get in trouble with the leadership. Not so with the Republicans. They were much more independent. But, say, on a bill we wanted to fight, let's assume that there are six non-committed votes, which means we can't find out how the senator is going to vote, or the senator has not decided how to vote. Either way, that's when we go to work *outside*. That's when McClure says, go to this lobbyist and that lobbyist and get his people active in Illinois or Arkansas or Iowa. Tell them that they can't wait; this and that senator has to hear from influential people in his state immediately—people who can persuade the fence sitters. That's where McClure's knowledge of the lobbyists paid off. He knew where to go. He knew who could be effective and who could not."[31]

The Colloquy. Morning hour in the Senate is free speech time. This is when Senator Smith can rise and give a speech complimenting Mrs. Virginia Jones from his home state for winning the National Chrysanthemum Association's top award for growing the most beautiful chrysanthemums. That speech will go in the *Congressional Record*, then both a video of the senator's speech and a copy of the *Record* will be sent to Mrs. Jones and the senator wins a big fan and, perhaps, a new big donor to his next campaign. And that is the way it goes, generally. The morning hour (and it may not always be in the morning) was typically a fluff period.

McClure decided to turn it into something else. With willing members of his steering committee, he decided to use the morning hour for colloquies to influence legislation. One of these colloquies would proceed something like this. After prepping the other senator(s), say on a bill he was co-sponsoring to ease some of the regulatory teeth of OSHA, he might rise, get recognized, then say, "Distinguished members of the Senate, I rise today to give you an example of how the Occupational Safety and Health Administration is overstepping the law that created it and how, by doing this, they are creating more rather than less hazards in the workplace. I know that most of you have been around construction sites and heard the loud, squealing beep that trucks emit when they are backing up. OSHA mandated this as a safety device to prevent workers behind the truck from getting accidentally run over. They now have made every truck owner install such devices. Well, that created another problem, at least for some OSHA inspector. This inspector went out on a construction job, listened to the loud, squealing beep and decided that the noise could be deleterious to a worker's hearing. So what did he recommend? Changing the volume or frequency of the beep? No. Removing the sounding device? No. The inspector recommended that the workers exposed to the sound should wear ear protectors. This, unfortunately, is OSHA's wisdom, and it doesn't matter that the original purpose of the beep is negated by the ear protectors."

Next, one of McClure's colleagues, say Strom Thurmond, rises and asks if the senator would yield to him. McClure yields, and Thurmond launches into a related story for which he has been prepped. In the meantime, in every senator's office there is a television covering the happenings on the Senate floor (before television, there was audio) and most staffers also have a monitor somewhere near where they are working. In addition, reporters in the press gallery, ordinarily bored by the typical morning hour fare, are perking up, listening to the colloquy. McClure conceived the colloquy as a force multiplier. With colloquies during the morning hour he could get his messages out and thereby attract more supporters for whatever he was promoting, which multiplied votes for or against legislation that senators otherwise might ignore. The technique worked brilliantly; he got his message out, recruited supporters, and he did not have to tie up the Senate when it was in regular session.

TOM HILL ON McCLURE

Practically every staffer interviewed for this book insisted on convincing the author of McClure's stellar personality qualities. One of those qualities was his great sense of humor, which (they claimed) his constituents in Idaho did not fully appreciate. The other was his ability to win the genuine affection of senators on both sides of the aisle. Two stories related by LA Tom Hill were meant to reinforce these points:

One day Senator Muskie from Maine was on the floor talking about how children in his home state were excused from school to pick up potatoes during the harvest season. When he finished, McClure, with a gleam in his eye, asked to be recognized. Then he rose and said, "I wish the honorable senator from Maine to know that in Idaho we also excuse our students during the potato harvest. However, only students in junior high or above are released because children younger than that cannot safely lift our Idaho potatoes. After that, McClure received a lot of good-natured chiding for breaking a Senate custom that forbids one senator from embarrassing another.

Another time Senator Jennings Randolph from West Virginia was on the floor telling his colleagues how terrible it was for timber companies to do clear-cutting and leave such ugly patches of devastation. Again, with a gleam in his eye, McClure asked to be recognized, then said, "I wonder if the honorable senator from West Virginia would consider the miles and miles of his home state that have been devastated by strip mining to be almost as bad as our clear cuts." According to Hill, Randolph sputtered and stammered and was never able to answer McClure's challenge. A bit later McClure's friend on the other side of the aisle, Hubert Humphrey [D-Minnesota], *came over, leaned down, and said softly, "Jimmy, you're a bad, bad boy."*

Courtesy Tod Neuenschwander

McClure talks with Darrel Owen, left, Frank Cushing and Tod Neuenschwander, durin a flight to a meeting in San Jaun Puerto Rico for duscussion on the possibility of granting statehood to that commonwealth.

The germane amendment. During the Lyndon Johnson administration, Congress authorized the creation of a National Commission on Reform of Federal Law. That was followed by the appointment of a distinguished panel of legal scholars, practicing lawyers and congressional representatives. The existing criminal code had evolved over the years as legislation accumulated and, according to the President's original message:

> *A number of our criminal laws are obsolete. Many are inconsistent in their efforts to make the penalty fit the crime. Many—which treat essentially the same crimes—are scattered in a crazy-quilt patchwork throughout our Criminal Code.*[4]

By the mid-1970s the commission finished its work, then the Senate Judiciary Committee took over and reported it to the Senate for a vote. It was controversial, but it passed. However, a similar effort in the House languished and the effort was stalled. New President Carter injected life back into the effort and the Senate Judiciary Committee eliminated some of the most controversial portions of the bill and reintroduced it, with Senator Ted Kennedy being its chief sponsor. Kennedy went to Senator Strom Thurmond and convinced him that the new code was not really new, that all the Commission had done was rewrite the existing code using modern language and clear language. Thurmond signed on as a co-sponsor. Then McClure got into the act.

Actually it should be said that McClure and Mike Hammond got into the act. And who was Mike Hammond? He was the counsel on the staff of the Senate Steering Committee, but according to several staffers who knew him and worked with him, if he was not a bona fide genius, he was a near-genius who had an incredible ability to read a bill and see things in it that ordinary mortals would miss. Said Paul Weyrich, former special aide to Senator Carl Curtis, "Mike had something like a heat sensor. He could go through a thousand-page bill and this sensor allowed him to zero in on minute sections that appeared innocent, but when examined closely revealed that they could do great damage." [5]

Mike Hammond waded through the thousand or more pages of the proposed new Federal criminal code—they called it the Criminal Recodification Bill—and was appalled by what he found. He could see that it was not just the same old laws written in modern language as Kennedy and others claimed. What he saw was egregious penalties for businesses that tripped over the myriad regulations that were harassing them, and blatant social engineering for which liberals were lusting, all in the guise of criminal law. One example he cited to the author was a law that said something to the effect that hospitals which claimed to do all routine surgeries would be subject to Federal prosecution and fines if they denied such surgery for any patient who requested it. "What was really meant, though not spelled out in so many words," Hammond said, "was that if a hospital did appendectomies, they could not deny any patient who came in requesting an abortion, and if they did, they could be prosecuted. The new code was just full of things like that."[6]

Hammond, almost in a panic with what he found in the bill, got to McClure and showed him what he found. Since the first Senate bill breezed through by a vote of 72-15, it looked to Hammond like it was nearly hopeless to wage an effort to stop it. *And the bill was scheduled for a vote the next afternoon.*

McClure and Hammond sat down and contemplated what they might do. And now, neither of them can remember who came up with the strategy to defeat it: Hammond now says, probably modestly, "It was the Senator's strategy,"[7] while McClure does not remember, but says, generously, "It was probably Hammond's idea."[8] Let the reader decide the magnitude of its brilliance.

Here is what they decided. Hammond would stay up all night and write amendments to the bill, but not just ordinary amendments. He would write amendments that were exactly like the laws from the original code. McClure, himself, would line up one or two others from the Steering Committee who would join him in his special effort the next afternoon.

Hammond worked most of the night (he says he slept on the Senate floor for awhile) and in an effort that has to be labeled "Herculean." he prepared, according to Weyrich, 108 amendments, each with a paragraph of explanation, though the word that got out the next morning was that three conservative senators were coming to the floor with fifty amendments to the bill.

Kennedy and his supporters took this information, which was deliberately leaked, and assumed that the three conservatives were going to filibuster the bill. Thoughts immediately turned to the number of votes that could be mustered to cut off the filibuster—to invoke Senate Rule 22 and vote cloture. With the previous vote on the bill 72-15 in favor of it, that seemed more than enough to get the necessary cloture vote of sixty. So there was little worry on the part of the bill's sponsors when they took their seats that afternoon.

But McClure and his two colleagues, Jeremiah Denton (R-Alabama) and Jesse Helms (R-North Carolina), were not going to filibuster. Instead McClure rose and announced something to the effect that, "As you all know, after a filibuster has been stopped by a cloture vote, only amendments that are germane to the proposed bill can be considered. Since some of us are preparing to debate this new Federal Recodification Bill, I am requesting that our distinguished parliamentarian rule as to whether the amendments we are proposing are germane to this bill. I present my first amendment to the parliamentarian. It is the exact same law that is in our present code and we need to know if the new law, reputed to be just a rewrite of the old law, is close enough to it for my amendment to be germane."

The parliamentarian examined McClure's amendment, then the comparable section of the new law. Then he declared that McClure's amendment was not germane and would not be in order if cloture was voted. McClure thanked him and presented his second amendment, with the same result. After achieving the same rulings on several amendments, Denton and Helms took over and the parliamentarian made the same rulings. Neither McClure nor Hammond remember how many of the amendments went to the parliamentarian, but the result was the same. Undoubtedly, there were a lot of senators who were shocked, especially those like Thurmond who had been sold the idea that the new bill was like the old one but with streamlined language. With a dramatic tactic, McClure and his two colleagues demonstrated to the whole Senate that this was a drastically different code for which they were being asked to vote.

Then, when there was a motion to proceed to the bill, McClure notified the chair that he was going to debate the motion—he was going to filibuster. From here on the story gets complicated, but in short, McClure did not actually stand up and talk for hours. Instead, supporters of the bill filed cloture and when it was supported by sixteen senators, the petition to shut off the filibuster had to ripen for two days. This let the Senate conduct other business, and it gave time for proponents and opponents to twist arms, mobilize lobbyists and get press coverage—the latter intensifying the controversy. The eventual result: the vote to proceed failed by a vote of 47 to 48—a vote that indicated supporters of the bill would be thirteen votes short of evoking cloture if McClure elected to filibuster the main bill. More significant, the vote was a dramatic turnaround from the previous 72-15 vote, so significant that the recodification bill was dropped and nothing like it has been considered by the Senate to this day.

Such wins, especially when you were a part of an embattled minority, were especially satisfying. Losses were different. They took something away. And in the case of one of McClure's losses, he believed that it also took something very valuable away from America.

McClure was a fan of nuclear energy. This was not because his brother happened to work in that industry. Nor was it because of the Idaho Nuclear Engineering Laboratory (INEL) that was based in the Arco desert of east central Idaho—an industry vital to the economy of the Blackfoot and Idaho Falls area. He was a fan of nuclear energy because, as a recognized energy expert—at least among congressmen—he felt certain that it was the answer to practically all of our future energy needs. Most people at the time realized that nuclear energy could be used to replace coal and natural gas for generating electricity; at this time, during the Carter years, sixty-seven nuclear reactors were producing roughly 12 percent of the nation's electrical supply. McClure's vision for nuclear energy was much broader. The world was never going to run out of oil, but it was going to run out of oil that was economical to recover. He knew from just his experience after the Arab embargo of 1973 that oil prices would rise, then decline as a greater supply was recovered, then advance again. He predicted this trend would continue, with oil prices advancing, then falling back a bit, then advancing some more as demand increased in developing countries of the world. He saw this trend continuing until technology created a new solution or the economy collapsed. He dreaded the latter—as a young man in the Great Depression he saw things that he did not want his children and especially his grandchildren to suffer. It was clear to him that this did not need to happen. The technology that would save the nation's economy was almost ready.

What McClure and every other energy expert knew was that electrical energy produced by nuclear reactors could be used along the sea shores to break the chemical bonds of water molecules, producing hydrogen and oxygen. That process, called electrolysis, was so simple that, using a photovoltaic cell for his electrical energy, McClure performed a demonstration of electrolysis on the Capitol steps for his Senate colleagues. What he knew was that hydrogen, produced by electricity from nuclear reactors, could become the perfect fuel when the price of oil recovery became economically unfeasible, as it was certain to do. By igniting the hydrogen in the cylinder of an internal combustion engine it would create an explosion duplicating that of vaporized gasoline. During the explosion, the same energy it took to split the water molecule would power the engine, and the recombined oxygen and hydrogen would create water—a much more desirable byproduct than the gasoline exhaust fumes that were polluting America's cities.

So to McClure, hydrogen was the perfect solution to our future energy needs. Nuclear energy was the means of reaching that solution.

Being a conservative, McClure was anything but pleased that Jimmy Carter was going to be running the country for at least four years. But there was one consolation. Carter was a graduate of the Naval Academy. And he was bright enough to be recruited by Admiral Hyman Rickover, the father of the nuclear submarine. People who knew Rickover called him a demanding old S.O.B, an irascible, nit-picking perfectionist. But his standards were admired by all, and the millions of hours submariners had been confined undersea with nuclear reactors practically in their bunks with them, proved beyond any doubt that nuclear energy could be produced and used safely. Jimmy Carter seemed to be proud of that heritage. Many times he told of the example Rickover provided for him after he went in for his recruiting interview and saw the motto on Rickover's desk: WHY NOT THE BEST? Indeed, why not the best? Carter claimed that this motto had guided him every day he was Governor of Georgia and it would guide him every day he was president. So McClure knew that Carter understood nuclear energy. He knew that Carter had lived with it in the confines of nuclear submarines. And with "why not the best?" as his beacon, he, more than any other political figure, even himself, would know that nuclear energy was the best solution to the vexing energy problem that was absolutely certain to come.

But McClure did not know Jimmy Carter. Carter was not a fan of nuclear energy. What was worse, he was a dedicated enemy of a new technique for producing nuclear energy, a technique that McClure felt was the answer to the future energy needs, not only of America, but of the whole world.

That answer was the fast breeder reactor, a prototype of which had been built and operated at the INEL. McClure explains his reasoning in one of his press releases:

> *. . .The fast breeder reactor can pull us out of the energy crisis because it is capable of producing more fuel than it uses. Therefore, the advantages of conventional nuclear reactors are multiplied considerably by breeder reactors. Conventional reactors must have Uranium-235 to operate. But this type of uranium is found in 0.7 percent of uranium ore. The rest of uranium, Uranium-238, is found in 99.3 percent of the ore. U-238 is useless to conventional reactors—but extremely valuable when used in breeder reactors. Breeder reactors can convert U-238 to Plutonium 239 and use it as a fuel. As a result, our nuclear stockpiles of spent fuel, which now number roughly 300,000 tons, can be used for fuel in breeders. It is easy to*

see the advantages of the breeder in this regard. That stockpile has an energy equivalent of eight times our coal reserves and 100 times our oil reserves. Its value, when converted to nuclear energy, would be $30 trillion worth of petroleum at 1978 prices. . .[9]

McClure was arguing for the fast breeder reactor because it was a solution to future energy shortages. A bonus, which should have pleased environmentalists was that such reactors could also use spent fuels, converting them to energy while producing fewer wastes. And the wastes from breeder reactors would have a half-life of 30-40 years, infinitely shorter than the 25,000-year half-life of wastes from normal reactors.

President Carter understood all of that. But he was concerned with the Plutonium-239 that is produced by the breeder reactor. His thinking was yes, that plutonium could be used for fuel but pure Plutonium-239 can also be used to make an atomic bomb. What happens if terrorists steal Plutonium-239 from a reactor? That potential threat is simply too dangerous for us to gamble producing it in breeder reactors.

What Carter was ignoring was some basic laws of physics. An engineer explains:

> *Plutonium-239 produces significantly more energy than Uranium-235.* **And the process continues to produce the additional isotopes Plutonium-240 and 241 and 242.** [emphasis added] *Plutonium is used in atomic bombs—the fact that it's pure Plutonium-239 that makes an atomic bomb work, and not the other three isotopes apparently didn't matter [to Jimmy Carter]. . .Never mind that in the real world, it is essentially impossible to separate out the Plutonium-239 from the other isotopes in sufficient purity to use it for bomb making. The British tried it, the Russians tried it, the French tried it, and we tried it, but nobody did it very well, even though we had the best scientists and all the money in the world to throw at it. . .If you try to make a bomb with such a mixture of Plutonium isotopes, forget about it—it won't work, ever. . .Unless you have pure Plutonium-239, your bomb will fizzle. So throwing away all that valuable nuclear fuel to prevent terrorists from making a bomb that won't work anyway is just plain dumb.*[10]

McClure's immediate concern was a fast breeder reactor that was in the initial stages of construction in Clinch River, Tennessee. This reactor was being built at government expense as a "stepping stone" prototype for commercial reactors that could later be used as a model for private utilities. However, in a press release in July, 1978, he had to acknowledge to his Idaho constituents that the Senate had voted to scrap the Clinch River project.

This was a huge disappointment. But McClure was just down, not out. And he had a scheme. It had to do with natural gas deregulation, a highly controversial topic at that time. For background, most of the natural gas being sold in the country at this time was price regulated by various state commissions. Those who sold natural gas were considered to be public utilities like phone companies and electricity producers. With prices regulated at artificially low prices, it was obvious to many senators and congressmen that this was killing incentives for natural gas exploration, thus threatening future production. President Carter happened to be on the side of those arguing for deregulation, although a great many Democrats opposed it because, they said, if the price of natural gas is deregulated, the gas companies will charge whatever they want and the public will be gouged. McClure, of course, was all for deregulation just on principle; also it would matter little to Idahoans because most of their natural gas was coming from Canada where the price was not regulated. However, he was keeping quiet about it because, by his count, he and his colleague, Pete Dominici (R-New Mexico), would yield the swing votes when the Energy and Natural Resources Committee voted to send the deregulation bill to the Senate floor. One of the Committee staffers who, because of his current position wishes to remain anonymous, explains what happened next:

> *Actually, the legislation involved a lot more than just natural gas deregulation; the title of the bill was the National Energy Act, which was actually four separate pieces of legislation. The Natural Gas Policy Act was one of them and it was the key to getting passage of the entire package. It was getting late in the legislative session and the theory was to get a deal made with President Carter so work could be done over the* [August] *recess. Then, after Labor Day, it could be finalized and run through* [with the other legislation]. *I had been working with James Schlesinger, President Carter's special energy adviser*[ii] *and we brokered a meeting that took place one evening at the White House. I remember that Domenici drove with McClure and before we went through the back gate they had me get down on the floor of the back seat because the reporters at the White House knew me, and if they had seen me, they would have known that it was a meeting on the Energy Act, which was big news at the time. When we got to the Roosevelt room, Carter,* [Vice President] *Mondale,* [Domestic Policy Advisor] *Stu Eisenstadt and Schlesinger were waiting. It only took about ten minutes to cut the deal, but it must have taken 30 minutes for everyone to agree on a word to describe what was going to happen to the Clinch River reactor. Finally, Carter sent Mondale to get a thesaurus and it was agreed that the word "discontinuation" would be used. Work would stop on Clinch River, but there was a commitment to support robust funding for three years*

> *for fast breeder research at the INEL and Los Alamos* [in Domenici's New Mexico]. *Also, there was to be a press embargo, but McClure was so concerned about Howard Baker* [(R-Tennessee) and Senate Majority Leader] *not finding out about the deal by some leak, he went into another room and telephoned him while we were at the White House. Then we left by the back gate and again I was relegated to the floor of the back seat so the press would not see me.*[11]

This meeting with Carter was probably in early August. A few weeks later, on Thursday night, August 17, while McClure was in Idaho at the Lewiston Airport waiting for a flight, he received a call from President Carter. In what he announced as a 10-minute call, he and the President finalized their deal. Carter would agree not to scrap the Clinch River breeder reactor, but construction would stop and it would be mothballed for three years. For that concession, McClure got Carter to agree to: (1) a full, expanded, three-year Liquid Metal Fast Breeder Reactor program involving total funding of over $1.5 billion, (2) a commitment not to veto an authorization of the full three-year program now, nor to veto the appropriations for the three-year program in this year's appropriations bill and the bills in the next two years, and (3) accept the full funding for the program through October of 1980. And in a subsequent press release he pointed out that ". . .it is possible that a decision could be made in 1981 to proceed with a [new] design at the existing Clinch River, Tennessee site, incorporating the technical advances developed during the three-year period."[12]

It is probably safe to speculate that McClure was smiling when he boarded his airplane that Thursday evening after Carter's call. And Mike Hathaway, when thinking back over his years with the senator, thought that getting this concession from Carter was one of the highpoints of McClure's career. "But," said Hathaway, "Carter reneged." Hathaway said:

> *Two years after the agreement a memo was produced in the White House saying that after the election, win or lose, Carter was going to do everything possible to kill the breeder reactor program. Staff managed to get a copy of that memo* [no comment on how] *and a copy was given to Steve Symms, Idaho's First District Congressman who was campaigning for Senator Frank Church's seat. Now Church was in Idaho Falls campaigning and he had two good nuclear people on his staff who should have been with him because he was going to be meeting with a lot of the INEL folks. But they were not there—I was told that someone on Church's staff told them to get out of the country. Well, I happened to be in Idaho Falls and in the audience when Church was giving a campaign speech. When it came time for questions, a reporter read parts of the memo and asked for Church's comments. You have to realize, this was shocking news to the INEL*

folks—the money funding much of their research was the result of the McClure/Domenici deal. The result was a disaster for Church. I'll never forget the look on his face—he was devastated by what his own president was doing to him. He fumbled and muttered—he was pathetic. And I really believe that this was a significant factor in his loss to Steve Symms in that election."[13]

Worse for McClure, the accident at the Three-Mile Island nuclear plant in Pennsylvania in March of 1979 turned out to be very bad news. Though there was no significant pollution and no injuries or deaths, the event was turned into a cataclysm by nuclear opponents and the media, and it was used stridently to sway public opinion against nuclear energy. After the Three-Mile Island "disaster," and after Carter's turnaround, the breeder reactor program was dead, at least in America. Jim McClure had won a battle but he ended up losing a war. And he laments it to this day.

Chapter 25 notes

i McClure was somewhat of an exception. Many lobbyists never get in to see senators; they concentrate on staffers. In another inside/outside fight, it would likely be the staffer who knows what lobbyists to mobilize.

ii Former Secretary of Defense under Nixon and Ford, and who became the first Secretary of Energy when the National Energy Act passed, creating the new Department of Energy.

Chapter 26

The Carter Years - Two

Right in the middle of the Carter years, McClure had a problem: he had to get re-elected.

Of course, it is not completely correct to say he *had* to get re-elected; he could have ended his political career and gone on to other endeavors. But, it is doubtful if that alternative crossed his mind. Why? Because he was having fun doing what he was doing. If that sounds frivolous, realize that those exact words were used by several of his staffers. Said Tod Neuenschwander, former press secretary and, later, administrative assistant, "To be very honest, Jim McClure totally enjoyed the legislative process and the many interactions with people. And I would even go beyond that. I would say that he truly enjoyed all of the intellectual challenges of being a United States senator. You have to realize: he was not the typical politician out running in front of cameras and seeking publicity. He loved the work that most other senators hated; he loved digging into the details of legislation. He loved challenging the minutiae of a bill. He got great satisfaction out of changing language to make a bill less damaging or more effective. Definitely, I'd say he was having fun."[1]

And said Phil Reberger, who would become McClure's campaign manager in 1978[i]: "Yes, McClure was having fun. Of course, my perspective is largely from Idaho, but I can tell you that he really enjoyed interacting with what he considered "his" people when he was in the State. I also think he was energized by knowing that in his position in the Senate he was where he could be really effective, not only to help Idaho people, but, as in his leadership in the energy fields, the whole country."[2]

McClure, himself, was a bit turned off by the word "fun" when he was asked the question—his Calvinist upbringing and conscience limiting him to more respectable terms such as "satisfying" and "fulfilling" to describe his feelings about his work in the Senate. But that does not really matter. In his first term he had proven to himself and his constituents that the U.S. Senate was where he *should* be and he was determined to do whatever he could to win another six-year contract from his Idaho people.

Which was not a problem because there was not a flock of Democratic candidates eager to get out and challenge him. Eventually, Idaho Democratic Party Chairman George Klein found a sacrificial lamb by the name of

From "Visiting Boise", Caxton Press
Dwight Jensen

Dwight Jensen. A brash, outspoken newscaster for Channel 2 in Boise at the time, Jensen admitted that he knew he was likely to get trounced by the popular McClure, but said he agreed to the challenge ". . .if he [Klein] could assure me that it wouldn't cost me any money."[3] (Jensen also said that he had to convince himself that he could mentally stand to lose.)

Looking back, Jensen believes he tried to run a good campaign, which he also said he enjoyed, but McClure campaigned with nearly the same intensity as in 1972 ("*We were not sure the media wouldn't feel that he was one of their own and start promoting him, but they did not do that. Also, I could never forgive myself if I lost a campaign by not working hard enough.*"[4]) and he gathered nearly 70 percent of the vote while carrying all forty-four of Idaho's counties. As his campaign manager Phil Reberger put it, "McClure got a grade of A+ for his first term from the voters of Idaho."[5] The only good news for Jensen was, as Klein promised, he was beaten without sacrificing any of his own funds.[ii]

McClure went back to the Senate, and he would have his time and energy devoted to a multitude of projects. The cheating of the Soviets on nuclear weapons that was being ignored by the Carter administration was high on his list. Also, he was deeply concerned about the fiscal irresponsibility of the Democrats that he believed was causing rampant inflation and soaring interest rates. However, it was his passion for the intelligent management of the nation's energy, water, and other natural resources which was foremost in his mind.

Energy was especially important to him in the mid and late '70s. The nation was still trying to recover from the aftermath of the Arab oil embargo, and even though he still believed a nuclear/hydrogen mix was the ultimate answer to America's energy independence, he was eager to support other measures that would contribute to that end. And in doing so he acquired a strange bedfellow that politics is said to create. J. Bennett Johnston was a socially moderate to liberal Democratic senator from Louisiana who was elected the same time as McClure and who served with him on the Energy and National Resources Committee. Johnston also had a keen interest in energy. Cynics like Howard Metzenbaum (D.Ohio), who also served on that committee and who had a deep-seated enmity for the big oil companies, would say that Johnston was only interested in energy because of his tie to the oil companies competing to drill under the offshore waters of

Louisiana. McClure did not accede to this cynical attitude. He and Johnston had engaged in numerous discussions about America's energy problems and, despite the "strange bedfellow" nature of their relations, they came to develop a mutual respect and friendship for each other. And they produced results. McClure said:

> *Bennett and I were both concerned about the nation's vulnerability if we ever experienced another embargo of the kind instituted by the Arabs in 1973. We talked a lot about that, and together we were able to come up with a brainchild that would provide, at least up to now, an emergency solution. We called it the Strategic Petroleum Reserve Bill, which was legislation that provided for underground storage sites in salt caverns along the Gulf Coast where an emergency supply of oil could be stored. Getting this legislation passed was not easy, particularly because of those who distrusted the oil companies and who wanted to use the strategic reserve to dampen out the supply-demand cycles that affected the price of gasoline to the consumer— their idea being that when the price of gasoline rose, oil could be pumped from the reserve to increase the supply and drive the price down. One of the very very important things we did in setting up this reserve was to mandate that it could not be used for economic purposes. We made a big fight over specific wording. As a compromise we used language that would let the executive branch decide when a supply interruption would justify emergency withdrawal of the reserve. This was one of the few examples of how a democracy can look ahead and enact measures to solve potential problems that may arise in the future. Democracy is notoriously short-sighted. Normally we react to emergencies; we don't plan for the long term.*[6]

Senator J. Bennett Johnston was not the only Democrat who became a strong ally in McClure's crusade to insulate the United States economy from an oil disruption. President Carter, whose policies McClure generally detested, became an ally when he proposed massive new funding for a government sponsored, government run Synfuels Corporation. To many Republicans this idea looked like a typical big-government boondoggle—a project that would stick the government's nose into a business that should best be left to private investors and private industry. But in this case, McClure did not side with his conservative brethren. He knew the synfuels history. He knew what had happened in World War II:

> *In 1944 General George S. Patton's Third Army was racing across southern France. In his haste to be the first U.S. commander to cross into Germany, however, Patton overextended his supply lines. His armored columns ground to a dead stop. Faced with the choice of*

> *waiting until he could be resupplied or draining the fuel of captured German vehicles, Patton chose the latter. His tanks and armored personnel carriers continued to steamroll toward Germany, powered by the German's own ersatz gasoline—synthetic fuel manufactured from coal...At the time more than 92 percent of Germany's aviation gasoline and half its total petroleum during World War II had come from synthetic fuel plants. At its peak in early 1944, the German synfuels effort produced more than 124,000 barrels per day. . .*[7]

He also knew that South Africa, isolated physically and socially, and with an economy extremely vulnerable to a punitive oil boycott, had been farsighted enough to create a strong and viable synfuels industry. If Nazi Germany could do it and South Africa could do it, McClure believed that it made good sense for his own country to do it.[iii] And, no, he was not enthusiastic about the idea of a government run business being a major supplier of synthetic fuel. He agreed with his fellow conservatives that this was a bad idea. What worried him was that, despite what the scientists and engineers in Nazi Germany and South Africa had done, the technology for converting the massive coal and oil shale deposits in the United States was not ready for a major production effort.

Faced with a serious disruption in the oil supply, the experts to whom he was listening said that it would take many years before the technology would be ready, even with a World War II Manhattan-type effort.[iv] More important, getting the technology ready was not a viable investment for any private company or companies. Potential profits to pay off the enormous debt for such research were not on any investor's screen. What McClure envisioned and what he led the congressional battle to achieve was a Synfuels Corporation that would use taxpayer funds to develop the technology that would be ready for private companies to use when the inevitable energy emergency arrived. He had no doubt then, and, thirty years later he still has no doubt that the country will face a severe energy crunch. However, like the nuclear energy future that he dreamed of, but which he lived to see languishing and moribund, so went his dreams for the birth of new synfuels technology. Yes, he and like-minded Senators and Representatives did get a Synfuels Corporation established while Carter was still president. However, it had barely gotten organized when the next President, Ronald Reagan, through machinations irrelevant to the McClure story, effectively scuttled the whole program. The question of whether that was wisdom or folly is yet to be answered.

It should be emphasized that McClure was not just interested in nuclear energy or fuel produced from coal and oil shale. In his words, "At that time no one knew whether it should be nuclear energy or geothermal energy or solar energy or wind energy or energy from biomass or whatever. In many ways I was a maverick among the conservatives in my own party, but I believed then and I believe now that it is a legitimate use of the taxpayers' money to fund research that can tell us the energy mix that will be best for the country—and by country, I mean what is best for the economy, the environment, and the health and safety of the American people. I would hate for anybody to believe that I was only interested in one or two kinds of energy; I was interested in exploring the potential of all forms of usable energy."[8]

He not only was interested in exploration, he was also interested in demonstration. It has already been mentioned how he held a solar energy electrolysis demonstration on the Capitol steps for his colleagues. He followed that up with a full-blown auto show, bringing every model of electric automobile that his staff could locate (probably including many that were home-garage, do-it-yourself, one-of-a-kind models) and displaying them outside the Capitol. One aide, Mike Hathaway, had to chuckle when he described how one of the models broke down before they could get it in the lineup. Even in his press releases, McClure was quick to admit that the technology was primitive and that there were a lot of potential problems with electric automobiles. Just the same, he also wanted his colleagues to know that he was dead serious about the need to encourage the kinds of research that might uncover a hidden potential of the electric car.

To prove that he was serious, McClure garaged his trusty 1969 turquoise and white Mustang convertible (the one famous among staffers for its screwdriver gear shift) and used his personal funds for a two-year lease of the only commercial electric car available at the time: a Bradley GTE, a sleek, two gull-winged door sports car. Actually, it was not a sports car in the performance sense; it just looked like it was designed for the race track. Said McClure:

> *I drove it every day, and I had to be really careful when I drove up to a cross walk because it was so quiet that pedestrians conditioned to the noise of a car to alert them did not know I was there. I got Idaho Power to loan me a meter that I installed in my garage so I could keep track of the power I used to charge the batteries—it would go about fifty miles on a charge, less if it was colder. Computing the residential electric rate at the time, and factoring in 1,000 deep cycles of the batteries before replacement—the batteries were expensive—the cost was about the same as a gasoline-powered car. But, it was fun to drive and, yes, I did take some of my colleagues for a ride in it. The only drawback was that it had no air conditioner, which was tough in the summer except when I drove to work in the early morning.*[9]

Energy was not a high profile issue for McClure's Idaho constituents, although it is doubtful if the Senator lost much sleep worrying about the time he was spending on the issue. He did feel that it was a critical issue for

Courtesy Ron Shiflett

McClure's electric van drew attention in Idaho and in Washington, D.C. Once Ron Shiflett spotted someone crawling around inside the van while it was parked underneath the Dirksen Office Building. The curious intruder turned out to be Senator John Glenn.

the nation, and since few of his colleagues were concerned enough to take the lead on such matters, he more or less assumed the role of Senate leader on energy by default. That is not meant to imply that there were not other senators interested in the energy problem. J. Bennett Johnson has already been mentioned as one such senator. Another was Senator Pete Domenici from New Mexico. McClure worked closely with both of them on numerous energy issues. Another Senator interested in energy was Henry "Scoop" Jackson (D-Washington) who was chairman of the Energy and Natural Resources Committee on which McClure was serving. McClure had a good personal relationship with Jackson even though they were strong antagonists on a number of issues. More important, however, was the fact that both of them were from the Northwest where there was a need to put ideological differences aside and work for the betterment of the region. And in the late Carter years, a major issue of that type had arisen.

The Columbia River Basin drains water from a vast area that includes the states of Montana, Idaho, Oregon and Washington as well as mountainous areas of Alberta and British Columbia in Canada. During the 20th century the Bureau of Reclamation and the Corps of Engineers constructed thirty-one dams on the Columbia and its tributaries. The primary purpose for this construction was to impound water that could be used for irrigation or to store water to prevent flooding. A bonus at each of the sites was a hydroelectric generating facility, which could provide low-cost power to Northwest customers and, in addition, create revenues that would come back into the U.S. Treasury to pay back the costs of the projects. A second bonus was the creation of a navigable waterway all the way to Lewiston, Idaho, which enabled wheat growers from Camas Prairie and the Palouse region of Idaho and Eastern Washington to ship their grain to the West Coast for a fraction of the cost by rail. A third bonus was the impounded water itself, which furnished recreation for hundreds of thousands of people in the region.

But there were negative side effects. The impounded waters also flooded centuries old Native American fishing villages. And the dams were

THE ELECTRIC VAN

Ron Shiflett was McClure's legislative assistant for energy at the time of the 1978 election. He tells the story of McClure's electric van:

McClure was dead serious about the need to demonstrate the value of electric cars. Just before his 1978 campaign I contacted a friend I'd gone to high school with in Virginia who worked for General Electric in Salem. Through him we got a lease on a Ford Econoline van that had been converted with an electric motor and batteries. We had JIM McCLURE FOR SENATE—ENERGY EFFICIENCY IN ACTION painted on the side, and Tod Neueschwander and I towed it out to Idaho. Then McClure or I would drive it in every parade and at every stop on the campaign trail. It had Virginia plates, but when we were in an Idaho town, I'd take them off so people wouldn't wonder about a vehicle from Virginia. One afternoon I happened to be on the freeway outside of Boise and without the plates. I saw blue lights flashing—a state trooper—and after he pulled me over, he said, "You don't have any plates." I explained what I was doing and he could see the Jim McClure writing on the side. We talked for several minutes, then he asked me what kind of a rig it was. I pulled the cap off the battery pack and he was fascinated with the technology. Then he asked me if he could take it for a spin. I agreed and he took off and here I am standing at the open door of his patrol car, blue lights still flashing. Finally, he shows up about 25 minutes later, a big grin on his face. He loved it and I never got a ticket.

Another story. I had driven the van to work and parked it in McClure's spot underneath the Dirksen Building. After work I went down to get it—it was late afternoon and not much light was down there—and I saw the sliding door open and a man crawling around inside. I could see he was wearing a suit and dress shoes. There was little security in those days and I was concerned because some of McClure's things were in it. I walked up and asked the man what he was doing. He raised up and introduced himself. "I'm John Glenn," he said. It was Senator John Glenn and he had pulled the cap off the battery pack and had been studying the technology. He went on to explain that the moon rover he had used for practice when he was an astronaut was also an electric vehicle. He was just fascinated with the technology and said that he agreed with McClure that electric vehicles needed to be in our future.

Courtesy Ron Shiflett

McClure arranged for numerous electric cars to be exhibited outside the Capitol. This GE-100 prototype drew interest from a number of congressmen and senators.

barriers to salmon and steelhead trout that had to swim upstream to the shallow waters where they were born before they could reproduce. And many believed that several species of these anadromous fish were heading toward extinction because of the dams.

In 1937 Congress established the Bonneville Power Administration (BPA) as the agency that would market and distribute the electric power produced by the growing number of dams in the Columbia drainage. Their mandated priority was to build transmission lines and market the power to public utilities—non-profit utilities owned by public entities such as municipalities, utility districts and co-ops. A second priority was to stimulate the growth of industry in the region, particularly aluminum smelters, an industry that required huge amounts of electricity and which could only flourish where such power was cheap. An abundance of low-cost power was also a boon to irrigators over the region who could now afford to use large quantities of electricity to pump water for application to their crops.

Low-cost power did everything the dam builders envisioned. The Northwest economy flourished as every major producer of aluminum established smelters in the region. Huge agricultural projects based upon cheap pumping costs began to appear, particularly in the dry central regions of Washington and Oregon. By the mid-'70s the cheap-power boom in the region was catching up with the supply and the BPA had to notify its customers that, if forced to purchase electricity on the open market from other producers, rates might have to rise dramatically. At the same time a regional group, the Pacific Northwest Utility Conference Committee, was forecasting a seven percent compounded growth rate in the use of electrical energy in the region. The reader is not likely to imagine the shock that such a prediction created among those who were running BPA. Peter Johnson, who took over as Administrator of BPA just as the price of power began escalating, said, "The forecasted rate of increase was shocking. It would have meant that we would need to build and bring on line a new nuclear power plant every year."

Dramatic growth in the region fueled by cheap power—that was a formula that brought joy to the hearts of congressional delegates in the region. But the rumblings about the days of low-cost power coming to an end had the opposite effect—it struck fear into their hearts. And the politician who was struck the hardest was the great public power advocate of the Northwest, Senator Henry Jackson from the state of Washington.

Scoop Jackson, as he was known to all of his colleagues, was not about to sit on the sidelines and let his beloved image of a public power-fed economic paradise become strangled by the supply-demand vagaries of the Northwest economy. Besides, he was chairman of the powerful Senate committee that had jurisdiction over the energy and resources of the region. He could do something about the problem. And he did. He initiated an all-encompassing piece of legislation titled the Pacific Northwest Electric Power Planning and Conservation Act. This was the formal name; it subsequently became known simply as the Northwest Power Act.

Enter Jim McClure, who was the second ranking Republican on Jackson's committee. McClure was suspicious of the legislation for several reasons. For example, a part of the Act specified that a Pacific Northwest Electric Power and Conservation Planning Council was to be established with two representatives to be appointed by each of the governors of Washington and Oregon. He strenuously objected to the exclusion of Idaho and Montana, both of which supplied water to the Columbia Basin. Said McClure;

> *They thought Idaho was a country cousin and didn't have much say on down-river rights. I managed to get four states involved by arguing for equal representation on the proposed Council. But that was a fight. It was played out mostly in committee in conversations between principals. I think the reason I won that fight was because they believed I could stop the legislation. It is easier to stop legislation than to pass it. Once you create chaos around a bill like that, it is not going to go. That was especially true with this legislation. There was a tension in Congress about the Northwest, a feeling that the federal government had already done too much to help that region. There was resentment because of the low-cost electricity in the region. Why should electricity be cheaper for those citizens than in the Northeast or Midwest? Some didn't think that was fair. Scoop Jackson knew that, and he also knew that unless the whole Northwest delegation was united, he was not going to get the legislation passed.*[10]

McClure also disagreed strenuously with Jackson and several others on the committee who wanted the council to be a governmental entity in the Northwest—an entity that could mandate how much electricity was needed, where it was needed, who would construct new facilities, how the facilities would be constructed, and who would build and own the transmission lines.[v] Said McClure:

> *I argued that the proposed council should be advisory only and not a regional government. We had a terrible time trying to write the*

Courtesy Frank Cushing

Ron Shiflett, left, and Tod Neuenschwander were two of McClure's key aides.

> *language that would declare whether the council would have binding authority or be advisory. I remember that Dan Evans, who had just completed three terms as governor of Washington, insisted that his delegation should hold out for the council to become a centralized planning authority that would make decisions with which all other agencies had to conform. I was equally insistent that appointed people on the council would have more authority than the states and that was not proper. We struggled with the language and finally solved the problem with a bit of ambiguity. I got the wording in that made it possible to pass the Act, language specifying that the council would have the authority to make plans and decisions and that other entities had to consider them. Dan Evans* [who was appointed to the first council and was its first president] *was never satisfied with that and there have been a lot of arguments about the power of the council since the passage of the Act* [in 1980].[11]

Then the demand for electricity collapsed and the planners who were touting a seven percent annual rate compounded had to go hide. The actual rate of growth was 1.5 percent, and the difference between prognostications and reality fueled the greatest public bond default in the history of the United States.

Chapter 26 notes

i. The reader may wonder: What happened to Jim Goller who managed the four previous campaigns? Goller felt that McClure had more need for him as his Chief of Staff and that Reberger, who had successfully managed a Senator's campaign in Virginia, was fully competent. Goller did confess, "I kept a close eye on the campaign."

ii. Jensen never returned to broadcasting; after the campaign he went back to college, earned an M.S. Degree, then taught journalism at Syracuse University and Marshall University. At the time of this interview he had retired and was living in Cazenovia, New York.

iii. McClure was also aware that gasoline from coal also had a higher energy density than petroleum gasoline, meaning that an airplane could fly farther with the same amount of fuel. He tried to get the Pentagon interested, touting extended range for their airplanes, but got no interest.

iv. The Manhattan Project was the pull-out-all-stops effort that created the atomic bomb.

v. The legislation also mandated that the Council must develop a "program to protect, mitigate and enhance fish and wildlife."

Chapter 27

New Roles

It is mid-October, 1980, and Senator Jim McClure is in Grangeville, Idaho. He has spent the whole day on Representative Steve Symms' campaign bus, shaking hands with constituents and making stump speeches extolling the virtues of his younger colleague. Symms, the First District congressman, is running against Frank Church, Idaho's senior senator. Handsome, personable, and with a self-deprecating sense of humor, Symms is, according to the latest poll, steadily cutting into Church's once significant lead. And having the popular McClure along with him is even more of a help. "I was kind of a bomb-thrower," Symms admitted twenty-five years later, "but McClure gave me credibility."[1]

It was well known in Washington that McClure was backing Steve Symms in his bid to unseat Frank Church. But, despite some sniping that Church had done against him,[i] McClure carefully avoided saying anything negative in return. Occasionally, with his staff, McClure would joke about the way Church would dress in three-piece suits and hob nob with his liberal supporters when he was in the East, and how he would change into cowboy clothes back in Idaho so he would look like a Westerner. But those comments were never meant for the public. McClure constantly admonished his staffers: "Don't do anything or say anything negative about Frank Church. We have to work with him and we *need* to work with him in order to do the best job of helping Idaho people."

And the best-laid schemes o' mice an 'men Gang aft agley. . .

An ABC Network news team happened to be covering the Symms campaign bus that October day, and prior to his taking the platform for a speech, they had fitted Symms with a wireless microphone. Promptly forgetting that he was hot-miked, Symms saw one of his "hard-core" supporters, John Brandt, in the audience and greeted him. Brandt, the owner of a hardware store in the nearby town of Stites, now remembers[2] that he asked Symms some questions, including one about Church and whether he had caused any damage to the CIA as the result of the bad publicity that resulted from the Church Committee hearings in 1975. He also remembers Symms suggesting that he ask that question of McClure if there was a question/answer period after his speech. Brandt agreed, and when the time came, McClure was asked the question.

McClure says the question surprised him. He also said, with a tone of sadness in his voice, that he really did not want to answer the question. "But it was a direct question," he admitted later, "and it is against my principles not to answer a direct question. So I answered him."

What follows is how McClure and Symms remember the event.

McClure:

In mid-December of 1975 I was returning from a visit to Israel when I stopped in Athens for a briefing by CIA Station Chief Richard Welch. After the briefing, which contained secret material I still do not wish to discuss, Welch opened up and began telling me how he felt about the actions of the Church Committee[ii]*, which made public many of the CIA's formerly secret activities, was undermining the morale of CIA personnel and also making their work more dangerous. Also, he specifically said that his own life was in danger because the revelations were bound to make his enemies more bold. I got the feeling that he was definitely afraid for his life, and that bothered me as I flew on back to Washington. I had been back a very short time when I got word that Richard Welch had been shot and killed by masked terrorists as he returned to his home with his wife after attending a Christmas party.*

> TOD NEUENSCHWANDER'S OBSERVATION
>
> *I was his press secretary and was with him in Grangeville when he told the Welch story. I heard the whole thing and I know the reaction was tough on Jim. He had known and worked with Frank Church for years, and although they saw most issues differently, they did come together on most Idaho issues, and there was always a mutual respect. I believe Jim's unplanned telling of the Welch story, although totally true, bothered him for several years.*

I had told Steve Symms that story and that is the story I repeated in Grangeville. I have never said that Frank Church released Welch's name or ever had any direct responsibility for Welch's death. I only passed on what Welch told me, that the information made public by his [Church's] *committee made our enemies more bold and more determined to commit reprisals and get even. I believed Welch then, and I still believe he was correct.*[3]

Symms:

In her newscast, Cassie [Catherine] *Mackin almost ignored the story that McClure told about the assassination of the Athens CIA chief. She thought the big story was about me planting a question in the audience. That's what made the news and I'm sure her purpose in doing that was to embarrass me. But it back-fired; people in Idaho didn't think anything about me planting a question, but her broadcast sure raised the consciousness of the Idaho voters regarding Church's role in the CIA hearings. It was all over Idaho.*

There was also a funny ending to this story. I was in a group of sixteen Republican senators who won that November—we were called the "Sweet 16," and after we were sworn in, there was a party for us at Howard Baker's [new majority leader] *home.*

All the press folks were standing outside and Cassie Mackin grabbed me for a comment. I thanked her profusely, and while the rest of the press listened, I told her that I wouldn't be there if it were not for her. She was flabbergasted and stammered to the other press folks that she had not taken sides in the election. I laughed; then told how her story about me planting a question in the campaign had gotten around in Idaho and how Idaho people would never have

WORLD NEWS TONIGHT (ABC)
October 13, 1980
(Transcript)

Catherine Mackin: *But Symms, traveling around Idaho with the state's conservative Senator James McClure, proved no slouch himself at gut level politics. After a speech at this rally, Symms, wearing a wireless microphone, could be heard in the audience staging a question damaging to Church.*

Steve Symms: *If they open this up to questions ask McClure that question in front of the TV guys. Get up and ask him.*

Catherine Mackin: *The man complied, asking whether Church was responsible for weakening the Central Intelligence Agency in the Congressional investigation Church led. Symms, in a good guy-bad guy routine, acted unaware the question would be asked and called on McClure to answer it.*

Steve Symms: *Alright, I'd rather see Jim McClure answer that question than me. He was in the Senate when the CIA things went on. Would you care to answer that, Jim? I think he played a big role in it personally, but. . .*

Catherine Mackin: *McClure then seemed to imply Church was responsible for the death of CIA agent Richard Welch, killed five years ago in Greece.*

Senator McClure: *And this man, who was the head of the CIA said, "It isn't so much what Church is saying, or even the fact that he's naming our agents or saying that what we've done is wrong. He called the CIA a rogue elephant running wild.* [Welch said] *But what he's doing is* [unintelligible to transcriber—McClure says he said "emboldening"] *the enemies of the United States, and he's going to get some of our people killed" Two weeks later that man was dead. The man I was talking to had been assassinated. He had forecast his own death. . .*

Catherine Mackin: *To survive this election, Senator Church has a most difficult balancing act—how to get by the assault of those right wing organizations that are helping Congressman Symms. . .how to overcome the genuine conservative tide that is sweeping all across this state. It won't be easy. Catherine Mackin, ABC News, Bogus Basin, Idaho.*

Courtesy Alan Timothy

McClure and Idaho Democratic Senator Frank Church. McClure drew fire when he criticized Church for his handling of Senate Foreign Relations Committee hearings on the CIA.

> *known about Frank Church and the CIA if it hadn't been for her. She about died of embarrassment and I loved it.*

Afterward, McClure was criticized for making the statement in Grangeville. Church's biographers claimed that "McClure. . .attributed Richard Welch's death to Church," while an editorialist said, ". . .when Church ran for re-election in 1980, Republican Senator Jim McClure of Idaho publicly blamed him for Welch's death."[4] Despite all of this, McClure, while wishing that he had not been asked Symm's question in Grangeville, has no regrets. He said, "It has always been my opinion that if Frank Church did not believe that his committee's release of CIA horror stories to the world would damage the reputation of the CIA, trigger the wrath of CIA critics, and cause reprisals, he was either naive or he did not care. If he had some other defense in his mind, we will never know it. And since he cannot defend himself, for the sake of his family I would rather let the matter drop."[iii 5]

The election of 1980 caused more than the defeat of Idaho's senior senator. It sent Jimmy Carter back to Georgia and brought Ronald Reagan to the White House.

It also changed the life of Senator Jim McClure. The "Sweet-16" new Republican senators, of which Steve Symms was one, changed the power structure in the Senate. The Republicans were now in the majority, which was the biggest swing since 1958 when Eisenhower was President. Robert Byrd (D-West Virginia) had to relinquish his position as Majority Leader and become Minority Leader. Howard Baker (R-Tennessee) became the new Majority Leader.

The progression was a bit more convoluted in the Energy and Natural Resources Committee. McClure had been the second ranking Republican on that committee. After the election, when it was known that the Republicans would be in charge during the next Congress, Senator Mark Hatfield (R-Oregon), who had been the ranking Republican on the committee, decided he would rather be chairman of the Senate Appropriations Committee on which he was also the ranking Republican. This moved McClure up a notch and enabled him to replace Scoop Jackson as chairman of the Energy and Natural Resources Committee.

McClure was also on the Senate Appropriations Committee and was the ranking Republican on the Subcommittee on Interior Appropriations. After the 1980 election, he became its chairman, which put him in a position where he had the power to influence the allotment of funds on many programs affecting Idaho.

He was also determined to get into a leadership position in the Senate, not as his staffers insist because of any desire for ego enhancement, but as Dick Thompson put it, ". . .so he would have more influence and more impact on what was going on."[6] Two years earlier he had run for conference chairman against Robert Packwood of Oregon and was defeated. He ran again after the 1980 election and beat Senator John Heinz (R-Pennsylvania).

And what is the conference over which he won the right to preside? In the Senate the organization that is made up of all the Democratic senators is called the "Caucus." Unlike the Idaho Senate where the organizations for both parties have the same name, in the U.S. Senate the Republicans call their organization the "Conference." As the elected chairman, McClure was the third-ranking Republican in the leadership hierarchy. Also, throughout the year, the chairman could call special meetings of the Conference when there were important issues to discuss—meetings over which the Chairman presided rather than the Majority Leader or Assistant Majority Leader (Whip).

Aside from the normal duties of a chairman such as setting priorities and meeting agendas, the Conference Chairman exerted great influence by having the authority to appoint senators to two special committees. One was the Republican Policy Committee[iv], which was influential in establishing Republican positions on major issues of the day. The other was the Committee on Committees, which was a select group of senators who made all other committee assignments. McClure had ideas on how he wanted to structure both committees, but Dick Thompson remembers that the Committee on Committees was the one he most wanted to influence.

McClure had been in the Senate for eight years and one of the problems he perceived was the way the membership on certain committees was stacked with liberal senators of both parties. According to Thompson, this was especially true of the Health and Welfare, and Education Committees, which were notorious among conservatives for the amount of liberal social legislation that came out of them. McClure wanted to change that. He wanted to move liberal Republican senators off those committees and he wanted them replaced by conservatives. Of course, he could not do that directly; he had no power to make individual committee assignments. However, by

McCLURE HELPS DEFUSE A POTENTIAL CRISIS
by Paul Weyrich

After George Bush was named as Reagan's vice-presidential candidate, he continued to knock some of Reagan's ideas, calling his economic plan "voodoo economics" and saying that Reagan was going too far in restricting abortions. McClure knew this was damaging because the press was making an issue of it, so he called a meeting of the Steering Committee and asked Bush to attend. At the meeting Paul Laxalt spoke first, before Bush arrived, and said that a potential disaster was brewing because the media coverage is going to be Bush vs Reagan instead of Reagan vs Carter. McClure made it very clear that he agreed, then Bush comes in and old Strom Thurmond says "I want to get right to the point." Then he tells Bush that Reagan is our nominee and we have to support him. Then [Jessie] Helms weighs in: "Your campaign is over and you have joined your opponents team. Your obligation is to support him."

Bush was silent as every senator there—sixteen or twenty of them—chastised him. Some were getting hot about it and McClure handled the situation deftly by injecting a little humor. He said to the senator, "Why don't you come back when you really feel strongly about this." Everybody laughed and that took the edge off. McClure went around to every senator, and when everybody had spoken, he wrapped up and summarized. "The major point here is you have ended your campaign and you cannot carry on as if you are still running." To my surprise—this was as tense an ordeal as I've every attended—Bush said, "I want to thank you for your candor. I must tell you I hadn't seen it the way you present it; I thought Reagan would allow a differing point of view and I see now that I was wrong. I assure you that you will see an entirely different approach from this minute forward. McClure ended the meeting and Bush went around and shook the hands of all the senators. And from that day forward, he was a team player. He never uttered a word against Reagan even though reporters continued to taunt him. I was not a Bush fan but my respect went up greatly after seeing how he handled that. And McClure was exactly the right person to preside over something that tense and emotional.

appointing the right people to the Committee on Committees, he could, indirectly, cause some changes of that type to occur.

When McClure won election to the Republican Conference, he had to vacate his chairmanship of the Senate Steering Committee. He also brought his staff director, Margo Carlisle, with him to manage the thirty-odd personnel who worked for the conference. According to Carlisle, she and McClure sat down and reviewed the activities of the conference, searching for ways to make the organization more effective. Together, they agreed that there was both wastage and duplication. The creation of newsletters had been a basic function. They agreed that there were better ways of getting publicity for senators. The preparation of analytical policy papers on such things as health care and energy was another function, but it was largely a duplication of efforts by the staff of the Policy Committee. With McClure's encouragement, Carlisle made significant changes in the activities of the conference. What senators really needed, they decided, was a means of getting live broadcasts, either radio or television, to stations in the their home states, with emphasis on *immediate* releases—releases that would be heard or seen at home no later than twenty-four hours after they were recorded. This meant that overnight delivery services had to be used, and it also meant that the use of satellite loads and downloads had to be developed. With this system Republican senators could stand up before the camera, explain what bills were coming out of their committees and why they were supporting them, and their constituents at home could watch them on their local channels that same evening.

One problem was the education of the senators in the art of extemporizing in short bites—a problem that McClure, himself, had difficulty solving. Tod Neuenschwander, McClure's long-time press secretary and later, administrative assistant, said, "McClure was a challenge. Ask him the time and he would tell you how a clock was made. I'd take some of his comments and try to edit them and I couldn't cut out a 60- or 90-second sound bite; they all ran together. I coached him and coached him—even Louise worked with him—and we finally educated him on how to do it."[7] Carlisle remembers that senators had difficulty, ". . .but we made significant progress and were able to greatly increase the output, especially to terribly news hungry states like New York."[8]

New committees and new chairmanships, and heavy new responsibilities—all of these added to the load of a senator who had seemingly been operating at maximum capacity before the 1980 election. But there was more to come.

Orval Hansen, McClure's University of Idaho classmate and former Idaho Second District Congressman[v] engineered one more appointment for his old friend. Hansen explains:

After I left Congress, President Ford appointed me to the board of the Kennedy Center for the Performing Arts, a place that was of a great interest to me because of my interest in such things and because of my wife who had been an actress for most of her life. That board has members appointed by the President and members appointed by the leadership of the House and the Senate. Each leader appoints five each, with the majority getting three positions, the minority getting two. The evening of the 1980 election, when I learned that the Republicans were going to gain control of the Senate, I remembered that Jim McClure had expressed an interest in being on that board. As soon as I realized that there would now be room for a third Republican, I called Tom Hill [a McClure legislative assistant] *and asked him to immediately get a letter to Howard Baker requesting an appointment. Tom drafted the letter, McClure flew in the next day and signed it, and it went to Baker. Nothing happened for quite a while. The story I heard was that Baker and Jim were on a trip to the Middle East when Baker said, "Jim, I'm going to appoint you to the Kennedy Center Board even though Ted Stevens* [R-Alaska] *desperately wants it. I'm appointing you because your letter came in first."*

Well, Roger Stevens was the chairman of the board and he was an old Democratic politician—he had once been finance chairman of the party, and before that, he had once lived under the most difficult circumstances, riding the rails and working in the wheat fields during the Depression before his fortune changed and he became wealthy enough to purchase the Empire State Building. To put it mildly, Stevens was not impressed with McClure being appointed—What interest would a conservative like McClure have in this institution? I suggested that he meet McClure, so we took a car and went up to the Senate where they got acquainted. It was Stevens' good fortune to have McClure on that board because he became a stalwart and a real champion of the Kennedy Center, and when they needed real help in appropriations and getting bills passed, Jim knew how to do that. He was a skilled and dedicated Board member. Roger saw Jim's value immediately and it wasn't too long after his appointment when he was named a member of the Executive Committee.[9]

McClure had his own comments on Roger Stevens and his reasons for wanting on the Kennedy Center Board:

My interest started in a negative sense. Roger Stevens was always pushing for money from Congress—that after assuring Congress that it wasn't going to cost taxpayers a dime for the Center to operate. Then he would come in asking for money. I didn't like that process. He would say that he needed the appropriation just for this year and that he would be okay next year. Then he would come in for more money. He was an emotional man—he once broke down and cried in my office—but I did not like doing business that way; it was dishonest. So I looked at the critical side of serving on that board. I had more than a slight suspicion that Roger Stevens was less interested in the financial aspect than he should have been—that he wasn't as careful as he should have been on the expense side. However, a good many members of Congress had been and were on that board but they put that up as a trophy and never attended. I always attended and participated, and I served on committees and worked at it.

Frankly, I turned the corner and the Center turned the corner. I discovered the richness of its programs—there were plays, dance, concerts—the American Film Institute was housed there, and I served on the Education Committee and encouraged outreach programs in the schools of the area, which enabled hundreds and hundreds of school kids to participate and benefit from the activities. I had some influence in getting the Idaho Vandaleers to perform there and I had some influence in broadening the role. I don't want to overstate my role, but I did help make sure jazz was a part of the program—I got Gene Harris there as a performer, and I supported making country music a part of the awards—that music is an American art form. It was fun and satisfying, and as I say, I turned the corner. I came to believe that the Center had programs that were worthy of and should have federal funding, and I worked to establish a permanent appropriation for it. [10]

Actually, McClure's work on the Kennedy Center Board was not his first excursion into the aesthetic world of Washington. Some time earlier his office was routinely visited by a "persistent lady" who brought homemade bagels for the staff, hoping that her generosity would be rewarded with a chance to speak to the Senator. Tom Hill, who enjoyed her bagels, found, after talking with her, just why she specifically wanted to talk to *his* senator. Hill remembers that she was or had been associated with an organization in Washington that had the mission of saving historic buildings, and McClure, being chairman of the subcommittee that appropriated funds for such purposes, was the man who could save a building that she cherished. One day, after one of her bagel visits, Hill's curiosity finally overcame his reluctance to leave the office during duty hours and he agreed to follow her just to see the edifice that was the object of her affection. Hill tells the rest of the story:

I walked with this lady a few blocks from our office to this huge old building known as the "Pension Building." It had been designed after the Civil War by Montgomery Meigs who had been the Union

Army's Quartermaster General—the man responsible for supplying nearly one-million troops and who had lost a son in the war. The building was meant to be both a memorial to the men who fought and died, and a building that would house the hundreds of clerks who would manage the pensions to be paid to widows and disabled veterans of that war.

When we got there, I was impressed with its size, and when we went inside, I was more impressed with the huge columns, the second largest indoor columns in the world after those of St. Peter's in Rome. Also impressive was the Great Hall, the largest indoor space in Washington and which had been the location for several presidential inaugural balls. But it was in a terrible state of disrepair. The roof was caving in and a big tarp was catching water that came through it. One thing she told me caught my attention. She explained how Meigs had designed it so all the workers would have light, and how a special ventilation system kept fresh air circulating for them. This shifted my mind to the energy problems we were having and how this old building had been designed for energy efficiency. I thought that might be the hook that would interest McClure so I went back and told him about it. He was interested and went with me for a look. It didn't take long for him to appreciate it and he was immediately sold on doing what he could to preserve the building. He ended up getting the initial appropriation that fixed the roof, then worked on subsequent funding that completely restored the building. It is now gorgeous inside and serves as the National Building Museum dedicated to American architecture and engineering. Also, the Great Hall has since been the site for several more inaugural balls. I'm proud that McClure was the key individual responsible for saving it and that I also had a small role by getting him interested.

McClure claims that he never heard of the bagels or the lady who brought them to his office, but does admit that he became enthusiastic about preserving the Pension Building after he saw it. Said he, "It was a magnificent piece of architecture, but in disrepair—so much so that it was a question whether it should be fixed up or torn down. Fortunately, there were groups of people outside of government interested in preservation so it was just a question of asking the right people. I did get the initial appropriation and worked with one of those groups—they had the information and the inspiration. Yes, I was anxious to help their effort, but, to put it into perspective, it wasn't a principal focus of mine at the time."[11]

What he did have in focus at that time was an art exhibit that he and his wife were promoting. Long before they had left Payette, Idaho, for Washington the two of them had been admirers of art produced by Idaho artists.

Every art show or exhibit in their region was sure to attract them, and they took pride in having pieces of Idaho art decorating their home. This interest continued when they went to Washington.[vi] One of their favorite weekend pastimes was to visit the National Gallery and other art exhibits in the Capitol and surrounding area. However, as they did this, they remember remarking to each other that the art they were seeing in those exhibits was not any better than that produced by artists back in Idaho. They cannot remember now who suggested it, but the outgrowth of their interest in Idaho artists was to invite some of them to send their works for display in the McClure offices—when he was in the House and, later, when he went to the Senate.

After the 1980 election, when McClure became the chairman of the Subcommittee on Interior Appropriations, he became acquainted with Dillon Ripley, secretary of the Smithsonian Institution, whose budget was controlled by the committee. Over a period of several months they also were seeing each other socially and Louise and Ripley's wife, Mary, became good friends. Sometime after that, when they were together, Jim or Louise—they do not remember which—asked Ripley if there was any chance they could get an Idaho art exhibit into the Smithsonian. Ripley liked the idea immediately but then grew skeptical when he thought of funding such a project—Louise now says that the Smithsonian was "on hard times" then. "What if we raise all the money needed to do it from Idaho contributors?" Ripley was then asked. "From that time on," said Louise, "Ripley became an enthusiastic supporter and Jim and I worked as a team to get the project accomplished. We just knew this would give a big boost to the Idaho art community."[12]

After that meeting, McClure called John Fery, CEO of the Boise Cascade Corporation whom he knew to be an avid collector of Idaho art. Fery, after hearing what the McClures had in mind, instantly signed on to the project and agreed to raise the necessary funds from donors in Idaho. With that commitment established, McClure felt secure enough to issue a press release announcing the project and inviting Idaho artists to participate:

> *Idaho's Senator Jim McClure announced today that the National Museum of American Art, a part of the Smithsonian Institution, is planning an exhibit of contemporary fine artists living and working in Idaho. "Those of us from Idaho know of the fine art produced in our state, and this is a great opportunity to let the rest of the country know," said McClure. The exhibit, which is just in the planning stages, will encompass paintings, drawings, prints, and sculptures, as well as some mixed media. Crafts will not be included in this exhibition. "I encourage all of the interested artists in Idaho to submit slides for the exhibit," McClure said, "and I hope that we will have a good response. . ."* [13]

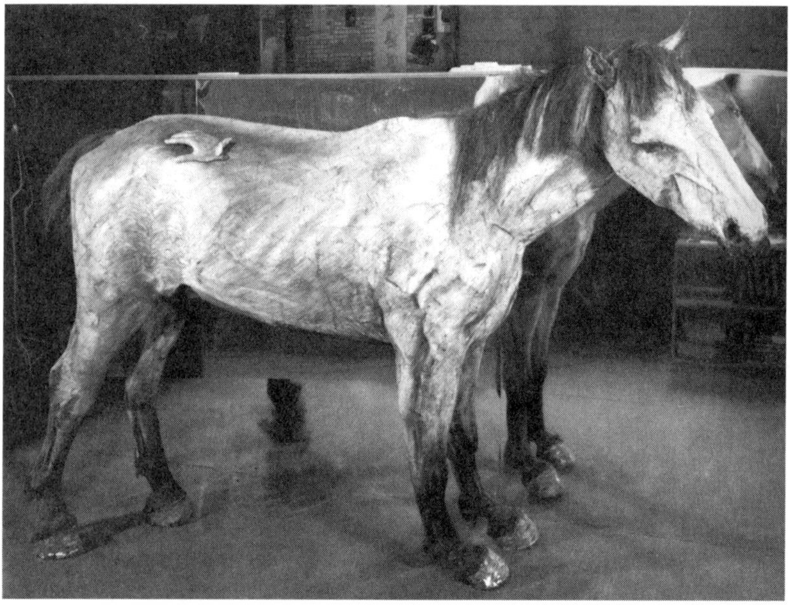

National Museum of American Art

"Horse" was the hit of SAWTOOTHS AND OTHER RANGES OF THE IMAGINATION, a display of Idaho art at the National Museum of American Art.

Enter Martha Solodky, McClure's legislative assistant for health, education and welfare issues. "Oh my God, yes." Solodky exclaimed, "He picked me to supervise that project and it consumed almost two years of my life! I did everything from addressing envelopes for the opening to getting huckleberries from Idaho to arranging for pianos to be rented and tuned to getting the catalog published in Idaho[7]and I even set up a 501C-3 so the donors could get a tax deduction. Not a day went by that I didn't spend several hours working on that art show."[14]

When the author first heard about this project, his first thought was that the McClure's had lost their minds. With 500 or more artists dreaming of having their work exhibited in the Smithsonian when only thirty or forty could be selected, the McClures had signed on to a venture that was sure to create enmity throughout the state, not only from the hundreds of rejected artists themselves, but from all of their relatives and boosters. But that did not happen, and for two good reasons. First, the Smithsonian put one of their art curators on the project, a "very gracious" lady named Barbara Shissler, who assumed the responsibility for selecting the art,[vii] an action that totally absolved the McClures from any association with the decisions. Second—and this came not only from the McClures, but from all the others interviewed—the art community was so thrilled that some of their deserving members would be exhibited in the Smithsonian that those whose works were not selected sincerely rejoiced for the talented ones whose were. "I cannot remember a single negative comment," said Gloria Brown, owner of Brown's Gallery in Boise who was a member of the Idaho steering committee that supervised the selection process. "Some of the traditional artists might have been a little disappointed because the Smithsonian curator wanted a wide variety of art and not many of their types could be selected, but, you know, artists in general have to learn to accept rejection—that goes with the territory. As for the McClures, I'm confident they received nothing but praise from the Idaho art community."[15]

And the result? Overall good. But the McClure's were a bit disappointed in some of the selections. "We are more traditional people," said Louise, "and some of that art was off-the-wall for us." Jim McClure added, "I remember saying, 'A lot of this stuff is not very good,' and Barbara replied, 'You're trying to chose art like the old masters, but nobody paints like Rembrandt and Reubens now. What we look for is the best of something else.' She didn't pick the kind we buy and hang on our walls, although she did have work from a few of our favorite artists. She also picked a paper mache sculpture of a six-foot horse. What a pain it was to get it and ship it to Washington, but it was probably the most popular thing at the show."[16]

"Do I ever remember Horse!" Solodky exclaimed when she was asked about the troubles with the piece. "First of all, we had to pay the artist's way up to Seattle where the piece was located because he insisted on supervising the packing and shipment. I was in trouble for awhile after getting funds for that. Then, after we got Horse back here, I got this call from Barbara Schissler at the Smithsonian, 'Martha,' she said, 'you've got to bring a gun and come over here. Horse has broken his leg and we have to take him out and shoot him.' What happened was when they were running rods down Horse's legs to support him, its weight pulled it over and one of the legs broke. But they patched him up and, I agree with the Senator, there were always more people around Horse than any of the other exhibits."[17]

The exhibit itself, titled SAWTOOTHS AND OTHER RANGES OF IMAGINATION, ran from November 1983 through February 1984 and by all who commented, it was a huge success. "At the reception," said Louise, "we had an all-Idaho buffet with smoked blue-back [Kokanee] salmon from Lake Pend 'Orielle, special potato skins created just for the occasion by Ore-Ida Foods, wine from Steve Symms' Idaho winery, and delicious Idaho huckleberry tart. A reporter from the *Washington Post* who described the reception said that most events of this type were deadly dull, but with the Idaho people he found good conversation, good music and good food. He also said that Idaho people really know how to let down and have fun."[18]

And what did it do for the Idaho art community? According to Gloria Brown, it was a real inspiration for hundreds of artists and it was a springboard for several of those whose works were exhibited to go on and become financially prosperous. Rod Kagan of the Sun Valley area, who had a sculpture in the show, said, "You just can't imagine what that kind of exposure means to an artist. Before my work was accepted for the exhibit, I was truly the struggling artist. I owe a great deal of gratitude to the McClures and John Fery for making that possible and helping me establish a long, satisfying and prosperous career. I'm kind of a loner and don't see the other artists who had things in the exhibit, but I'm sure many of them have to feel as I do."[1]

Chapter 27 notes

i. Because of McClure's steadfast belief that Arabs should be treated as fairly as Israelis, Church claimed that McClure was acting "like a water boy for radical Arabs."

ii. Senate Select Committee on Intelligence, begun in 1975 and chaired by Senator Frank Church, uncovered secret activities such as assassination plots against Castro—activities that caused Church to describe the agency as a "rogue elephant" on the rampage.

iii. Steve Symms confessed that had Church won that election it would have been much harder for the two senators to work together because of McClure's telling of that story.

iv. Dick Thompson left as McClure's Administrative Assistant in 1979 to become the staff director of the Republican Policy Committee—a better paying and more prestigious position.

v. Defeated by George Hansen in the 1974 Primary.

vi. Every year they commissioned an Idaho artist to paint a church, which they then reproduced and used to make their Christmas cards. Maintaining their Christmas card list, with as many as 5000 names, was a huge chore.

vii. McClure says that he had to fight with the Smithsonian people because he wanted everything done in Idaho and they couldn't believe anybody in Idaho could print a decent catalog. After he had the work done by Caxton Printers in Caldwell, he said they grudgingly agreed that it was a fine piece of work.

Chapter 28

The Pragmatist

In November, 1979, Iranian students took over the U.S. Embassy in Teh-ran, captured the staff and ended up holding fifty-two of them hostage for 444 days. As a result of this action, President Jimmy Carter froze Iranian assets in the U.S. and instituted a trade embargo. One result of that action, after the cutoff of Iranian oil shipments to the country, was another oil crisis even more severe than the one caused by the OPEC embargo of 1973. McClure staffers tell of taking turns going to all-night gasoline stations at three or four o'clock in the morning, then car pooling to work so they could avoid the three and four-hour lines that formed during daylight hours.

The hostages were released on President Reagan's first day in office and the trade embargo with Iran was lifted. Soon the oil supply logistics were normalized and the long gas lines eventually became a bitter memory to city dwellers who had been hit the hardest by the oil shortage. But Jim McClure did not let those memories fade. For years he had been thinking of the dire problems the country would face if there was a severe interruption in the petroleum supply. The long gas lines were just superficial blemishes. They were aggravating, but could be tolerated. What worried McClure was the malaise that would grow deep into the country's vital systems. He worried about the transport system—the trains and the hundreds of thousands of long-haul trucks that carried the fuel for our economic furnace. He worried about the millions of tractors and other motorized farm machinery that had to keep running to prevent the starvation of countless millions who were totally dependent upon American agricultural production. Gas lines were an inconvenience. Mis-allocation of fuel to the vital industries could be deadly and catastrophic to the nation.

And who in the United States of America had the most responsibility to see that such a catastrophe would not happen? Arguably the ultimate responsibility should fall on the shoulders of the U.S. president. And since 1973 and the passage of the Emergency Petroleum Allocation Act—a law that gave the president authority and guidelines for handling such an emer-gency—that responsibility was defined. But that law was to expire in 1981. And what would then happen if there was a severe shortage after that?

Enter the political ideologues. On the right the ideologues argued that the government had no business interfering with the free economy that supply-demand forces would, if left alone, take care of the problem. The leftist ideologues felt that such free marketers were as stupid as one would be leaving a loaded gun next to a suicide candidate. To them the renewal of the Emergency Petroleum Allocation Act—a law they felt was hopelessly weak and flawed—was the absolute minimum that should be accomplished. What they really wanted was a law that would put an emergency bureaucracy in place, equipped with detailed allocation plans for every commercial user of fuel, and already-printed fuel ration stamps for private consumers.

And where was McClure in this ideological stew? On the right side, of course. He had seen bureaucracies created, all with noble-sounding names, all with noble missions, all with leaders inspired to achieve noble deeds. And he had seen how these same bureaucracies soon degenerated into fiefdoms of waste, sloth, flaccidity, and an ever-increasing appetite for tax dollars to perpetuate their noble endeavors. So, yes, McClure believed in free-market solutions. He believed that economic forces would eventually level out the temporary mis-allocations that were bound to occur in an emergency. And he most certainly did not believe that his Idaho farmers and ranchers stood a snowball's chance of surviving under a fuel allocation bureaucracy dominated by eastern liberals beholden to the industrial base of their constituencies. McClure was a conservative, in his mind and in his soul. Liberal solutions were an anathema.

So what was the chairman of the Senate Energy and Natural Resource Committee going to do about the impending expiration of the Emergency Petroleum Allocation Act? Did he dare fight the liberal minority that wanted to create a paper bureaucracy to deal with a severe interruption of the nation's oil supply? Did he dare gavel down those who distrusted all oil companies and free-marketing advocates? And what if he was wrong? What if the supply-demand market forces did not solve mis-allocations before the economy tanked? With such a critical question in his sights, was he sure enough of his conservative convictions to risk the future of his country?

Weighty matters were these. In pondering them one had to have a forward vision. One had to call upon experience and an understanding of the way Americans would react in a potential crisis of the type under consideration. McClure confessed that his mental calculations at the time were dire, even dreadful. Without allocation authority or guidelines, a president could not act. McClure had lived through the bank panic of the Great Depression. He had seen the way desperate people reacted when their livelihood was threatened. And recently he had witnessed the mass protests in the streets of Washington triggered by Americans angry over civil rights issues and the Vietnam War. He strongly suspected that Americans were far less disciplined now than was the generation of Americans that had panicked during the Depression. Would the Americans of this generation, denied the right to purchase fuel for their trucks, tractors and cars, react with riotous

Courtesy Jim McClure

McClure with President Ronald Reagan and Vice President George Bush.

aggression? Might they even revolt against the government if nothing was done to solve their problem?

In McClure's mind the answers were yes and possibly. At the very least he envisioned that there would be a huge clamor for a fair allocation system to be developed by Congress. And he paled at thoughts of what kind of system might emerge from such a legislative frenzy. Would his Idaho farmers and ranchers, would his Idaho timber haulers and loggers, would ordinary Idaho citizens who had to drive forty and fifty miles for their necessities all be treated fairly by such hasty legislation? His conclusion? Doubtful, doubtful, doubtful. And to a question that had to have been is his mind: Would his fellow legislators, even the die-hard conservatives, fight off this legislative steamroller and vote for a free-market solution? Answer in his mind: it was doubtful. And the ultimate question: how would the newly minted, rock-ribbed conservative president react? Would President Reagan go on national television and declare that the government was going to stay out of the whole mess, that Americans must remain patient and let free-market forces get them their gasoline and diesel fuel?. Answer: It is doubtful.

McClure's mind envisioned panic of a high order among the populace. And he envisioned frenzy in a Congress prodded by the sword of a president frightened by mass protests and civil disobedience. And the victims of it all would be his farmers and ranchers, his timber haulers and loggers, and his constituents who by their geographic isolation would be marooned in their desert and mountain homes.

Undoubtedly, in the middle of a sleepless night, or while peering out the window of an airliner going to or from Idaho, or while bottled up in a traffic jam on Constitution Avenue, Senator James A. McClure of Idaho came to the only conclusion possible. He must do what a leader with his responsibility had to do. He could no longer listen to ideologues. He had to forget those purists who had sustained him ideologically during all his years in Congress. Americans in a panic were a menace. Freedom was a spirit that could be trampled in a mob. Conclusion: America must be controlled by the rule of law. And in this case, a law has to be in place and ready should events trigger a major fuel crisis. The president must have legislation that will give the administration authority and guidelines for allocating fuel in such a crisis.

And while coming down on this side of the issue, McClure felt that he could do better by his constituents and the nation by crafting such legislation while the nation was tranquil rather than having to do it with a mob biting at the heels of his colleagues. The need was time for contemplation, time for reflection, time for many parties to be heard, and most of all, time for crafting a bill with the legislative intent clear, unambiguous and not subject to the vagaries of judicial activists. McClure proceeded to engineer such a law through his committee knowing that many of his colleagues in the Steering Committee would be dead set against it. This had to be a disturbing thought for him at the time, but many years later he merely shrugged his shoulders. Said he, "I knew we could get a far better bill out of my committee then, rather than waiting for a crisis. That was my justification. I truly felt that I was doing the best for my constituents. That is all that mattered."[1]

As with his effort to establish a strategic petroleum reserve, and as with his effort to establish a government managed Synfuels Corporation, so the conservative McClure did sponsor, *"A bill to authorize the President to allocate supplies of crude oil and petroleum products during a severe petroleum supply shortage."*[2] He got this bill through the Senate; with like-minded representatives backing it, the bill then passed the House. After conference and mark-up, it passed both houses and was sent to President Reagan who then called Senator McClure and told him that he had to veto it. The government, he said, had no business getting involved in the American economy. Left alone, free market forces would solve the mis-allocations that would initially occur in such an emergency.

One of McClure's aides remembers the Reagan call and, generally, what the senator said in reply: "Well, Mr. President, let us hope that such an emergency does not happen on your watch."[3]

Roughly at the same time Reagan was vetoing McClure's emergency allocation legislation, his administration was quietly initiating steps that would doom McClure's long sought after Synfuels Corporation. So McClure the conservative, but who rightfully should be labeled a "pragmatic" conservative rather than a conservative ideologue, was to suffer two defeats on issues he believed were vital to the nation. And those defeats, in conjunction with the killing of the fast breeder reactor by the previous president, dealt blows to America's energy future that might become perilous. At least that is how McClure still feels about the three issues. As a consolation he can be comforted in knowing that there are now 692 million barrels of oil stored in America's strategic reserve that he was instrumental in creating.

After these defeats, his aides can remember their boss repeating a lament that America was burning up and squandering its most precious resource. "And he wasn't talking about the burning of petroleum resources," said Legislative Aide Tom Hill, "he was talking about time. Time was America's greatest resource back in the '80s, and McClure predicted that one day Americans would look back and wonder why they had squandered the time they had to develop energy independence. I think a lot of us now agree that McClure was probably right. We aren't even close to being energy independent now, and we certainly won't have time on our side if a real emergency hits us."[4]

Roughly when all of the above was happening, a new, bastardized acronym was being coined in the Pacific Northwest to describe another kind of impending, energy-related emergency. Whoops, slang for uh-oh!, evolved out of the acronym for Washington Public Power Supply System, or WPPSS. And WHOOPS was a descriptive acronym because the members of WPPSS, which consisted of municipal power companies, public utility districts and electricity coops, had embarked on a massive electric generation program designed to meet the annual seven percent growth rate that was projected for the region—a program that was, in the early '80s, becoming an uh! oh!, we-made-a-big-mistake-getting-into-this-kind-of-program venture.

Their big mistake was going in debt to finance the building of five new nuclear power plants. By the early '80s it was obvious to the WPPSS board of directors that units four and five, which they were directly financing, were not going to get finished before they ran out of money. The Bonneville Power Administration (BPA), the agency responsible for marketing and transmitting public power in the Northwest—mostly from hydroelectric facilities in the government dams that had been built in the region—was still financing units one, two and three, but their costs were escalating dangerously as they were becoming more and more behind schedule. In short, WPPSS was becoming WHOOPS.

Enter Peter Johnson, a Boise native, Dartmouth ski racer, former CEO of Trus-Joist Corporation, member of the Reagan transition team, and now the new Administrator of BPA. McClure had engineered the appointment of Johnson to that job (despite the pressure from Oregon Senator Mark Hatfield to appoint his own choice) and now Johnson, about three weeks into his new job, came to Washington to confer with McClure. He easily could have asked, with good justification: McClure, what the hell did you get me

Courtesy Peter Johnson

Peter Johnson led the Bonneville Power Administration.

into? But he was too much of a gentleman to do that. Instead, he and two of his aides gave McClure a gloom and doom briefing on what they felt was an impending disaster. Johnson describes what happened next:

> *We were in this small, private room—they called it the Vice President's Room—and I don't now remember how many senators were there, but I do remember Senator Scoop Jackson and the apparent warm relationship McClure had with him. Well, McClure listened to the briefing, grim faced, and when we finished, he turned to Jackson, whom he had just replaced as chairman, and said something to the effect, "Do you have any ideas about this situation?" That was a logical question since Jackson had been chairman when all of this started. Jackson broke into a big smile, looked at McClure and said, "Mr Chairman, this is now your responsibility. You used to throw hand grenades at me, now it is my turn to throw them back to you. It is now your watch and it is your problem." After that, I saw a change in Jim McClure. I saw a maturing right there. Of course, he didn't resolve the problem then because it was almost unsolvable. But he did agree to organize further studies and evaluations. He followed this up with several on-site visits and saw to it that a blue-ribbon panel was appointed to advise us. Really, he threw the whole weight of himself, his office and his intellect, which was considerable, into the challenge we faced.*[5]

Eventually units four and five were abandoned and WHOOPS defaulted on two and one-third billion dollars—the largest municipal bond failure in U.S. history. Shortly thereafter, for lack of debt financing, BPA mothballed units one and three but proceeded to finish Unit two (which was 98 percent completed) using the agency's cash flow. BPA's rates jumped over 100 percent. As prices of electricity went up, consumption went down, and growth projections dropped from seven to one and one-half percent a year. The Northwest Power Planning Council (NPPC) eventually voted to abandon units one and three.

Still a problem remained. Cheap electricity from BPA had, since the late 1930s, been the incentive for the aluminum industry to locate plants in the Northwest. Every major manufacturer of aluminum was located in the region, but all of them were in trouble when BPA had to raise their rates 900 percent. Faced with the possibility of these plants shutting down or moving to countries with cheaper electricity, Peter Johnson trekked to Washington to apprise McClure of the problem. According to Johnson, McClure listened patiently while he explained that there was a very high probability the region would lose half of the aluminum plants. Johnson said:

> *McClure listened and was totally expressionless, and when I finished my speech, he said, matter-of-factly, 'But Peter, that is not why you are there. Your job is to see that these plants don't leave.' Needless to say, I was taken aback, but he had also thrown me a challenge which I accepted at once. 'All right, I said, that is what we will do.' I went back and with my staff we came up with a concept of flexible rate pricing. This resulted in a formula that based the price of electricity on the world price of aluminum; as the price of aluminum rose, we charged more. In public forums throughout the region, we received a lot of input from the companies, utilities and consumers as we developed that plan. We promptly instituted it and enjoyed gratifying results for several years. Unfortunately, due to the world realities of the aluminum market, our success only postponed the closing of the less efficient aluminum plants in the Northwest.*[6]

Energy occupied a lot of McClure's time and attention in the early '80s. But he was also heavily involved in fiscal affairs of the country through his membership on the Joint Economic Committee. Like his conservative brethren, he was especially upset at the high interest rates and high inflation rate at the end of the Carter administration. Interest rates on credit card debt had skyrocketed to over 20 percent, while the inflation rate had gone from 4.9 percent during President Ford's last year to 12.5 percent at the end of Carter's term. McClure and his like-minded colleagues were sure that those high rates were responsible for the economic stagnation in the country, and the lack of growth in jobs. Carter had passed it all off as the result of oil price increases, poor harvests—in other words, bad luck. McClure thought otherwise. He felt that as inflation rose, American workers gradually assumed a greater share of the tax burden. With a disproportionate share of earnings going to the government in taxes, this money was being withheld from the economy, hence the economic stagnation that was upon the land. The way to solve the problem, McClure believed, was to cut taxes and put more money in people's pockets. Instead of going to the government, it would go into the economy, create more jobs and more earnings that eventually would bring more money into the Treasury for reducing the nation's debt.

McClure had an uphill battle selling this concept. Traditional economists made fun of what came to be called "supply-side" economics[i] But McClure was not listening to the traditional economists; he was listening to a UCLA economist named Art Laffer who was saying that traditional economists, when analyzing business cycles, place too much emphasis on the demand side of the equation and too little attention on the supply side. Laffer was saying that tax cuts, making more money available for spending, would stimulate the economy; traditional economists at the same time were preaching to Congress that they should raise taxes to reduce the national debt—that the national debt was the real cause of the economic stagnation in the country. "I just knew Laffer was correct, and so I sponsored a bill that would enact a series of tax cuts."

McClure's bill drew attention, not only from his Senate colleagues, but from some of his fellow conservatives in the House. One of them, a former professional football quarterback for the Buffalo Bills, became enthusiastic about what came to be called the "supply side" method of stimulating the economy and balancing the national debt. This was Representative Jack Kemp, and with his well-known name and celebrity status, McClure quickly agreed that Kemp's co-sponsorship of the bill, with his very recognizable name, would make his legislation more visible.[ii]

McClure's tax cut bill had to go through the Senate Finance Committee, and while it was there, Senator William Roth (R-Delaware) became enthusiastic about it. "That satisfied me," said McClure. "I could see that Bill Roth was going to be a strong advocate and would work the bill in his committee. I felt it was in good hands, so I urged him to take over sponsorship. It was a good move. He got it out of committee to the floor where it passed. Jack Kemp did the same in the House. Reagan signed it and the Kemp-Roth bill became law."[7]

The Kemp-Roth bill has become famous. Although traditional economists are said to have never endorsed supply-side economics, many who write about the '80s and '90s claim that the Reagan tax cuts, known at the time as "Reaganomics," were responsible for the longest period of economic expansion in recent American history. Some even claim that Reagan should be remembered for this legacy just as much as he has been remembered for his role in ending the Cold War.

Why has McClure not been given credit for initiating the supply side movement? McClure staffers, when asked that question, are adamant that their boss has been slighted in this matter. However, they quickly point out that even though their own feelings were hurt over their senator's oblivious position, that McClure had no regrets. Said one, "His ego was not in his job, and it never was. He could have cared less. He was genuinely pleased that Bill Roth got the credit."[8]

The people who could bring the most veracity to the claim that McClure had no ego to go with his job was the press that covered him. Said McClure:

> *Because of my position as chairman of the Conference, I usually had a meeting with the president at the White House every week.*

> *The press knew this and before I could even get to the press pool, Evans and Novak would come up and ask what went on with the president. I would say, 'I will tell you what I said to the president if you are interested, but I will not tell you what the president said.' I just wouldn't do it. I know a lot of others would; they would line up to meet the press and regale them with what they said and what Reagan said. That made great publicity at home and made them look bigger in the eyes of their constituents. But I never did it. Ever. Yes, I would always go before the press pool after these meetings, and I would gladly tell them what I said to the president. I'm sure they didn't like that, but they had to accept it.*[9]

McClure was challenged after making that statement. "That was easy for you to do—you didn't need that kind of publicity at home. But, a lot of those other senators did. They literally had to run for their political lives during each election. You did not. You carried all forty-four counties in your last election. There wasn't an opponent in the state who could even come close to beating you. Isn't that at least a part of the reason why you so cavalierly stiff-armed the press?"

After some hesitation, he replied, "Maybe that might have been part of it." Then he added, "I was lucky to have been serving Idaho people. I might not have lasted in some of the other states."[10]

Whether McClure could have been elected or remained elected in other states is a good question for a late night discussion with his friends. But, for this work we must avoid speculation and remain with McClure's history as it played out. And in that sequence he had to face another election campaign in 1984, one that he said "concerned" him, but one that he also admitted did not cause him great worry.

It is now time to meet his new opponent: Pete Busch.

Chapter 28 notes

i. Vice-President George H.W. Bush called it "voodoo" economics.

ii. McClure, after a recent trip to Washington D.C., said that he ran into Jack Kemp who chided him a bit for doing that. "That bill should have been the McClure-Kemp bill," Kemp said.

Chapter 29

WIN ONE, LOSE ONE

Pete Busch retired from the U.S. Marine Corps in 1976 as a lieutenant colonel. He had been a fighter pilot and had flown hundreds of missions in Vietnam during two tours of duty there, volunteering for his second tour after he had been shot down and rescued in North Vietnam. After release from active duty he came back to Lewiston, Idaho, where he had grown up. During those young years he became an Eagle Scout, and in his senior year of high school, was elected student body president.

Back in Lewiston he floundered while trying to adjust to civilian life. He first tried his hand at running a night club, but it failed financially. Next, he tried selling cars for a local Ford dealer, but that did not work out. Then he tried life insurance with the same result. Finally, he got a real estate license and was selling real estate in 1983 when he decided it was time to get into the public arena. In December of 1983 he announced that he was going to run against Jim McClure, and in an interview that accompanied his announcement he said:

> [I am running because] *I felt it was a shame that we, the people of Idaho, allow our senator to be influenced by special interest groups out of state. . .This is where the majority of Senator McClure's funds come from. We allow these special groups...to determine who will represent us in Washington D.C. . . .*

He also said in a press release that Democratic State Chairman, Mel Morgan, urged him to run against McClure, but in a recent interview, Morgan refutes that. Said Morgan, "Pete Busch was a really nice guy and I wished him well, but I can't remember ever urging him to run or even talking with him about it. I think he made up his mind to do that himself. I'll have to give him credit, he tried. I think he campaigned as hard as he knew how. But, he was a strict amateur. He wasn't able to attract many funds and, in my opinion, he was way out of his league trying to compete against Jim McClure. I think he would have done better two years later against Larry Craig."[1]

The McClure team campaigned as hard as ever even though polls showed that Busch had no chance of winning. The McClure bus made the rounds of the state, stopping at every town and city, and the candidate, as before, was the first one off the bus and the last one on. H. D. Palmer, who was McClure's press secretary at the time, remembers that the candidates had one debate, but it must have been a non-event because neither Palmer nor the candidate can remember anything about it. In sum, the 1984 campaign turned out not to be a race, but a runaway. McClure won 293,193 votes to his opponents 105,591. And, as in his 1978 election, he carried all forty-four of Idaho's counties. On November 7, 1984, Jim McClure knew he was going back to Washington, D.C. for another six-year term.

And what was going on in the new, third-term senator's mind? Many things, of course, but there was one issue that was dominant, and it was an issue that had been in his mind for the past year.

In the fall of 1983, Senate Majority Leader Howard Baker (R-Tennessee) announced that he would not be seeking re-election in 1984. This triggered a flurry of articles in the press, each author speculating on who might be running to replace Baker and the impact of various candidacies upon possible new heads of various Senate committees. One of the first of these articles was inspired by Dick Thompson, now staff director of the Republican Policy Committee, but formerly McClure's administrative assistant. Thompson said:

> *McClure doesn't know this to this day and he will probably be appalled by what I am about to say. But, just after Baker made his announcement, I went to Margo (Carlisle) and said, "You need to do something. You need to go to the steering committee and take a poll of who would support Jim McClure if he should decide to run for majority leader." She did that and there were several—I don't remember how many—who said they wanted Jim to run. I then called a reporter at the* Washington Times, *and without giving my name, told him about this poll of a "group of Republican senators." Of course, the results were skewed—the steering committee was made up of conservative senators who thought like McClure but I didn't tell the reporter that. Sure enough, two days later there was this big story about McClure being a possible candidate and already having lots of support.*[2]

About this same time a small group of McClure supporters showed up at his home in Arlington one evening. They included Thompson, Paul Weyrich, Tod Neuenschwander Margo Carlisle, Frank Cushing and Jim Goller. They came armed with three persuasive arguments: (1) We have a conservative Republican president and he is not getting the support he needs from the Senate. If you can get elected as majority leader, you know enough about the Senate workings to move his agenda in the 99th Congress; (2) Those senators elected in 1980 brought a Republican majority to the Senate. How they fare in the 1986 elections is critical and we are worried. The new majority leader

Courtesy Jim McClure

McClure discusses proposed legislation with Senate collegue Howard Baker, (R-Tennessee), right.

has to exert special effort to insure that every time a bill comes before the Senate that has re-election implications for one of them, that senator must manage the bill on the floor, must meet the press in the well each day the bill is before us, and when there are White House leadership meetings on the bill, that senator must go along and meet with the White House press corps afterwards; and (3) Through your leadership with the steering committee and conference you have already demonstrated to your colleagues that you have a strategic mind and know how to get things done.

Sometime during the arm-twisting presentations McClure was getting from his supporters, his wife, Louise, remembers interjecting some of her own comments. "First, I said to them, 'You know, I've never heard Jim say that he wanted this.' They became quiet, then I looked at Jim and said, 'Jim, do you want this? Or are you being pushed into this so others can bask in your glory?' Actually, I'm sure I wasn't quite that blunt about it, but that is the gist of what I said. Then I turned to them and said something to the effect, 'I'm not sure in my own mind that Jim wants this so I'll ask him right here. Jim, do you really want to run for majority leader?' Jim hesitated and then finally said, 'Well, I guess so.' It wasn't a real positive statement. It wasn't like he had a burning desire to do it."[3]

That evening McClure committed to a first step in running. He told the small group that he would immediately write to his colleagues seeking their advice on whether he should or should not run. "I can always back out if they don't support me," he said to them.[4]

Within days of that meeting the letters were ready. Following is the one that went to most of the senators:

December 8, 1983

Honorable Paula Hawkins
United States Senator
Washington, D. C. 20510

Dear Paula:

During the adjournment period, I intend to make the final decision as to whether or not I will be a candidate for the position of Majority Leader. Your advice in this regard is very important to me.

I am willing to serve. I am willing to make the leadership a shared responsibility with all Republican senators. But most of all, I want the leadership to reflect the views of the millions of Americans who affiliate with our Party. To a great extent, the actions of the Republican leadership in the Senate in the next two years will determine whether or not we maintain control after the crucial mid-term elections in 1986.

I am realistic enough to know that if I can't count on the support of my colleagues, there is no point in my running at all. No one should run just because they want the job. Therefore, I not only seek your advice, but I would also very much like your commitment to my candidacy should I make the decision to run. I will carefully weigh the advice that you and the others send me. If enough of you give me the green light, I will announce immediately upon our return to Washington in January. So, I need your response as soon as possible. Your letter will, of course, be held in complete confidence and your advice, positive or negative, greatly appreciated

Sincerely yours,

James A. McClure

There are a few replies to McClure's letter in the archives, none with firm pledges of support; however, he remembers getting enough positive verbal replies that he decided to run, if, of course, he won re-election the coming fall. Said McClure, "I announced early because I wanted to get some commitments before some others might decide to run. Also, I was hoping that my announcement might discourage some from jumping into the race.

Throughout the year, other senators entered the race. Robert Dole (R-Kansas) was one of the first. McClure: *As soon as he moved from the House to the Senate and started a campaign to defend Nixon, we knew that he was really running for the presidency.*[5] Then Ted Stevens (R-Alaska), the Assistant Majority Leader (Whip) announced. Thompson: *McClure was the only person I ever heard who said he liked him. Goldwater backed him saying, "He's the meanest man in the Senate and I want the toughest man in the Senate leading my party. You've got Robert Byrd on the other side and I want somebody who can handle him"—that was the gist.* Then Richard Lugar (R-Indiana) announced. Thompson: *I'm from Indiana and I happen to know that Dan Quayle* [Lugar's junior colleague] *wanted to support McClure but could not after Lugar announced. That cost us a vote.*

TOD NEUENSCHWANDER COMMENTS

I was his administrative assistant at the time and I distinctly remember that Jim McClure paid a personal visit to every Republican senator in their respective offices prior to the vote. He did seek their advice, he did ask for their support (at least that's what he told us) but he didn't buttonhole them and ask for a pledge. That's not Jim McClure. And I don't believe he did any horse trading. But I distinctly remember getting each of those meetings scheduled, and I know that every time he returned from one of the meetings, we would get his reaction. We kept a running vote tally leading up to the election, based mostly on Jim's one-one-one meetings.

My impression, beginning from that first meeting at the McClure's home, was that there was too much talk about what philosophical changes might be made if McClure won, and not enough time spent on nuts and bolts of campaigning for the job, vote counting, and getting him elected. But most of us, probably all of us gathered that evening, had never waged a "campaign" for Majority Leader, and we really didn't know how to proceed. And throughout, Jim insisted that it was a very personal decision by each senator, not a job one could campaign for. Apparently Bob Dole disagreed with that assessment.

At the last minute another senator announced and that was a blow to McClure. Said he, "I don't have any evidence, but I just know that Bob Dole talked Pete Domenici [R-New Mexico] into running, knowing that this would hurt my chances.[6]" Several senators, including McClure's friend Paul Laxalt from Nevada, had pledged support for McClure unless Domenici ran—saying to McClure that as chairman of the budget committee, Domenici had dispensed favors that needed to be repaid. "I'll definitely support you on the second ballot," McClure was told, "after I pay my debt to Pete."[7] Chick Hecht, the meek and mild junior senator from Nevada always did what Laxalt did. Consequently, Laxalt's defection meant the loss of two votes for McClure. Jeremiah Denton (R-Alabama), a strong McClure supporter, was also talked into supporting Domenici on the first round. The trouble with the Denton vote was that he made the decision just minutes before the election.

Courtesy John Rosholt.

Jim Goller, left, fires up the McClure team after the 1984 election. From right, Secretary of Energy Don Hodel, Jim and Louise McClure, Fran and Senator Steve Symms.

There was another factor that hurt McClure. Throughout the year articles in *The Washington Post* (May 29, 1984, the *Wall Street Journal* (June 3, 1984), the fall *Congressional Quarterly, The New York Times* (October 15, 1984), and *The Oil Daily* (October 22, 1984) did stories on the majority leader contest and how subtle political factors were going to influence the voting of the senators. The big factor affecting McClure, said the writers, was the problem of his replacement on the Senate Energy Committee if he became majority leader. The second ranking Republican was Lowell Weicher from Connecticut who had the dual onus of being hostile to most projects Western senators coveted and being an outspoken proponent of much social legislation that conservatives despised. There were many senators who did not want Weicher to succeed to that chair and some, like Don Nickels (D-Oklahoma) flatly told McClure, "There is no way I am going to vote for you because I can't stand the thought of Lowell Weicher heading the Energy Committee."[8] Nickles ended up voting for Lugar.

Another factor was a group of liberal to moderate senators who called themselves "The Gang of Six." They wanted to maximize their influence and their impact upon the election, but they couldn't make up their minds which man to support. Philosophically, they were closest to the one they liked the least, Ted Stevens. So, they invited each candidate to meet with them privately. One of the group, Senator Mark Hatfield (R-Oregon), told McClure, "I will be your advocate, but if the group decides to support someone else, I will support that man as well."[9] McClure felt his interview went extremely well and thought he had a chance to get their votes. Bob Dole, however, cleverly promised the Gang something tangible. As senate leader, he would get to name the chairman of the Senate Select Committee on Intelligence, and Dole promised to select a moderate. (He delivered on that promise, giving the nod to Minnesota's David Durenberger.) Until the Gang of Six endorsed Dole, the Kansas senator was not considered a factor in the majority leader's race.

After the general election in November, the Republican senators gathered in the Old Senate Chamber, McClure presiding as chairman of the conference. Dick Thompson was present (as was Margo Carlisle, conference staff director) taking notes. Here are some of his direct impressions:

> *At the beginning of the meeting I was bothered. Here they were, about to make one of the most important decisions of their whole career, and they came in laughing and kidding—nobody seemed to be serious. I was sitting next to Dan Quayle and he and Weicker were laughing, as were Al Simpson* [R-Wyoming] *and John Heinz* [R-Pennsylvania]. *They acted like this was some joke and I had the impression they weren't taking this as seriously as they should. It really irritated me because I was taking it seriously and others weren't. Then, just as the meeting started, the smoke alarm went off, and after that interruption, McClure, presiding, called for the nominations. Goldwater nominated Ted Stevens and I remember Weicker sitting near me was really irritated by Goldwater, saying, "That guy embarrasses me." Steve Symms then nominated McClure with a good speech. After that Quayle nominated his colleague, Lugar, then Jack Danforth* [R-Missouri] *nominated Dole, and* [Dan] *Evans* [R-Washington] *nominated Domenici. Of all the speeches given, Danforth's was the best, and in my notes I wrote "Good speech, too bad." After the nominating speeches, they voted by secret ballot. The ballots were handed to Bill Hildebrand, secretary of the Senate, and he gave them to Howard Greene, Secretary to the Republicans, who counted the votes. The results were then handed to Howard Baker and John Tower* [R-Texas] *who were the tellers. They looked them over, okayed them, then gave them to McClure who would announce the votes. He looked at them, not betraying any emotion, then announced the results: Dole 14, Stevens 12, Lugar 10, Domenici 9, and McClure 8. McClure had to announce that he, himself, was eliminated. It was the bravest performance I ever saw anyone give. He was magnificent. It was the shining moment of his whole career. I was so proud of*

him I had tears in my eyes. The senators were stunned. The frivolity ceased. Almost everyone had thought McClure would be the eventual winner, or that at least the final choice would be between Stevens and him. One McClure supporter, Gordon Humphrey [R-New Hampshire] *suggested that further votes be put off to another day, saying, "I wasn't prepared for this." But, with the media panting outside the door, that wasn't possible.*

After that, he continued to preside during the rest of the voting. The second round, the vote was Dole 17, Stevens 14, Lugar 12, Domenici 10. Domenici was out. Third round: Dole 20, Stevens 20, Lugar 13 and Lugar was out. Final round: Dole 28 and Stevens 25.

After the vote, I did an analysis for McClure that showed how the vote could have been different. I showed him that three of the first round votes that went to Domenici—Laxalt, Hecht, and Denton—should have gone to him, but all three had told McClure, "You're going to win anyhow, so after we give our payback votes to Pete, we'll go to you on the second ballot." Dole was cunning. He got Domenici into the race just for this purpose. However, if McClure had really buttonholed those three and told them he had to have their votes on the first round, Domenici would have been eliminated, which, by my count, would have jumped McClure up to 16 on the second ballot. Domenici had pledged his vote to McClure if he got eliminated, and McClure would have gotten most of his supporters. After the vote was over and we were walking out, Pete Domenici ran over while I was talking to McClure. He grabbed Jim's arm and said, "If I'd known this would be the outcome, I never would have run."

By my analysis, and it gets too complicated to put in a book, the final ballot could easily have been between Ted Stevens and McClure. What is amusing is that Ted Stevens called McClure after the meeting and said the same thing: "This race should have been between you and me; I represent the best of the moderate side of the party and you represent the best of the conservative wing. Since we both lost, let's take our wives out for dinner tonight." Ted picked them up and they had a great time and a great evening.[10] [ii]

Steve Symms now says that he had some doubts about McClure running and went to the point of suggesting, before the election, that McClure should run for the whip's position. According to Symms, McClure replied, "Steve, there is nothing wrong with reaching for the brass ring. Yes, I know it is going to be a stretch to get the job, but why not try? It won't hurt me to lose. I'll still have my chairmanship of the Energy Committee, and I'll still have my subcommittees on Appropriations where I can do Idaho some good."[11]

Looking back, McClure said:

I don't regret having done it, and I don't feel offended that I lost. Bob Dole did something right smart. He got Domenici to run because he knew that would split the votes into smaller pieces and take away some of my support, and it worked. However, I didn't campaign for the job as I should have. I could not bring myself to do the thing that I probably should have done. I didn't go to people personally and buttonhole them. I don't believe in doing that. It would have been embarrassing to them and it would have been embarrassing to me. I didn't want to put people on the spot. I didn't do it and I wouldn't do it. For me, it's the golden rule. I wouldn't have wanted to be buttonholed and so I would not do that to anyone else. Besides, my shoulders aren't built right. I would break my arm if I tried to pat myself on the back. I've always felt it is good to believe in yourself, but you don't have to brag about it.[12]

The above is from an interview with both Jim and Louise McClure. During that interview, Louise admitted that she had a gut feeling her husband was going to lose, and she also confessed that she had said that to Eb Gaines, one of their friends. Then Jim said that he had a confession to make:

I'm not sure if this is correct, but I think I had a feeling at that time that I wanted to begin leading a more normal life, one where I could spend more time with Louise. I knew the majority leader's job would have been all-consuming and I was prepared to make that adjustment. Perhaps I was also thinking that I should be less driven rather than more driven, and perhaps I had started thinking that I should retire at the end of that third term. I'm not at all sure that was true, but if it was, that would have made it easier for me to accept that defeat.

Some wise man once said that defeat isn't bitter if you don't swallow it. That is probably true and, in the case of Idaho's senior senator, it is doubtful if the glass of defeat ever got near his lips. Too much was at stake, particularly in his home state, and there was much work to do.

Chapter 29 notes

i. After announcing that he was going to run against Larry Craig in 1986, Pete Busch was killed while flying his airplane from north Idaho to Idaho Falls for a Truman Day dinner. Also killed in the crash was State Senator Terry Reilly from Canyon County who had announced for Lieutenant Governor.

ii. In his analysis Thompson also pointed out that the race had implications that went far beyond who would lead the Senate in the coming years. Without the forum afforded the Majority Leader, Bob Dole was unlikely to have been the Republican presidential nominee in 1996.

Chapter 30

Wilderness Struggles

. . .no good can ever result from any attempt to set one of these fiery zealots to rights, either in fact or principle. They are determined as to the facts they will believe, and the opinions on which they act. Get by them, therefore, as you would by an angry bull; it is not for a man of sense to dispute the road with such an animal.

Thomas Jefferson

We had a presumption that McClure knew his own sympathies were with the outdoors and Wilderness, but who was extremely shrewd in understanding that his base of constituents were way right of that. He had sympathies that, if uncontrolled, would not be politically astute. Therefore, we suspected that he consciously hired ideological staff people to insure that he didn't let his sympathies carry him too far.

Doug Scott
Northwest Representative
Sierra Club

By the late 70's Wilderness was really getting controversial in Idaho. For sure you didn't dare drop into a cowboy bar in Riggins or Salmon and say you were with the Sierra Club.

Doug Scott
Northwest Representative
Sierra Club

Idaho has never had many of the problems that have plagued other states. There was no looting or burning after Martin Luther King's assassination; there have been no tornadoes, hurricanes or major earthquakes to kill hundreds and decimate property; traffic jams that create parking lots out of freeways have been infrequent; forced school busing has never been an issue. But as Doug Scott suggests in one of the quotes above, it would not be wise to walk into a logger or cowboy bar and announce that you are a tree-hugger or a wolf advocate or that you are especially fond of spotted owls.

Nor would one want a bumper sticker on a car with such slogans as BAN SNOWMOBILES or ATV'S ARE A MENACE.

The majority of Idaho people have a genuine affection for the unique geography of their state. And many express that affection by their active involvement with the outdoors. In their spare time the active ones hike, fish, backpack, hunt, ski, 4-wheel, snowmobile, shoot, kayak, raft, ATV, mountain bike, horseback ride, and paraglide. Many others, particularly those who work outdoors every day, enjoy more passive communion with the outdoors, relaxing in a multitude of camps and campers, but almost always in one of the thousands of scenic byways the state affords.

Idahoans are also economically bonded, directly or indirectly, to their unique geography. They raise cattle and sheep, often using grazing allotments on the public lands. They log and produce lumber from the millions of acres of forest lands. They mine lead, zinc, silver and gold, and the Idaho phosphate deposits contribute in a major way to keeping America's farmlands ever-fertile for the production of food and fiber.

And Idahoans are passionate about their outdoor environment. They want it protected. They want its scenic values preserved. Most of all they want the freedom to carry on their activities on the public lands of Idaho, the lands managed by the Forest Service and the Bureau of Land Management, the land that comprises about two-thirds of the whole state. Yes, intellectually, they realize that these are public lands, theoretically owned by all the people in the United States. But there is also an unwritten territorial imperative in their souls that says, *Damnit, these lands are our lands; they are in Idaho and we should have some say in controlling them.* And therein lies a perpetual conflict. Idaho people do not have any direct control over two-thirds of their state. Their control is only indirect, through their four congressional delegates: two out of 435 representatives, and two out of 100 senators.

And Idahoans bombard their congressional delegates with their problems, their perceived solutions to problems, and their aspirations for the lands they know is not theirs. As these congressional delegates move around the state listening to their constituents, either in town meetings (where their attention may be half-hearted), or while campaigning (where they are listening more intently), or in formal hearings where the speaking and listening is ritualized, they are forever reminded that theirs is a spear-carrying job. They are the lancers who must mount their best steeds and wade into the bureaucracy of the patrons of the Idaho lands. They must fight for one man's grazing allotment. They must fight for a community of hunters that is trying to reverse the closure of a logging road they have used for decades. And they must try to untie the bureaucratic knots tying up a timber sale upon which the survival of an Idaho town depends.

All the while these spear carriers must charge through those who cheer and jeer. To those who cheer, the spear carrier is trying to save some poor rancher from ruin by Bureau of Land Management bureaucrats. To those who jeer, this fat-cat rancher, who has given the politician a big campaign contribution, is trying to get wealthy by ravaging federal lands while paying a fraction of the value of his grazing allotments. To the spear carrier trying to keep a logging road open, the cheering hunters want to name the road for him. Those who jeer want him to forever have the name of a salmon killer because the silt from the road is fouling the poor animals' conjugal grounds. Cheers for the town saver have to be very loud to drown out the jeers from those who yell that the spear carrier, because of alleged hidden campaign contributions, is only trying to save the predatory mill operator or the greedy lumber baron or the monopolistic, mega national pulp, paper and wood products corporation.

In the 1970s, when the cheers and jeers were growing ever-increasingly louder, Senator Jim McClure was becoming a veteran spear carrier. Laying his private sympathies aside (there may have been a grain of truth in Doug Scott's perception of McClure's sympathies—see opening quote), McClure generally responded to environmental problems, initially at least, on the side of the Idahoans who considered themselves threatened by the bureaucracies. He had staff members whose full time responsibilities were to investigate and resolve those conflicts. And when they needed the clout of his personal spear, he was always ready, even eager, to engage the leaders of the bureaucracies directly.

And what about those who said that his actions were a sham, that his real motive was to protect the fat cat or the big corporation because he was, as a recipient of their campaign contributions, beholden to them? His answer was always the same. The dialogue would go something like this:

> Critic: *You Republicans are all alike. What you are really doing is looking out for the big guy.*
>
> McClure: *You're right. I plead guilty.*
>
> Critic: *You could care less about the little guy.*
>
> McClure: *You're wrong. I plead not guilty.*
>
> Critic: *You can't be for both.*
>
> McClure: *I have to be.*
>
> Critic: *That's typical politician double talk.*
>
> McClure: *May I ask you a question*?
>
> Critic: *Yeah, I guess.*
>
> McClure: *Do you want to keep your job?*

Critic: *What's that got to do with it?*

McClure: *Everything. Do you want to get laid off and have to move someplace else to get another job?*

Critic: *That's a dumb question; who wants to get laid off; I've got a wife and two little kids to support.*

McClure: *So what is going to happen if the timber sale is delayed and the company you are working for has no logs?*

Critic: *We'll probably get laid off.*

McClure: *So who am I looking out for if I fight the Forest Service?*

Critic: (a shrug)

McClure: *I'm looking out for the big guy and the little guy, the owner and the worker.*

Critic: (another shrug)

McClure: (With a smile, teasing) *And the big guy contributed to my campaign.*

Critic: (shrugs again and walks away)

Dialogues like the preceding probably occurred hundreds of times throughout McClure's years of interacting with his constituents. And they did not vary between workers in mines, mills or industrial plants. "You bet I'm getting support from the corporations. If that money helps keep me in office, I can continue fighting for **your** jobs."

Over and over again McClure's opponents tried to brand him as a tool of the wealthy, and they used his campaign contributions in their rhetoric to discredit him. McClure probably never achieved the understanding for which he hoped—diehard Democrats had been believing in financial conspiracy since the days of William Jennings Bryan. But, of course, enough supporters saw through the rhetoric to give him his last two landslide victories; however, when he went back to Washington, he was constantly aware that he was just one of 100 and that the constituents of many other senators cared nothing for how the people of Idaho felt.

This was particularly true of wilderness issues. During the 1970s as the environmental forces grew, those hungry for more wilderness designations began focusing in on Idaho. During one particular crusade to turn the Gospel Hump region southeast of Grangeville into a wilderness, a move that would cost hundreds of jobs in Idaho County, compromise was finally reached thanks to Frank Church. According to Doug Scott, who worked that issue as the Northwest representative of the Sierra Club, Church called some other wilderness advocates and him into a Lewiston motel room and, while "polluting the room with a big, fat cigar that his wife, Bethine, kept telling him to put out,"[1] explained that the Gospel Hump issue was causing him a lot of trouble in the region, trouble that Scott interpreted as meaning, *Hey, I've got an election coming up in 1980 and this issue could be dangerous for me.* Scott eventually went into a series of closed sessions with Fred Hutchinson from Church's staff mediating between all sides of the controversy.[i] "We got out the maps, drew lines, and cut a deal," said Scott. "Those areas not designated as wilderness would be available for multiple use, including logging. It took awhile, with hearings in Idaho and lots of work in Washington, but eventually it was signed into law in February, 1978, with both Church and McClure supporting it. I learned a helluva lot working with those Grangeville people. I learned what it is like in those kinds of places. I now understand why small town rural West folks feel alienated from people like me."[2] [ii]

In the late 1970s the environmentalists were on a roll. Authors like Paul Ehrlich [iii] were projecting doomsday scenarios—*a billion or more people could die from starvation by the mid-80s*—thus energizing them and causing hordes of new believers to seek membership in the environmental organizations. All of that, combined with a sympathetic president in the White House and Democrats in control of the congress, meant that the golden moment had arrived when the environmental organizations' own spear carriers had to strike. And when they did, their lances were driven right into the heart of Idaho.

There was already a wilderness there, or almost a wilderness. Since the 1930s the Forest Service had administered the central part of Idaho which included much of the Salmon River and its Middle Fork tributary, as a "Primitive Area." Guides and outfitters, marketing their treks on that river by the more mysterious and romantic name, River of No Return, were well established with power boats and river camps by the '70s. Also, an enthusiastic Idaho state director of aeronautics had led the effort to establish and upgrade a series of aircraft landing fields in the Primitive Area—fields called "back country airstrips."

Enter Frank Church. By all accounts he had a deep love for the Primitive Area and, thus, was the one senator whom the Sierra Club and Wilderness Society believed could best get action on a new wilderness. It proved to be good synergism. Fred Hutchinson, a Church staffer (from Mud Lake, Idaho) working with leaders in the two organizations, coordinated the drafting of the Central Idaho Wilderness Act that Church introduced in the Energy and Natural Resources Committee.

Enter now Jim McClure who at the time was the second-ranking minority member on that committee. He immediately saw the complexities in the act, and, through his own comments and through witnesses he brought to the committee, he was able to delineate a series of issues he felt should be resolved through specific wording in the legislation. One issue loomed large: the back country airstrips. The environmental activists were adamantly opposed to them: *How the hell can you have a wilderness if you have airplanes landing and taking off?* Perhaps it is more correct to say they were livid, for it had already been established that motorized machines of any form—even chain saws—were *verboten* in wilderness areas. But, getting into the "back country" by airplane was not only essential for Idaho's booming tourist industry, it was one of those rights considered inalienable by Western private pilots, especially those in Idaho who had the highest per-capita ownership of general aviation airplanes outside of Alaska. In addition, Idaho activists were split on this issue. According to McClure the two key Idaho leaders, Ted Trueblood and Ernie Day, were not opposed to the back country airstrips. With Frank Church's support, McClure prevailed with language that allowed them to remain.

The second major issue was upstream water. The environmentalists insisted that, in order to maintain the pristine water in the wilderness, upstream water (water before it flowed into the wilderness) should be controlled by the federal government. McClure felt such a mandate would end up limiting downstream irrigation and development. But, more importantly, he believed—vehemently would not be too strong an adverb—that Idaho had sovereign rights over its own water and that the federal government had no right to be involved in any decisions as to its use. Church, undoubtedly realizing that water is the "third rail" in Idaho politics, agreed to support McClure on that issue and Idaho retained control of the upstream water.

A third issue was the hunting camps and power boats on the Salmon. The environmentalists wanted them all eliminated. The outfitters and guides, deeply concerned for their livelihood, argued for their retention. Again, Church went along with McClure in retaining them.

There were some other, smaller issues that McClure was able to resolve in his favor, but two major issues were still left—issues he opposed and Church supported.

One related to a cobalt deposit in the West Panther Creek drainage on the south side of the proposed wilderness. At the time this was the only large deposit of cobalt in the nation, and current supplies were mostly coming from Zambia and Zaire, two highly unstable African nations. After a fight, McClure was able to get language into the bill allowing cobalt mining in that area if the resource grew scarce and the nation needed it. However, the environmentalists got Church to also put language in that permitted mining only if it was conducted underground. This bothered McClure. He knew that such language effectively precluded any kind of mining.

The other issue was even more important to him. It was a favorite tactic of the environmentalists to lock up roadless areas into wilderness by legislation; then when logging companies bid on sales outside the boundaries, they would go to court with suits to stop, or at least, delay the harvesting of the timber. What McClure wanted written in this legislation had a generic term at the time; it was called "release language." Release language was wording actually in the bill that declared lands outside the boundaries of a Wilderness to be "multiple use" lands—lands that could be grazed, logged or mined. Also, the wording in the release language specifically made such lands immune to lawsuits of the type the environmentalists had been using. There was a battle over those two issues in the committee. McClure completely lost the first battle. The language relating to the cobalt deposits remained. As for the second battle, Church supporters "compromised"—their term—by putting release language in the committee report, but not in the legislation itself. McClure, calling that a sham, declared in a news release that he could not support a Wilderness bill that did not have release language in the legislation itself.

> KIT CAPLES KIMBALL ON THE BACK COUNTRY AIRSTRIPS
>
> *McClure convinced Frank Church and others to leave some of the airstrips in place in the new wilderness bill by doing his homework thoroughly, as was his style. He hired a pilot and the Senator and I took several days to fly into the primitive area and land on every back country airstrip. He assessed the need for the strip, what it allowed access to and took into account the environmental consequences of leaving it open. Armed with this information, he was able to make convincing arguments on why a majority of the landing strips should remain open. Needless to say, it was an awesome several days of work even though it was a bit scary at times.*

"Then we held hearings in Idaho," said McClure, "and these were made contentious by the numbers the environmental leaders urged to attend. I clearly remember the Boise hearing. I remember that Frank Church, while attending a Boise Chamber breakfast wore a suit and tie, but then, for the hearing, changed into Levis. We kidded about that. Also, because of the huge numbers wanting to testify, we had to cut the time down to just a few minutes for each person. But that didn't deter Carole King, the singer. She felt she was above all that. Church was gone—he only stayed a few minutes and left—so I was in charge, and when she went overtime, I gaveled her down. But she ignored me. I gaveled again and she ignored me. Finally I had to call for security to take her out. I remember her boyfriend at the time. He had long hair, was dressed in fringed buckskins, and had a knife in his belt. He just glared at me. I glared back, amused."

Back in the Senate, and after some of the language in the bill was fine tuned after the hearings, Church and McClure went at each other on the floor of the Senate. On November 20, 1979, McClure presented an amendment that would permit mining of cobalt in the West Panther Creek drainage, but with specific language requiring all necessary precautions to prevent adverse effect upon a herd of big horn sheep that lived in that habitat. Church argued against the amendment, saying that mining could be allowed but only as an underground operation. The semantics are confusing here (as they probably were to the senators), but, according to McClure, such a prohibition on mining method was enough to prevent cobalt mining from ever occurring in the drainage. McClure spoke eloquently, describing how 97 percent of cobalt was imported, but from unstable countries, and how huge amounts of cobalt were necessary for the production of jet engines and for the magnets in electric motors. But, it was time wasted. On mostly a party line vote, his amendment was defeated.

> JEFF CILEK ON JIM McCLURE
>
> I was the staffer who worked with McClure on the Appropriations Subcommittee on the Interior. One day we were in a meeting with Senator Robert Byrd and his staffer, and Byrd was being his obnoxious self, belittling McClure's argument that release language should be a part of any new wilderness bill. Finally, McClure looked at Byrd and said, "Bob, we don't want the West to be turned into another Appalachia." Byrd, who was extremely sensitive about the plight of his people in West Virginia's Appalachia, noticeably stiffened—I mean you could see the physical effect of McClure's remark. After that, Byrd was a changed person. His antagonism diminished, and he was more cooperative. I cite this as an example of the gift McClure had in coming up with just the right statements to get his point across to his opponents.

He then tried again with another amendment—one to put release language in the bill. Said McClure on the Senate floor:

> *. . .my Idaho colleague argued that release language on these areas would be sufficient if included in the report. I feel strongly that to provide for a truly meaningful release of areas no longer to be considered for wilderness, it is necessary to accomplish this by statute. . .*[3]

McClure failed again, and when the vote was taken on the Senate floor for the Central Idaho Wilderness Act (which included the River of No Return Wilderness), only McClure's conservative colleagues voted with him against it. Later a similar version passed the House, and after a conference and markup, at which McClure had no further luck in advancing his two key issues, the bill was sent to President Carter who signed it in July, 1980. Political observers later speculated that the fallout from Church's role was a factor that helped Steve Symms defeat him the following November. It is less speculative to observe that the Democratic Party lost a lot of their

Courtesy Jim McClure

McClure shares a humorous moment with President Ronald Reagan.

stalwarts in Idaho's First District because of the adverse effect of more restrictive logging in the areas *outside* the boundaries of the wilderness.

Years later those who detested McClure's politics took delight in emphasizing that he "opposed creating" the River of No Return Wilderness. The fine points of his opposition are left to moulder in the aftermath; he committed a sin and that is how it will always be. If that bothered McClure, he has let nobody know of it. Four years after his vote was cast, when Frank Church lay dying of cancer, McClure went to the floor of the Senate and introduced S.2354, A BILL To rename the "River of No Return Wilderness" in the State of Idaho as the "Frank Church—River of No Return Wilderness." While introducing the legislation, McClure said:

> *. . .I recognize that Frank Church performed with sincerity and skill the very difficult task of getting the River of No Return Wilderness, as well as other wilderness legislation passed through Congress. . .*[4]

McClure's bill was signed by President Reagan on March 1, 1984. Church died five weeks later.

Meanwhile, lumber mills from the Canadian border southward were being strangled. Largely, this was the result of restricted timber sales, but Canadian exports of lumber were also hurting the industry. The letters from distressed Idahoans—those who had lost their jobs and those who were about to—were poignant and plentiful. And the entire Idaho delegation was receiving them: Larry Craig in the First District, George Hansen in the Second District, and Idaho's junior Senator, Steve Symms. The angst of so many Idahoans was powerful motivation, and the four, led by McClure, decided to take on the challenge of solving the problem. Said McClure:

> *In the roadless areas outside the wilderness, there was so much uncertainty it was about to paralyze the logging industry. It was a big issue that was unresolved and we decided to take it upon ourselves to try and resolve it.*[5]

To start the resolution process, McClure issued a press release on March 16, 1983, that said:

> *. . .in a letter to Pat Ford, executive director of the Idaho Conservation League,* [he] *called on Idaho conservation groups to submit proposals for drafting an Idaho wilderness bill. . ."Other special interest groups have indicated that they are developing and will be sending me their recommendations for a statewide bill," McClure said in the letter. "I urge you to do the same."*
>
> *Challenging suggestions that an unannounced deadline exists for introducing wilderness legislation, McClure said, "I am not locked into any timetable. In fact, I have not yet made the final commitment to introduce such a bill."*
>
> *McClure said he would present the proposals by conservation groups——along with those of other interested groups—for public review before drafting any legislation. . .McClure offered both to meet with representatives from conservation groups after reviewing their proposals, and to send members of his staff to meetings of conservation groups at their request. . .*[6]

What McClure and the rest of the delegation wanted was to end the uncertainty. If there was to be more wilderness in the roadless areas of Idaho, so be it. Let us get on with it and get it designated. At the same time, for land that is not going to be set aside as wilderness, there should be release language that legally mandates multiple use management and precludes obstructive lawsuits.

In August, McClure conducted hearings in Boise, Lewiston, Idaho Falls and Coeur d'Alene where more than 700 people testified. Mike Field, a legislative assistant who attended the Idaho Falls hearing said:

> *My memory of that hearing is one of deep division. On the one side there were the producers—the loggers and the cowboys—folks*

> *who had been the only users of the public lands for as long as they could remember. On the other side were the environmentalists who had the lock-it-up mentality. The senator would draw both sides out at the meetings. He was really trying to understand all sides of the issue. Seldom did he express his own opinions. He was there to listen. However, there were other places where he did express himself. Remember, he was constantly traveling around the state holding town meetings. There he would freely discuss the issues as they came out. One of his major themes, which he repeated many times, was that the old ways are changing. To the producers* [cattlemen and loggers] *he stressed that the environment was going to have to be protected and you cannot continue to be successful in your business if you can't figure out ways to do this. To the environmentalists he urged that they start a dialogue with the producers and not go off on their own without understanding the other side. I observed the responses. I saw some of both sides listening. Now, twenty-five years later, I'm still working in the state and I can see the results of McClure's influence. The producers of the next generation have learned to protect the environment and still remain successful in business. And there is much better dialogue between producers and environmentalists.*[7]

Exactly one year from the day McClure asked for wilderness proposals from Idaho groups, he and the other members of the delegation issued a joint press release that said, in part:

> *. . ..After nearly a year of careful study and analysis, the Idaho Congressional Delegation today announced specific details of the Idaho Forest Management Act. . .the time has now arrived to come to a decision on the management of Idaho's roadless areas. Already, Idaho has 3,835,388 acres of Wilderness—more than any other state except Alaska. The bill proposed by the Delegation will add 526,064 additional acres to the National Wilderness Preservation System, for a statewide total of 4,361,452 acres. . .The Forest Service acreage that is not designated Wilderness shall be managed for multiple uses other than Wilderness, until and unless otherwise directed by an Act of Congress. . .*[8]

The delegation's Forest Management Act was introduced in both the House and Senate, and hearings were held over the next several weeks. In addition, two polls were taken of Idaho residents, one by a professional pollster that queried 500 Idahoans by telephone, and another taken by McClure as a result of a questionnaire mailed to his constituents. In the telephone poll, 54 percent *strongly* felt there was enough wilderness already and another 19 percent felt there was enough wilderness—73 percent overall, while those who felt strongly or not so strongly that there should be more wilderness was 22 percent. In McClure's questionnaire, with 13, 667 respondents, 53 percent favored no more wilderness, 10 percent favored additional wilderness as proposed in the delegation's Forest Management Act, 14 percent favored an additional 1,007,503 acres, and 21 percent favored an additional 4, 519,426 acres. And, in McClure's poll, to the question: Should lands not designated as wilderness be made available for multiple uses? Eighty-three percent favored multiple use. Then the thing most Idahoans dreaded happened. In August, 1984, two representatives, one from Wisconsin and the other from Pennsylvania, introduced legislation that would create 3.4 million acres of new wilderness in Idaho.

McClure was angry, and in a press release said:

> *I strongly object to this last-minute meddling in the legislative process. This is clearly an attempt to derail months of serious discussion and I hope it won't be taken seriously by those who have been negotiating in good faith for so long. . .I don't believe that persons who lack in-depth knowledge of the many complex land issues of a particular state should try to force themselves into the process at the last minute. . .*[9]

McClure and Larry Craig, First District Congressman, struggled for another two months, cajoling and compromising, then hit a brick wall in the person of Congressman John Seiberling (D-Ohio)[iv]. Urged on by various environmental groups, Seiberling rejected McClure and Craig's bottom line compromise, which would have put 810,000 acres in wilderness, set aside another 225,000 for wilderness study, placed another 700,000 acres in a long-range study, left 1,000,000 acres without a release designation, and released the remaining acres for multiple-use management. "All of these compromises were rejected," said McClure, "even though our final offer was probably more than what we should have offered. The inability to reach an agreement. . .comes down to a difference of opinion between Idahoans and a small national constituency in support of large additions of wilderness."[10]

And so died McClure and the delegation's one and one-half year effort to resolve the wilderness issue in Idaho.

Four years later Cecil Andrus, who had served two terms as Idaho governor and four years as Jimmy Carter's interior secretary, was running for another term as governor. As Andrus' press secretary, Marc Johnson, remembers it:

> *Wilderness was a negative issue for us because more people were anti-wilderness than were for it, and Andrus had the image of a wilderness advocate. To counter that we convinced our candidate to announce that, if elected, he would go to Jim McClure and the two*

Courtesy Eric Smallwood

Friendly opponents. McClure and Democrat Cecil Andrus worked together to hammer out a wilderness compromise plan.

of them would sit down and work out a compromise wilderness proposal. We were getting banged by the absolutely no more wilderness crowd. They were saying, "Don't back Andrus because he'll lock up the whole state. We felt that by letting it be known that we were going to work with McClure, this would convince folks that a new wilderness proposal would be reasonable.[11]

Andrus made the announcement after talking with McClure, and in December 1987, after Andrus was elected, the two of them met in the Governor's office and began their work on a joint proposal. Eighteen years later they got together again, accompanied by Marc Johnson, and recalled their partnership. What follows is a digest of their dialogue:

Author: *I heard that the two of you went into the Governor's office, chased out the staff, got down on your hands and knees, and began poring over maps.*

Andrus: *Nah, that is what we did a few years earlier when we were trying to work the kinks out of the Hells Canyon Recreation*

Area proposal. This time around we did it the civilized way; we spread maps out on the table.

Author: *Did you know the state well enough to do that?*

Andrus: (looking at McClure) *Yes, but how many days did we travel this state? He looked at some* [of it] *by himself; I looked at some by myself; and we traveled together lots of times.*

McClure: *But, we knew the state like the back of our hand. I know it sounds a bit far-fetched, but we both knew every drainage, every stream, every river.*

Andrus (joking): *So at hearings, when John Q farmer gets up and is worried about some rock on his hillside, we could identify what he was talking about.*

McClure (straight-faced): *We would know the hillside. But we might have trouble identifying the rock.*

Author: *Did you have kibitzers?*

Andrus: *Yeah, well, some of my supporters in the environmental community said, "All McClure wants to protect is the rock and ice. That's not good for anything else, anyway.*

Author: *Rock and ice?*

Andrus: *That used to be their buzz word for the high-altitude stuff. Anyway, we really knew those areas and I would tell those people, "You are crazy. The man is legitimately trying to work a way through this and we are going to find an answer.*

Author: *How much disagreement did you have?*

Andrus: *It took several months of give and take negotiations.* (Smiling) *And all of the Senator's press releases said that this was the McClure/Andrus proposal—his name was always first.*

McClure (smiling): *And all his press releases called it the Andrus/McClure proposal.* (Now serious) *In retrospect it would probably have been wise for me to have put the Andrus name first. Your name was associated favorably with wilderness. Mine was not. People might have assumed that it was your proposal and that I supported it.*

Andrus: *But anyway, we worked our tails off and you know what happened? The aginers. . .his aginers and my aginers cut our throats and we couldn't get anything past. And today, there are still 9.3 million acres out there that are in limbo.*

McClure: *We thought maybe we could carve out a middle and people would come together. Instead, we carved out the middle and they went apart.*

Andrus: *It was like an athletic contest. Each side wanted to win—no matter what.*

Author: *Were the organizations opposed—the Idaho cattlemen, Farm Bureau, Sierra Club, Wilderness Society?*

Andrus: *We started out with the organizations saying, "You know, this is great. You two fine statesmen just work all of this out." But then it was chippy, chippy, chippy as we went through the hearings, and we ended up getting our fannies kicked. I finally said at one point in time, "Blazes with you folks. I am through!*

PAT FORD ON COUNTER STRATEGY

After I got McClure's letter, I decided my main job was to bring leaders of various [environmental] *organizations together and figure out a response—a corporate response. When I did that, it was obvious that we all believed any bill that McClure would come up with would be a bad bill. We decided right then that we had to start working on how we were going to defeat it. We did respond with proposals, but with many more acres—three to four million—than he would ever propose.*

As a way to defeat his bill we went to work immediately on John Seiberling from Ohio. We made trips back to Washington to convince him that he should be a wilderness advocate for Idaho. We also got some supporters in Ohio to work on him. We put in a lot of work and the result was that we got him to agree to come to Idaho on a personal inspection—a Forest Service sponsored helicopter tour of all the proposed wilderness areas. We put on a real show the three days he was here. We had a big thank-you meeting party in Boise, a similar reception in Ketchum, and another one in Moscow or Coeur d'Alene, at all of which he received lots of applause. Then we did a dramatic thing. We knew that he would be landing at the Pioneer Cabin, which is above Ketchum, so we got about 100 supporters to hike up there and greet him when he arrived. It was like welcoming royalty, and he was both pleased and impressed. I think it made a big impression. We certainly pulled out all the stops to make him feel welcome.

Later when McClure and Seiberling got into negotiations on the bill, we were worried. Through a Seiberling aide we knew that Seiberling was wavering, but eventually Seiberling did win out. However, his aide said that it was very close.

Author: *But it was passed by the Energy and Natural Resources Committee.*

Andrus: *That was brute strength and awkwardness on his part. I mean, they weren't going to vote against one of their own.*

McClure: *Besides that, every one of them had had something in their own states that I had supported. I said, "I let you do in your state what you wanted; now it is time for you to let us do in our state what we want to do.*

Author: *And you elected not to introduce it on the floor of the Senate?*

McClure: *There wasn't any point in putting people through the agony of voting on that thing when the national environmental groups were all monolithically opposed to it. I don't think Cecil will disagree with me when I say this. Those issues on a national scale are relatively easy to predict. You ask a congressman from Florida to vote on a bill in Idaho and every congressman will have 50 or 100 people who will contact him on behalf of the preservation/wilderness/conservation side of the issue. He has nobody from his district on the other side. So, it becomes a very, very easy vote for him or her and that is the way most of those kinds of issues boil down in Congress.*

Andrus: *And I remember Jim calling me and he says, "Cecil, we are dead. We have had it." I said, "Are you sure?" Then he explained the situation and I said, "We are done."*[12]

This ended both McClure and Andrus' efforts to resolve the Idaho wilderness issue.

Many years later one of the leading wilderness leaders at the time of the McClure/Andrus proposal confessed to the author:

> *It is not uncommon for environmentalists like me to point a gun at our head and do things that are counterproductive to ourselves. We rationalize by saying that we are keeping bad things from happening. It is a powerful tool, but it doesn't work very well. Environmentalists have stopped a lot of bad things over the years. But, they have also missed a lot of opportunities. Frankly, we weren't mature enough to deal with Senator McClure. I know now that we could have reached an accommodation with him. He was our best opportunity to get something done because he was good at what he did. We missed an opportunity because we weren't ready for it. History is all about perfect hindsight.*[13]

Chapter 30 notes

i. The Forest Service was not represented. Said Scott, "The first thing we agreed on was that the Forest Service had to go."

ii. Scott also told of how he was hanged in effigy on a flatbed truck outside the Grangeville hearing, and how he was given sheriff's protection because of death threats.

iii. *The End of Affluence,* Paul Ehrlich, Ballantine Books, 1974.

iv. Chairman of the House Public Lands and National Parks Subcommittee.

Chapter 31

Farewell, Pink Cards

He says he really did not mind spending thirty-five out of fifty-two weekends in Idaho. Meetings with Idaho people recharged his enthusiasm for representing them. Nor did he mind the hundreds of hours he spent on airplanes. In fact, those hours were a treat because there were no telephone calls to make or receive, no staffers standing on one foot then the other urgently needing to confer with him. The airplane ride was a rare time of solitude for him; time to catch up on reading, time for contemplation, time to reflect and to peer ahead. And living out of a suitcase in motel room after motel room, and constantly having to reset his biological clock while flitting across the two-hour time-zone differential? He did not mind the suitcase living: *The rooms were generally clean and the beds generally good.* As for the time zones: *I didn't have a biological clock to reset. The only problem was getting into Boise at 10:30 p.m.—12:30 my time—and needing to stay up another two or three hours to talk.*[1]

But, oh, the Tuesday, Wednesday and Thursday evenings. They were wearing on him. More and more he was dreading them. And the wear and the dread was increasing with every week that passed. Could he get out of them? It was a tempting thought, but, no, he could not get out of them. Not and enjoy the camaraderie and respect of his colleagues. Without that he would have no more effectiveness as a United States Senator.

What were these Tuesday, Wednesday and Thursday evening millstones that were grinding him down? They were every United States senator's sustenance. Literally. Not one senator could survive without them. Because every senator is under constant threat. *There are always thousands and thousands of folks back home who are lusting to see you lose your job. And there are a few powerful folks back home who are ravenous to take your job away from you.* A United States senator's seat is one of the most precarious, threatened, tenuous—pick an adjective—positions a public servant can hold. And, yes, good work and good public relations have something to do with keeping foes in abeyance. But what every U.S. senator needs more than anything, what every senator absolutely must have for survival, what every senator must perpetually be in search of, is *money.* Lots of *money.* Hundreds and hundreds of thousands of dollars of *money*.

Over the years innovative senators and their supporters have made traditional entrepreneurs look like amateurs when it comes to hustling dollars for their campaigns. But who knows where or when the prince of all hustlers came up with a magic cash dispensary—one where those with lined pockets come to pant and paw for the opportunity to thrust their *money* into the hands of the senator.

So how does this senatorial cash dispensary work? It is a very simple mechanism. Bring some booze and some snacks with, ideally, some pretty ladies to serve them, to a large suite or small meeting room in one of the nice Washington hotels—the Mayflower and the Hilton are two favorites. Then the senator invites his buddies, usually of the same party, but with occasional mavericks of the other party, to "meet a few of my friends." Of course, what his "buddies" well know is that wives are not welcome (usually) and staffers are not welcome. So what is waiting, from six to nine o'clock on Tuesday evening, is one of the most powerful, exclusive, influential—pick another adjective—small groups of people on Planet Earth. There they are, Senator Stevens and Senator Dole and Senator Lugar and Senator Domenici and Senator Goldwater and. . . And there you are, you who have just shed some of the lining of your pockets. The senators are all yours. There is no staffer to stiff-arm you away, no secretary to invent an excuse why the senator is unavailable, no one with whom you have to waste time on small talk.

One-on-one you shake hands with these here-to-fore untouchables, discuss Kachina dolls with the senator from Arizona, the Indianapolis 500 with the senator from Indiana, and, with the senator from Alaska: *Oh, by the way, there is a gold dredging operation we're proposing that will be a great economic boon to the Inuits in your Katmai Peninsula—we've heard they are really poor and hard pressed, right?* And the noble public servants are genuinely warm and friendly and eager to listen to your every word. It is a miracle. An hour ago these exalted Knights of the Capitol Dome were dour-faced, harried commuters in the tunnel between the Senate and their office, surrounded and insulated by aides gesturing and gesticulating. Now they are relaxed, affable good old boys and girls, and you all, who have paid your admission fee, are now one of their clubbies—that is for the 30, or 45, or 60 minutes before they rush to another suite or another meeting room or, worse luck, another hotel for another one of these "fund raisers."

Yes, there are no euphemisms used in this entrepreneurial enterprise. They are called by the mundane name that tells what they are: fund raisers. And, for United States senators on Tuesday, Wednesday and Thursday evenings, they are as inevitable as the sunset and the sunrise. And as a senator, do you like them? For quite a while the senator from Payette, Idaho liked them. When he first came to the Senate, he was a sponge eager to be immersed. The folks who came to the fund raisers had more than the lining in their pockets. They had knowledge. They had useful information. And their

Courtesy Tod Neuenschwander

McClure, from his hotel room in Damascus, Syria, talks on a secure line with President George Bush on the night before he flew to Iraq to meet with Saddam Hussein. With McClure is his office Chief of Staff Tod Neuenschwander. The trip took place in April 1989, six months before Iraq invaded Kuwait.

sponsors had schooled them in the art and craft of explaining a point of view in the time it takes to down two sips from a scotch and soda. (For the record, McClure occasionally had a glass of wine but was more likely to drink 7-up over ice.) Just move around, meet as many of these information fountains as you can. And when the thirty or forty-five or sixty minutes are up, you have received an accelerated education. You know a little bit, or quite a bit, or, perhaps, a whole lot more about things you did not know much about when you left your office. And there is another fund raiser to attend this evening. And another one after that.

All of these senatorial shake-downs were interesting and educational to the new senator from Idaho. Well, maybe most of them fell into that category. At first, that is. The second year you go to them and you look around. You know this guy and that guy and the woman across the room. You know who they are and you pretty well remember what they are going to be telling you during the two sips of your scotch and soda. But, you realize that you need to hear it again. You need to refresh your memory. You need the review. And maybe there is something new that you should know. So you are your affable self. You smile and greet and listen. And, perhaps, there are new things to learn. And perhaps you want to extend the conversation and probe into unexplored territory. And perhaps not. Perhaps it is the same message, one that you can recite as efficiently as the messenger.

But, of course, there is a third year and a fourth year, and for McClure a ninth year and a twelfth year and a sixteenth year. That is longer than the man endured the teachings and preachings of his public school. And in the sixteenth year, on a Tuesday evening, you go to that same suite in the Mayflower Hotel, you look around at the bartender and the not-so-pretty ladies serving the finger food, and you steel yourself for the meeting, greeting and the two-sips from your drink incantations—for that is what they are now—from the those who have paid from their sponsor's gross profits to be there. And you may go to another one that same evening. And occasionally you must go to a third one. And the routine is repeated the following evening. And at six o'clock on Thursday morning, while it is dark, cold and raining outside, you sit on the edge of your bed putting on your shoes, and while your wife is lying half-dozing, half-awake on the other side of the bed, you mumble softly, "I don't think I can make myself go to another fund raiser tonight."

McCLURE LOSES JIM GOLLER

It was late 1986, just after Cecil Andrus was elected again as Idaho governor. As he was walking by the Boise Post Office he ran into Jim Goller and they began talking about Larry Mills, former speaker of the Idaho House of Representatives, who was now serving on the Northwest Regional Power Planning Council. It was well known at the time that Mills was suffering from some health problems and the discussion turned to who might be his replacement. Goller, who was going through a divorce at the time and who was looking for a change in his life, told Andrus that he would be interested in that job if Mills had to resign. According to Goller, Andrus agreed to give it some thought, and sometime later, while he was in Hawaii for some relaxation before starting the grind in January, Andrus called Goller and said, "If you're really serious, come in and talk to me when I get back." Goller did that and, to no one's surprise—Andrus was known for his middle-of-the-road way of working with Republicans—Goller got the appointment. "McClure was quite surprised," said Goller. "But I had a hunch he wasn't going to run again, and even if he did, he wouldn't need me—he would have been a shoo-in. Why did I do it? I wanted to do something else with my life and I had a real interest in the issues before the Council."

Mike Field replaced Goller and was called the Idaho assistant. He soon took another job and was replaced with Pat Sullivan.

Your wife stirs, blinks, ponders. Then, in the authoritative tone that she mastered while mothering three children, she says, "Jim, doesn't that tell you something?"[2]

Perhaps it did. He does not remember answering. However, it does not matter. There was work that had to be done that Thursday morning. The New York senators were at it again. They were doing everything in their power to get the Treasury and the Defense Departments to dump large quantities of their stored silver on the market so one of their big sponsors, Eastman Kodak, could stuff their maw with the metal at depressed prices. And Congressman Silvio Conte from Connecticut was doing the same thing for the silverware manufacturers in his home state. McClure could not allow that. At least he had to get with his First District Congressman, Larry Craig, in whose district the Idaho silver mines were located, and with their collective weight in the House and Senate, fight valiantly to prevent such sales. He and Larry Craig also had to lead a joint counteroffensive. Using every conceivable tactic they or anyone else could devise, he had to champion causes for which silver commemorative coins could be minted. Thousands of Idaho miners depended upon a healthy price for silver. And for the healthy price to exist, there had to be a healthy demand.

There were many other problems that kept McClure intensely occupied during the latter years of his third term. Despite significant setbacks, nuclear energy was still very much on his mind. Partly, of course, was because of the INEL in Idaho whose appropriations he had to guard assiduously. But partly it was because he had not given up on the promotion of new nuclear generation plants in the United States. Even though the last energy crisis was a fading memory to the public and a worn-out topic with the media, he was painfully aware that the country was burning its most precious resource: time—time that could be used in mastering the technology for fast-breeder reactor production of energy to be used in hydrolyzing water. (*Damnit, hydrogen produced by this method could be the ultimate, cheap, perfect source of energy for the next two centuries. Why are we wasting all this time and making ourselves vulnerable to those in the Middle East who hate us?*) Actually, Senator McClure was a mild spoken senator and probably did not even think such caustic thoughts. He was also a practical man and did not waste a lot of time with "what ifs" and "why nots." He just went about his business in his quiet way, especially after the 1986 election when Democrats once again took over leadership of the Senate and he lost his chairmanship of the Energy and Natural Resources Committee. As the ranking minority leader, now, he felt he should continue doing everything he could to further the development of nuclear energy.

It was tough going, however. Nuclear energy opponents had found the one issue that resonated with Americans, especially those who considered themselves intellectuals. The old issue, *nuclear reactors are dangerous*, was not registering any more. America's nuclear Navy had been safely transporting hundreds of thousands of sailors above and below the seas for thirty years. *But, ah, what about those horrible nuclear wastes that remain dangerous for a million years?* Good question. Of course, they did not remain dangerous for a million years, but hundreds, thousands, or millions—no one quibbled over the number.

The fact was that nuclear wastes remained dangerous for a long time, although that danger decreased precipitously after about sixty years. No one, least of all McClure, denied that nuclear wastes were a problem, but he was convinced that it was a solvable problem. And to augment his argument, not only did he become a student of the waste disposal technology as devised by American engineers, he traveled to Sweden and to France where he studied those country's technological solutions. The French solutions were especially interesting because that country, virtually without fossil resources, had made and was continuing to make vast investments in nuclear generation facilities and disposal technology. Here was no half-hearted, maybe we want this energy or maybe we do not, kind of approach. The French were serious and determined and McClure became an admirer of both their resolve and their technology.

Then he went to the Soviet Union with ten other members of the Senate Energy Committee. This was at the invitation of the Soviet legislature's Energy Committee and the purpose was to compare each country's energy problems. McClure was interested, of course, in the ways the Soviets were using technology. But, he was a lot more interested in meeting and discussing Soviet-American relations with the charismatic new leader, Mikhail Gorbachev. Was there a breath of fresh air blowing through the empire that had been our arch-enemy for the past forty-plus years? McClure was skeptical. Communists were Communists and he really did not expect that the country was going to change.

"Gorbachev was charming and very personable," said McClure, "but so was Nikita Khruschev.[i] My impression of Gorbachev was good, but I was cautious."[3]

The delegation did see that positive changes were flowing through the society. They visited the prestigious scientific city of Dubia, 75 miles north of Moscow and saw the renowned Flerov Laboratory and the particle accelerator where new atoms were discovered. *Yes, it was impressive, but it was in a remodeled old warehouse where the concrete floor was uneven, and when standing on the accelerator I could see poor welds and I'm not a weld expert. It was typical Soviet—the best and the worst together.*[4]

McClure asked for and was granted the opportunity to meet Andrei Sakharov, the Nobel Laureate who had been under house arrest for six years because of his outspoken demands for freedom. Said McClure in a telephone call to his administrative assistant:

> *I had one of the most extraordinary experiences in my life this evening talking at some length with Dr. Sakharov. . .You can't visit with* [him] *without understanding the tremendous force of his personality and the dedication that he has towards increasing the freedom of Soviet citizens within their own country. . .Dr. Sakharov and his wife, Yelena Bonner, are* [amazing] *personalities and it was a marvelous experience for me to be able to talk to him and to discuss with him some of the opportunities for improved relationships between the Soviet Union and the United States. . .*[5]

One of the most memorable experiences of McClure's life occurred the evening before the delegation was to fly out of Moscow. It was the evening before Easter and the delegation was allowed to attend services at an Orthodox Church. McClure remembers:

> *We were put on a bus and taken to this church where we were invited to join in the procession. There was a huge crowd and not just old people; there were many young people and young families. . . It was a two-hour service, from ten o'clock to midnight, and it was the tradition that everybody stands during the service—to sit would be an affront to God. However, they put our delegation with the choir, which was seated. It was inspiring to see those people able to worship in the old way—a great change from the way it had been under the Communists. From there we went to the airport on the bus, and while it was quiet, this younger man, our guide and translator, said in a rather soft voice, but so we could hear him, "Maybe the old ways were right." That whole experience was tremendously moving.*[6]

McClure came back still a skeptic. The delegation had been briefed by U.S. sources on a powerful radar site, which, because it was inside the country and not near its borders, was a violation of the ABM Treaty. That, and the fact that the American Embassy under construction was so embedded with listening devices it could never be used, caused McClure and his colleagues to wonder if Ronald Reagan's demand some months earlier, *Mr. Gorbachev, tear down this wall!*, would ever come to pass. "Never in my wildest dreams could I have imagined that the Berlin Wall would be torn down eighteen months later," said McClure.[7]

The trip to the Soviet Union was stimulating and informative, but the same old grind was waiting for him at home. Every afternoon, at five o'clock (or as close to five o'clock as he could get back to his office), he would pick up his 3"x 6" pink card, a card that most of the senators carried, on which his personal secretary would type his schedule for the evening and the following day. "We lived by those pink cards; all day long we would consult our pink card to see what we had to do next," McClure said later. "It wasn't unusual to have one side of the card covered with things you had to do, and when the schedule ran over on to the back of the card, you knew your life was totally out of control."[8]

On Tuesday, Wednesday and Thursday mornings there was often a breakfast of some kind—a prayer breakfast, a breakfast with the Chowder and Marching Society of which he had been a member since his first term in the House, and numerous organizational breakfasts. Then it was to the office with meetings of staff, perusal of important mail, the meeting and greeting of visitors, and then a rush to one or more committee and subcommittee meetings where he would again have to communicate with committee staff in the rushed time before or after formal proceedings. Often in the afternoon, after a luncheon meeting of some kind, he was on the Senate floor actively participating in debates on legislation he supported or opposed, then there would be more hurried meetings with staff. Sometime later he would get back to the office, deal with the fires that had to be put out, then grab his pink card and run to the first fund raiser that was on the schedule. And, occasionally, the evening activity would be of a different sort. Sometimes, wives would be welcome to dinners put on by various organizations like the National Rifle Association. "And one of the favorites," said McClure, "was the reception put on by the National Dairy Association. Kids were welcome at these receptions and they served many kinds of ice cream."[9]

One morning, probably in 1988 after returning from the Soviet Union, McClure lingered at the house and had breakfast with Louise. She saw that he was dawdling a bit and she believes she asked him, "Jim, are you all right?" According to her memory, he looked up at her and replied, "I just don't have any desire to go to work today." "Again, I replied to him, 'Jim, that ought to tell you something.' I really believe that his serious thinking about retiring from the Senate went back to this moment—I'm not sure it was in '88—it could have been in early '89. But, he was just getting sick of the battles. He loved the challenge of the legislation. He loved representing the people of Idaho. But not the never-ending fund raisers and the fights over natural resources that he was constantly losing. He had seen his kids grow up and get married and he thought of how he had missed doing things with them—fishing, and taking them to the places he remembered from his youth—doing the things a father wants to do. I think he felt guilty. And all of this was wearing him down. He fought the same battles year after year, and once he thought a battle was over, it would come up again. I think it began to drain his energy."[10]

Other thoughts were creeping into Jim McClure's mind about this time. One was of the rustic old cabin near McCall he had purchased in 1979. The back of the cabin looked out over Wagon Wheel Bay of Payette Lake, a view that would be hard to surpass anywhere in the United States. He loved that old cabin. Moreover, it was a challenge. It needed rewiring, replumbing, re-almost everything, which to Jim McClure (unlike most ordinary souls) presented an exciting challenge, a test of his do-it-yourselfer skills, a time sink away from telephones, conferences, fund raisers, and most of all, *away from the pink cards.*

> KEN McCLURE COMMENTS
>
> *You have to understand my dad to appreciate why he may have started thinking about leaving Washington. They sold their Payette house in 1973 and for several years they did not have a place in Idaho—he used his parents' home for his permanent address. He was lost when he had no place to putter or call home. He could never just sit. I remember when they vacationed a week at Hal Ryan's place—dad sided Hal's whole damned garage. He couldn't sit still. A beach vacation would have driven him nuts. When they finally bought the cabin in McCall, he replumbed it twice—that's a lot of hours living under that cabin. I remember in 1980 he took the bathroom out for a week and they had to use the one at their neighbors. I really think that his statement confessing that he was wondering if he should be less driven relates directly to that cabin. He wanted to spend more time with mom and he wanted a permanent home.*

What McClure did after that confessional breakfast with Louise reminds the author of a scene witnessed many times in the Basque Country of Spain and France, and on sheep ranches in Idaho where Basques were, for many years, employed as shepherds. Faced with a daunting challenge, or with a task they are reluctant to do (like slitting the throat of a lamb they have to butcher), they would invariably tuck in their shirt, hike up their pants, spit on their hands and rub them, then, with their chin thrust forward, proceed aggressively to the task at hand. By all accounts of those who worked for and with him at the time, metaphorically that is what Jim McClure did. No one but Louise knew that his interest was flagging. No one can remember any easing off, any downbeat words, any indication at all that he was tired of the battle.

And the battle went on. On one front were the natural resource issues. Laws had been passed that gave detailed guidelines to the Forest Service which called for the establishment of 10-year plans—plans that required environmental impact studies, endangered species studies, fish and wildlife habitat studies—studies that, when completed, were the basis for how National Forests and the districts within them would be managed. "When we passed the legislation that everyone agreed would provide for intelligent and balanced administration of the Forests, we thought the problem was solved," said McClure. "Shortly after that happened, we could see that there were those who had no intention of following the law. Soon the lawsuits started, and it was one after the other, all with the goal of upsetting the Forest plans. It was discouraging, but we fought on."[11]

On another front were some unusual battles—battles of single individuals against the capriciousness of the United States government.

One involved a Mountain Home Air Force Base contractor whose name is embargoed in the McClure archives because of sensitive personal information in the files. This contractor had his contract canceled for reasons that a later board of appeals ruled were wrongful and without cause. After his contract was terminated, they got another contractor to finish the work even though they admitted they had been wrong. No matter, the contractor suffered acute financial damage, was forced into a condition of insolvency where he could no longer obtain construction bonding, and, during the whole sordid mess, ended up losing his wife and all of his assets. And despite the board of appeals decision, the Air Force turned their back on the man and refused him the compensation to which he was entitled as an adjustment.

When McClure learned of this case, he did not hesitate; he put a rider on an appropriation bill to compensate him. However the Pentagon was opposed. McClure said:

> *The Pentagon appealed to the Minority Leader, Bob Dole, and he agreed to set up a meeting in his office with the Deputy Undersecretary of Defense—the number two person. She was just adamant that it would destroy the contracting procedures and set a precedent they couldn't live with. She did not persuade me that I was wrong. I got the appropriation through and the contractor got his money. It didn't make him whole; nothing could recreate what had been destroyed. At another meeting on this problem when a General was trying to talk me out of proceeding, I said to him, "I've always been respectful and proud of the uniform I wore, but I am not proud of it today." The General at least had the decency to look ashamed. Actually, he was there because it was his job; I don't think he felt right about it. This was an open and shut case of a little guy who had been destroyed by the Air Force and I think he knew as I did that they should have provided some compensation.*[12]

That same year McClure took on another fight for an individual who had been wronged by the government. A Coeur d' Alene resident, Pat Purvis, had won the contract to build the U.S. Pavilion for the 1962 Seattle World's Fair. The General Services Administration (GSA) that was overseeing the construction called for a number of changes requiring additional funds. However, the funds did not arrive and Purvis, responding to the need to finish the pavilion in time for the fair's opening, went ahead with the modifications on the word of GSA officials that he would be compensated. He finished on time, the fair opened, but Purvis was never compensated. After a protracted legal battle that forced Purvis into bankruptcy, the U.S. Court of Claims awarded a token sum that had to be paid to the bonding company and for legal fees. Purvis then got McClure involved who, after checking the legitimacy of the claim, wrote a Purvis relief bill and then recruited co-sponsors from the Northwest delegation. Twenty-five years after the wrong, McClure and Purvis stood in the Oval Office when President Reagan signed the relief bill saying, "There are two parts to government. One is seeing that government doesn't commit a wrong, and the other one is when the government does commit a wrong to see if we can correct it."[13]

The preceding fights were of little consequence except to the individuals involved. Earlier, McClure engaged in a battle that would have far-reaching consequences for Northern Idaho.

For decades the Milwaukee Railroad[ii] had a main line that ran from Chicago to Seattle, traversing the Panhandle of Idaho through the small town of Avery. The railroad's crack streamliner, *Hiawatha*, was a popular way for passengers to travel from the Midwest to the Pacific, and, for promotion purposes, the line was named the "Route of the Hiawatha." The line itself, constructed mainly by Chinese workers in the early 1900s, was a marvel of engineering, especially the ten tunnels and seven high trestles in the fifteen-mile stretch through the Bitterroot Mountains that separate Montana from Idaho. One of the tunnels, the Taft Tunnel, is 1.66 miles long and reportedly, when the builders met in the middle after starting on each end, they were less than two inches off.[14]

In 1977 the Milwaukee Railroad went bankrupt, and after several years of legal wrangling, its assets were put up for bid. The Edwards Investment Company, based in St. Maries, Idaho, successfully bid on the section of the line from St. Regis, Montana, to Avery, Idaho, and immediately began taking out the tracks and ties and selling them. Their goal was to convert the roadbed to a logging road, which they could use (their main business was logging) and on which they could charge tolls to others that would use it for timber hauling. However, there was a problem. Over the past years, as ties were changed, spikes and other metallic debris was left in the roadbed, and there was so much of it that it presented a hazard to tires. To solve this problem the company repeatedly graded the line and ran powerful magnets over it to attract the metal. About the time all of this expensive work was completed, the U.S. Forest Service entered the picture. Their attorneys declared that the Edwards Investment Company really did not own all of the road. Because the line was originally built utilizing land grants, a 1922 law declared that land not being used by a railroad would revert back to government ownership—and since the line traversed the Panhandle National Forest, that agency would now exert control. Also, almost as an insult, the Forest Service refused to allow the road to be used for logging (they said the trestles would not be safe for logging trucks even though heavy trains had been crossing them for decades and the company had paid for expensive engineering surveys to confirm their safety) and they only offered a token amount of compensation to the company for their land and extensive improvements. By then the company was nearly bankrupt and could not afford to sue. That is when they came to McClure who, after some investigation with Jim Goller and staffers Frank Cushing and Jeff Cilek, saw another underdog being abused by the federal bureaucracy. With Cushing and Cilek doing most of the legwork and negotiations over details, McClure eventually got a relief bill passed—a bill that provided substantial compensation but not entirely what the owners had spent.[iii] Since that time, the Forest Service has made a fifteen-mile stretch of the road into a hiking/biking trail that traverses the most spectacular part of the route, including the 1.66 mile tunnel between Idaho and Montana. And, Jim McClure, and staffers Frank Cushing and Jeff Cilek who spent many hours working on the project, can take pride that they not only saved the Edwards Investment Company, but that the company's improvements eventually made it possible for the now-named Hiawatha Trail to become one of the premier hiking/biking trails in the U.S.

The year 1988 brought another challenge. It was a presidential election year. Reagan's second term would be up and Washington insiders were speculating on who would replace him. His Vice President, George Herbert Walker Bush, had, since his chastisement by the Senate Steering Committee, been true to his word. Even his worst critics acknowledged that he had been completely faithful to Ronald Reagan during the two terms he served as Number Two. But could he get the nomination? Bush had little chance to demonstrate his leadership ability as a vice president; Reagan was a dominant personality and Bush cast only a faint shadow over the land. Some of the congressional conservatives were especially skeptical of Bush's seemingly mild personality. Would Bush have fired the striking air traffic controllers? Would Bush have bombed Ghadaffi in Libya? Would Bush have invaded Grenada? They had doubts.

The Republican senators also had one of their own who was seeking their party's nomination. It was their majority leader turned minority leader (after the 1986 election), Bob Dole. They had few doubts about his backbone. He had been a combat infantryman in World War II and had survived a serious wound. And in the Senate they knew he could be tough, even hard, when he had to be. Besides, they knew him a lot better than George Bush and they knew, as president, that he would work closely with him.

Then Jim McClure enters the picture. He and George Bush had been friends since the days when they were both freshman congressmen. And their wives had grown even closer over the years.[iv] At Bush's request, McClure agreed, along with Senator Mitch McConnell (R-Kentucky), a bright new rising star in the Senate, to co-chair the Committee to Elect George Bush. This move, according to Chief of Staff Tod Neuenschwander:

> *. . .sent a clear message to conservatives. . .that they could trust Bush, that Dole had no lock on GOP Senate support. Early on we set up regular meetings with the Bush campaign people to share*

Courtesy Jim McClure

McClure at lunch with President George Bush at the White House. Below, President Bush and wife Barbara, Ken, Louise and Jim McClure. The two men and their wives have remained close since leaving office.

information. . .and we would then get it out to the rest of the GOP senate offices. . .not to push them, but to keep them informed, keep them in the loop, let them know that Bush wanted to include them though they were working day to day with Bob Dole.

As the campaign wore on and it became more apparent that Bush would be the nominee, our efforts to coordinate the Republican senators became more important. GOP senators became increasingly eager to get on board with Bush...

McClure made some appearances for Bush. I remember him going to the regional GOP convention in Denver, and he played a role in the national convention as well. As I recall, he made several other speeches at various places around the country for Bush. During the GOP national convention in hot, steamy New Orleans, we set up an office that did little else than to make sure all GOP senators were taken care of and had the "message of the day" so all were speaking from the same page. McClure spoke at the convention, and although I can't remember exactly when, it was during the prime-time session.

All that support paid off very well when Bush was elected. McClure had almost complete access to the White House and the President. In typical McClure style, he never abused it, but it was always there.[15]

Bush was inaugurated in January 1989, but McClure was in Vienna, Austria, where, as a member of the Helsinki Commission on human rights, he was participating in a conference of thirty-five nations. Along with Secretary of State George Schultz and twenty other members of Congress, the conference was held to update the Helsinki agreement of 1975, especially to more accurately define human rights violations and to add stronger guidelines. Said McClure, "We wanted to ratchet up the temperature, increase the pressure, and sharpen the focus [on nations that were abusing human rights]. Of course, I was skeptical, but it was something worth doing. I've always believed that is better to do the right thing and not expect too much than it is to expect too much and see nothing but failure."[16]

When he returned from Europe, he landed in the middle of two battles, one he lost and one he won.

The new president was heavily engaged in getting his new cabinet officers confirmed in the Senate,[v] and with one of them he was encountering difficulty. Former Senator John Tower (R-Texas) had been nominated for secretary of defense, but the Democrats were aggressively fighting against him with accusations McClure considered malicious and mean-spirited. On the Senate floor, he said, "This is not the Senate's finest hour." Alluding to an FBI report that was supposed to have contained damning evidence against Tower, McClure said, "Where is the evidence. . .I have read the FBI report and the evidence simply is not there. What is there is allegation and anonymous, unsworn testimony...We all know what the real issue is here; it is a struggle for power, a struggle between a Democratic majority and a Republican president."[17] McClure and the president lost this battle. John Tower was not confirmed by the Senate.

McClure's other fight was with the Army Corps of Engineers. At stake was the annual migration of anadromous fish—salmon and steelhead—which had declined precipitously in the past decade. Over the years McClure had become a student of the problem, having had the advantage of listening to hundreds of hours of testimony by fish experts as well as several on-site tours of the Snake and Columbia River dams that were believed to be the major cause of the problem. As a result of this involvement, he and Senator Hatfield (R-Oregon) made sure there was money in the 1988 budget for certain remedial work at the dams, including fish by-pass construction, screens to prevent downstream migrating fingerlings from entering dam turbines, and flip lids. The Army Corps of Engineers, whose mission was to carry out the construction of these remedial measures, was supposed to have begun immediately. But it did not happen. By early 1989 it was obvious they were defying the mandate of Congress, and McClure decided he had to do something about it. He said:

> *I called a meeting in my office with the Army chief of engineers and the Walla Walla chief district engineer and made it quite clear that they had a right to their opinion—they believed that barging was the sole answer to the problem— but that Congress has a right to its opinion and that the last time I read the Constitution, Congress' opinion must prevail. They did not concede easily. They argued that what Congress approved was a waste of money. I knew better—I had studied the problem as much or more than they had—and their defiance made me angry. I made sure they understood who was in charge and they left, grudgingly agreeing to initiate the construction.*[18]

McClure's fight for dam modification funds and his subsequent arm-wrestling with the Corps of Engineers did not go unnoticed. That same year the Idaho Steelhead and Salmon Unlimited organization presented him with their annual award to the individual who made the greatest contribution toward protecting and rebuilding Idaho's anadromous fish runs. Said their executive coordinator, "Without him (McClure) we'd be twenty years getting done what he's done in the last two years. Senator McClure has taken the bull by the horns and moved it ahead. Otherwise I'd hate to think where we'd be."[19]

As the year 1989 passed, there was a certain number that Senator McClure admitted having on his mind quite often. When asked if the number was 65—that would be his age on December 27 of that year, he shook his head. "No, it was not the number 65, it was the number 72. I was thinking that if I ran and won another term I would be 72 when it was completed. That number bothered me. If I wanted to do something else with my life, I could still do it at 65. At age 72, my options would be a lot more limited."[20]

Both Jim and Louise believe that, as the year 1989 dwindled, their talks of retirement became more and more serious. They examined the factors quite objectively, as they did in their living room of their McCall cabin years later. As they remembered it, the fund raisers were the hardest on the senator. At this point he almost had to put a knife in his back to force himself to go meet and greet, and listen to the two sips of scotch and soda incantations that he could now repeat backwards.

Factor number two was the chronic frustration he was experiencing with natural resource issues. And probably "pain" should be added to the frustration, for it did pain him every time he learned that another timber mill was shutting down and releasing its workers. The Emmett Mill, one of the largest in the state, had shut down. The Horseshoe Bend Mill, another large one, had shut down as had the Council Mill, the whistle of which he had heard as a child. And it went on and on, from south Idaho to the Canada border. It was depressing to him to have fought so hard to keep some of those small communities alive, for practically all of them were one-industry towns. Of course, in many cases it was not legislative failure. Part of the problem, as mentioned in an earlier chapter, was Canadian imports; they were killing Northwest producers. Also, the battlefield had changed. It had moved from the Congress to the courts; it had moved from the spear carriers in the House and Senate to near-anonymous judges dressed in black. Most of all, the enemy—as he saw it—was awash in money, big money, money to pay high-priced lawyers that the struggling timber operators could not afford.

Factor number three was the atmosphere of the Senate. It had changed in the seventeen years he had been there. There was a term that almost everybody used to describe the earlier relationship of the members to each other: collegial. One definition of that term "characterized by camaraderie among colleagues" is a good description of the member relationships according to observers who knew it then. Of course, there were debates, even arguments and an occasional sharp word, but, inside the elevator, or alone together in the commuter tunnel, or at a secluded spot in the parking garage, apologies, or at least words spoken in a tone of appeasement would be spoken. Practical, if not personal, imperatives were at stake. Even if one did not *want* to get along, one *needed* to get along. You may need your opponent of today as your supporter tomorrow—that was a fact that every new senator was advised to learn.

But things had begun to get nasty in the Senate. What Hedrick Smith called "prickly politics"[vi] probably went up a notch during the Agnew/Nixon brouhahas, went up another notch during the Reagan administration when the Democrats replaced the Republicans as snipers, especially during the Iran-Contra Hearings, and, according to McClure, became even more nasty and personal when Bush tried to get his nominations through the Senate. In addition, said McClure, "There was also the growth of negative campaigning. For an opponent to be successful there was the need to tear the other person down. Whatever suggestions one candidate was making, it was the opponent's job to attack the person, not necessarily the suggestion. Back when I was in the State Senate, the fellows across the aisle were as good of friends as those on my side. In the House I worked closely with chairman and Democrat Wayne Aspinall—we got along very well together. In my early days in the Senate it was much the same. Then it began to change. I can't put a finger on real specific ways it changed; it just changed, and for the worst in my opinion."[21]

The preceding may have been the major factors, but there were minor factors as well. One of them was the looming campaign, the 1990 campaign. Even though he was sick of fund raisers, he knew that *he was going to have to start raising money for himself, big money, probably a million to a million and one-half dollars.* There was "some" money still in the kitty that could be used, but the huge majority of it had yet to be raised. According to Jim Goller, who was already at the Northwest Power Planning Council, "I think it would have been closer to one and one-half million he would have had to raise. It would have been work, but by this time McClure had a lot of supporters. McClure himself wouldn't have been of any help—he absolutely hated fund raising and fought us when we tried to get him to do it. But the money could have been raised if he had wanted to do it [run for a fourth term].[22]

> DICK THOMPSON ON THE CHANGE
>
> *When I came to work in Washington, it was a time when the Members of Congress were universally respected. And the top staff people were men and women who had made names for themselves in other areas—in business or academia, and they were topping off their careers by serving in Washington. And when the "giants" spoke on the Senate Floor (Richard Russell, Walter George, Everett Dirksen, etc.) people stopped what they were doing and went to the galleries to listen. Floor debate could actually alter the outcome of an issue. But over the years, it all changed, and I don't know why. There are no longer any "giants" in the Senate, and members are no longer civil to one another. No one has time to go to the Floor to listen to debate, and it wouldn't matter anyway. Staffers are mostly young people using the Congress as a stepping stone to higher paying jobs in the business world. It was partisan in the old days, but not partisan in the bitter, hate-driven way it is now. McClure's career happened to coincide with that change. Maybe it just wasn't fun for him anymore.*

At this point in the story, one thing needs to be said with emphasis. Jim McClure was and still is a very patient man, but there is one thing for which his threshold of toleration is near zero. That is for people who whine and complain and who are full of negative excuses. He cannot stand people like that, and, in respect to his musings over why he was thinking of not running again, he has a horror of thinking his comments might lead someone to think he was doing just that. And just in case an idea like that might be lingering in the reader's mind, he gave an example to try and counter such a conclusion. He said:

> *I don't think anybody but Louise knew how I felt at that time. I went to the fund raisers; I fought the natural resource battles; I continued to get along well with my colleagues. Most important, if I would have had any idea that a strong Democrat was going to run for my seat, I would never have given the slightest thought to retiring. I told the president* [Bush] *that one evening when we were at the cabin in McCall. It was around Christmas time and he called me there. "What's this I hear about you thinking of not running next year?" he asked. He then went on to twist my arm because he was afraid of losing a Republican seat in the Senate. I told him that if I perceived there was a chance a Democrat could get in, I wouldn't think of retiring. But I assured him there was no problem. At that time I assumed Larry Craig would run even though we had not talked about it. I knew there was nobody who could come close to beating Larry Craig and I told the president that. I say this to emphasize my level of feeling at the time. Yes, I was tired of the fund raisers and the pink cards and that other stuff, but not to the point where it was driving me from the Senate. I was not being driven by anything; I was doing the driving myself. To me it was just a question of which direction was I going to turn when I got to the intersection.*[23]

It was no secret that McClure was thinking about retiring from the Senate. Starting in the summer of 1989 he did not hesitate discussing the matter with reporters who were starting to bug him about his decision. *I'll admit that it is on my mind, but I have not made a decision.* That would paraphrase his usual comment. But even those close to him knew that he was telling the truth. Son Ken remembers that the family was having discussions about it when they visited with him at the cabin in August of that year. "I clearly remember sitting with them and discussing the pro's and con's. Once he said, 'One of the things we could do if I retired is buy an RV and just travel around the United States.' Mom quickly put a stop to that thinking. She said, 'If you do that, you go alone.' Mom liked being a senator's wife. It wasn't the prestige near as much as the things she was involved in and the people she associated with around Washington. It was stimulating for her. She liked her life and, personally, I think she was reluctant to give that up. But, she also knew how hard Dad was working and she didn't encourage him either way. She always felt it was his decision to make and she would go along with it."[24]

Idaho reporters continued to speculate throughout the autumn of 1989, some betting that he would retire, others betting that he would not. Then McClure re-hired Al Henderson who had managed his 1984 campaign.

That was seen as a sign that he was going to run. Also, money started flowing into his campaign fund and he had nearly $300,000 banked for used in the 1990 campaign. Then, in a interview in Boise in early December he said:

> *. . .The time is coming when I have to make a decision. I know that. It's past the time when I thought I would. I keep waiting for some flash of inspiration, and it hasn't come. I eat dill pickles and ice cream and go to bed thinking something will happen by the morning. It hasn't happened yet. . .*[25]

Three things deeply concerned McClure as 1989 drew to a close. One, it was not fair to delay a decision. If Larry Craig was going to run as his replacement, he had to get started immediately with his campaign, especially on a drive to raise at least a million and a half dollars. Two, it was not fair to send a dedicated worker like Al Henderson out raising money and planning a campaign that might not materialize. Three, he was already worried about his devoted, hard-working, loyal staffers who needed to know whether or not they were going to be out of a job the following year. They needed time to plan their lives.

BILL HALL'S PERSPECTIVE

One of McClure's long-time antagonists, Bill Hall of the *Lewiston Morning Tribune*, expressed some opinions about McClure and possible retirement in a July editorial. Said Hall:

Idaho Sen. Jim McClure has as light a case of Potomac fever as there is in the nation's capital. If anybody can walk away from the Senate at a rather tender age (by political standards), it is McClure. So it is no surprise that he is having some difficulty deciding whether he really wants to run one more time.

Any sane person would step down at this time in his career. Granted, not many members of Congress are sane about deciding when to hang it up. But if there is an exception, it is McClure. He is a down-to-earth, unpretentious man, surprisingly modest for a member of the most pompous club on earth. He may have the perspective on himself—and on life—to escape that madcap scene now rather than at some less flattering point in his career. . . And while McClure can probably go no farther [in Senate leadership], *he has already gone a long way. He has spent three terms. . .where he has been a respected if not a dazzling member, a workhorse more than a showhorse. He has been true to his state and to his conservative philosophy. And his worst critics think kindly of him as a person.*

He cannot improve on that. He can quit while he is ahead.

No wonder he is tilting toward retirement.

Finally, after the Christmas holidays, Senator James A. McClure made his decision. His chief of staff and closest associate (other than Goller), Tod Neuenschwander, eloquently comments on the lead up to that decision and the countdown to its announcement:

. . .The question of Jim McClure's possible retirement was endlessly debated. We debated with Jim, and we debated among the staff, with supporters, the press, everybody. But, really, nobody had a clue. . .Jim is the type of person whose mind was always two steps ahead of the rest of us. So he openly discussed retiring, I believe to draw the rest of us out. He did this with many issues, always asking questions so he could assimilate many points of view before making a decision. Even in this most personal of decisions, his method was no different.

To the very end, not one of us had any real indication which way he would go. Finally, as the pressure mounted in early 1990, we set a date for a public announcement. I was in Boise, working out of the Boise office. The press conference was scheduled for the following day. Still no clue from the McClures. They were up at the cabin in McCall. I remember calling them that afternoon for some direction, any direction. We had to prepare something for the next day.[vii] *Louise invited me up to spend the night. It wasn't until that evening, sitting in the cozy living room of their cabin, that Jim told me that he wasn't going to run again. Louise, ever direct and to the point, asked if I hadn't known anyway. I remember answering her very honestly, that despite all the speculation and discussion, I really hadn't had a clue until that very moment and that no one else did either. I think I was the first to know, other than possibly some of the family.*

We put together an early lunch in Boise for the following day . . .announcement day. Key members of the staff were invited. As I recall, Ken and Sally may have been there also. [they were] *Certainly Jim Goller, Pat Sullivan, H. D. Palmer and others were there. . .maybe twelve to fifteen people in all. McClure told them his decision. Then it was off to the press conference to make it public.*

Some have questioned whether it was burnout that kept Jim from running again. After eighteen years in the Senate and six in the House before that, he had every right to be burned out—and there may have been some burnout as the same old legislative issues seem to recycle themselves over and over again. But I give less weight to the question of burnout, than I do to Jim's unfailing love of Idaho, its people, its lifestyle, its very place.

I always thought Jim McClure was torn in two directions. On the one hand, as an extremely bright, intelligent man, he always thirsted for more answers, and therefore was always asking more questions, more than could ever be answered. He was a student of the nation and the world and was forever ingesting new information. The Senate and Washington D.C. quenched that intellectual thirst as he dealt with issues of enormous importance.

On the other hand, Jim McClure was always one with Idaho. As a non-native Idahoan it was difficult for me to grasp at first. But he never wasted a minute that he wasn't out of DC and back in the state. He tried and usually succeeded visiting all fourty-four counties at least every year. I know, I traveled with him for many years. And it was a killer schedule that he maintained throughout. Yet despite the horrible travel schedules and time away from family, he loved it. He was a changed person when he was in Idaho, and we could all feel it when he returned to DC. It was no secret; we knew he wanted to return to Idaho and, frankly, enjoy the rest of his life.[26]

Idaho has a way of affecting people like that, even those not lucky enough to have been native born.

Chapter 31 notes

i. Soviet leader after Stalin.

ii. The complete name was Chicago, Milwaukee, St. Paul and Pacific Railroad.

iii. McClure received a lot of flack from Idaho editorial writers for doing such a "special favor" for an "investment" company. Actually it was a logging company using "investment" as a name for their railroad line venture. McClure never wavered. He publicly declared that the Forest Service used appraisal values on just land and not the expensive improvements—the trestles, roadbed and tunnels—and that their appraisals were "ridiculously low." They did not get the full amount appropriated because the Graham-Rudman Law knocked down all appropriations by a percentage.

iv. Many years later, when Barbara Bush celebrated her 70th birthday, Jim and Louise were one of the couples invited to Kennebunkport for the party. Also, Tod Neuenschwander said, "I remember spending the better part of an entire day with George Bush and Jim and Louise McClure in a motel suite in Idaho Falls, and it was there that I learned first hand of the friendship between the Bushes and McClures.

v. McClure publicly expressed disappointment that Bush did not accept his recommendation that Peter Johnson, former BPA Administrator, be appointed as Secretary of Energy. Bush appointed retired Admiral James Watkins, former Chief of Naval Operations, instead.

vi. *The Power Game,* Hedrick Smith, Random House, 1988.

vii. H.D. Palmer, his press secretary who also was in Boise, said that he had two press releases written, one saying that he would run, the other saying that he was retiring from the Senate.

Epilogue

James A. McClure celebrated his 66th birthday just before he announced that he would be retiring from the United States Senate. And soon after that announcement the question that had bothered him before his retirement announcement began crowding his thoughts again: What am I going to do when I leave the Senate? He knew that he did not really want to retire, that is, quit working altogether. He knew he was not yet ready to prop his feet up and watch the sunsets on Payette Lake from his cabin near McCall. That was at least four or five years away. Yet when thoughts of a post-Senate career did emerge, feelings of guilt swept them away. Constantly he reminded himself (and probably his staff) that the people in Idaho had not elected him to a five-year term. *So quit thinking about another career. Do what the Idaho people elected you to do. Take your pink cards each day and continue to fight your battles.*

High on McClure's priority list was the Silver Valley in northern Idaho. Through the years he had been in Congress, he had done everything in his power to save those jobs in Idaho. For example, when Eastern congressmen fought to sell off the Treasury's silver stocks at bargain prices—actions that would have especially helped the Connecticut silverware manufacturers, but which would have been disastrous for the silver market—he countered those efforts by sponsoring legislation for the coinage of silver dollars. However, it was a losing battle. Silver prices tanked as did the other commodities from the mines: lead and zinc. In addition, the huge Bunker Hill smelter outside Kellogg was a notorious polluter and there were no technical fixes that were economically feasible. In 1981, Bunker Hill finally closed its mine, smelter and zinc plant idling 3,100 workers. Shortly thereafter the Star Mine closed, and then it was off again, on again for the other mines until the mid- to late-1980s when practically the entire mining industry of the area collapsed. This, of course, created an unemployment disaster which, according to local businessman and Economic Council member Dale Lavigne, ". . .resulted in 50 percent unemployment—that's not a government statistic because many of those people were off the unemployment rolls and ceased to be a statistic. It was just terrible. Many businesses closed and the ones that managed to stay open were hanging by their fingernails." [1]

What hope was there for the Silver Valley? The smelter area was declared a Superfund Site and the environmental recovery program would bring some money into the Valley. But what about the long-term future? Was there hope for a new major industry?

Community leaders did have a vision. It was based upon what they had observed in another area of Idaho. The world famous Sun Valley ski resort was booming at the time because it had grown out of its one-season past and had become a year-around recreational area catering to a variety of outdoor enthusiasts. The Silver Valley leaders said to themselves, "When the smelter site is cleaned up, this area will be a heck of a lot more beautiful than the Sun Valley area. Let's go for it. Let's get a ski resort going and build hiking trails and. . ." Dreams? Visions of grandeur? Perhaps. And perhaps not if the money can be raised to get a ski area started.

Then it dawned on them. *Ah ha! We have a senator whose heart is in this Valley. Let's get McClure working for us*. That inspiration succeeded. McClure and his staffers signed on and were soon cajoling and bludgeoning every funding source in the Federal bureaucracy that had anything to with economic disaster areas. *Get out to the Silver Valley and see what you can do to help them finance the gondola they need to develop a ski resort.* The bureaucrats obeyed, and they studied, and they wrote reports, and they ultimately turned the Senior Senator from Idaho down. It is not feasible, or it was not in our power to help, or… It was a long and sad story, but with a happy ending. Fed up with the FHA and all the other bureaucracies that had studied and declined to get involved, McClure got a direct appropriation of six million dollars through his Energy and Natural Resources Appropriations Subcommittee—a grant that would have to be matched locally—and the folks in the Silver Valley were ecstatic. McClure, the hero, had come through for them. And forget the pounding the man got from media across the country for using his muscle to get the fattest of all the pork that was dispensed in the year 1990. And forget that the people of the Valley almost lost their grant by being unable to match it. (It was saved when the citizens of Kellogg voted a two-million-dollar bond and the Swiss developer,Von Roll Transportation, agreed to match the rest.) Viewed by many as a classic boondoggle, the project teetered on the edge for several years, but as this is being written, 99 luxury condos on the mountain just sold in less than four hours after being placed on the market, and the area is becoming a premier recreation center exceeding the most grandiose dreams of Valley leaders.

The year 1990 was also the year of the bears and the wolves.

The grizzly bear is the most dangerous animal in North America. And in the late '80s the U.S. Fish and Wildlife Service was quietly reintroducing them in northern Idaho against the overwhelming opposition of the residents. At hearings throughout the state, opponents such as Explorer Scout leaders warned that no leader would dare take young people on wilderness treks in grizzly habitat, and that reintroduction of the grizzly would eliminate wilderness experiences for thousands of youngsters. *But we are not doing that,* claimed the bureaucrats. *We will not do that until we have the mandate of the people.*

Jim McClure and his staffers knew better. Hundreds of letters from constituents, some claiming visual sightings of grizzlies, claimed otherwise. Suspecting that the Fish and Wildlife people were lying to him when they claimed innocence, McClure put Legislative Assistant Carl Haywood on the trail of the agency to sleuth out the truth. Finally, after helicopter records were subpoenaed and examined in 1990, Haywood proved beyond doubt that the agency had lied to the Senator. They had been introducing grizzlies and admitted it when they were faced with the evidence. Quietly, the bears were removed.

The grey wolf is generally not a direct threat to humans, but it is an active predator of deer and elk, especially of their fawns and calves. And like humans they are also fond of beef and lamb. So what happens when, in 1989, the Fish and Wildlife Service wants to reestablish the wolf population of Yellowstone Park? Two sides quickly begin mobilizing their forces. On the cheering side, wolf recovery proponents like Congressman Major Owens (D-New York) wrote, "Nature has a way of striking a balance between animals and their food sources but, without wolves in Yellowstone, that balance has been disturbed."[2] On the anti-wolf side ranchers and cattlemen went to the courts to file injunctions against wolf recovery in the Park, claiming that once the wolves multiplied and left the Park, their livelihoods would be threatened. On their side were senators Malcolm Wallop of Wyoming and Conrad Burns of Montana who induced the Interior Department to pressure the National Park Service to stop distributing "Wolf Pac," a series of articles regarding wolves and the issues of reintroduction because they were t0o one-sided.

Then Senator McClure got involved. In an attempt to mediate the dispute between the acrimonious opponents, he introduced compromise legislation, saying before the Senate Subcommittee on Public Lands:

> *My bill is a sincere attempt to find a compromise solution that provides the means to re-establish wolf populations . . .while protecting the legitimate interests of ranchers, hunters, and others at the same time. Both sides must give a little in order to get a little; otherwise, the polarization and controversy will continue until one side or the other is forced to capitulate. Extremists on both sides continue to believe that they will prevail. I continue to hope we can find a way to prove them both wrong, and I believe this bill is the first step in doing just that.*[3]

McClure's legislation would have placed three breeding pairs of wolves in Yellowstone Park and in two wilderness areas of Idaho. However, once the wolf population grew to the point where it was spreading outside these "core" areas, it would be de-listed as an endangered species; that would allow state wildlife agencies to control the population and protect ranchers from depredation. As with the previous Andrus-McClure efforts at wilderness compromise, McClure's effort was torpedoed by forces not interested in compromise and he left the Senate with the issue unresolved. Five years later pro-wolf advocates won out in Congress and the courts, and currently possible wolf-pack depredation, especially of the Idaho elk herds, worries the retired Senator.

In this final year, McClure also made another trip to the Middle East with a Senate delegation. There he dined with presidents Assad of Syria, Mubarak of Egypt, King Hussein of Jordan and, following a hasty conference call with then President George Bush, endured a three-hour meeting with Saddam Hussein of Iraq. With the latter there were no comments from Hussein when he was questioned about the use of biological and chemical agents in the Iran-Iraq War and against his Kurdish minority population. And there was denial that his movement of Iraqi troops south toward Kuwait had any real significance. However, three months later Hussein's forces marched into Kuwait and took over its oil fields—an action that triggered the First Gulf War and arguably the second war in Iraq a decade later.

Louise McClure enjoyed a special honor during her husband's last year in office. This story started in Boise when the then-Mayor Dirk Kempthorne formed a committee to lobby for the naming of a new U.S. Navy ship after the famous *U.S.S. Boise*, a light cruiser that fought in battles off Guadalcanal in World War II. This committee, headed by retired Navy Captain Michael Everett, working with the entire Idaho congressional delegation, was successful and in October, 1990, Louise McClure was selected as sponsor of the Navy's newest fast-attack submarine. In her role as sponsor she traveled to Newport News, Virginia, and with her matrons of honor, Pat Kempthorne, wife of the Boise mayor, and Evelyn Little, long-time friend, at her side at the elegant ceremony, christened the new *U.S.S. Boise* with the traditional bottle of champagne.

As the months passed in 1990, the what-am-I-going-to-do-next question kept emerging. Of course, it was not only a question for the senator; practically every one of his forty-seven staffers[i] not only wanted another job, they *needed* another job. McClure said that he was not overly worried about this problem. "Everybody on the hill knew I had one of the best staffs. Yes, I was concerned for them but I was quite sure they could find jobs."[4]

But what was Jim McClure going to do? He and Louise had worked to eliminate all their debt in order to be ready for retirement. And from the job offers he got from law firms in Idaho, it seemed that he was destined to return to Idaho and take one of those positions. (Several Washington, D.C., firms approached him but he had no interest in trying to build a new client base in that city.) He was especially interested in the Givens Pursley firm to which his son, Ken, now belonged. Said McClure, "My father went into practice with his father-in-law and I went in with my father, so it seemed natural for me to join a firm where my son worked."

Then one day, probably in August or September, his two top staffers came into his office. "We need to talk with you, boss," they said.

It was Jack Gerard, his legislative director (who was raised on a farm near Mud Lake, Idaho) and Tod Neuenschwander, his chief of staff. Gerard, on his own initiative, had worked out a business plan that Neuenschwander instantly liked. It called for the two of them, with the senator, to establish a governmental relations consulting firm that would include the usual service of lobbying Congress, but, in addition, would furnish clients with advice on how to deal with various entities of the federal bureaucracy. Gerard and Neuenschwander had considerable experience dealing with those kinds of firms and felt that with their knowledge and McClure's impeccable reputation and his intricate knowledge of the Congress, it could be a very successful enterprise.

McClure looked over Gerard's business plan which consisted of three scenarios. Then he conferred with some friends who had joined such firms. He remembers that one of them was Howard Baker, former senator from Tennessee and a good friend. Baker encouraged him.

But there were two huge negatives on the other side of the proposal. First, he would have to postpone his return to Idaho. This really bothered him. He would have been gone from his native state for twenty-four years at the end of his term. His heart and soul were in Idaho and he longed to be there and away from the hustle-bustle of city life and in particular, the heat and humidity of the D.C. area. The other huge negative was that in order to start the new business, he would have to not only go back into debt, but would take on the largest debt of his life. Gerard's estimate was that the lease alone for the kind of office space they needed would be in the $13,000-$14,000 a month range and for a *minimum of five years*!

But there were positives on the tally sheet. If Gerard's projections were right on Scenario Two and especially on Scenario One, McClure had, for the first time in his life, the opportunity to make some serious money. Also, by staying in Washington, he could continue to serve on the boards of the Kennedy Center and the Smithsonian Institution—positions he especially enjoyed. Then there was the other half of the partnership. Louise was fond of their Washington, D.C. life. With boundless energy and great enthusiasm for anything in the graphic, musical, or performing arts, she would, by going back to Idaho, be giving up the kind of involved life she had grown to love.

Finally, after many talks with his two aides and probably a few hundred hours of mutual soul-searching with his marriage partner, he came to a decision that was agreeable with Gerard and Neuenschwander. Yes, he would join them in forming a governmental relations consulting firm. And, yes, he would sign the leases and debt agreements that would make him jointly liable for everything they would owe. But, the attraction of Idaho would not let him become a full-time partner in the enterprise. He would devote approximately half of his time to the new firm and he would spend roughly the same amount of time with Givens Pursley in Boise.

In January, 1991, Larry Craig was sworn in as the new United States Senator from Idaho and James A. McClure became an ex-senator. Shortly afterward the new firm of McClure, Gerard, and Neuenschwander, Inc., rented office space in a new building next to the Naval Memorial, a building eight blocks from the Capitol. To McClure this was "kind of scary." To Neuenschwander it was "a bit frightening." But Gerard said, "I was concerned but not overly so. I knew we would have to work very hard and that we would have to watch every penny that we spent. But we had an immense trust in each other. Each of us had unique talents. I had more of a businessman's mind than the others. Tod was great dealing with people and he knew lots of them. McClure was an issues guy. Confronted with a problem dealing with a government agency, he had great insight. He could predict the problems a client would encounter, and he could suggest creative solutions. We made a great team."[5]

They may have had a great team, but they got off to rocky start. The office they leased had not yet been built out; it was just a huge, empty room. Also, they had no furniture, no phones, nor office machines. Gerard remembers the three of them sitting around a folding card table and on beat-up chairs borrowed from Neuenschwander's basement. But they did have an all-star secretary/receptionist/office manager who became the "glue" that held them together. Susan Tackish, who had been one of McClure's personal aides when he was in the Senate, had, during his last year, found a good job at the Interior Department. But the three of them lured her away, telling her not to worry, that they, themselves, might not get paid *but we will always make sure that you get paid.*

Then they hit the pavement, or at least Gerard and Neuenschwander did—they all agreed that it was not McClure's place to go out and make cold calls on potential clients. Their tactics were to hold McClure in reserve. Should the other two find a client who was interesting in hearing more about their services, they would then take McClure to a pre-arranged luncheon.

All three of them thought their best opportunity lay with energy companies that would want their services, since McClure was so well known in that field and such companies were often ensnarled in the federal bureaucracy. To their surprise, this did not happen, at least right away. The very first client they landed was Coeur d'Alene Mines, a company based in the city of that name, and one with extensive holdings in South America. Not only did they do a lot of good work with this company, the administration recruited McClure for their board of directors, a position he held for the next fifteen years.

Neuenschwander now laughs when he reminisces about their first months in the new business. "We were using old doors laid across two-drawer filing cabinets for desks and we didn't dare bring potential clients to the office."[6] Gerard added: "But we made sure that Susan had a desk before anybody else. I don't know where we got it. We scrounged it somewhere. And I remember when we had the first clients scheduled to come in. We quickly rented a conference table and chairs so we would look respectable."[7]

"Within a month or two," recalls Neuenschwander, "a coalition of about half of the nation's electric utility companies also hired us to lobby against deregulation of the electric industry. I distinctly remember meeting with them just after we rented our conference table and chairs so we could host them in our office. And we co-represented the coalition with Patton, Boggs and Blow, the number one lobbying/law firm in D.C. with its hundreds of lawyers and support staff. That was pretty heady stuff for the four of us. That told me we would be respected. . .that we could make it."

Slowly they began to land other clients. And much needed cash. And with their cash they leased, then purchased nice office furniture, art for the walls, and all of the office machines they needed. After six months, they had an office that looked upscale and professional, and they were reasonably confident that they would be successful. After the first year, they were certain of it.

And they worked very hard. "Getting the clients was just the beginning," said Gerard. Getting the job done for the clients took a tremendous amount of time and work. Your mind was on their problems constantly, and in that respect it really was a 24/7 job. When we left at night, we wouldn't go home and relax. We took our client's problems home with us and in the middle of the night, we would wake up thinking of how we were going to solve them."[8]

Susan Tackish, whom Gerard claims was the one dodging the financial bullets that were fired at them the first six months, remembers working very long hours and the demands that were so great upon her that her husband had to leave his own work to take their son to the doctor when he was sick. "And don't forget the sad little plant we had at the beginning,"[9] she laughed when reminding Gerard of things he omitted when telling of their primitive office furnishings.

Their client list grew, as did their reputation, and, "By the end of the first year, said Gerard,"we had succeeded beyond our wildest dreams—and it continued to grow from there into a very successful business." Added

Neuenschwander, "We even had to turn down some clients. At one point I remember that the nudists came to us wanting our help. . .what was that organization. . .AANR, American Association of Nudist Recreation? Something like that. It seems the Park Service was closing down some of their clothing optional beaches. [laughing] We decided they weren't a fit for us."[10]

McClure, who was commuting to Boise mostly when Congress was not in session, was also establishing himself at Givens Pursley. "I told them I did not want to get involved in court cases, and they already had a fellow who specialized in water cases so I avoided his territory. And, yes, it was an enjoyable practice. I had knowledge that they needed and it worked out well for me."

"What was your most memorable client in Washington?" McClure was asked.

"Without a doubt it was the World Cup USA," he answered quickly. They were hosting the World Cup soccer playoff and they came to us with all kinds of problems. How could we get the U.S. Government to provide the necessary security? How could we do this and do that? One of their big problems was to get a commemorative coin minted, the proceeds from the sale of which they could use to help fund the event. As I remember it, they were on a very tight deadline, but I had been through that exercise many times and knew the key players, the problems and the pitfalls, and I was able to help them get their coin minted. And I got to know Pele [world famous soccer player]. The whole project was very satisfying."[11]

During those first years out of the Senate, McClure was asked to join several corporation boards. As mentioned, he joined the Coeur d'Alene Mining Corporation. He also joined the boards of The Williams Companies, Boise-Cascade Corp, and the Idaho Power Company. He was also involved with the Mountain States Legal Foundation and the University of Idaho in many capacities. With the latter he and Louise were very involved in energizing the yearly Lionel Hampton jazz festival.

In 1992, with their children grown and married, they sold their Arlington home and bought a condominium in the building where their D.C. office was located. *I then commuted to the office by elevator.* At the same time, he finally turned contractors loose to enlarge their cabin on Payette Lake. *No, I did not get involved in any of it; I let them do all the work.* After that Gerard and Neuenschwander found a good buy on a building across the street from one of the Senate office buildings. McClure gave them his blessings but elected not to invest—a decision he probably regrets, for when they sold the building several years later, it had experienced tremendous appreciation.

Originally, McClure told his partners that he would probably stay with them for three years. At the end of that period, he elected to stay one more year. Then, after that, he continued to do some work during the fifth year, but, as Neuenschwander put it, "His work with us just wound down in a natural way. There were no bumps in the road. He just became less and less involved in day to day matters. Fairly early on, we teamed with a D.C. law firm to help run a coalition aimed at improving and reforming the Endangered Species Act. Jim became its chairman. Later, even after he had pretty much settled in Idaho, he continued on as chairman—he felt that strongly about the issue. Individual biologists, just on their say so, were shutting down projects because of some mouse or snail they thought was endangered. Unfortunately, we ultimately failed in that endeavor even though we had strong bi-partisan support in the Congress."[12]

The next ten years of Jim McClure's life could be described as the near-perfect ride into a long sunset. Together 100 percent of the time now, Jim and Louise did about everything that they had always wanted to do. They traveled extensively. They visited and entertained their friends. They built a beautiful home in Boise designed for two families, a home they share with Ken, his wife, Sally, and granddaughters Emily and Katie. (And in one of the garages in that home is the restored 1969 Mustang convertible—no longer with a screwdriver gear shift—that McClure's staffers remember with affection.) After leaving the Kennedy Center board in Washington, the McClures became stalwart supporters of the arts in Idaho. Most of all, they enjoyed their cabin on Payette Lake, even in the winter when the snow was piled four-feet deep around them.

There was one bump in the road. In 2001, while on a ladder cleaning the rain gutters of his cabin, the ladder slipped and Jim fell and broke his arm and his leg at the ankle. Four years later he was still limping and in pain until fusion surgery finally enabled the bones in the ankle to heal.

Meanwhile numerous honors were bestowed upon him. An engineering building at the University of Idaho now bears his name. Also, the big federal building in Boise was dedicated on July 1, 2002 as the James A. McClure Federal Building.

He has been asked many times by his friends and supporters (as well as the author) to rank his achievements. He claims that his answer is always the same: "That is impossible for me. I just don't live in the past."[13] Then, when badgered, he expounds with more or less meaningless generalizations. However, there is another way to judge the man and his achievements. That is to watch his eyes when he recalls his history. When discussing one issue—his role in establishing the SNRA—his eyes seem to light up more than normal and he definitely becomes more animated in his speech, as he does when he talks about the Sawtooth Society in which he is still an active board member. Chalk that issue up as at least a probable most significant achievement. However, he did one other thing that may end up making him a true hero in the nation. If terrorists had been successful recently in destroying a key element in the Saudi oil infrastructure, or if this should happen in the future, the Strategic Petroleum Reserve that he and Senator Bennett Johnston fought to establish could make a huge difference in preventing an economic catastrophe. To this issue he says, modestly, "Let's just hope that all our work in establishing that [strategic reserve] is forever in vain."[14]

So how will Senator Jim McClure be remembered? What will be his reputation a hundred years from now? Many people have commented on that question. But interestingly the words that seemed most profound and most appropriate for concluding this biography came from one of McClure's long-time opponents who labels himself as a "liberal." While pre-interviewing Bill Hall, former editor of the *The Lewiston Morning Tribune* in respect to what he thought should be in a McClure biography, Hall said this about the man:

> *Jim McClure is a nice guy. He always was and always has been. I think he was born for the job. . . I don't think I've ever seen a member of the Idaho congressional delegation who epitomizes so much the people of Idaho, and when I say that, of course, I mean the majority. You could not disagree with Jim McClure on practically anything without disagreeing with the majority of the people of Idaho. Damnit.* [15]

Epilogue notes

i. 21 in his D.C. Senate office, 11 in his Idaho offices, 12 on his Energy Committee—most of whom he had hired and who would not want to work for others, and 3 on his Appropriations Subcommittee.

Appendix One

Big shots, bandits and some good guys—
Offhand comments of Jim McClure on some of the important personalities he has known during his political career

Idahoans

Bob Smylie

I knew Bob Smylie very well from his years as Idaho attorney general, then as governor. However, I first met him when I was Payette County prosecuting attorney and program chairman of the Kiwanis Club where he was invited as a speaker. Later, as assistant majority leader in the Idaho Senate, I met with him on a regular basis.

I would characterize Bob Smylie as an old time politician in the sense that he ran a political organization for his own benefit and alienated a good many people within the party when his interests were apparently counter to the interests of the party. He expected political support for the decisions he made whether it was granting a savings and loan charter or buying insurance for a state agency or activity. His most effective term was his last one when he provided leadership on very tough issues. Throughout his tenure he did a great deal to improve workman's compensation laws. He and I were on opposite sides on the sales tax but he was successful in getting that adopted. Not untypical of politicians, he had a very large ego. You can't think about Bob Smylie without thinking of his wife, Lou, who was a very great help to him in every respect—a great lady.

Don Samuelson

I first met Don when he was running a sporting goods store in Sandpoint and was first elected to the State Senate from Bonner County. We became good friends as he and I shared an apartment at the 1961 session for a time before our wives came to Boise. Don was a very intense person who had trouble doing routine things such as learning the way to move a bill on the floor of the Senate—what do you say, when do you say it, when do you make a motion. Like, what is the procedure that is used? He cared nothing for the procedure; he was always thinking of the end result. The same thing was true when he was speaking—thinking ahead to the end result. Very honest, very hard working, and was in many respects a very good governor—but his public relations skills were not up to the task. Ruby Samuelson was a fine first lady whom I think everyone loved.

Cecil Andrus

We became acquainted in the 1961 session of the Legislature when he was a freshman senator from Clearwater County and I was a freshman senator from Payette County. Cece was one of the younger members of the Senate. We have become friends over the years despite the fact that we have differed politically. Cece is very gregarious and likeable. When he was Secretary of the Interior in President Carter's cabinet he took positions he said were what Carter wanted even though they were not then widely supported in Idaho. I sometimes wonder how much was Carter and how much was Andrus. There is no doubt that Eastern preservationist interests were happier with him as Secretary than were his old logging buddies in Orofino.

John Evans

He became governor from his elected post of lieutenant governor when Cece Andrus left to become Secretary of the Interior. He was never one of the strongest leaders of Idaho, but a very decent person.

Phil Batt

The Batt family is one of the strongest agribusiness families in southwestern Idaho. Phil calls himself an onion farmer, but his farming interests are much broader than that. He was very instrumental in my first election to Congress, and has remained a personal friend over all the years since. He makes jokes about his short stature, but he is in every way a big man—a man who can be elected governor of our state and be successful, and still enjoy playing his clarinet in a small combo can't be all bad. His tenure as governor was exactly what you would expect: terse, taut, and economical.

Tom Boise

A legend in Idaho politics, a man whom I met but did not know well was a powerhouse in Democrat politics and who affected politics for years. His effectiveness grew from his detailed knowledge of the desires and prejudices of Idaho political figures—he was a student of politics and the people involved in it.

Lloyd Adams

Was a Republican kingmaker who was greatly respected by people in both parties and who worked hard and effectively for or against things that seemed important to him. We clashed once over bank closing hours. He won, I lost, but eventually I won when legislation was finally passed that allowed banks to remain open for normal business hours. He represented Idaho banking interests with a tremendous influence on Idaho legislation.

K.C. Barlow

When I arrived in the State Senate in 1961, there were a few old bulls that led the herd. K. C. Barlow was one. From Burley, he was a man of tremendous ability and great integrity. He had the respect of all who knew him, and was in every way a real force in the Legislature.

Tom Heath, Franklin County

He was one of the great characters as well as one of the genuine leaders in the State Senate when I arrived, especially in agriculture, and the sugar industry in particular. In business circles, especially, he was admired and respected. He also had a great sense of humor, and often lightened the mood in the debates.

Jack Murphy

A young lawyer from Shoshone, he was elected president pro-tem of Senate, and was a very effective organizer and leader whom I got to know well, especially when I became assistant majority leader. I worked closely with him and others of the leadership team in the legislature. Unfortunately, his death removed him from the political scene too early.

George Blick

George was from Castleford, a potato farmer, food processor, and a legislative leader who was a great friend. I remember in particular the way he would lean back, take a cigar from his mouth, roll it between his fingers, and half-drawl a question or an answer or a comment. Very capable and very steady.

Pete Cenarrusa

He almost defies any summary and needs no introduction to Idahoans. One of the most popular and durable of the state's leaders in its history. A very principled man with absolute total integrity that makes people warm to him and like him. He and Freda have been very close personal friends for many years.

George Hansen

I first met George when he was running for the U.S. Senate against Frank Church in 1962. One of the best campaigners the state has ever seen. He could shake more hands, ring more doorbells, write more press releases, greet more people than anyone else I have known. He was a very staunch conservative who was elected to Congress in 1964 and was a great help when I arrived in 1967. His political downfall came with the passage of campaign finance laws which required meticulous record keeping. It just wasn't in George's way of working to keep the kind of records required because he was too busy campaigning.

Orval Hansen

One of the brightest men to serve Idaho. Only the second student to graduate from the University of Idaho with a straight 4.0 grade average. An Idaho Falls native who served at a time the most conservative elements in Idaho politics held their greatest sway. Their sometimes personal attacks on Orval's positions led him to a confrontation with them, which resulted in his defeat at the end of his second term. Orval's commitment to public service did not end with that election. He has remained very active in a variety of public and semi-public efforts, an example being his staunch support of the Sawtooth Society. He and June remain close friends.

Dirk Kempthorne

First came to my attention as a young government relations representative for FMC in Pocatello, but really arrived on the scene when he was elected mayor of Boise. He was a very popular and effective mayor who, when he decided to run for the Senate, I was very happy to support. It did not surprise me that he decided he would rather be back in Idaho in the office of governor, because he is much more comfortable as an executive than he was as a member of the Senate.

Louise Shadduck

If there is any better public servant around I don't know who it is. She spent a lifetime in a whole variety of different ways in being one of the best citizens this state has ever known. Dedicated, able, and consistent, she is just a marvel.

Len Jordan

He was kind of my father in politics—an example of a man I looked up to as the kind of person who ought to be occupying public office. Successful sheep man, governor, and senator—altogether a marvelous human being. No comment about him could be complete without mentioning his wife, Grace. Her book, *Home Below Hells Canyon* is still one of my favorites.

Larry Craig

I've known him since his days as student body president at the University of Idaho. An able, hard-working son of a ranching family who has done extremely well in his Senate career.

Perry Swisher

He is one of the most interesting personalities that I have encountered in my years in public life. Perceptive, off-beat, sometimes acerbic, and often insightful, he is one of the better observers of the political scene in Idaho. And I am glad to call him a friend.

National Figures

Lyndon B. Johnson

He was president when I first went to Washington as an insignificant first-term Republican congressman. I could have not been treated more courteously by LBJ and his White House staff. I never experienced his arm-twisting, finger-jabbing, coercive leadership that so many have mentioned.

Richard Nixon

He is one of the most tragic figures in politics because his presidency ended in a scandal that obscures much of the positive leadership he provided. I share the opinion that he had more than a touch of paranoia. He simply could not trust the American people enough to level with them, but he was absolutely brilliant in his grasp of world affairs. Henry Kissinger has been given too much credit and Nixon too little credit for their foreign policy management.

Gerald Ford

He was the Republican leader in the House and I got to know him very well. He stumbled once on the steps of Air Force One, the presidential airplane, and was forever after characterized by the press as something much less than the athlete he had been. Jerry Ford was a good, solid, decent person and a more than adequate president.

Jimmy Carter

Jimmy Carter has been known as a master of detail, but unable to see the larger picture. I think I agree with that judgment. I like him, personally, but had strong disagreements with him over energy policy.

Ronald Reagan

As you might expect, I think Ronald Reagan was one of our finest presidents. A superb story teller, a great communicator, and a lot of fun to be with. His optimism helped Americans restore their faith in our country. He led the fight to keep the Communists from taking over the film industry in Hollywood and started his life-long battle against the Evil Empire. His leadership undoubtedly brought about the fall of the Soviet Union much earlier than might have otherwise been the case.

George Herbert Walker Bush

He was elected to Congress and arrived in Washington at the same time as I. He and Barbara became our friends from that time. I have been close to him through his presidency and our wives remain very close friends today. If he has a flaw, it lies in his inability to brag about his own achievements or to find personal fault in others. The latter has also been a great strength. It helped him build personal relationships sorely missing in Washington today. The bitter partisanship of today's political warring could benefit from his example. It is also the basis of the personal relationships with foreign leaders that contributed to the great foreign policy successes forged by him and Secretary Jim Baker.

John McCormick

He was Speaker of the House of Representatives when I first served in the House. I never knew him well. He appeared to be a relatively colorless person until taking the floor, a relatively rare occurrence for the Speaker. Then you could see the fire that had made him an effective leader for the Democrats.

Carl Albert

In ways, Carl Albert's rise to be Speaker of the House was surprising and unexpected. Diminutive in stature, unimposing in appearance, he simply did not look the part. But anyone who could not look further would misjudge the man. He shocked many people when he gaveled down those whom he did not wish to hear speak at the Democratic National Convention in 1968. "For what reason does the delegate rise?" he would ask, and when the delegate responded that he wished to speak on a topic Albert did not wish to hear, he would respond, "The delegate is not recognized for that purpose" and gavel him down. He ran the House of Representatives in exactly the same way. Anyone who believed it was a democratic exercise never noticed how Carl ran the house. Anyone who believes that the House, or the Senate for that matter, are democratic institutions would be wrong. They are to a degree (and somewhat by necessity) autocratic. The rules which are written to guarantee individual members rights are used to deprive members of their individual rights.

Melvin Laird

Mel Laird was then, as he has been over the years since, a leader in whatever group he was working. He has always had the capacity to influence others by his knowledge and his ability to persuade people to his point of view. That was evident when I first knew him and was evident over the years since. In Washington circles he is acknowledged as one of the people who count. His advice and counsel have been called on by numerous organizations and leaders. In any discussion in Washington when you are thinking of whom you would like to have involved on your side, Mel Laird's name would be sure to come up.

Wayne Aspinall

Democratic Congressman from Colorado and chairman of the House Committee on Interior and Insular Affairs, Aspinall had a reputation as a crotchety old curmudgeon when I first arrived on the committee. But, no one could have been a better friend to me. He learned very quickly that I viewed Western land and resource issues much as he did, and that I would be an ally in the committee. We forged a very good working relationship and I learned to admire and respect him very much. In the decades of the '50s and '60s no one had more sway over Western public land issues than Wayne Aspinall.

John Saylor

Republican congressman from Pennsylvania, he was the senior Republican on the Interior Committee when I joined it. It was unusual to have an Easterner on that committee because it was nearly always dominated by those from the West where the public lands are located. He became a spokesman for the emerging environmental movement and was often at odds with most of the Republican members of the committee. He educated me in the politics of the national environmental movement and although we often disagreed, he became a good friend.

Tom Foley

Tom Foley, Democrat Congressman from Spokane, Washington, had been an aide to Senator Scoop [Henry] Jackson. He was a leading voice for agriculture in the House and we worked very closely on issues which affected the Palouse area wheat farmers. The facts that his district bordered Idaho and that we shared common problems threw us together in dealing with many issues. We also traveled together on the business of the Interior Committee. Much more liberal than his district, Tom, nevertheless, managed to represent that agricultural district and its interests. His liberalism led to his election as Speaker of the House, but did not serve him well in his much more conservative district.

Morris "Mo" Udall

Mo Udall became a congressman from Arizona when his older brother, Stewart, then the congressman, became Secretary of the Interior. He was one of the most engaging personalities with whom I served. A great wit and good story teller. The Udall brothers wanted to build a dam in Marble Canyon in the Grand Canyon of the Colorado but, failing in that, both became spokespersons for the national environmental movement.

Cliff Hansen

Cliff was a gentleman in every respect and was one of the most popular senators in Washington. He was always courteous to other senators and their staffs. He accomplished a great deal simply because he was so well liked by everyone. He and Martha are still great favorites with Louise and me.

Frank Church

I had worked hard to defeat Frank Church for years before I was elected to Congress, although I did not know him personally. In the six years I was in the House of Representatives I had almost no contact with him because he traveled in circles that I did not. When I was elected to the Senate, it was obvious that he and I would have to work together on Idaho issues, and we did. I think it is fair to say that I did more of the detail work on Idaho wilderness designations because I was more intimately acquainted personally with the facts. But it was a good working relationship. I never did, however, have any more personal relationship than that. I believe he practiced the kind of politics that I do not like, characterized by the attitude that you do what you have to do to get elected so you can do what you want to do after you are elected. In Church's case that meant convincing Idahoans that he was less liberal than he actually was. When he became chairman of the Foreign Relations Committee, he had enough exposure in the national press that he could no longer as easily conceal his liberalism from Idahoans and this led to his ultimate defeat.

Barry Goldwater

I first met Barry Goldwater at the Republican National Convention in 1964. I was an alternate delegate and he was the odds on favorite with the Idaho delegation for nomination for president. Nelson Rockefeller was also seeking the nomination. Bob Smylie supported Rockefeller and the people who controlled the Republican Party in Idaho at that time very nearly refused to allow him to be a delegate. I felt that as governor he was entitled to go and he did, but they extracted a promise from him before permitting that to happen that he would not be very active and he was therefore somewhat quiet in his support of Rockefeller.

Goldwater was the undoubted leader of the conservative wing of the party and his book *Conscience of a Conservative* was the bible of the movement. That election, of course, is history as his campaign simply did not catch fire with the majority of the American people. He was the hero of the conservatives then and remained so until Ronald Reagan emerged. He was elected again to the Senate and I worked with him and his staff on many many issues. His greatest influence on policy in those later years was in defense policy. He was very easy to work with and we became very good friends. He never lost his personal appeal and was always highly regarded by all of us. I think it is fair to say that having been a presidential candidate he never returned to being just a senator.

Russell Long

It was hard for me to see Russell Long as the heir of the Long political dynasty of Louisiana; having read about Huey Long I guess I expected something different. Russell was a gregarious, likeable and energetic fellow that I instinctively liked, but I have never discounted the fact that Louisiana politics are in very little measure like Idaho. He was chairman of the Finance Committee, which writes tax legislation, and I had many contacts with him discussing the impact of various taxes on our citizens. Russell also carved out a very large area of authority over social policy and I guess our differences were even greater there. Despite our differences we were good friends.

Sam Nunn

Sam Nunn was expected to rise to the stature of his predecessor, Richard Russell, and worked very hard in that direction. Sam was a very serious and hard-working member of the Senate and far less partisan than many of the Democrats. He had a good sense of humor, but what struck me most forcefully was his characteristic serious demeanor. Respected on both sides of the aisle, he became noted for expertise in defense matters. The only serious disagreement I had with him in any personal way was his opposition to John Tower, when Tower was nominated to be Secretary of Defense. I have always thought there was more than just a little personal jealousy involved because John Tower had a larger reputation as a defense expert at that time.

John Tower

John Tower was physically one of the smallest men in the Senate, but had a large reputation. Unfortunately, the reputation had several parts. One as an expert on defense, one as a staunch conservative from Texas, one as a tough politician, one as liking the women too well, and one of perhaps drinking too much. But, there was no doubt that John was a force to be reckoned with. Blunt, outspoken, and tenacious, he made himself felt in whatever debate he entered.

Lloyd Bentsen

Lloyd Bentsen was a man with immense personal charm, but also a man of tremendous ego. It was said of him that he could strut sitting down. Not because of, but despite his very apparent ego, we were friends and worked well together, but Lloyd was one of those very partisan Democrats forged in the inferno of Texas politics which, unfortunately, detracted somewhat from our ability to become closer.

Daniel Patrick Moynihan

Pat Moynihan, undoubtedly, was a very bright man, but somehow he didn't live up to the advance billing as far as I was concerned. Very likeable and easy to get along with, very much involved in a number of issues of importance, he was somewhat overshadowed by his florid rhetoric. In spite of that, he contributed a great deal to the dialogue on important issues. I have the feeling that he might well have taken more moderate positions on some issues if he had represented another state rather than New York. I know that it is the responsibility of a senator to represent the views of his constituents, but Moynihan almost made an excuse of it, particularly on western land issues. He said to me on more than one occasion, "Jim, you may be right but I simply can't do it."

Jacob Javits

Jacob Javits was the quintessential New Yorker. I have never seen him more animated than when exclaiming about the virtues of New York City. He was a powerful senator who assumed that he should be powerful because he was from New York City. By my standards an extreme liberal and we had almost no working relationship.

Henry "Scoop" Jackson

He was chairman of the Senate Interior Committee on which I served. This committee had jurisdiction over most public land management issues, and I spent much of my time and energy there. After all, two-thirds of the state of Idaho is owned by the federal government. When the energy crisis hit the U.S., the committee took on energy policy as well, and I became very involved in that. Scoop was willing to see the federal government exercise broader discretionary powers—quite the opposite of my views—which led to several disagreements. (His ardent unquestioning support for Israel affected his views on energy policy as well as foreign policy.) Although we disagreed, we respected each other. Scoop was well-read and could expound on historical trends better than most. Ours was a friendly working relationship.

Bob Dole

I first knew Bob Dole in the House before he was elected to the Senate. I don't have many clear impressions of him during those first years, but after he was elected to the Senate, he became one of the most outspoken defenders of President Nixon. He has as quick a wit as I have ever seen, but so quick it sometimes got him in trouble. The wit also often times had a sharp edge, which led his critics to dub him the "hatchet man." I have never thought of his wit as mean spirited, but there is no doubt that he could cut. He was undoubtedly a man with "presence;" when he entered the room, you noticed. It was obvious even then that he was very ambitious and intended to move up. That is not a fault. He was the leader for Republicans in formulating farm policy and I worked with him very directly on some of those issues. He and I clashed only when we both ran for Republican leader after Howard Baker retired. We remained friends, however, and I still have great respect for him.

Howard Metzenbaum

For a long time I did not like Howard, but after traveling with him, I got to know him better and to appreciate his human side—and he did have one. I think a little of his character was revealed by the dark suspicions that he had of everyone else. I don't believe a person could be that untrusting if he, himself, were completely trustworthy, but he was always sure that everyone else was trying to put something over on him, and it was his duty to find out what it was. Coming from Ohio, he was a product of labor union politics in that state. And in committee he was a constant thorn in my side.

John Glenn

John Glenn has always puzzled me because I would expect something different from an ex-Marine and a man of strong religious practice. And somehow he didn't seem to fit the mold. The astronaut fame may have overpowered other impressions or perhaps it was the friendship that had developed between him and JFK, but he was something of a mystery to me. However, we enjoyed their friendship and his wife, Annie, is one of the most delightful persons Louise and I have known. We are both very fond of her.

Edmund Muskie

I liked Ed very much. He tended to be somewhat dark and somber but he had a sense of humor. His attitude toward U.S. businesses was something I couldn't stand—he believed they were all evil and the only way they were going to do what they were supposed to do was to hold their feet to the fire. He had no hesitation at all in penalizing them for what he was sure they must have done. His staff person on the Public Works Committee was extremely left-wing. Aside from those problems I got along well with him and enjoyed kidding him about Maine's small potatoes.

Hubert Humphrey

Hubert Horatio Humphrey—I have a mental picture of him that I will never be able to forget. I see him in long shorts and a walking stick leading a group of Blue-Bird girls. That is not completely fair to him, but his effervescent personality was always a joy. Our political views seldom matched except sometimes in foreign policy, but I enjoyed him as did everyone else.

Robert Packwood

Bob Packwood was one of the most active minds in the Senate. He was an acknowledged expert on tax policy and was always trying to organize the Republicans to do a more effective job. It is too bad that personal problems limited his career.

Mark Hatfield

Mark and Antoinette Hatfield are perhaps the closest couple to Louise and me. We traveled together and Antoinette and Louise are very close. Although we have much in common, our political views don't coincide because he is in the liberal wing of the Republican Party. His views fit Multnomah Country [western Oregon] better than Malheur County [eastern Oregon].

Robert Byrd

Robert C. Byrd—and he insists that it is "Robert" and not "Bob"—a man whose personal history demands respect, but who has no close friends in the Senate. I have no doubt that he has genuine concern for the people of West

Virginia, but I believe his reputation as an historian of the Senate is overvalued. We traded positions as chairman or ranking minority member on the Appropriations Committee's Subcommimittee on Interior and Related Agencies. His interest was almost solely on what was in it for West Virginia. Broader questions he pretty much left to me. We worked well together.

Mike Mansfield

Mike Mansfield was a superb leader of the Senate, greatly respected on both sides of the aisle. He often was the oil that calmed troubled waters. He was always quiet and measured, but could be very firm. One of the genuinely likeable senators.

He kept the Senate on a much more even keel, and the partisanship in the Senate really erupted when Mike retired.

Joe Biden

Joe Biden is an enigma. Sometimes he appears to be a statesman and at other times he is flippant to the point of childishness. It is hard to place a value on someone who goes from one pole to the other so frequently.

Ted Kennedy

Ted Kennedy is a real challenge for me because one of the worst faults of the political system I see today is the tendency to personalize disagreements. By that I mean the tendency to condemn a person with whom you disagree rather than confronting the policy differences, and in that respect Ted brings out the worst in me. He seems to believe that if he just shouts louder, he will be more persuasive. I got to the point that when he started ranting on the floor of the Senate, I would simply leave the room. Logic is not increased by raising the decibel level.

Dick Cheney

Dick Cheney is still one of my most admired political figures. Calm, unflappable, and steady, I have thought he has been one of our most effective leaders and find it amazing that the political left has chosen to attack him so relentlessly.

Strom Thurmond

What can you say about Strom Thurmond except to review his personal history? County judge, colonel in the OSS dropped behind the lines before D-day and beyond, governor of his state, senator, candidate for president of the United States—all before I graduated from college—and then to serve with him was indeed a privilege. One of the attendants in the Senate gym asked me one day to guess which senator pressed the most iron. My mind immediately turned to someone like ex-football player Al Gore. He said I was wrong—it was Strom Thurmond!

Jesse Helms

Jesse Helms was a close friend in the Senate and a political ally in many fights. I didn't always agree with his viewpoints or his tactics, but I always admired his consistency and moral purpose. He kept the focus on so-called social issues to the benefit of all of us, I believe. He was a true southern gentleman in all my dealings with him, and I regard him with a great deal of affection.

William Fulbright

Fulbright's reputation in the field of foreign policy was well established long before I arrived in the Senate. After I had traveled to the Middle East, he and I found that we shared opinions that led us to a closer personal relationship, but that shared opinion—that there are two sides to the Israeli/Palestinian question—led to his defeat in his next election.

Ted Stevens

Ted Stevens earned his reputation as a pugnacious and tenacious legislator. A good many people were understandably afraid of his temper, and I think that detracted from his stature in the Senate. Alaska and Idaho have many of the same issues and that led to our collaboration. He was and remains a friend.

John McCain

I knew John McCain by reputation but came to know him personally when he served as the U.S. Navy escort officer on one of our Senate trips. Certainly, I don't have to add the observation that he is known as something of a maverick, but that strength of character and independence was probably what enabled him to survive his years as a POW in Vietnam. He would be more effective if he could learn how to be more of a team player.

Al Gore

I believe the public probably now sees Al Gore more in the light that I saw him: a big, good-looking, college football player of some political background and talent, but not nearly as important as he saw himself. A man of unlimited ambition but with limited resources.

Howard Baker

A friend of mine once remarked about Howard Baker that "Howard wants to be president but didn't know why." Howard did not use his position to push his own personal agenda but used his great talent in working with people to bring out their best and to make it possible to work together. He was a very good and effective leader of the Republicans in the Senate. He was and remains a very good friend and I admire him very highly.

Henry Kissinger

Henry Kissinger served Richard Nixon in a very important way, but I believe he has been given too much credit for foreign policy during that time. There is no doubt of his influence, but I am convinced that Nixon was the architect of his own foreign policy. Kissinger was distrusted by many conservatives because of his conviction that the Cold War could not be won and that we must learn to live with the Soviet Union. I was given the task of introducing him at the Republican Convention because there was a substantial fear that there would be a demonstration against him. The convention manager, of course, wanted to avoid that. I don't believe Kissinger ever forgave me for a somewhat tepid introduction.

Ed Meese

Ed Meese was much more than just one of Ronald Reagan's loyal lieutenants; he was doggedly and persistently following his own agenda, which just happened to coincide with Reagan's. He and I had occasion to work together on a number of personnel issues for the administration, and the only tension that ever developed was when I insisted on naming candidates for the federal court system in Idaho and the 9th Circuit Court of Appeals. He eventually was able to convince himself that we were pursuing the same objectives, and acquiesced. You could never overestimate the strength of his convictions or his influence in the Reagan administration.

Casper Weinberger

Cap Weinberger was one of my favorites. From the Office of Management of Budget, Secretary of Defense, trusted advisor on a wide range of issues, Cap was an effective part of the Reagan administration. Not as well known was his great sense of humor. I always enjoyed him.

George Schultz

He was a man of immense self assurance, which sometimes appeared to me to be inflexible dogmatism. He was a man with a great reputation and ability, but I was never able to get beyond his reserve and feel any close personal relationship.

David Stockman

David Stockman was undoubtedly one of the bright young men of that era. He certainly knew the numbers when it came to the federal budget. However, his judgment of priorities was not necessarily the same as the majority of Republicans. Being director of OMB is a nearly impossible task at best, and he did a more than credible job.

Roger Mudd. [CBS anchor]

One of the genuinely likeable newsmen. He did not engage in personalities nor attempt to expose or destroy the people he was reporting about. In that regard he stands out in my memory in contrast with many who have followed him. I still trust him and respect his judgment. Hedrick (Rick) Smith is another journalist I trusted and respected.

David Broder

David Broder is undoubtedly one of the more cerebral writers. That does not mean, however, that he was always right. He has always been absolutely consistent in refusing anything that will appear to influence his writing. He would not even allow me to pay for a cup of coffee we shared while interviewing. He is consistently liberal to the point of failing to understand the more conservative viewpoints he was exposed to when he was out of Washington D.C. I think, however, that he is an honest liberal.

Arthur Burns

I became well acquainted with Arthur Burns when he was chairman of the FED when I was serving on the Joint Economic Committee. He had a deliberate demeanor as a witness, which always amused me. He was always careful in his answers, and when he needed a little more time to phrase his response, he would load and light his pipe, and after a puff or two, give his response. He appealed to my vanity by letting me know that my questions were very good and my understanding very perceptive. You have to like a man like that.

Bill Simon

Bill Simon, then the Secretary of the Treasury, was one of the most intense personalities with whom I worked. Very very focused and direct, with little time for obvious pleasantries, he was impatient with the political posturing that he ran into all around him. He was intellectually honest and very able.

Billy Graham

He is one of the most outstanding Americans of our time. His is a household name, and he has appeared on television so often that there is instant recognition of who he is and what he stands for. He conducted his crusade in Russia and made some very flattering comments about Russian leadership with which I strongly disagreed. I wrote him a letter in which I protested what I thought were comments misleading the public about the character of the leaders of Russia. I will never know if he ever received the letter because I never received a reply.

Jerry Falwell

I became acquainted with Jerry Falwell personally through some conservative political contacts we shared. I believed then that he needed better advice about politics than he was revealing in his public statements. He very nearly accepted my advice as to political assistance which he could get, but very soon decided to distance himself from direct political action. I think he could have become much more effective if he had tried to learn more about how to involve himself politically. Instead, he allowed himself to be marginalized, although I am sure his own view is somewhat different.

Pat Robertson

Pat Robertson has allowed himself to be diminished by events rather than broadening to a wider influence. I am sure that he can look around himself and be very satisfied with what he has accomplished in his lifetime. It would be very easy to become self-satisfied and inward looking. It is too bad that he didn't look beyond his immediate circles to find ways to involve himself more broadly. I think he would have avoided some of the mistakes that narrowed his appearance in the eyes of others, positioning him on the fringes.

Appendix One

International Figures

Moammar Ghadaffi

Meeting Ghadaffi in Libya was an interesting experience if only for the setting. He had a very large room arranged like a tent in the desert, with carpets on the floor and carpet covered benches around the edge. Aside from the setting, Ghadaffi was an interesting man, himself. I couldn't figure out whether he was intelligent or simple. I do know he had attended Sandhurst Military Academy in Great Britain, but I believe that he had severe mental problems. There was an unnatural brightness in his eyes and a nervousness in his physical actions. He was somewhat famous for copying Mao Tse-Tung's *Little Red Book* by publishing a *Little Green Book* of his own sayings. I read a portion of his little book and the sayings were simple to the point of childishness. I don't know whether that was calculated for his audience or a measure of his intellect.

Saddam Hussein

Just shortly before Desert Storm I was in a small group of senators who went to the Middle East. We wanted to include Iraq on our itinerary but were told that Saddam Hussein would not see us. When we were in his office in Cairo, Hosni Mubarak said that we should see Hussein. We told him that we were informed we could not see Saddam Hussein. Mubarak said, "I'll take care of that," and picked up the phone. After a few minutes of rapid fire conversation, he hung up the phone and said, "That's taken care of; he will see you."

When we landed in Baghdad, we were told that Hussein was not in the city but was in Northern Iraq in Mosul (the Biblical city of Nineveh) and that we would meet him there. We were also told that our U.S. airplane would not be permitted to fly to Mosul, but we would travel in an Iraqi aircraft. We didn't very much like that idea, but we had no choice if we wanted to see him. Howard Metzenbaum, a practicing Jew and an ardent supporter of Israel, was understandably very very nervous and wasn't at all sure that he would be permitted to leave the country. However, we did make the trip and met with Saddam Hussein in a hotel which he had commandeered for his stay in Mosul. Saddam was dressed in military uniform and surrounded by military personnel. Our meeting lasted about an hour and we all took part in the conversation (even Metzenbaum). But, I don't think we accomplished a thing. Hussein was very calm, spoke very quietly, listened intently, and never raised his voice, nor did he argue with us. In short, he was inscrutable.

King Hussein of Jordan

I met him on several occasions, both in Washington and in Amman. He justified his reputation as a great friend of the United States and was an eloquent spokesman for the people of his region. Short, physically fit, urbane, and intelligent, he survived because of the fierce loyalty of his army. The last time I saw him was at a small private dinner in the palace in Jordan where I was seated beside his American wife, Queen Noor, and Louise was seated by the King. I had not known the Queen although I was well acquainted with her father,

Najeeb Halaby (we were both on the board of the Wolftrap Farm Park for the Performing Arts).

King Faisal of Saudi Arabia

In the early 1970s Saudi Arabia was just beginning its transformation. Riyadh was more ancient than modern, and in that setting the magnificence of the Royal Palace seemed almost an anomaly. The setting was magnificent, the furnishings were ornate, and displayed great wealth in the midst of a city of mud buildings, piles of rubbish, and garbage. The King, himself, was a tall, gaunt figure with piercing black eyes and a commanding presence. I had a very good discussion about the Arab view of the Israeli problem. Faisal was very direct that the United States would have problems throughout the Middle East until the Israeli-Palestinian conflict was solved. And that has certainly proven to be true. I remember in particular mentioning the status of Jerusalem and his reply that, if we got to that point, that would be easy to solve. Obviously, we haven't yet come to that point.

Anwar Sadat, President of Egypt

Of all the world leaders I have met, Anwar Sadat was the most impressive. He had been a colonel in the Army during the revolt against British rule, and a relatively minor figure under Nasser's leadership. But, there was no doubt of his abilities or his stature as leader of Egypt after Nasser.

I first met him at his summer offices at the Barrages, a British installation in the Nile Delta where the flow of the Nile was controlled. They were old British buildings, large and well-maintained, but cooler in the summer than in the city. I will never forget the way he dealt with Senator Jacob Javits. Javits, of course, was a very outspoken supporter of Israel, and critic of all things Arab. During our visit, he would make some comment which revealed his attitudes and Sadat would smile and say, "Now Jacob," and completely diffuse the situation.

In Washington, D.C., after the Camp David accord had been reached, both Begin and Sadat separately met with groups of senators and the contrast between the two was remarkable. Begin was short, intense, and dwelled on every small detail, while Sadat was looking at the broad picture with confidence in the future. Begin looked like a pettifogger and Sadat looked like a statesman. It was a great tragedy when Sadat was assassinated by a member of the Muslim Brotherhood in his own Army.

Menachem Begin, Prime Minister of Israel

The nation of Israel was born in strife. The struggle against British rule in Palestine was marked by violence we have since come to call acts of terrorism. Menachem Begin was very much involved in that period of struggle for an independent Jewish nation. I always found him to be unable to escape attitudes which had enabled him to fight for his people in the establishment of his country. I did not think he was particularly impressive except by his record.

Shimon Peres, Prime Minister of Israel

Perez was an Israeli leader who clearly saw that some accommodation had to be reached with the Palestinians and worked toward that end. This, of course, was not acceptable to the most fanatic Zionists. He was, I believe, open with his views, both in public and in private conversations.

Yitzhak Rabin, Israeli Prime Minister after Begin.

Rabin was a relative hard-liner compared to Perez, but certainly much more flexible than Begin. He was well received in Washington and there was no doubt that there was a slight thaw but no concessions to the Palestinians. He was assassinated in 1995, after I left the Senate.

Aerial Sharon

The most intractable and most inflexible of the Israeli figures when I first knew him. He reminded me of other right-wing radical leaders such as LaPen in France. He had been an outstanding general, but the war was not over as far as he was concerned. I found him extremely dogmatic and impossible to reason with. It was a great surprise to me, and many others I'm sure, when he announced his willingness to remove settlements from Gaza. He had been one of the most militantly in favor of expanding Israel with settlements in Palestinian territory. While I welcome that change, I can't help but note that it was a unilateral decision which did not involve any discussion with the Palestinians.

Yasser Arafat, Head of the PLO

Yasser Arafat was a very unattractive person and the Palestinians would have been better served by a different spokesman. There is no doubt, however, that he had the support of the majority of his people. His faction appeared radical to most casual observers, but he was moderate when compared to George Habash, the leader of the Popular Front for the Liberation of Palestine. I spent an uncomfortable two hours with the PFLP when I was in Libya. I believe it was impossible for Arafat to make concessions and to have survived as leader of the Palestinians.

Helmut Kohl, Chancellor of Germany

Kohl was a big, hearty fellow with a booming voice and a lumberjack handshake. I instantly liked him and had confidence in what he said. U.S. German relationships were very warm and friendly during that period of time. He was chancellor when the Berlin Wall fell and he had the very difficult task of reuniting East Germany with West Germany.

John Paul II

I talked to the Pope in private sessions (in a small group) a couple of times. I think the public has an image of him as a gentle, benign wise presence. That is even more apparent when talking with him. It was special and a privilege each time. I think there is no doubt of his great influence on events throughout the Western World.

Margaret Thatcher

Margaret Thatcher was known as the "Iron Lady." The reputation was earned by her actions in leading Great Britain away from the excesses of a Socialist government. In person she was crisp and emphatic, but not at all shrill. She was always immaculately dressed and very gracious. When we asked her what advice she could give to President Reagan, she replied, "I didn't go far enough fast enough."

Ahmed Zaki Yamani

Zaki was an American educated (NYU + Harvard Law Degree) Oil Minister for the Kingdom of Saudi Arabia. He was one of the young technocrats, not of the Royal Family, who were the administrators of a more modern kingdom. We visited in his home in Jiddah, which was modern and opulent. At the time we visited, it was unusual to have men and women in the same room at social events, but that was the practice of young Saudis at that time. I think it may have been a liberalization trend that has been reversed, but I don't know that. He also had a big library of video. Yamani invited me to visit him at his summer home in Taif, but I was never able to do so. He wanted to take me on a camel ride in the desert, too, but that never happened either.

Hisham Nasir

He was another of the young technocrats running the country. When I first knew him, he was Deputy Minister of Planning, but has since become Minister of Planning and replaced Yamani as Oil Minister. He has a masters degree from UCLA and knows the West very well.

Prince Bandar

A longtime Saudi ambassador to the United States. He is married to one of King Faisal's daughters and was educated at the Royal Air Force College and Johns Hopkins University. He was a very effective spokesman for his country and looked after their interests very well. He is a gregarious and very likeable fellow who has many friends in Washington, D.C.

Prince Saud

The Foreign Minister of Saudi Arabia and a member of the Royal Family. He was in a more minor post in the government when I first knew him. A graduate of Princeton University, he still holds the school record for goals scored on the soccer team. He is tall, thin and intense. A very attractive man. He has also been quite outspoken about U.S. support for Israel.

Vaclav Havel

A playwright in Soviet dominated Czechoslovakia and an active dissident during the Cold War. When I was visiting in Czechoslovakia I had the opportunity to meet him even though he was in hiding at the time. There was nothing in his personal appearance or presence that led me to believe that he would emerge as the first elected president of Czechoslovakia and the first elected president of the new Czech Republic. You could not, however, miss the dedication that propelled him into the leadership of the dissident movement. He literally risked his life for what he believed.

Leonid Brezhnev

When a group of us visited the Soviet Union, we had the opportunity for a meeting with Brezhnev. He obviously had been briefed well and tagged me as a Western senator. Upon being introduced he remarked, "Oh, the cowboy." He knew where I was from but not much about me. He was a genial, hail-fellow-well-met, whom I thought would be a formidable candidate running for office in the United States. With his bushy eyebrows and genial attitude you could almost forget that he was the head of a ruthless and repressive government.

Anatoly Dobrynin

Long time Soviet Ambassador to the United States, he was almost a fixture in the diplomatic corps. He was genial and well liked, but kept very closely to the official line, which meant that I did not trust him at all.

Mikhail Gorbachev

I did not know him personally although I was in groups that met with him on two or three occasions. As the face of a new Soviet Union, he was very hard to figure. It was his stated aim to preserve Communism by modernizing it. If that was his purpose, he found that granting a little freedom started events that he could not control.

Andre Sakarov

The leading Soviet dissident when I made my last official trip to the country. His immense reputation preceded him and there was a natural tendency to measure him in person against the reputation. None of the passion in his exposition of Soviet barbarity was evident in talking with him. I got the impression that while he was an outspoken critic of the Soviet system, he was no particular friend of the United States.

Mikhail Suslov

The leading Communist ideologue from the days of the Revolution. During our visit to the Soviet Union in 1975, we held our meeting with our Soviet counterparts in a very large room in the Kremlin. There was a long table down the center of the room and we would march in from one side of the room and take our places at the table, and the Soviet group would march in from the other end of the room and take their places opposite us at the table. The conversation and exchanges went on for a couple of hours with quite a lot of give and take. Obviously, we did not concede to them and they certainly did not concede to us on points that were raised. But, it was a civil exchange. At the conclusion of the meeting, however, Suslov came in, and standing at the end of the table, delivered a virulent attack, telling us what a rotten bunch of Capitalist thugs we were. And on that note the meeting ended. I was impressed, but negatively.

Hafez el-Assad, President of Syria

Assad had the reputation for being a very tough man in the old tribal sense. He was an autocratic leader, but I found him very likeable and very easy to talk with. He was not known to have that persona.

I have to tell you about a private dinner I had with Assad in Damascus—Mike Hathaway was with me—where I was reminded of a lesson that I had not learned well enough. I was seated across the table from a man and his wife and remarked on the beautiful ring she was wearing. It was an ornate dinner ring with sapphires. The husband immediately asked her to remove her ring, which she did, then he gave it to me. I had heard that you need to be careful in making compliments but I had forgotten. Of course, I could not accept the ring, but I couldn't be so impolite to refuse it. Our ambassador to Syria was at the dinner and I later gave it to him. He said he would take care of it for me. Afterward I remembered a story that had been told to me of one of our people complimenting an Arab and his wife on the baby she was carrying and the father gave him the baby.

End Notes

Prologue

[1] Dawn Mattmiller, September 12, 2000.

[2] Bruce Hickey, September 28, 2000.

[3] Bob Robson, September 11, 2000.

[4] Hank Crowley, October 28, 2000.

[5] Dick Kading, October 31, 2000.

[6] Bob Robson, September 11, 2000.

[7] Dawn Mattmiller, February 5, 2001.

[8] Dick Bieber, January 6 and February 7, 2001.

[9] Ibid.

[10] Ibid.

[11] Dick Bieber, April 10, 2001.

[12] Dick Bieber, February 7, 2001.

[13] Billy Grammer, February 1, 2001.

[14] Dick Bieber, January 6, 2001.

[15] Percy "Perk" Lyda, February 2, 2001.

[16] Dick Bieber, January 6, 2001.

[17] Billy Grammer, February 1, 2001.

[18] Dick Bieber, February 7, 2001.

[19] Ibid.

[20] Duane Williams, September 29, 2000.

[21] Dick Bieber, February 7, 2001.

[22] Dawn Mattmiller, February 5, 2001.

Chapter 1: The McClures

[1] *The Civil War: Red River to Appomattox*, Shelby Foote, pg 874.

[2] Bud Barkdoll, Franklin County Historical Society, May 8, 2001

[3] Robertson McClure to Catharine McClure, March 9, 1865. Original in possession of Elsie Glenn Kaiser, Rt. 3, Box 204, Rich Hill, Missouri 64779

[4] *The Civil War: Red River to Appomattox*, Shelby Foote, pg 900-901

[5] Mrs. Fay to Catharine McClure, July 4, 1865, in possession of Elsie Glenn Kaiser, Rt. 3, Box 204, Rich Hill, Missouri 64779

[6] Terry Reimer, Research Coordinator, National Museum of Civil War Medicine

[7] Fannett Township Plat, 1868, Franklin County Historical Society, Chambersburg, Pennsylvania.

[8] James Laughery Paul, Pennsylvania's Soldiers Orphan Schools, Giving a Brief Account of The Origin of The Late Civil War, The Rise and Progress of The Orphan System, And Legislature Enactments Relating Thereto: With Brief Sketches and

Engravings of The Several Institutions, With Names of Pupils Subjoined. Harrisburgh: Lane S. Hart 1877. Family History Library Book 974.8 J3pa

[9] Randy Bell, May 21, 2001.

Chapter 3: Will and Marie

[1] Jim McClure November 10, 1999.

[2] Textbox information on Intermountain Institute from Derig, Betty *Roadside History of Idaho*, 1996, pp 233-234.

[3] Dates and locations of Will McClure's Army service are in a "Memo Book" in the possession of Ray McClure. Camp Dick as a concentration camp from Military Aviation Activities in Texas, World Wars I and II, Robert E. Hays, Jr. M.A. thesis, University of Texas, 1963. Confirmation of WW I flying training sequence by Dr. Edward Coffman, Lexington, KY, an authority on WW I Army aviation, interview June 29, 2001

[4] University of Idaho Registrar's Office.

[5] Raymond McClure August 15, 2000 and Jean Parton June 7, 2001

[6] Adams County Leader December 28, 1923.

[7] Jim McClure July 31, 2000.

[8] *History of Idaho*, Beal and Wells, Volume II, pg 243.

[9] Jean Parton June 7, 2001.

[10] Fred Rabinau August 15, 2000.

[11] Ken and Ila "Ike" Frazier August 16, 2000.

[12] Warren McCain July 2, 2001.

[13] Lucie Cobb Lingel, September 15, 2001.

[14] Mary Meechan Davis, August 15, 2000. Her older sister later confirmed that Mary's memory of the cross-burning was correct..

[15] Ila "Ike" Frazier and her husband, Ken, August 15, 2000.

[16] Jean Parton June 7, 2001.

[17] Raymond McClure August 15, 2000.

Chapter 4: Jamie

[1] Ray McClure August 15, 2000.

[2] Jim McClure September 19, 2001.

[3] Grandfather stories were repeated in several interviews with Jim McClure on November 10, 1999 and September 13 and 19, 2001.

[4] Ray McClure August 15, 2000.

[5] Ibid.

[6] Jim McClure November 10, 1999

[7] Fred Rabinau August 15, 2000.

[8] Ray McClure October 3, 2001.

[9] Jim McClure November 10, 1999

[10] Jim McClure October 4, 2001.

[11] Ray McClure, August 15, 2000.

[12] Jim McClure September 19, 2001.

[13] Jean Parton June 7, 2001.

[14] Harold Preston September 17, 2001.

[15] Dave Bivens September 20, 2001.

[16] Jim McClure November 10, 1999.

[17] Ibid.

[18] Jim McClure September 13, 2001.

[19] Harold Preston September 17, 2001.

Chapter 5: Mac

[1] Harold Preston September 17, 2001

[2] Ibid.

[3] Ibid.

[4] Jim McClure 10-23-01.

[5] Harold Preston September 17, 2001.

[7] Jim McClure September 19, 2001.

[8] Harold Preston September 17, 2001.

[9] Jim McClure September 19, 2001.

[10] Harold Preston September 17, 2001.

[11] Ibid.

[12] Jim McClure September 19, 2001.

[13] Ibid.

[14] Ibid.

[15] Ibid.

[16] Ibid.

[17] Ibid.

Chapter 6: Aviation Cadet

[1] Jim McClure September 19, 2001.

[2] Ibid.

[3] Ibid.

[4] Ken Snyder, National Museum of Naval Aviation, Pensacola, Florida, November 21, 2001.

[5] Jim McClure September 19 and November 28, 2001.

[6] Ibid.

[7] Ibid.

[8] Ibid.

[9] Ibid.

[10] Ken Snyder, November 21, 2001.

[11] Textbox: David Levy, local historian, Norman, Oklahoma, November 30, 2001.

[12] Jim McClure September 19 and November 28, 200l.

[13] Ibid.

[14] Ibid.

[15] Ibid.

[16] Ibid.

[17] Ibid.

[18] Ibid.

[19] *The Last Great Victory*, Stanley Weintraub, Konecky & Konecky, 1995, pp 204-205.

[20] *The Second World War,* Martin Gilbert, Henry Holt, 1989, page 703.

[21] Jim McClure September 19 and November 28, 2001.

Chapter 7: Law Student

[1] Jim McClure, October 4, 2001.

[2] *West's Encyclopedia of American Law*, G.I. Bill & Prentice Hall Documents Library: The GI Bill of Rights.

[3] Ray Rigby, December 10, 2001.

[4] Roger Vincent, December 11, 2001.

[5] Glen Lockery, December 11, 2001 and December 29, 2001.

[6] Louise McClure, October 4, 2001.

[7] Roger Vincent, December 11, 2001.

[8] John Jordan, December 12, 2001.

[9] Jim McClure, October 4, 2001.

[10] Bill Sweet, December 27, 2001.

[11] Louise McClure, December 28, 2001.

[12] Norman Logan, December 11, 2001.

[13] Jim and Louise McClure, December 28, 2001.

[14] Bob Yost, December 27, 2001.

[15] Jim McClure, November 11, 2001.

[16] Duane Miller, December 16, 2001.

[17] Louise McClure, October 4, 2001.

[18] Duane Miller, December 16, 2001.

[19] Jim and Louise McClure, December 28, 2001.

[20] Ibid.

[21] Ellomae Holden DeMond, January 17. 2002.

[22] Ibid.

[23] Ibid.

[24] Ellomae Holden DeMond, January 17, 2002.

Chapter 8: The Lawyer

[1] Textbox: HARMON KILLEBREW. From interviews with Ron Manser January 15, 2001 and Tobe Massingill October 30, 2002.;

[2] Jim McClure, January 10, 2002.

[3] Mike Felton, February 4, 2002.

[4] Ibid.

[5] Gilbert Norris, January 28, 2002.

[6] Jeanette Rutan, January 11, 2002.

[7] Louise McClure, January 15, 2002.

[8] Jeanette Rutan, January 11, 2002.

[9] Jim McClure, January 15, 2002.

[10] Jim McClure, January 10, 2002.

[11] Ibid.

[12] Ibid.

[13] Ron Manser, January 15, 2002.

[14] Jim McClure, January 15, 2002.

[15] Marilyn McClure Roach, February 4, 2002.

[16] Jeanette Rutan, January 11, 2002.

[17] Jim McClure, January 15, 2002.

Chapter 9: The Legislator

[1] Jim McClure, March 6, 2002.

[2] Ibid.

[3] *The Idaho Statesman*, January 2, 1961.

[4] Jim McClure, March 11, 2002. Telegram in the legislative papers of Jim McClure, University of Idaho. The telegram is dated 5:35 p.m., January 19, 1961.

[5] Jim McClure, March 11, 2002.

[6] *The Sand Pebbles*, Richard McKenna, Harper and Row, 1962, pp 3-4.

[7] Jim McClure, March 11, 2002.

[8] Jim Goller, March 26, 2002.

[9] Perry Swisher April 3, 2002.

[10] Watt Prather, December 12, 2001.

[11] Jim McClure, February 6, 2002.

[12] Jim McClure, March 26, 2002.

[13] Marilyn McClure Roach, February 2, 2002.

[14] Ibid.

[15] In interviews with Bob Robson (September 11, 2000 and February 26, 2002), the Kellogg attorney who was instrumental in ousting the Mine, Mill, and Smelter Workers Union in Shoshone County, he declared that President Clark of that union had openly declared himself to be a Communist.

[16] Joint interview with Shirley and Cliff Massingill, January 12, 2002.

[17] FIRST STRIKE OPTIONS AND THE BERLIN CRISIS, SEPTEMBER 1961, NEW DOCUMENTS THE KENNEDY ADMINISTRATION, National Security Archive Electronic Briefing Book No. 56, William Burr, Editor, September 25, 2001.

[18] *The Idaho Statesman*, January 26, 1963.

[19] Jim McClure, August 1, 2002.

[20] Jim McClure, December, 2001.

[21] *The Idaho Statesman,* January 10, 1963.

[22] Ibid.

[23] *The Idaho Statesman*, February 9, 1963.

[24] *The Idaho Statesman*, February 27, 1963.

[25] Jim McClure, July 27, 2002.

[26] Joint interview with Jim McClure and Jim Goller, December 15, 1999.

[27] For an interesting and detailed account of this rift in the Republican Party and how it led to Don Samuelson's embarrassing defeat of Smylie when he ran for a fourth term, Chapters Six and Seven of Paradox Politics, Randy Stapilus, Ridenbaugh Press, 1988, is highly recommended.

[28] Jim McClure, August 1, 2002.

[29] Pete Cenarrusa, October 1, 2002.

[30] Cleora Murphy, in a telephone conversation, October 2, 2002, confirmed Cenarrusa's memory of attendees and the substance of the agreement that was made.

[31] Perry Swisher, October 2, 2002.

[32] Phil Batt, October 4, 2002.

[33] Jim McClure, October 4, 2002.

[34] *The Idaho Statesman*, January 4, 1965.

[35] Updated report to the Independent-Enterprise, Legislative Papers, McClure Collection, University of Idaho.

[36] Ibid.

[37] *The Independent-Enterprise*, January 7, 1965.

[38] *The Independent-Enterprise*, January 28, 1965.

[39] Ibid.

[40] *Idaho Falls Post-Register*, March 25, 1985.

[41] Jim McClure, October 8, 2002.

[42] Textbox on Condominium Statute.

[43] Joint interview with Jim McClure and Jim Goller, December 15, 1999.

[44] Interview with Jim and Louis McClure, March 3, 2002.

[45] In an interview March 15, 2002, Bill Schroeder confirmed that he and McClure had talked about a joint practice.

[46] Joint interview with Jim and Louise McClure, March 3, 2002.

Chapter 10: Fate Opens a Door

[1] *Independent-Enterprise*, March 18, 1965.

[2] Jim McClure, November 15, 2002.

[3] In casual conversations with Jim McClure he repeatedly used these words to describe his reaction, and, later, when he announced in his hometown paper that he was thinking of running (Independent-Enterprise, February 16, 1966), these were the exact words he used in the press release.

[4] Jim McClure, February 6, 2002.

[5] Joint interview with Jim and Louise McClure, March 3, 2002.

[6] Joint interview with Jim McClure and Jim Goller, December 15, 1999.

[7] *The Idaho Statesman*, February 3, 1966.

[8] Ibid.

[9] Ibid.

[10] Ibid.

[6] Footnote: Bart Brassey , June 14, 2001.

[11] Jim Goller, November 18, 2002.

[12] Jim McClure, November 15, 2002.

[13] Jim Goller, November 4, 1999.

Chapter 11: The Candidate

[1] Jim McClure , August 1, 2002.

[2] Ibid.

[3] Jim Goller, March 27, 2002.

[4] Joint interview with Jim McClure and Jim Goller, December 15, 1999.

[5] Pete Wilson, November 24, 2002.

[6] Alice Nelson, November 26, 2002.

[7] Dolly Hartman, November 26, 2002.

[8] Ruthie Johnson, June 6, 2000.

[9] Berne Jensen, Decembe4 27, 2000.

[10] Bob Robson, December 1, 2002.

[11] Textbox, Marty Peterson, November 2, 2000.

[12] Joint interview with Jim McClure and Jim Goller, December 15, 1999.

[13] Patty Wendstrom Franden, November 25, 2002.

[14] Joint interview with Jim McClure and Jim Goller, December 15, 1999.

[15] Ibid.

[16] Textbox Vietnam, Jim Goller, December 4, 2002.

[17] Paradox Politics, Stapilus, Randy, Ridenbaugh Press, Boise, 1988, pg. 126.

[18] Textbox, Jim Harris, November 1, 2000.

[19] Jim McClure and Jim Goller, December 15, 1999.

[20] Ibid.

[21] Jim McClure and Jim Goller, December 15, 1999.

[22] Scootch Harper Pankonin, July 17, 2000.

[23] Jim McClure and Jim Goller, December 15, 1999.

[24] Ibid.

[25] Scootch Harper Pankonin, July 17, 2000.

[26] Jim Goller, March 27, 2002.

[27] Patty Wendstrom Franden, November 25, 2002.

[28] Jim McClure and Jim Goller, December 15, 1999.

[29] Ibid.

[30] Ibid.

[31] Ibid.

Chapter 12: From Payette to Washington, D.C.

[1] Goller and McClure, December 15, 1999.

[2] Ibid.

[3] Jim McClure, May 1-3, 2002.

[4] David McClure, July 23, 2003.

[5] Ken McClure, December 15, 1999.

[6] Ibid.

[7] Marilyn McClure Roach, December 19, 2002.

[8] Ibid.

[9] Ibid.

[10] Ken McClure, December 15, 1999.

[11] Jim McClure, May 2, 2002

Chapter 13: The Deluge

[1] Special collections, Box 4, Folder 52, McClure Archives.

[2] Dick Thompson, July 22, 2003.

[3] Scootch Harper Pankonin, July 17, 2000.

[4] McClure and Goller, December 15, 1999 and McClure, May 1, 2002.

[5] McClure and Goller, December 15, 1999.

[6] Dick Thompson, August 22, 2003.

[7] Scootch Harper Pankonin, July 17, 2000.

[8] Dick Thompson, August 22, 2003.

[9] Jim McClure, January 11, 2003.

[10] Jim McClure, May 1, 2002.

[11] Jim Goller, August 21, 2003.

Chapter 14: The Committeeman

[1] Sam Steiger quoted in *A Rage for Justice*, John Jacobs, 1995, University of California Press, pg 221.

[2] Ibid, pg 220.

[3] Lee McElvain, Majority Counsel as quoted in Wayne Aspinall and the Shaping of the American West, Steven C. Schulte, 2002, University Press of Colorado, pg 267. Also confirmed in interviews with Lloyd Meeds (February 7, 2003) and Lee McElvain (September 29, 2003).

[4] Comment from two former observers of the Interior Committee who wish to remain anonymous.

[5] Lloyd Meeds, February 7, 2003.

[6] Lee McElvain, February 3, 2003.

[7] Memo to members of the Committee on Interior & Insular Affairs, April 10, 1967. University of Idaho Archives.

[8] Jim McClure, May 1-3, 2002.

[9] Ibid for the McClure statement. The staffer asked for no attribution.

[10] Quote and textbox: Telephone interview with Dick Thompson, January 8, 2004.

Chapter 15: The Congressional Balancing Act

[1] Jim McClure, December 20, 2003.

[2] Dick Thompson, January 21, 2004.

[3] Jim Goller, January 21, 2004.

[4] Louise McClure, January 5, 2004.
Textbox. Marilyn McClure Roach diary quoted in November 1, 2005 letter to author.

[5] Ibid.

[6] Marilyn McClure Roach, January 7, 2004.

[7] Jim McClure, January 5, 2004.

[8] Marilyn McClure Roach, January 7, 2004.

[9] Louise McClure, January 26, 2004
.

Chapter 16: The Pace Increases

[1] *The Lewiston Morning Tribune*, October 18, 1967.

[2] Jim Goller, February 12, 2004.

[3] Jim McClure, February 11, 2004.

[4] Letter March 26, 1968 to Mrs. Rita Albers from Jim McClure.

[5] John Swayne, February 21, 2004.

[6] Lee McElvain, December 3, 2003.

[7] Dick Thompson, March 9, 2004.

[8] Tom Foley, December 3, 2003.

[9] Lloyd Meeds, February 7, 2003.

[10] Marilyn McClure Roach, February 26, 2004.

[11] A Rage for Justice, John Jacobs, University of California Press, 1995, pp 209-210
Textbox: Tom Schabot to the author, August 1999.

[12] Jim Goller, February 12, 2004.

[13] Jim Goller, March 31, 2004.

[14] Jim McClure, March 31, 2004.

[15] Letter from Frank Church, June 4, 1968, University of Idaho Archives.

[16] *Meridian News-Times*, July 25, 1968.

[17] McClure Archives, University of Idaho.

[18] Dick Thompson, July 11, 2001.

[19] Jim Goller, April 2, 2004.

[20] Ibid.

[21] Jim McClure, April 5, 2004.

[22] Textbox, Dorothy Hanford, April 7, 2004.

Chapter 17: An Environmental Challenge

[1] Ronald Bailey, "Silent Spring at 40," Reason June 12, 2002.

[2] Ibid.

[3] Jim McClure January 8, 2005.

[4] JIM McCLURE REPORTS, Summer 1969 Newsletter.

[5] Ibid.

[6] Ibid.

[7] File 33-1322, date obliterated, McClure archives, University of Idaho.

[8] Letter to A.J. Teske, June 19, 1969, McClure archives, University of Idaho.

[9] Bill Brauner, Caldwell, May 11, 2004.

[10] *Lewiston Morning Tribune*, July 23, 1970.

[11] Memo from McClure to Goller.

[12] Lee McElvain, February 3, 2003.

[13] Orval Hansen, July 29, 2004.

[14] Ibid.

[15] Lee McElvain, January 14, 2005.

[16] Orval Hansen, July 29, 2004.

[17] Ibid.

[18] Gray Reynolds, July 28, 2004 and January 17, 2005. Textbox Kit Caples Kimball, June 2, 2006.

[19] Ibid.

[20] *Congressional Record*, January 26, 1972.

[21] Orval Hansen, July 29, 2004.

[22] Congressional Record, January 26, 1972.

[23] Ibid.

[24] Jim McClure, May 11, 2004.

[25] *Congressional Record*, August 2, 1972.

[26] Jim McClure, January 21, 2005.

[27] Essay by Orval Hansen given to the author July 29, 2004.

Chapter 18: A New Opportunity

[1] Orval Hansen, July 29, 2004.

[2] *Weiser American*, March 15, 1971.

[3] Jim Goller, January 20, 2005.

[4] Ibid.

[5] Ibid.

[6] Press release, August 24, 1971, McClure Archives.

[7] Letter from Jack Stockton, McCall, Idaho, McClure Archives.

[8] Letter from A. John Gaige, Boise, Idaho, McClure Archives.

[9] Letter from Mr. And Mrs. John B. Dean, Boise, Idaho, McClure Archives.

[10] Letter from Curtis Larson, Lewiston, Idaho, McClure Archives.

[11] Letter from V.C. McKenzie, Boise, Idaho, McClure Archives

[12] Letter from Waldo E. Jones, Fruitland, Idaho, McClure Archives.

[13] Letter from W.T. "Bill" Marineau, Moscow, Idaho, McClure Archives.

[14] Letter from J.A. Stewart, Blackfoot, Idaho, McClure Archives.

[15] Letter from Abe McGregor Goff, Moscow, Idaho, McClure Archives.

[16] Jim Goller, January 17 and January 28, 2005.

[17] Jim McClure, January 23, 2005.

[18] Jim Goller, January 28, 2005.

[19] *North Idaho Press*, November 17, 1971.

[20] The Coeur d'Alene, Idaho *Press*, November 4, 1971.

[21] Sally McClure, November 28, 2003.

[22] Louise McClure, November 28, 2003.

[23] Jim McClure, November 28, 2003.

Chapter 19: Getting the Nomination

[1] Marvin Esch, February 2, 2005.

[2] Jim McClure, January 30 and February 3, 2005.

[3] Dick Thompson phone conversation, February 3, 2005.

[4] Jim McClure, February 3, 2005.

[5] Dick Thompson, February 5, 2005.

[6] Ruthie Johnson, February 2, 2005.

[7] Jim McClure, February 1, 2005.

[8] Jim Goller, January 29, 2005.

[9] Jim Goller, February 9, 2005.

[10] Chris Carlson, February 23, 2003

[11] *The Idaho State Journal*, Pocatello, November 21, 1971

[12] Letter to Mr. Ross Burrup, Blackfoot, Idaho, June 15, 1972.

[13] Jim McClure, August 15, 2004.

[14] Ibid.

[15] Jim Golller, February 9, 2005.

[16] Jim McClure, February 1, 2005.

[17] Jim Goller, February 11, 2005.

[18] Press release to the *Bonners Ferry Herald*, July 20, 1972.

[19] *Lewiston Morning Tribune*, June 18, 1972.

Chapter 20: The Great Race

[1] Chris Carlson, February 14, 2005.

[2] William E. "Bud" Davis, February 15, 2005.

[3] Ibid.

[4] Jay Shelledy, February 18, 2005.

[5] Ibid.

[6] Ibid.

[7] Textbox, Jay Shelledy, February 18, 2005, confirmed by Bill Hall same date.

[8] William E. "Bud" Davis, February 15, 2005.

[9] Jay Shelledy, February 18, 2005.

[10] Statement by George Hansen regarding the Idaho United States Senatorial Primary Election of 1972, McClure Archives 88-3269

[11] Jim McClure, February 14, 2005.

[12] Nancy Carlile, February 15, 2005.

[13] Jim McClure, February 14, 2005.

[14] Vernon Clinton, undated memo, McClure archives 88-3266.

[15] Chris Carlson, August 22, 1972.

[16] *Twin Falls Times News*, August 6, 1972.

[17] Robert A. Wright, *The New York Times*, October 31, 1972.

[18] Jim Goller, letter, 9-22-05.

[19] P.T. "Pete" Rathbone, February 18, 2005.

[20] *The Blackfoot News*, October 31, 2005.

[21] Blanche Evans Sorenson, February 8, 2005.

[22] William E. "Bud" Davis, February 13, 2005.

[23] Jay Shelledy, February 18, 2005.

[24] Jim McClure, February 14, 2005.

[25] Jay Shelledy, February 18, 2005.

[26] Jim Goller, February 9 and February 18, 2005.

[27] P.T. "Pete" Rathbone, February 18, 2005.

Chapter 21: Freshman Senator

[1] Dick Thompson, July 10, 2001.

[2] Scootch Pankonin, July 17, 2000.

[3] Dick Thompson, July 15, 2004.
Textbox. Margo Carlisle, January 26, 2005.

[4] Jim and Louise McClure, February 24, 2005.

[5] Mike Hathaway, February 23, 2005. The author was unable to find a copy of this speech in the archives.

[6] Ibid.

[7] Margo Carlisle, January 28, 2005.

[8] Dick Thompson, July 15, 2004.

[9] Jim McClure, February 24, 2005.

[10] Mike Hathaway, February 23, 2005.

[11] Brian Trumbore, "The Arab Oil Embargo of 1972-74," StocksandNews.com

[12] Jim McClure, February 24, 2005.

[13] Herman F. Eilts, February 25, 1905.

[14] Mike Hathaway, February 24, 2005.
Textbox: Jim Norell, March 15, 2005

[15] Ibid.

[16] Jim McClure, February 24, 2005.

[17] Mike Hathaway, February 24, 2005.

[18] Jim McClure, February 24, 2005.

[19] Mike Hathaway, February 24, 2005.

[20] Jim McClure, March 7, 2005.

Chapter 22: Gold, Clean Air and the Rise to Leadership

[1] Jim McClure, March 11, 2005.

[2] Jim Norell, March 15, 2005.

[3] Dick Thompson, March 11, 2005.

[4] Mike Hathaway, February 25, 2005.

[5] Jim McClure, February 28, 2005.

[6] Mike Hathaway, February 25, 2005.

[7] Ibid.

[8] Jim Norell, March 15, 2005.

[9] Dick Thompson, March 11, 2005.

[10] Paul Weyrich, March 14, 2005.

Chapter 23: Embattled Minority

[1] Related to the author by Tillie Arnold, one of Hemingway's closest friends.

[2] Jim McClure, March 22, 2005.

[3] Jim Norell, March 15, 2005.

[4] Jim McClure, March 22, 2005.

[5] Margo Carlisle, March 26, 2005.

[6] Jim Norell, March 15, 2005.

[7] James A. McClure News Release May 12, 1975, 154-5965.

[8] Margo Carlisle, March 26, 2005.

[9] Ibid.
Footnote. Bureau of Labor Statistics; Monthly Labor Review February 1, 1988: Some recollections of a brief tenure.

[10] Press Release, December 29, 1975, 154-5965
Textbox. Jeff Cilek, March 10, 2006. *Congressional Record*—Senate, March 22, 1979.

[11] *Lewiston Morning Tribune*, December 21, 1975.

Chapter 24: Another Tragedy

[1] Jim Goller, April 12, 2005.

[2] Jim Norell, March 15, 2005.

[3] Nancy Carlile, August 24, 2004.

[4] Jim Goller, April 15, 2005.

• Textbox, Ruthie Johnson, June 6, 2000.
• Textbox. Nancy Carlile, April 25, 2005
• Textbox. Letter from Dick Thompson, May 1, 2005.
• Textbox: Nancy Carlile, August 24, 2004.

5 Jim Goller, April 15, 2005.

6 Debbie Field, April 8, 2005.

7 Nancy Carlile, August 24, 2004.

8 Jim McClure, April 15, 2005.

9 Tod Neuenschwander. June 5, 2002.

10 Jim Goller, April 15, 2005.

Chapter 25: The Carter Years

1 Margo Carlisle, April 21, 2005.

2 Jim McClure, April 18, 2005.
• Textbox, Debbie Field, April 15, 2005.

3 Margo Carlisle, April 20, 2005.

4 Buffalo Criminal Law Review, Vol. 2.1:45, pg 94.

5 Paul Weyrich, March 28, 2005.

6 Mike Hammond, April 2, 2005.

7 Ibid.

8 Jim McClure, April 4, 2005.

9 Press release to Idaho Weekly Newspapers, week of July 3, 1978. Archives 654-17814.
• Textbox, TomHill, June 14, 2005.

10 Nuclear Energy III — Nuclear Waste and Breeder Reactors—Myth and Promise, Robert G. Williscroft, June 4, 2004, thedeadhand.com

11 Anonymous, May 3, 2005.

12 Press release, September 1, 1978. Archives 655-17815

13 Mike Hathaway, April 21, 2005.

Chapter 26: The Carter Years - Two

1 Tod Neuenschwander, May 12, 2005.

2 Phil Reberger, May 12, 2005.

3 Dwight Jensen, May 19, 2005.

4 Jim McClure,

5 Phil Reberger, May 12, 2005.
• Textbox. Source: U.S. Department of Energy, Office of Fossil Energy, Strategic Petroleum Reserve Storage Sites.

6 Jim McClure, May 7, 2005.
• Textbox: Senator J. Bennett Johnston, June 6, 2005

7 U.S. Department of Energy, Office of Fossil Energy, The Early Days of Coal Research.
• Textbox: Ron Shiflett, June 18, 2005.

8 Jim McClure, June 7, 2005.

[9] Jim McClure, June 7, 2005.

[10] Ibid.

[11] Ibid.

Chapter 27: New Roles

[1] Steve Symms, June 15, 2005.

[2] John Brandt, June 22, 2005.

[3] Jim McClure, June 16, 2005.

[4] Steve Symms, June 15, 2005.
• Textbox: ABC World News Tonight, The Transcript Company, Burbank, CA.

[5] LeRoy Ashby and Rod Gramer, *Fighting the Odds: The Life of Senator Frank Church*, Washington State University Press, 1994, pp 600. Chris Mooney, *American Prospect*, November 5, 2001.

[6] Jim McClure, June 17, 2005.
• Textbox. Paul Weyrich, March 28, 2005.

[7] Dick Thompson, June 14, 2005.

[8] Tod Neuenschwander, June 5, 2002.

[9] Margo Carlisle, January 28, 2005.

[10] Orval Hansen, June 29, 2004.

[11] Jim McClure, June 23, 2005.
• Textbox: Abbreviated from Kathryn Jacob, Historic Traveler.com, pp 26-29, Fall 2001 issue, a publication of the PRIMEDIA History Group.

[12] Jim McClure, June 23, 2005.

[13] Jim and Louise McClure, June 27, 2005.

[14] McClure press release, June 22, 1982.

[15] Martha Solodky, June 27, 2005.

[16] Gloria Brown, June 27, 2005.

[17] Jim and Louise McClure, June 27, 2005.

[18] Martha Solodky, June 27, 2005.

[19] Jim and Louise McClure, June 27, 2005.
• Textbox: Barbara Shissler Nosanow, June 29, 2005.

[20] Rod Kagan, June 28, 2005.

Chapter 28: The Pragmatist

[1] Jim McClure, June 14, 2005.

[2] Bill Summary & Status for the 97th Congress, S.1503, thomas.loc.gov.

[3] Tom Hill, June 13, 2005.

[4] Ibid.

[5] Peter Johnson, May 1, 2005.

[6] Ibid.

[7] Jim McClure, June 27, 2005.

[8] Dick Thompson, July 11, 2001.

[9] Jim McClure, June 27, 2005.

[10] Ibid.

Chapter 29: Win One, Lose One

[1] Mel Morgan, July 6, 2005.

[2] Dick Thompson, August 13, 2001.

[3] Louise McClure, July 15, 2005.

[4] Jim McClure, July 15, 2005.

[5] Ibid.

[6] Ibid.

[7] Dick Thompson, August 13, 2001.

[8] Ibid.

[9] Dick Thompson, July 18, 2005.

[10] Ibid.

[11] Steve Symms, July 16, 2005.

[12] Jim McClure, July 15, 2005.

Chapter 30: Wilderness Struggles

[1] Doug Scott, January 22, 2003.

[2] Ibid.
• Textbox. Kit Caples Kimball, June 2, 2006.

[3] *Congressional Record*—Senate, November 20, 1979.

[4] *Congressional Record*—Senate, February 27, 1984.
• Textbox. Fred Hutchinson, August 3, 2005.

[5] Jim McClure, July 24, 2005.

[6] Press Release, McClure archives, March 16, 1983.

[7] Mike Field, July 25, 2005.

[8] Press Release, McClure archives, March 16, 1984.

[9] Press Release, McClure archives, August 2, 1984.

[10] Press Release, McClure archives, October 11, 1984.
• Textbox. Pat Ford, July 26, 2005.

[11] Joint interview Cecil Andrus, Jim McClure and Marc Johnson, July 7, 2005.

[12] Ibid.

[13] Anonymous.

Chapter Thirty-one: Farewell, Pink Cards

[1] Jim and Louise McClure, August 1, 2005.

[2] Ibid.
• Textbox: Jim Goller, August 10, 2005.

[3] Jim McClure, August 6, 2005.

[4] Ibid.

[5] Press release April 6, 1988, McClure archives.

[6] Jim McClure, August 6, 2005.

[7] Jim and Louise McClure, August 1, 2005.

[8] Ibid.

[9] Ibid.

[10] Ibid.

[11] Ibid.

[12] Ibid.

[13] Quoted in McClure press release, April 27, 1988. McClure archives.

[14] Frank Cushing, June 23, 2005.

[15] Tod Neuenschwander, August 6, 2005.

[16] Jim McClure, August 8, 2005.

[17] Quoted in McClure press release March 9, 1989. McClure archives.

[18] Jim McClure, August 8, 2005.

[19] Quoted in McClure press release February 15, 1989. McClure archives.

[20] Jim and Louise McClure, August 1, 2005.

[21] Jim McClure, August 10, 2005.

[22] Jim Goller, August 10, 2005.

[23] Jim and Louise McClure, August 1, 2005.

[24] Ken McClure, August 15, 2005.

[25] Randy Stapilus, *The Idaho Statesman*, December 10, 1989.
• Textbox. Bill Hall, *Lewiston Morning Tribune*, July 20, 1989.

[26] Tod Neuenschwander, August 18, 2005.

Epilogue

[1] Dale Levigne, April 18, 2006

[2] Congressman Major Owens quoted in USDA Forest Service Proceedings RMRS-P-VOL-2. 2000, pg 68.

[3] PR 90:133 September 19, 1990.

[4] Jim McClure, March 28, 2006.

[5] Joint interview with Jack Gerard and Susan Tackish, April 14, 2006.

[6] Tod Neuenschwander, March 29, 2006.

[7] Joint interview with Jack Gerard and Susan Tackish, April 14, 2006.

[8] Ibid.

[9] Ibid.

[10] Tod Neuenschwander, March 29, 2006.

[11] Jim McClure, March 28, 2006.

[12] Tod Neuenschwander, March 29, 2006.

[13] Jim McClure, March 28, 2006.

[14] Ibid.

[15] Bill Hall, October 15, 1999.

The Author

William L. Smallwood, a 53-year resident of Idaho, began his career as a high school teacher and subsequently authored numerous science ttextbooks. In the mid 1980s he began writing for the general public. He wrote the candidate guide books on the three service academies, two books on air combat in the Gulf War (*Warthog* and *Strike Eagle*, *The Idaho Hemingway*, as well as many video documentaries and magazine articles. He resides in Sun Valley and Wickenburg, Arizona.

Index

Y

Z

Other Western
Biographies
from

Caxton Press

Sixty-Four Years as a Writer
by Bill Gulick
ISBN 0-87004-453-2, 368 pages, paper, illustrated, $16.95

J. R. Simplot
A Billion the Hard Way
by Louie Attebery
ISBN 0-87004-399-4, 288 pages, cloth, photos, $24.95

Cool North Wind
Morley Nelson's Life With Birds of Prey
by Stephen Stuebner
ISBN 0-87004-426-5, 458 pages, cloth, photos, $24.95

Hobbled Stirrups
Jane Burnett Smith, Bronc Rider
by Jane Burnett Smith
ISBN 0-87004-454-0, 440 pages, paper, illustrated, $17.95

Elegant Soul
The Life and Music of Gene Harris
by Janie Harris with Bob Evancho
ISBN 0-87004-445-1, 280 pages, color, paper, illustrated, $24.95

For a free catalog of Caxton titles write to:

CAXTON PRESS
312 Main Street
Caldwell, Idaho 83605-3299

or

Visit our Internet web site:

www.caxtonpress.com

Caxton Press is a division of THE CAXTON PRINTERS, Ltd.